Societies in Late Medieval Prussia: Ethnicities

From the moment that Prussia entered the world of the crusade movement and the zone of Western European external expansion in the 13th century, and was quickly dominated by the Teutonic Order, the new Prussian Land created by the Order became a transitional area and a frontier country. A significant aspect of Prussia's character was ethnic diversity and a consequent multiculturalism.

This collective volume takes up the subject of ethnicity in Prussia between the 13th and 16th centuries and shows several other aspects of this phenomenon in a region on the outskirts of late medieval Europe. Lithuanians arriving from the east, Poles migrating from the south and Curonians living in the north-eastern peripheries come to light, but the volume also analyses issues of interethnic relations, both in the so-called 'period of conquest' (13th century) and at the turn of the Middle Ages and the Early Modern period (15th/16th centuries). Also, the issue of linguistic differentiation among the predominantly German-speaking brothers of the Teutonic Order, previously unnoticed in historiography, although difficult to grasp, is presented.

Eight papers offer a new contribution to the subject of multiethnicity in late medieval Prussia. The book is partly the outcome of the panel *The Multiculturalism of Prussia in the Late Middle Ages: Ethnic Groups, Elites, Ideas* organised in 2022 at the Congress of Polish Medievalists in Katowice, in connection with the implementation of the research project *The Historical-Geographical Dictionary of Prussia in the Middle Ages and at the Dawn of the Early Modern Period, vol. 1: Lower Prussia, vol. 2: Ermland*, funded by the polish National Programme for the Development of the Humanities (no. 11H160151 84).

Krzysztof Kwiatkowski is an associate professor in the Institute of History and Archival Sciences at the Nicolaus Copernicus University in Toruń. His research interests include military and social history of the Middle Ages as well as the history of the Teutonic Order and history of Prussia. He publishes especially on topics related to the military affairs of Prussia and the Prussian branch of the Teutonic Order in the late Middle Ages. Since 2013, he has been a co-organizer of the biennial international conference 'Ordines Militares. Colloquia Torunensia Historica' devoted to the military orders.

Radosław Biskup is an associate professor in the Institute of History and Archival Sciences at the Nicolaus Copernicus University in Toruń. His research focuses on the history of the Baltic Zone in the Middle Ages, especially ecclesiastical developments in the Prussian branch of the Teutonic Order. A special priority in his research is given to editing sources for the ecclesiastical history of medieval Prussia. He is also the chairman of the scientific council of the publishing series 'Ecclesia clerusque temporibus medii aevi'.

Studies in Medieval History and Culture

Recent titles include

Light, Privacy, and Neighbors
Windows in Late Medieval and Early Modern London
Janet S. Loengard

Medieval Iceland. Politics, Patronage and Power
Sverrir Jakobsson

Medieval Work, Worship, and Power
Persuasive and Silenced Voices
Edited by Abigail P. Dowling, Nancy Ann McLoughlin, and Tanya Stabler Miller

Continuity and Change in Medieval East Central Europe
Social, Ruling and Religious Transformations
Edited by Dušan Zupka

Remembering England: Cultural Memory in the Sagas of Icelanders
Matthew Firth

Sexuality in Medieval Poland in a European Context
Karolina Morawska

The Emergence of the Nobility in East Central Europe between the Eighth and Thirteenth Centuries
Edited by Robert Antonín and Jiří Macháček

Societies in Late Medieval Prussia: Ethnicities
Edited by Krzysztof Kwiatkowski and Radosław Biskup

For more information about this series, please visit:
https://www.routledge.com/Studies-in-Medieval-History-and-Culture/book-series/SMHC

Societies in Late Medieval Prussia: Ethnicities

Edited by Krzysztof Kwiatkowski and Radosław Biskup

LONDON AND NEW YORK

First published 2026
by Routledge
4 Park Square, Milton Park, Abingdon, Oxon OX14 4RN

and by Routledge
605 Third Avenue, New York, NY 10158

Routledge is an imprint of the Taylor & Francis Group, an informa business

© 2026 selection and editorial matter, Krzysztof Kwiatkowski and Radosław Biskup; individual chapters, the contributors

The right of Krzysztof Kwiatkowski and Radosław Biskup to be identified as the authors of the editorial material, and of the authors for their individual chapters, has been asserted in accordance with sections 77 and 78 of the Copyright, Designs and Patents Act 1988.

All rights reserved. No part of this book may be reprinted or reproduced or utilised in any form or by any electronic, mechanical, or other means, now known or hereafter invented, including photocopying and recording, or in any information storage or retrieval system, without permission in writing from the publishers.

For Product Safety Concerns and Information please contact our EU representative GPSR@taylorandfrancis.com. Taylor & Francis Verlag GmbH, Kaufingerstraße 24, 80331 München, Germany.

Trademark notice: Product or corporate names may be trademarks or registered trademarks, and are used only for identification and explanation without intent to infringe.

British Library Cataloguing-in-Publication Data
A catalogue record for this book is available from the British Library

ISBN: 978-1-032-82086-6 (hbk)
ISBN: 978-1-032-82087-3 (pbk)
ISBN: 978-1-003-50287-6 (ebk)

DOI: 10.4324/9781003502876

Typeset in Sabon
by KnowledgeWorks Global Ltd.

Contents

List of Figures · vii
List of Tables · viii
List of Abbreviations · ix
Notes on Contributors · xiv

1 Introduction · 1
KRZYSZTOF KWIATKOWSKI AND RADOSŁAW BISKUP

2 *The Chronicle of the Prussian Land* as Evidence of Multiethnicity in 13th- and Early 14th-Century Prussian Towns · 18
MATTHEW FRANK STEVENS

3 Old-Prussians as Co-Creators of Teutonic Order's Rulership and Members of the New Society in Late Medieval Prussia · 44
ALICJA DOBROSIELSKA

4 Native Identities after the Crusades: The Archaeology of Ethnicity in Medieval Prussia · 58
ALEKSANDER PLUSKOWSKI, MACIEJ KARCZEWSKI, AND MAŁGORZATA KARCZEWSKA

5 Curonians and the Teutonic Order: Settlement and Military Structures on the Outskirts of Late Medieval Prussia · 81
KRZYSZTOF KWIATKOWSKI

6 Migration of Rural Settlers (esp. Lithuanians) to Eastern Prussia in the 15th/16th Century · 113
GRISCHA VERCAMER

7 Polish Nobility in Royal Prussia 1454–1506: Status, Position, and Migrations 152
SOBIESŁAW SZYBKOWSKI

8 The Functioning of Mendicant Orders in Multi-Ethnic Communities in the Territory of the Teutonic Order in Prussia and in Royal Prussia until the Beginning of the 16th Century 180
RAFAŁ KUBICKI

9 Teutonic Order and German Dialects under Special Consideration of the Prussian Branch in the Late Middle Ages 206
PIOTR GOTÓWKO

Index 239

List of Figures

4.1 Part of the map of the "Districtus Lecenzis" by Józef Naronowicz-Naroński showing the location of *Stasswin* (Staświny), the surrounding villages and *Letzen* (Lötzen) in 1663. Staatsbibliothek, Berlin.   63
4.2 Dress accessories from the late medieval cemetery in Równina Dolna representing Western and native Prussian influences (Kętrzyn County, Warmian-Masurian Voivodeship): (a–d) brooches; (e) bear claw set in bronze fitting with metal plates; (f) pendant with bells. Archaeology Department, Museum of Warmia and Mazury in Olsztyn, Poland. Author: Jarosław Sobieraj. Reproduced with permission.   67
6.1 Administrative boundaries in the eastern commanderies (Balga, Brandenburg and Königsberg) in Prussia around 1400)   115
6.2 Settlement of the Great Wilderness (until 1507–1519)   119
6.3 Settlement of the Great Wilderness (1540)   123
8.1 Mendicant Friaries in Royal Prussia and in Teutonic Order's Prussia about 1525   185

List of Tables

6.1	Demographic calculation according to the results of the agrarian reform around 1400	124
6.2	Tapiau district in 1539/1540	135
9.1	Representation of different dialects among all the Prussian brethren 1310–1351	214
9.2	'Tongues' of the most important members of the Teutonic Order in Prussia 1351–1400	216

List of Abbreviations

Primary Sources (archival):

AGAD, MK = Warszawa. Archiwum Główne Akt Dawnych, Metryka Koronna.
APByd = Bydgoszcz. Archiwum Państwowe w Bydgoszczy
APG = Gdańsk. Archiwum Państwowe w Gdańsku
APT = Toruń. Archiwum Państwowe w Toruniu
BCz., TN = Kraków. Biblioteka Czartoryskich w Krakowie, Teki Naruszewicza.
GStA PK, XX. HA, EM = Berlin. Geheimes Staatsarchiv Preußischer Kulturbesitz, XX. Hauptabteilung, Etats-Ministerium
GStA PK, XX. HA, OBA = Berlin. Geheimes Staatsarchiv Preußischer Kulturbesitz, XX. Hauptabteilung, Ordensbriefarchiv.
GStA PK, XX. HA, OF = Berlin. Geheimes Staatsarchiv Preußischer Kulturbesitz, XX. Hauptabteilung, Ordensfolianten
GStA PK, XX. HA, Ostpr. Fol. = Berlin. Geheimes Staatsarchiv Preußischer Kulturbesitz, XX. Hauptabteilung, Ostpreußische Folianten

Primary Sources (published):

ÄChO = 'Die ältere Chronik von Oliva.' Edited by Theodor Hirsch. In SRP, vol. V, edited by Theodor Hirsch, Max Toeppen, and Ernst Strehlke, 594–624. Leipzig: Hirzel, 1874.
ASP = *Acten der Ständetage Preussens unter der Herrschaft des Deutschen Ordens.* Edited by Max Toeppen. Vol. I, *Die Jahre 1233–1435.* Leipzig: Duncker & Humblot, 1878. Vol. V, *1458–1525*, Leipzig: Duncker & Humblot, 1886.
CDP = *Codex diplomaticus Prussicus. Urkunden Sammlung zur älteren Geschichte Preussens aus dem Königl. Geheimen Archiv zu Königsberg nebst Regesten.* Edited by Johannes Voigt. Vol. I. Königsberg: Verlag der Gebrüder Bornträger, 1836. Vol. II. Königsberg: Verlag der Gebrüder Bornträger, 1842. Vol. III. Königsberg: Verlag der

Gebrüder Bornträger, 1848. Vol. IV. Königsberg: Verlag der Gebrüder Bornträger, 1853. Vol. V. Königsberg: Wilhelm Koch, 1857. Vol. VI. Königsberg: Wilhelm Koch, 1861.

CEVMDL = *Codex epistolaris Vitoldi Magni Ducis Lithuaniae 1376–1430*. Pars I–II. Edited by Antoni Prochaska. Monumenta medii aevi historica res gestas Poloniae illustrantia VI = Wydawnictwa Komisji Historycznej Akademii Umiejętności w Krakowie 23. Cracoviae: Sumptius Academiae Literarum Crac., 1882.

CDW = *Codex diplomaticus Warmiensis oder Regesten und Urkunden zur Geschichte Ermlands*. Vol. I, *Urkunden der Jahre 1231–1340*, Edited by Carl Peter Woelky and Johann M. Saage. MHW I/I. Meinz: Franz Kirchheim, 1860. Vol. II, *Urkunden der Jahre 1341–1375 nebst Nachträgen von 1240–1340*, Edited by Carl Peter Woelky and Johann M. Saage. MHW I/II. Meinz: Franz Kirchheim, 1864. Vol. III, *Urkunden der Jahre 1376–1424 nebst Nachträgen*. Edited by Carl Peter Woelky. MHW I/V. Braunsberg and Leipzig: Eduard Peter, 1874. Vol. IV, *Urkunden der Jahre 1424–35 und Nachträge*. Edited by Victor Röhrich, Franz Lidtke, and Hans Schmauch. MHW I/IX. Braunsberg: Druck der Ermländischen Zeitungs- und Verlagsdruckerei, Selbstverlag des Vereins, 1935.

Dusburg (T) = 'Petri de Dusburg Chronicon terre Prusie.' Edited by Max Toeppen. In SRP, vol. I, edited by Theodor Hirsch, Max Toeppen, and Ernst Strehlke, 3–219. Leipzig: S. Hirzel, 1861.

Dusburg (S/W) = Petri de Dusburg *Chronica Terre Prussie*/Peter von Dusburg, *Chronik des Preußenlandes*, trans. and Edited by Klaus Scholz and Dieter Wojtecki. Ausgewählte Quellen zur deutschen Geschichte des Mittelalters 25. Darmstadt: Wissenschaftliche Buchgesellschaft, 1984.

Dusburg (W) = Petrus de Dusburg: *Chronica terrae Prussiae*. Edited by Jarosław Wenta and Sławomir Wyszomirski, Monumenta Poloniae Historica. Nova Series, vol. XIII. Kraków: Polska Akademia Umiejętności, 2007.

Dusburg (W/W) = Piotr von Dusburga, *Kronika ziemi Pruskiej*. Edited by Jarosław Wenta. Translated by Sławomir Wyszomirski. Toruń: Wydawnictwo Naukowe Uniwersytetu Mikołaja Kopernika, 2011.

FTAP = 'Franciscani Thorunensis Annales Prussici (941–1410).' Edited by Ernst Strehlke. In SRP, vol. III, edited by Theodor Hirsch, Max Toeppen, and Ernst Strehlke, 13–388. Leipzig: Verlag von S. Hirzel, 1866.

Grunau = *Simon Grunau's preussische Chronik*. Edited by Max Perlbach. Vol. I. Leipzig: Verlag Duncker & Humblot, 1876.

Jeroschin = 'Di Kronike von Pruzinlant des Nicolaus von Jeroschin.' Edited by Ernst Strehlke. In SRP, vol. I, edited by Theodor Hirsch, Max Toeppen, and Ernst Strehlke, 291–624. Leipzig: S. Hirzel, 1861.

List of Abbreviations xi

Jeroschin (F) = *The Chronicle of Prussia by Nicolaus von Jeroschin: A History of the Teutonic Knights in Prussia, 1190–1331.* Edited by Mary Fischer. Crusade Texts in Translation 20. London: Routledge, 2016.

LECUB = *Liv-, est- und kurländisches Urkundenbuch nebst Regesten.* Sec. 1, vol. I, *1093–1300*. Edited by Friedrich G. v. Bunge. Reval: Commission bei Kluge und Ströhm, 1853. Sec. 1, vol. II, *1301–1367*. Edited by Friedrich G. v. Bunge. Reval: Commission bei Kluge und Ströhm, 1855. Sec. 1, vol. III, *I. Nachträge zu den zwei ersten Bänden. II. Fortsetzung von 1368–1393*. Edited by Friedrich G. v. Bunge. Reval: Commission bei Kluge und Ströhm, 1857. Sec. 1, vol. IV, *1394–1413*. Edited by Friedrich G. v. Bunge. Reval: Commission bei Kluge und Ströhm, 1859. Sec. 1, vol. V, *1414 – Mai 1423*. Edited by Friedrich G. v. Bunge (Riga: Verlag von Nikolai Kymmel, 1867; Sec. 1, vol. IX, *1436–1443*. Edited by Hermann Hildebrand. Riga/Moskau: Verlag von J. Deubner, 1899.

LRCh = *Livländische Reimchronik mit Anmerkungen, Namenverzeichnis und Glossar.* Edited by Leo Meyer. Paderborn Verlag von Ferdinand Schöningh, 1876.

LWB = 'Die littauischen Wegeberichte.' Edited by Theodor Hirsch. Beilage I to: 'Die Chronik Wigands von Marburg. Originalfragmente, lateinische Übersetzung und sonstige Überreste.' In SRP, vol. II, edited by Theodor Hirsch, Max Toeppen, and Ernst Strehlke, 662–711. Leipzig: Verlag von S. Hirzel, 1863.

MRPS = *Matricularum Regni Poloniae Summaria, excussis codicibus, qui in Chartophylacio Maximo Varsoviensi asservantur.* Edited by Theodorus Wierzbowski. Pars I, *Casimiri regis tempora complectens (1447–1492)*. Varsoviae: Typis Officinae C. Kowalewski, 1905. Pars II, *Iohannis Alberti regis tempora complectens (1492–1501)*. Varsoviae: Typis Officinae C. Kowalewski, 1907. Pars III, *Alexandri regis tempora complectens (1501–1506)*. Varsoviae: Typis Officinae C. Kowalewski, 1908. Pars IV, *Sigismundi I regis tempora complectens (1507–1548)*, vol. 1, *Acta cancellariorum, 1507–1548*. Varsoviae: Typis Officinae C. Kowalewski, 1910. Pars IV, *Sigismundi I regis tempora complectens (1507–1548)*, vol. 2, *Acta vicecancellariorum, 1507–1535*. Varsoviae: Typis Officinae C. Kowalewski, 1912.

MTB = *Das Marienburger Tresslerbuch der Jahre 1399–1409*, ed. Erich Joachim. Königsberg: Verlag von Thomas & Oppermann, 1896.

PommUB = *Pommerlisches Urkundenbuch.* Edited by Max Perlbach. Danzig: Westpreussischen Geschichtsverein, 1882.

Posilge = 'Johanns von Posilge, Officials von Pomesanien Chronik des Landes Preussen (von 1360 an, forgesetzt bis 1419).' Edited by Ernst Strehlke. In SRP, vol. III, edited by Theodor Hirsch, Max Toeppen, and Ernst Strehlke, 13–388. Leipzig: Verlag von S. Hirzel, 1866.

PUB = *Preußisches Urkundenbuch. Politische (allgemeine) Abteilung.* Vol. I, part 1, *1206–1256*. Edited by Rudolph Philippi and Carl P. Woelky. Königsberg: Hartungsche Verlagsdruckerei, 1882. Vol. I, part 2, *1257–1309*. Edited by August Saraphim. Königsberg: Hartungsche Verlagsdruckerei, 1909. Vol. II, *1309–1335*, part 1, *1309–1324*. Edited by Max Hein and Erich Maschke. Königsberg/Pr.: Gräfe und Unzer, 1932. Vol. II, *1309–1335*, part 2, *1325–1335*. Edited by Max Hein and Erich Maschke. Königsberg/Pr.: Gräfe and Unzer, 1939. Vol. III, part 1, *1335–1341*. Edited by. Max Hein. Königsberg/Pr.: Im Kommisionsverlag: Gräfe and Unzer, 1944. Vol. III, part 2, *1342–1345*. Edited by Hans Koeppen. Marburg: N. G. Elwert Verlag, 1958. Vol. III, *Nachträge*. Edited by Hans Koeppen. Marburg: N. G. Elwert Verlag, 1961. Vol. IV, *1346–1351*. Edited by Hans Koeppen. Marburg: N. G. Elwert Verlag, 1960. Vol. IV, *Nachträge*. Edited by Hans Koeppen. Marburg: N. G. Elwert Verlag, 1964. Vol. V, part 1, *1352–1356*. Edited by Klaus Conrad. Marburg: N. G. Elwert Verlag, 1969. Vol. V, part 2, *1357–1361*. Edited by Klaus Conrad. Marburg: N. G. Elwert Verlag, 1975. Vol. VI, part 1, *1362–1366*. Edited by Klaus Conrad. Marburg: N. G. Elwert Verlag, 1975. Vol. VI, part 2, *1367–1371*. Edited by Klaus Conrad. Marburg: N. G. Elwert Verlag, 2000.

Rowell = Rowell Stephen C., 'Smulkos žinios iš XV amžiaus Klaipėdos (apie 1400–1525 m.),' *Acta Historica Universitatis Kleipedensis* 11 (2005) (*Klaipėdos visuomenės ir miesto struktūros*): 47–69.

SHGZCh = *Słownik historyczno-geograficzny ziemi chełmińskiej w średniowieczu*. Prepared by Krystyna Porębska and Maksymilian Grzegorz. Edited by Marian Biskup. Wrocław, Warszawa, Kraków, Gdańsk: Zakład Narodowy im. Ossolińskich – Wydawnictwo, 1971.

SLVA = *Senās Latvijas vēstures avoti*. Part 2. *1238–1256 g*. Edited by Arveds Švābe, Latvijas vēstures avoti II. Rīgā: Latvijas Vēstures institūta apgādiens, 1940.

Türkensteuer = *Die Türkensteuer im Herzogtum Preußen 1540*. Vol. 2, *Memel – Tilsit*. Edited by Hans H. Diehlmann. Sonderschriften des Vereins für Familienforschung in Ost- und Westpreußen e.V. 88/2. Hamburg: Selbstverlag des Vereins für Familienforschung in Ost- und Westpreußen, 2006. Vol. 3, *Ragnit, Insterburg, Georgenburg, Saalau*. Edited by Hans H. Diehlmann. Sonderschriften des Vereins für Familienforschung in Ost- und Westpreußen e.V. 88/3. Hamburg: Selbstverlag des Vereins für Familienforschung in Ost- und Westpreußen, 2008.

UBBC = *Urkundenbuch des Bisthums Culm*. Edited by Carl P. Woelky, Vol. I, *Das Bisthum Culm unter dem deutschen Orden 1243–1466*. Neues Preußisches Urkundenbuch. Westpreussischer Theil 2: Urkunden der Bisthümer, Kirchen und Klöster. Danzig: Commissionsverlag von Theodor Bertling, 1885. Vol. II, *Das Bisthum*

Culm unter Polen 1466–1774. Neues Preußisches Urkundenbuch. Westpreussischer Theil 2: Urkunden der Bisthümer, Kirchen und Klöster. Danzig: Commisionsverlag von Theodor Bertling, 1885.

UBBP = *Urkundenduch zur Geschiche des vormaligen Bisthums Pomesanien*. Edited by Hermann Cramer. Vol. I. Marienwerder: Im Selbstverlag des Historischen Vereins für den Regierungs-Bezirk, Marienwerder, 1884. Vol. III. Marienwerder: Im Selbstverlag des Historischen Vereins für den Regierungs-Bezirk, Marienwerder, 1886.

UBBS = *Urkundenbuch des* Bisthums *Samland*. Edited by Carl P. Woelky and Hans Mendthal, Neuses Preußisches Urkundenbuch. Ostpreußischer Theil. Leipzig: Duncker & Humblot, 1891.

USF = *Urkundenbuch der alten sächsischen Franziskanerprovinzen*. Vol. I, *Die Observantenkustodie Livland und Preußen*. Edited by Leonhard Lemmens. Düsseldorf: Kommissionsverlag von L. Schwann, 1912.

Wigand (Z/K) = Wigand von Marburg. *Cronica nova prutenica*. Edited by Sławomir Zonenberg and Krzysztof Kwiatkowski. Toruń: Towarzystwo Naukowe w Toruniu, 2017.

Book Series, Journals, Reference Works:

APB = *Altpreußische Biographie*
FTNT= Fontes Towarzystwa Naukowego w Toruniu
KMW = *Komunikaty Mazursko-Warmińskie*
MHW = Monumenta Historiae Warmiensis oder Quellensammlung zur Geschichte Ermlands
SRP = *Scriptores rerum Prussicarum. Die Geschichtsquellen der Preussischen Vorzeit bis zum Untergange der Ordensherrschaft*
ZH = *Zapiski Historyczne*

Notes on Contributors

Radosław Biskup, Uniwersytet Mikołaja Kopernika w Toruniu, Poland

Alicja Dobrosielska, Towarzystwo Naukowe Pruthenia, Olsztyn, Poland

Piotr Gotówko, Université de Fribourg/Universität Freiburg, Switzerland

Małgorzata Karczewska, Ośrodek Badań Europy Środkowo-Wschodniej, Białystok, Poland

Maciej Karczewski, Ośrodek Badań Europy Środkowo-Wschodniej, Białystok, Poland

Rafał Kubicki, Uniwersytet Gdański, Gdańsk, Poland

Krzysztof Kwiatkowski, Uniwersytet Mikołaja Kopernika w Toruniu, Poland

Aleksander Pluskowski, University of Reading, United Kingdom

Matthew Frank Stevens, Swansea University, United Kingdom

Sobiesław Szybkowski, Uniwersytet Gdański, Gdańsk, Poland

Grischa Vercamer, Universität Passau, Germany

1 Introduction

Krzysztof Kwiatkowski and Radosław Biskup

The ethnic diversity in Prussia during the late Middle Ages is one of the issues quite frequently noted in scholarly publications, not only from the 19th century but also from the beginning of the 21st.[1] During the 13th century, the land of Baltic Old-Prussians, Scalovians and Yotvingians/Sudovians was initially taken under military control by the Teutonic Order, and in the following decades, a new socio-political entity under the preponderant leadership of the Order was created, which finally split into two parts after a long internal war in the middle of the 15th century. This ended the domination of the Order in the Prussian Land.[2] Questions about ethnicity were asked in various contexts in relation to each of these three sub-periods of the late Middle Ages in Prussia. However, the issue still remains insufficiently researched, evidenced by the fact that so far it has not been the subject of a monograph-length publication.

From the beginning of the formation of modern Prussian historiography at the beginning of the 19th century, which co-founded the academic discipline of 'critical history', a picture emerged of the tripartite nature of the Prussian Land regarding ethnicity during the late Middle Ages. This rested on the basis of systematically investigated historical sources. This triplex picture consisted of newcomers from the German-speaking countries of the Holy Roman Empire (Germ. *Reich*) arriving from the 1230s, especially intensively between the 1280s and 1320/1350s. The second element were the Slavic populations. These people lived from the 8th to 9th centuries in the areas on the right bank of the bend of the Vistula River, where its course transitions from the middle to the lower reaches (the later Culmer Land/Chełmno Land, Germ. Kulmerland, Pol. ziemia chełmińska), and in the eastern areas of the vast land of Pomerania (Pol. Pomorze, Germ. Pommern) located on the left bank of the lower Vistula's reaches. Completing this relatively simple mosaic were the indigenous Balts, whom crusaders and Western settlers had been encountering in the vast areas stretching eastwards from the lower Vistula to the lower and middle reaches of the Nemunas. These people were referred to as Prussians, an exegenic ethnonym, although today it is doubtful if they shared a common identity.[3] To distinguish them from the later inhabitants of the Prussian Land, among whose elites a new Prussian identity was gradually

DOI: 10.4324/9781003502876-1

formed between the 14th and 17th centuries, these Baltic people are consistently referred to in the present volume as (native) Old-Prussians.[4]

Such an established narrative about this ethnic triad in the Prussian Land in the late Middle Ages was perpetuated throughout the entire 19th and the first half of the 20th centuries initially by German-speaking scholars and subsequently by Polish- and Lithuanian-speaking historians. Studies by Christian Krollmann, Bruno Schumacher, Henryk Łowmiański, Karol Górski and Gerard Labuda, among others,[5] can be cited here. This narrative is still present to some extent in the simplified narrative about late medieval Prussia.

This tripartite picture of ethnic affairs in late medieval Prussia was created and then perpetuated in a 'cultural climate' of growing nationalism and cultural chauvinism. The peak point came during the interwar period (1918/1919–1939), although the influence of these cultural currents was present in research until the 1970s–1980s, especially in Polish, Lithuanian and East German historiography. This was partly overlaid after 1945 by dialectic materialism and from it derived paradigm of Marxist historical dialecticism.[6]

Within the framework of these historiographical currents which were heavily ideologized and subordinated to political demands of the times, three detailed images were created which, due to their simplicity of interpretation, even grew into stereotypical *clichés* in the following decades. They can still be encountered in places, although now only on the margins of the main scholarly (and popular scientific) discourse.

Nationalistically minded German (mainly Prussian) scholars promoted a narrative according to which settlers arriving from the 'West' countries were the carriers of civilizational progress and higher, German culture (referred to by the term *Kulturträger*), and this fact alone justified the conquest and violence in building new socio-political structures in Prussia. Hand in hand with such interpretations went their anachronistic understanding of the phenomenon of collective identity, erroneously attributing national identity to the late medieval clergy, nobles, burghers and peasants which, in this case, meant belonging to the German people, supposedly predestined to dominance.

In turn, in the antagonistically-oriented circles of Polish scholars and, in the course of time, also Lithuanian historians, equally nationalistic as their Prussian and German adversaries, presented in their publications the concepts of a far-reaching, and sometimes even almost total, physical elimination of the indigenous Baltic population carried out in the course of the conquest of Prussia by the Teutonic Order. According to these concepts, this process was to take place under the leadership of this religious corporation conceived by these historians as a tool of alleged German expansionism (so-called *Drang nach Osten*), which was equally anachronistically interpreted as a medieval phase of a centuries-old phenomenon going beyond a single historical epoch.

The third narrative, which took on the form of a stereotypical *cliché* over time, was the assumption by Polish researchers of the 'Polishness' of the areas of the later Culmer Land, and, at times, of other areas located on the southern fringes of Prussia. These historians also emphasized the original belonging of Eastern Pomerania to 'Polish statehood' which, in turn, was linked to the attribution to the local Pomeranian Slavic population of the alleged possession of a Polish identity. Again, this was treated anachronistically as a national identification.

All three of these narratives thus imposed interpretations which significantly hindered the undertaking of more objective research removed from ideological dogmatism. At the same time, they perpetuated the above-described image of only three ethnicities that made up the ethnic diversity of late medieval Prussia.

Epistemologically, this picture that emerged was based primarily on the settlement studies.[7] Although the source materials have not been preserved uniformly for all regions of the Prussian Land, due to their relatively large number, they allow for in-depth research. Such studies have been undertaken for several decades and have already yielded a number of significant results.[8] It is still necessary to verify the results of earlier settlement studies of the late 19th and first half of the 20th centuries conducted under the influence of the above-mentioned ideology of nationalism. Moreover, the progressive recognition of sources produced in the late Middle Ages in Prussian towns creates potential for analysis of ethnic issues in various aspects, although problems of interpretation arise quite often.[9] It has not yet been adequately exploited.

Although the 'classical' tripartite picture of the ethnic mosaic of Prussia in the late Middle Ages presented above remains the essential framework,[10] it must be supplemented by a whole series of additional elements that significantly diversify the mosaic. Indeed, because of research undertaken since the 1960s, this picture is gradually being completed and thus the mosaic is more nuanced. To the previously known Dutch settlers of Preußisch Holland (today Pasłęk) in the first half of the 14th century[11] or groups of Ruthenians on the eastern and southeastern edges of Prussia from the last quarter of this century,[12] there have been new findings of Dutch and Zeelanders in the area of Żuławy Wiślane (Germ. Großes Werder),[13] the organized hinterland of English merchants in Gdańsk (former Danzig),[14] or the captive Tatar settlements near Ragnit (today Neman).[15] The study of some issues has been in-depth, such as Mazovian/Masurian settlement in the southeastern regions of Prussia in the second half of the 15th and early 16th centuries,[16] works on Curonians on the Curonian Spit and around Memel (today Klaipėda) during the 15th century,[17] and Lithuanians in the northeastern parts of the country.[18] Urban studies have yielded a varied picture of the immigration of settlers from a non-native-speaking cultural background to some Prussian centres, revealing the presence of Silesian, Westphalian or German Wendish groups there.[19] More recently, the question of the presence of the Jewish population in the Prussian dominion (Germ. *Herrschaft*) of the Teutonic Order has been hotly debated.[20] A number of issues still remain only hinted at, or analyzed only in certain aspects, such as the immigration of the Polish population from Kuyavia and Greater

Poland to Royal Prussia after 1454/1466,[21] or the aforementioned immigration of Lithuanian settlers to the eastern districts of the Prussian Land beginning in the last quarter of the 15th century.[22]

The above thematic studies of ethnicity in the Prussian Land include in its basic form research of the ethnic structure of communities living in a given area. Here, one deals mainly with issues of settlement and place naming (onomastics). Above this base level, the phenomenon of ethnicity encompasses a vast set of other issues, primarily social and anthropological, in addition to religious, legal and economic ones. In this field, historians dealing with late medieval Prussia can also already show some concrete achievements. The 'liberation' from the vapours of nationalist ideology, which has been outlining since the 1960s, has allowed researchers to begin to see not only the mere presence of various ethnicities among the inhabitants of Prussia and to locate in detail the geographical distribution of their settlements in different parts of the country along with perceiving the temporal dynamics of settlement processes. As part of these new research trends, the participation of representatives of various ethnic groups in social life and the process of creating local culture have also begun to be noted.

The most important achievements have been worked up in recent decades by Prussian historiography (still created mainly by German- and Polish-speaking researchers, albeit not exclusively) with regard to the Baltic autochthons. This can be somewhat emblematically called the 'discovery of the Old-Prussians' in late medieval Prussia. From the early 1960s, it slowly began to be noticed that the activity of the Teutonic Order in Prussia as the main ruler and preponderant political factor was not based solely on newcomers primarily of Germanic origins.[23] To this day, it has already been irrefutably demonstrated that numerous indigenous people of local, predominantly Baltic origin, participated in the shaping of a new socio-political reality in Prussia under the ruling leadership of the Order, which began from about the middle of the 13th century. The new local dominions (Germ. *Herrschaften*) of the Order, the Prussian bishops, and their diocesan chapters were multiethnic social and political entities. It was no longer just the mere presence of Baltic autochthons as residents living 'side by side' with these newcomers from the 'West', who were only to be 'silent' witnesses to the building of new power structures and social and cultural institutions by Western settlers. The active participation of the indigenous people in the creation of this 'new world' and 'new country', both in the 13th and subsequent centuries, was recognized and established without any doubt.[24] Only the scope and the various increasingly numerous aspects of this participation were analyzed, as well as its significance for the overall social, economic and cultural changes taking place at that time. Inhabitants of Prussia descended from Old-Prussian ancestors are noted today as active participants in a variety of interactions and appear in multiple social roles. The same 'turn', albeit to a lesser extent, can be applied to the Slavic populations living in the western and southern parts of late medieval Prussia. More and more detailed studies bring further evidence of this active participation of the Pomeranian, Polish and Mazovian communities in the social and cultural life of the Prussian Land.[25]

Nevertheless, it is still probably too early to attempt a comprehensive assessment of the magnitude of the impact that individual ethnicities in particular and the ethnic diversity of Prussia in general had on the social life and cultural phenomena and processes taking place in late medieval Prussia. Further in-depth research is needed bringing more and more material documenting various aspects of the existence of individual ethnic communities in the country.

New research stripped of the old nationalist burdens and other ideological ballasts (e.g. the paradigm of cultural superiority of the Western world conceived as a cultural-civilizational formation based solely on Judeo-Christian and Greco-Roman cultural models) should, at the same time, avoid the tendency to completely reverse the perspective. This would suggest a top-down interpretation of new and old source materials using the categories of cultural 'victim' and cultural 'perpetrator'. Thus, one should consider the validity of the question of whether the social and cultural reality of late medieval Prussia could be studied using the 'postcolonial studies' paradigm fashionable in recent years. After all, contrary to past opinions, late medieval Prussia was not a colonial country. It was a country in which colonizers, i.e. settlers, were present at various times, not only from the West, but also from the South and from the East (and probably also from the North). However, it did not have the character of a colony.[26] The new reality of the Prussian Land was shaped not only by colonizers and their descendants, but also by those whom the newcomers found there. Just as the images of 'brave German colonists' bringing 'high Christian culture' to the local 'primitive pagan Balts' were rightly removed from historiographical debates as incorrect, so too does the image of 'peaceful, sowing, plowing and breeding' Slavs or Balts succumbing to the onslaught of foreign weapons by 'cruel crusaders' and then 'subjected to exploitation by the victors' require revision. It seems that in the case of the ethnic issues of late medieval Prussia, one should rather still prioritize baseline detailed research over attempts at general overviews subordinated to the latest interpretive paradigms. Such detailed research should be based on a thorough analysis of the most extensive source base, especially archival ones, conducted in the context of settlements, toponomastics, anthroponomastics, sociotopography and a long series of other issues concerning the multiple fields of human interactions. Other fields might include the 'production of culture' and the 'social construction of reality'. The question is, of course, whether there will still be scholars willing to continue such baseline research.

In this postulate formulated above, all eight studies presented in this volume fit in. Each of them is devoted to a single aspect of the phenomenon of ethnicity in late medieval Prussia between the first half of the 13th and the first half of the 16th centuries. The first four chapters deal with the issue of Baltic autochthons in the Prussian Land. Their reading quickly makes it clear that despite the numerous studies already made, some of which have been cited above, the number of specific issues related to the population of Baltic origin in Prussia of the Teutonic Order's period and hitherto still insufficiently investigated, sometimes extremely superficially, is still very large.

Matthew F. Stevens conducts an analysis of one of the primary narrative sources produced in late medieval Prussia, the chronicle of Peter von Dusburg. His chapter mines the chronicle information on the ethnic diversity of Prussian towns in the 13th and first half of the 14th centuries. While this is not the first reading of this chronicler's narrative in the context of issues of cultural otherness,[27] his study presents a comprehensive thematization of the presence of native (Baltic and Slavic origins) town dwellers in Dusburg's work.

Corresponding with this chapter is the work of Alicja Dobrosielska who, based on the results of her previous research published in Polish, focuses on the phenomenon of cooperation between two generations of Old-Prussians and the Teutonic Order during the period of the conquest of the country by the Order. She also primarily uses the chronicle of Peter von Dusburg and supplements it with diplomatic material (i.e. documents, Germ. *Handfesten*). Using such source materials, she seeks to capture the continued persistence of the analysed phenomenon in the generations immediately following the end of the conquest era, investigating a number of Balts attested in sources from different regions of the country. In doing so, she draws on Reinhard Wenskus' pioneering research of the 1970s and 1980s, complementing it with further case studies and findings.

Three archaeologists, Aleksander Pluskowski, Maciej Karczewski, and Małgorzata Karczewska, deal with the question of the identity of the Baltic indigenous people, investigating it based on archaeological sources. This is another publication that is the aftermath of their long-term research on the transformation of settlement, in addition to social cultural structures framed in close connection with geo-environmental conditions.[28] The authors focus, in particular, on the phenomenon of the transformation of the identity of the indigenous inhabitants of Prussia, which took place following the 13th-century conquest of the country by the Teutonic Order. They analyse archaeological evidence providing information on the material dimensions of these transformations leading to the gradual cultural assimilation of the indigenous people into the new social and cultural world shaped as a result of the conquest. They show how material culture was used to maintain or blend ethnic identities, while highlighting the gradual Germanization and Polonization of indigenous Old-Prussian communities.

The next chapter by Krzysztof Kwiatkowski deals with the question of the military character of the Curonian settlements in the Memel area, which only came under the rule and administration of the Prussian branch of the Teutonic Order in 1328. Due to the relatively small amount of source material, the author employs a comparative method, juxtaposing the Curonian group settled after 1328 at the Order's castle in Memel with the similar groups of the Scalovians/Schalvians, who were located by the Order's brethren between the late 13th and late 14th centuries in one and then four other defensive settlements near Ragnit. This comparison makes it possible (in a situation where the few surviving written sources yield only circumstantial information) to study the range of military functions that the Curonians performed in the late 14th and early 15th centuries (and probably earlier) in the military structures created by the Teutonic Order in the north-eastern and eastern edges of Prussia. This study is another contribution to the analysis of the active participation of indigenous people in the shaping and maintenance of the military structures of the Order's authority in Prussia.[29]

The Baltic population in Prussia, albeit occurring as newcomers, is devoted to a thorough study by Grischa Vercamer. Referring to Hans and Gertrud Mortensen's unfinished and unpublished pre-World War II research, he presents the question of the influx of Lithuanian-speaking people into the eastern regions of Prussia beginning in the last quarter of the 15th century. He emphasizes the large size of this phenomenon, as a result of which the population in these parts of the country probably doubled within two generations from the turn of the 15th century. He also points out the actions of the local officials of the Order and, after 1525, Prussian dukes who invited Lithuanian settlers, while at the same time keeping administrative control of the new settlement to a minimum. Vercamer's chapter is a classic settlement study which shows the great variety of detailed questions encountered by researchers dealing with ethnic issues. However, based on his extensive experience in settlement research,[30] Vercamer outlines very vividly the problems of interpretative and, consequently, epistemological nature with which historians of settlements in the late Middle Ages and at the beginning of the early modern era are confronted.

The study of Sobiesław Szybkowski takes up the issue of the immigration of Poles and Mazovians to Royal Prussia during the so-called Thirteen Years' War (1454–1466) and in the following decades up to the beginning of the 16th century. He reveals the *milieu* of commanders of the mercenary troops fighting during the war in the service of the King of Poland, who, after the end of the conflict, received Prussian starosties in pledge. The second group receiving similar benefits were representatives of the Polish political elite, especially from the regions adjacent to Prussia, i.e. Kuyavia, Dobrzyń Land and Greater Poland, which are well known to the author.[31] Based on an in-depth analysis of written sources on a number of cases of Polish and Mazovian migrants in Prussia, Szybkowski outlines the mechanisms of this phenomenon. As in many other types of complex social processes of the Middle Ages, or pre-industrial societies more broadly, it turns out that, in the first instance, it was the family, as well as the big family (Germ. *Geschlecht*, Pol. *ród*) and the circle of friends (including comrades-in-arms in the case of the mercenaries) that constituted mainframes on the basis of which the migration process increased its dynamics and assumed increasing intensity.

The issues of coexistence of people belonging to different ethnicities in late medieval Prussia are also analysed by Rafał Kubicki. Based on his own existing research,[32] he deals with the ethnic diversity of monastic communities in mendicant orders and their functioning in a multiethnic social environment. Regarding the second topic, Kubicki presents the pastoral activities carried out both in towns (where the German-speaking population dominated, but the Polish and Old-Prussian populations were also present) and in rural areas (where the dominance of a German-speaking population did not exist). In the first part of the study, he analyses the composition of mendicant convents in Prussia and their relationship to the ethnic structure of the towns and administrative districts within which alms collections for the local monastery were conducted. Kubicki's observations of the presence in the monasteries of monks speaking both medieval German languages, i.e. Middle Upper German and Middle Lower German, which reflected the adaptation of the convents to the real ethnolinguistic situation in the areas where they conducted their preaching activities are noteworthy.

This under-recognized issue of ethnolinguistic differentiation of the German-speaking populations of late medieval Prussia is also addressed in the closing chapter by Piotr Gotówko. The author considers the issue of linguistic (in particular, dialectic) diversity of members of the Teutonic Order arriving in Prussia from the German-speaking countries of the *Reich*. It should be noted that in previous prosopographical research on the Order, the theme of their linguistic diversity has remained absent.[33] So far, the regional differentiation has been analysed which, as Gotówko seems to suggest, was smaller than the dialectological one. He tries to show how substantial significance the different ethnic origins within the German-speaking 'culture circle' had on the course of official careers of individual Order's brethren in Prussia. In contrast to the former nationalist views promoting the existence of a unified 'German nation', Gotówko shows the considerable size and scope of these differences expressed, among other things, in the linguistic field. Of course, in such an outlined research context, questions must arise about the possibility of juxtaposing the place of origin of individuals with the language or dialect they use, and the latter with their ethnic identity. This methodological approach proposed by Gotówko should generate discussion. Nevertheless, one cannot take away from attempts to interpret the phenomenon of linguistic diversity among the German-speaking brethren of the Teutonic Order, as Gotówko made, some potential for creating platforms for further exchange of opinions and views.

The intention of the collection of studies presented here is to focus more closely on several selected aspects of multiethnicity in late medieval Prussia which corresponded to the research interests of the historians and archaeologists invited to participate in the project. The editors of the volume hope that this goal has been satisfactorily achieved. The eight selected studies should bring new insights into medieval societies and settlement collectives in that country lying on the southeastern shores of the Baltic Sea. With its new look at various ethnic and ethnocultural groups, it is hoped that they have the potential to inspire further scholarly discussions on various aspects of ethnic and ethnolinguistic diversity in Prussia and, as a result, to further in-depth understanding of the late medieval history of this country.

Notes

1 *Cf.* e.g. Johannes Voigt, *Geschichte Preussens von den ältesten Zeiten bis zum Untergange der Herrschaft des Deutschen Ordens*, vol. III, *Die Zeit vom Frieden 1248 bis zur Unterwerfung der Preussen 1283* (Königsberg: Gebrüder Bornträger, 1828); vol. VI, *Die Zeit des Hochmeisters Konrad von Jungingen, von 1393 bis 1407. Verfassung des Ordens und des Landes* (Königsberg: Gebrüder Bornträger, 1834); Bruno Schumacher, *Geschichte Ost- und Westpreußens*, Der Göttinger Arbeitskreis 322 (Würzburg: Holzner Verlag, 1977, 6th ed.); Sylvain Gouguenheim, *Les chevaliers teutoniques* (Paris: Tallandier, 2007); Klaus Militzer, *Die Geschichte des Deutschen Ordens*, Kohlhammer-Urban-Taschenbücher 713 (Stuttgart: Kohlhammer, 2012, 2nd ed.).
2 *Cf.* short overview of the history of Prussia in the late Middle Ages by Jürgen Sarnowsky, *Der Deutsche Orden*, Beck'sche Reihe 2428 (München: C.H. Beck, 2007); also Aleksander Pluskowski, *The Archaeology of the Prussian Crusade. Holy War and Colonisation* (London, New York: Routledge, 2022, 2nd ed.).
3 *Cf.* e.g. Jan Powierski, 'Rola Zakonu Krzyżackiego w wiekach XIII–XVI,' in *Stosunki polsko-niemieckie w historiografii*, part I, *Studia z dziejów historiografii polskiej i niemieckiej*, ed. Jerzy Krasuski, Gerard Labuda, and Antoni W. Walczak, Studium Niemcoznawcze Instytutu Zachodniego 25 (Poznań: Instytut Zachodni, 1974), 327–361 (reprinted in *Zakon krzyżacki a Polska w średniowieczu. IV Konferencja Wspólnej Komisji Podręcznikowej PRL–RFN Historyków 16–22 IX 1973 r., Warszawa. V Konferencja Wspólnej Komisji Podręcznikowej PRL–RFN 19–23 IX 1974 r., Toruń*, ed. Marian Biskup, Materiały Konferencji Wspólnej Komisji Podręcznikowej PRL–RFN II (Poznań: Instytut Zachodni, 1987), 53–64); Schumacher, *Geschichte*, 72, 77–78; Christian Krollmann, 'Die Herkunft der deutschen Ansiedler in Preußen,' *Zeitschrift des Westpreußischen Geschichtsvereins* 54 (1912): 1–105; Stanisław Zajączkowski, *Podbój Prus i ich kolonizacja przez Krzyżaków*, Dzieje Prus Wschodnich 1, Prusy Krzyżackie (Toruń: Kasa im. Mianowskiego/Warszawa: Instytut Popierania Nauki, 1935), 34–35, 38.
4 Erich Maschke, 'Preußen. Das Werden eines Deutschen Stammesnamens,' *Ostdeutsche Wissenschaft. Jahrbuch des Ostdeutschen Kulturrates* 2 (1955): 116–156 (reprinted in id., *Domus hospitalis Theutonicorum. Europäische Verbindungslinien der Deutschordensgeschichte. Gesammelte Aufsätze aus den Jahren 1931–1963*, Quellen und Studien zur Geschichte des Deutschen Ordens 10 (Bonn, Godesberg: Wissenschaftliches Archiv, 1970), 158–187); Marian Biskup, 'Etniczno-demograficzne przemiany Prus Krzyżackich w rozwoju osadnictwa w średniowieczu (o tzw. nowym plemieniu Prusaków),' *Kwartalnik Historyczny* 98, no. 2 (1991): 45–67; Janusz Małłek, 'Regionale Identität und die ethnischen und konfessionellen Minderheiten in frühneuzeitlischem Preußen,' in *Nationale, ethnische Minderheiten und regionale Identitäten in Mittelalter und Neuzeit*, ed. Antoni Czacharowski (Toruń: Uniwersytet Mikołaja Kopernika, 1994), 125–135.
5 From overviews *cf.* Christian Krollmann, *Politische Geschichte des Deutschen Ordens in Preußen*, Ostpreußische Landeskunde in Einzeldarstellungen (Königsberg i. Pr.: Gräfe und Unzer, 1932); Karol Górski, *Państwo krzyżackie w Prusach* (Gdańsk, Bydgoszcz: Instytut Bałtycki, 1946); id., *Zakon krzyżacki a powstanie państwa pruskiego* (Wrocław, Warszawa, Kraków, Gdańsk: Zakład Narodowy im. Ossolińskich, 1977, 1st ed.); Gerard Labuda, 'Zwycięstwo ustroju wczesnofeudalnego na Pomorzu Wschodnim (1120–1310),' in *Historia Pomorza*, vol. I, *do roku 1466*, ed. Gerard Labuda, part I (Poznań: Wydawnictwo Poznańskie,

1972, 2nd ed.), 346–580; and publications cited in endnotes 1 and 3; from monographic studies *cf.* e.g. Krollmann, 'Die Herkunft,' 1–105; id., 'Zur Besiedlungs-Geschichte und Nationalitätenmischung in den Komtureien Christburg, Osterode und Elbing,' *Zeitschrift des Westpreußischen Geschichtsvereins* 64 (1923): 3–41; id., 'Die deutsche Besiedlung des Ordenslandes Preussen,' *Prussia. Zeitschrift für Heimatkunde und Heimatschutz* 29 (1931): 250–268; Henryk Łowmiański, *Polityka ludnościowa Zakonu Niemieckiego w Prusach i na Pomorzu* (Gdańsk, Bydgoszcz, Szczecin: Instytut Bałtycki, 1947) (reprinted in id., *Prusy – Litwa – Krzyżacy*, prep. Marceli Kosman, Klasycy Historiografii (Warszawa: Państwowy Instytut Wydawniczy, 1989), 125–178).

6 *Cf.* Wolfgang Wippermann, *Der Ordensstaat als Ideologie. Das Bild des Deutschen Ordens in der deutschen Geschichtsschreibung und Publizistik*, Einzelveröffentlichungen der Historischen Kommission zu Berlin 24 = Publikationen zur Geschichte der Deutsch-Polnischen Beziehungen 2 (Berlin: Colloquium Verlag, 1979); Jörg Hackmann, *Ostpreussen und Westpreussen in deutscher und polnischer Sicht. Landeshistorie als beziehungsgeschichtliches Problem*, Deutsches Historisches Institut in Warschau, Quellen und Studien 3 (Wiesbaden: Otto Harrassowitz, 1996); Marian Biskup, 'Die polnische Geschichtsschreibung zum Deutschen Orden,' in *Zwischen Konfrontation und Kompromiß. Oldenburger Symposium "Interethnische Beziehungen in Ostmitteleuropa als historiographisches Problem der 1930er Jahre"*, ed. Michael Garleff, Schriften des Bundesinstituts für Ostdeutsche Kultur und Geschichte 8 (München: Oldenbourg, 1995), 73–94.

7 *Cf.* e.g. Karl Kasiske, *Die Siedlungstätigkeit des Deutschen Ordens im östlichen Preußen bis zum Jahre 1410*, Einzelschriften der Historischen Kommission für ost- und westpreußische Landesforschung 5 (Königsberg i. Pr.: Gräfe und Unzer, 1934).

8 *Cf.* e.g. Heide Wunder, *Siedlungs- und Bevölkerungsgeschichte der Komturei Christburg 13.–16. Jahrhundert*, Marienburger Ostforschungen 28 (Wiesbaden: Otto Harrasowitz, 1968); Peter Germershausen, *Siedlungsentwicklung der preußischen Ämter Holland, Liebstadt und Mohrungen vom 13. bis zum 17. Jahrhundert*, Wissenschaftliche Beiträge zur Geschichte und Landeskunde Ostmitteleuropas 87 (Marburg/Lahn: J. G. Herder-Institut, 1970).

9 *Cf.* Theodor Penners, *Untersuchungen über die Herkunft der Stadtbewohner im Deutsch-Ordensland Preußen bis in die Zeit um 1400*, Deutschland und der Osten 16 (Leipzig: S. Hirzel, 1942); Hartmut Boockmann, 'Zur ethnischen Struktur der Bevölkerung deutscher Ostseestädte,' in id., *Wege ins Mittelalter. Historische Aufsätze* (München: C.H. Beck, 2000), 123–132.

10 *Cf.* e.g. new publication from the last two decades: Jürgen Sarnowsky, 'Preußen und Rhodos als multiethnische Gesellschaften des 15. Jahrhunderts,' *Beiträge zur Geschichte Westpreußens* 20/21 (2006/2008): 175–187.

11 Theodor Wichert, 'Die Gründung der Stadt Pr. Holland. Kritik und Darstellung,' *Altpreußische Monatsschrift* 36 (1899): 563–586; Robert Helwig, *Die Geschichte der Stadt Pr. Holland*, Wissenschaftliche Beiträge zur Geschichte und Landeskunde Ostmitteleuropas 46 (Marburg/Lahn: J. G. Herder-Institut, 1961, 2nd ed.).

12 Hans & Gertrud Mortensen, *Die Besiedlung des nordöstlichen Ostpreussens bis zum Beginn des 17 Jahrhundert*, part II, *Die Wildnis im östlichen Preußen, ihr Zustand um 1400 und ihre frühere Besiedlung*, Deutschland und der Osten 8 (Leipzig: Verlag von S. Hirzel, 1938).

13 Wiesław Długokęcki, *Osadnictwo na Żuławach w XIII i początkach XIV w.* (Malbork: Muzeum Zamkowe, 1992); id., 'Dzieje miasta Pasłęka w latach 1297–1454,' in *Pasłęk. Z dziejów miasta i okolic 1297–1997*, ed. Józef Włodarski (Pasłęk: Zarząd Miasta i Gminy, 1997), 255–266.

14 Marian Biskup, 'Pod panowaniem krzyżackim – od 1308 r. do 1454 r.,' in *Historia Gdańska*, vol. I, *do roku 1454*, ed. Edmund Cieślak (Gdańsk: Wydawnictwo Morskie, 1985, 2nd ed.), 384, 386, 409 and 521–525.
15 Krzysztof Kwiatkowski, 'The Muslim People of Desht-i Qipchaq in Fifteenth-Century Prussia,' in *Fear and Loathing in the North: Jews and Muslims in Medieval Scandinavia and the Baltic Region*, ed. Cordelia Heß and Jonathan Adams (Berlin, Boston: De Gruyter, 2015), 141–170.
16 Grzegorz Białuński, *Osadnictwo regionu Wielkich Jezior Mazurskich od XIV do początków XVIII wieku – starostwo leckie (giżyckie) i ryńskie*, Rozprawy i Materiały Ośrodka Badań Naukowych im. Wojciecha Kętrzyńskiego w Olsztynie 159 (Olsztyn: Ośrodek Badań Naukowych im. Wojciecha Kętrzyńskiego w Olsztynie, 1996); id., *Kolonizacja "Wielkiej Puszczy" (do 1568 roku) – starostwa piskie, ełckie, straduńskie, zelkowskie i węgoborskie (węgorzewskie)*, Rozprawy i Materiały Ośrodka Badań Naukowych im. Wojciecha Kętrzyńskiego w Olsztynie 204 (Olsztyn: Ośrodek Badań Naukowych im. Wojciecha Kętrzyńskiego w Olsztynie, 2002); Janusz Małłek, 'Migracje ludności niemieckiej, polskiej i litewskiej na ziemie pruskie w XIII–XVIII wieku,' KMW 4/242 (2003): 431–441.
17 Dainius Elertas, 'XVI a. visuomenės siluetas šiaurinėje Kuršių nerijos dalyje,' *Res Humanitariae* 15 (2014): 17–67.
18 Arthur Hermann, 'Die Besiedlung Preußisch-Litauens im 15.–16. Jahrhundert in der deutschen und litauischen Historiographie,' *Zeitschrift für Ostforschung* 39, no. 3 (1990): 321–341; Bernhart Jähnig, 'Litauische Einwanderung nach Preußen im 16. Jahrhundert. Ein Bericht zum dritten Band von Hans und Gertrud Mortensen,' in *Zur Siedlungs- und Bevölkerungs- und Kirchengeschichte Preussens*, ed. Udo Arnold, Tagungsberichte der Historischen Kommission für ost- und westpreußische Landesforschung 12 (Lüneburg: Verlag Nordostdeutsches Kulturwerk, 1999), 75–94; Jūratė Kiaupienė, 'Die litauischen Forschungen zu den litauisch-deutschen Beziehungen des 15. bis 19. Jahrhunderts,' in *Deutschland und Litauen. Bestandsaufnahmen und Aufgaben der historischen Forschung*, ed. Norbert Angermann and Joachim Tauber (Lüneburg: Verlag Nordostdeutsches Kulturwerk, 1995), 45–54.
19 Cf. e.g. Tomasz Jasiński, 'Imigracja westfalska do Prus w okresie późnego średniowiecza (XIII–XV wieku),' in *Niemcy – Polska w średniowieczu. Materiały z konferencji naukowej zorganizowanej przez Instytut Historii UAM w dniach 14–16 XI 1983 roku*, ed. Jerzy Strzelczyk (Poznań: Instytut Zachodni, 1986), 105–118 (German version: 'Die westfälische Einwanderung in Preußen im Spätmittelalter,' in *Zur Siedlungs- und Bevölkerungs- und Kirchengeschichte Preussens*, ed. Udo Arnold, Tagungsberichte der Historischen Kommission für ost- und westpreußische Landesforschung 12 (Lüneburg: Verlag Nordostdeutsches Kulturwerk, 1999), 95–110).
20 Cordelia Hess, *The absent Jews: Kurt Forstreuter and the historiography of medieval Prussia* (New York, Oxford: Berghahn Books, 2017).
21 Bartosz Drzewiecki, *Szlachta województwa chełmińskiego w latach 1454–1772. Mobilność społeczna i terytorialna* (Warszawa: DiG, 2014).
22 Cf. endnote 18.
23 Cf. Reinhard Wenskus, 'Die gens Candein. Zur Rolle des prußischen Adels bei der Eroberung und Verwaltung Preußens,' *Zeitschrift für Ostforschung* 10, no. 1 (1961): 84–103 (reprinted in id., *Ausgewählte Aufsätze zum frühen und preußischen Mittelalter. Festgabe zu seinem 70. Geburtstag*, ed. Hans Patze (Sigmaringen: Jan Thorbecke Verlag, 1986), 435–454); id., 'Der deutsche Orden und die nichtdeutsche Bevölkerung des Preußenlandes mit besonderer Berücksichtigung der Siedlung,' in *Die Deutsche Ostsiedlung des Mittelalters als Problem der europäischen Geschichte*, ed. Reinhard Wenskus, Vorträge und Forschungen XVIII

(Sigmaringen: Jan Thorbecke Verlag, 1975), 417–438 (reprinted in id., *Ausgewählte Aufsätze*, 353–374).
24 *Cf.* e.g. Grzegorz Białuński, 'Bando – pleban pasłęcki. Przyczynek do kariery Prusów w państwie zakonu krzyżackiego,' in *Ad fontes. Studia ofiarowane Księdzu Profesorowi Alojzemu Szorcowi w siedemdziesięciolecie urodzin*, ed. Zoja Jaroszewicz-Pieresławcew and Irena Makarczyk (Olsztyn: Pracownia Wydawnicza "ElSet", 2006), 52–59; id., 'Prus Wapel. Przyczynek do udziału Prusów w kolonizacji krzyżackiej,' *Masovia* 13 (2010): 37–42; id., 'Uwagi o karierze Prusów w państwie krzyżackim,' *Studia z Dziejów Średniowiecza* 19 (2015): 15–26; Alicja Dobrosielska, *Opór – oportunizm – współpraca. Prusowie wobec zakonu krzyżackiego w dobie podboju*, Monumenta literaria Prussiae, Seria C: Monografie 7 (Olsztyn: Oficyna Wydawnicza Pruthenia, 2017); ead., 'Uwagi o udziale Jaćwięgów w kolonizacji krzyżackiej,' *Pruthenia* 5 (2010): 113–131; ead., 'Uwagi o współpracy Prusów z zakonem krzyżackim w dobie podboju (1233–1283),' *Rocznik Działdowski* 9 (2014): 81–99.
25 *Cf.* Michał Targowski, *Na prawie polskim i niemieckim. Kształtowanie się ziemskiej własności szlacheckiej na Pomorzu Gdańskim w XIII–XVI wieku*, Szlachta i ziemiaństwo na ziemiach dawnej Rzeczypospolitej (Warszawa: DiG, 2014).
26 *Cf.* Krzysztof Kwiatkowski, 'Zakon niemiecki w późnośredniowiecznych Prusach i jego tamtejsze władztwo – XX-wieczna wizja Karola Górskiego,' *Rocznik Działdowski* 9 (2014): 136–164.
27 *Cf.* Vera I. Matuzova, '"Chronika zemli Prusskoj" Petra iz Dusburg v kul'turno-istoričeskom kontekste,' *Balto-slavânskie issledovaniâ* (1985) [print: 1987]: 102–118; ead., 'Mental Frontiers: Prussians as Seen by Peter von Dusburg,' in *Crusade and Conversion on the Baltic Frontier, 1150–1500*, ed. Alan V. Murray (Abington, New York: Routledge: 2001), 253–259; Edith Feistner, 'Krieg und Kulturkontakt: Zur ‚Ethnologie' der Prussen und Litauer bei Peter von Dusburg und Nikolaus von Jeroschin,' in *Mittelalterliche Kultur und Literatur im Deutschordensstaat in Preussen: Leben und Nachleben*, ed. Jarosław Wenta, Sieglinde Hartmann, and Gisela Vollmann-Profe, Sacra Bella Septentrionalia 1 (Toruń: Wydawnictwo Naukowe UMK, 2008), 529–539; Waldemar Rozynkowski, 'Chrzest pogan w świetle Kroniki Piotra z Dusburga,' in *Teologia i liturgia chrztu od starożytności do czasów nowożytnych*, ed. Andrzej M. Wyrwa and Janusz Górecki (Poznań: Poznańskie Towarzystwo Przyjaciół Nauk, 2015), 313–324.
28 Pluskowski, *The Archaeology*; *Environment, colonization, and the Baltic crusader states: Terra Sacra I*, ed. Aleksander Pluskowski (Turnhout: Brepols, 2019); *Ecologies of crusading, colonization and religious conversion in the medieval Baltic. Terra Sacra II*, ed. Aleksander Pluskowski (Turnhout: Brepols, 2019).
29 *Cf.* Krzysztof Kwiatkowski, *Zakon niemiecki jako "corporatio militaris"*, part I, *Korporacja i krąg przynależących do niej. Kulturowe i społeczne podstawy działalności militarnej zakonu w Prusach (do początku XV wieku)* (Toruń: Wydawnictwo Naukowe Uniwersytetu Mikołaja Kopernika, 2012); id., *Wojska zakonu niemieckiego w Prusach 1230–1525 (korporacja, jej pruskie władztwo, zbrojni, kultura wojny i aktywność militarna)* (with cooperation of Maria Molenda) (Toruń: Wydawnictwo Naukowe Uniwersytetu Mikołaja Kopernika, 2016).
30 *Cf.* Grischa Vercamer, *Siedlungs-, Verwaltungs- und Sozialgeschichte der Komturei Königsberg im Deutschordensland Preußen (13.–16. Jahrhundert)*, Einzelschriften der Historischen Kommission für ost- und westpreußische Landesforschung 29 (Marburg/Lahn: N. G. Elwert Verlag, 2010).
31 *Cf.* e.g. Sobiesław Szybkowski, *Kujawska szlachta urzędnicza w późnym średniowieczu (1370–1501)* (Gdańsk: Wydawnictwo Uniwersytetu Gdańskiego, 2006); id., *Kościeleccy ze Skępego herbu Ogon i ich protoplaści. Studium z*

dziejów późnośredniowiecznej rodziny możnowładczej (Gdańsk: Wydawnictwo Uniwersytetu Gdańskiego, 2018).
32 Cf. e.g. Rafał Kubicki, *Środowisko dominikanów kontraty pruskiej od XIII do połowy XVI w.* (Gdańsk: Wydawnictwo Uniwersytetu Gdańskiego, 2007); id., 'Mendicant Friaries in the Dominion of the Teutonic Order in Prussia and in Royal Prussia after 1466 until the Reformation,' ZH 81, no. 4 (2016): 83–99.
33 Cf. Dieter Wojtecki, *Studien zur Personengeschichte des Deutschen Ordens im 13. Jahrhundert*, Quellen und Studien zur Geschichte des östlichen Europa 3 (Wiesbaden: Franz Steiner Verlag, 1971); Klaus Scholz, *Beiträge zur Personengeschichte des Deutschen Ordens in der ersten Hälfte des 14. Jahrhunderts. Untersuchungen zur Herkunft livländischen und preußischen Deutschordensbrüder* (Münster: Westfälischen Wilhelms-Universität, 1971); Maciej Dorna, *Die Brüder des Deutschen Ordens in Preußen 1228–1309. Eine prosopographische Studie*, transl. Martin Faber (Wien, Köln, Weimar: Böhlau Verlag, 2012).

Secondary Sources

Białuński, Grzegorz. 'Bando – pleban pasłęcki. Przyczynek do kariery Prusów w państwie zakonu krzyżackiego.' In *Ad fontes. Studia ofiarowane Księdzu Profesorowi Alojzemu Szorcowi w siedemdziesięciolecie urodzin*, edited by Zoja Jaroszewicz-Piereslawcew and Irena Makarczyk, 52–59. Olsztyn: Pracownia Wydawnicza "ElSet", 2006.
Białuński, Grzegorz. *Kolonizacja "Wielkiej Puszczy" (do 1568 roku) – starostwa piskie, ełckie, straduńskie, zelkowskie i węgoborskie (węgorzewskie)*. Rozprawy i Materiały Ośrodka Badań Naukowych im. Wojciecha Kętrzyńskiego w Olsztynie 204. Olsztyn: Ośrodek Badań Naukowych im. Wojciecha Kętrzyńskiego w Olsztynie, 2002.
Białuński, Grzegorz. *Osadnictwo regionu Wielkich Jezior Mazurskich od XIV do początków XVIII wieku – starostwo leckie (giżyckie) i ryńskie*. Rozprawy i Materiały Ośrodka Badań Naukowych im. Wojciecha Kętrzyńskiego w Olsztynie 159. Olsztyn: Ośrodek Badań Naukowych im. Wojciecha Kętrzyńskiego w Olsztynie, 1996.
Białuński, Grzegorz. 'Prus Wapel. Przyczynek do udziału Prusów w kolonizacji krzyżackiej.' *Masovia* 13 (2010): 37–42.
Białuński, Grzegorz. 'Uwagi o karierze Prusów w państwie krzyżackim.' *Studia z Dziejów Średniowiecza* 19 (2015): 15–26.
Biskup, Marian. 'Etniczno-demograficzne przemiany Prus Krzyżackich w rozwoju osadnictwa w średniowieczu (o tzw. nowym plemieniu Prusaków).' *Kwartalnik Historyczny* 98, no. 2 (1991): 45–67.
Biskup, Marian. 'Pod panowaniem krzyżackim – od 1308 r. do 1454 r.' In *Historia Gdańska*, vol. I, *do roku 1454*, edited by Edmund Cieślak, 337–627. Gdańsk: Wydawnictwo Morskie, 1985, 2nd edition.
Biskup, Marian. 'Die polnische Geschichtsschreibung zum Deutschen Orden.' In *Zwischen Konfrontation und Kompromiß. Oldenburger Symposium "Interethnische Beziehungen in Ostmitteleuropa als historiographisches Problem der 1930er Jahre"*, edited by Michael Garleff, 73–94. Schriften des Bundesinstituts für Ostdeutsche Kultur und Geschichte 8. München: Oldenbourg, 1995.
Boockmann, Hartmut. 'Zur ethnischen Struktur der Bevölkerung deutscher Ostseestädte.' In id., *Wege ins Mittelalter. Historische Aufsätze*, 123–132. München: C.H. Beck, 2000.
Długokęcki, Wiesław. 'Dzieje miasta Pasłęka w latach 1297–1454.' In *Pasłęk. Z dziejów miasta i okolic 1297–1997*, edited by Józef Włodarski, 255–266. Pasłęk: Zarząd Miasta i Gminy, 1997.

Długokęcki, Wiesław. *Osadnictwo na Żuławach w XIII i początkach XIV w.* Malbork: Muzeum Zamkowe, 1992.
Dobrosielska, Alicja. *Opór – oportunizm – współpraca. Prusowie wobec zakonu krzyżackiego w dobie podboju.* Monumenta literaria Prussiae, Seria C: Monografie 7. Olsztyn: Oficyna Wydawnicza Pruthenia, 2017.
Dobrosielska, Alicja. 'Uwagi o udziale Jaćwięgów w kolonizacji krzyżackiej.' *Pruthenia* 5 (2010): 113–131.
Dobrosielska, Alicja. 'Uwagi o współpracy Prusów z zakonem krzyżackim w dobie podboju (1233–1283).' *Rocznik Działdowski* 9 (2014): 81–99.
Dorna, Maciej. *Die Brüder des Deutschen Ordens in Preußen 1228–1309. Eine prosopographische Studie*, transl. Martin Faber. Wien, Köln, Weimar: Böhlau Verlag, 2012.
Drzewiecki, Bartosz. *Szlachta województwa chełmińskiego w latach 1454–1772. Mobilność społeczna i terytorialna.* Warszawa: DiG, 2014.
Elertas, Dainius. 'XVI a. visuomenės siluetas šiaurinėje Kuršių nerijos dalyje.' *Res Humanitariae* 15 (2014): 17–67.
Feistner, Edith. 'Krieg und Kulturkontakt: Zur ‚Ethnologie' der Prussen und Litauer bei Peter von Dusburg und Nikolaus von Jeroschin.' In *Mittelalterliche Kultur und Literatur im Deutschordensstaat in Preussen: Leben und Nachleben*, edited by Jarosław Wenta, Sieglinde Hartmann, and Gisela Vollmann-Profe, 529–539. Sacra Bella Septentrionalia 1. Toruń: Wydawnictwo Naukowe UMK, 2008.
Germershausen, Peter. *Siedlungsentwicklung der preußischen Ämter Holland, Liebstadt und Mohrungen vom 13. bis zum 17. Jahrhundert.* Wissenschaftliche Beiträge zur Geschichte und Landeskunde Ostmitteleuropas 87. Marburg/Lahn: J. G. Herder-Institut, 1970.
Gouguenheim, Sylvain. *Les chevaliers teutoniques.* Paris: Tallandier, 2007.
Górski, Karol. *Państwo krzyżackie w Prusach.* Gdańsk, Bydgoszcz: Instytut Bałtycki, 1946.
Górski, Karol. *Zakon krzyżacki a powstanie państwa pruskiego.* Wrocław, Warszawa, Kraków, Gdańsk: Zakład Narodowy im. Ossolińskich, 1977, 1st edition.
Hackmann, Jörg. *Ostpreussen und Westpreussen in deutscher und polnischer Sicht. Landeshistorie als beziehungsgeschichtliches Problem.* Deutsches Historisches Institut in Warschau, Quellen und Studien 3. Wiesbaden: Otto Harrassowitz, 1996.
Helwig, Robert. *Die Geschichte der Stadt Pr. Holland.* Wissenschaftliche Beiträge zur Geschichte und Landeskunde Ostmitteleuropas 46. Marburg/Lahn: J. G. Herder-Institut, 1961, 2nd edition.
Hermann, Arthur. 'Die Besiedlung Preußisch-Litauens im 15.–16. Jahrhundert in der deutschen und litauischen Historiographie.' *Zeitschrift für Ostforschung* 39, no. 3 (1990): 321–341.
Hess, Cordelia. *The absent Jews: Kurt Forstreuter and the historiography of medieval Prussia.* New York, Oxford: Berghahn Books, 2017.
Jasiński, Tomasz. 'Imigracja westfalska do Prus w okresie późnego średniowiecza (XIII–XV wieku).' In *Niemcy – Polska w średniowieczu. Materiały z konferencji naukowej zorganizowanej przez Instytut Historii UAM w dniach 14–16 XI 1983 roku*, edited by Jerzy Strzelczyk, 105–118. Poznań: Instytut Zachodni, 1986 (German version: 'Die westfälische Einwanderung in Preußen im Spätmittelalter.' In *Zur Siedlungs- und Bevölkerungs- und Kirchengeschichte Preussens*, edited by Udo Arnold, 95–110. Tagungsberichte der Historischen Kommission für ost- und westpreußische Landesforschung 12. Lüneburg: Verlag Nordostdeutsches Kulturwerk, 1999).
Jähnig, Bernhart. 'Litauische Einwanderung nach Preußen im 16. Jahrhundert. Ein Bericht zum dritten Band von Hans und Gertrud Mortensen.' In *Zur Siedlungs- und Bevölkerungs- und Kirchengeschichte Preussens*, edited by Udo Arnold, 75–94. Tagungsberichte der Historischen Kommission für ost- und

westpreußische Landesforschung 12. Lüneburg: Verlag Nordostdeutsches Kulturwerk, 1999.
Kasiske, Karl. *Die Siedlungstätigkeit des Deutschen Ordens im östlichen Preußen bis zum Jahre 1410.* Einzelschriften der Historischen Kommission für ost- und westpreußische Landesforschung 5. Königsberg i. Pr.: Gräfe und Unzer, 1934.
Kiaupienė, Jūratė. 'Die litauischen Forschungen zu den litauisch-deutschen Beziehungen des 15. bis 19. Jahrhunderts.' In *Deutschland und Litauen. Bestandsaufnahmen und Aufgaben der historischen Forschung*, edited by Norbert Angermann and Joachim Tauber, 45–54. Lüneburg: Verlag Nordostdeutsches Kulturwerk, 1995.
Krollmann, Christian. 'Die deutsche Besiedlung des Ordenslandes Preussen.' *Prussia. Zeitschrift für Heimatskunde und Heimatschutz* 29 (1931): 250–268.
Krollmann, Christian. 'Die Herkunft der deutschen Ansiedler in Preußen.' *Zeitschrift des Westpreußischen Geschichtsvereins* 54 (1912): 1–105.
Krollmann, Christian. *Politische Geschichte des Deutschen Ordens in Preußen.* Ostpreußische Landeskunde in Einzeldarstellungen. Königsberg i. Pr.: Gräfe und Unzer, 1932.
Krollmann, Christian. 'Zur Besiedlungs-Geschichte und Nationalitätenmischung in den Komtureien Christburg, Osterode und Elbing.' *Zeitschrift des Westpreußischen Geschichtsvereins* 64 (1923): 3–41.
Kubicki, Rafał. 'Mendicant Friaries in the Dominion of the Teutonic Order in Prussia and in Royal Prussia after 1466 until the Reformation.' ZH 81, no. 4 (2016): 83–99.
Kubicki, Rafał. *Środowisko dominikanów kontraty pruskiej od XIII do połowy XVI w.* Gdańsk: Wydawnictwo Uniwersytetu Gdańskiego, 2007.
Kwiatkowski, Krzysztof. 'The Muslim People of Desht-i Qipchaq in Fifteenth-Century Prussia.' In *Fear and Loathing in the North: Jews and Muslims in Medieval Scandinavia and the Baltic Region*, edited by Cordelia Heß and Jonathan Adams, 141–170. Berlin, Boston: De Gruyter, 2015.
Kwiatkowski, Krzysztof. *Wojska zakonu niemieckiego w Prusach 1230–1525 (korporacja, jej pruskie władztwo, zbrojni, kultura wojny i aktywność militarna)* (with cooperation of Maria Molenda). Toruń: Wydawnictwo Naukowe Uniwersytetu Mikołaja Kopernika, 2016.
Kwiatkowski, Krzysztof. 'Zakon niemiecki w późnośredniowiecznych Prusach i jego tamtejsze władztwo – XX-wieczna wizja Karola Górskiego.' *Rocznik Działdowski* 9 (2014): 136–164.
Labuda, Gerard. 'Zwycięstwo ustroju wczesnofeudalnego na Pomorzu Wschodnim (1120–1310).' In *Historia Pomorza*, vol. I, *do roku 1466*, edited by Gerard Labuda, part I, 346–580. Poznań: Wydawnictwo Poznańskie, 1972, 2nd edition.
Łowmiański, Henryk. *Polityka ludnościowa Zakonu Niemieckiego w Prusach i na Pomorzu.* Gdańsk, Bydgoszcz, Szczecin: Instytut Bałtycki, 1947 (reprinted in id., *Prusy – Litwa – Krzyżacy*, prep. Marceli Kosman, 125–178. Klasycy Historiografii. Warszawa: Państwowy Instytut Wydawniczy, 1989).
Małłek, Janusz. 'Migracje ludności niemieckiej, polskiej i litewskiej na ziemie pruskie w XIII–XVIII wieku,' KMW 4/242 (2003): 431–441.
Małłek, Janusz. 'Regionale Identität und die ethnischen und konfessionellen Minderheiten in frühneuzeitlischem Preußen.' In *Nationale, ethnische Minderheiten und regionale Identitäten in Mittelalter und Neuzeit*, edited by Antoni Czacharowski, 125–135. Toruń: Uniwersytet Mikołaja Kopernika, 1994.
Maschke, Erich. 'Preußen. Das Werden eines Deutschen Stammesnamens,' *Ostdeutsche Wissenschaft. Jahrbuch des Ostdeutschen Kulturrates* 2 (1955): 116–156 (reprinted in id., *Domus hospitalis Theutonicorum. Europäische Verbindungslinien der Deutschordensgeschichte. Gesammelte Aufsätze aus den Jahren 1931–1963*, 158–187. Quellen und Studien zur Geschichte des Deutschen Ordens 10. Bonn, Godesberg: Wissenschaftliches Archiv, 1970).

Matuzova, Vera I. '"Chronika zemli Prusskoj" Petra iz Dusburg v kul'turno-istoričeskom kontekste.' *Balto-slavânskie issledovaniâ* (1985) [print: 1987]: 102–118.
Matuzova, Vera I. 'Mental Frontiers: Prussians as Seen by Peter von Dusburg.' In *Crusade and Conversion on the Baltic Frontier, 1150–1500*, edited by Alan V. Murray, 253–259. Abington, New York: Routledge, 2001.
Militzer, Klaus. *Die Geschichte des Deutschen Ordens*. Kohlhammer-Urban-Taschenbücher 713. Stuttgart: Kohlhammer, 2012, 2nd edition.
Mortensen, Hans & Gertrud. *Die Besiedlung des nordöstlichen Ostpreussens bis zum Beginn des 17 Jahrhundert*. Part I, *Die preußisch-deutsche Siedlung am Westrand der Großen Wildnis um 1400*. Deutschland und der Osten 7. Leipzig: Verlag von S. Hirzel, 1937. Part II, *Die Wildnis im östlichen Preußen, ihr Zustand um 1400 und ihre frühere Besiedlung*. Deutschland und der Osten 8. Leipzig: Verlag von S. Hirzel, 1938.
Penners, Theodor. *Untersuchungen über die Herkunft der Stadtbewohner im Deutsch-Ordensland Preußen bis in die Zeit um 1400*. Deutschland und der Osten 16. Leipzig: S. Hirzel, 1942.
Perlbach, Max. 'Zur Geschichte des ältesten Großgrundbesitzes im Deutschordenslande Preußen. Dietrich von Dypenow und Dietrich Stange.' *Altpreußische Monatsschrift* 39 (1902): 78–124.
Pluskowski, Aleksander. *The Archaeology of the Prussian Crusade. Holy War and Colonisation*. London, New York: Routledge, 2022, 2nd edition.
Powierski Jan. 'Rola Zakonu Krzyżackiego w wiekach XIII–XVI.' In *Stosunki polsko-niemieckie w historiografii*, part I, *Studia z dziejów historiografii polskiej i niemieckiej*, edited by Jerzy Krasuski, Gerard Labuda, and Antoni W. Walczak, 327–361. Studium Niemcoznawcze Instytutu Zachodniego 25. Poznań: Instytut Zachodni, 1974 (reprinted in *Zakon krzyżacki a Polska w średniowieczu. IV Konferencja Wspólnej Komisji Podręcznikowej PRL–RFN Historyków 16–22 IX 1973 r., Warszawa. V Konferencja Wspólnej Komisji Podręcznikowej PRL–RFN 19–23 IX 1974 r., Toruń*, edited by Marian Biskup, 53–64. Materiały Konferencji Wspólnej Komisji Podręcznikowej PRL–RFN II. Poznań: Instytut Zachodni, 1987).
Rozynkowski, Waldemar. 'Chrzest pogan w świetle Kroniki Piotra z Dusburga.' In *Teologia i liturgia chrztu od starożytności do czasów nowożytnych*, edited by Andrzej M. Wyrwa i Janusz Górecki, 313–324. Poznań: Poznańskie Towarzystwo Przyjaciół Nauk, 2015.
Sarnowsky, Jürgen. *Der Deutsche Orden*. Beck'sche Reihe 2428. München: C.H. Beck, 2007.
Sarnowsky, Jürgen. 'Preußen und Rhodos als multiethnische Gesellschaften des 15. Jahrhunderts.' *Beiträge zur Geschichte Westpreußens* 20/21 (2006/2008): 175–187.
Schumacher, Bruno. *Geschichte Ost- und Westpreußens*. Der Göttinger Arbeitskreis 322. Würzburg: Holzner Verlag, 1977, 6th edition.
Szybkowski, Sobiesław. *Kościeleccy ze Skępego herbu Ogon i ich protoplaści. Studium z dziejów późnośredniowiecznej rodziny możnowładczej*. Gdańsk: Wydawnictwo Uniwersytetu Gdańskiego, 2018.
Szybkowski, Sobiesław. *Kujawska szlachta urzędnicza w późnym średniowieczu (1370–1501)*. Gdańsk: Wydawnictwo Uniwersytetu Gdańskiego, 2006.
Targowski, Michał. *Na prawie polskim i niemieckim. Kształtowanie się ziemskiej własności szlacheckiej na Pomorzu Gdańskim w XIII–XVI wieku. Szlachta i ziemiaństwo na ziemiach dawnej Rzeczypospolitej*. Warszawa: DiG, 2014.
Voigt, Johannes. *Geschichte Preussens von den ältesten Zeiten bis zum Untergange der Herrschaft des Deutschen Ordens*. Vol. III, *Die Zeit vom Frieden 1248 bis zur Unterwerfung der Preussen 1283*. Königsberg: Gebrüder Borntrāger, 1828. Vol. VI, *Die Zeit des Hochmeisters Konrad von Jungingen, von 1393 bis 1407. Verfassung des Ordens und des Landes*. Königsberg: Gebrüder Borntrāger, 1834.

Wenskus, Reinhard. 'Der deutsche Orden und die nichtdeutsche Bevölkerung des Preußenlandes mit besonderer Berücksichtigung der Siedlung.' In *Die Deutsche Ostsiedlung des Mittelalters als Problem der europäischen Geschichte*, edited by Reinhard Wenskus, 417–438. Vorträge und Forschungen XVIII. Sigmaringen: Jan Thorbecke Verlag, 1975 (reprinted in id., *Ausgewählte Aufsätze zum frühen und preußischen Mittelalter. Festgabe zu seinem 70. Geburtstag*, edited by Hans Patze, 353–374. Sigmaringen: Jan Thorbecke Verlag, 1986).

Wenskus, Reinhard. 'Die gens Candein. Zur Rolle des prußischen Adels bei der Eroberung und Verwaltung Preußens.' *Zeitschrift für Ostforschung* 10, no. 1 (1961): 84–103 (reprinted in id., *Ausgewählte Aufsätze zum frühen und preußischen Mittelalter. Festgabe zu seinem 70. Geburtstag*, edited by Hans Patze, 435–454. Sigmaringen: Jan Thorbecke Verlag, 1986).

Wichert, Theodor. 'Die Gründung der Stadt Pr. Holland. Kritik und Darstellung.' *Altpreußische Monatsschrift* 36 (1899): 563–586.

Wippermann, Wolfgang. *Der Ordensstaat als Ideologie. Das Bild des Deutschen Ordens in der deutschen Geschichtsschreibung und Publizistik*. Einzelveröffentlichungen der Historischen Kommission zu Berlin 24 = Publikationen zur Geschichte der Deutsch-Polnischen Beziehungen 2. Berlin: Colloquium Verlag, 1979.

Wojtecki, Dieter. *Studien zur Personengeschichte des Deutschen Ordens im 13. Jahrhundert*. Quellen und Studien zur Geschichte des östlichen Europa 3. Wiesbaden: F. Steiner, 1971.

Wunder, Heide. *Siedlungs- und Bevölkerungsgeschichte der Komturei Christburg 13.–16. Jahrhundert*, Marienburger Ostforschungen 28. Wiesbaden: Otto Harrassowitz, 1968.

Zajączkowski, Stanisław. *Podbój Prus i ich kolonizacja przez Krzyżaków*. Dzieje Prus Wschodnich 1, Prusy Krzyżackie. Toruń: Kasa im. Mianowskiego/Warszawa: Instytut Popierania Nauki, 1935.

2 The *Chronicle of the Prussian Land* as Evidence of Multiethnicity in 13th- and Early 14th-Century Prussian Towns*

Matthew Frank Stevens

This chapter argues that the main narrative source for the Teutonic Order's conquest and settlement of Prussia, the early 14th-century Latin *Chronicon terrae Prussiae* by Peter von Dusburg, which was translated to Middle High German verse and extended by his contemporary Nicolaus von Jeroschin, contains fragmentary but valuable information regarding the presence of non-Germans in the region's early urban settlements.[1] This evidence predates most early municipal records of Prussian towns, which exist in abundance only from the later 14th century and are broadly inconclusive regarding the openness of Prussian towns to non-Germans, leading to extensive debate. Peter and Nicolaus' chronicles typically provide details which are suggestive, rather than conclusive, of the multiethnic character of urban settlements. But when put in the broader context of late medieval northern European colonisation, they provide an unparalleled insight into the varied character of non-German, and particularly Old-Prussian, participation in the first century and more or urban life in Prussia.

The conquest, colonisation and Christianisation of Old-Prussian territories by the Teutonic Order from 1231 onwards, as a renewal and extension of earlier Polish efforts (see below), resulted in the contemporaneous co-existence of overlapping cultural spheres – native-pagan and Germanic-Christian – each comprised its own particular symbolic universe of faith and socio-political order.[2] Thus, Alicja Dobrosielska has recently characterised the progressive reception and integration of native Old-Prussians into the Germanic-Christian sphere over the following century as a "migration to a new world", a migration which was as much mental as physical in nature.[3] At the same time, within the Germanic-Christian cultural sphere, the legal model and social form of the chartered town was introduced into conquered Old-Prussian territories from almost the inception of the Teutonic Order's

---

* The author would like to thank Professor Stephen Rigby (Manchester University) and Dr Gregory Leighton (Muzeum Zamkowe w Malborku/Malbork Castle Museum) for their insightful comments on previous drafts of this chapter, all remaining errors being the author's alone.

DOI: 10.4324/9781003502876-2

crusading activities, with the issue of a foundation charter to the fledgeling communities of Kulm (today Chełmno) and Thorn (today Toruń) in 1233.[4] Urban foundations were not only physical spaces within which selected residents enjoyed specified privileges of self-government and self-regulation but also imported to Prussia the germ of the "cosmopolis", an already venerable concept of, in Keith Lilley's words, "a dualism between the social and spatial ordering of both city and cosmos which defined and reinforced social and spatial boundaries in urban landscapes".[5] That is to say, urbanisation introduced a place within which the physical location of people and structures corresponded to their perceived spiritual and social value, with the powerful/wise and holy at the centre, the honourable merchant townsfolk dwelling around them, and the craftsmen and labourers at its periphery.[6] From the point of view of both the native Old-Prussian and the Polish settler, the chartered town, positioned within the German-Christian sphere and founded implicitly or explicitly (see below) for the habitation of a German, mercantile colonial elite, comprised a world within a world. Navigating urban spaces would have required Old-Prussian incomers and, to a lesser extent Polish settlers, to attain a degree of Germanic-Christian cultural literacy greater than that stemming from their extra-urban experience of conquest and absorption into the surrounding socio-political milieu of the Teutonic Order. Equally, the local social contexts embodied by Old-Prussian and Polish extra-urban populations inevitably influenced the character of early Prussian towns. Thus, historians have long sought to find and to interpret evidence of non-German, and especially native Old-Prussian, interactions with urban environments.

I

Historiographical Context

The historiography of ethnicity in medieval Prussian towns has tended to focus on municipal records, which generally survive in abundance only from the late 14th century onwards. Historians have most often followed one of two main lines of inquiry. First, from the early 20th century onwards, German and Polish scholars focused on the evidence of personal names in municipal records in order to establish the relative proportion of Germanic, Slavic or Old-Prussian inhabitants in towns, particularly those attaining access to civic privileges as burghers.[7] This research tended, explicitly or implicitly, to investigate the degree to which the character of medieval Prussian towns could be associated with modern nation-states. However, from the 1960s, historians have retreated from such nationalist perspectives. And attention has been drawn to the unreliability of personal-name data, which only allow the identification of general trends in urban ethnic composition and typically reflect only the upper strata of urban residents.[8]

The second main line of scholarly inquiry has investigated the social and legal frameworks of the participation of native Old-Prussians in post-conquest society.⁹ Reinhard Wenskus, for example, surveyed the relative freedom of Old-Prussian nobles and free tenants to integrate into landholding and administrative structures as subjects of the Order or of the bishops of Ermland, noting their ability to emigrate to towns such as Christburg (today Dzierzgoń).¹⁰ Exploring urban migration, Guido Kisch's research on town law in medieval Prussia analysed 13th-century town charters and elaborated on previously unappreciated differences between citizens, residents and guests – typically, but not exclusively, termed *cives*, *habitatores/incolae* and *forenses* – accepting that while a few non-Germans probably became citizens, many non-Germans likely fell within the category of "residents".¹¹ Guests were those staying temporarily in the town for trade, worship, entertainment or other reasons.

Citizens, particularly in times of rapid urban expansion, comprised a narrow, privileged stratum at the top of the urban social hierarchy. Kisch speculated that in Prussian towns in general, and in Königsberg (today Kaliningrad) specifically, while the intent of a charter's grantor – the Order or bishops of Ermland – may have been for townspeople principally to comprise Germanic incomers, "It seems that a not inconsiderable part of the population of Königsberg was of Old-Prussian descent, and the German element advanced most slowly in the early days of settlement", pointing to a Henniko Prutenus among witnesses to the 1286 charter of the old town, seemingly a citizen.¹² Kisch also used legal texts to show that among new arrivals to urban foundations who sought to become residents, Old-Prussians had a different legal position from that of Germanic incomers, with the latter often being referred to as pilgrims (*peregrini*) until the later 14th century.¹³ He argued that the "general place of jurisdiction" of Germanic residents and incomers was the town court, where they would have laid legal actions. And the place of jurisdiction of Old-Prussian residents and incomers remained the local court of the Teutonic Order, even after they had permanently migrated from village to town.¹⁴

Old-Prussians straddled the resident-guest distinction, which was at any rate only developing at the end of the 13th century as colonisers from German lands began to arrive in increasing numbers.¹⁵ A so-called 'Prussian paragraph', reserving jurisdiction over lawsuits laid by Old-Prussians to the territorial lord (i.e. the Teutonic Order or bishop of Ermland), appears in town-foundation charters from this time, beginning with those granted to Marienburg (today Malbork) and Königsberg in 1286.¹⁶ Roman Czaja has recently shown that this 'Prussian paragraph' is to be found in more than half of Prussian town charters. Nuancing Kisch's view, he has argued that it typically applied only to Old-Prussians from extra-urban communities visiting the town as "guests", rather than Old-Prussian citizens or residents, and noted that it sometimes expressly excluded those subject to other feudal lords, including the Old-Prussian nobility.¹⁷ He asserts that the paragraph was principally intended to protect the rights of the territorial lord (Germ. *Landesherr*) from municipal encroachment rather than to encourage ethnic exclusivity.[18] Similarly, Hartmut Boockman argued that when legislation limiting the access of guests to municipal law appeared in the late 14th century, it did not explicitly single out Old-Prussians and Slavs, and was principally economic in character rather than ethnically exclusionary in character; that is, it was designed mainly to preserve rural labour supply.[19] However, a lack of explicit discrimination does not obviate the innately discriminatory character of laws enumerating ethnic groups (e.g. distinguishing Old-Prussians from Germans) or creating a predictably disparate impact (e.g. requiring letters of recommendation not readily available to Old-Prussians in order to attain citizenship; see below). Thus, despite the arguments of Kisch and Boockman, as recently as the 1990s some German and Polish historians have maintained that Old-Prussians had no right to settle in towns as legally enfranchised burghers, despite the absence of any explicit prohibition on Old-Prussians becoming urban residents or citizens before 1417 and 1418, respectively.[20]

New Approaches

One cause of this disagreement regarding the relative openness of Prussian towns to non-German and especially Old-Prussian participation in urban life has been historians' failure to distinguish between active and passive discrimination when assessing the evidence, generally that of municipal records. Active discrimination is typically the singling out of a group for disadvantageous treatment, as in the 1417 and 1418 prohibitions on Old-Prussians becoming residents or citizens, noted above.[21] Passive discrimination occurs when no such explicit prohibition exists, and yet individuals within one subculture (e.g. ethnic Germans) discriminate by limiting interaction with and input from other groups (e.g. Old-Prussians, via the 'Prussian paragraph').[22] The intensity of passive discrimination increases as the internal integration of a subculture increases, with the social insulation of subgroups in a pluralistic society providing a "powerful structure that fosters discriminatory behaviour against outgroups".[23]

As Prussian towns, like the Teutonic *Ordensland* itself, became more firmly established and German immigration to Prussia increased from the late 13th century, creating a more insulated German elite – that is, one less dependent on non-German human and material capital –, passive discrimination against non-Germans increased. This was periodically catalysed to become active discrimination by calamity. This could be martial calamity, such as rebellion against Order's rule. For example, when Christburg was re-founded after its destruction in the Second, or "Great", Prussian Uprising of 1260–1274 ethnic restrictions were laid on "(Old-)Prussians not remaining in the said city", suggesting that some had already freely settled there.[24] Or it could be an economic calamity, such as the dislocation experienced in late 15th-century Prussian towns following the 1466 Second Peace of Thorn, when the butchers' and bakers' guilds of Thorn and Kulm forbid Polish membership.²⁵ This reasoning underpins the argument recently made by Roman Czaja and Matthew Frank Stevens, that a common pattern of native-coloniser relations can be seen in the post-conquest towns of both Prussia and Wales.²⁶ In both cases, native (and in Prussia, Polish) urban participation was initially welcomed in fledgeling towns that were in immediate need of human and material capital, but this was followed both by top-down discrimination by territorial lords in the wake of native rebellion and, later, by bottom-up discrimination by ethnically German or English urban populations under economic strain, typically after the mid-14th-century Black Death.

The appearance of the 'Prussian paragraph', even if not actively directed against existing ethnically Old-Prussian urban dwellers, was a fruit of passive discrimination. It was indicative of the emergence of a growing sensitivity by territorial lords and, from the 15th century, by urban elites, to perceived adverse consequences, such as the depletion of rural labour reserves, of Old-Prussian and occasionally even German rural migration to urban communities.²⁷ As demonstrated by the 'Prussian paragraph', by the 14th century the cosmopolis had manifested itself, with the Germanised urban community positioned at its moral and spatial core and the rural, non-German population on or beyond its periphery. This was in some cases true socially, with letters of recommendation from German points of departure allowing German immigrants an expedited entry into the citizen stratum. The facility was all but unavailable to rising non-Germans and yet potentially a prerequisite for burgher rights, as in Thorn Old Town from 1389.²⁸ It could also be true spatially, with aspirational non-German, ethnically mixed and humble-origin migrants potentially needing to make an economically significant spatial journey. This was one from residing in labourer- and craftsmen-dominated suburbs to the merchant-dominated old town if they were to integrate into town's uppermost stratum, as at Elbing (today Elbląg) and Thorn. Janusz Tandecki has characterised the arrival of non-Germans, initially concentrated in town suburbs, as "non-legal immigration" ("nicht legale Immigration") with such migrants seemingly not being on a path towards entry into the town's legal franchise as citizens.²⁹ Thus, it is unsurprising that while some Poles and Old-Prussians did enter the urban sphere as citizens and residents, in doing so they become difficult to distinguish in the historical record from the dominant German-speaking population, or subculture, as, for example, when they adopted German names like Elbing citizen Thomas Westval *Polonus* (the Pole).³⁰

As Klaus Militzer stressed, working to fit in to the dominant German subculture in pursuit of prosperity and adopting aspects of a German identity need not have necessitated eschewing an Old-Prussian or Polish identity.³¹ Nevertheless, the reality of passive discrimination would suggest that Alicja Dobrosielska's interpretation of the integration of the Old-Prussian nobility into the post-conquest landed elite, while innovative in attempting to offer an Old-Prussian perspective, is too optimistic. She has suggested that, in the

13th century, the Teutonic Order sought only the "modernisation of traditional (Old-)Prussian culture" and that at least some of the Old-Prussian nobility found this "quite an attractive direction of change".[32] Non-Germans' experiences doubtless encompassed a mixture of both discriminatory pressures and socio-economic inducements to integrate and assimilate that differed radically across social strata.

A second cause of disagreement regarding the relative openness of Prussian towns to non-German participation in urban life is the paucity of municipal evidence for the first century of rule of the Teutonic Order in Prussia, and a failure to contextualise adequately the evidence we do have within a northern European colonial frame. The paucity of 13th-century municipal evidence has left it open to debate whether the German attitude towards non-German participation in urban life shifted from initial acceptance to eventual intolerance or was simply one of intolerance and exclusion from the start, an attitude which was increasingly articulated in law. As indicated above, Czaja and Stevens have recently made a case for the former, based on a comparison of the Prussian experience with contemporary Welsh evidence.[33] This suggests that the 13th century would have been the period of greatest fluidity between rural and urban habitation for non-Germans in Prussia, before sustained German immigration from the late 13th century insulated the urban German subculture from explicit reliance on non-German human and material capital.[34]

A means by which to overcome the paucity of municipal records in the early period has been demonstrated by Dobrosielska, whose work on the Old-Prussian nobility has comprised a critical rereading of the main narrative sources for the early history of Prussia, Peter von Dusburg's *Chronicon terrae Prussiae* and Nicolaus von Jeroschin's extended translation of it to Middle High German verse. This chapter seeks to arrive at an understanding of the relative openness of Prussian towns to non-German participation by addressing three main issues. First, it expands the range of urban evidence by following Dobrosielska's lead and revisiting von Dusburg and von Jeroschin's narrative texts. Second, it places the evidence for the presence of non-Germans in Prussian towns within a broader context of northern European urban colonisation, looking to near contemporaneous Wales, Ireland and Livonia. Finally, it seeks to take into account the possibility of passive discrimination across the various strata of non-Germans in towns when interpreting evidence of their inclusion and exclusion. This approach is intended to address the openness of early Prussian towns to non-Germans as being more than a binary issue of their presence or absence and instead offers a more gradated view of different non-German experiences.

Employing Dusburg's chronicle, as translated and expanded by Jeroschin, requires us to understand the character of the text. Peter von Dusburg was a priest of the Teutonic Order who was probably writing in Königsberg in the years from 1324 to 1330, finishing his chronicle in 1326 just under a century after the Order's first urban foundations at

Thorn and Kulm.[35] As Rasa Mažeika has shown in her recent re-evaluation of the text, Dusburg's chronicle had three aims.[36] The first was to offer a history of the deeds of famous men, namely the Teutonic Knights and visiting crusaders, whose achievements were to be "memorialised for posterity". Its second aim was to promote the Order beyond and within its lands, perhaps even being intended to provide inspirational and entertaining readings at the meals of the ordinary Teutonic Knights.[37] To enhance this promotional aspect, Grand Master Luther von Braunschweig commissioned his chaplain at Marienburg, Nicolaus von Jeroschin, to produce his German verse translation, which was "more verbose and passionate in tone".[38] The third aim was ideological, namely, in Eric Christiansen's words, "to create and affirm a sense of historical mission", as a contest between good and evil, but also, as stressed by Mažeika, to affirm that the Order's ongoing actions comprised "justifiable warfare" on behalf of the papacy.[39]

The content of the *Chronicon terrae Prussiae* is arranged as a series of episodes relating events, some miraculous, which are placed in a generally chronological order. Beyond extolling the virtues of the Teutonic Order and its knights, the text also fawns over visiting crusaders, is ambivalent towards Poles, and is openly hostile towards native Old-Prussians, apart from when a more sympathetic portrayal of Old-Prussian pagans is useful to the chronicler's immediate narrative or overarching discourse, as when they appear as loyal converts (see below).[40] The Order's urban foundations are rarely mentioned unless they have a role within the volume's central story of martial conflict and achievement, more rarely still dose it mention townspeople. Interpretation of the chronicle as a source for urban history requires us to look past the central narrative so as to interpret the implications of details secondary to it and to examine how its references to non-Germans fit in with its broader laudatory discourse of the Teutonic Order's triumph. In each instance, a consideration of the historical context, both Prussian and more broadly northern European (e.g. Livonia, Wales and Prussia) is essential. Dusburg's chronicle, and Jeroschin's expansion of it, had to be credible within the mental framework of its contemporary audience. It was located within a matrix of common knowledge (e.g. history/legend), received wisdom (e.g. social attitudes, including ethnic stereotypes) and Christian belief (e.g. the intertwined mundane and miraculous) as well as elements that we would now consider "fictional" but which would not have been perceived as such by contemporaries.[41] This framing, together with Dusburg's probable use of older chronicle and documentary sources, means that the content of his chronicle does not necessarily become more factually accurate, as we might see it, when approaching his own time.[42] It does, however, project his own preconceptions back in time. This is discussed in more detail below, in the conclusion, but first it is necessary to set out and to contextualise the evidence provided by Dusburg and Jeroschin of non-German participation in urban life.

II

Poles

Poles both took part in early crusading activities in Culmer Land (Germ. *Kulmerland*) and helped to settle it, especially before the destruction of much of the Old-Prussian population in the Second Prussian Uprising of 1260–1274 which would make way for significant Germanic immigration. Some scant colonisation probably accompanied increasingly organised Polish efforts to subdue and to Christianise southwestern Old-Prussian areas from the mid-12th century.[43] In 1222, Duke Conrad of Mazovia donated 23 castles and 100 villages, in the area that had probably been depopulated by recent Old-Prussian raids, to Christian, the papally appointed leader of the Christian mission in Prussia from 1209 and first bishop of Prussia from 1215.[44] At the time of the initial entrance of the Teutonic Order into *Kulmerland*, in 1231, "this land was largely inhabited by the Slavic Mazovian populations, including Slavic elites".[45] It is within this context of the partial Slavic colonisation of *Kulmerland*, and not that of a raw Prussian wilderness, that Thorn and Kulm, the earliest town foundations of the Teutonic Order, received their location privileges designed to attract German settlers in December 1233.

The clientele of these and other early urban foundations must, for much of the 13th century, have been primarily a mixture of Poles and Old-Prussians prior to the arrival of substantial numbers of German immigrants following the Second Prussian Uprising. Poles would have possessed a cultural frame much closer to the ideological outlook of the new urban cosmopolis being created through German urban colonisation and were probably themselves initial inhabitants of the Order's towns. When Peter von Dusburg writes of the 1234 construction of the town of Marienwerder (today Kwidzyn) (*De edificacione civitatis Insule sancte Marie*), following the conquest of lands immediately north of *Kulmerland*, he begins by emphasising the participation of the burgrave of Magdeburg in the effort. But he indicates that the construction of the town was undertaken by a large number of knights and men-under-arms brought by "many princes" who accompanied the burgrave to Marienwerder, most of whom were from Polish lands, "namely from Poland: Duke Conrad [of Mazovia], [his son Kazimerz] Duke of Kuyavia, Henry [the Bearded] Duke of Krakow and of Wrocław [Prince of Silesia, and his son, Henry the Pious], [...] Duke [Władysław] Odonic of Gniezno [Prince of Greater Poland] and many other noble and important men [...]".[46] Marian Dygo has suggested that the participation of Duke Conrad in this 1233/1234 campaign against the Old-Prussians, ending in the building of Marienwerder, was a shield against the duke's potential complaints that the Teutonic Order had overstepped their agreed authority in *Kulmerland* by founding Thorn and Kulm some months earlier.[47] The men involved in building Marienwerder, and particularly some part of the lesser Polish men-under-arms they would have brought with them, would have expected to have been given a stake in the urban space they helped physically to define, or perhaps redefine from earlier Old-Prussian use, for the inducement of future urban settlement.[48] Martial ability was expected of early urban residents. The so-called 'Kulm law', as articulated in 1233, burdened burgher estates with military service similar to that of German ministerial properties, and townspeople-knights formed a numerically significant and politically influential group.[49]

The grant of urban plots to the conquerors' administrators, prominent soldiers and skilled labourers was common in other spheres of urban colonisation, such as Wales and Ireland, and it is unrealistic that Poles would have been excluded ab initio. In Wales, for example, at the immediate-post-conquest founding of Denbigh ca. 1282, at least a marshal, a steward and three masons were made initial burgesses under town founder and Earl of Lincoln, Henry de Lacy.[50] Likewise, at Ruthin ca. 1282, at least a mason, a "beloved squire" and a serjeant received borough property from town founder and Justiciar of Chester, Reginald de Grey.[51] Irish evidence tends to be indirect but convincing. For example, in 1169, Robert FitzStephen, having subdued Wexford but yet facing Irish armies, is reported by Gerald of Wales to have exhorted his war band of only about 500 mercenaries, mostly from south Wales, by saying "we are come hither, not for the sake of pay or plunder, but indeed by the promise of towns and lands, to be granted to us and our heirs forever".[52] Place-name and tenure data from Kildare and the east of Ireland indicate numerous early settlements named for Welshmen reflecting a "nucleus [...] provided by mercenary soldiers", often with burgage tenure and elements of an urban constitution that served to attract subsequent colonists.[53]

In and around *Kulmerland*, the presence of Polish colonists and the importance of Polish participation to the success of the Teutonic Order's early conquests probably lent permeability to the boundary between urban and rural spheres for Poles. After the founding of Marienwerder, on 19 October 1235, a contract agreed between Duke Konrad and the Teutonic Order required princely Polish knights to surrender their free rural estates in *Kulmerland* and to receive them back from the Order burdened with military service; many did so and, in any case, this would not have affected Poles holding recently created and already-so-burdened urban estates.[54] As William Urban has pointed out, as early as the 1240s Polish knights, "less well known, but more numerous" than German vassals and merchants, "were sent into Kulm by the bishop of Kuyavia to hold fiefs from his lands there, many of these went into the service of the Teutonic Knights".[55] Peter von Dusburg reports an incident during the Second Prussian Uprising that speaks to the commonality of Poles without and within urban settlements. In the midst of a 1263 raid by the Sudovian leader Skomand on the town of Kulmsee (today Chełmża), a traitorous Polish knight called *Ninerik*, following a plan agreed with the rebel leader, was able to ride freely into the town as it was put under siege. Even as the townspeople rushed to defend their walls, he ascended unchallenged to the battlements where he signalled the enemy with two horn blasts, frightening

The Chronicle of the Prussian Land *as Evidence of Multiethnicity* 27

the townspeople, before he was apprehended and later executed as an enemy collaborator.[56] The plausibility of this plan and its near success indicate that Poles were recognisably different to Old-Prussians in appearance and manner, and were welcome to traverse urban space. It is not coincidence that the following entry in Dusburg's episodic *Chronicon terrae Prussiae*, on "the wickedness of the Old-Prussians who could speak German", is a continuation of the theme of inability to tell friend from foe should the enemy dishonestly present himself visually, or in this latter case audibly, as a Christian.[57] In this instance, Heinrich Monte, the rebel Natangian leader who had been raised among the brother-knights, calls out in German to Christians hiding from his forces in woods and swamps, inducing them to show themselves so that they may be captured or killed. The Polish knight's integration into the urban environment parallels Monte's linguistic fluency. Following the revolt, Polish settlement continued to increase as, from the 1270s, later bishops of Kuyavia further encouraged the immigration of Polish settlers who would be required to pay "Peter's pence", a tax levied only on Polish territories.[58] The tide of German immigration would rise rapidly only in the latter part of the century, ultimately eclipsing Polish immigration and resulting in the arrival of an estimated 10,000 to 15,000 colonists by the turn of the 14th century.[59]

Old-Prussians

Best known among the native Old-Prussians who accepted Christian conversion and integrated into the new society created by Teutonic conquest are the Old-Prussian nobles, as recently reassessed by Alicja Dobrosielska.[60] A subset of these took a step further than simply migrating to the post-conquest "new world" of the Teutonic Order's dominion (Germ. *Herrschaft*) and entered into nascent urban spaces. Peter von Dusburg notes, for example, that early in the Second Prussian Uprising there was a "zealous and faithful" Christian Old-Prussian called Girdaw, from a wealthy and respected family, who lived in Barthia and possessed a castle likewise known as *Girdowia*.[61] The area had been pacified by the knights in 1251 and subsequently Girdaw had converted to Christianity, presumably converting the wider household.[62] Subject to repeated attack or siege by his rebellious neighbours, Girdaw chose to burn down his castle and fled to the knight-brothers in Königsberg with all his household and *familia*, with Dusburg reporting that many of his progeny still lived in his day (i.e. the 1320s), going by the name of Rendalia.[63] Königsberg itself, founded after 1255, would be destroyed in the uprising and eventually re-founded by Kulm law in 1286, Girdaw's progeny apparently being present throughout.[64]

Henryk Łowmiański, writing in the early 20th century, characterised Girdaw's move to Königsberg as reflective of a transitory relocation of Old-Prussian nobles to fortified points as commanders in times of war.[65] Yet, Dusburg's indication of the subsequent family name of Girdaw's progeny as a contemporary reference-point intended to lend credibility to his account speaks to a more permanent move, particularly as von Dusburg was writing in Königsberg.⁶⁶ Jeroschin's subsequent embellishment of the story, to the credit of Girdaw and by extension his living progeny, does likewise.⁶⁷

In a similar entry entitled "Concerning the war of the brothers and citizens of Elbing", Dusburg recounts that, during the same Second Prussian Uprising, "some noble Pogesanians [...] [remaining true to the faith] [...] although few [...] leaving their paternal inheritance, came with all of their household and *familia* to the brothers at Elbing, adhering to them".⁶⁸ These "virtuous men", as von Jeroschin calls them may, like Girdaw, have entered the citizen stratum of urban life. Here too von Jeroschin embellishes the episode, adding that "they have since remained loyal and upright supporters of the brothers", presumably in Elbing.⁶⁹

Dusburg similarly blurs the distinction between resident and guest in a series of episodes relating to the 1271 siege of Christburg. In the first, a force of Pogesanians attacked a certain castle situated next to Christburg which was inhabited by faithful Pomesanians (*castrum situm juxta ipsum, in quo fideles Pomesani habitabant*), capturing and killing all those who could not take refuge in the castle (*castrum*) of Christburg itself; von Jeroschin calls this castle "a refuge nearby where Christian Pomesanians usually retreated in times of war".⁷⁰ In the following episode, Dusburg describes how a force of knight-brothers intending to counter Old-Prussian rebels came to the aid of Christburg, and "found the brothers and townspeople there already armed and prepared" (*venerunt fratribus et civibus de Cristburgk jam in armis paratis in auxilium*).⁷¹ Heading off to confront the enemy, this relief force was ambushed near the river Sorge and fled back to Christburg where the pursuing Old-Prussians won three strongholds, "the town, the castle of the Pomesanians and the outer fortifications of the [brothers'] castle".⁷² Jeroschin here describes the Old-Prussian element as "a refuge used by the local peasants".⁷³

This "castle" or "refuge" next to Christburg, as described by Dusburg and Jeroschin, surely served as a suburb of the town containing non-German residents. As stressed by Roman Czaja, 40%–60% of the population of medieval cities comprised local migrants or longer-distance, often higher-status, immigrants.⁷⁴ In a pattern common to medieval European urbanisation, but bearing an extra layer of significance in multiethnic colonised zones (e.g. Prussia, Wales and Ireland), when access to full participatory rights in the spatial core of medieval towns and cities was restricted, unprivileged migrants and immigrants tended to cluster in suburbs. The subsequently filtered physically, legally and socially into town interiors. Such figuratively or literally "extramural" communities sometimes gave rise to additional, legally constituted towns such as New Town Elbing or New Town Thorn, which long-continued to house comparatively lower-status inhabitants than the older urban core. For example, in New Town Elbing, in the 14th century, as much as 65% of residents came from within the Teutonic Order's lands, most commonly from the surrounding Elbing Plateau, and between 5% and 7%

of the population was Slavic or Old-Prussian.[75] Within Elbing certain streets and suburbs contained concentrations of Polish residents, while just beyond the Elbing's municipal area was a so-called 'hackelwerk' community of Slav fishermen obliged to provide certain services to the local Teutonic Order's commander, such as wood chopping and harvesting.[76]

Decades earlier, at the time of the siege of Christburg, when rural German and Slavic immigration was yet nascent there, the residents of the neophyte Christian Pomesanian "castle" or "refuge" next to Christburg would undoubtably have been, at least in part, an urban-migrant community. As recently argued for the better-documented English colonisation of Wales and Ireland, such ethnic enclaves were a typical by-product of externally imposed urbanisation by a privileged minority who dominated the new, legally defined town space.[77] For example, the English urban plantation of Flint, in Wales, constructed from 1277 and granted a charter of liberties in 1284, was in 1294–1295 destroyed by Welsh rebellion, apart from the castle.[78] As the diminished English-immigrant community tried to rebuild in 1296–1297 they petitioned the king to complain that "Welsh villeins have bought land in the town and bake and brew, contrary to their charter and custom".[79] As Militzer noted of poly-ethnicity in later 14th- and 15th-century Prussian and Livonian towns, giving as examples Elbing and Riga, significant numbers of non-German natives acted as servants and menial labourers.[80] To this, one might add that the suburban spaces within which these not-fully-enfranchised people often lived were transitional spaces occupied en route to fuller urban assimilation. Their contribution to town life, as labourers and consumers, was crucial to the success of colonial communities from the beginning even though their motivating aspirations to greater equality and associated prosperity were anathema to the legal and social exclusivity that defined new urban plantations.

This context, and the seemingly contradictory actions of natives it inspired, is essential to understanding another part of Dusburg's story of the 1271 siege of Christburg. The town was reduced to only the stronghold of the brothers, defended by a handful of knights and their servants. Dusburg reports that then a Pomesanian Old-Prussian named Sirenes, who was imprisoned in Christburg castle "on account of offences he had committed", broke free of his shackles so as to take up sword and lance and to stand against the rebel Old-Prussians on the castle drawbridge "fearless like a lion" until the castle gate could be closed.[81] While it impossible to confirm, it is probable that, even if exaggerated, these were the actions of a man with a vested interest in the settlement, perhaps as a resident. Certainly, native people in other colonial contexts could be integrated into the privileged urban community and similarly favoured allegiance to the town over their ethnic group, despite a general context of ethnic discrimination. For example, Madog Crach, a prosperous Welsh resident of the English urban plantation of Harlech, was listed as one of the men defending the castle there in 1295 after the town was sacked in a Welsh uprising.[82] Similarly, in 1408, the Welsh burgess and sometime bailiff of Brecon, Thomas ap David, received praise for organising the recent defence of the borough during the nationwide revolt of Owain Glyndŵr; in 1411 he witnessed the borough's new charter that explicitly banned Welsh burgesses while regarding present burgesses, like Thomas himself, "as English".[83]

Almost immediately after recounting the story of Sirenes, Dusburg's chronicle includes a related episode entitled "About the difficulty of bringing provisions to the castle of Christburg". In this, he recounts that the failure to resupply successfully the besieged castle led to such extreme hunger that the brothers told the "loyal Pomesanians who had stayed with them" to withdraw from the castle least they should die of hunger, without prejudice to their rights and liberties (*jure et libertate*).[84] Some Pomesanians left while others stayed; some of them must have been the same Pomesanians descried earlier as having fled to the brothers from the Pomesanian castle next to Chistburg.[85] Those with defined rights and liberties may have been exclusively rural Old-Prussian nobles but it is probable that some were Old-Prussians who had attained citizen status in Christburg as was associated with military-service obligations under Kulm law, by which the town would be re-established in 1288 with ethnic restrictions laid only on "(Old-)Prussians not remaining in the said city".[86] As earlier indicated, von Dusburg reports that the knight brothers, upon first coming to the aid of Christburg, found the citizens of Christburg "armed and prepared" to fight.[87]

Further down the social hierarchy from citizens and resident artisans were the Old-Prussian servants, beggars and slaves whom Dusburg mentions, and who may well have been counted among the "visitors" identified by Kisch in town law (see above).[88] For example, in 1262, "a certain (Old-)Prussian" in Königsberg predicted that the knight-brothers would defeat the unbaptised Sambian Old-Prussians on St Vincent's day (22 January), earning him public ridicule; he promised that if it did not come true they could strike off his head.[89] The victory, of course, came to pass.

This story only works if the Old-Prussian, described by von Jeroschin as an "old Prussian", is regularly present in Königsberg for rumour and ridicule to spread, and indeed for the promised punishment to be meted out should he be wrong. The existence of this precise "old Prussian" – perhaps a beggar given his implied lack of social standing – is less important than the chronicler's assumption that contemporaries would be familiar with the trope of the old Old-Prussian convert, some years after local conquest, passing his final days in the town.[90] One must keep in mind that Königsberg had been founded on the site of a pre-existing Old-Prussian village, the Order routinely reusing earlier castle and artisan settlements to site urban foundations.[91] Hence, at least some Old-Prussians dwelling in and around urban spaces, especially recent town foundations, were likely to have been locals from the immediate vicinity rather than aspirational migrants.

Old-Prussian, and later Lithuanian, servants or slaves living involuntarily in towns would also have comprised a significant part of the urban community, and they are alluded to by Dusburg. For example, he attributes the sacking of Brandenburg (today Ushakovo) in Prussian *Niederland* around 1270 to an Old-Prussian slave girl (*mulier Pruthena servilis condicionis*) who, in contrast to the Old-Prussian saviour of Christburg, betrayed the castle to native rebels.[92] Slavery, or a state of unfreedom closely approximating it, was commonplace in Prussia at this time, with women and children, as human capital, chief among the spoils of war; slavery would cease only in the 15th century.[93] As Anti Selart has discussed, within the neighbouring Scandinavian world "the majority of slaves served in the domestic sphere, and on agricultural estates they toiled alongside tenants and hired workers", with the situation in Prussia and Livonia being much the same.[94]

Direct evidence of slavery in early Prussian towns is generally lacking, but the fragmentary evidence of slavery in the towns of the Order's Livonian territories, as identified by Selart, is suggestive. "Thirteenth-century Riga town law mentions that a child of a free man and a slave is free, but the mother remains in slavery", meaning the situation was sufficiently common to warrant regulation.[95] At Reval (today Tallinn) "townspeople bought thralls [i.e. slaves], as in 1370 [...] when a citizen of Reval bought a woman of heathen descent in Narva".[96]

Dusburg's *Chronicon terrae Prussiae* mentions the capture of Old-Prussians or Lithuanians following Christian victories more than thirty times, such references typically being phrased similar to "having killed countless men, they devastated the land by fire and plunder and led off the women and children as captives".[97] While some captives were ransomed, many were sold by the Teutonic Order or its allies to German colonists or native Old-Prussians, or even to Ruthenians, Lithuanians or Samogitians, with at least a smattering of captives taken to Western Europe.[98] Selart cautions that, in line with contemporary Christian and missionary thinking, "slavery" in the Baltic was perhaps not a permanent condition.[99] But whatever the exact extent of the unfreedom of Dusburg's oft-mentioned captive women and children, some of these displaced people must have ended up in Prussian towns. Immigrants in the Middle Ages, as so often in the modern period, tended predominately to be single men, that is, men in need of wives, a reality that calls to mind Riga's early regulation that the children of free men and "slave" women should be free.

The relationships that may have existed between slavery – or close approximations to it – conversion, marriage and sexual activity are murky in the 13th century. By way of context, the 1249 Treaty of Christburg between the Order and the neophyte Christian Old-Prussian nobility, at least some of whom found their way into new towns (see above), banned the selling of daughters into marriage, along with the buying of a wife for one's self or one's son, and the inheriting of a father's wife by his son.[100] The regulation about the buying and selling of wives, which is referred to by the Order as "a custom that we understand to have arisen among them" (i.e. the Old-Prussians; *talis inter ipsos consuetudo, sicut intelleximus, inolevit*), is followed immediately by a statement that henceforth only the issue of marriages in accordance with Canon law were to be considered legitimate heirs.[101] At the same time, with respect to all Christians, the pope had declared that conversion entitled slaves to attend church and to receive the sacraments, but not to manumission.[102] As acknowledged by Riga's law, potentially ambiguous scenarios arose among Germans and non-Germans alike involving variously the purchase, conversion, manumission and marriage of non-German women. Church law unequivocally allowed for one's path from slave to wife, so long as there was consent, while in the Levant, Frankish crusaders' concubinage and marriage with local women is well attested.[103]

Of tantamount importance to the Church was not the ethnic purity of the offspring of colonists, but rather the perpetuation of the Christian community, even should the typical gender-imbalance in favour of men among crusaders and colonists be reversed. This is highlighted by von Dusburg in an episode relating to early Kulm, predating even the 1249 Treaty of Christburg's attempt to bring neophyte Old-Prussian nobles in the fold of the Order. The first part of this episode takes place in 1244, after the disastrous Battle near Lake Rensen in which the fighting-age men of Kulm were nearly wiped out. "When the bishop of Kulm saw that the town was desolate of men, for all had been slain in the conflict, he enjoined the widows, for the remission of all their sins, to marry their manservants (*famulus suos*) lest the continuation of the faith there be imperilled".[104] The need to invoke the remission of sins suggests that these manservants would, in normal times, have been seen as undesirable marriage partners; the implication being that the widows would be making a sacrifice on a par with crusaders, who had received the remission of sins for their activities in the Baltic since 1147.[105] The widows' manservants may have been lower-status Germans or Poles, but, in the context of the townsmen's demise, they were likely most often neophyte Old-Prussians. The contention that servants in early Prussian towns were often native Old-Prussians is supported not only by Militzer's observation from municipal records that this was the case by the later 14th century (see above), but also by the broader context of contemporary northern-European colonisation.[106] For example, in the English colonial foundations of Wales and Ireland, native Welsh and Irish were well or even disproportionately represented among servants.[107]

The second part of the episode describes how two women on the way to church each spotted a handsome but ragged servant (*famulus*) in the marketplace playing dice among others (*inter alios*). The first tells her maid to take the servant to her house. The second, hearing this, more speedily sends her maid to fetch the servant to her own house where he is finely dressed and immediately contracted in marriage to the second woman. This leads to a rift between the women. The anecdote ends by pointing out that the servant was a German born in Halle, and would prove unequalled in "honesty", "wisdom" and "virtue" (*honestas*, *sapientia* and *virtus*). Nicolaus von Jeroschin's translation of this episode contains embellishments. The most important are the details that the servant in questions was a young man, or "boy" (Germ. *Knabe*), and that he had been playing dice among a group of "peasants" (*in der bûvin schar*), perhaps Old-Prussians.[108]

The blunt discourse of the overall episode, perhaps told with humorous intent, is that of two widows each desperately working to avoid the negative fate of marrying their manservant by conniving to wed a handsome young German boy. The boy's explicit identification as a German and the emphasis placed on his honest virtue, in context, imply an interethnic discourse. This contrasts "virtue", expounded by Dusburg at the start of his chronicle as chief among the crusaders' weapons (both offensive and defensive), and the recurrent theme of the treachery of non-Germans. Here, the contrast alludes to treachery as orchestraited in the chronicle's preceeding episodes by Duke Świętopełk of Pomerelia, who stirred many Old-Prussians to rebellion against the Christians, causing the death of Kulm's menfolk.[109] In a town bereft fitting – that is German – marriage partners, the ragged boy from Halle was suddenly an object of desire.

Conclusion

Both Peter von Dusburg's *Chronicon terrae Prussiae* and Nicolaus von Jeroschin's expansion of it unquestionably provide evidence of Polish and Old-Prussian participation in urban life in Prussia from its very inception. The episodes examined here do not comprise a comprehensive survey of direct or oblique references to non-Germans in urban settings, but rather are those most indicative of resident non-Germans. The evidence is not unproblematic. It must be read in the comparative context of urban colonisation elsewhere in northern Europe and through the lens of Dusburg's and Jeroschin's own early 14th-century sense of what made a credible story, something shaped by interethnic discourse. This latter point is important when considering descriptions of early or mid-13th-century events that transpired before significant German immigration and an improved security situation sufficiently insulated the dominant German subculture so as to allow widespread passive discrimination. For example, would Nicolaus von Jeroschin's embellished tale of Kulm's two widows competing in desperation for a German mate – who coincidentally was of exceptionally honest character – and feuding thereafter have been perceived in the same way by an earlier audience? Perhaps earlier versions of this story focused more on the humorous feud than the ethnic identity and character of the boy. By the time of the chronicle's composition the 'Prussian paragraph', surely an indicator of passive, if not active, discrimination, had for decades been included in at least half of town charters.

Fortunately, the validity of the argument set out here is not dependent upon whether or not the interpretation of all of the episodes cited above is convincing. Rather, it is dependent upon whether or not enough of them are convincing to warrant the conclusion that Prussian towns were indeed initially open to non-German participation in urban life. Indeed, it is not even a question of the existence of specific Poles or Germans cited in Dusburg's episodes. The key issue is rather the credibility of those characters' presence and actions in urban environs to a 14th-century audience, despite that audience's potential familiarity with the subsequent restrictions laid on non-German participation in urban life. If the episodes related were credible in the 14th century, might not an even greater diversity of non-German participation have been possible in the early or mid-13th century?

Further, if one admits that the *Chronicon terrae Prussiae* demonstrates an openness to non-German participation in early Prussian towns, it also demonstrates a necessity to move beyond a binary view of towns as open or closed to non-Germans, much as Militzer advocated a need to cease thinking of identity in binary German versus non-German terms.[110] As shown by Dusburg, Old-Prussians probably existed in early Prussian towns in social positions ranging from those of citizens to domestic servants or even slaves. This was a continuum not wholly incomparable to that later to encompass the extremes both of prosperous free Native Americans or Black people, and of slaves, on the streets of early modern towns in the Americas.[111] Just as Alicja Dobrosielska has employed Dusburg's chronicle to move forward discussion of native Old-Prussians' experiences of the conquest and reorganisation of rural Prussia, the evidence set out here moves forward discussion of non-Germans during the first century of urban life in Prussia.[112]

Notes

1 Dusburg (T), 21–219; Jeroschin, 303–624; Jeroshin has been translated into English; see Jeroschin (F).
2 Alicja Dobrosielska, *Opór – oportunizm – współpraca. Prusowie wobec zakonu krzyżackiego w dobie podboju* (Olsztyn: Oficyna Wydawnicza Pruthenia, 2017), 152.
3 Dobrosielska, *Opór*, 152.
4 *Przywileje lokacyjne Torunia*, ed. Karola Ciesielska (Toruń: Towarzystwo Miłośników Torunia/Towarzystwo Naukowe Organizacji i Kierownictwa "Dom Organizatora", 2008).
5 Keith Lilley, 'Mapping cosmopolis: moral topographies of the medieval city,' *Environment and Planning D: Society and Space* 22 (2004): 681.
6 Lilley, 'Mapping cosmopolis,' 685.
7 For a summary of research on this theme before the mid-1950s, see Erich Keyser, 'Die Herkunft der städtischen Bevölkerung des Preußenlandes im Mittelalter,' *Zeitschrift für Ostforschung* 6, no. 4 (1957): 539–557.
8 Krzysztof Mikulski, 'Struktura etniczna mieszkańców i status społeczny ludności pochodzenia polskiego w Toruniu od końca XIV do połowy XVII wieku,' *Roczniki Historyczne* 63 (1997): 119–121; Tomasz Jasiński, *Przedmieścia średniowiecznego Torunia i Chełmna* (Poznań: Uniwersytet im. Adama Mickiewicza, 1982), 70–77; Dieter Heckmann, 'Zuwanderung und Integrationsprobleme in Königsberg in Mittelalter und früher Neuzeit,' in *Probleme der Migration und Integration im Preußenland vom Mittelalter bis zum Anfang des 20. Jahrhunderts*, ed. Klaus Militzer (Marburg: N.G. Elwert Verlag, 2005), 78–84.

9   For example, on Christburg, see Heide Wunder, *Siedlungs- und Bevölkerungsgeschichte der Komturei Christburg (13.–16. Jahrhunderts)*, Marburger Ostforschungen 28 (Wiesbaden: Otto Harrassowitz, 1968), 77–88, 245–252.
10 Reinhard Wenskus, 'The Teutonic Order and the non-German population of Prussia (with particular reference to the settlement process),' in *The North-East Frontiers of Medieval Europe: The expansion of Latin Christendom in the Baltic Lands*, ed. Alan V. Murray (Farnham: Ashgate, 2014), 309–318 (towns at 317–318).
11 Guido Kisch, *Studien zur Rechts- und Sozialgeschichte des Deutschordenslandes* (Sigmaringen: Jan Thorbecke Verlag, 1973), 19–86.
12 Kisch, 45–52, quote at 45.
13 Kisch, 46–52 (Old-Prussians), 53–63, 74–75 *(peregrini)*.
14 Kisch, 51–52, 73–74.
15 Kisch, *Studien*, 68; Marian Biskup, 'Das Problem der ethnischen Zugehörigkeit im mittelalterlichen Landesausbau in Preussen,' *Jahrbuch für die Geschichte Mittel- und Ostdeutschlands* 40 (1991): 9–10.
16 The paragraph varies greatly, but the 1286 Königsberg example reads as follows: *Volumus siquidem statuentes, ut si Prutheni vel Sambite nostri homines seu cuiuscumque condicionis de familia nostre domus ex quacumque causa se in prefata civitate mutuo offenderint, vulneraverint aut occiderint vel quicquam aliud iudicio dignum commiserint, a nemine quam a nostris fratribus debeat iudicari. Si autem Pruthenus aut Sambita seu cuinscumque condicionis homo de nostra familia aliquem civem vel quempiam Theuthonicum in predicta civitate occiderit, vulneraverit, percusserit aut verbis offenderit, talis offensa sive excessus iudicetur per predicte iudicem civitatis, cf.* PUB, I/2: 309 no. 483.
17 Roman Czaja and Matthew Frank Stevens, 'The place of native populations in the chartered towns of conquered regions: Wales and Prussia as a comparative case study,' in *Towns on the Edge in Medieval Europe: The Social and Political Order of Peripheral Urban Communities from the Twelfth to Sixteenth Centuries*, eds. Matthew Frank Stevens and Roman Czaja (Oxford: Oxford University Press, 2022), 34–37.
18 Czaja and Stevens, 37.
19 Hartmut Boockman, 'Zur ethnischen Struktur der Bevölkerung deutscher Ostseestädte,' in *Der Ostseeraum – historische Elemente einer wirtschaftlichen Gemeinschaft*, ed. Klaus Friedland (Lübeck: Industrie und Handelskammer, 1980), 17–28.
20 Peter Erlen, *Europäischer Landesausbau und mittelalterliche deutsche Ostsiedlung. Ein struktureller Vergleich zwischen Südwestfrankreich, den Niederlanden und dem Ordensland Preussen* (Marburg: J. H. Herder-Institut, 1992), 172; Alojzy Szorc, *Dominium Warmińskie 1243–1772* (Olsztyn: Wydawnictwo Pojezierze, 1990), 276.
21 This applied to Old-Prussian subjects of the Teutonic Order, *cf.* ASP, I: 309, 317.
22 Harry Kitano, 'Passive discrimination: the normal person,' *The Journal of Social Psychology* 70 (1966): 23.
23 Kitano, 23 (quote), 30–31.
24 Wunder, *Siedlungs-*, 62, no. 283: *Verumtamen Pruteni in prefata civitate non manentes nostris iudiciis in suis causis quibuscumque sint astricti.*
25 Czaja and Stevens, 'The place of native populations, 43.
26 Czaja and Stevens, 21–45.
27 Czaja and Stevens, 37, 41–43.
28 Janusz Tandecki, 'Probleme der Migration und der Integration der Nurbürger in Thorn im Mittelalter und in der frühen Neuzeit,' in *Probleme der Migration und Integration im Preussenland vom Mittelalter bis zum Anfang des 20. Jahrhunderts*, ed. Klaus Militzer (Marburg: N. G. Elwert Verlag, 2005), 60–61; Roman

Czaja, 'Migration und Integration in die Stadt Elbing in Mittelalter und in der frühen Neuzeit,' in *Probleme*, ed. Militzer, 43–44.
29 Tandecki, 'Probleme der Migration,' 60 (Thorn); Czaja, 'Migration und Integration,' 45–48 (Elbing: Slavs in the *Hackelwerk* fishing settlement south of the city or the northern suburb near Lastadie).
30 Boockman, 'Zur ethnischen Struktur,' 19.
31 Klaus Militzer, 'Problem der Migration und Integration sozialer Gruppen in Prußenland,' in *Probleme*, ed. Militzer, 33–34; Czaja and Stevens, 'The place of native populations,' 26.
32 Dobrosielska, *Opór*, 153–154. See also Chapter 3 in this volume.
33 Czaja and Stevens, 'The place of native populations,' 21–45.
34 Czaja and Stevens, 30–31.
35 Jarosław Wenta, 'Wstęp,' in Piotr von Dusburga, *Kronika ziemi Pruskiej*, ed. Jarosław Wenta, trans. Sławomir Wyszomirski (Toruń: Wydawnictwo Naukowe Uniwersytetu Mikołaja Kopernika, 2011), xv–xviii.
36 Rasa Mažeika, 'Violent victims? Surprising aspects of the just war theory in the chronicle of Peter von Dusburg,' in *The Clash of Cultures on the Medieval Baltic Frontier*, ed. Alan V. Murray (London: Routledge, 2016), 123–124.
37 The latter, readings aspect is Mažeika's contested assertion ('Violent victims?,' 123–124). The former aspect is broadly accepted; see Arno Mentzel-Reuters, *Arma spiritualia. Bibliotheken, Bücher und Bildung im Deutschen Orden* (Wiesbaden: Harrassowitz Verlag, 2003), 20–26, 75.
38 Eric Christiansen, *The Northern Crusades* (London: Penguin, 1997, 2nd ed.), 224.
39 Christiansen, 225; Mažeika, 'Violent victims?,' 137. For a general survey of von Dusburg's ideology, see Janusz Trupinda, *Ideologia krucjatowa w kronice Piotra z Dusburga* (Gdańsk: Officina Ferberiana, 1999).
40 Mažeika, 'Violent victims?,' 124 footnote 7 (a review of the main historiography).
41 See Monika Otter, 'Functions of fiction in historical writing,' in *Writing Medieval History: Theory and Practice for the Post-Traditional Middle Ages*, ed. Nancy Partner (London: Bloomsbury Academic, 2005), 109–130.
42 Wenta, 'Wstęp,' xxiii–xxv.
43 László Pósán, 'Prussian missions and the invitation of the Teutonic Order into Kulmerland,' in *The Crusades and the Military Orders: Expanding the Frontiers of Medieval Latin Christianity*, eds. Zsolt Hunyadi and József Laszlovszky (Budapest: Central European University, 2001), 429–436.
44 Pósán, 434; *Przywileje lokacyjne*, 76 ("23 castles, 100 villages, the estates of the former voivod, the duke's villages and forests near Gruta, villages of Czarnowo and Papowo, which belonged to the bishop of Płock").
45 Krzysztof Kwiatkowski, 'The relations of the Teutonic Order in Prussia with the local nobility in the 13th-early 16th century. Scope of issues, research state and research perspectives,' in *Noblesses et ordres militaires. Réseaux, familles, pouvoirs*, eds. Anne Brogini and Germain Butaud, Cahiers de la Méditerranée 104 (Nice: Institut des Sciences Humaines et Sociales du CNRS, 2022), 121.
46 Dusburg (T), 57–58 (quotation); Jeroschin, 354–355 (transl.: Jeroschin (F), 75–76); Marian Dygo, 'Początki i budowa władztwa zakonu krzyżackiego (1226–1309),' in *Państwo zakonu krzyżackiego w Prusach. Władza i społeczeństwo*, eds. Marian Biskup and Roman Czaja (Warszawa: Wydawnictwo Naukowe PWN, 2008), 65.
47 Dygo, 'Początki,' 75.
48 Aleksander Pluskowski, *The Archaeology of the Prussian Crusade: Holy War and Colonisation* (Routledge: Abingdon, 2013), 121.
49 Dygo, 'Początki,' 76 ("Znaczącą liczebnie i wpływową politycznie grupę stanowili mieszczanie-rycerze.").
50 D. Huw Owen, *The Lordship of Denbigh, 1282–1543* (Cardiff: University of Wales Press, 2024), chapter 7.

51 Andrew D. M. Barrell and Michael H. Brown, 'A settler community in post-conquest rural Wales: the English of Dyffryn Clwyd, 1294–1399,' *Welsh History Review* 17 (1995): 336–337; Robert Ian Jack, 'Records of Denbighshire lordships: II. – the lordship of Dyffryn Clwyd in 1324,' *Denbighshire Historical Society Transactions* 17 (1968): 13, 15.
52 *Geraldus Cambrensis: The Conquest of Ireland*, eds. and trans., Thomas Forester and Thomas Wright (Cambridge, Ontario: In Parentheses Publications, 2001), 20.
53 Annette Jocelyn Otway-Ruthven, 'The Character of Norman settlement in Ireland,' in *Historical Studies*, vol. 5, ed. J. L. McCracken (London: Bowes & Bowes, 1965): 79; William Sherlock, 'The original Anglo-Norman settlers in County Kildare,' *Kildare Archaeological Society Journal* 3 (1899–1902): 290–299.
54 Dygo, 'Początki,' 76.
55 William Urban, *The Prussian Crusade* (Chicago: Lithuanian Research and Studies Center, 2000, 2nd ed.), 156.
56 Dusburg (T), 128; Jeroschin, 475–476 (transl.: Jeroschin (F), 174–175).
57 Dusburg (T), 128–129; Jeroschin, 476 (transl.: Jeroschin (F), 175).
58 Urban, *The Prussian Crusade*, 118.
59 Pluskowski, *The Archaeology*, 104 (here citing Danielle Buschinger and Mathieu Olivier, *Les Chevaliers Teutoniques* (Paris: Ellipsis, 2007), 131).
60 Dobrosielska, *Opór*, 149–195.
61 Dusburg (T), 109; Jeroschin, 442–443 (transl.: Jeroschin (F), 147).
62 Gottfried Trampenau, 'Geschichte der Burg Gerdauen,' in *Der Kreis Gerdauen. Ein ostpreußischen Heimatbuch*, ed. Oskar-Wilhelm Bachor (Würzburg: Holzner Verlag, 1968), 79–82.
63 Dusburg (T), 109; Jeroschin, 443 (transl.: Jaroschin (F), 147). Gerdauen subsequently became the property of the Order, which constructed there a stone castle in the 14th century, around which a town subsequently grew.
64 Roman Czaja, 'Towns and Urban Space in the State of the Teutonic Order in Prussia,' in *The Teutonic Order in Prussia and Livonia. The political and ecclesiastical structures, 13th–16th Century*, eds. Roman Czaja and Andrxej Radzimiński (Toruń: Towarzystwo Naukowe w Toruniu/Köln, Weimar, Wien: Böhlau Verlag, 2015, 2015), 80.
65 "Pruscy nobiles, przebywający w grodach z powodu okoliczności wojennych w charakterze dowódców, „kasztelanów""‚ *cf.* Henryk Łowmiański, *Studja nad początkami społeczeństwa i państwa litewskiego*, vol. 2 (Wilno: Towarzystwo Przyjaciół Nauk w Wilnie, 1932), 217.
66 Dusburg (T), 109; Wenta, 'Wstęp,' xv–xviii.
67 Jeroschin, 443 (transl.: Jeroschin (F), 147). The most recent academic edition of Dusburg notes that neither Girdaw nor the Rendalia family have been identified in other contemporary documents, but this is unremarkable given the paucity of sources, *cf.* Dusburg (W/W), 113.
68 Dusburg (T), 129; Jeroschin, 476 (transl.: Jeroschin (F), 175).
69 Jeroschin, 476 (transl.: Jeroschin (F), 175).
70 Dusburg (T), 120; Jeroschin, 462–463 (transl.: Jeroschin (F), 163).
71 Dusburg (T), 120; Jeroschin, 462–463 (transl.: Jeroschin (F), 163).
72 Dusburg (T), 121; Jeroschin, 463 (transl.: Jeroschin (F), 163).
73 Jeroschin, 463 (transl.: Jeroschin (F), 164).
74 Czaja, 'Migration und Integration', 41.
75 Czaja, 45.
76 Czaja, 45–46.
77 Sparky Booker and Matthew Frank Stevens, "Irishtowns' and 'Welsh Streets': Ethnic Enclaves Within the Towns of Colonial Ireland and Wales in a Northern-European Colonial Context,' in *Towns on the Edge in Medieval Europe: The Social and Political order of Peripheral Urban Communities from the Twelfth*

to *Sixteenth Centuries*, eds. Matthew Frank Stevens and Roman Czaja (Oxford: Oxford University Press), 46–72.
78 Ian Soulsby, *The Towns of Medieval Wales* (Chichester: Philmore, 1983), 135–136.
79 *Calendar of Ancient Petitions Relating to Wales*, ed. William Rees (Cardiff: University of Wales Press, 1975), 178.
80 Klaus Militzer, 'Polyethnizität und Migration in baltischen Städten,' in *Vieler Völker Städte: Polyethnizität und Migration in Städten des Mittelalters – Chancen und Gefahren*, eds. Kurt Ulrich Jäschke and Christhard Schrenk (Heilbronn: Stadtarchiv Heilbronn, 2012), 104, 108.
81 Dusburg (T), 121; Jeroschin, 463 (transl.: Jeroschin (F), 164).
82 John Griffiths, 'Documents relating to the rebellion of Madoc, 1294–5,' *Bulletin of the Board of Celtic Studies* 8 (1935–1937): 150; Keith Williams-Jones, *The Merioneth Lay Subsidy Roll, 1292–3* (Cardiff: University of Wales Press, 1976), 65–66.
83 Robert Rees Davies, 'Brecon,' in *Boroughs of Medieval Wales*, ed. Ralph Alan Griffiths (Cardiff: University of Wales Press, 1978), 66–67; John Alban and W.S. Kenneth Thomas, 'Charters of the borough of Brecon, 1276–1517,' *Brycheiniog* 25 (1992–1993): 46–47.
84 Dusburg (T), 122; Jeroschin, 464–445 (transl.: Jeroschin (F), 165).
85 Dusburg (T), 120; Jeroschin, 462–443 (transl.: Jeroschin (F), 163).
86 Wunder, *Siedlungs-*, 62; Kisch, *Studien*, 49, argues, that the wording of the charter does not exclude Old-Prussians as burghers (point curtesy of Roman Czaja); Dygo, 'Początki,' 76.
87 Dusburg (T), 120; Jeroschin, 462–443 (transl.: Jeroschin (F), 163).
88 Kisch, *Studien*, 19–86.
89 Dusburg (T), 103; Jeroschin, 436 (transl.: Jeroschin (F), 141).
90 Parallel, recent analysis of better-documented colonial America has stressed how "porous and permeable" the urban frontier was, with numerous short and long-term Native American town residents, *cf.* Colin Calloway, *The Chiefs Now in This City: Indians and the Urban Frontier in Early America* (Oxford: Oxford University Press, 2021), 4.
91 Biskup, 'Das Problem,' 6.
92 Dusburg (T), 115; Jeroschin, 454–455 (transl.: Jeroschin (F), 157).
93 Anti Selart, 'Slavery in the eastern Baltic in the 12th–15th centuries,' in *Serfdom and Slavery in the European Economy, 11th–18th Centuries*, ed. Simonetta Cavaciocchi (Florence: Firenze University Press, 2014), 351. A similar situation prevailed under crusader rule in the Levant, see John Gillingham, 'Crusading warfare, chivalry, and the enslavement of women and children,' in *The Medieval Way of War: Studies in Medieval Military History in Honor of Bernard S. Bachrach*, ed. Gregory Halfond (London: Routledge, 2016), 133–151.
94 Selart, 'Slavery,' 353.
95 Selart, 363.
96 Selart, 357.
97 Dusburg (T), 136; Jeroschin, 493–494 (transl.: Jeroschin (F), 190). Notably, Jeroschin's translation typically emphasises the capture of captives and plunder, especially women and children. Sometimes von Jeroschin adds mention of captives where Dusburg omits it (e.g. Dusburg (T), 58; Jeroschin, 355 (transl.: Jeroschin (F), 76)). Sometimes he elaborates on Dusburg, for example, expanding "a thousand prisoners" to become "more than one thousand women and children" (Dusburg (T), 138; Jeroschin, 496–497 (transl.: Jeroschin (F), 193). See also Sven Ekdahl, 'The treatment of prisoners of war during the fighting between the Teutonic Order and Lithuania,' *The Military Orders*, vol. 1, Malcolm Barber (London: Routledge, 1994), 265–267; Kurt Villads Jensen, 'Prisoners of war in the Baltic in the XII–XIII centuries,' *E-strategica* 1 (2017): 285–295.

98 Selart, 'Slavery,' 360; Werner Paravicini, *Die Preußenreisen des europäischen Adels*, vol. 2, Beihefte der Francia 17/2 (Sigmaringen: J. Thorbecke, 1995), 100–110 (booty).
99 Selart, 'Slavery,' 361–362.
100 Selart, 362.
101 PUB, I/1: 161 no. 218. For a survey of the social shift from slave to wife in a Mediterranean context see, Rena N. Lauer, 'From slave to wife: manumission and marriage in Venetian Crete,' *Medieval People* 36 (2021): 107–132.
102 Selart, 'Slavery,' 362.
103 Gratian's *Decretum*, Causa 29, Questio 2, surveyed in context by Anders Winroth, 'Neither slave nor free: theology and law in Gratian's thoughts on the definition of marriage and unfree persons,' in *Medieval Church Law and the Origins of the Western Legal Tradition: A Tribute to Kenneth Pennington*, eds. Wolfgang P. Müller and Mary E. Sommar (Washington, DC: Catholic University Press, 2006), 97–109; Gillingham, 'Crusading warfare,' 142.
104 Dusburg (T), 74; Jeroschin, 386–387 (transl.: Jeroschin (F), 101).
105 Iben Fonnesberg-Schmidt, *The Popes and the Baltic Crusades, 1147–1254* (Leiden: Brill, 2007), 27–37.
106 Militzer, 'Polyethnizität,' 104, 108.
107 Matthew Frank Stevens, *Urban Assimilation in Post-Conquest Wales: Ethnicity, Gender and Economy in Ruthin, 1282–1348* (Cardiff: University of Wales Press, 2010), 218 (fig. 5.4), 254; id., 'Anglo-Welsh towns of the early fourteenth century: a survey of urban origins, property-holding and ethnicity,' in *Urban Culture in medieval Wales*, ed. Helen Fulton (Cardiff: University of Wales Press, 2012), 145; Sparky Booker, *Cultural Exchange and Identity in Late Medieval Ireland: The English and Irish of the Four Obedient Shires* (Cambridge: Cambridge University Press, 2018), 76, 249.
108 Dusburg (T), 74; Jeroschin, 387 (transl.: Jeroschin (F), 101–102).
109 Dusburg (T), 67, 69, 71, and 73; Jeroschin, 328, 335–341 (virtue), 371, 374, 379–380, and 383–384 (treachery) (transl.: Jeroschin (F), 51, 59–62 (virtue), 89, 92, 96, and 99 (treachery)).
110 Militzer, 'Problem der Migration,' 33–34.
111 Dusburg (T), 109, 115; Jeroschin (F), 147, 157.
112 Dobrosielska, *Opór*, passim.

Primary Sources

Acten der Ständetage Preussens unter der Herrschaft des Deutschen Ordens. Vol. I, *Die Jahre 1233–1435*. Edited by Max Toeppen. Leipzig: Verlag von Duncker & Humblot, 1878.

Calendar of Ancient Petitions Relating to Wales. Edited by William Rees. Cardiff: University of Wales Press, 1975.

The Chronicle of Prussia by Nicolaus von Jeroschin: A History of the Teutonic Knights in Prussia, 1190–1331. Edited by Mary Fischer. Crusade Texts in Translation 20. London: Routledge, 2016.

Geraldus Cambrensis: The Conquest of Ireland. Edited by Thomas Forester and Thomas Wright. Cambridge, Ontario: Parentheses Publications, 2001.

Nicolaus von Jeroschin. 'Kronike von Pruzinlant.' Edited by Ernst Strehlke. In SRP, vol. I, edited by Theodor Hirsch, Max Toeppen, and Ernst Strehlke, 303–624. Leipzig: Hirzel, 1861.

Petri de Dusburg. 'Chronica terre Prussie.' Edited by Max Toeppen. In SRP, vol. I, edited by Theodor Hirsch, Max Toeppen, and Ernst Strehlke, 21–219. Leipzig: Hirzel, 1861.

Preußisches Urkundenbuch. Politische (allgemeine) Abteilung. Vol. I, part 1, *1206–1256.* Edited by Rudolph Philippi and Carl P. Woelky. Königsberg: Hartungsche Verlagsdruckerei, 1882.

Preußisches Urkundenbuch. Vol. I, part 2, *1257–1309.* Edited by August Saraphim. Königsberg: Hartungsche Verlagsdruckerei, 1909.

Przywileje lokacyjne Torunia. Edited by Karola Ciesielska. Toruń: Towarzystwo Miłośników Torunia/Towarzystwo Naukowe Organizacji i Kierownictwa "Dom Organizatora", 2008.

Secondary Sources

Alban, John, and W. S. Kenneth Thomas. 'Charters of the borough of Brecon, 1276–1517.' *Brycheiniog* 25 (1992–1993): 31–55.

Barrell, Andrew D. M., and Michael H. Brown. 'A settler community in post-conquest rural Wales: the English of Dyffryn Clwyd, 1294–1399.' *Welsh History Review* 17 (1995): 332–355.

Biskup, Marian. 'Das Problem der ethnischen Zugehörigkeit im mittelalterlichen Landesausbau in Preussen.' *Jahrbuch für die Geschichte Mittel- und Ostdeutschlands* 40 (1991): 3–25.

Boockman, Hartmut. 'Zur ethnischen Struktur der Bevölkerung deutscher Ostseestädte.' In *Der Ostseeraum – historische Elemente einer wirtschaftlichen Gemeinschaft*, edited by Klaus Friedland, 17–28. Lübeck: Industrie und Handelskammer, 1980.

Booker, Sparky and Matthew Frank Stevens. '"Irishtowns" and "Welsh Streets": ethnic enclaves within the towns of colonial Ireland and Wales in a northern-European colonial context.' In *Towns on the Edge in Medieval Europe: The Social and Political order of Peripheral Urban Communities from the Twelfth to Sixteenth Centuries*, edited by Matthew Frank Stevens and Roman Czaja, 46–72. Oxford: Oxford University Press, 2022.

Booker, Sparky. *Cultural Exchange and Identity in Late Medieval Ireland: The English and Irish of the Four Obedient Shires.* Cambridge: Cambridge University Press, 2018.

Buschinger, Danielle, and Mathieu Olivier. *Les Chevaliers Teutoniques.* Paris: Ellipsis, 2007.

Calloway, Colin. *The Chiefs Now in This City: Indians and the Urban Frontier in Early America.* Oxford: Oxford University Press, 2021.

Christiansen, Eric. *The Northern Crusades.* London: Penguin, 1997, 2nd edition.

Czaja, Roman and Matthew Frank Stevens. 'The place of native populations in the chartered towns of conquered regions: Wales and Prussia as a comparative case study.' In *Towns on the Edge in Medieval Europe: The Social and Political Order of Peripheral Urban Communities from the Twelfth to Sixteenth Centuries*, edited by Matthew Frank Stevens and Roman Czaja, 21–45. Oxford: Oxford University Press, 2022.

Czaja, Roman. 'Towns and urban space in the State of the Teutonic Order in Prussia.' In *The Teutonic Order in Prussia and Livonia. The political and ecclesiastical Structures 13th–16th century*, edited by Roman Czaja and Andrzej Radzimiński, 79–107. Toruń: Towarzystwo Naukowe w Toruniu/Köln, Weimar, Wien: Böhlau Verlag, 2015.

Czaja, Roman. 'Migration und Integration in die Stadt Elbing in Mittelalter und in der frühen Neuzeit.' In *Probleme der Migration und Integration im Preussenland vom Mittelalter bis zum Anfang des 20. Jahrhunderts*, edited by Klaus Militzer, 39–51. Marburg: N.G. Elwert Verlag, 2005.

Davies, Robert Rees. 'Brecon.' In *Boroughs of Medieval Wales*, edited by Ralph Alan Griffiths, 47–70. Cardiff: University of Wales Press, 1978.

Dobrosielska, Alicja. *Opór – oportunizm – współpraca. Prusowie wobec zakonu krzyżackiego w dobie podboju*. Olsztyn: Oficyna Wydawnicza Pruthenia, 2017.
Dygo, Marian. 'Początki i budowa władztwa zakonu krzyżackiego (1226–1309).' In *Państwo zakonu krzyżackiego w Prusach. Władza i społeczeństwo*, edited by Marian Biskup and Roman Czaja, 53–78. Warszawa: Wydawnictwo Naukowe PWN, 2008.
Ekdahl, Sven. 'The treatment of prisoners of war during the fighting between the Teutonic Order and Lithuania.' In *The Military Orders*, vol. 1, edited by Malcolm Barber, 263–269. London: Routledge, 1994.
Erlen, Peter. *Europäischer Landesausbau und mittelalterliche deutsche Ostsiedlung. Ein struktureller Vergleich zwischen Südwestfrankreich, den Niederlanden und dem Ordensland Preussen*. Marburg: J. H. Herder-Institut, 1992.
Fonnesberg-Schmidt, Iben. *The Popes and the Baltic Crusades, 1147–1254*. Leiden: Brill, 2007.
Gillingham, John. 'Crusading warfare, chivalry, and the enslavement of women and children.' In *The Medieval Way of War: Studies in Medieval Military History in Honor of Bernard S. Bachrach*, edited by Gregory Halfond, 133–151. London: Routledge, 2016.
Griffiths, John. 'Documents relating to the rebellion of Madoc, 1294–5.' *Bulletin of the Board of Celtic Studies* 8 (1935–1937): 147–159.
Haak, Avri. 'Local characteristics of the medieval Livonian town.' In *The Baltic Crusades and Societal Innovation in Medieval Livonia, 1200–1350*, edited by Anti Selart, 232–260. Leiden: Brill, 2022.
Heckmann, Dieter. 'Zuwanderung und Integrationsprobleme in Königsberg in Mittelalter und früher Neuzeit.' In *Probleme der Migration und Integration im Preussenland vom Mittelalter bis zum Anfang des 20. Jahrhunderts*, edited by Klaus Militzer, 78–84. Marburg: N.G. Elwert Verlag, 2005.
Jasiński, Tomasz. *Przedmieścia średniowiecznego Torunia i Chełmna*. Poznań: Uniwersytet im. Adama Mickiewicza, 1982.
Jack, Robert Ian. 'Records of Denbighshire lordships: II. – the lordship of Dyffryn Clwyd in 1324.' *Denbighshire Historical Society Transactions* 17 (1968): 7–53.
Jensen, Kurt Villads. 'Prisoners of war in the Baltic in the XII–XIII centuries.' *E-strategica* 1 (2017): 285–295.
Keyser, Erich. 'Die Herkunft der städtischen Bevölkerung des Preußenlandes im Mittelalter.' *Zeitschrift für Ostforschung* 6, no. 4 (1957): 539–557.
Kisch, Guido. *Studien zur Rechts- und Sozialgeschichte des Deutschordenslandes*. Sigmaringen: Jan Thorbecke Verlag, 1973.
Kitano, Harry. 'Passive discrimination: the normal person.' *The Journal of Social Psychology* 70 (1966): 23–31.
Kwiatkowski, Krzysztof. 'The relations of the Teutonic Order in Prussia with the local nobility in the 13th – early 16th century. Scope of issues, research state and research perspectives.' In *Noblesses et ordres militaires. Réseaux, familles, pouvoirs*, edited by Anne Brogini and Germain Butaud, 119–146. Cahiers de la Méditerranée 104. Nice: Institut des Sciences Humaines et Sociales du CNRS, 2022.
Lauer, Rena N. 'From slave to wife: manumission and marriage in Venetian Crete.' *Medieval People* 36 (2021): 107–132.
Lilley, Keith. 'Mapping cosmopolis: moral topographies of the medieval city.' *Environment and Planning D: Society and Space* 22 (2004): 681–698.
Łowmiański, Henryk. *Studja nad początkami społeczeństwa i państwa litewskiego*, vol. 2. Wilno: Towarzystwo Przyjaciół Nauk w Wilnie, 1932.
Mažeika, Rasa. 'Violent victims? Surprising aspects of the just war theory in the chronicle of Peter von Dusburg.' In *The Clash of Cultures on the Medieval Baltic Frontier*, edited by Alan V. Murray, 123–137. London: Routledge, 2016.

Mentzel-Reuters, Arno. *Arma spiritualia. Bibliotheken, Bücher und Bildung im Deutschen Orden.* Wiesbaden: Harrassowitz Verlang, 2003.
Mikulski, Krzysztof. 'Struktura etniczna mieszkańców i status społeczny ludności pochodzenia polskiego w Toruniu od końca XIV do połowy XVII wieku.' *Roczniki Historyczne* 63 (1997): 11–130.
Militzer, Klaus. 'Polyethnizität und Migration in baltischen Städten.' In *Vieler Völker Städte: Polyethnizität und Migration in Städten des Mittelalters – Chancen und Gefahren*, edited by Kurt Ulrich Jäschke and Christhard Schrenk, 101–116. Heilbronn: Stadtarchiv Heilbronn, 2012.
Militzer, Klaus. 'Problem der Migration und Integration sozialer Gruppen in Prußenland.' In *Probleme der Migration und Integration im Preussenland vom Mittelalter bis zum Anfang des 20. Jahrhunderts*, edited by Klaus Militzer, 11–38. Marburg: N. G. Elwert Verlag, 2005.
Otter, Monika. 'Functions of fiction in historical writing.' In *Writing Medieval History: Theory and Practice for the Post-Traditional Middle Ages*, edited by Nancy Partner, 109–130. London: Bloomsbury Academic, 2005.
Otway-Ruthven, Annette Jocelyn. 'The character of Norman settlement in Ireland.' In *Historical Studies*, vol. 5, edited by J. L. McCracken, 7–84. London: Bowes & Bowes, 1965.
Owen, D. Huw. *The Lordship of Denbigh, 1282–1543.* Cardiff: University of Wales Press, 2024.
Paravicini, Werner. *Die Preußenreisen des europäischen Adels.* Part 2. Beihefte der Francia 17/2. Sigmaringen: Jan Thorbecke Verlag, 1995.
Pluskowski, Aleksander. *The Archaeology of the Prussian Crusade: Holy War and Colonisation.* Routledge: Abingdon, 2013.
Pósán, László. 'Prussian missions and the invitation of the Teutonic Order into Kulmerland.' In *The Crusades and the Military Orders: Expanding the Frontiers of Medieval Latin Christianity*, edited by Zsolt Hunyadi and József Laszlovszky, 429–448. Budapest: Central European University, 2001.
Selart, Anti. 'Slavery in the eastern Baltic in the 12th–15th centuries.' In *Serfdom and Slavery in the European Economy, 11th–18th Centuries*, edited by Simonetta Cavaciocchi, 351–364. Florance: Firenze University Press, 2014.
Sherlock, William. 'The original Anglo-Norman settlers in County Kildare.' *Kildare Archaeological Society Journal* 3 (1899–1902): 290–299.
Soulsby, Ian. *The Towns of Medieval Wales.* Chichester: Philmore, 1983.
Stevens, Matthew Frank. *Urban Assimilation in Post-Conquest Wales: Ethnicity, Gender and Economy in Ruthin, 1282–1348.* Cardiff: University of Wales Press, 2010.
Stevens, Matthew Frank. 'Anglo-Welsh towns of the early fourteenth century: a survey of urban origins, property-holding and ethnicity.' In *Urban Culture in medieval Wales*, edited by Helen Fulton, 137–162. Cardiff: University of Wales Press, 2012.
Szorc, Alojzy. *Dominium Warmińskie 1243–1772.* Olsztyn: Wydawnictwo Pojezierze, 1990.
Tandecki, Janusz. 'Probleme der Migration und der Integration der Nurbűrger in Thorn im Mittelalter und in der frühen Neuzeit.' In *Probleme der Migration und Integration im Preussenland vom Mittelalter bis zum Anfang des 20. Jahrhunderts*, edited by Klaus Militzer, 53–69. Marburg: N. G. Elwert Verlag, 2005.
Trampenau, Gottfried. 'Geschichte der Burg Gerdauen.' In *Der Kreis Gerdauen. Ein ostpreußischen Heimatbuch*, edited by Oskar-Wilhelm Bachor, 79–82. Würzburg: Holzner Verlag, 1968.
Trupinda, Janusz. *Ideologia krucjatowa w kronice Piotra z Dusburga.* Gdańsk: Officina Ferberiana, 1999.
Urban, William. *The Prussian Crusade.* Chicago: Lithuanian Research and Studies Center, 2000, 2nd edition.

Wenskus, Reinhard. 'The Teutonic Order and the non-German population of Prussia (with particular reference to the settlement process).' In *The North-East Frontiers of Medieval Europe: The expansion of Latin Christendom in the Baltic Lands*, edited by Alan V. Murray, 307–327. Farnham: Ashgate, 2014.

Wenta, Jarosław. 'Wstęp.' In Piotr von Dusburga, *Kronika Ziemi Pruskiej*, edited by Jarosław Wenta, translated by Sławomir Wyszomirski, vii–xli. Toruń: Wydawnictwo Naukowe Uniwersytetu Mikołaja Kopernika, 2011.

Williams-Jones, Keith. *The Merioneth Lay Subsidy Roll, 1292–3*. Cardiff: University of Wales Press, 1976.

Winroth, Anders. 'Neither slave nor free: theology and law in Gratian's thoughts on the definition of marriage and unfree persons.' In *Medieval Church Law and the Origins of the Western Legal Tradition: A Tribute to Kenneth Pennington*, edited by Wolfgang P. Müller and Mary E. Sommar, 97–109. Washington, DC: Catholic University Press, 2006.

Wunder, Heide. *Siedlungs- und Bevölkerungsgeschichte der Komturei Christburg (13–16. Jahrhundert)*, Marburger Ostforschungen 28. Wiesbaden: Otto Harrassowitz, 1968.

3 Old-Prussians as Co-Creators of Teutonic Order's Rulership and Members of the New Society in Late Medieval Prussia

Alicja Dobrosielska

Old-Prussians, who in the Middle Ages inhabited the area between the Vistula and Memel (Nemunas) Rivers to the south of the Baltic Sea, and the territory comprising the swamps by the Drwęca, Narew, and Biebrza Rivers (42,000 km² altogether), were not a coherent ethnic group. They were divided into many autonomic tribes or even smaller territorial units (their population was about 170,000 people). In the times of conquest (1230–1295), the inhabitants of those lands most likely did not identify themselves as Old-Prussians, but rather as Natangians, Sambians, Pomesanians, Yotvingians, etc.[1] Before the Teutonic Order came to the Old-Prussian lands with a vision of establishing their own authority, the locals did not have to make ultimate choice between their former societal organization, beliefs, or lifestyle, and the new Western cultural system imposed by the crusading movement. To a large extent, the conquest led to polarized attitudes among the local population, giving way to two camps: the ones who, regardless of their loss, put up a fight to maintain the old pagan world, and the ones who accepted the system imposed by the Teutonic Order, seeing in it not as a threat but rather as a chance to change their past lifestyle.

As Peter von Dusburg noted, the Teutonic Order offered free domains to Old-Prussians of wealthy and noble houses (*nobiles*), so that they could live in conformity to with their previous social status. However, to those who did not originate from such houses (*communis populi*), the Teutonic Order offered work in service of the knights.[2] What was an absolute condition of both obtaining/maintaining the status and having a possible way of promotion, also for the enslaved people, was the acceptance of baptism and faithfully supporting the Order. When speaking of the locals who supported the knights in the time of peace, Dusburg employed the term: *cooperatio*.[3] The chronicle is not the only one written source where it is possible to find examples of accepting the Teutonic Order's cultural system by Old-Prussians or taking various actions in favour of the Order. On cooperative Old-Prussians, it can be read in a later translation of Dusburg's chronicle into Middle High German rhymes by Nikolaus von Jeroschin[4]; some new information is also given by *Chronica Olivensis*,[5] *Descriptiones terrarum*,[6] as well as source documents of bestowals.[7]

DOI: 10.4324/9781003502876-3

In this chapter, I discuss the issue of Old-Prussian cooperation with the Teutonic Order, understood as a conscious action in favour of the latter. What I am interested in is not the course of the conquest, nor its military aspect. Rather, I provide here forms of the cooperation to present and understand the active role of the locals who not only got involved in the construction of the Teutonic Order's authority, but also became a part of the newly forming society.

The Cooperation of Old-Prussians

In the available source material, it is possible to find some accounts that provide us insight into the various forms of cooperation between Old-Prussians and brethren of the Teutonic Order. When considering the degree of involvement, it is possible to list the following forms of cooperation: that done in secret from 'the own kind'; overt declaration of allegiance to the Order and subsequent actions carried out in favour of it; and participation in military campaigns at the Teutonic Knights' side against other local people.

There is some information that the locals covertly provided leaders of the Teutonic Order's army with some data on territories they were to conquer, or the army, who protected those lands. For example, the Order was informed on the headcount of an army of Sambians by Gedune, an Old-Prussian nobleman, father of Wissegaud from Medenau (today Logvino), from the house of Candeyn, who knew all advantages of warriors in Sambia. It was by the initiative of the Order, however voluntarily, that Gedune met Ottokar II, the king of Bohemia, in 1254 before the Order's attack on the lands of Sambians. The king showed Gedune his army, consisting of armed men from Bohemia and Brandenburg, as well as numerous pilgrims from Meissen, Saxony, Thuringia, and Austria, and asked him whether he would defeat the Sambians with such forces. When Gedune saw the king's forces, he responded that with such an army he would beat the Prussians effortlessly.[8] What adds credibility to Dusburg's report is the fact that a similar event appears in the 13th-century *Descriptiones terrarum*. Here, a wealthy Sambian man, not mentioned by his name, meets Ottokar II of Bohemia and, furthermore, adopts the name of the Christian sovereign at his baptism.[9] It seems that the wealthy man may be identified as Gedune. It can be added that, in 1261, Gedune was bestowed some land on very favourable conditions, according to which the Order could not seize his land without any compensation in the form of better lands and most of all – without his consent to such a transaction.[10] Together with his sons, he was also mentioned among the *Witings* (Old-Prussian: *wītingis* 'a nobleman', Germ. *Witinge*). These were men who were faithful to the Teutonic Order. The list referring to Gedune was issued on 10 August 1299 by Berthold von Brühaven, the Commander of Königsberg,[11] which also confirms their cooperation with the Order.

The above case of cooperation between the house of Candeyn and the Teutonic Order was not a sparse one; there are many similar accounts to be found on the pages of the chronicle by Peter von Dusburg. For example, we can consider the example in which Heinrich Zuckschwert asked an Old-Prussian man, who had reported to the knights on an impending attack against them, how to avoid it and what to do with the rebels. The man advised coming back to his people with an army. The view of fully armoured and battle-ready Teutonic Knights was to frighten the Old-Prussians and, thereby, discourage them from the rebellion.[12]

The Teutonic Order could count on help and support of the Old-Prussians secretly working for them even in the hardest times. When the knights, surrounded by the Old-Prussians in the castle of Christburg (today Dzierzgoń), were close to starvation and cut off from supplies, a noble man named Samile came to rescue them,[13] as he lived among the Old-Prussians but secretly held to the new religion.[14] When the Old-Prussians discovered that they punished him severely, they poured boiling water into his mouth and scorched his body by fire. Then, as he was hardly alive, they passed him to the Order, where he miraculously recovered.[15] Another act of aid for the Teutonic Knights involved boring holes in Old-Prussian boats with a bit, which was most likely done by a local man, although Peter von Dusburg does not provide his name. The man repeated that action many times until the Old-Prussians, tired by constant repairs and their costs, were forced to stop destroying boats of the Teutonic Order.[16] The events took place during the siege of the castle of Königsberg (today Kaliningrad), which could not be captured by assault by the Old-Prussians, so they used boats to obstruct food deliveries to the crew of the castle.

There is a story of a very effective Old-Prussian cooperant preserved in *Chronicon terrae Prussiae*. In 1239, warriors of Pogesania, Warmia, Natangia, and Barthia organized themselves to fight commonly with the Order's forces and attacked the castle of Balga (today Bal'ga). The situation of its inhabitants was not good, so the knights gathered more and more often at their meetings in search of the right 'cure'. They were helped by an Old-Prussian named Pomanda, originating from Natangia. Pomanda had secretly adopted Christianity and, in consultation with the Teutonic Order, went back to his people, where he pretended that he was an enemy of the Order and talked them into entrusting their commandership to him. Pomanda led the Old-Prussian army into an ambush prepared by the knights and all the Old-Prussians commandeered by him were slain.[17] On the same events, it can be read in *Chronica Olivensis*[18]: Pomanda, a fresh neophyte, was to be bribed with numerous gifts by the prince Otto of Brunswick.

Such secret activities involved high risks. After all, the Old-Prussians who undertook them functioned in their native communities that actively opposed the Teutonic Order (particularly in the first years of the conquest). Those who were discovered to be working in the interests of the Order were subjected to long tortures and death, as shown by the case of Samile. Most likely, such risky adventures were not spontaneous but effected from previous contacts and established relations between both parties. According to Peter von

Dusburg's narrative, Samile was secretly baptized. It is hard to say to what extent hidden supporters of the new social order occurred within Old-Prussians, but it does not seem to be a scarce phenomenon.

Many Old-Prussians openly advocated the Teutonic Order and became its supporters. Many times, such locals played the roles of guides and point men. The Old-Prussian named Trisko not only surrendered the freshly reinforced stronghold of Wehlau (today Znamensk),[19] but also led the Teutonic Order's army to the land of Wohnsdorf (today Kurortnoye), as he perfectly knew the roads leading to it.[20] Skomand, the Yotvingian chieftain, was also a Teutonic Order's guide,[21] and, in the summer of 1284, showed the Order's army, led by Land Master Konrad von Thierberg, the way to the castle of Hrodna.[22] Nikolaus von Jeroschin presents Skomand's significantly greater role played in that raid as beyond that of just a guide. He clearly stresses Skomand's active participation in destroying and plundering the vicinity of Hrodna, after the castle town was conquered.[23] One year after raid, the Land Master bestowed to Skomand and his three sons, Rukals, Gedete, and Galms, the village of *Steynio*, the adjacent meadow of *Penkoweo*, and the field of *Labalaucs*. All those domains were located near Landsberg (today Górowo Iławeckie).[24]

In 1262, Stanteko, a Prussian who allied himself with the Order, warned the Order's army from an ambush. At that time, the castle of Königsberg was besieged by the Sambian army. Counts Wilhelm IV von Jülich and Engelbert I von der Mark came to help the besieged. However, they did not start their fight with the Old-Prussians right away, instead deciding to delay their attack on the castle to the next day. At dawn, it turned out that the Prussians abandoned the siege and barred the way for the Teutonic Order's army. Suspecting an ambush, the commanders started to withdraw the army and sent their Prussian point men to the front. One of them, the aforementioned Stanteko, came across Sambian guards and came back, heavily wounded, and, holding a naked sword covered in blood, informed of the ambush.[25] It is possible that Stanteko may be identified with the son of Grande from the land of Laptau (today Muromskoye) mentioned in a document issued by the commander of Königsberg in 1299.[26]

The most numerous examples of Old-Prussians acting in favour of the Teutonic Order present open and active military support of the Order's forces. Peter von Dusburg provides about forty cases that required the utmost involvement of the locals. Numerous Old-Prussians gave proof of their adherence to the Order in the Battle of Durbe (13 July 1260). Some of them enjoyed profound respect and trust of the Teutonic Knights. Pipin, a great enemy of the Order, defeated the knights painfully many times.[27] However, his son, Matto, was described by Peter von Dusburg as *nobilis vir de Pomesania*,[28] who adopted the name of Hermann when baptized.[29] Matto was not only close to Heinrich Botel, the commander of the Teutonic Order's army, but also advised him on tactics. When asked how to attack the enemy, he recommended leaving the horses and launching an infantry attack, so that retreat would be impossible.[30] In 1260, Matto's possession of the domains of

Trist, *Trumpe*, and *Sobis* near Riesenburg (today Prabuty) was confirmed by the Pomesanian bishop Albert, which seems to be connected with his participation the Battle of Durbe, as well as his obligation to military service, and his duty to pay recognition rent in the form of one pound of wax and one Cologne denarius.[31] Contrary to his father, Matto appears to be a devout Christian, loyal to the Teutonic Order.[32]

As the castle of Beisleiden (today Bezledy), located in the forest of *Kertene* near Bartenstein (today Bartoszyce), was besieged by Yotvingians, Nadrovians, and Scalovians, the crew of the castle were encouraged to fight by Nameda of the house of Montemin, mother of Posdraupot. According to Dusburg, she was to say to her sons that she regretted giving birth to them, as they did not want to fight against warriors of the Old-Prussian tribes. Those words must have brought their desired effect because Nameda's sons and the rest of the crew started to fight and killed, as it is noted by Dusburg, over two thousand people.[33] In the nearby caste of Bartenstein, the Order's men were helped by an Old-Prussian called Tropo, who might be identified with a nobleman of the same name mentioned in the Land Master's bestowal of 1262,[34] and Miligedo, who was so brave that the Old-Prussians compared his death to killing a half of the besieged crew.[35] In 1339, Grand Master Dietrich von Altenburg granted to Miligedo's three descendants: knight (*miles*) Santung, his brother Perdor, and his nephew Gedethe, a privilege on the Magdeburg law for three villages of *Torpine* (later Topprienen, today Toprzyny), *Gelayne* (later Gallehnen, today Gałajny), and *Dulsyenkysus* (later Dulsen/Dulzen, today Dulsin), whose area was 122 *mansos*.[36]

What is characteristic for the locals is their faithful abiding with the Teutonic Order's forces in the battlefield even in the hardest times. For instance, during one of the Order's attacks in Lithuania, Curonians stood against the knights of the Order and attacked them from behind, although they were considered to be the faithful ones before. But two men of Old-Prussian lands stayed with the knights; one of them, the Sambian man called Sklodo from Quedenau (today Severnaya Gora),[37] father of Nalub, reached out to his relatives and friends so that they gave their lives in the name of the new faith and their Order's brothers in arms.[38]

Finally, one more example from Peter von Dusburg's chronicle may be provided, as it may be interpreted as an expression of the locals' extreme attachment to the Teutonic Knights. Naudiota, son of Jodute, a Sambian nobleman who was elected by the Old-Prussians to be the leader of their uprising of 1295, betrayed his comrades and disclosed all the information on the uprising and its organizers, by which he led to the failure of the uprising.[39]

The neophytes' contributions in the fight are confirmed in the texts of bestowals; it is particularly visible in the documents dating back to the first years of the Second Prussian Uprising (1260–1274), mostly in bestowals for Sambians. When offering domains to them, their contributions to the Christian faith and believers during the uprising are also stressed, as well as the toils, hardships, and dangers that they had to suffer when defending the knights and Christianity. In the bestowal to Wargule, it was written that he suffered hard times for the knights and the Christian faith.[40] Similarly, in the bestowal to Tyrune, it may be read of his contribution to the Church during his apostasy.[41] Finally, the bestowal to Kerse and Nekarkis says that in the light of their deeds, they deserved both the Church's and the Order's gratitude.[42]

The supporters of the Teutonic Order's include mostly Old-Prussian noblemen. They make almost 80% of the cooperation cases described by Peter von Dusburg: e.g. Pomanda caused a defeat of his tribesmen when fighting for the castle of Balga,[43] and Trisko surrendered the castle town of Wehlau and led the Teutonic Order's army to the land of Wohnsdorf.[44] During the Second Prussian Uprising, the majority of the noblemen were faithful to the Order: e.g. a group of Pogesanian noblemen took shelter from their tribesmen at the Teutonic Knights in Elbing (today Elbląg)[45]; a man called Girdaw defended the castle of Gerdauen (today Zheleznodorozhny) for a long time[46]; noblemen Miligedo and Troppo defended the stronghold of Bartenstein[47]; and Samile (or Namile) from Pomesania rescued the Teutonic Knights besieged in Christburg.[48] Even sons of the Old-Prussians killed by the Order's brethren cooperated closely with them later: Matto, son of the nobleman Pipin,[49] may serve as an example here. Peter von Dusburg writes that Pipin was at first fixed to a horsetail and then hanged on a tree.[50] Another, equally scary, way of killing Pipin may be found in *Chronica Olivensis*. It can be read there that Pipin's viscera were torn out of him and nailed to a tree, after which he was made to run around the tree until he dropped dead.[51] Regardless of the way that Pipin was slain in reality, his son was faithful to the Teutonic Order.

People cooperating with the Teutonic Knights may also be found among common (i.e. non-noble) Prussians. For example, a subject of the Warmian chieftain Glappo treacherously turned him to the Order.[52] It should be added that the cooperation was common in all the Old-Prussian lands, however, it peaked in tribal Pomesania and Sambia, which may be connected with that fact that inhabitants of those lands' established contacts with the Western culture earlier and the influence of that culture was much stronger (which includes mixed Slavic/Old-Prussian and Scandinavian/Old-Prussian settlement).

Consequences of the Cooperation

Neither of the social strata of that newly formed authority, ranging from knighthood to clergy and bourgeoisie, was closed to Old-Prussians. This can be confirmed by specific source examples.[53] The locals were promoted to the status of knight – e.g. Tessim from Geisseln, Glabune, Glausote, Nadruwe, Hannus Schayboth, Jodute, Noer, or Dietrich Skomand[54] – and then to the status of the Prussian nobility (the 15th–16th century) – e.g. the houses von Pfeilsdorf, von Lehndorf,[55] and most likely von Diebes.[56] Altogether, at least several dozens of such houses may have been given, for example: Perbandt, Schlubutt, Lesgewang, Packmohr, or Kalkstein.[57]

It is possible to find descendants of Old-Prussians among clergymen, whether as priests in parishes or monks. The example of Brother John can be given here, as he was a custody in the Franciscan Order in Braunsberg (today Braniewo) in 1318 and was described as a native Old-Prussian (*fratre Johanne pruteno*).[58] In 1326, Albertus Pruthenus was a parson in Wormditt (today Orneta).[59] Then, Bando, son of Stenion of the house of Tessymid, was a parson in Preußisch Holland (today Pasłęk) and, furthermore, held the post of a Teutonic Order's prosecutor in the Warsaw Trial of 1339.[60] Saul, son of Milutin,[61] and Hojko of Konojady[62] were ones of the Grand Master's notaries. The status of a knight-brother of the Teutonic Order was achieved by Zacharias von Sparwein; possibly Johannes von Waplitz (today Waplewo), from the house of Tessymid (15th century)[63]; Zancirmo/Santirme, the House Commander (Germ. *Hauskomtur*) of Schönsee (today Kowalewo Pomorskie) (1317–1319); Glabune in the convent of Danzig (today Gdańsk) (1349); Leykot, in the convent of Schlochau (today Człuchów) (1344), a Procurator (Germ. *Pfleger*) of Friedland (today Pravdinsk) (1346), and the Fish Master (Germ. *Fischmeister*) of Schlochau (1347–1348).[64] There are also known cases of Old-Prussians who were town councillors or inhabitants. The list of town councillors includes Heinrich Crattegalbe in Bartenstein (1356), Johannes Pruthenus (Pruse) in the New Town Elbing, or Henniko Pruthenus (1286) and Claus Witing (1360) in Königsberg.[65] It is sure that a list of townsmen include Glinde Pruthenus, Nycolaus *dictus Pyrgune*, Hannus Merun, Glabune, and Barthus Nyvirgalt.[66] The list also includes members of the house of Zamehl, who were descendants of the aforementioned Old-Prussian Samile: Jacob settled down in Marienburg (today Malbork), and then John, his descendant, moved to Elbing.[67]

It is also possible to mention Old-Prussians who held various offices in the Teutonic Order's territorial rulership (Germ. *Landesherrschaft*), including that of an advocate (Germ. *Vogt*) or a bailiff (Germ. *Kämmerer*). One strong example of this can be seen in the house of von Packmohr: their surname 'Packmohr' meant 'bailiff' in the Old-Prussian language.[68] The house of Tessymid should also be mentioned here: Albert (Wajsyl?), an owner of domains in today's Krupin near Christburg, was a *Kämmerer* there.[69] The office of a *Kämmerer* in Heilsberg (today Lidzbark Warmiński) was also held by Merun/Marune Nakie (1346, 1349). Merun previously served as a *familiaris* of the *Vogt* of Pogesania.[70] Some Old-Prussians holding the high lay office of a bishop's *Vogt* may also be found in Ermland: Brulando (1280), Rapoto (1287), and then Otto von Russen (1305–1313), son of the Old-Prussian called Juncter.[71] The office of burgrave was another popular administrative post that could be obtained by Old-Prussians: for instance, the burgrave of the chapter castle in Allenstein (today Olsztyn), Nikolaus Kunras *de Kyrpeyn*, was given ten lans of land nearby on the Prussian law.[72]

In the times of the conquest, as well as after it, a significant role was played by interpreters (*interpreti*). These figures were also called *tolks* from Old-Prussian. Without their work, any actions in favour of the Teutonic Order would be strongly hindered, if possible at all. The sources provide numerous examples of such people as for instance Jacob, an interpreter in Balga, in 1289,[73] Albertus in Christburg.[74] The function of an interpreter persisted in the following centuries as well.[75] The name of Leonard von Sparw(e) may be given here, as he was an interpreter of the Prussian language in the convent of Balga in 1386.[76] Johannes Peytune who was an interpreter of the Bishop of Ermland/Warmia in 1342 may serve here as another example.[77]

There are no estimations, ever rough ones, on the share of the locals and their descendants in the structure of particular social strata. There are only some initial percentages for the towns. The available data show that descendants of Old-Prussians in Bartenstein could make 9% of its inhabitants, in the New Town Elbing – 7%, and in Marienburg, Braunsberg, and the Old Town Elbing – 3%.[78]

Conclusions

Accepting the Teutonic Order's 'cultural offer' being baptized, and starting the cooperation made Old-Prussians be active co-creators of the newly built Order's territorial rulership. It was not a short process; the conquest itself took more than 50 years. In that time, as well as in the following centuries, numerous Old-Prussians and their descendants were actively involved in the formation of this territory. They became Christians, received donations of land, obtained knight's belts, finished schools (learnt to read and write, and some were graduated from universities), received priestly orders, and held offices of Teutonic Order's notaries, *Vogt*s, *Kämmerer*s, burgraves, etc. Some of them inhabited towns, of which they became citizens and councillors.

The presented examples of the Old-Prussians, who cooperated with the Teutonic Order in the time of conquest in 13th century, as well as their descendants in 14th and 15th centuries, who found themselves in the new social, economic, and political order, even if they are not numerous (not because of the sources lack in them, but because they require some deeper research), demonstrate that the indigenous Prussians were active actors of the social life under the Teutonic Order's authority, and did not play a marginal role in the new society formed in the Prussian Land.[79]

Translated by Jarosław Solmiński

Notes

1 Erich Maschke, 'Preußen. Das Werden eines deutschen Stammesnamens,' in *Domus hospitalis Teutonicorum. Europäische Verbindungslinien der Deutschordensgeschichte. Gesammelte Aufsätze aus den Jahren 1931–1963*, ed. Erich Maschke (Bonn, Bad Godesberg: Verlag Wissenschaftliches Archiv GMBH, 1970), 158–187; Albert L. Ewald, *Die Eroberung Preussens durch die Deutschen*, Book I, *Berufung*

und Grundung (Halle/Saale: Verlag der Buchhandlung des Weisenhauses, 1872); Book II, *Die erste Erhebung der Preussen und die Kämpfe mit Swantopolk* (Halle/Salle: Verlag der Buchhandlung des Weisenhauses, 1875); Book III, *Die Eroberung des Samlandes, des östlichen Natangens, östlichen Bartens und Galindens* (Halle/Salle: Verlag der Buchhandlung des Weisenhauses, 1884); Book IV, *Die große Erhebung der Preussen und die Eroberung der östlichen Landschaften* (Halle/Salle: Verlag der Buchhandlung des Weisenhauses, 1886); Marian Biskup, 'Etniczno-demograficzne przemiany Prus krzyżackich w rozwoju osadnictwa w średniowieczu (o tzw. nowym plemieniu Prusaków),' *Kwartalnik Historyczny* 98, no. 2 (1991): 45–67; Dariusz A. Sikorski, *Instytucje władzy u Prusów w średniowieczu (na tle struktury społecznej i terytorialnej)* (Olsztyn: Edycja wspólna Towarzystwa Naukowego i Ośrodka Badań Naukowych im. Wojciecha Kętrzyńskiego, 2010), 49–57.
2 Dusburg (W).
3 Dusburg (W), 189 (pars III, cap. 220). I have discussed the issue of the Old-Prussian cooperation with the Teutonic Order in my previous publication, see Alicja Dobrosielska, *Opór – oportunizm – współpraca. Prusowie wobec zakonu krzyżackiego w dobie podboju* (Olsztyn: Oficyna Wydawnicza Pruthenia, 2017), 149–194.
4 Jeroschin, 291–624.
5 ÄChO, 594–624.
6 Marvin L. Colker, 'America rediscovered in the Thirteenth Century?' *Speculum* 54, no. 4 (1979): 712–726; Karol Górski, '*Descriptiones Terrarum* (Nowo odkryte źródło do dziejów Prus w XIII wieku),' ZH 46, no. 1 (1981): 7–16; *Spotkanie dwóch światów. Stolica apostolska a świat mongolski w połowie XIII wieku. Relacje powstałe w związku z misją Jana di Piano Carpiniego do Mongołów*, ed. Jerzy Strzelczyk (Poznań: Wydawnictwo Abos, 1993), 290–301.
7 The bestowals given to Old-Prussians have been collected and published in the following publications: a.o. PUB, I–VI; CDW, I–IV; UBBS; UBBP I.
8 Dusburg (W), 102 (pars III, cap. 71).
9 Górski, '*Descripiones Terrarum*,' 8.
10 Reinhard Wenskus, 'Die gens Candein. Zur Rolle des preußischen Adels bei der Eroberung und Verwaltung Preußens,' in id., *Ausgewälte Aufsätze zum frühen und preußischen Mittelalter*, ed. Hans Patze (Sigmaringen: J. Torbecke, 1986), 435–447.
11 PUB, V/2: 449 no. 718.
12 Dusburg (W), 206–207 (pars III, cap. 249).
13 Alicja Dobrosielska, 'Elbląska rodzina Zamehl. Przyczynek do trwania pruskiej tożsamości,' *Pruthenia* 2 (2006): 94–102.
14 Dusburg (W), 146–147 (pars III, cap. 145).
15 Sławomir Jóźwiak, *Wywiad i kontrwywiad w państwie zakonu krzyżackiego w Prusach* (Malbork: Muzeum Zamkowe w Malborku, 2004), 215–222.
16 Dusburg (W), 122 (pars III, cap. 102).
17 Dusburg (W), 66–67 (pars III, cap. 26).
18 ÄChO, 598.
19 Dusburg (W), 104–105 (pars III, cap. 73).
20 Dusburg (W), 105 (pars III, cap. 74).
21 For more information on Skomand, see Martin Rouselle, *Woria, Der Kreis Pr. Eylau südlich des Stablack und der Eylauer Heide zur Zeit des Ritterordens und der preußischen Herzöge* (Königsberg: Kreisgemeinschaft Pr. Eylau, 1924), 11–12; Grzegorz Białuński, *Studia z dziejów rycerskich i szlacheckich rodów pruskich (XIII–XVI wiek)*, part 1 (Olsztyn: Edycja wspólna Towarzystwa Naukowego i Ośrodka Badań Naukowych im. Wojciecha Kętrzyńskiego w Olsztynie oraz Towarzystwa Naukowego Pruthenia, 2012), 169–195; Wiesław Długokęcki, 'Instytucja wodzostwa u Prusów w XIII wieku,' in: *Instytucja „wczesnego*

państwa" w perspektywie wielości i różnorodności kultur, ed. Jacek Banaszkiewicz, Michał Kara, and Henryk Mamzer (Poznań: Ośrodek Badań Pradziejowych i Wczesnośredniowiecznych Instytutu Archeologii i Etnologii PAN w Poznaniu, 2013), 373–375.
22 Dusburg (W), 190–191 (pars III, cap. 223).
23 Jeroschin, 516.
24 PUB, I/2: 297–298 no. 464; Białuński, *Studia z dziejów*, 181–195.
25 Dusburg (W), 119–120 (pars III, cap. 98).
26 PUB, I/2: 448 no. 718; more abaut relationship between the Teutonic Order and the Sambian nobility, see Grischa Vercamer, *Siedlungs-, Sozial- und Verwaltungsgeschichte der Komturei Königsberg in Preußen (13.–16. Jahrhundert)*, Einzelschriften der Historischen Kommission für Ost- und wespreußische Landesforschung 29 (Marburg: N. G. Elwert Verlag, 2010), 45–116; Wiesław Długokęcki, 'Das Verhältnis des Deutschen Ordens zum sämlandischen Adel im 13. und frühen 14. Jahrhundert.' *Questiones Medii Aevi Novae* 28 (2023): 174–209.
27 Białuński, *Studia z dziejów*, 203–208.
28 Dusburg (W), 55 (pars III, cap. 7).
29 ÄChO, 597.
30 Dusburg (W), 110 (pars III, cap. 84).
31 UBBP I: 6 no. VI. For the history of Matto's descendants and his domains, see Białuński, *Studia z dziejów*, 204–208.
32 Dusburg (W), 55 (pars III, cap. 7).
33 Dusburg (W), 162–163 (pars III, cap. 174).
34 PUB, I/2: 141 no. 173. The bestowal is a proof that wealthy freemen could possess and did possess lands in various tribal territories; see Wenskus, 'Die Gens Candain,' 88.
35 Dusburg (W), 130 (pars III, cap. 119).
36 PUB, III/1, 183–184 no. 255: *Domino Santungen nostro Militi atque Perdor fratrii suo necnen Gedethen filio fratris eorum [...]*.
37 Sklodo, the Old-Prussian *Witing* from Quedenau, is listed together with his son Nalub as faithful to the Teutonic Order during the Prussian Uprising in a document issued by the Commander of Königsberg in 1299, *cf.* PUB, I/2: 449 no. 718; UBBS, 34 no. 64 (from 1258), 38 no. 72 (from 1261).
38 Dusburg (W), 110–111 (pars III, cap. 84).
39 Dusburg (W), 214–215 (pars III, cap. 262).
40 UBBS, 38 no. 72.
41 PUB, I/2: 128–129 no. 155.
42 PUB, I/2: 120 no. 140.
43 Dusburg (W), 67 (pars III, cap. 26).
44 Dusburg (W), 104–105 (pars III, cap. 73–74).
45 Dusburg (W), 159 (pars III, cap. 168).
46 Dusburg (W), 127 (pars III, cap. 113).
47 Dusburg (W), 130 (pars III, cap. 119).
48 Dusburg (W), 146–147 (pars III, cap. 145).
49 Dusburg (W), 55 (pars III, cap. 7), 110 (pars III, cap. 84).
50 Dusburg (W), 55 (pars III, cap. 7).
51 ÄChO, 597.
52 Dusburg (W), 139–140 (pars III, cap. 136).
53 Grzegorz Białuński, 'Uwagi o karierze Prusów w państwie krzyżackim,' *Studia z Dziejów Średniowiecza* 19 (2015): 15–26.
54 Białuński, *Studia z dziejów*, 59, 67–69, 88, 123–127, 183, 195, 218, and 223.
55 Białuński, *Ród Prusa Kleca ze szczególnym uwzględnieniem rodziny von Pfeilsdorfów-Pilewskich* (Malbork: Muzeum Zamkowe w Malborku, 2006), 41–42, 48–50.

56 Białuński, *Studia z dziejów*, 98–110.
57 Białuński, 6–21.
58 CDW I: 324 no. 188; *cf.* Stanisław Achremczyk and Alojzy Szorc, *Braniewo* (Olsztyn: Ośrodek Badań Naukowych im. Wojciecha Kętrzyńskiego w Olsztynie, 1995), 153.
59 CDW I: 379 no. 224; *cf.* Aniela Olczyk, *Sieć parafialna biskupstwa warmińskiego do roku 1525* (Lublin: Towarzystwo Naukowe Katolickiego Uniwersytetu Lubelskiego, 1961), 31, 33, 50, and 80.
60 Białuński, *Studia z dziejów*, 62–68; Marcin Sumowski, 'The Priest in the Multilingual Church. Language as an Aspect of the Functioning of the Lower Clergy in Late Medieval Prussia,' *Acta Historica Universitatis Klaipedensis* 41 (2020): 54, 57–61.
61 Martin Armgart, *Die Handfesten preußischen Oberlandes bis 1410 und ihre Aussteller. Diplomatische und prospographische Untersuchungen zur Kanzleigeschichte des Deutschen Ordens in Preußen*, Veröffentlichungen aus den Archiven Preußischer Kulturbesitz 2 (Köln, Weimar, Wien: Böhlau Verlag, 1995), 226–229.
62 According to Grzegorz Białuński, he came from the house of Klec; see Białuński, *Ród Prusa Kleca*, 89–92.
63 Białuński, *Studia z dziejów*, 11, 119.
64 Reinhard Wenskus, 'Das Ordensland Preußen als Territorialstaat des 14. Jahrhunderts,' in id., *Ausgewählte Aufsätze*, 338.
65 Marzena Pollakówna, 'Zanik ludności pruskiej,' in *Szkice z dziejów Pomorza*, ed. Gerard Labuda (Warszawa: Książka i Wiedza, 1958), 189; Theodor Penners, *Untersuchungen über die Herkunft der Stadtbewohner im Deutsch-Ordensland Preussen bis in die Zeit um 1400*, Deutschland und der Osten. Quellen und Forschungen zur Geschichte ihrer Beziehungen 16 (Leipzig: Hirzel, 1942), 86, 122, and 167.
66 Penners, *Untersuchungen*, 168.
67 Dobrosielska, 'Elbląska rodzina,' 94–102; Białuński, 'Uwagi o karierze,' 25.
68 Reinhard Wenskus, 'Kleinverbände und Kleinräume bei den Prussen des Samlandes,' in id., *Ausgewählte Aufsätze*, 250.
69 CDW III: 104 no. 139.
70 CDW II: 69 no. 65, 142 no. 141; *cf.* Anton Kolberg, 'Die ältesten Kämmerer und Kammerämter in Ermland. Aus den Nachlaßpapieren des Domvicars Dr. Woelky,' *Zeitschrift für die Geschichte und Altertumskunde Ermlands* 9 (1891): 580; Grzegorz Białuński, 'Pruskie związki terytorialno-osadnicze w dorzeczu środkowej Łyny w XIII wieku,' KMW 1/243 (2004): 13.
71 For the examples, see Jan Ptak, *Wojskowość średniowiecznej Warmii* (Olsztyn: Ośrodek Badań Naukowych im. Wojciecha Kętrzyńskiego w Olsztynie, 1997), 95–96; Marzena Pollakówna, *Osadnictwo Warmii w okresie krzyżackim* (Poznań: Instytut Zachodni, 1953), 71; CDW I: 33–44 nos. 56–57, 43 no. 75, 44–45 no. 77b, 82–83 no. 149.
72 CDW II: 547–548 no. 512; Ptak, *Wojskowość*, 96.
73 PUB, I/2: 334 no. 531.
74 PUB, I/2: 433–434 no. 690.
75 Krzysztof Kwiatkowski, *Zakon niemiecki jako „corporatio militaris"*, part I, *Korporacja i krąg przynależących do niej. Kulturowe i społeczne podstawy działalności militarnej zakonu w Prusach (do początku XV wieku)*, Dzieje Zakonu Niemieckiego 1 (Toruń: Wydawnictwo Naukowe Uniwersytetu Mikołaja Kopernika, 2012), 323–325.
76 Białuński, *Studia z dziejów*, 11.
77 CDW II: 13–14 no. 13.

78 Marian Biskup, 'Rozkwit państwa krzyżackiego w Prusach,' in Marian Biskup and Labuda, *Dzieje zakonu krzyżackiego w Prusach. Gospodarka – społeczeństwo – państwo – ideologia* (Gdańsk: Wydawnictwo Morskie, 1986, 1st ed.), 323; Pollakówna, 'Zanik,' 188, 189.
79 Karin Friedrich, *Inne Prusy. Prusy Królewskie i Polska między wolnością a wolnościami (1569–1772)*, trans. Grażyna Waluga (Poznań: Poznańskie Towarzystwo Przyjaciół Nauk, 2005), 29–41.

Primary Sources

'Die ältere Chronik von Oliva.' Edited by Theodor Hirsch. In SRP, vol. V, edited by Theodor Hirsch, Max Toeppen, and Ernst Strehlke, 594–624. Leipzig: Hirzel, 1874.

Codex Diplomaticus Warmiensis oder Regesten und Urkunden zur Geschichte Ermlands. Vol. I, *Urkunden der Jahre 1231–1340*. Edited by Carl P. Woelky and Johann M. Saage. MHW I/I. Meinz: Franz Kirchheim, 1860.

Codex Diplomaticus Warmiensis oder Regesten und Urkunden zur Geschichte Ermlands. Vol. II, *Urkunden der Jahre 1341–1375 nebst Nachträgen von 1240–1340*. Edited by Carl P. Woelky and Johann M. Saage. MHW I/II. Meinz: Franz Kirchheim, 1864.

Codex Diplomaticus Warmiensis oder Regesten und Urkunden zur Geschichte Ermlands. Vol. III, *Urkunden der Jahre 1376–1424 nebst Nachträgen*. Edited by Woelky. MHW I/V. Braunsberg, Leipzig: Eduard Peter, 1874.

Nikolaus von Jeroschin. 'Die Kronike von Pruzinland des Nicolaus v. Jeroschin.' Edited by Ernst Strehlke. In SRP, vol. I, edited by Theodor Hirsch, Max Toeppen, and Ernst Strehlke, 291–624. Leipzig: Hirzel, 1861.

Petrus de Dusburg, *Chronica terrae Prussiae*. Edited by Jarosław Wenta and Sławomir Wyszomirski, Monumenta Poloniae Historica. Nova Series XIII. Kraków: Polska Akademia Umiejętności, 2007.

Preußisches Urkundenbuch. Politische (allgemeine) Abteilung. Vol. I, part 2, 1257–1309. Edited by August Saraphim. Königsberg: Hartungsche Verlagsdruckerei, 1909.

Preußisches Urkundenbuch. Politische (allgemeine) Abteilung. Vol. III, part 1, 1335–1341. Edited by Max Hein. Königsberg: Im Kommisionsverlag: Gräfe and Unzer, 1944.

Preußisches Urkundenbuch. Politische (allgemeine) Abteilung. Vol. V, part 2, 1357–1361. Edited by Klaus Conrad. Marburg: N. G. Elwert Verlag, 1975.

Urkundenbuch des Bisthums Samland. Edited by Carl P. Woelky and Hans Mendthal, Neuses Preußisches Urkundenbuch. Ostpreussischer Theil. Leipzig: Duncker & Humblot, 1891.

Urkundenbuch zur Geschiche des vormaligen Bisthums Pomesanien. Edited by Hermann Cramer. Vol. I. Marienwerder: Im Selbstverlag des Historischen Vereins für den Regierungs-Bezirk, Marienwerder, 1884.

Secondary Sources

Achremczyk, Stanisław and Alojzy Szorc. *Braniewo*. Olsztyn: Ośrodek Badań Naukowych im. Wojciecha Kętrzyńskiego w Olsztynie, 1995.

Armgart, Martin. *Die Handfesten preußischen Oberlandes bis 1410 und ihre Aussteller. Diplomatische und prospographische Untersuchungen zur Kanzeleigeschichte des Deutschen Ordens in Preußen*. Veröffentlichungen aus den Archiven Preußischer Kulturbesitz 2. Köln, Weimar, Wien: Böhlau Verlag, 1995.

Białuński, Grzegorz. *Studia z dziejów rycerskich i szlacheckich rodów pruskich (XIII–XVI wiek)*. Part 1. Olsztyn: Edycja wspólna Towarzystwa Naukowego i Ośrodka Badań Naukowych im. Wojciecha Kętrzyńskiego w Olsztynie oraz Towarzystwa Naukowego Pruthenia, 2012.
Białuński, Grzegorz. *Ród Prusa Kleca ze szczególnym uwzględnieniem rodziny von Pfeilsdorfów-Pilewskich*. Malbork: Muzeum Zamkowe w Malborku, 2006.
Białuński, Grzegorz. 'Uwagi o karierze Prusów w państwie krzyżackim.' *Studia z Dziejów Średniowiecza* 19 (2015): 15–26.
Białuński, Grzegorz. 'Pruskie związki terytorialno-osadnicze w dorzeczu środkowej Łyny w XIII wieku.' KMW 1/243 (2004): 3–17.
Biskup, Marian. 'Etniczno-demograficzne przemiany Prus krzyżackich w rozwoju osadnictwa w średniowieczu (o tzw. nowym plemieniu Prusaków).' *Kwartalnik Historyczny* 98, no. 2 (1991): 45–67.
Biskup, Marian, 'Rozkwit państwa krzyżackiego w Prusach.' In Marian Biskup and Gerard Labuda, *Dzieje zakonu krzyżackiego w Prusach. Gospodarka – społeczeństwo – państwo – ideologia*, 264–352. Gdańsk: Wydawnictwo Morskie, 1986, 1st edition.
Colker, Marvin L. 'America rediscovered in the Thirteenth Century?' *Speculum* 54, no. 4 (1979): 712–726.
Długokęcki, Wiesław. 'Instytucja wodzostwa u Prusów w XIII wieku.' In *Instytucja „wczesnego państwa" w perspektywie wielości i różnorodności kultur*, edited by Jacek Banaszkiewicz, Michał Kara, and Henryk Mamzer, 355–387. Poznań: Ośrodek Badań Pradziejowych i Wczesnośredniowiecznych Instytutu Archeologii i Etnologii PAN w Poznaniu, 2013.
Długokęcki, Wiesław. 'Das Verhältnis des Deutschen Ordens zum sämlandischen Adel im 13. und frühen 14. Jahrhundert.' *Questiones Medii Aevi Novae* 28 (2023): 167–215.
Dobrosielska, Alicja. *Opór – oportunizm – współpraca. Prusowie wobec zakonu krzyżackiego w dobie podboju*. Olsztyn: Oficyna Wydawnicza Pruthenia, 2017.
Dobrosielska, Alicja. 'Elbląska rodzina Zamehl. Przyczynek do trwania pruskiej tożsamości.' *Pruthenia* 2 (2006): 94–102.
Ewald, Albert L. *Die Eroberung Preussens durch die Deutschen*. Book I, *Berufung und Grundung*, Halle/Saale: Verlag der Buchhandlung des Weisenhauses, 1872. Book II, *Die erste Erhebung der Preussen und die Kämpfe mit Swantopolk*, Halle/Salle: Verlag der Buchhandlung des Weisenhauses, 1875. Book III, *Die Eroberung des Samlandes, des östlichen Natangens, östlichen Bartens und Galindens*, Halle/Salle: Verlag der Buchhandlung des Weisenhauses, 1884. Book IV, *Die große Erhebung der Preussen und die Eroberung der östlichen Landschaften*, Halle/Salle: Verlag der Buchhandlung des Weisenhauses, 1886.
Friedrich, Karin. *Inne Prusy. Prusy Królewskie i Polska między wolnością a wolnościami (1569–1772)*. Translated by Grażyna Waluga. Poznań: Poznańskie Towarzystwo Przyjaciół Nauk, 2005.
Górski, Karol. 'Descriptiones Terrarum (Nowo odkryte źródło do dziejów Prus w XIII wieku.' ZH 46, no. 1 (1981): 7–16.
Jóźwiak, Sławomir. *Wywiad i kontrwywiad w państwie zakonu krzyżackiego w Prusach*. Malbork: Muzeum Zamkowe w Malborku, 2004.
Kolberg, Anton. 'Die ältesten Kämmerer und Kammerämter in Ermland. Aus den Nachlaßpapieren des Domvicars Dr. Woelky.' *Zeitschrift für die Geschichte und Altertumskunde Ermlands* 9 (1891): 573–584.
Kwiatkowski, Krzysztof. *Zakon niemiecki jako "corporatio militaris"*. Part I, *Korporacja i krąg przynależących do niej. Kulturowe i społeczne podstawy działalności militarnej zakonu w Prusach (do początku XV wieku)*. Dzieje Zakonu Niemieckiego 1. Toruń: Wydawnictwo Naukowe Uniwersytetu Mikołaja Kopernika, 2012.

Maschke, Erich. 'Preußen. Das Werden eines deutschen Stammesnamens.' In *Domus hospitalis Teutonicorum. Europäische Verbindungslinien der Deutschordensgeschichte. Gesammelte Aufsätze aus den Jahren 1931–1963*, edited by Erich Maschke, 158–187. Quellen und Studien zur Geschichte des Deutschen Ordens 10. Bonn, Bad Godesberg: Wissenschaftliches Archiv, 1970.

Olczyk, Aniela. *Sieć parafialna biskupstwa warmińskiego do roku 1525*. Lublin: Towarzystwo Naukowe Katolickiego Uniwersytetu Lubelskiego, 1961.

Penners, Theodor. *Untersuchungen über die Herkunft der Stadtbewohner im Deutsch-Ordensland Preussen bis in die Zeit um 1400*. Deutschland und der Osten. Quellen und Forschungen zur Geschichte ihrer Beziehungen 16. Leipzig: Hirzel, 1942.

Pollakówna, Marzena. *Osadnictwo Warmii w okresie krzyżackim*. Poznań: Instytut Zachodni, 1953.

Pollakówna, Marzena. 'Zanik ludności pruskiej.' In *Szkice z dziejów Pomorza*, edited by Gerard Labuda, 160–207. Warszawa: Książka i Wiedza, 1958.

Ptak, Jan. *Wojskowość średniowiecznej Warmii*. Olsztyn: Ośrodek Badań Naukowych im. Wojciecha Kętrzyńskiego w Olsztynie, 1997.

Rouselle, Martin. *Woria, Der Kreis Pr. Eylau südlich des Stablack und der Eylauer Heide zur Zeit des Ritterordens und der preußischen Herzöge*. Königsberg: Kreisgemeinschaft Pr. Eylau, 1924.

Sikorski, Dariusz A. *Instytucje władzy u Prusów w średniowieczu (na tle struktury społecznej i terytorialnej)*. Olsztyn: Edycja wspólna Towarzystwa Naukowego i Ośrodka Badań Naukowych im. Wojciecha Kętrzyńskiego, 2010.

Spotkanie dwóch światów. Stolica apostolska a świat mongolski w połowie XIII wieku. Relacje powstałe w związku z misją Jana di Piano Carpiniego do Mongołów. Edited by Jerzy Strzelczyk. Poznań: Wydawnictwo Abos, 1993.

Sumowski, Marcin. 'The Priest in the Multilingual Church. Language as an Aspect of the Functioning of the Lower Clergy in Late Medieval Prussia.' *Acta Historica Universitatis Klaipedensis* 41 (2020): 53–71.

Vercamer, Grischa. *Siedlungs-, Sozial- und Verwaltungsgeschichte der Komturei Königsberg in Preußen (13.–16. Jahrhundert)*. Einzelschriften der Historischen Kommission für Ost- und wespreußische Landesforschung 29. Marburg: N. G. Elwert Verlag, 2010.

Wenskus, Reinhard. 'Die gens Candein. Zur Rolle des preußischen Adels bei der Eroberung und Verwaltung Preußens.' In id., *Ausgewählte Aufsätze zum frühen und preußischen Mittelalter. Festgabe zu seinem 70. Geburtstag*, edited by Hans Patze, 435–454. Sigmaringen: J. Thorbecke, 1986.

Wenskus, Reinhard.'Das Ordensland Preußen als Territorialstaat des 14. Jahrhunderts.' In id., *Ausgewählte Aufsätze zum frühen und preußischen Mittelalter. Festgabe zu seinem 70. Geburtstag*, edited by Hans Patze, 317–352. Sigmaringen: J. Thorbecke, 1986.

Wenskus, Reinhard. 'Kleinverbände und Kleinräume bei den Prussen des Samlandes.' In id., *Ausgewählte Aufsätze zum frühen und preußischen Mittelalter. Festgabe zu seinem 70. Geburtstag*, edited by Hans Patze, 245–298. Sigmaringen: J. Thorbecke, 1986.

4 Native Identities after the Crusades

The Archaeology of Ethnicity in Medieval Prussia

Aleksander Pluskowski, Maciej Karczewski, and Małgorzata Karczewska

Introduction

The military conquest of Prussian lands between 1230 and 1283 saw the creation of a new society, governed by the Teutonic Order, bishops and their cathedral chapters. German- and Polish-speaking migrants came to live alongside the surviving native population, some of whom were relocated by the new regime. According to the earliest detailed account of Prussia, produced by Peter von Dusburg, a priest of the Teutonic Order writing in the early 14th century, there were ten native peoples (the terms *gentes* and *naciones* are used) who lived in distinct geographical regions.[1] Written sources from the crusading period also indicate the existence of territorial sub-divisions within these regions. For example, ten native districts of Pomesania are referred to in documents relating to the division of territory between the Teutonic Order and bishops in 1250.[2] In the early 13th century, before the onset of the crusades, there were an estimated 170,000 native Old-Prussians. A century later, this number had been reduced to an estimated 90,000, with 15,000 Germans and 30,000 Poles making up the new, composite population of the annexed territories.[3]

This was partly the result of fifty years of warfare, although the impact on the native population in Prussia varied regionally. Sudovia was depopulated, whilst the largest concentration of native Old-Prussians in the post-crusade period could be found in Sambia. In fact, this region had been the focus of resettlement for large numbers of Sudovians, who were also dispersed elsewhere throughout Prussia. Some of the surviving Old-Prussian elites, including those who were resettled, were permitted to retain certain privileges in exchange for obedience to the new regime, but the native peasantry remained servile.[4] This provided the Order with the means of repopulating regions devastated by warfare, incorporating them into the new social system established by the crusades and distancing them from Lithuania. But the demographic changes were also the result of protracted external migration which began in earnest in western Prussia in the 1290s. Subsequent waves of migration would drive the establishment of new urban and rural settlements. The 'Great Wilderness' (Germ. *Große Wildnis*) of eastern Prussia – the frontier

DOI: 10.4324/9781003502876-4

with Samogitia and the Grand Duchy of Lithuania – began to be colonised from the 1320s and then more extensively from the 1370s.[5] Much of this later movement was internal, led by second and third generations of settlers, although substantial external migrations into Prussia took place in the later 15th century from Poland, when Mazovians were invited to settle in parts of south-eastern Prussia.[6] Many migrants came to live in close proximity to native Old-Prussian communities or inhabited the same settlements. But the in some regions, native settlements came under the governance of the Prussian law (*Iura Pruthenorum*), of which the earliest surviving example can be dated to 1340.[7] This, along with the separate treatment of non-Germans (i.e. Old-Prussians and Slavs) in some urban jurisdictions, must have contributed to a sense of cultural segregation. In the early 15th century, the Order began to regulate the migration of rural Old-Prussians to villages and towns governed by German laws. The aim was not to create ethnic segregation, but rather to prevent a drain of valuable labour from the countryside, which would have had an economic impact of both the Order's revenue and that of the towns. In the second half of the 15th century, legislation restricting access to non-Germans was passed in small towns, again as a measure of protection by groups of artisans grappling with the effects of economic stagnation.[8]

Whilst society in medieval Prussia was defined, in part, by segregation and cultural distinction based on language, customs and even variability in religious practices, it was also increasingly defined by assimilation. Over time, as a result of societal reorganisation under the new regime, disenfranchisement and contact with migrants, native individuals and communities gradually became 'Germanised' and, in the southern parts of Prussia, 'Polonised'. This entailed the adoption of the incoming culture's language, customs and religion, including personal names. By the turn of the 15th century, around 20% of the native peasants in Sambia had Christian names, and the proportion was around 50% amongst the free population, i.e. those of higher social status. By the mid-15th century, native names were rarely used in Prussia.[9] As a result of this, the ethnic character of the population of Prussia gradually changed. German became the prevalent language across the region and would develop its own high and low dialects. In the region which became known as Masuria, a separate Polish dialect developed from the 15th century with German and Old-Prussian loanwords, and this formed the basis for a new, composite identity.[10] By this time, the term 'Prussia' became widely used to refer to all of the Order's territories and all of its inhabitants were described as 'Prussian', irrespective of what language they spoke.[11] This included annexed Pomerania, which had a substantial population of Poles and Kashubians. Nonetheless, distinctions between native Old-Prussians and those with external ancestry continued to be recognised and were noted in 16th- and 17th-century chronicles, such as Simon Grunau's *Preussische Chronik* and Matthäus Prätorius' *Deliciae Prussicae, oder Preussische Schaubühne*. The native language was no longer spoken by the end of the 17th century, essentially marking the end of Old-Prussian as a living identity.[12]

This outline of post-crusade native Old-Prussian culture is based on written sources produced solely by the region's Christian elites, in the absence of an indigenous literary tradition. The archaeological record for the post-crusade period in Prussia may also offer alternative windows on native identities. But to what extent is it possible to identify deliberately constructed identities in the post-crusade period on the basis of material culture? This is not a straightforward question, as native identities continued to transform, even as they were essentialised by the new regime. This chapter reviews the existing evidence for the material expressions of these identities, drawing on interpretative frameworks developed for medieval Livonia and Wendish lands. It provides the first comprehensive discussion of the materiality of native identity in post-crusade Prussia, and offers a framework for future research.

Material Culture and Ethnicity in the Medieval Baltic

Archaeologists have long debated the problematic relationship between material culture and different forms of identity, including ethnicity. In broad terms, ethnicity can be defined as a self-conscious identity constructed by a group based on subjective beliefs in common origins and shared cultural and biological traits, contrasted with those of other groups. It can be twinned with other types of identity, such as religious affiliation.[13] The discussion around the problematic material correlates of ethnicity has been most intensive and developed for the Migration Period and Early Middle Ages in Europe.[14] In the case of the Later Medieval Period, where there are more abundant written sources, most discussions of ethnicity have focused on the identification of Jewish communities, except in Iberia and parts of the Balkans where there have been ongoing debates regarding the material traces of multiple ethno-religious groups. In the Baltic Sea region, the material traces of native ethnic identities have been examined for Wendish lands (north-east Germany),[15] Livonia (Latvia and Estonia)[16] and Finland,[17] whilst the existence of a shared, inter-regional German Hanseatic identity has also been proposed on the basis of shared material culture.[18] These studies have demonstrated the potential for interpreting mundane items such as ceramics in the context of multicultural identities, but also the pitfalls inherent in looking for material signifiers of ethnicity.

Native identities, which may have included ethnic affiliations, have been linked with evidence for continuity in architecture, dress accessories, ceramic forms and burial rites in regions conquered by Christian forces. These have been juxtaposed with cultural elements introduced by migrants. But to what extent were these actively used to define ethnic boundaries? For example, imported stoneware vessels are recognised as a characteristic feature of Hanseatic urban culture by the end of the 13th century, visibly associated with migrating German communities. But at the same time, in Livonian towns, stoneware vessels were consumed by both migrant and native communities, suggesting these were not used to mark ethnic boundaries by urban populations. Their absence from native rural sites until the 16th century is likely to reflect some form of intersectionality: socio-economic status, segregation from urban economic systems and perhaps a form of cultural resistance.[19] The same can be said for the almost complete absence of evidence for cleavers, based on cut marks on animal bone, from the so-called 'Liv quarter' in Riga, in comparison to the area of the castle. There is nonetheless evidence for the limited use of cleavers, a tool introduced by migrants, suggesting at least a minimal transfer in technology. This perhaps reflects the presence of what Nils Blomkvist termed 'reagents' who interacted and moved between both cultures.[20] Cultural hybridity is a key tenet of post-colonial theory, which has been increasingly applied to medieval frontier societies. This has challenged essentialist definitions of identity, such as in the case of German mercantile communities in Åbo (Fin. Turku).[21]

Archaeologies of Old-Prussian Identities

The native groups and sub-groups in Prussia referred to in historical sources are more difficult to identify archaeologically. Distinctive groups are most evident in the Iron Age and Migration Period within the historical bounds of Prussia, largely on the basis of their cemeteries. Four main Old-Prussian groups are recognised within the broader West Balt region during the Migration Period: the Sambian-Natangian group, the Elbląg group, the Olsztyn group and the Sudovian culture. For the early medieval period, archaeologists defer to the regional names mentioned in later sources, whose boundaries are typically defined by rivers. In regions with excavated cemeteries, distinctions in funerary culture are evident between named groups like the Sambians, Scalovians and Sudovians.[22] In contrast, the general absence of such cemeteries in the historical territory of Galindia has hindered the archaeological identification of a distinct group within these regions.[23] The most visible inter-regional differences are defined by the political landscape, marked by the remains of earthen strongholds and their associated settlements.[24] The regional chronology of these structures remains vague, and is the focus of an ongoing project.[25] Material culture within early medieval Prussia is nonetheless distinctive from neighbouring Western Balt and Slavic regions, particularly in terms of ceramics and metalwork.[26]

The crusading period marks a visible archaeological hiatus in Prussia. Native political centres were abandoned, new ones constructed using a different architectural tradition, planned towns were established and built up with timber-framed and brick/field stone housing, churches and monasteries were built and different manufacturing technologies were introduced, most visible in the production of new types of ceramics fired in kilns in a reductive atmosphere. There is also evidence for new types of tools, such as heavy steel-tipped cleavers which are evident from distinct cut marks on animal bone and later medieval/early modern examples.[27] These new material forms, from buildings to ceramics, have traditionally been interpreted as reflecting the presence of substantial numbers of migrants from diverse social backgrounds. Some have been associated with coming from specific regions, on the basis of analogous finds.[28] The archaeology (including architectural history) of the post-crusade period in Prussia, ca. 1283–1525, is then largely defined by the continued development of these various cultural elements.

Ceramics and Identity

The defining material culture of settlers during and after the crusading period is reduction fired ceramics referred to as 'greyware'. This is a type of wheel-thrown pottery mass-produced in German towns from the end of the 12th century.[29] Its discovery in archaeological deposits within the historical bounds of Prussia has been associated with the presence of migrants at sites where both pre- and post-crusade phases are evident. For example, at Stary Dzierzgoń, wheel-thrown "traditional" ceramics, dating from the start of the 12th century to the early decades of the 13th century, are followed stratigraphically by greyware dated to the 14th century.[30] The first appearance of greyware ceramics at sites in Prussia is typically regarded as the earliest date of incoming migrants, or at least the establishment of imported technology associated with migrant potters which provided a market for a diverse range of new vessel types. This cultural relationship has been reinforced by the discovery of a ceramic kiln and associated timber building in the north-east of the Old Town Elbing (today Elbląg), dated to the 1280s. Here, 82,451 ceramic fragments of wheel-thrown, mostly flat-bottomed greyware, were recovered. On the basis of the ceramic forms, it was suggested the potter came from Thuringia via Silesia or from Upper Saxony.[31] In this respect, greyware from crusading period Prussia has been treated by archaeologists as an ethnic marker, but was it recognised as such at the time?

More complex forms of ceramic consumption have been identified at the opposite end of the Teutonic Order's Prussian Land, in 13th- and 14th-century archaeological contexts in Klaipėda (then Memel). Here, the discovery of local-produced wheel-turned ceramics, alongside greyware and imported tableware, has been connected to the presence of local people, interacting with German migrants. At nearby Žardė, a native settlement which was occupied until at least the mid-13th century, both greyware and locally produced ceramics were found, whilst imports were absent.[32] The continued production and dominant role of local wares suggests that the new kiln technology was not adopted, and that greywares were produced by migrant potters in Klaipėda and obtained through trade. The ambiguity regarding Žardė's final phase of occupation prevents a diachronic perspective on native engagement with migrant technology. However, a longer ceramic sequence from a native settlement in eastern Prussia has been found in Staświny in north-east Poland. This is a rare example of an archaeologically investigated transition from a pre-crusade Old-Prussian lauks (the smallest unit of native settlement consisting of a few families) to a late medieval settlement which sheds further light on native agency and imported ceramic traditions.

Ceramic Transitions in Staświny

The present-day village of Staświny was established in 1475 under the name Eisermühl by Bernhard von Balzhofen, the commander of the Teutonic

Order's Brandenburg convent.³³ It appears to have replaced the nearby settlement micro-region, most probably the Old-Prussian lauks, with its principal settlement on Święta Góra (*Heiliger Berg* or *Pruzzenhöhe*, later *Święta Góra* ('Sacred Hill')).³⁴ Święta Góra is situated on an extended morainic elevation to the north of the village. The final phase of occupation of Święta Góra (Site 1) could be dated from the end of the 10th/start of 11th until the 13th or potentially 14th century. The end phase was radiocarbon-dated to the first half of the 13th century and associated with fragments of greyware ceramics. The site's toponym suggests a sacred function, but no archaeological traces could be linked to this. Nonetheless, the surrounding landscape contains toponyms incorporating the Old-Prussian word svin, namely Lake *Swinteseyte* (today Święcajty), the village of Stasswinnen (today Staświny), a meadow located near this village which until the 19th century was called Lake *Stasswin* (Stasswienen See, today Łąki Staświńskie) and a small river called Stasswin (today Staświnka). In the 16th century, the Old-Prussian linguistic appellation *Stas Swins* referred to 'this sacred [place]' (Figure 4.1).³⁵

Figure 4.1 Part of the map of the "Districtus Lecenzis" by Józef Naronowicz-Naroński showing the location of *Stasswin* (Staświny), the surrounding villages and *Letzen* (Lötzen) in 1663. Staatsbibliothek, Berlin.

Excavations in the central area of the village (Site 73) aimed to investigate whether there was any continuation in occupation between the native Sacred Hill site and the later village founded by the Teutonic Order. The excavation demonstrated that settlement began in the central area of the village in the 13th century, and continued into the period of the historically attested foundation. Within the remains of a building connected with iron and glass production (providing a link with the village's medieval name Eisermühl), occupation layer 5 contained artefacts, mainly ceramic fragments that were analogous to those found at the Święta Góra site. A fragment of wood from occupation layer 12 was radiocarbon dated to ca. 1414–1458. This evidence suggested the village established in 1475 was not a new foundation, but rather the reorganisation of the existing Old-Prussian lauks by the Teutonic Order.[36] This most probably resulted in significant changes in the layout and appearance of the village and its associated field systems. The first church in the vicinity was built three kilometres to the south at Milken (today Miłki) in the last decades of the 15th century, most likely in ca. 1481.[37] These foundations reflect a broader trend of increasing settlement in the Great Wilderness, following the cessation of hostilities with Poland-Lithuania.

One of the outcomes of the coexistence of the Old-Prussian population in Staświny, with the Slavic population that arrived from Mazovia in 1475, and in the following years, was the introduction of new ceramic vessels. Their range of forms, style and firing technology corresponds to late medieval Mazovian pottery. These were pots with defined rims. In the assemblage of late medieval kitchenware from Staświny, there is a visible transition from hand-made to wheel-thrown vessels, with the simultaneous disappearance of admixtures of finely crushed granite and sand added into the clay. These vessels were fired in conditions that resulted in their surfaces having a variable and uneven colour, ranging from dark brown to grey. This relatively low level of technological change, compared to, for example greyware vessels introduced already in the 13th century, indicates that these pots derived from local, rural workshops, probably managed by potters from northern Mazovia. This should not come as a surprise, as historical sources indicate that the settlers in Staświny and the neighbouring villages, such as Czyprki, Konopki, Lipińskie and Wyszowate were members of the nobility from northern Mazovia, originating from the Wisna Land and the vicinity of Łomża.[38] Far less common, technologically advanced, greyware pottery must have appeared in Staświny around the same time as vessels bearing all the hallmarks of Mazovian pottery. These vessels, especially greyware jugs, formed a separate set of tableware.[39]

The ceramic sequence from Staświny demonstrates that technology associated with urban centres in Prussia, originating from the eastern regions of the Holy Roman Empire in the 13th century, was consumed by the native community in this sparsely populated area of the Teutonic Order's territory. The ceramics first appear in the Święta Góra settlement in the mid-13th century, during the crusading period. They are then found in the village following its reorganisation in the later 15th century. Locally produced forms disappear, suggesting that either native Old-Prussians are relying on purchasing vessels from the new influx of migrant potters settling the region, or that the new technology was adopted in native villages. Until a kiln site is discovered in such a context, this cannot be confirmed. However, as has been argued for Livonia, it suggests the adoption of new ceramic forms in Prussia reflected availability and affordability, rather than a conscious expression of ethnic identity. There is no evidence that greyware was "resisted" by native communities. This is also suggested by the ceramic sequence from Elbing, which in its earliest phases includes locally produced Old-Prussian and Pomeranian pottery, but within a short time this is superseded by greyware and imported wares, with the continuing presence of native Old-Prussians evident from written sources.[40] It is also suggested by the inclusion of greyware ceramics in burials that have been identified as those of native Old-Prussians.

Expressing Native Identity in Death

The treatment of the dead in post-crusade period Prussia, provides more compelling material evidence for constructions of native ethnicity. The choice of particular funerary rites and the inclusion of specific sets of grave goods are widely regarded as a deliberate act, intended to communicate social meanings to onlookers and to contribute to the memorialisation of the dead. Native individuals have been identified in one urban cemetery at Barczewko (Germ. Alt-Wartenburg), and of those rural cemeteries that have been excavated, the case for native identities in Równina Dolna (Germ. Unterplehn), Bezławki (Germ. Bäslack) and Znamensk (Germ. Alt Wehlau) will be briefly examined, in turn.

Barczewko

The only urban context that Old-Prussians have been identified in archaeologically to date is the site of Barczewko II. This has been associated with the urban colony of Alt-Wartenburg, founded in the 1320s and destroyed by a Lithuanian army in 1354. Excavations in the cemetery uncovered burials in coffins, oriented west-east following normative Christian custom and with few grave goods which included belt buckles, rings and knives. Some graves also contained deposits of one or more coins. In one grave belonging to a female child, a star-shaped brooch typical of Old-Prussian jewellery was discovered, along with five bronze appliqués in the form of a stylised flower decorating headgear (interpreted as a headband or veil), a miniature glazed jug, coins and a greyware ceramic fragment. The deliberate inclusion of a ceramic fragment has been interpreted as a new type of burial rite associated with Old-Prussian neophytes – converts to Christianity. Here, it attests to the presence of local people in early urban colonies, which are otherwise only evident from Old-Prussian names mentioned in town documents.[41]

Równina Dolna

The cemetery of Równina Dolna was in use in the 13th and 14th centuries (and some have argued into the 15th century), where German and later Polish excavations uncovered a total of around 250 burials which, on the basis of the finds, have been interpreted as those of the Old-Prussian population. All the bodies were inhumed, many in coffins, and a number were buried with elaborate sets of grave goods. There was also evidence for pits filled with charcoal and ash, and some graves included deposits of charcoal. The presence of lead crosses, amulets with bear teeth set in bronze fittings and necklaces incorporating the Order's coins with the inscription *Ave Maria* has led to suggestions this was site where neophytes were already being buried, although both German and Polish excavations identified a broad range of grave orientations. Finds of weapons, including three swords, daggers, spearheads and axes, as well as spurs, point to the presence of the privileged Old-Prussian elites who were permitted to retain their arms. All the ceramics found at the site were greyware, which reflects the swift adoption of this tableware by the native population attested at other sites in former Prussia.

Influences from two cultural areas are evident in the dress accessories and bodily adornments: ring buckles with zigzag patterns or rosette applications, rosette brooches, star-shaped brooches or single-edged daggers with disc knobs can be connected with Western or Western-Central Europe, representing the latest in international fashion. However, the diversity in pendants, bear claw amulets and horseshoe brooches is Balt in origin (see Figure 4.2a–f).

The most striking Balt dress accessories are represented by metal sheet diadems that would have been worn on the forehead in the manner of a head-dress. These were found in situ on the cranium in one burial. A similar diadem sheet was found during excavations of the earthen rampart of the nearby castle located to the south-east, leading to suggestions the local Old-Prussian aristocracy were possibly residing here. A further example was also reported in the late medieval Sambian cemetery of Gerdauen (today Zheleznodorozhny).[42] *Totenkrone*-type necklaces (an Old-Prussian variant that was also popular amongst other Balt and Finno-Ugric groups) were found in three burials at Równina Dolna, most likely those of women, and the remains of silk, alongside wool and linen, again point to the presence of the native elite.[43] The abandonment of the cemetery most likely coincided with the start of internments in the local parish churchyard, far from the former burial site.

Bezławki

Excavations of the cemetery (Site 15) situated in the vicinity of the medieval and present-day settlement uncovered sixty burials, oriented west-east. The village was established in 1371, and burials appear to have begun soon after and continued until the end of the 15th/start of the 16th century. A large

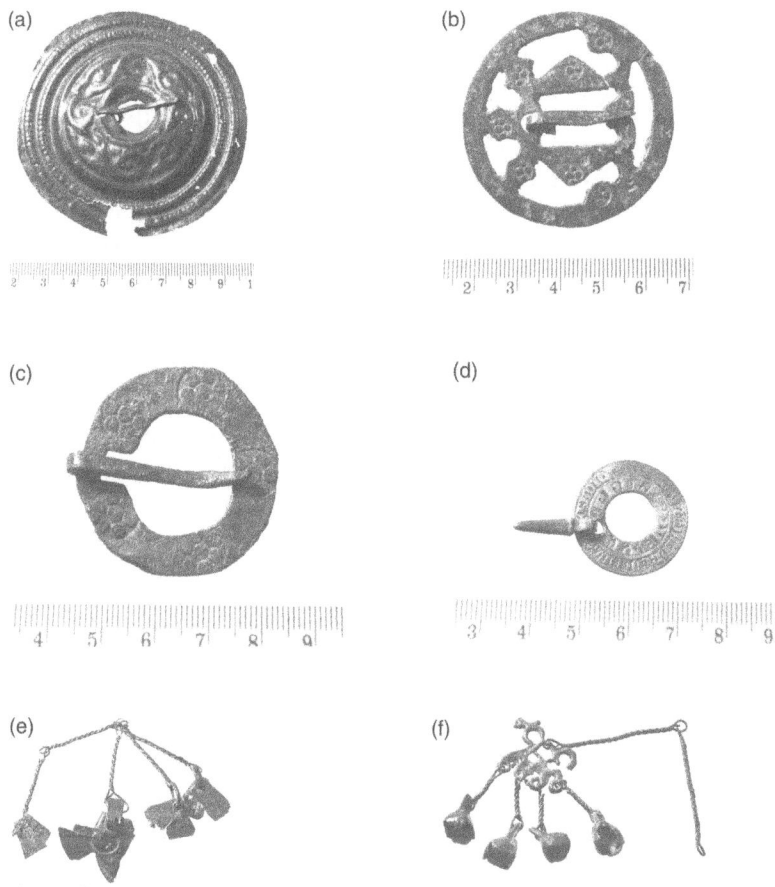

Figure 4.2 Dress accessories from the late medieval cemetery in Równina Dolna representing Western and native Prussian influences (Kętrzyn County, Warmian-Masurian Voivodeship): (a–d) brooches; (e) bear claw set in bronze fitting with metal plates; (f) pendant with bells. Archaeology Department, Museum of Warmia and Mazury in Olsztyn, Poland. Author: Jarosław Sobieraj. Reproduced with permission.

part of the cemetery had been destroyed by subsequent development, but 230 graves containing some 300 individuals were uncovered. Most burials were completely unfurnished, but in nine, there were individual fragments of greyware ceramics within the grave fill, with one exception where two fragments were discovered. In several graves, eggshells from chickens were found, referencing perhaps both pre-Christian and Christian symbolism associated with resurrection.[44] In a few instances fragments of burnt clay were also discovered. A total of 43 coins, most of which dated to the 14th and 15th centuries, were found at the site. The majority had been deposited with buried individuals. Other grave goods included belt buckles, knives, brooches and scissors, as well as single ceramic fragments.[45] Coins were also found at Site II, where they appear to have been deposited from the mid-15th century and were interpreted as reflecting both votive deposits and trade-related losses in the church. These findings are not unusual, and are attested in churches in other parts of northern Europe.[46] The cemetery at Bezławki provides an example of the end stage of the homogenisation of funerary customs in rural Prussia. The deposition of coins in graves would endure as a funerary custom in Masuria until the first half of the 20th century.[47]

Alt Wehlau (Znamensk)

The cemetery at Alt Wehlau is located near Znamensk in eastern Sambia, within the former Teutonic Order's commandery of Königsberg.[48] Here, excavations uncovered some 372 burials dating from the mid-13th century to the start of the 17th century.[49] The Order had built a castle nearby and in 1361 a church was constructed within the bounds of the cemetery. Its foundations truncated and destroyed earlier graves, although there was no evidence for the deliberate removal of artefacts. The church would itself be demolished by the time of the cemetery's abandonment. However, of those post-crusade native cemeteries which have been investigated, the one at Alt Wehlau is the only one with a confirmed church, which may reflect attempts by the diocesan authorities to suppress perceived pagan customs, or to define the cemetery as a Christian burial ground. Burials dating to the 13th and 14th centuries were interpreted as belonging to Old-Prussians who served as the castle garrison, a practice recorded in the Order's documents.

Burials at this site featured a variety of personal adornments, which included a range of dress accessories and bodily adornments found in other Old-Prussian cemeteries, including *Totenkrone*,[50] individual and strung glass beads, brooches, bronze and silver rings, bone combs and bracelets. Graves dated to the 14th century included bags containing silver bracteates minted by the Teutonic Order, cross pendants attached to necklaces and bear claws set in bronze with a pair of trapezoid pendants, echoing similar combinations of items found in Równina Dolna. Male burials were furnished with weapons, particularly javelin- and spear-heads, some of which were broken and bent, and in two instances swords, with burned and broken blades. In around 40% of burials dating to the 13th and 14th centuries, there were associated pits containing fragments of charcoal, bird bones and wheel-thrown ceramics. In one burial, the discovery of a buckle possibly decorated with the Order's cross and a stylised image of the mythical companion of the Old-Prussian god Perkunas has been interpreted as representing a fusion of the two cultures.[51] By the 15th century, the range of grave goods noticeably decreases in both male and female burials.

Regime change in Prussia saw the rapid cessation of the main indicators of pagan funerary rites – cremation and the ritual deposition of animals, especially horses.[52] There are occasional reported findings of post-crusade cremation burials, such as at Stabławki (Germ. Stablack) dating to the 15th century,[53] and in Dobre Miasto (Germ. Guttstadt) where the cremains were dated by the accompanying later medieval sword.[54] In the description of the borders of the diocese of Sambia from the years 1322 and 1331, there are also references to native cremation cemeteries.[55] However, in the large post-crusade cemeteries that have been excavated the rite is absent. The practice of ritual animal killing by Old-Prussians in the post-crusade period is mentioned in written sources, but there is no firm evidence this continued in cemeteries. Where animal bones have been reported at sites such as Alt Wehlau, these deposits may represent food offerings but it is not possible to determine if the animals were deliberately killed for funerary purposes or if portions of meat were simply brought to the cemetery.

Instead, expressions of identity became focused on the adornments of individuals in death. Excavations of post-crusade cemeteries in the historical territories of Prussia and Livonia have identified comparable trends, albeit with regional differences reflecting the tempo of social and religious change.[56] In both regions, 'native dress' has been identified as a deliberate and socially conservative means of displaying social identity. These funerary choices would have also intersected with ethnic identity, with German counterparts most evident in urban contexts.[57] When this eventually changed amongst local elites, the most visible carriers of this identity, it most likely reflected the adoption of Western-Central European fashions. This is already evident in the adoption of greyware ceramics, which features in all the cemeteries surveyed above. In other words, these archaeological tendencies reflect the material expressions of Germanisation that are widely understood to have transformed native Old-Prussian culture.

In the territory of modern Latvia elaborate dress accessories characteristic of the Iron Age are no longer deposited in graves by the late 13th century, whilst southern Estonia and eastern Latvia remained conservative, retaining earlier traditions. In the easternmost parts of Livonia, the only noticeable change in funerary practices was the gradually abandoned of cremation, whilst gender-based furnished burials continued.[58] This is also the case in Lithuania, with archaeological evidence for cremation ending by the mid-15th century. Here, the late appearance of bear claw pendants, also in predominantly female burials, has been interpreted a little differently – as a potential signifier of Christianisation, albeit one reinterpreted using an existing native symbol.[59] In the case of Prussia, by the mid-15th century, luxurious and impractical objects such as the *Totenkrone*-type necklace and bear claws pendants, which have been found in five post-crusade cemeteries in Prussia typically in association with female burials, were no longer being deposited with the dead.

In summary, identifying archaeological traces that would have been recognisable as 'ethnically native Old-Prussian' by people at the time are solely – and in some cases tentatively – confined to inhumation burials in the post-crusade period. These have been found in cemeteries that appear to have been exclusively used by native communities, and in those shared with migrants or those of migrant-descent.

Conclusion

The ethnic diversity of post-crusade Prussia is difficult to identify archaeologically, largely because almost no villages occupied by the pre-crusade native population have been extensively excavated. The sites at Staświny and Święta Góra represents a rare example of a native settlement complex in Prussia with an occupation sequence stretching from the pre-crusade to post-medieval period, where artefacts used on a daily basis have been recovered. But to what extent would ethnic labels have been attributed to material culture? The ceramic record for medieval Prussia can provide a valuable lens on technological and cultural change during and after the crusading period, but there is no evidence that an ethnic identity was mapped onto pottery. Instead, this provides a window on the tempo of cultural transformation at the scale of individual settlements. The evidence from Staświny, the first detailed analysis of a ceramic assemblage from a native Old-Prussian rural site spanning the pre- to post-crusade periods, suggests that the reorganisation of native rural settlements integrated them within the Teutonic Order's economic system. This is also confirmed by the regular deposits of coins in graves associated with Old-Prussians.

In contrast, clothing and bodily adornments buried with the dead bring us closer to what it meant to be recognised as a native Old-Prussian, in a society where visual display was a fundamental means of social communication. This changed over time, both in how the dead were presented and where they were interred. Furnished burials in the post-crusade period, with distinctive jewellery that represented both the continuity of past customs and hybridity, incorporating new forms of material culture, have been plausibly interpreted as the graves of Old-Prussians. Some reflect a renegotiation of power relations following regime change, but more recently, all have been interpreted as the graves of neophytes. Although defined by cultural hybridity, but they were precursors to the adoption of normative and relatively homogenous Christian funerary practices, evident in the urban cemeteries dominated by the migrant culture. The abandonment of native cemeteries and the relocation of burials to churchyards such as the one at Bezławki or Barczewko was a step towards the homogenisation of late medieval rural Old-Prussian society. This shift in burial location ultimately severed connections with the ancestral dead – an important source of familial and dynastic identities, firmly connected to a sense of place.

The tempo of these changes was slow and the memory of ancestral burial grounds endured for several generations. Written sources from different regions of Prussia point to the continued practice of burial away from churches, in earlier cemeteries.⁶⁰ Where there is evidence for the establishment of native cemeteries during or after the crusading period, such as at Alt Wehlau and Równina Dolna, new mortuary rites were introduced negotiating the process of religious transformation. Studies of long-term trends in burial rites in Livonia indicate that ascribing simplistic religious labels to the treatment of the dead is problematic.⁶¹ Instead, changes in fashion and consumption have been revealed to be major drivers in the patterning of grave goods. However, dress plays an important role in the visual construction of ethnic identity, and the persistence of Old-Prussian jewellery and bodily adornments suggests a conscious choice was made to maintain some visible difference from the migrant population.

In order to further our understanding of the material dimensions of native Old-Prussian identities, two approaches can be suggested. Firstly, the application of isotopic and genetic analyses to skeletal material from archival and future cemetery excavations is a crucial next step for characterising the population of post-crusade Prussia.⁶² Secondly, archaeologists should consider investigating rural settlements in more detail. Some of these may still be inhabited, in which case Lewis' strategy for targeted excavation in collaboration with local communities would prove beneficial.⁶³ Given the prevalence of excavated cemeteries, especially on the Sambian Peninsula, related settlements and religious sites – both sacred natural sites and Christian structures such as chapels and churches – could be the focus of future, targeted excavations. This would also be complemented by environmental data, which would provide additional proxies for the range and intensity of human activity in the associated landscape. The overarching framework for such an approach is essentially provided by landscape archaeology, which we argue has the potential to significantly further our understanding of the Old-Prussian population following the Teutonic Order's conquest.

Notes

1 Dusburg (W), 4 (Prologus), 50 (pars I, cap. 3) (*cf.* transl.: Dusburg (W/W), 5, 43–44). Peter describes Prussia as being made up of eleven regions, as he includes the Mazovian frontier castellany centred on Culm, which he refers to as depopulated. The terms native and indigenous are used interchangeably in this chapter, whilst acknowledging they can have specific and divergent meanings in other contexts.
2 Seweryn Szczepański, *Pomezania. Na styku świata pogańskiego i chrześcijańskiego* (Olsztyn: Instytut Północny w Olsztynie, 2019), 42–97.
3 Gerard Labuda, 'Powstanie i rozwój państwa krzyżackiego w Prusach,' in Marian Biskup and Gerard Labuda, *Dzieje zakonu krzyżackiego w Prusach. Gospodarka – Społeczeństwo – Państwo – Ideologia* (Gdańsk: Wydawnictwo Morskie, 1986, 1st ed.), 177–178; Marian Biskup, 'Etniczno-demograficzne przemiany Prus Krzyżackich w rozwoju osadnictwa w średniowieczu,' *Kwartalnik Historyczny* 98, no. 2 (1991): 133.
4 Joachim Stephan, 'Prusowie w gospodarstwie krzyżaków,' in *Gospodarka ludów morza bałtyckiego starożytność i średniowiecze. Mare Integrans: Studia nad dziejami wybrzeży Morza Bałtyckiego*, eds. Michał Bogacki, Maciej Franz, and Zbigniew Pilarczyk (Toruń: Wydawnictwo Adam Marszałek, 2009), 317–325.

5 Wiesław Długokęcki, 'Społeczeństwo wiejskie,' in *Państwo zakonu krzyżackiego w Prusach. Władza i społeczeństwo*, ed. Marian Biskup and Roman Czaja (Warszawa: Wydawnictwo Naukowe PWN, 2008), 460–494.
6 Grzegorz Białuński, *Osadnictwo regionu Wielkich Jezior Mazurskich od XIV do początku XVIII wieku – starostwo leckie (giżyckie) i ryńskie*, Rozprawy i Materiały Ośrodka Badań Naukowych im. Wojciecha Kętrzyńskiego w Olsztynie 159 (Olsztyn: Ośrodek Badań Naukowych im. Wojciecha Kętrzyńskiego, 1996), 45.
7 Józef Matuszewski, *Iura Prutenorum* (Toruń: Państwowe Wydawnictwo Naukowe, 1963), 14–15; Długokęcki, 'Społeczeństwo wiejskie,' passim.
8 Roman Czaja and Mathew Frank Stevens, 'The place of native populations in the chartered towns of conquered regions. Wales and Prussia as a comparative case study,' in *Towns on the Edge in Medieval Europe: The Social and Political Order of Peripheral Urban Communities from the Twelfth to Sixteenth Centuries*, eds. Mathew Frank Stevens and Roman Czaja (Oxford: Oxford University Press, 2022), 21–45.
9 Anti Selart, 'A new faith and a new name? Crusades, conversion, and baptismal names in medieval Baltics,' *Journal of Baltic Studies* 47, no. 2 (2016): 179–196.
10 Andrzej Sakson, *Mazurzy, społeczność pogranicza* (Poznań: Instytut Zachodni, 1990).
11 Antoni Czacharowski, 'Toruń średniowieczny (do roku 1454),' in *Toruń dawny i dzisiejszy: zarys dziejów*, ed. Marian Biskup (Warszawa: Państwowe Wydawnictwo Naukowe, 1983), 72.
12 Algirdas Sabaliauskas, *We the Balts* (Vilnius: Science and Encyclopaedia Publishing), 70.
13 Sian Jones, *The Archaeology of Ethnicity. Constructing Identities in the Past and Present* (London: Routledge, 1997).
14 For example, Florin Curta, 'Some remarks on ethnicity in medieval archaeology,' *Early Medieval Europe* 15, no. 2 (2007): 159–185; id., 'Medieval archaeology and ethnicity: Where are we?,' *History Compass* 9, no. 7 (2011): 537–548; Jacek Bojarski, 'Ethnic or cultural identity? The problem of elite burials in early medieval cemeteries of the Chełmno – Dobrzyń zone,' in *Gruppenidentitäten in Ostmitteleuropa. Auf der Suchen nach Identität*, eds. Bogusław Dybaś and Jacek Bojarski (Göttingen, Vandenhoeck & Ruprecht, 2021), 47–70
15 Magdalena Naum, 'Re-emerging frontiers: Postcolonial theory and historical archaeology of the borderlands,' *Journal of Archaeological Method and Theory* 17 (2010): 101–131.
16 Arvi Haak, 'Problems in defining ethnic identity in medieval towns of Estonia on the basis of archaeological sources,' in *Today I Am Not The One I Was Yesterday: Archaeology, Identity, and Change*, eds. Arvi Haak, Valter Lang, and Mika Lavento (Tartu: Tartu Ülikool, 2015), 19; Heiki Valk, 'Finnic language islands in eastern Latvia: Archaeological background and perspective', *Eesti Ja Soome-Ugri Keeleteaduse Ajakiri* 12, no. 2 (2021): 95–122.
17 Timo Ylimaunu, Sami Lakomäki, Titta Kallio-Seppä, Paul R. Mullins, Risto Nurmi, and Markku Kuorilehto, 'Borderlands as spaces: Creating third spaces and fractured landscapes in medieval Northern Finland,' *Journal of Social Archaeology* 14, no. 2 (2014): 244–267.
18 David Gaimster, 'A parallel history: the archaeology of Hanseatic urban culture in the Baltic c. 1200–1600,' *World Archaeology* 37 (2005): 408–423; Magdalena Naum, 'Migration, identity and material culture: Hanseatic translocality in the medieval Baltic Sea,' in *Comparative Perspectives on Past Colonisation, Maritime Interaction and Cultural Integration*, eds. Lene Melheim, Håkon Glørstad, and Zanette Tsigaridas Glørstad (Sheffield: Equinox, 2016), 129–148.
19 Erki Russow, *Importkeraamika Lääne-Eesti linnades 13.–17. sajandil* (Tallinn: Tallinna Raamatutrükikoda, 2006), 207.

20 Rowena Banerjea, Monika Badura, Uldis Kalējs, Aija Cerina, Krzysztof Gos, Sheila Hamilton-Dyer, Mark Maltby, Krish Seetah, and Aleks Pluskowski, 'A multi-proxy, diachronic and spatial perspective on the urban activities within an indigenous community in medieval Riga, Lativa,' *Quaternary International* 460, no. 1 (2017): 3–21.
21 Visa Immonen, 'Defining a culture: the meaning of Hanseatic in medieval Turku,' *Antiquity* 81, no. 313 (2007): 720–732.
22 Ludwika Jończyk, 'The last Yotvingian pagans. The case of the Mosiężysko Cemetery in Northeast Poland,' in *From Paganism to Christianity. Burial Rites During the Transition Period*, ed. Rytis Jonaitis and Irma Kaplūnaitė (Vilnius: Lietuvos istorijos institutas, 2024), 219–243.
23 Wojciech Nowakowski, '"Kurhany Jaćwięgów" – kilkadziesiąt lat naukowego mitu,' *Światowit* IX (L), Fasc. B (2012): 181–192; id., 'Jaćwieskie cmentarzysko warstwowe (?) w miejscowości Burdyniszki, na Suwalszczyźnie,' in *Studia z dziejów cywilizacji. Studia ofiarowane profesorowi Jerzemu Gąssowskiemu w pięćdziesiątą rocznicę pracy naukowej*, ed. Andrzej Buko (Warszawa: Instytut Archeologii Uniwersytetu Warszawskiego, 1998), 119–123; Ludwika Jończyk, 'Niemcowizna, st. 1, woj. podlaskie. Badania w roku 2011,' *Światowit* IX (L), Fasc. B, (2011): 319–322; id., 'Szurpiły, st. 8 ("Mosiężysko"), woj. podlaskie. Badania w roku 2011,' *Światowit* IX (L), Fasc. B (2011): 349–353; Ludwika Sawicka, 'Szurpiły, st. 8 ("Mosiężysko"), woj. podlaskie. Badania w latach 2008–2010,' *Światowit* VIII (XLIX), Fasc. B (2011): 263–268; Marcin Engel and Jerzy Siemaszko, 'Jaćwieskie cmentarzysko ciałopalne w Krukówku, pow. suwalski. Okoliczności odkrycia i opis znalezisk,' *Studia Archaeologica Sudauica* 2 (2019): 299–309.
24 Maciej Karczewski, 'Environment, Settlement and Economy of the West Baltic Tribes in the Roman Period,' *Archaeologia Lituania* 7 (2006): 54–65; Tomasz Nowakiewicz, 'Galindia in the Viking Age – New Shape of the Culture,' in *Transformatio Mundi: The Transition from the Late Migration Period to the Early Viking Age in the East Baltic*, ed. Mindaugas Bertašius (Kaunas: Kaunas University of Technology, Department of Philosophy and Cultural Science, 2006), 161–172.
25 Timo Ibsen, 'Burgwälle als Archive der Siedlungsforschung: Ein neuer Ansatz zur Datierung von Burgwällen im Baltikum am Beispiel von Apuolė in Litauen,' *Archäologisches Korrespondenzblatt* 48, no. 2 (2018): 241–263; id., 'Spatial and temporal distribution of hillforts on the Sambian peninsula in Russia,' in *Fortifications in their Natural and Cultural Landscape: From Organising Space to the Creation of Power*, eds. Timo Ibsen, Kristin Ilves, Birgit Maixner, Sebastian Messal, and Jens Schneeweiß (Bonn: Habelt-Verlag, 2022), 141–166.
26 Roman Shiroukhov, 'Western Balts between the Vikings and Crusades. The Development of the Southeast Baltic Region in the 10th–13th centuries according to the Archaeological Data,' *ZBSA Jahresbericht* (2016): 68–71.
27 Krish Seetah, Aleksander Pluskowski, Daniel Makowiecki, and Linas Daugnora, 'New Technology or Adaptation at the Frontier? Butchery as a Signifier of Cultural Transitions in the Medieval Eastern Baltic,' *Archaeologia Baltica* 20 (2013): 84–101.
28 Aleksander Pluskowski, *The Archaeology of the Prussian Crusade* (London: Routledge, 2013, 1st ed., 2022, 2nd ed.)
29 Hartwig Lüdtke, 'Grauware des 12. Bis 15. Jahrhunderts,' in *Handbuch zur mittelalterlichen Keramik in Nordeurope*, eds. Hartwig Lüdtke and Kurt Schietzel (Neumünster: Wachholtz Verlag, 2001), 83–173.
30 Joanna Jezierska, 'Analiza ceramiki ze Starego Dzierzgonia, stan 1.,' in *Wielokulturowy obiekt warowny na Górze Zamkowej oraz gród cyplowy w Starym Dzierzgoniu*, ed. Daniel Gazda (Warszawa: Trzccia Strona, 2018), 155 184, 161–163

31 Grażyna Nawrolska, 'Handicrafts in medieval Elbląg,' in *Lübecker Kolloquium zur Stadtarchäologie im Hanseraum V: Das Handwerk*, eds. Ilka Hillenstedt a.o. (Lübeck: Schmidt-Römhild, 2006), 393–416, 396–400.
32 Edvinas Ubis, 'Archaeological data as evidence of cultural interaction between the Teutonic Order and local communities: problems and perspectives,' *Archaeologia Baltica* 25 (2018): 164–176.
33 Białuński, *Osadnictwo*, 56–57. For details of the archaeology see: Małgorzata Karczewska and Maciej Karczewski, 'Grodzisko Święta Góra w Staświnach w Krainie Wielkich Jezior Mazurskich. Archeologia archiwalna i nowa,' KMW 2/256 (2007): 131–163; Aleksander Pluskowski, Marc Jarzebowski, Małgorzata Karczewska, and Maciej Karczewski, 'Sites in Prussia: the historical and archaeological background,' in *Environment, Colonization and the Baltic Crusader States*, ed. Aleksander Pluskowski (Turnhout: Brepols, 2019), 257–292.
34 Małgorzata Karczewska, Maciej Karczewski, and Aleksander Pluskowski, 'Późnośredniowieczna i wczesnonowożytna wieś Staświny w komturii brandenburskiej (Polska NE) w świetle źródeł archeologicznych,' in *Materiały do archeologii Warmii i Mazur*, ed. Sławomir Wadyl, Maciej Karczewski, and Mirosław Hoffmann (Warszawa: Instytut Archeologii Uniwersytetu Warszawskiego/ Białystok: Instytut Historii i Nauk Politycznych Uniwersytetu w Białymstoku, 2015), 195, fig. 2.
35 Robert Klimek, 'Pogańskie kamienne ołtarze Prusów,' in *Zjawiska magiczno-demoniczne na tle dawnych ziem pruskich na tle porównawczym*, ed. Kazimierz Grążawski and Jan Gancewski (Olsztyn: Wydawnictwo Uniwersytetu Warmińsko-Mazurskiego, 2014), 47–66, 64–65.
36 Białuński, *Osadnictwo*, 56, 79.
37 Małgorzata Karczewska, Maciej Karczewski, Robert Kempa, and Ewa Pirożnikow, *Miłki. Monografia krajoznawcza gminy mazurskiej* (Białystok, Miłki: Wydawnictwo Kwadrat, 2005), 108.
38 Białuński, *Osadnictwo*, 81–83.
39 Małgorzata Karczewska, Maciej Karczewski, and Aleksander Pluskowski, 'Późnośredniowieczna i wczesnonowożytna wieś Staświny,' 200–201, fig. 8.
40 Grażyna Nawrolska, 'Przemiany kulturowe w XIII-wiecznym Elblągu efektem spotkania tradycji i obcych wpływów,' *Archaeologia Historica Polona* 21 (2013): 79–99.
41 Arkadiusz Koperkiewicz, 'Nowe porządki, stare obyczaje? Wyjątki z praktyk pogrzebowych pruskich neofitów na przykładzie Bezławek,' in *Zjawiska magiczno-demoniczne*, eds. Grążawski and Gancewski, 17–46; id., 'Barczewko – a cemetery of the first settlers in Southern Warmia against the background of medieval inhumation necropolises in Teutonic Prussia,' *Archaeologia Historica Polona* 28 (2020): 199–228; id., 'Anno 1354 Kynstute, Algard ... festinant in Wartenberg. O trudnych początkach Barczewa,' in *Homini, qui in honore fuit. Księga pamiątkowa poświęcona śp. Profesorowi Grzegorzowi Białuńskiemu*, eds. Alicja Dobrosielska, Aleksander Pluskowski, and Seweryn Szczepański (Olsztyn: Towarzystwo Naukowe Pruthenia, 2020), 303–304.
42 Norbert Goßler and Christoph Jahn, 'Die archäologischen Untersuchungen am spätmittelalterlichen Gräberfeld und am Burgwall von Unterplehnen, Kr. Rastenburg (Równina Dolna, pow. Kętrzyński) zwischen 1827 und 1940 – Ein Rekonstruktionsversuch anhand der Materialien im Berliner Bestand der Prussia-Sammlung (ehem. Königsberg/Ostpreußen),' *Acta Praehistorica et Archaeologica* 45 (2013): 230.
43 Romuald Odoj, 'Sprawozdanie z prac wykopaliskowych przeprowadzonych w Równinie Dolnej, pow. Kętrzyn w 1956 i 1957 r.,' *Rocznik Olsztyński* 1 (1958): 117–156; id., Sprawozdanie z prac wykopaliskowych w miejscowości Równina Dolna, pow. Kętrzyn, *Wiadomości Archeologiczne* 23 (1960): 177–196.

44 Arkadiusz Koperkiewicz, '"Zmartwychwstanie neofity" czyli pierwsi chrześcijanie w okolicach Świętej Lipki,' in *Święta Lipka: perła na pograniczu ziem, kultur i wyznań*, part 2, eds. Aleksander Jacyniak and Edgar Sukiennik (Kętrzyn: Labrita, 2020), 51.
45 Arkadiusz Koperkiewicz, 'Cmentarzysko w Bezławkach (stanowisko XV). Badania w latach 2010–11,' in *Bezławki – ocalić od zniszczenia. Wyniki prac interdyscyplinarnych prowadzonych w latach 2008–2011*, ed. Arkadiusz Koperkiewicz (Gdańsk: Wydawnictwo Uniwersytetu Gdańskiego, 2013), 137–152.
46 Borys Paszkiewicz, 'La monnoye des Prussenayres – monety z Bezławek,' in *Bezławki*, ed. Koperkiewicz, 183–219.
47 Max Töppen, *Wierzenia mazurskie*, eds. Anna Szyfer, Władysław Ogrodziński, Paweł Błażewicz, and Jerzy M. Łapo (Dąbrówno: Oficyna Wydawnicza Retman, 2008), 127; Janusz Bohdanowicz, 'Wyposażanie zmarłych,' in *Komentarze do Polskiego Atlasu Etnograficznego*, vol. V, *Zwyczaje, obrzędy i wierzenia pogrzebowe*, ed. Janusz Bohdanowicz (Wrocław: Polskie Towarzystwo Ludoznawcze, 1999), 105.
48 Vladimir I. Kulakov and A. A. Valuev, 'Veluva (Alt-Wehlau), ein heidnischer Friedhof im christlichen Nadrauen,' *Eurasia Antiqua. Zeitschrift für Archäologie Eurasiens* 2 (1996): 493–499; A. A. Valuev, 'Alt Wehlau – "Pogańskie" cmentarzysko na obszarze chrześcijańskich Prus w świetle badań archeologicznych,' in *Archeologia ziem pruskich. Nieznane zbiory i materiały archiwalne. Ostróda 15–17 X 1998*, eds. Mirosław Hoffmann and Jarosław Sobieraj (Olsztyn: Stowarzyszenie Naukowe Archeologów Polskich. Oddział w Olsztynie, 1999), 397–400.
49 A. A. Valuev, S. A. Denisov, and K. N. Skvorcov, 'Amulety-podveski «medvezhij kogot'» iz pogrebenij XIII–XV vv. nekropolja Al't-Velau,' *KSIA* 264 (2021): 290–306.
50 Although Ludwika Jończyk and Karol Żołędziowski dispute the identification of these fragments from this site, see Ludwika Jończyk and Karol Żołędziowski, 'Elite Burden. *Totenkrone*-Type Necklaces from the 'Mosiężysko' Cemetery in Szurpiły,' *Światowit* LX (2021): 59–75.
51 Vladimir V. Kulakov, 'Sudavy na Sambii v XIII–XIV vv.,' *Vestnik Arkheologii, Antropologii i Etnografii* 53, no. (2021): 91–98.
52 Roman Shiroukhov, 'Prussian graves in the Sambian Peninsula, with imports, weapons and horse harnesses, from the tenth to the thirteenth century: The question of the warrior elite,' *Archaeologia Baltica* 18 (2012): 224–25.
53 Stanisław Chmielewski, 'Czy pruski grób ciałopalny z XV wieku? (Próba interpretacji opisu znaleziska z 1703 r.),' *Rocznik Olsztyński* 5 (1963): 295–319.
54 Mirosław Hoffmann, 'Theodor Josef Blell,' *Borussia* 7 (1993): 186.
55 Seweryn Szczepański, 'Surkapurn and Kreken: The phenomenon of name and place and the organisation of sacred space in Prussia using archaeology and other sources,' in *Ecologies of Crusading, Colonisation and Religious Conversion in the Medieval Eastern Baltic*, ed. Aleksander Pluskowski (Turnhout: Brepols, 2019), 175–184.
56 For a summary of Livonia see Aleksander Pluskowski and Heiki Valk. 'Conquest and Europeanisation: the archaeology of the crusades in Livonia, Prussia and Lithuania,' in *The Crusader World*, ed. Adrian Boas (London: Routledge, 2016), 568–592.
57 Magdalena Naum, 'Multi-ethnicity and material exchanges in late medieval Tallinn,' *European Journal of Archaeology* 17, no. 4 (2014): 656–677.
58 Eugenijus Svetikas, 'XIV a. pabaigos – XV a. amule-tai iš apkaustyto lokio nago Lietuvos Didžiojoje Kunigaikštystėje ir kaimyniniuose kraštuose,' *Lietuvos Archeologija* 34 (2009): 171–210.
59 Tatjana Berga. *Augšdaugavas 14.–17. gadsimta senvietas: no Krāslavas līdz Slutiškiem* (Riga: Latvijas vēstures institūts, 2007).

60 Szczepański, 'Surkapurn and Kreken,' 182.
61 Vitolds Muižnieks, 'The co-existence of two traditions in the territory of present-day Latvia in the 13th–18th centuries. Burial in dress and in a shroud,' in *The Archaeology of Death in Post-Medieval Europe*, ed. Sarah Tarlow (Berlin: de Gruyter, 2015), 89–110.
62 Koperkiewicz, 'Nowe porządki,' 21.
63 Carenza Lewis, 'Test pit excavation within currently occupied rural settlements: results of the University of Cambridge CORS project in 2011,' *Medieval Settlement Research* 28 (2013): 42–56.

Primary Sources

Piotr von Dusburga, *Kronika ziemi Pruskiej*. Edited by Jarosław Wenta. Translated by Sławomir Wyszomirski. Toruń: Wydawnictwo Naukowe Uniwersytetu Mikołaja Kopernika, 2011.

Secondary Sources

Banerjea, Rowena, Monika Badura, Uldis Kalējs, Aija Cerina, Krzysztof Gos, Sheila Hamilton-Dyer, Mark Maltby, Krish Seetah, and Aleks Pluskowski, 'A multi-proxy, diachronic and spatial perspective on the urban activities within an indigenous community in medieval Riga, Lativa.' *Quaternary International* 460, no. 1 (2017): 3–21.
Berga, Tatjana. *Augšdaugavas 14.–17. gadsimta senvietas: no Krāslavas līdz Slutiškiem*. Riga: Latvijas vēstures institūts, 2007.
Białuński, Grzegorz. *Osadnictwo regionu Wielkich Jezior Mazurskich od XIV do początku XVIII wieku – starostwo leckie (giżyckie) i ryńskie*. Rozprawy i Materiały Ośrodka Badań Naukowych im. Wojciecha Kętrzyńskiego w Olsztynie 159. Olsztyn: Ośrodek Badań Naukowych im. Wojciecha Kętrzyńskiego, 1996.
Biskup, Marian. 'Etniczno-demograficzne przemiany Prus Krzyżackich w rozwoju osadnictwa w średniowieczu.' *Kwartalnik Historyczny* 98, no. 2 (1991): 129–150.
Labuda, Gerard. 'Powstanie i rozwój państwa krzyżackiego w Prusach.' In *Dzieje zakonu krzyżackiego w Prusach. Gospodarka – Społeczeństwo – Państwo – Ideologia*, edited by Marian Biskup and Gerard Labuda, 96–263. Gdańsk: Wydawnictwo Morskie, 1986, 1st edition.
Bohdanowicz, Janusz. 'Wyposażanie zmarłych.' In *Komentarze do Polskiego Atlasu Etnograficznego*, vol. V, *Zwyczaje, obrzędy i wierzenia pogrzebowe*, edited by Janusz Bohdanowicz, 105. Wrocław: Polskie Towarzystwo Ludoznawcze, 1999.
Bojarski, Jacek. 'Ethnic or cultural identity? The problem of elite burials in early medieval cemeteries of the Chełmno – Dobrzyń zone.' In *Gruppenidentitäten in Ostmitteleuropa. Auf der Suchen nach Identität*, edited by Bogusław Dybaś and Jacek Bojarski, 47–70. Göttingen: Vandenhoeck & Ruprecht, 2021.
Chmielewski, Stanisław. 'Czy pruski grób ciałopalny z XV wieku? (Próba interpretacji opisu znaleziska z 1703 r.).' *Rocznik Olsztyński* 5 (1963): 295–319.
Curta, Florin. 'Some remarks on ethnicity in medieval archaeology.' *Early Medieval Europe* 15, no. 2 (2007): 159–185.
Curta, Florin. 'Medieval archaeology and ethnicity: Where are we?' *History Compass* 9, no. 7 (2011): 537–548.
Czacharowski, Antoni. 'Toruń średniowieczny (do roku 1454).' In *Toruń dawny i dzisiejszy: zarys dziejów*, edited by Marian Biskup, 31–131. Warszawa: Państwowe Wydawnictwo Naukowe, 1983.

Czaja, Roman and Mathew Frank Stevens. 'The place of native populations in the chartered towns of conquered regions. Wales and Prussia as a comparative case study.' In *Towns on the Edge in Medieval Europe. The Social and Political Order of Peripheral Urban Communities from the Twelfth to Sixteenth Centuries*, edited by Mathew Frank Stevens and Roman Czaja, 21–45. Oxford: Oxford University Press, 2022.

Długokęcki, Wiesław. 'Społeczeństwo wiejskie.' In *Państwo zakonu krzyżackiego w Prusach. Władza i społeczeństwo*, edited by Marian Biskup and Roman Czaja, 460–494. Warszawa: Wydawnictwo Naukowe PWN, 2008.

Engel, Marcin and Jerzy Siemaszko. 'Jaćwieskie cmentarzysko ciałopalne w Krukówku, pow. suwalski. Okoliczności odkrycia i opis znalezisk.' *Studia Archaeologica Sudauica* 2 (2019): 299–309.

Gaimster, David. 'A parallel history: the archaeology of Hanseatic urban culture in the Baltic c. 1200–1600.' *World Archaeology* 37 (2005): 408–423.

Haak, Arvi. 'Problems in defining ethnic identity in medieval towns of Estonia on the basis of archaeological sources.' In *Today I Am Not The One I Was Yesterday: Archaeology, Identity, and Change*, edited by Arvi Haak, Valter Lang, and Mika Lavento, 13–27. Tartu: Tartu Ülikool, 2015.

Hoffmann, Mirosław. 'Theodor Josef Blell.' *Borussia* 7 (1993): 185–187.

Ibsen, Timo. 'Burgwälle als Archive der Siedlungsforschung: Ein neuer Ansatz zur Datierung von Burgwällen im Baltikum am Beispiel von Apuolė in Litauen.' *Archäologisches Korrespondenzblatt* 48 no. 2 (2018): 241–263.

Ibsen, Timo. 'Spatial and temporal distribution of hillforts on the Sambian peninsula in Russia.' In *Fortifications in their Natural and Cultural Landscape: From Organising Space to the Creation of Power*, edited by Timo Ibsen, Kristin Ilves, Birgit Maixner, Sebastian Messal, and Jens Schneeweiß, 141–166. Bonn: Habelt-Verlag, 2022.

Immonen, Visa. 'Defining a culture: the meaning of Hanseatic in medieval Turku.' *Antiquity* 83 no. 313 (2007): 720–732.

Jezierska, Joanna. 'Analiza ceramiki ze Starego Dzierzgonia, stan 1.' In *Wielokulturowy obiekt warowny na Górze Zamkowej oraz gród cyplowy w Starym Dzierzgoniu*, edited by Daniel Gazda, 155–184. Warszawa: Trzecia Strona, 2018.

Jończyk, Ludwika. 'Niemcowizna, st. 1, woj. podlaskie. Badania w roku 2011.' *Światowit* IX (L), Fasc. B (2011): 319–322.

Jończyk, Ludwika. 'Szurpiły, st. 8 ("Mosiężysko"), woj. podlaskie. Badania w roku 2011.' *Światowit* IX (L), Fasc. B (2011): 349–353.

Jończyk, Ludwika. 'The last Yotvingian pagans. The case of the Mosiężysko Cemetery in Northeast Poland.' In *From Paganism to Christianity. Burial Rites during the Transition Period*, edited by Rytis Jonaitis and Irma Kaplūnaitė, 219–243. Vilnius: Lietuvos istorijos institutas, 2024.

Jończyk, Ludwika and Karol Żołędziowski. 'Elite burden. *Totenkrone*-type necklaces from the 'Mosiężysko' cemetery in Szurpiły.' *Światowit* LX (2021): 59–75.

Jones, Sian. *The Archaeology of Ethnicity. Constructing Identities in the Past and Present*. London: Routledge, 1997.

Karczewska, Małgorzata and Maciej Karczewski, 'Grodzisko Święta Góra w Staświnach w Krainie Wielkich Jezior Mazurskich. Archeologia archiwalna i nowa.' *KMW* 2/256 (2007): 131–163.

Karczewska, Małgorzata, Maciej Karczewski, Robert Kempa, and Ewa Pirożnikow. *Miłki. Monografia krajoznawcza gminy mazurskiej*. Białystok, Miłki: Wydawnictwo Kwadrat, 2005.

Karczewska, Małgorzata, Maciej Karczewski, and Aleksander Pluskowski, 'Późnośredniowieczna i wczesnonowożytna wieś Staświny w komturii brandenburskiej (Polska NE) w świetle źródeł archeologicznych.' In *Materiały do archeologii Warmii i Mazur*, edited by Sławomir Wadyl, Maciej Karczewski, and

Mirosław Hoffmann, 195–203. Warszawa: Instytut Archeologii Uniwersytetu Warszawskiego/Białystok: Instytut Historii i Nauk Politycznych Uniwersytetu w Białymstoku, 2015.

Karczewski, Maciej. 'Environment, settlement and economy of the West Baltic tribes in the Roman Period.' *Archaeologia Lituania* 7 (2006): 54–65.

Klimek, Robert. 'Pogańskie kamienne ołtarze Prusów.' In *Zjawiska magiczno-demoniczne na tle dawnych ziem pruskich na tle porównawczym*, edited by Kazimierz Grążawski and Jan Gancewski, 47–66. Olsztyn: Wydawnictwo Uniwersytetu Warmińsko-Mazurskiego, 2014.

Koperkiewicz, Arkadiusz. 'Cmentarzysko w Bezławkach (stanowisko XV). Badania w latach 2010–11.' In *Bezławki – ocalić od zniszczenia. Wyniki prac interdyscyplinarnych prowadzonych w latach 2008–2011*, edited by Arkadiusz Koperkiewicz, 137–152. Gdańsk: Wydawnictwo Uniwersytetu Gdańskiego, 2013.

Koperkiewicz, Arkadiusz. 'Nowe porządki, stare obyczaje? Wyjątki z praktyk pogrzebowych pruskich neofitów na przykładzie Bezławek.' In *Zjawiska magiczno-demoniczne na terenie dawnych ziem pruskich na tle porównawczym*, edited by Kazimierz Grążawski and Jan Gancewski, 17–46. Olsztyn: Wydawnictwo Uniwersytetu Warmińsko-Mazurskiego, 2019.

Koperkiewicz, Arkadiusz. '"Zmartwychwstanie neofity" czyli pierwsi chrześcijanie w okolicach Świętej Lipki.' In *Święta Lipka: perła na pograniczu ziem, kultur i wyznań*, part 2, edited by Aleksander Jacyniak and Edgar Sukiennik, 28–61. Kętrzyn: Labrita, 2020.

Koperkiewicz, Arkadiusz. 'Barczewko – a cemetery of the first settlers in Southern Warmia against the background of medieval inhumation necropolises in Teutonic Prussia.' *Archaeologia Historica Polona* 28 (2020): 199–228.

Koperkiewicz, Arkadiusz. 'Anno 1354 Kynstute, Algard ... festinant in Wartenberg. O trudnych początkach Barczewa.' In *Homini, qui in honore fuit. Księga pamiątkowa poświęcona śp. Profesorowi Grzegorzowi Białuńskiemu*, edited by Alicja Dobrosielska, Aleksander Pluskowski, and Seweryn Szczepański, 285–308. Olsztyn: Towarzystwo Naukowe Pruthenia, 2020.

Kulakov, Vladimir V. and A. A. Valuev, 'Veluva (Alt-Wehlau), ein heidnischer Friedhof im christlichen Nadrauen.' *Eurasia Antiqua. Zeitschrift für Archäologie Eurasiens* 2 (1996): 493–499.

Kulakov, Vladimir V. 'Sudavy na Sambii v XIII–XIV vv.' *Vestnik Arkheologii, Antropologii i Etnografii* 53, no. 2 (2021): 91–98.

Lewis, Carenza. 'Test pit excavation within currently occupied rural settlements: results of the University of Cambridge CORS project in 2011.' *Medieval Settlement Research* 28 (2013): 42–56.

Lüdtke, Hartwig. 'Grauware des 12. Bis 15. Jahrhunderts.' In *Handbuch zur mittelalterlichen Keramik in Nordeuropa*, edited by Hartwig Lüdtke and Kurt Schietzel, 83–173. Neumünster: Wachholtz Verlag, 2001.

Matuszewski, Józef. *Iura Prutenorum*. Toruń: Państwowe Wydawnictwo Naukowe, 1963.

Muižnieks, Vitolds. 'The co-existence of two traditions in the territory of present-day Latvia in the 13th–18th centuries. Burial in dress and in a shroud.' In *The Archaeology of Death in Post-Medieval Europe*, edited by Sarah Tarlow, 89–110. Berlin: de Gruyter, 2015.

Naum, Magdalena. 'Re-emerging frontiers: Postcolonial theory and historical archaeology of the borderlands.' *Journal of Archaeological Method and Theory* 17 (2010): 101–131.

Naum, Magdalena. 'Multi-ethnicity and material exchanges in late medieval Tallinn.' *European Journal of Archaeology* 17, no. 4 (2014): 656–677.

Naum, Magdalena. 'Migration, identity and material culture: Hanseatic translocality in the medieval Baltic Sea.' In *Comparative Perspectives on Past Colonisation,*

Maritime Interaction and Cultural Integration, edited by Lene Melheim, Håkon Glørstad, and Zanette Tsigaridas Glørstad, 129–148. Sheffield: Equinox, 2016.
Nawrolska, Grażyna. 'Handicrafts in medieval Elbląg.' In *Lübecker Kolloquium zur Stadtarchäologie im Hanseraum V: Das Handwerk*, edited by Ilka Hillenstedt a.o., 393–416. Lübeck: Schmidt-Römhild, 2006.
Nawrolska, Grażyna. 'Przemiany kulturowe w XIII-wiecznym Elblągu efektem spotkania tradycji i obcych wpływów.' *Archaeologia Historica Polona* 21 (2013): 79–99.
Nowakiewicz, Tomasz. 'Galindia in the Viking Age – New Shape of the Culture.' In *Transformatio Mundi: The Transition from the Late Migration Period to the Early Viking Age in the East Baltic*, edited by Mindaguas Bertašius, 161–172. Kaunas: Kaunas University of Technology, Department of Philosophy and Cultural Science, 2006.
Nowakowski, Wojciech. '"Kurhany Jaćwięgów" – kilkadziesiąt lat naukowego mitu.' *Światowit* IX (L), Fasc. B (2012): 181–192.
Nowakowski, Wojciech. 'Jaćwieskie cmentarzysko warstwowe (?) w miejscowości Burdyniszki, na Suwalszczyźnie.' In *Studia z dziejów cywilizacji. Studia ofiarowane profesorowi Jerzemu Gąssowskiemu w pięćdziesiątą rocznicę pracy naukowej*, edited by Andrzej Buko, 119–123. Warszawa: Instytut Archeologii Uniwersytetu Warszawskiego, 1998.
Odoj, Romuald. 'Sprawozdanie z prac wykopaliskowych przeprowadzonych w Równinie Dolnej, pow. Kętrzyn w 1956 i 1957 r.' *Rocznik Olsztyński* 1 (1958): 117–156.
Odoj, Romulad. 'Sprawozdanie z prac wykopaliskowych w miejscowości Równina Dolna, pow. Kętrzyn.' *Wiadomości Archeologiczne* 23 (1960): 177–196.
Paszkiewicz, Borys. 'La monnoye des Prussenayres – monety z Bezławek.' In *Bezławki – ocalić od zniszczenia. Wyniki prac interdyscyplinarnych prowadzonych w latach 2008–2011*, edited by Arkadiusz Koperkiewicz, 183–219. Gdańsk: Wydawnictwo Uniwersytetu Gdańskiego, 2013.
Pluskowski, Aleksander. *The Archaeology of the Prussian Crusade*. London: Routledge, 2013, 1st edition, 2022, 2nd edition.
Pluskowski, Aleksander, Marc Jarzebowski, Małgorzata Karczewska, and Maciej Karczewski, 'Sites in Prussia: the historical and archaeological background.' In *Environment, Colonization and the Baltic Crusader States*, edited by Aleksander Pluskowski, 257–292. Turnhout: Brepols, 2019.
Pluskowski, Aleksander and Heiki Valk. 'Conquest and Europeanisation: the archaeology of the crusades in Livonia, Prussia and Lithuania.' In *The Crusader World*, edited by Adrian Boas, 568–592. London: Routledge, 2016.
Russow, Erki. *Importkeraamika Lääne- Eesti linnades 13.–17. Sajandil*. Tallinn: Tallinna Raamatutrükikoda, 2006.
Sabaliauskas, Algirdas. *We the Balts*. Vilnius: Science and Encyclopaedia Publishing, 1993.
Sakson, Andrzej. *Mazurzy, społeczność pogranicza*. Poznań: Instytut Zachodni, 1990.
Sawicka, Ludwika. 'Szurpiły, st. 8 ("Mosiężysko"), woj. podlaskie. Badania w latach 2008–2010.' *Światowit* VIII (XLIX), Fasc. B (2011): 263–268.
Seetah, Krish, Aleksander Pluskowski, Daniel Makowiecki, and Linas Daugnora. 'New technology or adaptation at the frontier? Butchery as a signifier of cultural transitions in the medieval eastern Baltic.' *Archaeologia Baltica* 20 (2013): 84–101.
Selart, Anti. 'A new faith and a new name? Crusades, conversion, and baptismal names in medieval Baltics.' *Journal of Baltic Studies* 47, no. 2 (2016): 179–196.
Shiroukhov, Roman. 'Prussian graves in the Sambian Peninsula, with imports, weapons and horse harnesses, from the tenth to the thirteenth century: The question of the warrior elite.' *Archaeologia Baltica* 18 (2012): 224–225.
Shiroukhov, Roman. 'Western Balts between the Vikings and Crusades. The development of the southeast Baltic region in the 10th–13th centuries according to the archaeological data.' *ZBSA Jahresbericht* (2016): 68–71.

Stephan, Joachim. 'Prusowie w gospodarstwie krzyżaków.' In *Gospodarka ludów morza bałtyckiego starożytność i średniowiecze. Mare Integrans: Studia nad dziejami wybrzeży Morza Bałtyckiego*, edited by Michał Bogacki, Maciej Franz and Zbigniew Pilarczyk, 317–325. Toruń: Wydawnictwo Adam Marszałek, 2009.

Svetikas, Eugenijus. 'XIV a. pabaigos – XV a. amule-tai iš apkaustyto lokio nago Lietuvos Didžiojoje Kunigaikštystėje ir kaimyniniuose kraštuose.' *Lietuvos Archeologija* 34 (2009): 171–210.

Szczepański, Seweryn. *Pomezania. Na styku świata pogańskiego i chrześcijańskiego*. Olsztyn: Instytut Północny w Olsztynie, 2019.

Szczepański, Seweryn. 'Surkapurn and Kreken: The phenomenon of name and place and the organisation of sacred space in Prussia using archaeology and other sources.' In *Ecologies of Crusading, Colonisation and Religious Conversion in the Medieval Eastern Baltic*, edited by Aleksander Pluskowski, 175–184. Turnhout: Brepols, 2019.

Töppen, Max. *Wierzenia mazurskie*, edited by Anna Szyfer, Władysław Ogrodziński, Paweł Błażewicz, and Jerzy M. Łapo. Dąbrówno: Oficyna Wydawnicza Retman, 2008.

Ubis, Edvinas. 'Archaeological data as evidence of cultural interaction between the Teutonic Order and local communities: problems and perspectives.' *Archaeologia Baltica* 25 (2018): 164–176.

Valk, Heiki. 'Finnic language islands in eastern Latvia: Archaeological background and perspective.' *Eesti Ja Soome-Ugri Keeleteaduse Ajakiri* 12, no. 2 (2021): 95–122.

Valuev, A. A. 'Alt Wehlau – "Pogańskie" cmentarzysko na obszarze chrześcijańskich Prus w świetle badań archeologicznych.' In *Archeologia ziem pruskich. Nieznane zbiory i materiały archiwalne. Ostróda 15–17 X 1998*, edited by Mirosław Hoffmann and Jarosław Sobieraj, 397–400. Olsztyn: Stowarzyszenie Naukowe Archeologów Polskich. Oddział w Olsztynie, 1999.

Valuev, A. A., S. A. Denisov, and K. N. Skvorcov. 'Amulety-podveski «medvezhij kogot'» iz pogrebenij XIII–XV vv. nekropolja Al't-Velau.' *KSIA* 264 (2021): 290–306.

Ylimaunu, Timo, Sami Lakomäki, Titta Kallio-Seppä, Paul R. Mullins, Risto Nurmi, and Markku Kuorilehto, 'Borderlands as spaces: Creating third spaces and fractured landscapes in medieval Northern Finland.' *Journal of Social Archaeology* 14, no. 2 (2014): 244–267.

5 Curonians and the Teutonic Order

Settlement and Military Structures on the Outskirts of Late Medieval Prussia

Krzysztof Kwiatkowski

Introduction: Research Issue and Methodology

Military matters were one of the cultural fields of participation of Baltic indigenous peoples in the establishing and subsequent functioning of the Teutonic Order's rulership/dominion (Germ. *Herrschaft*) in Prussia. Researchers on the issue have begun to recognize this fact starting in the 1970s, studying armaments, military equipment, technical and, to a lesser extent, technological borrowings, and developments in combat technique.[1] At this point, however, it should be made clear that this phenomenon extends far beyond the material aspects of military affairs. It also concerns the social and organizational or structural dimensions of the military matters in the Teutonic Order's dominion and, more broadly, in the Prussian Land as a whole. Some aspects of this phenomenon were noted as early as the 19th century,[2] and have been more extensively studied in recent decades.[3] However, this does not mean that the subject has been completely exhausted.

One such issue that has been poorly researched so far is the phenomenon of indigenous Baltic collectivities in the military structures of the Order's dominion in Prussia, existing in the form of compact settlement communities, which supplied the Order's armies with their armed members. They were, however, not individual armed men sent for the duration of military action, as the landowners (also of Baltic origin) did, but organized groups of armed men or even entire armed contingents continuously delivered to the Order's people for small military actions or to the Order's armies for military expeditions. Of these, two clearly ethnically marked collectivities existed for a relatively long period of more than one century. These were the Baltic indigenous Scalovians/Schalvians[4] living on the lower reaches of the Nemunas River, and the southern Curonians living near Memel (today Klaipėda). The military significance of both of these collectivities to the rulership of the Prussian branch of the Teutonic Order was devoted to two subsections of my dissertation published more than ten years ago,[5] and to a separate paper on Scalovians/Schalvians published recently.[6] The aim of this study is to present the results of my former, as well as latter, complementary research on the functioning of the Curonians in the dominion of the Livonian and Prussian branches of the Teutonic

DOI: 10.4324/9781003502876-5

Order in a military context. It will address questions concerning the nature of the Curonian settlement near Memel during the Teutonic Order's period, its relationship to the Order, its military functions and, finally, its importance in the military structures of the Order's rulership. This is a research questionnaire very similar to the one recently applied to the Scalovians/Schalvians. However, the number of sources at the disposal of a researcher approaching such an outlined issue is relatively small. Therefore, the comparative method and the reasoning and interpretations based on it will play an important role during the analysis.

Curonia/Courland, Curonians and the Teutonic Order

Curonians as an ethnocultural entity has been studied for several decades now and this issue has a very large number of publications in the fields of archaeology, anthropology and history.[7] Curonian communities came into contact with members of the Teutonic Order in the late 1230s when, following the incorporation of the Livonian Order of the Knights of Christ into the Teutonic Order in 1237, it was the latter that took the lead in military activity in the areas between the lower Daugava and lower Nemunas, and had been taking steps to bring the Curonians under its authority in the first half of the 1240s.[8] From the beginning of the 1250s, the Bishops of *Curonia*/Courland were also gradually becoming viable rulers in the area, although already in 1245 they received only a third of the entire country of the Curonians (*Curonia*) as their dominion as a result the decision of the papal legate William of Modena. The remaining two-thirds fell to the Teutonic Order, in contrast to land divisions between the Order and the other bishops in Livonia.[9] In the second half of 1252, an army of the Order's Livonian branch erected Memel castle[10] near the mouth of the Dange River (Lit. Danė) into the Curonian Lagoon. The castle was rebuilt in a slightly different location in 1253 after the destruction of the first stronghold.[11] Shortly after this, already ca. 1254/1257, a town of the same name was founded by the Land Master of Livonia and the bishop of *Curonia*/Courland.[12] The subsequent uprising of the Curonians in 1260 nearly abolished the rule of the Order and the bishops over almost the entire area for several years, with an exception being Memel itself.[13] In the second half of the 1260s, the Teutonic Knights and the bishops of *Curonia* succeeded in reestablishing their rulership over the country of the Curonians, which was confirmed by a collective agreement concluded with them in the summer of 1267.[14] For the following six decades, the pacified Curonians living in the (nominally) Christian country of Courland were in the orbit of influence and ruling interests of both the Livonian branch of the Teutonic Order and the bishops, with the Order being the main ruling power in the region. The southern part of *Curonia*/Courland, still sparsely inhabited, was only marginally controlled by both the Order and the bishops of Courland.

In 1328, the Order's leadership, headed by Grand Master Werner von Orseln, decided to transfer control over the Memel convent from the

Livonian branch to the Prussian branch of the Teutonic Order.[15] Memel castle and the commandery administered from it then became part of the Prussian dominion of the Order, albeit still part of the Diocese of Courland. This administrative change basically meant the division of the Curonians' country into two unequal parts between two branches of the Order. The administrative responsibilities of the Memel castle and convent extended north and northeast to the course of the Heilige Aa River and to the middle and upper reaches of the Minge River, while the main part of *Curonia*/Courland lying further north continued to be under the authority of the Livonian branch of the Order. The boundary drawn in 1328 by no means coincided with the limits existing between the five 'pre-Christian' southern Curonian settlement regions (*Ceclis, Duvzare, Megowe, Pilsaten* and *Lamotina*), but divided into unequal parts the areas of the two most northern ones, namely *Duvzare* and the most extensive of them, *Ceclis*. Roughly a third of the hitherto southern Curonian areas fell within the Prussian commandery of Memel, while two-thirds remained under the administration of the Livonian branch of the Order (within the commandery of Goldingen (today Kuldīga)). In both parts of southern *Curonia*, there were areas belonging to the dominion of the bishops of Courland. They retained the lands assigned to them in 1253 during the divisions of areas within the Diocese of Courland.[16] In the summer of 1392, the bishop of Courland ceded his portions of land not only in the Prussian part of the former *Curonia* to the Order, but also a little further north, while retaining full diocesan jurisdiction in these areas.[17] The peace treaty between the Teutonic Order and the Kingdom of Poland and the Grand Duchy of Lithuania in 1422 (known as the Treaty of Lake Melno) resulted in the demarcation of the Prussian-Lithuanian border. As a result, the area of the Memel commandery was significantly reduced, while a sizable portion of the former south *Curonia* area became part of Samogitia within the Grand Duchy of Lithuania.[18] The political, administrative and ecclesiastical situation in these frontier areas continued until the dissolution of the territorial rulership of the Order in Prussia in 1525.[19]

Curonians and the Prussian-Samogitian-Lithuanian Transition Zone (Frontier)

To take a comparative look at the issue of the Curonians in the military structures of the Teutonic Order's dominion, it is necessary to juxtapose several fundamental conditions and aspects of their existence in the Memel area and the Scalovians/Schalvians in the vicinity of Ragnit (today Neman). Such juxtaposition reveals far-reaching similarities. In the 13th–14th centuries, both indigenous collectivities inhabited areas covered by vast forests known as the 'Great Wilderness' (*Grosse Wildnis*). During that time, these areas were situated on the outskirts of the two regions of Prussia and Livonia, which were gradually developed at the time according to the civilizational models and cultural patterns of 'Western' countries. The flora-rich forests, together with the extensive hydrological network of smaller and larger rivers, numerous swamps, marshes and floodplains created difficult geo-environmental conditions for communication and compact, permanent settlement.[20]

The conventual castles erected in these areas by the Teutonic Order, namely Memel and Ragnit, lacked a developed settlement base in the form of villages with a dominant agricultural economy and/or livestock farming. In the geographic structure of the Order's administration, both castle complexes were relatively large strongholds, significantly separated spatially from the main developed regions and from the nearest neighbouring large fortified points. This geographic seclusion throughout the period of almost uninterrupted wars with Lithuania (the Grand Duchy of Lithuania), which lasted from roughly the 1260s to 1422, significantly increased the level of threat to both castles from hostile military actions. In this context, the aforementioned lack of a larger settlement base had a negative impact on the military potential of the strongholds during the period studied in this chapter, and in a number of different aspects.

Firstly, both castles had constant difficulties in obtaining sufficient numbers of armed men to defend the fortifications during military threats.[21] Secondly, they were unable to independently organize a sufficient number of labourers to work on the expansion, reconstruction or repair of fortification elements and equipment within their own fortified complexes.[22] Thirdly, they had an inadequate production base in relation to their large needs, which was necessary to supply the crews of the two castle complexes. These crews consisted of the Order's conventual brethren and accompanying groups of servitors (*gesinde*), i.e., servants (*dienere*), squires (*jungen*), and knechts (*knechte*), probably also specialized shooters (*schotczen*) and *Witinge*. All these people had a constant need for food, clothing, everyday equipment, armaments, horses and military equipment.[23] Fourthly, and finally, even in terms of basic food requirements, both castles were dependent on the delivery of grain and other food materials. And yet, the military importance of Memel and Ragnit castles for the Teutonic Order in Prussia and Livonia in the face of military confrontations with Samogitians and Lithuanians during the 14th century was considerable. Both strongholds performed various functions, starting with their role as communication stages for troops, contingents or entire armies, and their status as important points covering communication routes (especially the route on which messengers with correspondence between the dignitaries of the Prussian and Livonian branches of the Order passed through here).[24] Both were also permanent military bases sending guards (*warten*), scouts, secret agents, and armed groups of so-called *Strutters* (Germ. *Struttere*) into the wooded Prussian-Samogitian-Lithuanian transition zone (frontier). They also functioned as permanent and heavily fortified defence points ensuring the maintenance of the Order's armed and force presence on this constantly 'hot' (i.e. active) frontier.[25]

The Scalovians/Schalvians formed a collectivity with a distinctly homogeneous ethnic character and a high level of internal cohesion. They initially settled in the last decade of the 13th century in a specially erected Schalauerburg castle located near Ragnit which, over the course of the 14th century, either grew or was divided into several settlement groups. These groups inhabited fortified settlements (so-called *Hackelwerke*) in the second half of the 14th century and were maintained on a permanent basis by the Teutonic Order, who supplied them with food, clothing, various types of equipment and perhaps also weapons. They also received domestic animals from the Order, the breeding of which was one of the bases for meeting basic subsistence needs. In return, members of these communities performed various kinds of services to the Order, including, above all, military service, which took various forms. In this latter aspect, the Scalovians/Schalvians were an effective military tool of the Order in the so-called 'Lithuanian War' fought from the end of the 13th to the beginning of the 15th century in the specific conditions of the Prussian-Samogitian-Lithuanian frontier.[26] With the end of the armed conflict between the Order and the Grand Duchy of Lithuania in 1422, the military significance of the Schalvians began to regress markedly.

It was not only the above-mentioned geo-environmental, settlement, administrative, military and economic factors that made the living conditions of the Curonians in the Memel area similar to the Scalovians/Schalvians in the vicinity of Ragnit. Both ethnocultural groups also shared certain sociocultural elements which were apparent among them when they came into contact with the Teutonic Order and, more broadly, with the Latin world. Indeed, archaeological research developed in recent decades (especially with regard to the Curonian areas and, to a slightly lesser extent, to Scalovia), indicates the existence of a separate social elite in both groups in the 11th–13th centuries. These people probably lived in fortified settlements and were the carrier of a warrior culture, demonstrated militarily especially in the case of the Curonians by intensive pirate activity on the Baltic Sea.[27] Moreover, written sources on the Curonians in the 13th century bring information on the relationship between this warrior culture and their religious culture.[28] It is difficult to determine whether both groups somehow distinguished themselves from neighbouring Baltic ethnocultural communities in this period in terms of the intensity of military activity. In the case of the Curonians, however, it would be appropriate to note the strong interactions and influence of the warrior culture of the Scandinavian newcomers during the 9th–12th centuries.[29]

It should be noted that the phenomenon of depopulation of southern *Curonia* during the 13th century,[30] indicated by researchers as early as the first half of the 20th century, must have entailed a decrease in intensity of military activity of the remaining population there. Moreover, the military operations of the Teutonic Order in *Curonia* and Scalovia in the second half of the 13th century undoubtedly contributed to the reduction in the military activity of the local elite, eliminating part of them as a result of either physical extermination or forcing them to emigrate to another regions. The existence of an oral tradition regarding the warrior elite in these communities, built in part on the memory of earlier times, is, however, very likely in the 13th and 14th centuries among the Scalovians and Curonians, although as yet unambiguously unproven archaeologically. A further analysis based on written sources will show the continuation of these cultural patterns among the Curonians up to the first half of the 15th century.

Curonians in the Vicinity of Memel Castle

The similarities between the Curonians and Scalovians/Schalvians in the 13th–14th centuries presented so far provide strong reasons to expect Curonian settlements in the vicinity of Memel castle, which would have had, to some extent, a military nature during this period. Both in the second half of the 13th century and throughout the 14th century, the Teutonic Order's need to have compact settlement groups which could provide a military contingent (or at least armed groups to strengthen the military potential of Memel castle) was constant. It was similar to the situation that existed in the area around Ragnit. What do the relatively few surviving source accounts provide in this regard?

First of all, surviving documents directly or indirectly indicate the existence of a permanent Curonian settlement in the Memel area in the mid-13th century.[31] It should also be noted that from the very beginning of the Memel castle in 1252, two of the Order's advocates (Germ. *Vögte*) for *Curonia* are attested.[32] One of these men held his office in the then newly erected stronghold, since he is mentioned there evidentially in the summer of 1258.[33] Other brothers-officials with this title appear in the written sources even earlier, namely 1253, probably 1255, and then in 1291.[34] Meanwhile, it is known that *Vögte* were officials in the Livonian branch of the Order established by its authorities to bring the indigenous population under control and to manage the military contingents provided by them.[35] Additionally, the document confirming the April 1253 agreement between the Teutonic Order and the bishop of *Curonia*/Courland attests to the importance of the *Vögte* of *Curonia* in organizing the Curonian military contingents in the Order's armies.[36]

Indeed, the number of references to Curonian contingents attached to the Order's armies in the 13th century in chronicle sources is considerable. Their participation is attested in at least 15 military actions between ca. 1245 and 1290.[37] Regarding the last campaign in 1290, the legal sources also mention the Curonians referred to as 'villagers' (*rurenses*), whom the Livonian land master could call into his army against the Lithuanians.[38] While it is likely that most of the Curonian contingents came from the northern parts of the country, which was more densely populated at the time, it can be assumed that there were also Curonians from the Memel area among them. Thus, it can be seen that Curonian military service to the Livonian branch of the Teutonic Order was an established practice, dating back to the first half of the 13th century.[39] All of these evidences provide strong indications in favour of the existence among the Curonians of a warrior culture present in the first decades of the Teutonic Order's rule, and thus the continuation of old cultural patterns in this ethnocultural group. Moreover, it is difficult to challenge the claim that a large part of the Curonian population in the second half of the 13th century continued to live in the sphere of pre-Christian cults. There are sources indicating that this situation persisted at least until the first quarter of the 15th century.[40]

The existence in Memel of one or, at least two, *Vögte* set up by the Order for the country of the Curonians[41] indicates unequivocally that the region was by no means completely depopulated in the mid-13th century. This means that the Curonian uprising of the early 1260s and the resulting several years of suppressing it did not result in the complete depopulation of southern *Curonia*. There was still a permanent settlement there at the end of the 13th century, although undoubtedly less dense than in the northern part of the country.

Chronicle references relating to the 1250s and 1260s also have a similar meaning regarding a Curonian settlement in the Memel area.[42] Although a document dated 27 April 1261 indicates that the Curonians had abandoned some settlements at the time of their rebellion against the Order's rule,[43] in light of later accounts it should be assumed that there was no complete depopulation of the already relatively sparsely populated southern *Curonia*. Numerous Curonians are also mentioned, albeit unnamed, as witnesses to a document issued by Memel commander Gottfried and Memel *Vogt* Thitmar on 6 January 1291. The issuers of the document confirmed the division of the dominion of the bishop of *Curonia*/Courland between him and the local diocesan chapter.[44]

Preserved written sources even indicate the existence of settlement points in southern *Curonia* that performed central functions for the surrounding settlement. Several strongholds used by indigenous people are attested in the Memel area. There are references to a total of about eight settlements. The first two appear in a document dated 5 April 1253, which mentions the castle (*castrum*) of *Mutine* located on the Dange River and the castle district (*castellatura*) of *Poys*.[45] In a document dated 27 July 1258, the following *castellaturae* are mentioned: *Mutine, Poys, Ackete, Creten, Duwirstene, Palangen* and *Kalaten*.[46] Furthermore, the castles (*castra*) at *Poys* and *Sarden*, as well as the *castellatura* of *Creten*, appear in the charter of 6 January 1291.[47] The vast majority of these, as many as seven, were centres of *castellaturae* and three of them are referred to as castles.[48] Of these, the first five were located in the *Pilsaten* (today Pilsotas) area, while the next three were situated in the *Megove* (today Mėguva) area.[49] In addition, Vladas Žulkus points to the existence of seven more Curonian strongholds in the *Pilsaten* area, with it so far unknown whether they were still functioning in the mid-13th century. The existence of a significant number of strongholds in the vicinity of Memel is a strong indication of the presence of local Curonian mighty people in this area as late as the mid-13th century.[50]

Several written source accounts show the functioning of a warrior culture in the Curonian collectivities also in the later period, when the Memel commandery already belonged to Prussia. The military activities of the Curonians from the northern (Livonian) part of *Curonia*/Courland in the area of this commandery were referred to by the term 'military expedition' (*herwert*). These were sometimes organized without the knowledge of the Teutonic Order's dignitaries in Livonia, as reported in a letter from the commander of Memel to the Grand Master, dated 12 December 1408.[51] Another expedition of the Curonians from the northern *Curonia*/Courland to Samogitia is also attested at the end of June, probably 1432, with indications that it was undertaken by them independently (i.e., without the participation of the Order's brethren).[52] This information clearly shows that the looting expeditions undertaken in Samogitia were still an important part of the Curonians activity in the first half of the 15th century. This conforms with the military profile of the activities of various communities present in this northern part of the turbulent Prussian-Samogitian-Lithuanian frontier.[53] Although they refer to the Curonians from the northern part of *Curonia*/Courland, there is no indication that the Curonians from the southern (Prussian) part of the country were then operating under different cultural patterns. Moreover, the author of the continuation of the chronicle written by Detmar von Lübeck explicitly mentions the Curonians, as the only ethnocultural group, in the army of the Livonian branch of the Teutonic Order that attacked Samogitia in February 1399. This could be interpreted as a reminiscence of the special importance attributed at the time among the Order's members to this group in a military context.[54] The Flemisch nobleman and envoy, Guillbert de Lannoy, travelled through *Curonia*/Courland in October 1413. He reported on the funeral customs of the Curonians, according to which the corpse of the deceased was burned at the stake dressed in the best attire and equipped with weapons. This example further indicates the continuity of warrior culture in this ethnos.[55] Archaeological studies also confirm the persistence of pre-Christian burial customs among the Curonians until the 16th century.[56] Thus, based on the premises presented above, it is possible to formulate a hypothesis that the Curonians, until the first half of the 15th century, functioned largely on the basis of patterns of warrior culture under low control by the Teutonic Order, with their military activity conducted in support of it as well as autonomously.[57]

Curonians at Memel Castle

There is a lack of source information regarding the organizational frameworks of Curonians' military service to the Order. Vladas Žulkus saw here the functioning of the same mechanisms that the Order introduced in Prussia and Livonia, where there was a gradual granting of landed estates to indigenous peoples in exchange for a commitment to military service.[58] This opinion is accurate regarding the northern part of *Curonia*/Courland. In the case of southern *Curonia*/Courland, however, it seems that it can be cautiously assumed that here no such redistribution of land took place. Such assumptions suggest the above-mentioned similarities between the conditions in which the Curonians and the Scalovians/Schalvians functioned. For the Curonian areas south of the Heilige Aa River, there is almost a complete lack (with one exception)[59] of attestations of the granting of landed property by the Order, the bishops of Courland, or the diocesan chapter of Courland (after 1291) to individuals in exchange for military service.[60] Perhaps, then, did the few southern Curonians, like the Scalovians/Schalvians, join the Order's armies not as single armed men (and landowners), but in compact groups (of warriors)?

Such an interpretation could be supported by the account of Peter von Dusburg, a priest and chronicler of the Teutonic Order, who narrates the military events in the spring of 1323. It indicates that at least some part of the southern Curonians living in the Memel area, who were formally Christians at the time, had their own strongholds. These are described by Peter von Dusburg as 'three neophyte castles lying around' (*tria circumjacencia castra neophitorum*). They were to be destroyed that year either by Lithuanian forces coming from Samogitia or the Samogitians themselves during an invasion of southern *Curonia*.[61] During this invasion, the attackers also burned down the town of Memel, located right next to the castle.[62] Nikolaus von Jeroschin, a priest of the Order who translated Dusburg's chronicle to Middle High German, characterized these strongholds as 'shelter castles' (*vlîhûsir*, Germ. *Fliehenburgen, Fluchtburgen*). This would suggest that they were not permanently garrisoned fortified points, but only places where the local population took shelter during an enemy invasion. This is also how the nature of these strongholds has been interpreted in previous scholarly publications.[63] In light of Helene Dopkewitsch's research, it would therefore be appropriate to identify these anonymous fortified points with *castellaturae/burchsukungen*.[64] Vladas Žulkus proposed the identification in the Memel area of two such *castellaturae* with strongholds located at Laistai (*Lassiten*) and Purmaliai (*Mutina/Mutene/Mutone*).[65] The question arises, however, whether the small size of those two hillforts (Lit. *Piliakalniai*) makes it possible to interpret these fortified points as *Fluchtburgen*. In the case of Laistai, it seems problematic, even if this stronghold were to be treated together with neighbouring Žardė hillfort (*Sarden*)[66] as one settlement complex, as archaeologists have already done.[67] Likewise, it proves difficult to search for these three Curonian *vlîhûsir* mentioned 1323 among others of the aforementioned eight strongholds from the documents of 1253, 1258 and 1291. Only in Eketė (*Akutte/Ackete*) is there an extensive hillfort that may have been the remains of a stronghold that served as *Fluchtburg*. So far, however, it has been insufficiently investigated archeologically.[68] This stronghold was situated 10 km away from Memel castle, which would correspond well with the designation of the *vlîhûsir* from 1323 as lying in the vicinity of Memel (*circumjacentia*). Even the well-researched hillfort in Palanga, located on modern-day

Birutė Hill (Lit. Birutės kalnas), may raise doubts as a potential *vlihûsir* mentioned in Dusburg and Jeroschin's chronicles, for it occupied a relatively small area (although the entire settlement complex was much larger). Its existence in the early 14th century is not fully clear.[69] However, it cannot be ruled out that the refuge centres included small-sized wooden castles and accompanying settlements, such as Palanga or the Žardė/Laistai settlement complex.[70] Regardless, it remains possible that the Lithuanian or Samogitian army in 1323 did not destroy all the Curonian strongholds in the Memel area. Hans and Gertrud Mortensen believed that after the Lithuanian/Samogitian invasion of 1323, the Curonians may have been resettled directly under the Memel castle, forming a settlement (*suburbium*) adjacent to the castle there.[71] In my opinion, this is very likely, and is reminiscent of a similar, albeit later, action taken by the Prussian branch of the Teutonic Order with the Scalovians/Schalvians after 1365. The difference, however, is that Scalovians/Schalvians were concentrated not in one, but in three settlement points. Over time this developed into four fortified settlement points.[72] Whether all the Curonians living south of the Heilige Aa River were settled nearby the Memel castle is impossible to determine. However, it can be cautiously assumed that, like the Scalovians/Schalvians in Ragnit and at other settlement points, the Memel Curonians lived in a probably fortified settlement located in the immediate vicinity of the Order's castle, which had the character of a *Hackelwerk*.[73] This is indicated by written sources from the first half of the 15th century.

The extensive gap in the written sources for the period between 1323 and the early 15th century makes it impossible to determine the dynamics of the Curonian settlement at Memel castle. Archaeological research has not contributed anything concrete here either, due to the far-reaching destruction of the layers during various later construction works and the sheer fragmentary nature of the extent of the excavations. Curonians in Memel are attested several times in written sources only from the first and second quarters of the 15th century, with much of it dated only approximately. A letter from the first decade of the 15th century, perhaps dated 16 March 1409, indicates that the Curonians from the Livonian part of *Curonia*/Courland wanted to settle in Memel, and, at the same time, that their number at Memel castle was not then very large.[74] In turn, it is known from another letter that ca. 1425–1440, the Memel Curonians suffered great losses as a result of a fire in the town of Memel.[75]

Military Services of the Curonians at Memel Castle to the Teutonic Order

The surviving sources unequivocally point to the performance of various services by the Curonians at Memel castle for the benefit of the Teutonic Order, specifically the commander of Memel. The aforementioned letter, probably from 16 March 1409, refers to *hern dinst* – 'service to the lords', i.e., the Orders brethren.[76] That at least some part of the Curonian living next to Memel castle performed this service using weapons is indirectly attested to by a letter of the commander of Memel dated 4 September either 1400, 1406 or 1417, in which the sender informs that all the Curonians, in addition to the Order's members, Orders's *dienere* and burghers of Memel, are ill and therefore he has no armed men at his disposal.[77] In light of the analogy to the Scalovians/Schalvians in the Ragnit area and relative to the observations made earlier regarding the Curonian warrior culture, it can be assumed that the Curonian group living at the Memel castle had at least to some extent the character of a military settlement. It is impossible to say conclusively whether these indigenous people provided a compact and ethnically homogeneous armed contingent for the Memel commander's military expeditions, but it is quite likely. It is also difficult to determine the size of this collectivity, although given the size of the Scalovians/Schalvians groups,[78] it does not seem to have been larger than ca. 100–200 people, leaving aside its probable temporal fluctuations.[79]

It is very likely that the military functions of the Curonians at Memel were in part identical to those carried out by the Schalvians from the area around Ragnit. A letter from the commander of Memel dated 28 June, most likely 1432, reports that the Order's official sent his *Gesinde*, namely *dienere* and guides (*lietmanne, geleitsluwte*),[80] into the 'Great Wilderness', who carried out reconnaissance activities and marked out current communication routes (namely paths, places for camps and passages through rivers, streams, marshes and inter-lake straits). In 1409, one of the Memel Curonians accompanied the Grand Master on his journey from Memel to Ragnit, most likely just as a guide, for which he received the substantial sum of two *Marks*.[81] Several such guides from Memel are attested to in a list of paths in the 'Great Wilderness' (the so-called 'Wegeberichte') dating back more than a generation earlier, namely to the fourth quarter of the 14th century.[82] Their activities in the Curonian areas are also attested to for the 13th century in the 'Livonian Rhymed Chronicle'.[83] It is difficult to doubt that among these *geleitsluwte* were local Curonians, familiar with both the local geographical and topographical conditions, as well as the language of the population of the 'Great Wilderness' areas. They would have had the best understanding of the current situation. Another source, from the first quarter of the 15th century, also attests to the maintenance of guides by the commander of Memel.[84] The juxtaposition of these data allows us to conclude that the practice existed for a longer period, and given the broader Prussian context,[85] it can be assumed that it had a metric dating back to the mid-13th century. Among the *Gesinde* of the Memel's commanders were also translators (*tolke*), sometimes also taking on the task of guides.[86]

The source material reveals yet another function of the Curonians settled at Memel castle. The letter of the commander of Memel from ca. 1400–1420, cited earlier, indicates that this dignitary maintained men who served as guards (*wachen*), also known as *warten*.[87] This service consisted of patrolling and observing the main paths and road routes in the vast areas of the 'Great Wilderness' and, in the event of noticing the movement of hostile armed groups or entire troops, informing the Order's official (in this case the commander of Memel) as quickly as possible.[88] Again, using the analogy of the same function carried out by the Schalvians, and considering the small number of *dienere* and shooters (*schotczen*) at Memel castle, it can be assumed that at least some part of the armed men carrying out these *wachen* were Curonians. It is also difficult to doubt that guards (*warten*) were maintained in the areas to the east, northeast and southeast of Memel, although in the absence of sources, nothing more can be said about their detailed locations.

A final form of military service performed was the transportation of letters of the Order's officials. Curonians living in Memel are attested in the letter sent by the commander of Memel in 27 May 1409 as messengers carrying letters of Memel commander to the Livonian part of *Curonia*/Courland.[89] However, the same source clearly indicates that this was not an old custom at the time.[90] Probably due to the permanently inadequate number of *Gesinde* at the Memel castle, the commanders were forced, around the turn of the 14th and 15th centuries, to enlist Curonians from the adjacent *Hackelwerk* for such communication tasks as well.

The Curonian collectivity living at the Memel castle thus performed a number of military functions towards the Order, and in this sense, their settlement was largely military in nature. All of these are also attested to in the case of the Scalovians/Schalvians, and this is another attestation of the far-reaching analogies occurring between the two groups.

This was not, however, a group of people comprising only men or adults. From a letter dated to ca. 1425–1440, it is clear that male Curonians living in the Memel *Hackelwerk* had wives and children. In addition to their military service for the Order, at least some of them were engaged in fishing.[91] However, nothing concrete can be said about the social structure of this group. Thus, it remains an open question to what extent their social life was based on ancestral structures, and to what extent on 'small, nuclear families'. It remains unclear how far the above-mentioned warrior culture of the Baltic ethnocultural groups, including the Curonians, was based on kin (in anthropological terminology: 'large families'), while in recent decades the image of these social bodies has changed, at least partially. This new line of research focuses on, namely, their cognatic, and not agnatic, character, as assumed earlier, especially regarding the Lithuanian collectivities in the 13th century.[92]

One of the letters of the commander of Memel addressed to the Order's Grand Marshal, dating from ca. 1400–1420, contains important information concerning the relationship between the Order and the Memel Curonians. This source indicates that they perceived themselves at the time as closely associated with the Order's corporation. The commander informed the letter's addressee of the complaints made to him in Memel of how these Balts lived without sufficient means of subsistence and, in this difficult situation for them, they demanded that the Order provide them with the same assistance as the Schalvians had received two years earlier.[93] From the further contents of the letter, it appears that the commander intended to give each of them one bushel of flour. Thus, this source account allows to assume that the Curonians, like the Schalvians, may have been supported by the Order's brethren with grain, flour, bread, peas, and perhaps other foodstuffs, as partially confirmed by the records of the Order's 'Treasurer's Book' from 1399–1409.[94] They also sometimes received cash assistance.[95] Whether, as in the case of the Schalvians, they also received horses, livestock and clothing, and perhaps weapons remains impossible to verify. In light of the many parallels observed so far between both collectivities, however, this is not out of the question.

Other Curonian Groups in Southern *Curonia*

Memel was not the only settlement point where a group of Curonians lived in the first quarter of the 15th century. Another group was settled probably in the 1360s in a castle settlement (*suburbium*) in Windenburg, located about 40.5 km south of Memel.[96] They are also attested there four decades later, in 1404[97] and in 1410–1411, as having suffered as a result of the invasions (or raids) by Lithuanian forces during the 1409–1411 war.[98] Another settlement point where sources at the beginning of the 15th century indicate the existence of the Curonians was the Rossitten castle, located on the Curonian Spit. This stronghold was probably erected before 1372 and attested to unequivocally in 1423.[99] Confirmations of the Curonians' presence there date back to 1409[100] and 1423.[101] However, the nature of the settlement and the types of daily activities of the Curonians at the castles in Windenburg and Rossitten remain very unclear. Given the similarities of the geographic, geo-environmental, military, settlement and economic conditions occurring between Memel and especially Windenburg,[102] one would expect that this settlement collectivity was similar to the Memel group and its members also performed services of a military nature in relation to the Order. This remains only an assumption.

Conclusions

Summarizing the analyses carried out above, the Baltic indigenous populations of the southern part of *Curonia* were harnessed by the Teutonic Order, first its Livonian and then its Prussian branch, to the military structures created by this ecclesiastical corporation. Particularly since the concentration of at least some of the local population in the *Hackelwerk* beside Memel castle, which probably took place after 1323, the local commanders used the Curonians to perform a variety of military services. These services could have several forms, ranging from the transportation of letters, which was important in the context of communication, to serving as guides and especially as guards/*wachen* in areas of the 'Great Wilderness'. They also likely served in the military contingents issued by the Memel commander for war expeditions. Despite the few numbers of the Curonians settled at Memel castle, probably not exceeding 50 armed men, in view of the peculiar conditions in which the castle and the Teutonic Order's convent there functioned, this group to some extent supplemented the military potential of that stronghold. However, due to considerable military importance of the Memel castle for the Order during the wars with Lithuania from the last quarter of the 13th century to the first quarter of the 15th century, the incorporation of the southern Curonians into the military structures of the Order's dominion in the northeastern outskirts of Prussia had an undeniably significant value on the scale of the entire Prussian Land during this period.

Notes

1 *Cf.* e.g. Andrzej Nadolski, 'Niektóre elementy bałto-słowiańskie w uzbrojeniu i sztuce wojennej Krzyżaków,' *Pomorania Antiqua* 5 (1974): 165–172; id., 'Influence balto-slaves dans l'armament des Chevaliers Teutoniques,' in *Berichte über den II. Internationalen Kongress für Slawische Archäologie, Berlin 24.–28. August 1970*, vol. III, eds. Joachim Herrmann and Karl-Heinz Otto (Berlin: Akademie-Verlag, 1974), 33–36; Andrzej Nowakowski, *Arms and armour in the medieval Teutonic Order's State in Prussia*, Studies on the History of Ancient and Medieval Art of Warfare II (Łódź: Oficyna Wydawnicza MS, 1994); Sven Ekdahl, 'Das Pferd und seine Rolle im Kriegsführung des Deutschen Orden,' in *Das Kriegswesen der Ritterorden im Mittelalter*, ed. Zenon H. Nowak, Ordines Militares. Colloquia Torunensia Historica VI (Toruń: Uniwersytet Mikołaja Kopernika, 1991), 29–47; id., 'Horses and Crossbows: Two Important Warfare adventages of the Teutonic Order in Prussia,' in *The Military Orders*, vol. 2, *Welfare and Warfare*, ed. Helen Nicholson (Aldershot a.o.: Ashgate, 1998), 119–151.

2 Johannes Voigt, *Geschichte Preussens von den ältesten Zeiten bis zum Untergange der Herrschaft des Deutschen Ordens*, vol. III, *Die Zeit vom Frieden 1248 bis zur Unterwerfung der Preussen 1283* (Königsberg: Verlag der Gebrüder Bornträger, 1828), 420–443; Lothar Weber, *Preussen vor 500 Jahren in culturhistorischer, statistischer und militärischer Beziehung nebst Special-Geographie* (Danzig: [s.n.], 1878), 612, 614, 615 and 622.

3 Among the most recent works on topic *cf.* e.g. Grischa Vercamer, 'Man darf die schlafenden Hunde nicht wecken. Die militärische, soziale und politische Bedeutung der Freien im östlichen Ordensland Preußen für den Deutschen Orden,' in *Beiträge zur Militärgeschichte des Preussenlandes von der Ordenszeit bis zum Zeitalter der Weltkriege*, ed. Bernhart Jähnig, Tagungsberichte der Historischen Kommission für ost- und westpreußische Landesforschung 25 (Marburg: N.G. Elwert Verlag, 2010), 53–74; id., 'Die Freien im Deutschordensland Preußen als militärischer Rückhalt Ende des 14. – Anfang des 15. Jahrhunderts,' in *Tannenberg – Grunwald – Žalgiris 1410. Krieg und Frieden im späten Mittelalter*, eds. Werner Paravicini, Rimvydas Petrauskas, and Grischa Vercamer (Wiesbaden: Otto Harrassowitz, 2012), 175–189; Krzysztof Kwiatkowski, *Zakon niemiecki jako "corporatio militaris"*, part I, *Korporacja i krąg przynależących do niej. Kulturowe i społeczne podstawy działalności militarnej zakonu w Prusach (do początku XV wieku)* (Toruń: Wydawnictwo Naukowe Uniwersytetu Mikołaja Kopernika, 2012).

4 This English-language text distinguishes between two ethnonyms, which in German are rendered by the single term: *Schalauer*. Namely, the members of the tribal ethnocultural group until the 1270s–1280s inhabiting the land of Scalovia (*Scalovia*) in accordance with the existing naming tradition are referred to

as 'Scalovians'. Their descendants in the following decades already beyond the old, destroyed tribal forms, and incorporated into the new structures of the Teutonic Order's rulership, are described by the term 'Schalvians'. This is derived from the German version of the ethnonym. My intention is to capture and reflect terminologically the transformations that took place among the collectivities of Old-Prussian autochthons, who, during the Teutonic Order's period of rule, were subject to transformations going in the direction of acculturation to a new ethnic Prussian community composed of elements of mainly Baltic, Germanic and Slavic origins. For the same reason, in the text, it will be distinguished between *Curonia* and Courland, with the former toponym describing the country inhabited by the indigenous Curonians (Lat. *Curones*, Germ. *Kuren*), which, starting in the 13th century, slowly began to be changed under the influence of German-speaking newcomers and took the form of early modern Courland in the 16th century.

5 Kwiatkowski, *Zakon niemiecki*, 434–445; *cf.* also id., *Wojska zakonu niemieckiego w Prusach 1230–1525 (korporacja, jej pruskie władztwo, zbrojni, kultura wojny i aktywność militarna)* (with cooperation of Maria Molenda) (Toruń: Wydawnictwo Naukowe Uniwersytetu Mikołaja Kopernika, 2016), 116, 212, 218, 288, 332, 473, and 481.

6 Id., 'Schalauer – ein baltisches Element in der militärischen Organisation der Herrschaft des Deutschen Ordens in Preußen' in *Das Militärwesen im Deutschen Orden. Vorträge der Tagung der Internationalen Historischen Kommission zur Erforschung des Deutschen Ordens in Debrecen 2022*, ed. László Pósán, Quellen und Studien zur Geschichte des Deutschen Ordens 96 = Veröffentlichungen der Internationalen Historischen Kommission zur Erforschung des Deutschen Ordens 24 (Ilmtal-Weinstraße: VDG, 2025), 48–74.

7 *Cf.* especially the study by Vladas Žulkus, *Kuršiai Baltijos jūros erdvėje. Monografija* (Vilnius: "Versus Aureus" leidykla, 2004), here further detailed publications.

8 Philipp Schwartz, *Kurland im dreizehnten Jahrhundert bis zum Regierungsantritt Bischof Edmund's von Werd* (Leipzig: Verlag von E. Bidder, 1875), 49–50; Erich Chudzinski, *Die Eroberung Kurlands durch den Deutschen Orden im 13. Jahrhundert* (Borna: R. Niske, 1917), 16–26; and especially recently Alexander Baranov, 'Die Frühzeit des Deutschen Ordens in Livland und die Eroberung Kurlands. Ein peripheres Tätigkeitsfeld?' in *Livland – eine Region am Ende der Welt. Forschungen zum Verhältnis zwischen Zentrum und Peripherie im späten Mittelalter/Livonia – a Ragion at the Ende of the World. Studies on the Relations between Centre and Periphery in the Later Middle Ages*, ed. Anti Selart and Matthias Thumser, Quellen und Studien zur baltischen Geschichte 27 (Köln, Weimar, Wien: Böhlau Verlag, 2017), 315–345; also Anti Selart, 'Die Eroberung Livlands (12. und 13. Jahrhundert),' in *Das Baltikum. Geschichte eines europäischen Region*, vol. 1, *Von der Vor- und Frühgeschichte bis zum Ende des Mittelalters*, ed. Karsten Brüggemann, Detled Henning, Konrad Maier, and Ralph Tuchtenhagen (Stuttgart: Hiersemann Verlag, 2018), 197. Regarding the location of *Curonia* and the demographic expansion of the Curonians, *cf.* Žulkus, *Kuršiai*, 37–65; also id., 'Kurland. Die Grenzen und die nordlichen Landschaften in 8.–13. Jahrhundert,' *Archaeologia Baltica* 6 (2006): 88–103.

9 LECUB, 1/I: 237–238 no. 181 (the papal confirmation can be found in LECUB, 1/I: 239 no. 182); *cf.* Schwartz, *Kurland*, 54; Gustav A. Donner, *Kardinal Wilhelm von Sabina. Bischof von Modena 1222–1234. Päpstlicher Legat in den nordischen Ländern (†1251)*, Societas Scientiarum Fennica, Commentationes Humanorum Litterarum II/5 (Helsingfors: A.-G. F. Tilgmann, 1929), 291–292; Heinz von zur Mühlen, 'Livland von der Christianisierung bis zum Ende seiner Selbständigkeit (etwa 1180–1561),' in *Deutsche Geschichte im Osten Europas. Baltische Länder*, hrsg. v. Gert von Pistohlkors (Berlin: Siedler Verlag, 1994), 65;

Jan-Erik Beuttel, 'Kurland (ecclesia Curoniensis/Quironiensis),' in *Die Bischöfe des Heiligen Römischen Reiches 1198 bis 1448. Ein biographisches Lexikon*, ed. Erwin Gatz with cooper. of Clemens Brodkorb (Berlin: Duncker & Humblot, 2001), 311; Andrzej Radzimiński, 'Church Divisions of Livonia,' in *The Teutonic Order in Prussia and Livonia. The Political and Ecclesiastical Structures 13th–16th C.*, ed. Roman Czaja and Andrzej Radzimiński (Toruń: Towarzystwo Naukowe w Toruniu/Köln, Weimar, Wien: Böhlau Verlag, 2015), 258, 264. The actual division of the country was made on 4–5 April 1253, *cf.* LECUB, 1/I: 321–327 no. 248, 327–329 no. 249 (= SLVA, II: 335–336 no. 359); also LECUB, 1/I: 334–337 no. 253 (= SLVA, II: 346–350, no. 371); LECUB, 1/I: 357–358 no. 276, 404–405 no. 316.

10 *Cf.* a.o. Vladas Žulkus, *Klaipėdos senojo miesto raidos modelis. Leidinys parengtas remiantis Klaipėdos senamiesčio ir piliavietės archeologiniais tyrinėjimais* (Vilnius: Spauda, 1991), 7; id., *Viduramžių Klaipėda. Miestas ir pilis Archeologija ir istorija* (Vilnius: Leidykla "Žara", 2002), 28; Dietmar Willoweit, *Die Wirtschaftsgeschichte des Memellandes*, vol. I, Wissenschaftliche Beiträge zur Geschichte und Landeskunde Ost-Mitteleuropas 85/I (Marburg/Lahn: Johann Gottfried Herder Institut, 1969), 43–44; Tomasz Torbus, *Die Konventsburgen im Deutschordensland Preußen*, Schriften des Bundesinstituts für ostdeutsche Kultur und Geschichte 11 (München: R. Oldenbourg Verlag, 1998), 195, 535; Andres Kasekamp, *A History of the Baltic States*, Palgrave Essential Histories (Basingstoke, New York: Palgrave Macmillan, 2010), 17; among the older relevant works *cf.* a.o. Arthur Semrau, 'Beiträge zu Topographie der Burg und Stadt Memel im Mittelalter,' *Mitteilungen des Coppernicus-Vereins für Wissenschaft und Kunst zu Thorn* 37 (1929): 92–94; Erich Zurkalowski, 'Studien zur Geschichte der Stadt Memel und der Politik des Deutschen Ordens,' *Altpreussische Monatsschrift* 43 (1906): 155–165; Johannes Sembritzki, *Geschichte der Königlich Preussischen See- und Handelstadt Memel* (Memel: Verlag von F. W. Siebert, 1900), 14–16; Voigt, *Geschichte Preussens*, III: 67–73.

11 Vladas Žulkus, 'Klaipėdos istorijos ir topografijos bruožai XIII–XVII a. (Archeologijos duomenimis),' in *Klaipėdos miesto ir regiono archeologijos ir istorijos problemos*, ed. Alvydas Nikžentaitis and Vladas Žulkus, Acta historica universitatis Klaipedensis II (Klaipėda: KU Vakarų Lietuvos ir Prūsijos Istorijos Centras, 1994), 7, 9; id., 'Entwicklungslinien der Stadt Memel von der Gründung bis zur Mitte des 17. Jahrhunderts,' in *Memel als Brücke zu den baltischen Ländern. Kulturgeschichte Klaipėdas vom Mittelalter bis ins 20. Jahrhundert*, ed. Bernahrt Jähnig, Tagungsberichte der historischen Kommission für ost- und westpreußische Landesforschung 26 (Osnabrück: fibre Verlag, 2011), 19; Torbus, *Die Konventsburgen*, 195.

12 Žulkus, *Viduramžių Klaipėda*, 28; id., 'Klaipėdos istorijos,' 7, 9; id., 'Entwicklungslinien,' 19; Roman Czaja, 'Towns and Urban Space in the State of the Teutonic Order in Prussia,' in *The Teutonic Order*, ed. Czaja and Radzimiński, 80, 90; for the older works *cf.* Kurt Forstreuter, 'Memel und Lübeck im Mittelalter,' *Mitteilungen des Vereins für die Geschichte von Ost- und Westpreußen* 11, no. 4 (1937): 50; Erich Maschke, 'Das mittelalterliche Memel im baltisch-preussischen Raum,' *Mitteilungen des Vereins für die Geschichte von Ost- und Westpreußen* 2, no. 4 (1928): 54–55.

13 Chudzinski, *Die Eroberung Kurlands*, 60–64; Radzimiński, 'Church Divisions,' 264–265.

14 LECUB, 1/I: 508–509 no. 405; *cf.* Chudzinski, *Die Eroberung Kurlands*, 64–72; Max Toeppen, 'Excurs über die Verschreibungen des Ordens für Stammpreussen im 13. Jahrhundert,' in SRP, vol. I, Beilage 8 to 'Petri de Dusburg Chronicon terre Prussie' (Leipzig: Verlag von S. Hirzel, 1861), 254; Erich Maschke, *Der Deutsche Orden und die Preussen. Bekehrung und Unterwerfung in der preußisch-baltischen*

Mission des 13. Jahrhunderts, Historische Studien 176 (Berlin: Verlag Emil Ebering, 1928), 47–48.
15 *Preußisches Urkundenbuch. Politische (allgemeine) Abteilung*, vol. II: *1309–1335*, part 1: *1309–1324*, ed. Max Hein and Erich Maschke (Königsberg/Pr.: Gräfe und Unzer, 1932), 408–409 no. 617 (= LECUB, sec. 1, vol. II, *1301–1367*, ed. Friedrich G. von Bunge (Reval: Commission bei Kluge und Ströhm, 1855), 226–229 no. 733); *cf.* also LECUB, 1/II: 263 no. 745; *cf.* Bernhart Jähnig, 'Der Deutschordensstaat Preußen – die großen Hochmeister des 14. Jahrhunderts,' in *Die "Blüte" der Staaten des östlichen Europa im 14. Jahrhundert*, ed. Marc Löwener, Deutsches Historisches Institut Warschau. Quellen und Studien 14 (Wiesbaden: Harrassowitz Verlag, 2004), 58; Sławomir Jóźwiak, *Centralne i terytorialne organy władzy zakonu krzyżackiego w Prusach w latach 1228–1410. Rozwój – Przekształcenia – Kompetencje* (Toruń: Wydawnictwo Uniwersytatu Mikołaja Kopernika, 2001, 1st ed.), 127; Sembritzki, *Geschichte der Königlich Preussischen See- und Handelsstadt Memel*, 30–31; id., *Geschichte des Kreises Memel* (Memel: F. W. Siebert, 1918), 7.
16 *Cf.* endnote 9.
17 LECUB, sec. 1, vol. III, *I. Nachträge zu den zwei ersten Bänden. II. Fortsetzung von 1368–1393*, ed. Friedrich G. von Bunge (Reval: Commission bei Kluge und Ströhm, 1857), 673–678 no. 1319.
18 Robert Krumbholtz, 'Samaiten und der Deutsche Orden bis zum Frieden am Melno-See,' *Altpreußische Monatsschrift* 27 (1890): 23–24, 25; Hans Mortensen, *Litauen. Grundzüge einer Landeskunde*, Osteuropa Institut in Breslau, Quellen und Studien, 5. Abt.: Geographie und Landeskunde 1 (Hamburg: L. Friederichsen & Company, 1926), 40; Hans & Gertrud Mortensen, *Die Besiedlung des nordöstlichen Ostpreussens bis zum Beginn des 17 Jahrhundert*, part II, *Die Wildnis im östlichen Preußen, ihr Zustand um 1400 und ihre frühere Besiedlung*, Deutschland und der Osten 8 (Leipzig: Verlag von S. Hirzel, 1938), fig. 3 between p. 220 and 221; Roman Czaja and Zenon H. Nowak, 'An Attempt to Characterise the State of the Teutonic Knights in Prussia,' in *The Teutonic Order*, ed. Czaja and Radzimiński, 18.
19 Sławomir Jóźwiak, 'Kryzys władzy terytorialnej,' in *Państwo zakonu krzyżackiego w Prusach. Władza i społeczeństwo*, ed. Marian Biskup and Roman Czaja (Warszawa: Wydawnictwo Naukowe PWN, 2008), 342; and especially Julius Weise, *Herzog Erich von Braunschweig, der letzte Komtur des Deutschordens zu Memel* (Königsberg/Pr.: Ostpreussische Druckerei und Verlagsanstalt A.-G., 1908), 173–212. There was, however, a brief "intermezzo" in the years 1455–1468, when the commandery of Memel was pawned to the Livonian branch of the Order, *cf.* Kurt Forstreuter, 'Die preußische Kriegsflotte im 16. Jahrhundert,' *Altpreußische Forschungen* 17, no. 1 (1940): 70 (reprinted in id., *Beiträge zur preussischen Geschichte im 15. und 16. Jahrhundert*, Studien zur Geschichte Preussens 7 (Heidelberg: Quelle & Meyer, 1960), 90–91); Willoweit, *Die Wirtschaftsgeschichte*, 53–54
20 For scholarly views on the matter *cf.* Hans Mortensen, 'Die landschaftliche Bedeutung der Ausdrücke Wildnis, Wald, Heide, Feld usw. in den Quellen des deutschen Nordostens,' in *Vom deutschen Osten. Max Friedrichsen zum 60. Geburtstag*, ed. Herbert Knothe, Veröffentlichungen der Schlesischen Gesellschaft für Erdkunde und des Geographischen Instituts der Universität Breslau 21 (Breslau: Marcus, 1934), 127–142; also Friedrich Mager, *Der Wald in Altpreussen als Wirtschaftsraum*, vol. I, Ostmitteleuropa in Vergangenheit und Gegenwart 7/I (Köln, Graz: Böhlau Verlag, 1960), 145–154; and Karl Kasiske, 'Die Wildnis und ihre Besiedlung,' in *Der Deutsche Ritterorden. Seine politische und kulturelle Leistung im deutschen Osten*, ed. Erich Maschke and Karl Kasiske (Berlin: Deutscher Verlag fur Politik und Wirtschaft, Otto Jamrowski, 1942), 137.

21 GStA PK, XX. HA, OBA, no. 28196 (= edition: Rowell, 56–7 no. 10; dated to Spring, ca. 1400–1410); OBA, no. 4908 (3 March 1428); *cf.* also MTB, e.g. 117 lines 16–17 (year 1401), 152 lines 8–10 (year 1402), 176 lines 35–36 (year 1402), 219 lines 36–39 (year 1403), 231 lines 8–10 (year 1403), 232 lines 9–10 (year 1403); 584 lines 1–3 (year 1409), 587 lines 6–7 (year 1409), 592 lines 34–35 (year 1409); OBA, no. 28199 (2 August [1402 or 1413 or 1419]); OBA, no. 899, Bl. 1r (year 1406); OBA, no. 1319 (probably 30 June 1409); OBA, no. 1117 (= edition: CEVMDL, I: 191–192 no. 424; 26 August 1409); OBA, no. 28504 (ca. 1400–1420); OBA, no. 28641 (4 September, ca. 1410–1420); OBA, no. 1687, Bl. 2v (14 April 1412); GStA PK, XX. HA, OF 6, p. 6–7 (10 Februar 1413); OBA, no. 2026a (ca. 1413–1431); OF 13, p. 559 (25 December 1432). The Memel convent itself was not numerous, evidenced ca. 1412–1414 with 11 brethren, including 9 lay brothers, while in 1420 with 10 Order's members, *cf.* OBA, no. 1809 (ca. 1412–1414); OBA, no. 3189 (24 June 1420); Sławomir Jóźwiak, 'Liczebność konwentów zakonu krzyżackiego w Prusach w pierwszej połowie XV wieku,' ZH 72, no. 1 (2007): 10 (which incorrectly states that 7 or 8 brothers lived in the castle ca. 1411–1414). The castle was unable to withstand major Samogitian attacks, having fallen prey to them probably in 1379 and 1393, barely avoiding a similar fate in 1402, *cf.* Wigand (Z/K), 422 (cap. 250); FTAP, 110–111, 257; Posilge, 110–111, 189, 257; *cf.* a.o.: Heinrich A. Kurschat, *Das Buch vom Memelland. Heimatkunde eines deutschen Grenzlandes* (Oldenburg: Siebert, 1968), 151, 246, and 248; Kurt Forstreuter, 'Memel – Lage und Umland,' in id., *Wirkungen des Preussenlandes. Vierzig Beiträge*, Studien zur Geschichte Preußens 33 (Köln, Berlin: Grote, 1981), 373–374; Torbus, *Die Konventsburgen*, 535.

22 Regarding various construction works in the Memel castle *cf.* Posilge, 189 (year 1393); MTB, 22 lines 20–22 (year 1399), 35 lines 36–37 (year 1399), 117 lines 21–23 (year 1401), 128 lines 11–12 (year 1401), 137 lines 3–5 (year 1402); 257 lines 35–37 (year 1403), GStA PK, XX. HA, OBA, no. 775, Bl. 1r, 2r (year 1403 or 1404); OBA, no. 899, Bl. 1r (year 1406); MTB, 388 lines 38–39 (year 1406), 400 lines 14–15 (year 1406), 423 lines 4–6 (year 1407), 487 line 35 (year 1408), 539 lines 35–37 (year 1409), 556 lines 2–5 (year 1409), OBA, no. 1045 (20 Januar 1409); OBA, no. 1204 (most probably 31 March 1409); OBA. no. 1687, Bl. 2r–v (14 April 1412); OBA, no. 1690 (probably 30 April 1412); OBA, no. 27902 (ca. 1400–1420); OBA, no. 28141 (ca. 1410–1430); OBA, no. 28148 (ca. 1410–1430); OBA, no. 28184 (= edition: Rowell, 62–63 no. 17, which vaguely dates the text to the period before 1457); it was more probably composed 26–30 June, ca. 1411–1430); OBA, no. 28186 (ca. 1400–1420); OBA, no. 28187 (= edition: Rowell, 63–64 no. 18; 24 January, ca. 1400–1410); OBA, no. 28188 (= edition: Rowell, 64 no. 19, s. 64; ca. 1400–1420); OBA, no. 28189 (= edition: Rowell, 65 no. 20; ca. 1400–1420); OBA, no. 28190 (= edition: Rowell, 65–66 no. 21; 25 August, ca. 1400–1430); OBA, no. 28194 (ca. 1400–1420); OBA, no. 28197 (= edition: Rowell, 48–49 no. 2; 21 February [1407]); OBA, no. 28200 (= edition: Rowell, 66–67 no. 22; ca. 1420–1440); OBA, no. 28201 (= edition: Rowell, 57 no. 11; [19–24] May, ca. 1400–1420); OBA. no. 28504 (ca. 1400–1420); OBA, no. 28579 (ca. 1410–1430); OBA, no. 28812 (ca. 1410–1430); OBA, no. 2026a (ca. 1413–1431); OBA, no. 2358 (19 June 1416); OBA, no. 5097 (= edition: ASP, I: 519–520 no 391; 31 May 1429); OBA, no. 5140 (23 July 1429); OBA, no. 5176 (16 September 1429).

23 For Memel, this state of affairs is clearly attested to by a letter from an unknown brother of the Order who served as the commander there ca. 1412, from which it is known that he had received customary money from the Livonian land master in previous years. These payments, of unknown amount, constituted support of considerable importance for the maintenance of the Order's house and castle facilities, *cf.* GStA PK, XX. HA, OBA, no. 1778; also *cf.* OBA, no. 28199 (2

August [1402 or 1413 or 1419]). Numerous other source records have a similar meaning, and also testify the financial support of the Memel commandery by the Order's treasurer, as well as various expenses related to organizing the necessary works and transport of people, as well as bringing in materials, various types of equipment and horses, cf. MTB, e.g. 47 lines 26–27 (year 1400), 93 lines 16–21 (year 1400), 116 lines 40–41 (year 1401), 117 lines 21–23 (year 1401), 118 lines 24–26 (year 1401), 137 lines 1–3, 5–7 (year 1402), 138 lines 15–16 (year 1402), 162 lines 5–8 (year 1402), 176 lines 13–15 (year 1402), 183 lines 10–11 (year 1402), 192 lines 3–6 (year 1402), 194 lines 32–33, 35–37 (year 1402), 209 lines 8–10, 11–13 (year 1403), 239 lines 39–40 (year 1403), 248 lines 12–18 (year 1403), 250 lines 17–19 (year 1403), 252 lines 13–16 (year 1403), 255 lines 13–16 (year 1403), 258 lines 2–3 (year 1403), 274, lines 5–8 (year 1403), 276 lines 25–28 (year 1403), 277 lines 16–18 (year 1403), 291 lines 17–19, 22–24 (year 1404), 297 lines 10–13 (year 1404), 327 lines 8–10 (year 1404), 333 lines 4–6 (year 1405), 365 line 13 (year 1405), 374 lines 6–9 (year 1406), 390 line 41 – 391 line 2 (year 1406), 391 lines 4–8, 12–13, 15 (year 1406), 407 lines 37–41 (year 1406), 407 line 41 – 408 line 2 (year 1406), 408 lines 2–5, 10–14 (year 1406), 413 lines 2–4 (year 1407), 426 lines 38–40 (year 1407), 427 line 3–4 (year 1407), 428 lines 3–4 (year 1407), 454 lines 3–11, 17–20 (year 1408), 522 lines 29–35 (year 1409), 529 lines 27–28 (year 1409), 533 lines 4–6 (year 1409), 538 lines 1–2 (year 1409), 582 lines 10–12 (year 1409); OBA, no. 775, Bl. 2v (year 1403 or 1404); OBA 1204 (most probalby 31 March 1409); LECUB, 1/IV: 662 no. 1795 (27 Mai 1409); OBA, no. 1144 (13 September [1409]); LECUB, 1/IV: 833 no. 1928 (ca. 1412); OBA, no. 1687, Bl. 2r-v (14 April 1412); GStA PK, XX. HA, OF 6, p. 6–7 (10 Februar 1413); OBA, no. 2643 (ca. 1415–1417); OBA, no. 28204 (= edition: Rowell, 67 no. 23; 22 September, ca. 1411–1430); OBA, no. 28504 (ca. 1400–1420); OBA, no. 28565 (ca. 1400–1420); OF 13, p. 558–559 (25 December 1432).

24 Cf. 'E 34. Die Postwege des Deutschen Ordens in der ersten Hälfte des 15. Jahrhunderts,' in *Unter Kreuz und Adler. Der deutsche Orden im Mittelalter. Ausstellung des Geheimen Staatsarchivs Preußischer Kulturbesitz anläßlich des 800jährigen Bestehens des Deutschen Ordens*, ed. Friedrich Benninghoven (Mainz: Hase & Koehler, 1990), 111–112; Dieter Heckmann, '"Der Samaitische Strand". Beobachtungen zur Rechtsqualität einer Verkehrsverbindung zwischen den Deutschordensherrschaften Preußen und Livland vom 15. bis zum frühen 16. Jahrhundert,' in *Deutschordensgeschichte aus internationaler Perspektive. Festschrift für Udo Arnold zum 80. Geburtstag*, eds. Roman Czaja and Hubert Houben, Quellen und Studien zur Geschichte des Deutschen Ordens 85 (Ilmtal-Weinstraße: VDG, 2020), 83–85; Alfred Koch, 'Die deutsche Post im Memelland. Historischer Rückblick auf die Entwicklung des Postwesens 1230-1945,' *Archiv für Deutsche Postgeschichte* 1–2 (1961): 10 (although with a huge number of anachronisms); Kurt Forstreuter, 'Das Volk der Kurischen Nehrung,' in id., *Wirkungen des Preussenlandes*, 288. Among the numerous source references to the role of Memel in maintaining communication between Prussia and Livonia cf. e.g. GStA PK, XX. HA, OBA, no. 1071 (= edition: LECUB, 1/IV: 662–663 no. 1795; [27 May 1409]); LECUB, 1/V: 638–639 no. 2474 (with the wrong date 12 May 1420, *recte*: 25. April 1421); OBA, no. 27881 (= edition: Rowell, 60–61 no. 15; [19–24] October [ca. 1411–1420], the date of 1458 proposed by the editor is too late).

25 Regarding the awareness of the importance of the Memel castle among the Order's brethren and the need to constantly support its maintenance cf. GStA PK, XX. HA, OBA, no. 1842; cf. also a.o. OBA, no. 1690 (probably 30 April 1412); OBA, no. 2064 (29 April 1414); OBA, no. 4908 (3 March 1428); OBA, no. 28197a (= edition: Rowell, 49–50 no. 3; [2–7] November, ca. 1430–1440); OBA, no. 28544

(= edition: Rowell, 54 no. 8; 28 June, ca. 1420–1432); *cf.* Kwiatkowski, *Zakon niemiecki*, s. 444. It was similar in the case of the town of Memel, *cf.* LECUB, 1/ III: 666 no. 1317. The implementation of these control and protection tasks was particularly problematic. A document of the Bishop of Courland, Otto, dated 30 June 1392 and certifying the division of areas in southern (Prussian) *Curonial* Courland between him and the Prussian branch of the Order, clearly indicates that shortly before its issuance, neither the bishop nor the Order had the potential to effectively defend the Baltic Sea coastline in this section, causing many Christians to fall prey to pagan (probably Samogitian) attacks in the beach zone, *cf.* LECUB, 1/III: 674 no. 1319.

26 *Cf.* Kwiatkowski, *Wojska*, 32–33, 116, 228, and 251–254 (Ekskurs 26).

27 Regarding the Curonians *cf.* Žulkus, *Kuršiai*, 152–153, 158–161, 171, and 175–176; id., 'Settlements and Piracy on the Eastern Shore of the Baltic Sea: The Middle Ages to Modern Times,' *Archaeologia Baltica* 16 (2011) (*Settlements and Towns*): 61, 62–63, and 64–65; Arturas Mickevičius, *Normanai ir Baltai IX– XII a.* (Vilnius: "Versus Aureus" leidykla, 2004), 63–65, 66–67; Nils Blomkvist, 'East Baltic Vikings – with particular consideration to the Curonians,' in *Praeities puslapiai: archeologija, kultūram visuomenė. Skiriama archaelogo prof. habil. dr. Vlado Žulkus 60-ties metų jubiliejui ir 30-ties metų mokslinės veiklos sukakčiai* (Klaipėda: Klaipėdos universiteto leidykla, 2005), 73–90; also Andris Šnē, 'Warfare and Power in the Late Pregistoric Societies in the Territory of Latvia (tenth to 12th Centuries),' *Archaeologia Baltica* 8 (2007) (*Weapons, Weaponry and Man (In memoriam Vytautas Kazakevičius)*): 260; *cf.* also chronicle information about the servitors (*knechte, gesinde*) of the Curonians in the mid-13th century, indicating indirectly the existence of a layer of the mighty people among them, LRCh, 108 lines 4712–4717; 157 line 6861; regarding the Scalovians *cf.* Ugnius Budvydas, 'About Some Aspects of Scalvian Armament on the Basis of Investigations in Viešvilė Cemetery,' *Archaeologia Baltica* 8 (2007) (*Weapons, Weaponry and Man (In memoriam Vytautas Kazakevičius)*), 211; Kwiatkowski, 'Schalwen,' 51–54.

28 HLCh, 158 line 12–13 (cap. XXIII, 4) (even if there is likely narrative, stylistic hyperbole here); LRCh, 57 lines 2477–2486; 59 lines 2541–2542, 2560 (probable chronicler's hyperbole); 61 lines 2639–2640, 2649–2650; 95 lines 4139–4141; 96 lines 4181–4184; 109 lines 4748–4755; 111, 4812–4828 (also a rhetorical construction of the chronicler, but referring to reality); 123 lines 5370–5371; 205 lines 8968–8970; 209 lines 9114–9116; 268 lines 11745–11746.

29 *Cf.* Žulkus, *Kuršiai*, 141–148, 176, and 210; Mickevičius, *Normanai*, 87–103, 108–140, and 149–153.

30 It resulted from the gradual emigration of the local population to the north, which began as early as the 11th century, *cf.* Yanis Asaris, 'O severnykh territoriakh rasselenia kurshei v X–XIII vv. (po materialam mogilnikov).' in *Vakarų baltai: etnogenezė ir etninė istorija*, ed. Regina Volkaitė-Kulikauskienė (Vilnius: Lietuvos istorijos instituto leidykla, 1997), 201–205; Žulkus, *Kuršiai*, 40–42; earlier especially Mortensen, *Die Besiedlung*, 127, 131–132, 134–135, and 138 (but he dated it only to the 13th century).

31 LECUB, 1/I: 319–320 no. 246 (April 1253), 329 no. 249 (5 April 1253, whereby it is uncertain whether the *infeodati* […] *in terra Ceclis* mentioned in this document were local Curonians or, perhaps, incomers from other parts of Livonia. The document also mentions *seniores et discretiores terrarum* – the next evidence for the existence of not only individual settlers, but entire collectivities that may even have been the character of communities), 334–337 no. 253 (29 July 1253, here also mentioned *leenlude in deme lande to Cecklis*); *cf.* Mortensen, *Die Besiedlung*, 122, 142. A document, dated 5 April 1253, lists as many as 87 settlement toponyms, which in itself makes a strong argument for the existence of a population in these areas that carried this toponymic tradition; another document dated 29 July 1253

is of similar significance. For the last decade of the 13th century, *cf.* LECUB, 1/I: 663 no. 533 (9 May 1290, *castellatura Ampilten* (former Germ. Impelt, today Lit. Ipiltis)), 673–674 no. 540 (6 Januar 1291); *cf.* Mortensen, *Die Besiedlung*, 114.

32 LECUB, 1/I: 298 no. 236 (29 July 1252), 307–308 no. 241 (19 Oktober 1252); *cf.* Klaus Militzer, 'The list of dignitaries and officials of the Brothers of the Sword and the Teutonic Order in Livonia,' in *The Teutonic Order*, eds. Czaja and Radzimiński, 353; Lutz Fenske and Klaus Militzer, *Ritterbrüder im livländischen Zweig des Deutschen Ordens*, Quellen und Studien zur baltischen Geschichte 12 (Köln, Weimar, Wien: Böhlau Verlag, 1993), 113 (no. 64), 317 (no. 393), 684–685 (no. 920); Janusz Tandecki, 'Administrative divisions of the territory of the Teutonic Orders in Livonia,' in *The Teutonic Order*, eds. Czaja and Radzimiński, 187.

33 LECUB, 1/I: 416–417 no. 329 (27 July 1258), 417–418 no. 330 (27 July 1258); Fenske and Militzer, *Ritterbrüder*, 617 (no. 836).

34 LECUB, 1/I: 314 no. 244 (February 1253), 319–320 no. 245 (8 February 1253), 370 no. 285 (27 August 1255), 673–674 no. 540 (6 Januar 1291); *cf.* Militzer, 'The list,' 353; Fenske and Militzer, *Ritterbrüder*, 167 (no. 158), 601 (no. 813), 684–685 (no. 920).

35 LRCh, 96–97 lines 4187–4202; 113–114 lines 4942–4950; 121–122 lines 5290–5294; 164 lines 7153–7154; 205 lines 8951–8972; 208 lines 9067–9075; 209 lines 9119–9122, 9141; 216 lines 9431–9434; 245 lines 10728–10730; *cf.* Ernst Dragendorff, *Ueber die Beamten des Deutschen Ordens in Livland während des XIII. Jahrhunderts* (Berlin: Goedecke & Gallinek, 1894), 53–54, 60–62; for 13th-century Prussia *cf.* Jóźwiak, *Centralne*, 64–66.

36 LECUB, 1/I: 329–330 no. 250; *cf.* Helene Dopkewitsch, 'Die Burgsuchungen in Kurland und Livland vom 13.–16. Jahrhundert,' *Mitteilungen aus der livländischen Geschichte* 25, no. 1 (1933–1937): 16; von zur Mühlen, 'Livland,' 99. The fact that Latin political entities in Livonia were already trying to gain their military support among the Curonians for expeditions against the 'pagans' in the late 1220s is attested to by two treaties concluded on 28 December 1229 and 17 January 1230, respectively, by papal legate Balduin of Alna with part of the Curonian communities living in the region of the lower and middle reaches of the Windau River (Lit. and Let. Venta), and the 1230 treaty of the convent of the Church of Riga and the Order of the Knights of Christ in Livonia with the Curonians located further east, *cf.* LECUB, 1/I: 136 no. 103 (papal confirmation: LECUB, 1/I: 160 no. 114), 127 no. 104, 138 no. 105). This practice was maintained in the new political situation by the Teutonic Order as well.

37 These were the defensive campaign in *Curonia* ca. 1245 (*cf.* LRCh, 57 lines 2477–2483), the Samogitian expedition ca. 1254–1255 (*cf.* LRCh, 96 lines 4181–4193; 98 lines 4298–4299); the expedition at Memel in 1257 (*cf.* LRCh, 103 lines 4482–4488; 104 lines 4507–4508), two defensive campaigns in *Curonia* in 1259 (*cf.* LRCh, 109 lines 4730–4740, 4748–4755; 110 lines 4783–4785; 111, 4812–4828, 4835–4839, 4849–4852; 112 lines 4857–4863; 114 lines 4968–4970), a campaign in Semigallia in 1259 (*cf.* LRCh, 123, lines 5366–5372; 125 lines 5433–5434), the summer campaign in *Curonia* in 1260 (*cf.* Dusburg (T), 97 (lib. III, cap. 84); Jeroschin, 425 lines 10584–10592; LRCh, 130 lines 5601–5603, 5630–5631; 130–131 lines 5642–5643), the Curonian campaign ca. 1261 (*cf.* LRCh, 136 lines 5921–5923), the expedition against the stronghold of *Gresen* ca. 1264 (*cf.* LRCh, 166 lines 7225–7227), the Lithuanian campaign of 1279 (*cf.* LRCh, 191 lines 8334–8337), the expedition of the *Vogt* of Goldingen Johann von Ochtenhausen ca. 1279 (*cf.* LRCh, 205 lines 8968–8970; 206 lines 9004–9005; 207, lines 9022–9023; 208 lines 9091–9092, 9097–9098), the expedition of the commander of Goldingen to Semigallia ca. 1279 (*cf.* LRCh, 209 lines 9112–9125), a defensive campaign ca. 1289 (cf. LRCh, 254 lines 11131–11132), other military activities in *Curonia* ca. 1289 (*cf.* LRCh, 262 lines 11451–11454),

and the Lithuanian campaign of 1290 (*cf.* LRCh, 267, lines 11680–11686; 268 lines 11745–11746).
38 LECUB, 1/I: 671 no. 538.
39 *Cf.* Dragendorff, *Ueber die Beamten*, 61–62; Indriķis Šterns, 'Iezemiešu loma Senlatvijas pakļaušanā vācu varai,' *Latvijas Vēstures Institūta Žurnāls* 1 (46) (2003): 38–42, 46; Kaspars Kļaviņš, 'The Significance of the Local Baltic Peoples in the Defence of Livonia (Late Thirteenth – Sixteenth Centuries),' in *The Clash of Cultures on the Medieval Baltic Frontier*, ed. Alan V. Murray (Farnham: Ashgate, 2009), 325–326; Linda Kaljundi, 'Neophytes as actors in the Livonian crusades,' in *Making Livonia. Actors and Networks in the Medieval and Early Modern Baltic Sea Region*, eds. Anu Mänd and Marek Tamm (London, New York: Routledge, 2020), 108–109; Juhan Kreem, 'Der Deutsche Orden in Livland: die Heiden, Landvolk und Undeutsche in der livländischen Heeresverfassung,' in *L'Ordine Teutonico tra Mediterraneo e Baltico incontri e scontri tra religioni, popoli e culture/Der Deutsche Orden zwischen Mittelmeerraum und Balticum. Begegnungen und Konfrontationen zwischen Religionen, Völker und Kulturen. Atti del Convegno internazionale, Bari–Lecce–Brindisi, 14–16 settembre 2006*, eds. Hubert Houben and Kristjan Toomaspoeg (Galatina: Mario Congedo Editore, 2008), 239–241; Selart, 'Die Eroberung Livlands,' 199–200.
40 As late as 1413 the Flemisch traveller and diplomat, Guillebert de Lannoy, attests to the pagan customs of the Curonians, *cf. Oeuvres de Ghillebert de Lannoy, voyageur, diplomate et moraliste*, ed. Charles Potvin (Louvain: Imprimerie de P. et J. Lefever, 1878), 30; *cf.* also Vladas Žulkus, 'Heidentum und Christentum in Litauen im 10.–16. Jahrhundert,' in *Rom und Byzanz im Norden. Mission und Glaubenswechsel im Ostseeraum während des 8.–14. Jahrhunderts. Internationale Fachkonferenz der Deutschen Forschungsgemeinschaft in Verbindung mit der Akademie der Wissenschaften und der Literatur, Mainz, Kiel, 18.–25. September 1994*, vol. II, ed. Michael Müller-Wille (Mainz: Akademie der Wissenschaften und der Literatur/Stuttgart: F. Steiner, 1998), 151–152, 155–156.
41 The second *Vogt* of *Curonia* is attested in Goldingen, *cf.* LRCh, 205 lines 8951–8953.
42 LRCh, 103–104 lines 4461–4526 (year 1257), 109–112 lines 4730–4876 (year 1259), 156 lines 6787–6792 (ca. 1262), 160 lines 6977–6982 (year 1263), 160–161, lines 6983–7018 (year 1263), 161–162 lines 7019–7058 (year 1263), 162 lines 7059–7071 (year 1263).
43 LECUB, 1/1: 460–462 no. 362.
44 LECUB, 1/I: 672–674 no. 540.
45 LECUB, 1/I: 327–328 no. 249.
46 LECUB, 1/I: 417 no. 329.
47 LECUB, 1/I: 673–674 no. 540.
48 Dopkewitsch, 'Die Burgsuchungen,' 1–2, 4, 5–11, 14–16, 19–21, 23–24, and 35–41; *cf.* Žulkus, *Kuršiai*, 66–69. Helene Dopkewitsch has shown that the term *castellatura*, whose Middle High German equivalent was the term *burchsukung*, referred to separate areas organized by Baltic autochthons for defence in case of hostile invasions. They dated back to pre-Christian times and were a form of spatial organization of neighbourhood settlement communities of the Balts. The identification of all of the eight centres mentioned above has already been done with a high degree of certainty in historiography: *Poys* – Giruliai (former Germ. Plantage), *Mutina/Mutene/Mutone* – Purmaliai, *Akutte/Ackete* – Eketė (former Germ. Ekitten), *Kalaten* – Kalotė (former Germ. Kollaten), *Sarden* – Žardė (former Germ. Szarde), *Creten* – Ėgliškiai-Anduliai (former Germ. Krottingen), *Duwirstene/Dwiristis* – today not existed settlement (former Lit. Virkštininkai, Germ. Groß Wirsteniken), *Palangen* – Palanga (former Germ. Palangen).
49 *Cf.* Žulkus, *Kuršiai*, 45–50.
50 Žulkus, *Kuršiai*, 47 (map no. 8).

51 LECUB, 1/IV: 647 no. 1778; *cf.* also LECUB, 1/IV: 650 no. 1782.
52 GStA PK, XX. HA, OBA, no. 28544 (= edition: Rowell, 54–55 no. 8; 28 June, ca. 1420–1432); *cf.* Mortensen, *Die Besiedlung*, 228 footnote 1009.
53 GStA PK, XX. HA, OBA, no. 28201 (= edition: Rowell, 57 no. 11; [19–24] May, ca. 1400–1420); OBA, no. 28205 (= edition: Rowell, 67–68 no. 24; April–May, ca. 1400–1420); OBA, no. 28199 (2 August [1402 or 1413 or 1419]); OBA, no. 27872 (= Rowell, 52–53 no. 6; ca. 1435); OBA, no. 28475 (ca. 1412–1432); OBA, no. 2026a (ca. 1413–1431); in this regard *cf.* Sembritzki, *Geschichte der Königlich Preussischen See- und Handelsstadt Memel*, 36–37.
54 'Erste Fortsetzung der Detmar-Chronik von 1395–1399', in *Die Chroniken der niedersächsischen Städte. Lübeck*, vol. II, ed. Karl Koppmann, Die Chroniken der deutschen Städte vom 14. bis ins 16. Jahrhundert 26 (Leipzig: Verlag von S. Hirzel, 1899), 108 lines 8–11; regarding this expedition and the transmission of written sources for it, *cf.* Krzysztof Kwiatkowski and Gregory Leighton, 'Ein Heerzugsbericht des Deutschen Ordens aus dem Staatsarchiv Thorn: Inhalts-, Datum- und Kontextanalyse,' *Preußenland* 14 (2023): 62–77.
55 *Oeuvres de Ghillebert de Lannoy*, ed. Potvin, 30.
56 Žulkus, *Kuršiai*, 193.
57 Vladas Žulkus pointed out only the lower degree of integration of the local Curonian nobles into the structures created by the Teutonic Order compared to the Prussian territories, *cf.* Žulkus, *Kuršiai*, 196. However, it should be emphasized that it was first of all the insignificant extent of the Order's control over the area of southern *Curonia* that was one of the essential factors of that weak integration observed by the Lithuanian archaeologist.
58 Žulkus, *Kuršiai*, 200.
59 LECUB, 1/I: 319–320 no. 246; *cf.* Žulkus, *Kuršiai*, 204.
60 Meanwhile, estates under fief law in northern Courland are known as early as 1253 and 1258, *cf.* LECUB, 1/I: 320–322 no. 247, 410–411 no. 322.
61 Dusburg (T), 187 (lib. III, cap. 344); Jeroschin, 601 lines 25816–25823.
62 Dusburg (T), 187–188 (lib. III, cap. 344); Jeroschin, 601 lines 25816–25835.
63 *Cf.* Max Toppen in Dusburg (T), 187 footnote 3 on pp. 187–188; Mortensen, *Die Besiedlung*, 123, 127, and 142–143; regarding this category of strongholds, although with respect to the Slavic cultural circle, *cf.* Sebastian Brather, 'Zwischen "Fluchtburg" und "Herrensitz". Sozialgeschichtliche Interpretationen früh- und hochmittelalterlicher Burgwälle in Ostmitteleuropa,' *Archaeologia Baltica* 6 (2006): 41–43.
64 Dopkewitsch, *Die Burgsuchungen*, 5–16.
65 Žulkus, *Kuršiai*, 200 (here further publikations).
66 Jonas Genys, 'Žardė – Pilsoto žemės prekybos ir amatų centras', in *Lietuvininkų kraštas: monografija*, ed. Norbertas Vėlius (Kaunas: Litterae Universitatis, 1995), 108–127.
67 Žulkus, *Kuršai*, 90, 92, and 107; id., 'Zur Frühgeschichte,' 198.
68 Algimantas Merkevičius, 'Eketės (Klaipėdos raj.) piliakalnio tyrinėjimaj,' in *Archeologiniai ir etnografiniai tyrinėjimai Lietuvoje 1972 ir 1974 metais*, ed. Adolfas Tautavičius and Vitalis Morkūnas (Vilnius: Lietuvos TSR Mokslų Akademijos Istorijos Institutas, 1974), 15–19; Romas Jarockis, 'Eketė Iron Age and Early Medieval Hill-Fort Settlement Comlex. Aerial Archaeology and Remote Sensing,' *Archaeologia Baltica* 9 (2008): 8–14; *cf.* also Žulkus, *Kuršai*, 89–90, 98, 100, 106, and 107; id., 'Zur Frühgeschichte der baltischen Stadt,' in *Burg – Burgstadt – Stadt. Zur Genese mittelalterlicher nichtagrarischer Zentren in Ostmitteleuropa*, ed. Hansjürgen Brachmann, Forschungen zur Geschichte und Kultur des östlichen Mitteleuropa (Berlin: Akademie Verlag: 1995), 198.
69 Vladas Žulkus, *Palanga in the Middle Ages. Ancient settlements*, transl. Vijolė Arbas (Vilnius: "Versus Aureus", 2007), especially 58–61, 367–372; id., *Kuršiai*,

116–118; id., 'Zur Frühgeschichte,' 196–198; 'Palanga,' https://piliakalniai.lt/objektai/827 (with reference list), accessed 5 December 2024.
70 Id., *Kuršai*, 90, 92; id., 'Zur Frühgeschichte,' 198.
71 Mortensen, *Die Besiedlung*, 150, 222.
72 Cf. Kwiatkowski, 'Die Schalauer,' 56–58.
73 Cf. Žulkus, *Kuršiai*, 205, 213. *Hackelwerk*s from the northern part of Courland and in Semigallia in the 13th century are attested in written sources, cf. LRCh, 209 lines 9144, 9152; 210 line 9169; 216 line 9457; 221 line 9576; 222 line 9589; 252 lines 11010, 11017, and 11045; 253 lines 11060, 11074; 256 line 11222; 258 lines 11290, 11293; 259 lines 11337, 11355, and 11361; 262 lines 11458, 11474, and 11487; 270 lines 11820, 11822.
74 GStA PK, XX. HA, OBA, no. 1238.
75 GStA PK, XX. HA, OBA, no. 28195.
76 GStA PK, XX. HA, OBA, no. 1238.
77 GStA PK, XX. HA, OBA, no. 28641.
78 Cf. Kwiatkowski, 'Die Schalauer,' 61–62.
79 According to the account of the so-called Pomezanian official, during the attack of the Samogitians on the town of Memel and castle in the autumn of 1393, about 60 people and 1 brother of the Order were killed, cf. Posilge, 189. Among the former, one should also see some number of Curonians.
80 GStA PK, XX. HA, OBA, no. 28544 (= edition: Rowell, 54–55 no. 8).
81 MTB, 548 lines 15–17.
82 'Die littauischen Wegeberichte,' (hereafter cited as: LWB) ed. Theodor Hirsch, Beilage I to 'Die Chronik Wigands von Marburg. Originalfragmente, lateinische Übersetzung und sonstige Überreste,' in SRP, vol. II (Leipzig: Verlag von S. Hirzel, 1863), 664 (W. 1) (*Maldenne/Moltenne Eywan* in year 1387), probably also 665 (W. 2) (*Eywon Spandenne/Spandeme*), 667 (W. 4) (*Greyne* in year 1388), 667 (W. 5) (*Gintil*).
83 LRCh, 55 line 2376; 97 line 4213; 209 line 9126; 267 line 11694.
84 GStA PK, XX. HA, OBA, no. 28205 (= edition: Rowell, 67–68 no. 24; April–May, ca. 1400–1420).
85 Cf. Kwiatkowski, *Zakon niemiecki*, 322–323, 330; id., *Wojska*, 267, 269–270.
86 LWB, 666 (W. 3) (*Gayline* in year 1384); cf. Kwiatkowski, *Zakon niemiecki*, 323; id., *Wojska*, 270.
87 GStA PK, XX. HA, OBA, no. 28156 (= edition: Rowell, 58 no. 12); cf. attestations of *warten* in 13th-century *Curonia*, LRCh, 57 line 2469; 112 line 4896; 114 line 4986; 118 line 5150; 120 line 5207; 138 line 6017; 212 lines 9249, 9266, and 9274; 241 line 10567; cf. also guards accompanying the army in the field, LRCh, 98 lines 4261, 4264, and 4272; 115 lines 5010, 5026.
88 Cf. Kwiatkowski, *Wojska*, 269.
89 LECUB, 1/IV: 662 no. 1795.
90 LECUB, 1/IV: 662 no. 1795.
91 GStA PK, XX. HA, OBA, no. 28195; cf. also OPChLP, 257 (year 1402); MTB, 487 lines 35–36 (year 1408), 548 lines 9–10 (year 1409).
92 Marius Ščavinskas, 'Some Comments on the Formation of Medieval Warriors in Baltic and Finnish Societies (in the 12th and Early 13th Centuries),' *Acta Historica Universitatis Klaipedensis* 37 (2018): 44–52, 53–56; id., 'Some notes on the issue of the development of Balt society in the ninth to the 13th centuries in the context of the socio-political structures of the Baltic region,' *Archaeologia Baltica* 19 (2013): 86–97; Rimvydas Petrauskas, 'Socialiniai pokyčiai Lietuvoje valstybės formavimosi laikotarpiu/Der soziale Wandel bei der litauischen Staatsbildung,' in *Lietuvos valstybės susikūrimas europiniame kontekste*, ed. Rimvydas Petrauskas (Vilnius: "Versus Aureus" leidykla, 2008), 161–166, 171–172/185–191, 197–198; Mickevičius, *Normanai*, 59–61 (in all these publications earlier studies on this theme).

93 GStA PK, XX. HA, OBA, no. 28156 (= edition: Rowell, 58 no. 12); *cf.* Mortensen, *Die Besiedlung*, 222 footnote 978.
94 MTB, 176 lines 18–21 (year 1402), 188 lines 15–22 (year 1402).
95 MTB, 180 lines 36–37 (year 1402), 261 lines 25–27 (year 1403), 487 lines 35–36 (year 1408), 488 lines 3–4 (year 1408), 490 line 24 (year 1409), 548 lines 9–10 (year 1409).
96 The castle was erected in 1360, *cf.* Wigand, 270 (cap. 125); *cf.* also Kurt Forstreuter, 'Die Entwicklung der Nationalitätenverhältnisse auf der Kurischen Nehrung,' *Altpreußische Forschungen* 8 (1931): 48; Mortensen, *Die Besiedlung*, 223; and Andrzej Gierszewski, 'Mierzeja Kurońska i Zalew Kuroński w średniowieczu (do 1525 r.),' (PH Diss., Uniwersytet Gdański, 2015), 58, 72.
97 MTB, 287 lines 19–20; *cf.* also 488 lines 17–18 (year 1408).
98 Staatsarchiv Königsberg, OF 5b, p. 335 (missing); cited after: Mortensen, *Die Besiedlung*, 222–223.
99 'Hermanni de Wartberge Chronicon Livoniae,' ed. Ernst Strehlke, in SRP, II: 102; GStA PK, XX. HA, OBA, no. 4216, Bl. 2r; *cf.* also LWB, 665 (W. 2), 667 (W. 4, 2 Februar 1388), 674 (W. 1, year 1395); MTB, 248 lines 16–18 (year 1403), 257 lines 35–36, 37–38 (year 1403), 297 lines 10–12 (year 1403), 337 lines 26–28 (year 1405), 397 lines 5–7 (year 1406), 487 line 41 – 488 line 1 (year 1408), 490 line 23 (year 1408); Krzysztof Kwiatkowski, 'Neue Quellen aus dem Kreis des Deutschen Ordens zum Krieg von 1409–1411 (Teil 1),' ZH 75, no. 4 (2010): 81 no. 3; *cf.* also Forstreuter, 'Die Entwicklung,' 48, 54–55.
100 MTB, 548 lines 3–4 (year 1409); probably also 487 line 41 – 488 line 1 (year 1408).
101 GStA PK, XX. HA, OBA, no. 4216, Bl. 2r; *cf.* Mortensen, *Die Besiedlung*, 221; Forstreuter, 'Die Entwicklung,' 54–55; Grischa Vercamer, *Siedlungs-, Sozial- und Verwaltungsgeschichte der Komturei Königsberg in Preußen (13.–16. Jahrhundert)*, Einzelschriften der Historischen Kommission für ost- und westpreußische Landesforschung 29 (Marburg: N. G. Elwert Verlag, 2010), 411 (Anhang, Quellen, no. 5, however, with an erroneous reading); *cf.* also Wiesław Długokęcki, 'Odbudowa osadnictwa, kolonizacja i przemiany wsi w państwie krzyżackim (1411–1525),' in *Państwo zakonu krzyżackiego*, ed. Biskup and Czaja, 381; Gierszewski, 'Mierzeja Kurońska,' 62–64.
102 *Cf.* MTB, 116 lines 40–41.

Primary Sources

Berlin, Geheimes Staatsarchiv Preußischer Kulturbesitz, XX. Hauptabteilung, Ordensbriefarchiv, nos. 775, 899, 1045, 1071, 1117, 1144, 1204, 1238, 1319, 1687, 1690, 1778, 1809, 1842, 2026a, 2064, 2358, 2643, 3189, 4216, 4908, 5097, 5140, 5176, 27872, 27881, 27902, 28141, 28148, 28156, 28184, 28186, 28187, 28188, 28189, 28190, 28194, 28195, 28196, 28197, 28197a, 28199, 28200, 28201, 28204, 28205, 28475, 28504, 28544, 28565, 28579, 28641, 28812.
Berlin, Geheimes Staatsarchiv Preußischer Kulturbesitz, XX. Hauptabteilung, Ordensfolianten 6, 13.
Acten der Ständetage Preussens unter der Herrschaft des Deutschen Ordens. Edited by Max Toeppen. Vol. I, *Die Jahre 1233–1435*. Leipzig: Duncker & Humblot, 1878.
'Erste Fortsetzung der Detmar-Chronik von 1395–1399.' In *Die Chroniken der niedersächsischen Städte. Lübeck*. Vol. II, edited by Karl Koppmann, 71–114. Die Chroniken der deutschen Städte vom 14. bis ins 16. Jahrhundert 26. Leipzig: Verlag von S. Hirzel, 1899.

'Franciscani Thorunensis Annales Prussici (941–1410).' Edited by Ernst Strehlke. In SRP, vol. III, edited by Theodor Hirsch, Max Toeppen, and Ernst Strehlke, 13–388 (source edition at 57–316). Leipzig: Verlag von S. Hirzel, 1866.

Heinrici Chronicon Livoniae/Heinrichs livländische Chronik. Edited by Leonid Arbusow and Albert Bauer. Monumenta Germaniae Historica, Scriptores rerum Germanicarum in usum scholarum ex MGH separatim editi. Hannover: Hahnsche Buchhandlung, 1955, 2nd edition.

'Hermanni de Wartberge Chronicon Livoniae.' Edited by Ernst Strehlke. In SRP, vol. II, edited by Theodor Hirsch, Max Toeppen, and Ernst Strehlke, 9–116 (source edition at 21–116). Leipzig: Verlag von S. Hirzel, 1863.

'Johanns von Posilge, Officials von Pomesanien Chronik des Landes Preussen (von 1360 an, forgesetzt bis 1419).' Edited by Ernst Strehlke. In SRP, vol. III, edited by Theodor Hirsch, Max Toeppen, and Ernst Strehlke, 13–388 (source edition at 79–388). Leipzig: Verlag von S. Hirzel, 1866.

'Di Kronike von Pruzinlant des Nicolaus von Jeroschin.' Edited by Ernst Strehlke. In SRP, vol. I, edited by Theodor Hirsch, Max Toeppen, and Ernst Strehlke, 291–624 (source edition at 303–624). Leipzig: S. Hirzel, 1861.

Kwiatkowski, Krzysztof. 'Neue Quellen aus dem Kreis des Deutschen Ordens zum Krieg von 1409–1411 (Teil 1).' ZH 75, no. 4 (2010): 67–111.

'Die littauischen Wegeberichte.' Edited by Theodor Hirsch. Beilage I to: 'Die Chronik Wigands von Marburg. Originalfragmente, lateinische Übersetzung und sonstige Überreste.' In SRP, vol. II, edited by Theodor Hirsch, Max Toeppen, and Ernst Strehlke, 662–711 (source edition at 664–708). Leipzig: Verlag von S. Hirzel, 1863.

Liv-, est- und kurländisches Urkundenbuch nebst Regesten. Sec. 1, vol. I, 1093–1300. Edited by Friedrich G. v. Bunge. Reval: Commission bei Kluge und Ströhm, 1853.

Liv-, est- und kurländisches Urkundenbuch nebst Regesten. Sec. 1, vol. II, 1301–1367, edited by Friedrich G. v. Bunge. Reval: Commission bei Kluge und Ströhm, 1855.

Liv-, est- und kurländisches Urkundenbuch nebst Regesten. Sec. 1, vol. III, *I. Nachträge zu den zwei ersten Bänden. II. Fortsetzung von 1368–1393*, edited by Friedrich G. v. Bunge. Reval: Commission bei Kluge und Ströhm, 1857.

Liv-, est- und kurländisches Urkundenbuch nebst Regesten. Sec. 1, vol. IV, 1394–1413, edited by Friedrich G. v. Bunge. Reval: Commission bei Kluge und Ströhm, 1859.

Liv-, est- und kurländisches Urkundenbuch nebst Regesten. Sec. 1, vol. V, *1414 – Mai 1423*, edited by Friedrich G. v. Bunge. Riga: Verlag von Nikolai Kymmel, 1867.

Livländische Reimchronik mit Anmerkungen, Namenverzeichnis und Glossar. Edited by Leo Meyer. Paderborn Verlag von Ferdinand Schöningh, 1876.

Oeuvres de Ghillebert de Lannoy, voyageur, diplomate et moraliste. Edited by Charles Potvin. Louvain: Imprimerie de P. et J. Lefever, 1878.

'Petri de Dusburg Chronicon terre Prusie.' Edited by Max Toeppen. In SRP, vol. I, edited by Theodor Hirsch, Max Toeppen, and Ernst Strehlke, 3–219 (source edition at 21–219). Leipzig: S. Hirzel, 1861.

Preußisches Urkundenbuch. Politische (allgemeine) Abteilung. Vol. II, 1309–1335, part 1, *1309–1324*, edited by Max Hein and Erich Maschke. Königsberg/Pr.: Gräfe und Unzer, 1932.

Rowell Stephen C., 'Smulkos žinios iš XV amžiaus Klaipėdos (apie 1400–1525 m.),' *Acta Historica Universitatis Kleipedensis* 11 (2005) (*Klaipėdos visuomenės ir miesto struktūros*): 47–69.

Senās Latvijas vēstures avoti. Part 2. *1238.–1256 g.* Edited by Arveds Švābe, Latvijas vēstures avoti II. Rīgā: Latvijas Vēstures institūta apgādiens, 1940.

Wigand von Marburg. *Cronica nova prutenica.* Edited by Sławomir Zonenberg and Krzysztof Kwiatkowski. Toruń: Towarzystwo Naukowe w Toruniu, 2017.

Secondary Sources

Asaris, Yanis. 'O severnykh territoriakh rasselenia kurshei v X–XIII vv. (po materialam mogilnikov).' In *Vakarų baltai: etnogenezė ir etninė istorija*, edited by Regina Volkaitė-Kulikauskienė, 199–208. Vilnius: Lietuvos istorijos instituto leidykla, 1997.

Baranov, Alexander. 'Die Frühzeit des Deutschen Ordens in Livland und die Eroberung Kurlands. Ein peripheres Tätigkeitsfeld?' In Livland – eine Region am Ende der Welt. Forschungen zum Verhältnis zwischen Zentrum und Peripherie im späten Mittelalter/Livonia – a Ragion at the Ende of the World. Studies on the Relations between Centre and Periphery in the Later Middle Ages, edited by Anti Selart and Matthias Thumser, 315–345. Quellen und Studien zur baltischen Geschichte 27. Köln, Weimar, Wien: Böhlau Verlag, 2017.

Beuttel, Jan-Erik. 'Kurland (ecclesia Curoniensis/Quironiensis).' In *Die Bischöfe des Heiligen Römischen Reiches 1198 bis 1448. Ein biographisches Lexikon*, edited by Erwin Gatz in cooper. of Clemens Brodkorb, 311. Berlin: Duncker & Humblot, 2001.

Biermann, Felix, Cecilia Hergheligiu, Heidrun Voigt, Marc Bentz, and Ottilie Blum. 'Das Gräberfeld des 13. bis 15. Jahrhunderts von Stangenwalde bei Rossitten auf der Kurischen Nehrung – Auswertung der Materialien im Berliner Bestand der Prussia-Sammlung (ehemals Königsberg/Ostpreußen).' *Acta Praehistorica et Archaeologica* 43 (2011): 215–346.

Blomkvist, Nils. 'East Baltic Vikings – with particular consideration to the Curonians.' In *Praeities puslapiai: archeologija, kultūram visuomenė. Skiriama archaelogo prof. habil. dr. Vlado Žulkus 60-ties metų jubiliejui ir 30-ties metų mokslinės veiklos sukakčiai*, 71–93. Klaipėda: Klaipėdos universiteto leidykla, 2005.

Brather, Sebastian. 'Zwischen "Fluchtburg" und "Herrensitz". Sozialgeschichtliche Interpretationen früh- und hochmittelalterlicher Burgwälle in Ostmitteleuropa.' *Archaeologia Baltica* 6 (2006): 40–57.

Budvydas, Ugnius. 'About Some Aspects of Scalvian Armament on the Basis of Investigations in Viešvilė Cemetery.' *Archaeologia Baltica* 8 (2007) (*Weapons, Weaponry and Man (In memoriam Vytautas Kazakevičius)*): 205–213.

Chudzinski, Erich. *Die Eroberung Kurlands durch den Deutschen Orden im 13. Jahrhundert*. Borna: R. Niske, 1917.

Czaja, Roman. 'Towns and Urban Space in the State of the Teutonic Order in Prussia.' In *The Teutonic Order in Prussia and Livonia. The Political and Ecclesiastical Structures 13th–16th Century*, edited by Roman Czaja and Andrzej Radzimiński, 79–107. Toruń: Towarzystwo Naukowe w Toruniu/Köln, Weimar, Wien: Böhlau Verlag, 2015.

Czaja, Roman and Zenon H. Nowak. 'An Attempt to Characterise the State of the Teutonic Knights in Prussia.' In *The Teutonic Order in Prussia and Livonia. The Political and Ecclesiastical Structures 13th–16th C.*, edited by Roman Czaja and Andrzej Radzimiński, 13–30. Toruń: Towarzystwo Naukowe w Toruniu/Köln, Weimar. Wien: Böhlau Verlag, 2015.

Długokęcki, Wiesław. 'Odbudowa osadnictwa, kolonizacja i przemiany wsi w państwie krzyżackim (1411–1525).' In *Państwo zakonu krzyżackiego w Prusach. Władza i społeczeństwo*, edited by Marian Biskup and Roman Czaja, 375–383. Warszawa: Wydawnictwo Naukowe PWN, 2008.

Donner, Gustav A. *Kardinal Wilhelm von Sabina. Bischof von Modena 1222–1234. Päpstlicher Legat in den nordischen Ländern (†1251)*. Societas Scientiarum Fennica, Commentationes Humanorum Litterarum II/5. Helsingfors: A.-G. F. Tilgmann, 1929.

Dopkewitsch, Helene. 'Die Burgsuchungen in Kurland und Livland vom 13.–16. Jahrhundert.' *Mitteilungen aus der livländischen Geschichte* 25, no. 1 (1933–1937): 1–108.
Dragendorff, Ernst. *Ueber die Beamten des Deutschen Ordens in Livland während des XIII. Jahrhunderts*. Berlin: Goedecke & Gallinek, 1894.
Ekdahl, Sven. 'Das Pferd und seine Rolle im Kriegsführung des Deutschen Orden.' In *Das Kriegswesen der Ritterorden im Mittelalter*, edited by Zenon H. Nowak, 29–47. Ordines Militares. Colloquia Torunensia Historica VI. Toruń: Uniwersytet Mikołaja Kopernika, 1991.
Ekdahl, Sven. 'Horses and Crossbows: Two Important Warfare Advantages of the Teutonic Order in Prussia.' In *The Military Orders*, vol. 2, *Welfare and Warfare*, edited by Helen Nicholson, 119–151. Aldershot a.o.: Ashgate, 1998.
'E 34. Die Postwege des Deutschen Ordens in der ersten Hälfte des 15. Jahrhunderts.' In *Unter Kreuz und Adler. Der deutsche Orden im Mittelalter. Ausstellung des Geheimen Staatsarchivs Preußischer Kulturbesitz anläßlich des 800jährigen Bestehens des Deutschen Ordens*, edited by Friedrich Benninghoven, 111–112. Mainz: Hase & Koehler, 1990.
Fenske, Lutz and Klaus Militzer. *Ritterbrüder im livländischen Zweig des Deutschen Ordens*. Quellen und Studien zur baltischen Geschichte 12. Köln, Weimar, Wien: Böhlau Verlag, 1993.
Forstreuter, Kurt. 'Die Entwicklung der Nationalitätenverhältnisse auf der Kurischen Nehrung.' *Altpreußische Forschungen* 8 (1931): 239–261.
Forstreuter, Kurt. 'Memel – Lage und Umland.' In id., *Wirkungen des Preussenlandes. Vierzig Beiträge*, 370–382. Studien zur Geschichte Preußens 33. Köln, Berlin: Grote, 1981.
Forstreuter, Kurt. 'Memel und Lübeck im Mittelalter.' *Mitteilungen des Vereins für die Geschichte von Ost- und Westpreußen* 11 (1936): 50–56.
Forstreuter, Kurt. 'Die preußische Kriegsflotte im 16. Jahrhundert.' *Altpreußische Forschungen* 17, no. 1 (1940): 58–123 reprinted in id., *Beiträge zur preussischen Geschichte im 15. und 16. Jahrhundert*, 73–164. Studien zur Geschichte Preussens 7. Heidelberg: Quelle & Meyer, 1960).
Forstreuter, Kurt. 'Das Volk der Kurischen Nehrung.' In id., *Wirkungen des Preussenlandes. Vierzig Beiträge*, 280–296. Studien zur Geschichte Preußens 33. Köln, Berlin: Grote, 1981.
Genys, Jonas. 'Žardė – Pilsoto žemės prekybos ir amatų centras.' In *Lietuvininkų kraštas: monografija*, edited by Norbertas Vėlius, 108–127. Kaunas: Litterae Universitatis, 1995.
Gierszewski, Andrzej. 'Mierzeja Kurońska i Zalew Kuroński w średniowieczu (do 1525 r.).' PhD Diss., Uniwersytet Gdański, 2015.
Heckmann, Dieter. '„Der Samaitische Strand'. Beobachtungen zur Rechtsqualität einer Verkehrsverbindung zwischen den Deutschordensherrschaften Preußen und Livland vom 15. bis zum frühen 16. Jahrhundert.' In *Deutschordensgeschichte aus internationaler Perspektive. Festschrift für Udo Arnold zum 80. Geburtstag*, edited by Roman Czaja and Hubert Houben, 83–92. Quellen und Studien zur Geschichte des Deutschen Ordens 85. Ilmtal-Weinstraße: VDG, 2020.
Jarockis, Romas. 'Eketė Irin Age and Early Medieval Hill-Fort Settlement Complex. Aerial Archaeology and Remote Sensing.' *Archaeologia Baltica* 9 (2008): 8–14.
Jähnig, Bernhart. 'Der Deutschordensstaat Preußen – die großen Hochmeister des 14. Jahrhunderts.' In *Die "Blüte" der Staaten des östlichen Europa im 14. Jahrhundert*, edited by Marc Löwener, 45–63. Deutsches Historisches Institut Warschau. Quellen und Studien 14. Wiesbaden: Harrassowitz Verlag, 2004.
Jóźwiak, Sławomir. *Centralne i terytorialne organy władzy zakonu krzyżackiego w Prusach w latach 1228–1410. Rozwój – Przekształcenia – Kompetencje*. Toruń: Wydawnictwo Uniwersytetu Mikołaja Kopernika, 2001, 1st edition.

Jóźwiak, Sławomir. 'Kryzys władzy terytorialnej.' In *Państwo zakonu krzyżackiego w Prusach. Władza i społeczeństwo*, edited by Marian Biskup and Roman Czaja, 332–356. Warszawa: Wydawnictwo Naukowe PWN, 2008.
Jóźwiak, Sławomir. 'Liczebność konwentów zakonu krzyżackiego w Prusach w pierwszej połowie XV wieku.' ZH 72, no. 1 (2007): 7–21.
Kaljundi, Linda. 'Neophytes as actors in the Livonian crusades.' In *Making Livonia. Actors and Networks in the Medieval and Early Modern Baltic Sea Region*, edited by Anu Mänd and Marek Tamm, 93–112. London, New York: Routledge, 2020.
Kasiske, Karl. 'Die Wildnis und ihre Besiedlung.' In *Der Deutsche Ritterorden. Seine politische und kulturelle Leistung im deutschen Osten*, edited by Erich Maschke and Karl Kasiske, 137–140. Berlin: Deutscher Verlag für Politik und Wirtschaft, Otto Jamrowski, 1942.
Kļaviņš, Kaspars. 'The Significance of the Local Baltic Peoples in the Defence of Livonia (Late Thirteenth – Sixteenth Centuries).' In *The Clash of Cultures on the Medieval Baltic Frontier*, edited by Alan V. Murray, 321–340. Farnham: Ashgate, 2009.
Koch, Alfred. 'Die deutsche Post im Memelland. Historischer Rückblick auf die Entwicklung des Postwesens 1230–1945.' *Archiv für Deutsche Postgeschichte* 1–2 (1961): 3–38.
Kreem, Juhan. 'Der Deutsche Orden in Livland: die Heiden, Landvolk und Undeutsche in der livländischen Heeresverfassung.' In *L'Ordine Teutonico tra Mediterraneo e Baltico incontri e scontri tra religioni, popoli e culture/Der Deutsche Orden zwischen Mittelmeerraum und Balticum. Begegnungen und Konfrontationen zwischen Religionen, Völker und Kulturen. Atti del Convegno internazionale, Bari–Lecce–Brindisi, 14–16 settembre 2006*, edited by Hubert Houben and Kristjan Toomaspoeg, 237–251. Galatina: Mario Congedo, 2008.
Kuhn, Walter. *Geschichte der deutschen Ostsiedlung in der Neuzeit*. Vol. II, *Das 15. bis 17. Jahrhundert (Landschaftlicher Teil)*. Ostmitteleuropa in Vergangenheit und Gegenwart 1/II. Köln, Graz: Böhlau-Verlag, 1957.
Krumbholtz, Robert. 'Samaiten und der Deutsche Orden bis zum Frieden am Melno-See.' *Altpreußische Monatsschrift* 26 (1889): 193–258, 461–484; 27 (1890): 1–84, 193–227.
Kwiatkowski, Krzysztof. 'Schalauer – ein baltisches Element in der militärischen Organisation der Herrschaft des Deutschen Ordens in Preußen.' In *Das Militärwesen im Deutschen Orden. Vorträge der Tagung der Internationalen Historischen Kommission zur Erforschung des Deutschen Ordens in Debrecen 2022*, edited by László Pósán, 48–74. Quellen und Studien zur Geschichte des Deutschen Ordens 96 = Veröffentlichungen der Internationalen Historischen Kommission zur Erforschung des Deutschen Ordens 24. Ilmtal-Weinstraße: VDG, 2025).
Kwiatkowski, Krzysztof. *Wojska zakonu niemieckiego w Prusach 1230–1525 (korporacja, jej pruskie władztwo, zbrojni, kultura wojny i aktywność militarna)* (with cooperation of Maria Molenda). Toruń: Wydawnictwo Naukowe Uniwersytetu Mikołaja Kopernika, 2016.
Kwiatkowski, Krzysztof. *Zakon niemiecki jako "corporatio militaris"*. Part I, *Korporacja i krąg przynależących do niej. Kulturowe i społeczne podstawy działalności militarnej zakonu w Prusach (do początku XV wieku)*. Toruń: Wydawnictwo Naukowe Uniwersytetu Mikołaja Kopernika, 2012.
Kwiatkowski, Krzysztof and Gregory Leighton. 'Ein Heerzugsbericht des Deutschen Ordens aus dem Staatsarchiv Thorn: Inhalts-, Datum- und Kontextanalyse.' *Preußenland* 14 (2023): 62–77.
Labuda, Gerard. 'Entstehung und Entwicklung des Deutschordensstaates in Preussen.' In Marian Biskup and Gerard Labuda, *Die Geschichte des Deutschen Ordens in Preußen. Wirtschaft–Gesellschaft–Staat–Ideologie*, 115–290. Klio in Polen 6. Osnabrück: fibre Verlag, 2000.

Lohmeyer, Karl. 'Das Wort "Baude" im Marienburger Traßlerbuch, seine Herkunft und seine Bedeutung.' *Mitteilungen der Litauischen litterarischen Gesellschaft 5*, no. 25–30 (1911): 57–67.
Mager, Friedrich. *Der Wald in Altpreussen als Wirtschaftsraum*. Vol. I, Ostmitteleuropa in Vergangenheit und Gegenwart 7/I. Köln, Graz: Böhlau Verlag, 1960.
Maschke, Erich. *Der Deutsche Orden und die Preussen. Bekehrung und Unterwerfung in der preußisch-baltischen Mission des 13. Jahrhunderts*. Historische Studien 176. Berlin: Verlag Emil Ebering, 1928.
Maschke, Erich. 'Das mittelalterliche Memel im baltisch-preussischen Raum.' *Mitteilungen des Vereins für die Geschichte von Ost- und Westpreußen 2*, no. 4 (1928): 53–66.
Merkevičius, Algimantas. 'Eketės (Klaipėdos raj.) piliakalnio tyrinėjimaj.' In *Archeologiniai ir etnografiniai tyrinejimai Lietuvoje 1972 ir 1974 metais*, edited by Adolfas Tautavičius and Vitalis Morkūnas, 15–19. Vilnius: Lietuvos TSR Mokslų Akademijos Istorijos Institutas, 1974.
Mickevičius, Arturas. *Normanai ir Baltai IX–XII a*. Vilnius: "Versus Aureus" leidykla, 2004.
Militzer, Klaus. 'The list of dignitaries and officials of the Brothers of the Sword and the Teutonic Order in Livonia.' In *The Teutonic Order in Prussia and Livonia. The Political and Ecclesiastical Structures 13th–16th C*., edited by Roman Czaja and Andrzej Radzimiński, 347–375. Toruń: Towarzystwo Naukowe w Toruniu/Köln, Weimar, Wien: Böhlau Verlag, 2015.
Mortensen, Hans. 'Die landschaftliche Bedeutung der Ausdrücke Wildnis, Wald, Heide, Feld usw. in den Quellen des deutschen Nordostens.' In *Vom deutschen Osten. Max Friedrichsen zum 60. Geburtstag*, edited by Herbert Knothe, 127–142. Veröffentlichungen der Schlesischen Gesellschaft für Erdkunde und des Geographischen Instituts der Universität Breslau 21. Breslau: Marcus, 1934.
Mortensen, Hans. *Litauen. Grundzüge einer Landeskunde*. Osteuropa Institut in Breslau, Quellen und Studien, 5. Abt.: Geographie und Landeskunde 1. Hamburg: L. Friederichsen & Company, 1926.
Mortensen, Hans & Gertrud. *Die Besiedlung des nordöstlichen Ostpreussens bis zum Beginn des 17 Jahrhundert*. Part II, *Die Wildnis im östlichen Preußen, ihr Zustand um 1400 und ihre frühere Besiedlung*. Deutschland und der Osten 8. Leipzig: Verlag von S. Hirzel, 1938.
von zur Mühlen, Heinz. 'Livland von der Christianisierung bis zum Ende seiner Selbständigkeit (etwa 1180–1561).' In *Deutsche Geschichte im Osten Europas. Baltische Länder*, edited by Gert von Pistohlkors, 25–172. Berlin: Siedler Verlag, 1994.
Nadolski, Andrzej. 'Influence balto-slaves dans l'armament des Chevaliers Teutoniques.' In *Berichte über den II. Internationalen Kongress für Slawische Archäologie, Berlin 24.–28. August 1970*, vol. III, edited by Joachim Herrmann and Karl-Heinz Otto, 33–36. Berlin: Akademie-Verlag, 1974.
Nadolski, Andrzej. 'Niektóre elementy bałto-słowiańskie w uzbrojeniu i sztuce wojennej Krzyżaków.' *Pomorania Antiqua 5* (1974): 165–172.
Nowakowski, Andrzej. *Arms and armour in the medieval Teutonic Order's State in Prussia*. Studies on the History of Ancient and Medieval Art of Warfare II. Łódź: Oficyna Wydawnicza MS, 1994.
Petrauskas, Rimvydas. 'Socialiniai pokyčiai Lietuvoje valstybės formavimosi laikotarpiu/Der soziale Wandel bei der litauischen Staatsbildung.' In *Lietuvos valstybės susikūrimas europiniame kontekste*, edited by Rimvydas Petrauskas, 160–183/184–211. Vilnius: "Versus Aureus" leidykla, 2008.
Radzimiński, Andrzej. 'Church Divisions of Livonia.' In *The Teutonic Order in Prussia and Livonia. The Political and Ecclesiastical Structures 13th–16th C*., edited by Roman Czaja and Andrzej Radzimiński, 253–288. Toruń: Towarzystwo Naukowe w Toruniu/Köln, Weimar, Wien: Böhlau Verlag, 2015.

Schwartz, Philipp. *Kurland im dreizehnten Jahrhundert bis zum Regierungsantritt Bischof Edmund's von Werd*. Leipzig: Verlag von E. Bidder, 1875.
Selart, Anti. 'Die Eroberung Livlands (12. und 13. Jahrhundert).' In *Das Baltikum. Geschichte eines europäischen Region*, vol. 1, *Von der Vor- und Frühgeschichte bis zum Ende des Mittelalters*, edited by Karsten Brüggemann, Detled Henning, Konrad Maier, and Ralph Tuchtenhagen, 159–209. Stuttgart: Hiersemann Verlag, 2018.
Sembritzki, Johannes. *Geschichte der Königlich Preussischen See- und Handelstadt Memel*. Memel: Verlag von F. W. Siebert, 1900.
Sembritzki, Johannes. *Geschichte des Kreises Memel*. Memel: F. W. Siebert, 1918.
Semrau, Arthur. 'Beiträge zu Topographie der Burg und Stadt Memel im Mittelalter.' *Mitteilungen des Coppernicus-Vereins für Wissenschaft und Kunst zu Thorn* 37 (1929): 89–116.
Seraphim, Ernst. *Livländische Geschichte von der "Aufsegelung" der Lande bis zur Einverleibung in das russische Reich. Ein Hausbuch*. Vol. 1, *Die Zeit bis zum Untergang livländischer Selbständigkeit*. Reval: Verlag von Franz Kluge, 1897, 2nd edition.
Ščavinskas, Marius. 'Some Comments on the Formation of Medieval Warriors in Baltic and Finnish Societies (in the 12th and Early 13th Centuries).' *Acta Historica Universitatis Klaipedensis* 37 (2018): 41–61.
Ščavinskas, Marius. 'Some notes on the issue of the development of Balt society in the ninth to the 13th centuries in the context of the socio-political structures of the Baltic region.' *Archaeologia Baltica* 19 (2013): 82–101.
Širouchov, Roman. 'Kuršių nerijos ankstyvųjų viduramžių archeologiniai paminklai. Kuršių ir prūsų kontaktų zonos klausimas.' *Res Humanitaire* 15 (2014): 115–143.
Šnē, Andris. 'Warfare and Power in the Late Prehistoric Societies in the Territory of Latvia (tenth to 12th Centuries).' *Archaeologia Baltica* 8 (2007) (*Weapons, Weaponry and Man (In memoriam Vytautas Kazakevičius)*): 254–262.
Šterns, Indriķis. 'Iezemiešu loma Senlatvijas pakļaušanā vācu varai.' *Latvijas Vēstures Instittūta Žurnāls* 1, no. 46 (2003): 34–48.
Tandecki, Janusz. 'Administrative Divisions of the Territory of the Teutonic Orders in Livonia.' In *The Teutonic Order in Prussia and Livonia. The Political and Ecclesiastical Structures 13th–16th C.*, edited by Roman Czaja and Andrzej Radzimiński, 183–197. Toruń: Towarzystwo Naukowe w Toruniu/Köln, Weimar, Wien: Böhlau Verlag, 2015.
Toeppen, Max. 'Excurs über die Verschreibungen des Ordens für Stammpreussen im 13. Jahrhundert.' In SRP, vol. I, Beilage 8 to 'Petri de Dusburg Chronicon terre Prussie', 254–269. Leipzig: Verlag von S. Hirzel, 1861.
Torbus, Tomasz. *Die Konventsburgen im Deutschordensland Preußen*. Schriften des Bundesinstituts für ostdeutsche Kultur und Geschichte 11. München: R. Oldenbourg Verlag, 1998.
Vaškevičiūtė, Ilona. 'Tautų kraustymosi ir baltų genčių sklaidos laikotarpis.' In *Lietuvijos istorija*, vol. II, *Geležies amžius*, edited by Gintautas Zabiela, 173–297. Vilnius: Baltų lankų leidyba, 2007.
Vercamer, Grischa. 'Die Freien im Deutschordensland Preußen als militärischer Rückhalt Ende des 14. – Anfang des 15. Jahrhunderts.' In *Tannenberg – Grunwald – Žalgiris 1410. Krieg und Frieden im späten Mittelalter*, edited by Werner Paravicini, Rimvydas Petrauskas, and Grischa Vercamer, 175–189. Wiesbaden: Otto Harrassowitz, 2012.
Vercamer, Grischa. 'Man darf die schlafenden Hunde nicht wecken. Die militärische, soziale und politische Bedeutung der Freien im östlichen Ordensland Preußen für den Deutschen Orden.' In *Beiträge zur Militärgeschichte des Preussenlandes von der Ordenszeit bis zum Zeitalter der Weltkriege*, edited by Bernhart Jähnig, 53–74. Tagungsberichte der Historischen Kommission für ost- und westpreußische Landesforschung 25. Marburg: N.G. Elwert Verlag, 2010.

Voigt, Johannes. *Geschichte Preussens von den ältesten Zeiten bis zum Untergange der Herrschaft des Deutschen Ordens*. Vol. III, *Die Zeit vom Frieden 1248 bis zur Unterwerfung der Preussen 1283*. Königsberg: Verlag der Gebrüder Bornträger, 1828.
Weber, Lothar. *Preussen vor 500 Jahren in culturhistorischer, statistischer und militärischer Beziehung nebst Special-Geographie*. Danzig: s.n., 1878.
Weise, Julius. *Herzog Erich von Braunschweig, der letzte Komtur des Deutschordens zu Memel*. Königsberg/Pr.: Ostpreussische Druckerei und Verlagsanstalt A.-G., 1908.
Willoweit, Dietmar. *Die Wirtschaftsgeschichte des Memellandes*. Vol. I. Wissenschaftliche Beiträge zur Geschichte und Landeskunde Ost-Mitteleuropas 85/I. Marburg/Lahn: Johann Gottfried Herder Institut, 1969.
Zabiela, Gintautas. 'Ikivalstybnis ir baltų genčių sąjungų laikotarpis.' In *Lietuvos istorija*, vol. II, *Geležies amžius*, edited by Gintautas Zabiela, 413–467. Vilnius: Lietuvos istorijos institutas, 2007.
Zurkalowski, Erich. 'Studien zur Geschichte der Stadt Memel und der Politik des Deutschen Ordens.' *Altpreussische Monatsschrift* 43 (1906): 155–165.
Žulkus, Vladas. 'Entwicklungslinien der Stadt Memel von der Gründung bis zur Mitte des 17. Jahrhunderts.' In *Memel als Brücke zu den baltischen Ländern. Kulturgeschichte Klaipėdas vom Mittelalter bis ins 20. Jahrhundert*, edited by Bernahrt Jähnig, 13–34, Tagungsberichte der historischen Kommission für ost- und westpreußische Landesforschung 26. Osnabrück: fibre Verlag, 2011.
Žulkus, Vladas. 'Heidentum und Christentum in Litauen im 10.–16. Jahrhundert.' In *Rom und Byzanz im Norden. Mission und Glaubenswechsel im Ostseeraum während des 8.–14. Jahrhunderts. Internationale Fachkonferenz der Deutschen Forschungsgemeinschaft in Verbindung mit der Akademie der Wissenschaften und der Literatur, Mainz, Kiel, 18.–25. September 1994*, vol. II, edited by Michael Müller-Wille, 143–161. Mainz: Akademie der Wissenschaften und der Literatur/ Stuttgart: F. Steiner, 1998.
Žulkus, Vladas. 'Klaipėdos istorijos ir topografijos bruožai XIII–XVII a. (Archeologijos duomenimis).' in *Klaipėdos miesto ir regiono archeologijos ir istorijos problemos*, edited by Alvydas Nikžentaitis and Vladas Žulkus, 5–16. Acta historica universitatis Klaipedensis II. Klaipėda: KU Vakaru Lietuvos ir Prūsijos Istorijos Centras, 1994.
Žulkus, Vladas. *Klaipėdos senojo miesto raidos modelis. Leidinys parengtas remiantis Klaipėdos senamiesčio ir piliavietės archeologiniais tyrinėjimais*. Vilnius: Spauda, 1991.
Žulkus, Vladas. 'Kurland. Die Grenzen und die nordlichen Landschaften in 8.–13. Jahrhundert.' *Archaeologia Baltica* 6 (2006): 88–103.
Žulkus, Vladas. *Kuršiai Baltijos jūros erdvėje. Monografija*. Vilnius: "Versus Aureus" leidykla, 2004.
Žulkus, Vladas. *Palanga in the Middle Ages. Ancient Settlements*. Translated by Vijolė Arbas. Vilnius: "Versus Aureus", 2007.
Žulkus, Vladas. 'Settlements and Piracy on the Eastern Shore of the Baltic Sea: The Middle Ages to Modern Times.' *Archaeologia Baltica* 16 (2011) (*Settlements and Towns*): 58–71.
Žulkus, Vladas. *Viduramžių Klaipėda. Miestas ir pilis Archeologija ir istorija*. Vilnius: Leidykla "Žara", 2002.
Žulkus, Vladas. 'Zur Frühgeschichte der baltischen Stadt.' In *Burg – Burgstadt – Stadt. Zur Genese mittelalterlicher nichtagrarischer Zentren in Ostmitteleuropa*, edited by Hansjürgen Brachmann, 190–206. Forschungen zur Geschichte und Kultur des östlichen Mitteleuropa. Berlin: Akademie Verlag: 1995.
Žulkus, Vladas and Linas Daugnora. 'What Did the Order's Brothers Eat in the Klaipėda Castle? (The Historical and Zooarchaeological Data).' *Archaeologia Baltica* 12 (2009): 74–87.

6 Migration of Rural Settlers (esp. Lithuanians) to Eastern Prussia in the 15th/16th Century*

Grischa Vercamer

This chapter will focus on migration to Eastern Prussia in the Late Middle Ages and Early Modern Age, particularly in the 15th and 16th centuries. Three big ethnic groups in particular come into question: Germans, Lithuanians and Poles. From the beginning, the twelve tribes of the Old-Prussians were the original inhabitants of the region, hence the later name 'Prussians'.[1] The migration of German-speaking people up to the beginning of the 15th century will only be touched lightly, as it petered out in the first decades of this century. The end of this migration wave is generally associated with the crisis of the Teutonic Order after the Battle of Tannenberg/Grunwald/Žalgiris (1410). Generally spoken, research on external immigration of German-speaking people (13th/14th century) and the later internal migration from within the Order's territory made very good progress in the cause of the 20th century.[2] Based on the specific form of the *kulmische* villages (in the sources: *kulmische Dörfer*),[3] for which the foundation charters are almost completely preserved for many commanderies (Germ. *Komtureien*), it is easy to see that a wave of German settlement took place in the 14th century in particular and under the precise guidance of the Order's leadership – starting in the western commanderies of Prussia and gradually advancing to the eastern commanderies.[4] It is important to emphasize this: after the conclusion of the conquest and the subsequent Prussian uprisings (by 1283, all Old-Prussian territories had been completely subjugated), the Order was keen to leave the subjugated Old-Prussian population in their village structures wherever it was possible. The Old-Prussian population was by then considered to be Christianized, even if only superficially in many places, and early on the Order organized the Old-Prussian settlements in smaller administrative units (Germ. *Kammerämter*) and established a system of levies. Conversely, this meant that the systematic settlement of German-speaking peoples either established new villages in between the Old-Prussian settlements or developed new settlement areas. Definitely, the German-speaking settlers did not

---

* This chapter was realized and financed by the funds in a DFG-project (DFG-Projektnummer: 543627402).

DOI: 10.4324/9781003502876-6

displace the Old-Prussian villages. In my own research, resulting from my PhD on the commandery of Königsberg (today Kaliningrad), the most important *Komturei* in the eastern part of Prussia, I was able to conclude from onomastic material of the 14th century that the *kulmische* villages – previously always interpreted as ethnically purely German – were also inhabited by Old-Prussian freemen (Germ. *Freie*, who had to perform military service) and wealthier Old-Prussian farmers.[5] Consequently, ethnic mixtures were to be found in many *kulmische* villages, even if the majority of the peasants were certainly of German origin. The prerequisite may be supposed to have been that the Old-Prussians spoke German.[6] The key point about these ethnic mixtures seemed to be that as early as in the 14th century both the central and the regional leadership of the Teutonic Order and the predominantly German-speaking communities of the *kulmische* villages were open to such an assimilation of the Old-Prussian rural population. To have it in modern terms, there is no evidence of any kind of racism or ethnic discrimination. In the 16th century, acculturation processes took place anyway (Old-Prussian slowly died out as a language of its own), so that from this period onwards one can speak of a slow 'new tribe formation' (Germ. *Neustammbildung*) towards an overall population called 'Prussian' in the old settlement areas (except for the Great Wilderness regions).[7]

Geographically, this German-Prussian settlement and German migration to the eastern areas of the Order's territory, which formed more or less the rest of the smaller Order's territory after the Second Peace of Thorn (1466), can be seen primarily as a settlement movement in the closer regions near the Baltic Sea until the early 15th century. It is no coincidence that the larger towns (Danzig (today Gdańsk), Elbing (today Elbląg), Braunsberg (today Braniewo), Frauenburg (today Frombork), Königsberg) were all located within the coastal area of the Baltic Sea, while smaller towns located somewhat inland (such as Tapiau (today Gvardeysk) or Insterburg (today Chernyakhovsk)) never developed any supra-regional importance but actually remained 'agricultural towns' until the early 16th century.[8] Other smaller urban centres in the inland regions, initially founded as fortifications, such as Gerdauen (today Zheleznodorozhny) (1398), Allenburg (today Druzhba) (1400) or Nordenburg (today Krylovo) (1405), underline the Order's efforts to slowly advance the settlement work further inland. This strategy of the Order can be seen quite clearly (see Figure 6.1) if one looks at the administrative boundaries of the eastern commanderies (Balga (today Bal'ga), Brandenburg (today Ushakovo) and Königsberg, Ragnit (today Neman)) and the diocese of Ermland/Warmia[9] – all of them look like tubes running inland from the Baltic Sea in a south-easterly movement, thus very well representing the advance of the respective settlement movements. As already mentioned above, the Order had on a large scale to abandon his settlement plans in the freshly developed regions (the so-called 'wilderness areas', see below) after 1410 and to concentrate primarily on its old settlement areas – some of which were vastly deserted after the military conflicts around this time. German-speaking settlers from the Holy Roman

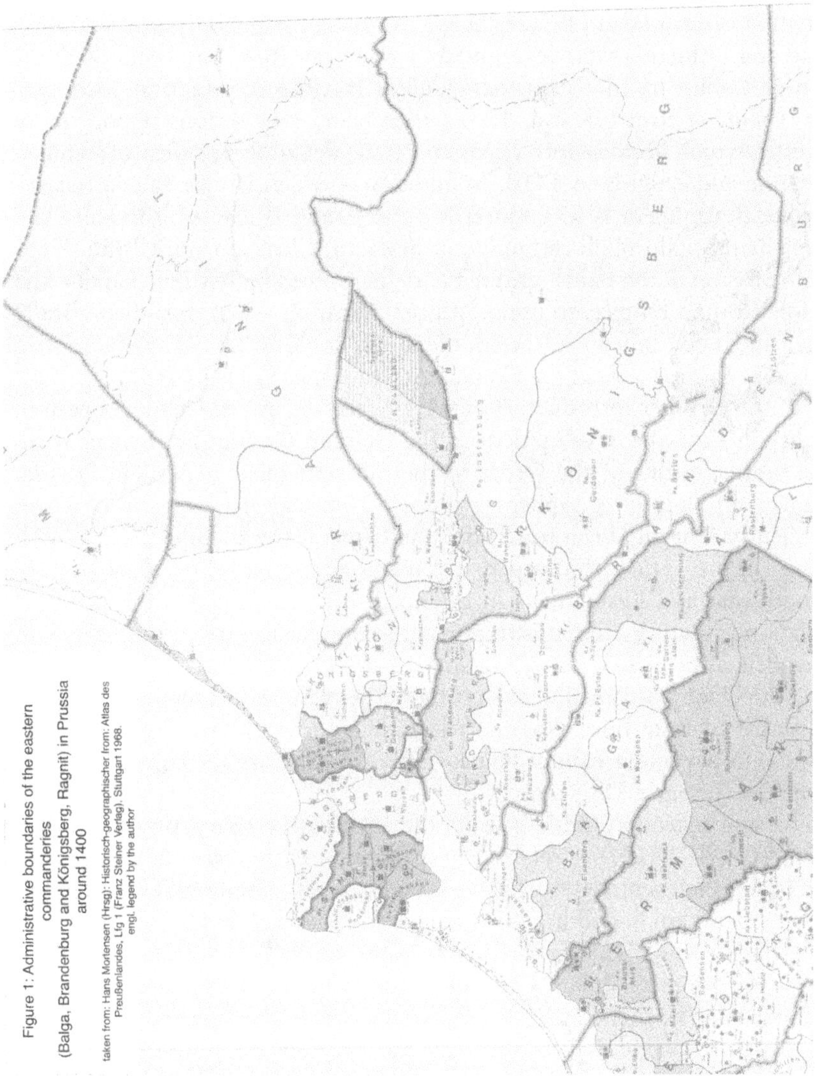

Migration of Rural Settlers (esp. Lithuanians) to Eastern Prussia 115

Figure 1: Administrative boundaries of the eastern commanderies (Balga, Brandenburg and Königsberg, Ragnit) in Prussia around 1400

taken from: Hans Mortensen (Hrsg.): Historisch-geographischer Atlas des Preußenlandes, Lfg 1 (Franz Steiner Verlag), Stuttgart 1968. engl. legend by the author

Figure 6.1 Administrative boundaries in the eastern commanderies (Balga, Brandenburg and Königsberg) in Prussia around 1400)

Empire no longer came from abroad, and also the important internal Prussian migration from within the Order's territory came to a standstill, precisely because major desertification processes had occurred as part of the conflict with the Kingdom of Poland and the Grand Duchy of Lithuania.[10] In addition to demographic and economic-fiscal factors in the period after 1410 there was another fundamental political and ecclesiastical reason for this: with the coronation of Lithuanian Prince Jogaila as Polish King Władysław II (1386), Poland and Lithuania were less united by one ruler (this only began with the Union of Lublin in 1569) but nevertheless in close cooperation with each other (Union of Krewo/Krėva, 1385), thus being very serious opponents of the Order, which became very apparent by the devastating defeat of Tannenberg/Grunwald/Žalgiris in 1410. In addition – which is why the ecclesiastical-political argument is so important – the Grand Duchy of Lithuania had become de jure (although certainly not de facto) Christian since 1386.[11] The Order's mission in the Baltic, granted and guaranteed by both the Papacy and the Holy Roman Empire, to initiate Christianization – was thus theoretically fulfilled and a continued presence of the Order could be (and was) questioned throughout Europe, e.g. at the Council of Constance (1414–1418).[12]

With these rather introductory remarks – as it is not the main concern of this chapter – on the development of the German-Prussian settlement work of the first centuries of the Order in the old settlement regions in Prussia, we move on to a large, peripheral regions within the Order's territory which until then had hardly been touched by settlement: the so-called 'Great Wilderness'. In the 15th/16th century, it was settled piecemeal by Mazovians in the south-east and Lithuanians in the north-east, leading to a considerable population growth.[13] Here it is important to emphasize: this took place with the explicit approval of the leadership of the Order (later the administration of the Duchy of Prussia), even if the settlement by Lithuanian settlers in the districts of Insterburg, Ragnit, Tilsit (today Sovetsk) and Memel (today Klaipėda) in particular cannot be proven very well from the sources (see below) before the early 16th century.

To have it in geographical terms: in the 14th/15th century, the 'Great Wilderness' (*Große Wildnis* – referred to as such as early as in the source language of the 14th century)[14] was a very wide, largely uninhabited border belt (approx. 50–60 km in width) which separated Prussia from the Duchy of Mazovia (which, from 1351 onwards, was occasionally in a vassal relationship with the Kingdom of Poland) and the Grand Duchy of Lithuania. Sparsely populated (and if, then rather by charcoal burners, beekeepers and similar rural classes who practised forestry), it ran between the borders of the old settlement area on an approximate line (from north-east to south-west) of the Order castles of Labiau (today Polessk), Insterburg, Gerdauen, Rhein (today Ryn), Ortelsburg (today Szczytno), Neidenburg (today Nidzica) and the political border of eastern Prussia, which had been established in the Treaty of Lake Melno in 1422.[15] This huge area thus comprised the later administration units (again from north-east to south-west) of Memel, Tilsit, Rossitten (today

Rybachi), Ragnit, Labiau, Georgenburg (today Mayovka), Saalau (today Kamenskoe), Taplacken (today Talpaki), Insterburg, Gerdauen, Nordenburg, Angerburg (today Węgorzewo), Barten (today Barciany), Stradaunen (today Straduny), Lötzen (today Giżycko), Rastenburg (today Kętrzyn), Lyck (today Ełk), Rhein, Seehesten (today Szestno), Johannisburg (today Pisz), Ortelsburg.

Just a few words on the development of the wilderness in the early period of the Order: the Yatvingians (Sudovians), probably the most powerful and therefore the most resistant among the Old-Prussian tribes during the Order's period of conquest, had settled in these areas until the 13th century (in the north also the Scalovians). These tribes were completely wiped out in the battles with the Order in the late 13th century or – as the chronicler Peter von Dusburg reported in his chronicle of 1326 – individual groups migrated to Lithuania or into the Rus'.[16] In the 14th century, both the Grand Duchy of Lithuania and the Teutonic Order carried out annual looting campaigns there. In the sources, the Order referred to these as 'Prussian' or 'Lithuanian journeys' (Germ. *Preußenreisen*, *Litauerreisen*). Any colonization of the wilderness during this period was of course vehemently hampered by these regular campaigns. Both the Order and the bishopric of Ermland/Warmia made painstaking attempts to found castles and towns there, in order to facilitate later rural settlement. A fine example of this practice is the town of Alt-Wartenburg (today Barczewko, north-east of Allenstein (today Olsztyn)): founded in 1325 by the bishop of Ermland/Warmia and, although it was located next to a castle, completely destroyed in 1354 during a Lithuanian invasion, it was rebuilt only decades later at a different location. Today it is one of the very few late medieval urban wastelands in Prussia – and therefore an eldorado for archaeologists.[17]

After 1410 in particular, German-Prussian settlement in these expansion areas was once again significantly more difficult and ultimately failed altogether – the reasons for this have already been mentioned above. Interestingly, from the 1420s and 1430s on, the Order practised a new, innovative migration practice – first in the southern regions (bordering on the Polish Duchy of Mazovia), as Mazovian-Polish freemen (petty noblemen) and peasants were now increasingly settled in the area of the later administrative districts of Rhein, Johannisburg, Lyck (today Ełk) and Lötzen.[18] To a certain extent, this new migration strategy had two prerequisites: (1) The border to Mazovia and Lithuania was finally established by the Treaty of Lake Mełno (1422) and was therefore undisputedly linear for the first time.[19] (2) Especially in the 15th century, the Duchy of Mazovia, in search of a powerful position of its own, vacillated back and forth between the Teutonic Order and the Kingdom of Poland, therefore becoming a suitable partner for the Order.[20]

This Mazovian-Polish immigration has been extremely well researched since the important studies by Hans and Gertrud Mortensen, Eckhard Jäger, and Reinhard Wenskus as part of the work on the *Historical-Geographical Atlas of the Prussian Land* (*Historisch-geographischer Atlas des Preußenlandes*),[21] and then, especially in the 2000s, by Grzegorz Białuński.[22] The results of these works should be recapitulated here, starting with the work on the *Atlas*: the

Mazovian peasants and freemen tended to found small, irregular hamlets (which is still partly reflected by the settlement pattern today), in contrast to the planned, *culmisch*-like common land villages (Germ. *kulmische Angerdörfer*). The dynamics of the Mazovian settlement work, always with the consent of the leadership of the Order, becomes very much obvious in chronological and numerical terms from the partial map of issue 8 of the *Atlas* (Map 8a: "Settlement of the Great Wilderness until 1507/19") (see Figure 6.2): the yellow (sovereign hides/*Hufen* of Freemen) and black (sovereign peasant holdings) squares represent the Mazovian-Polish immigration. The numbers given in the squares even indicate the number of hides (1 hide corresponds to 16.8 hectares). If these squares are semi-transparent, this means that they were founded before the Thirteen Years' War (i.e. before 1454). Clear accumulations of these squares can be seen for the period 1410–1453 in the later administrative district of Rhein (north of Lake Spirding) and in the later district of Johannisburg (around today's Biała Piska, i.e. directly on the border of the Mazovian duchy). Only some settlements can be found also in the later districts of Lyck and Stradaunen. There, all of these are yellow squares, i.e. Mazovian freemen (Pol. *drobna szlachta*) who received charters (*Handfesten*) in the Order's territory in order to establish peasant tenants on their (sometimes considerable) estates – the size varied from 10–60 hides, averaging around 30 hides.

The settlement significantly intensified after 1466 (as can be seen from the map, now it concerns the non-transparent squares there), as further freemen villages were founded, and occasionally the hides of Mazovian noblemen (who continued to have their headquarters in Mazovia) were added.[23] From this time onwards, the Order also carried out its own settlement programmes with Mazovian-Polish peasants (visible by the black colouring of the squares), as many sovereign peasant villages were now established in the indicated districts (some of them of an average size like *kulmische* villages, i.e. 50–60 hides). The re-establishment of the commandery of the Rhein (1477), which was now permanent, whereas before it had only existed for a short time twice (1393 and 1422), vividly illustrates the changing importance of the southern wilderness districts for the Order.[24]

Grzegorz Białuński's research contributed many more details and subtleties to these general lines of Mazovian settlement. Firstly, he shows that an interest in the borders to Mazovia (and thus settlement issues) existed as early as under Grand Masters Luther von Braunschweig (1331–1335) and Dietrich von Altenburg (1335–1341).[25] He therefore sees the beginnings of Mazovian settlement in the district of Johannisburg (about which *pars pro toto* I would like to go into more detail while skipping the districts of Lyck, Stradaunen, Neuhoff (today Zelki) and Angerburg, which he also took into account) as early as in the 14th century. However, he can only establish the first real evidence from the archive collections *Ordensbriefarchiv* and *Ordensfolianten* in Geheimes Staatsarchiv in Berlin for the early 15th century (namely the visitation report of the Johannisburg district of 1424)[26] – here he lists 16 designated settlement locations of Mazovian settler entrepreneurs, some of which held

Migration of Rural Settlers (esp. Lithuanians) to Eastern Prussia 119

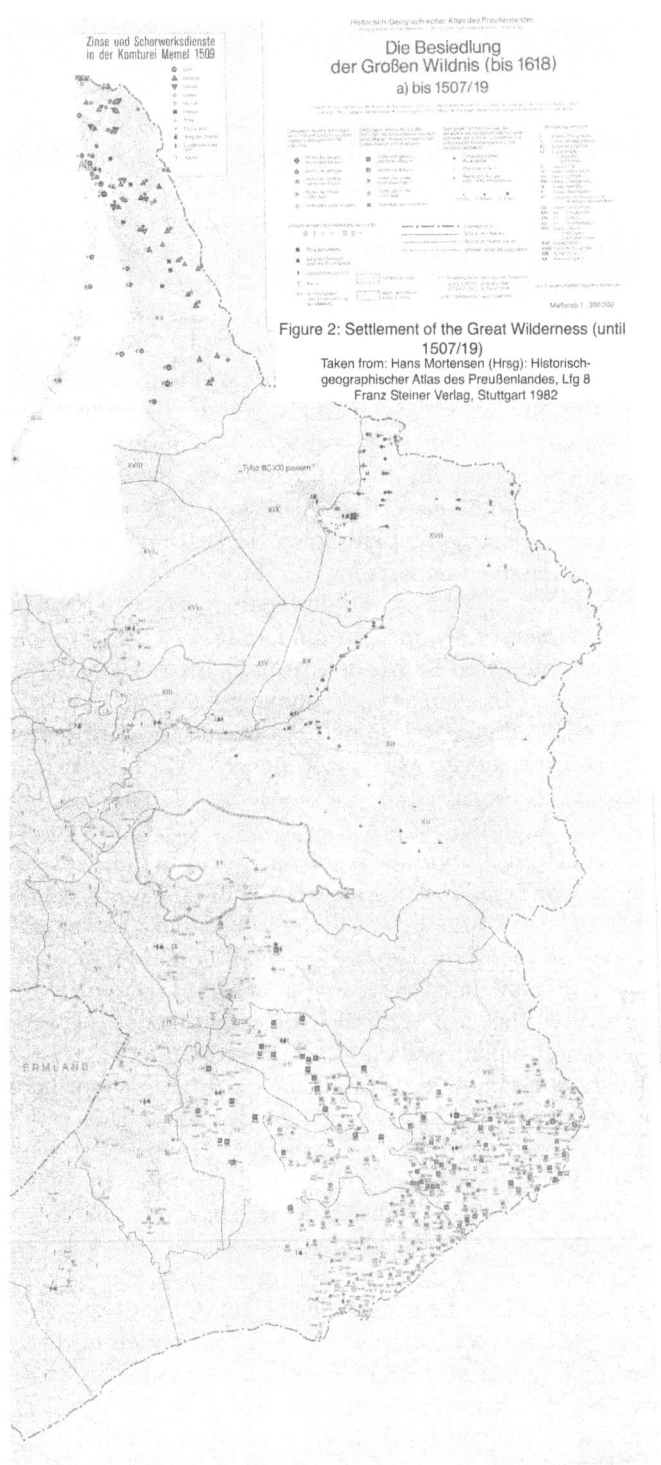

Figure 6.2 Settlement of the Great Wilderness (until 1507–1519)

large property titles (60–100 hides).²⁷ As Johannisburg was granted a town charter in 1451 – although the locator and village mayor (Germ. *Schulze*) was a German, not a Pole, named Lorenz Allmann – Białuński assumes that the settlement system in the district was already well advanced. For the period up to 1465, he can identify 77 settlements – including 6 tax villages (Germ. *Zinsdörfer*) and 69 military service estates (Germ. *Dienstgüter*).²⁸ For the period up to 1525, 38 settlements can be added (one *Zinsdorf* and 37 *Dienstgüter*). By 1579, for which we have an important source – a Church visitation register – another 31 settlements were added, so that by then we have a total of 149 settlements in the district. Białuński emphasizes that settlement activity in the Johannisburg district during the Ducal period appears to have slowed down considerably compared to the time of the Order (but increased, in contrast to this, in the Stradaunen and Angerburg districts). The predominance of *Dienstgüter* over *Zinsdörfer* can also be confirmed for the other districts, as mentioned above – by 1575, he counted a total of 564 settlements in all districts of the south-eastern (former) wilderness under examination, 62% of which were *Dienstgüter* (with some villages of noblemen), while only 28.5% could be classified as *Zinsdörfer*.²⁹ In hard figures, until 1466, we speak of a predominantly Mazovian-Polish population of initially only 3,420 people (0.7 inhabitants/km²), then, around 1525, of 16,112 people (i.e. 3.4 inhabitants/km²) and of 45,685 people around 1568. He was furthermore able to ascertain that Lithuanians also immigrated to the southern districts, although they were fully Polonized in the course of the 16th century in particular (in some cases as late as in the 17th century). In terms of numbers, Germans played a minor role in the settlement process in this region, but they were able to occupy prominent positions (office holders, nobility, townspeople). By far, the largest proportion of the settlement of these southern offices in the wilderness was made up of Mazovian-Polish migrants, which explains the later Polonization of the other ethnic groups and the formation of the Masuria region. In the 15th century, the small nobility (Pol. *szlachta*) and the knighthood predominated as settlers, later joined by numerous peasants; Białuński estimated that in 1568, 50% were peasants, 25% were freemen (including some noblemen), and around 25% were other rural classes.

With these findings in mind, I would like to turn to the northern districts in the wilderness and to the Lithuanian migration in the 15th/16th century – thus to the main focus of this chapter. The married couple Gertrud (historian) and Hans Mortensen (geographer) researched this topic for many decades (1920s–1960s). For political reasons, however, they were unable to complete their planned four-volume work on the settlement of north-eastern Prussia up to the beginning of the 17th century (precisely to the year 1618 – the exact end of Lithuanian settlement) at the height of their research at the end of the 1930s.³⁰ Just two (of four planned) volumes, which furthermore only outlined the conditions for the later migration, were published at that time.³¹ The last two volume manuscripts (approx. 600 pages), which deal with the central question of the actual Lithuanian settlement in a very focused manner and close to the sources, are only available as manuscripts at Geheimes

Staatsarchiv Preußischer Kulturbesitz in Berlin – they were revised several times by Mortensens until the 1960s, as can be seen from various handwritten marginal notes – but they were never published. I will be publishing these volumes in the near future (I transcribed them once in their entirety and added an index) and would therefore like to present the most important findings from these two volume manuscripts on Lithuanian immigration below.[32]

Before I present the work in more detail, I would like to briefly discuss the political implications in the 1910s/1920s, which may ultimately have motivated the Mortensens to deal so intensively with the subject. The Lithuanian migration in the 16th century is a good example of how a historical phenomenon can become a political issue. When Lithuania gained independence in 1918, the Lithuanians insisted – based on the false assumptions of the linguistic works of Königsberg linguist Adalbert Bezzenberger[33] – that Prussian Lithuania (sometimes also called Lithuania Minor, today the eastern half of Kaliningrad Oblast) had since the beginning been populated by Lithuanians. With this argument, which was never properly scientifically proven, the young Lithuanian state claimed the territory of 'Lithuania Minor' for itself.[34] Consequently, the Lithuanian side assumed later on that the work of Hans and Gertrud Mortensen, which proved the migration of Lithuanians to the eastern part of Prussia in the 16th century in particular, was pure hypothesis: "Die 'litauische Einwanderertheorie' von Mortensens beruht lediglich auf Annahmen. Eine solche Annahme ist, dass die Wildnis ein menschenleeres Gebiet war, so dass dort eine Neubesiedlung großen Ausmaßes, wie es die Theorie fordert, notwendig und möglich war". ("Mortensen's 'Lithuanian immigrant theory' is based solely on assumptions. One such assumption is that the wilderness was an area devoid of people, so that new, large-scale settlement, as the theory demands, was necessary and possible".)[35] The cited author, Martynas Gelžinis (1907–1990), was still mistaken in his posthumous publication (1996), stating that Mortensens had not published their third volume after the war "aus Mangel an Material" ("for lack of material").[36] It must be emphasized that it was rather the meticulousness of the couple that led to the standstill of the almost completed work on the third/forth volume – especially after the premature death of Hans Mortensen († 1964).[37]

Eventually, after Gertrud Mortensen's death in 1992, the still unpublished manuscript was given to Geheimes Staatsarchiv Preußischer Kulturbesitz in Berlin as the Mortensen *Nachlass*. The Word document transcribed by me comprises a total of 510 pages (Times New Roman, 12 p., 1.5 line spacing), so it is a really weighty work that has been divided into seven large chapters. In terms of content, the whole thing makes a 'well-rounded impression', but unfortunately there is no overarching table of contents, so I cannot tell for sure whether further chapters should have been added. However, the chapter headings indicate that two further volumes (i.e. volumes 3 and 4) were planned in addition to the two already published volumes.

1 The colonization of the wilderness. The immigration of Lithuanians and Curonian to East Prussia (175 pages – 2 appendices: tables).

2 The family, settlement and land structure of the non-German population (comparison with West and South Germany) (74 pages).
3 The importance of agrarian reforms for settlement and economic structure (21 pages).
4 Stagnation and decline of the settlement (32 pages).
5 Reasons for the population decline. Effects on the settlement structure. Fundamentals of the desertification problem (32 pages).
6 The Germans' share in the recolonization of the wilderness (20 pages).
7 Special phenomena in the course of settlement: Desertification processes – estate development – new German settlers (155 pages).

The quantitative weighing makes it easy to recognize what the Mortensens were particularly interested in (1) The immigration of the Lithuanian population (the Curonian formed a small, vanishing part)[38] until 1618 (Chapter 1). (2) The family structures of these ethnic groups (Chapter 2). (3) The difference between a cash rent based rule (Germ. *Grundrentenherrschaft*) and a manorial regime based on the exploitation of the demesne land, by using the compulsory services of unfree tenants (Germ. *Gutsherrschaft*) in Prussia (Chapter 7). I would like to focus on these aspects in the following.

The way in which the Old-Prussian population perceived the Lithuanian immigrants in Prussia in the 15th/early 16th century can perhaps be well summarized by the complaints of the former keeper of the Teutonic Order in Insterburg, Philipp von Creutz. In 1525, he clearly lamented the general state of affairs in what was now Ducal Prussia after he had lost his office and his castles: *und das meine* [his estates – G. V.] *nicht weiter durfen gebrauchen, wen alsz viel ich mit dem munde verzehrt, und nicht weniger vor eigen gehalten, alsz wer ich ein Littaw* ("and that my [estates] could no longer be used by me, only as much as I can eat with my mouth, and held no more as if I were a Lithuanian")[39] – "As if I were a Lithuanian"! He must have been referring to the Lithuanian immigrants who had already migrated to Prussia for one–two generations during Philip's time. The Lithuanian peasants were therefore obviously considered poor by this former knight of the Order (and presumably by the Prussian population in general) – this aspect will be taken up again in the conclusion at the end of the chapter.

In general, alongside the Poles from the Duchy of Mazovia (see above), the Lithuanians were the largest ethnic migrant group from the late 15th up to the early 17th century. They were attracted by the better living and economic conditions in the Great Wilderness[40] compared to their Lithuanian homeland. It is interesting to note that there is a clear geographical separation between these two ethnic groups in their settlement movements: Mazovian-Poles migrated into the south-eastern wilderness areas and Lithuanians into the north-eastern parts – a broad settlement-free area between Goldap (today Gołdap) and Marggrabowa (Treuburg, today Olecko), i.e. in the Angerburg and Stradaunen districts, is clearly visible on the topical map of the eighth issue of the historical-geographical atlas of Prussia of 1540 (see Figure 6.3).[41]

Migration of Rural Settlers (esp. Lithuanians) to Eastern Prussia 123

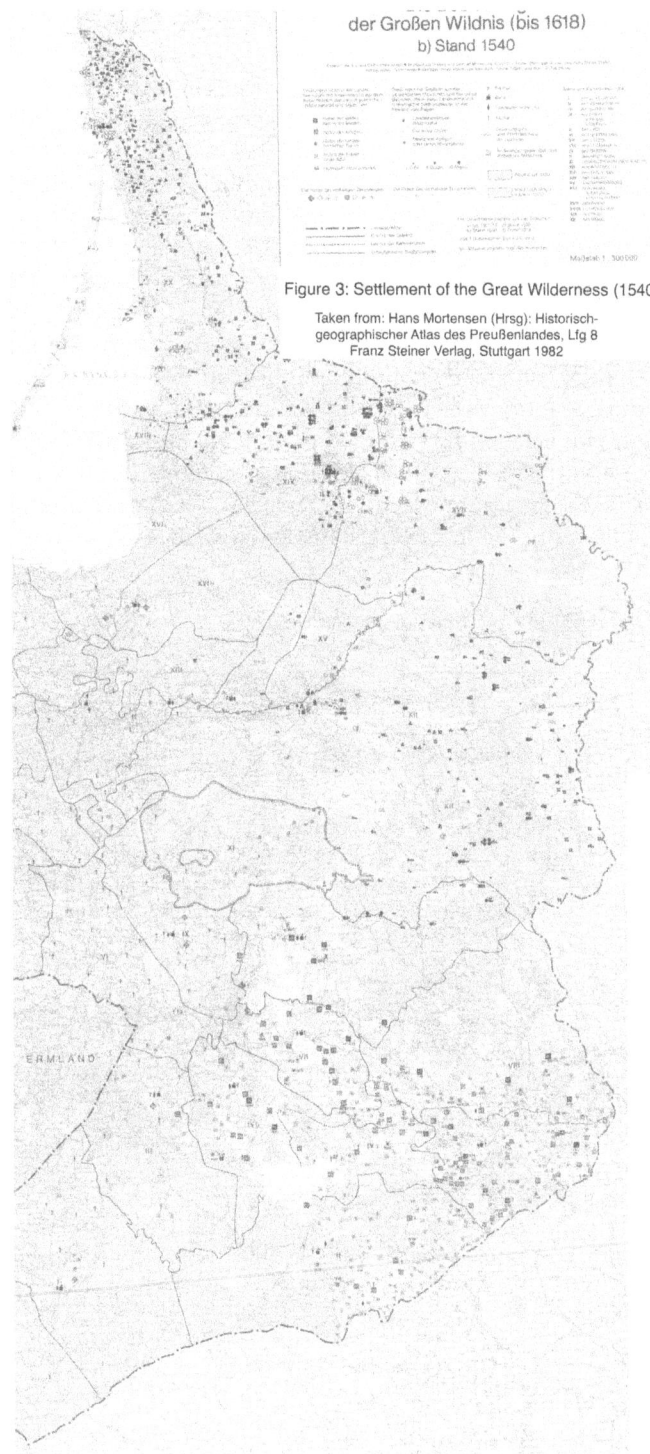

Figure 6.3 Settlement of the Great Wilderness (1540)

I will now reflect chronologically on the Lithuanian immigration: the first verifiable settlements of Lithuanians already existed in the early 14th century. They were clearly named as 'Lithuanians' in the administrative sources of the Order.[42] At that time, they were most likely religious refugees[43] from the Grand Duchy of Lithuania. In terms of numbers, there are only 31 charters for the Königsberg commandery in the period from 1311 to 1401 that were dedicated to Lithuanians. They were settled as lesser freemen with Prussian law and with holdings of two to six *haken* (hooks – each 11.2 hectares).[44]

A series of charters (Germ. *Handfesten*) was issued by the Landmeister in the *Kammeramt* of Labiau.[45] The Lithuanians there settled on their own – the separation from the Old-Prussian freemen may have been initiated by the Order or by the Lithuanians themselves, this cannot be clarified. Basically, they were settled under similar conditions to those that applied to the Old-Prussian freemen, i.e. they had to build castles and perform military service.

In order to compare the still small number of Lithuanian charters in the 14th century with the total population of the largest commandery in eastern Prussia (Königsberg), the following statistics (see Table 6.1) should be taken

Table 6.1 Demographic calculation according to the results of the agrarian reform around 1400

Area	Prussian peasant population	Kulm peasant	Large estates	Free population
Insterburg	18 peasants	–	–	19 freemen
Tapiau	72 peasants	556 farmers (1112.5 hides)	–	53 freemen
Gerdauen	86 peasants	318 farmers (636.6 hides)	416 hides (approx. 200–300 farmers)	97 freemen
Wehlau	83 peasants	–	541 hides (270–360 farmers)	48 freemen
Residential village	104 peasants	–	197 hides[46]	87 freemen
Nadrauen/ Nadrovia	28 peasants	–	200 hides (100–133 farmers)	42 freemen
Overall: adjoining Wilderness areas	391 peasants	874 farmers	570–793 farmers	346 freemen
Samland/Sambia	1340 peasants	approx. 100 farmers	approx. 100 hides (50–80 farmers)	360 freemen
Overall: Königsberg Commandery	1731 peasants	974 farmers	620–873 farmers	706 freemen

into account: at the end of the 14th century, there lived around 3500 peasants and around 700 freemen in the commandery of Königsberg. The statistics clearly show that the expansion in the wilderness areas around 1400 was still mainly carried out in the form of *kulmische* villages, where German settlers were mainly to be found, and by German and Prussian freemen as settlement entrepreneurs.

The Lithuanian immigrants were therefore still a very small minority at that time. In addition to the few Lithuanian settlements, we still find isolated Lithuanian freemen (presumably boyars – Lithuanian petty noblemen) who were integrated into Prussian freemen villages. At around 1400 there are several villages in Samland (Sambia Peninsula), where Lithuanians lived alongside Prussians as freemen or even as unfree peasants (Litauischdorf (today: Zorino), Wolkeniten (today: did not survive), Ankrehnen (today: Perovo), Wargenau (today: Malinovka), Schöntritten (today: Krasnoe). All in all, however, one would agree with Gertrud and Hans Mortensen who spoke of a rather 'insignificant settlement effect' of the Lithuanians in the other administrative areas of the Order at this time.[47] Incidentally, it can be assumed that the Lithuanian freemen served the Order as scouts, spies and guides – similar to some Prussian experts of the Great Wilderness. There are (few) references to this in the sources, e.g. in 1333, a Lithuanian was specifically exempted from guard duty in the wilderness (*custodia Litwinorum in solitudine*).[48]

For almost the entire 15th century, it can be stated that there were no more charters concerning Lithuanian settlements in the Königsberg commandery – after 1410 the trend of the 14th century was definitely interrupted.[49] An interesting example can be cited for the year 1443. In this year, *haben die Littawen unde Samaythen dem grosfursten geclaget, wie en etczliche gesinde her ins land unde ouch ken Lieffland entlieffen, die man en nicht widerkeren welde, unde clagen sunderlich uber den kompthur von rangnith. So bitte der herre grosfurste, das man die entlowffen lewte unde gesinde widerkere [...]* ("the Lithuanian and Samogitians [most probably: boyars] complained to the Grand Duke of Lithuania about how a lot of their servants escaped [to Prussia] and were not returned [by Prussian officials], especially they complained about the commander of Ragnit. Therefore, the Grand Duke requested the Order that they should return the escaped servants [...]").[50] The Lithuanian requests to the Order to send back Lithuanian defectors already played a role in the disputes between Lithuanian Grand Duke Alexander Vytautas (1392–1430) and the Order at the beginning of the 15th century.[51] The number of these defectors can hardly be overestimated.[52] In the course of the 15th century, such requests were repeatedly made by the Lithuanian side – the defections must therefore have taken place continuously, but we cannot quantify them in numbers.[53] In the 1480s, Grand Master Martin Truchsess von Wetzhausen (1477–1489) pointed out in an undated letter to a Lithuanian legation that the extradition of Lithuanian defectors would mean the greatest harm to body and soul for the defectors concerned.[54] This Grand Master had already issued a provision in 1478 that peasants who came in from *bawszen* ('outside') *lands* (i.e. immigrants) or *fremde lantleute* ('foreign people'), who *qwemen in disse lande* ("came to this land") enjoyed full freedom of movement and were allowed to settle wherever they pleased – whether under the Order's authority or under the bishop's or among the greater freemen or in towns.[55] At the same time, the Order was cautious: Evidently a prejudice existing among the population against allegedly burning, murdering and stealing Lithuanian defectors. In a Grand Master's decree of 1478 Lithuanians were forbidden to carry guns and lighters, and any person in Prussia was authorized to take them from them.[56] Furthermore, the Order tried to convince the Lithuanian Grand Dukes and officials that it had also no interest in the Lithuanian defectors, as they would not behave well in the country.[57]

At the end of the 15th century, there is increasing evidence that Lithuanians were settled in the wilderness on uncultivated land and that mass immigration was now gathering pace: Not long before 1492, for example, the field of *Saszlaucken* (later Germ. Sesslacken, today Pridorozhnoe) was occupied with great effort and labour by six or seven *Gesinde* (Lithuanian settlement units), for which the locator *Narcko* or *Narckaw* was promised two tax and two free hides, which he received in 1492.[58] Further examples are Mehlauken (today Zales'e), Kraupischken (today Ul'janovo) which also probably arose as Lithuanian wilderness settlements around 1500.[59] As well *Kulligkehmen* (later Germ. Prussischken, today Lipovo)[60] is a good example. Land was probably cleared there in 1497, as a Lithuanian Prusella from *Colicklaucken* (*der geburt ausz Sameiten* – "born in Samogitia") mentioned in a petition from 1544[61] that he had come to the land of Prussia as a young man at the time when the *hoffmeister* (Grand Master) died in the Wallachia (i.e. in 1497) and that he had begun *nach meiner artt in der wiltnusz zu arbeiten gefliessen, do ich itzundt wone, aus welcher wiltnusz ir sieben fur mir entlauffen, den sie haben den grossen beumen und strauch nicht konnen gerathen [...] ich sollte die wiltnusz arbeiten [...] vor denselbigen bedimpten plan wiltnusz gegeben vier ochsen [...] vier tonen honingk, das ich mochte ausroden strauch und brucher, das ich meinem vihe hew machen [...] ich sollte roden acker und wiesen zumachen, so viell ich konde [...]* (paraphrased: "He had begun to work and clear in the wilderness. Apparently seven 'carts' [settlers?] got away from him, because they could not cope with the hard circumstances. Apparently, he gave four oxen and four tons of honey for his land. He was instructed to clear as much as he could").[62]

Another example: In 1554, when the captain of Tilsit intended to establish a farm or sheep farm near *Linkuhnen*, but the people of Linkuhnen (today Rschewskoje) resisted: *an den orten [...], da wir wonen, vus unsere erbe, die wir zu Linkonen, sampt vnsern eltern und voreltern aus wildem walde vnd raucher wurczel mitt harter arbeyt gerottet, zugericht vnd gebawet, hinwegk nehmen will [...]* (paraphrased: "In the places [...] where we now live we cultivated together with our parents and grandfathers from the wild forest [...] with hard work [...]").[63] This also indicates that the village was founded around 1500, probably even earlier.[64]

The *Historical-Geographical Atlas* illustrates in detail the settlement patterns in the wilderness districts up to 1507/1519 (see Figure 6.2). However, it should be emphasized that the material in the various districts is not homogeneous enough to allow for a precise demographic calculation or to see exactly how the dynamics of settlement proceeded according to the natural landscape division[65] – this can only be done for the situation in 1540, which I discuss below. Nevertheless, it is already possible to identify certain settlement centres in the early 16th century. In the Memel district (here also Curonian settlements), the loose Lithuanian settlement was already spread over the entire area, in the Ragnit and Tilsit districts the settlement was concentrated in the area around the castles of Ragnit and Tilsit, while in the Insterburg district (and Georgenburg on the other side) it can be clearly seen how the Lithuanian settlements, starting from the main centre of Insterburg, advanced along the rivers Inster and Angerapp. We are therefore observing very much an inland settlement dynamic, starting from the centres of the old settlement (and not from the borders).

I will proceed to the Lithuanian migration to the Duchy of Prussia around the mid-16th century, which can be traced much better than the earlier phases. With the so-called Turk tax registers (Germ. *Türkensteuerregister*) of 1539/1540 (compiled due to the danger posed by the Ottomans), we have a first-class demographic source for Prussian settlement and population history which really does cover all districts (see Figure 6.3).[66] The Lithuanian settlement in the wilderness is thus very precisely visible here, and we can make clear statements about the demographic development: In 1540, the total number of Lithuanians and Curonians in the wilderness in northern Prussia who began to settle there over the course 50–75 years amounted to around 4,000 families, including the approximately 250–300 families who took over Old-Prussian settlement land, i.e. did not clear new land.[67] The majority of the Curonians worked as fishermen and their number is clearly limited compared to the Lithuanians in the Memel district. Since the figures are based on Lithuanian families, the number of individuals was probably around 20,000–30,000. Of these 4,000 families, only about one-third (approx. 1,300 families) can be counted as really new immigrants around 1540, while two-thirds can be traced back to natural population growth and internal migration within Prussia over approx. two generations, which Mortensens were able to reconstruct well on the basis of the settlement expansion. If we compare these population figures with the largest commandery in the eastern part of the Order (Königsberg) around the year 1400 – where we had identified more or less 3,500 peasant families and 700 freemen families (see Table 6.1) – we can see that the Lithuanian migration in the first half of the 16th century meant a significant population growth for the region (more or less one-third of the population).

The Lithuanian settlement movement started from the old settlement areas during the time of the Order and did not begin at the Lithuanian border (sic!) – this is an extremely important finding from Mortensens' manuscript[68]:

"Nirgends haben wir das Bild, dass die der politischen Grenze gegen Litauen nahen Gebiete die ältesten besiedelten sind, wie es bei einer wirklichen siedlungsmäßigen 'Wanderung längs der Flüsse' von Osten her der Fall sein müsste. Hier hat uns das geographische Bild des Jahres 1540 getäuscht. In Wirklichkeit erfolgt die erste Ansiedlung auf preußischem Altland und in unmittelbarer Anlehnung an das preußisch deutsche Siedlungsland bzw. die Burgen und schiebt sich von da aus, den günstigen Siedlungslinien, also besonders den Flüssen folgend, nach allen in Frage kommenden Seiten vor. Es entsteht auf diese Weise in einem bestimmten Stadium das Bild, als ob die Siedlung von Osten her längs der Flüsse erfolgt sein könnte [i.e. directly from Lithuania, which Mortensens regarded as false, author's note]. Dieses Stadium war um 1540 ungefähr erreicht".[69] So, in the early phase (around 1500), the Lithuanian immigration did not yet reach the actual wilderness, but the Lithuanians initially started from the existing German-Prussian settlements (including the surrounding areas of the castles at Insterburg and Ragnit). The thesis repeatedly put forward by Lithuanian scholars, that Lithuanian settlement had always been present in 'Minor Lithuania', must be clearly rejected as being simply false. In the sources, the immigrating Lithuanians as a mass phenomenon only can be traced back to around the year 1500, which Mortensens proved *in detail*.

By the dynamic settlement movement up to 1540, which the Mortensens painstakingly reconstructed in their unpublished manuscript and their later atlas work, we can state that the Lithuanians were initially under the control of the Order administration (later Ducal administration) and that they were immediately attached to the existing settlement land – presumably also to avoid border conflicts. In the beginning, the Lithuanian settlements were rather small, not comparable to the *kulmisch* villages. They were divided into *Gezinse* (alternatively also called *Gesinde*), 1–5 *Gezinsen* comprising one bigger village unit. A *Gezinse* was, in turn, divided into several *Brote* (breads) – in total, a *Gezinse* therefore formed an average of 5–10 farm units. A *brot*, in turn, corresponded to a farm unit (whereby the father's family house and the sons with their core families, who could live in different houses on the farm area, were grouped together).[70] A *Gezinse* was therefore most likely a Lithuanian community of property, represented to the outside by one settler, i.e. the eldest or first settler.[71]

To sum it up to this point: By 1540, the area of the Great Wilderness had been settled loosely though relatively extensively with Lithuanians and Mazovian Poles during the time of the Order and later in the Duchy of Prussia. However, it is striking that there was hardly any infrastructure in the wilderness districts around 1540. There was neither a large parish network (although this changed in the second half of the 16th century)[72] nor an economic network (mainly represented by *Kretzmer/Krüge*, i.e. inns, where the local trade was happening).[73] Most of the town foundations in the region (with the exception of Tilsit in 1552, Goldap in 1570 and Insterburg in 1583) did not take place until much later – under Prussian King

Friedrich Wilhelm I.[74] The total number of thirteen *Schulzenämter*, i.e. small administrative offices for a couple of Lithuanian settlements (comparable to the Prussian *Kammerämter*), can be found individually before 1540 and then, suddenly, all of them in 1554 for the *Hauptamt* Insterburg.[75] With regard to the Prussian nobility (which developed in the late 15th/16th century), it can be stated that their new estates were mainly located in the old settlement areas, while there was hardly any nobility in the Lithuanian wilderness districts.[76] The Lithuanian petty nobility (boyars) was generally not settled, or they lost their titles in the wilderness of Prussia.[77] All in all, it was large, peasant family groups that had migrated to eastern Prussia or the Great Wilderness over the last 50–80 years (since around 1470).[78]

The individual settlements and waves of migration in the second half of the 15th century and the first half of the 16th century must have been quite uncoordinated, if not to say 'wild', and it is not easy to provide concrete figures here. For the district of Ragnit a unique source is available from the beginning of the 16th century, the Ragnit house book (*Hausbuch*),[79] which records the land purchases by Lithuanians from 1504 up to 1544. The register consists purely of Lithuanian settlements, as the name material clearly shows. It was only at this time that the Teutonic Order must have realized that Lithuanian immigration and internal Lithuanian migration had reached such a degree that the requested land did not have to be given away for free but could also be sold.[80] When the new Lithuanian settlers bought the land from the Order/Duke, usually they paid oxen as a currency.[81] This clearly shows that, at least from the 16th century onwards, it must have been wealthier settlers who pushed ahead the land expansion in Prussia.[82] If we summarize the sales data in the house book, we count 300 oxen for new colonization plus remote expansion and 1,550 oxen for land expansion and local expansion by 1540 – the local internal expansion is therefore much bigger than the remote expansion. The Mortensens were able to calculate about 35 pre-documentary (charter-given) settlements for the beginning of the district, assuming a total size of 85 *Gesinde* or 500 oxen. They calculated that two oxen corresponded to one *Brot* (once again: a Lithuanian farm unit with a father and his adult sons), and one *Gesinde* was created of approx. three *Brote* (i.e. six oxen). Of course, these are only estimations for the Ragnit district. Based on the *Türkensteuerregister* for the district, we can determine 1,050 peasants and 98 single people in 1540, which roughly corresponds to the estimated number of land sales paid for in oxen.

In the following I am going try to answer questions about the origin of the Lithuanian migrants, the motives for their immigration, their economic situation and taxes raised by authorities.

Where did the majority of Lithuanian migrants actually come from? Anton Salys assumed in 1930[83] that they were crown peasants from the Samogitian wilderness who came to Prussia a little before 1529 (because the situation of the peasants in Prussia had improved considerably at this time).

The Mortensens were able to identify the beginning of the massive Lithuanian migration (see above) much earlier, at around the year 1500. Salys assumed that they had come from the Lithuanian wilderness areas and therefore simply had to be listed under cross-border 'internal migration'. The Mortensens, however, were able to prove that the Lithuanian wilderness near the border had not yet been settled at all at this time (see above).[84] Therefore, the migrants must inevitably have come from the old Lithuanian settlement areas. Nevertheless, some of the sources refer to them as *Szemaites*, but there are also indications that they came from the areas on the lower Dubissa River and on the western bank of the Nevėžis River (i.e. from the middle landscape between Aukštaitija and Samogitia (Žemaitija)). The main migration route was probably via the Memel River. The settlement was also due to active recruitment by Prussian and Lithuanian frontier commuters, some of whom worked on behalf of the Order and later the Duke and actively approached farmers in Lithuania.[85]

Which reasons do the Mortensens give for this migration in their work? They rule out religious reasons (especially the Reformation, which quickly found its way into the Duchy of Prussia), due to the still generally rudimentary anchoring of the Christian faith in the Lithuanian population (so that sufficient knowledge of the confessional disputes cannot be assumed).[86] They also reject overpopulation in Lithuania as a starting point – the clearest evidence against this is the Lithuanian Grand Duke's reclaiming of emigrants (because their lands in Lithuania were lying waste). The only really plausible reason is probably the worsening situation of the Lithuanian peasants.[87] In the 16th century, all four sovereignties in the greater region (Poland, Lithuania, Prussia, and Livonia) were struggling with overcoming the early modern agrarian depression and with retaining the peasants, but the Order/Duchy of Prussia seemed to have picked the best strategies for this – personal freedom and lower taxes may be supposed to have played a major role. A vivid example of this is provided by the statements of two boyars from the district of Jurbarkas (in Samogitia) who settled near *Aesernicken* (Eszeruppen near Willuhnen, today not existing) They reported that the peasants *inn Sameythen vnnd am Koniglichen theill* [i.e. Aukštaitija] *vonn der huben 8 Mark zinczen vnnd werden mit zoellen hoch beschweret, musten gleichwoll fur ihre freyheit alles thun, was man sie heisset vnnd wurden offtmalsz vber disz alles wohl zerpleuet vnnd zurschlagen* ("peasants in Samogitia and in the royal part (i.e. Aukštaitija) were being taxed 8 marks for one hide and had to do everything they were called upon to do for their freedom, and were nevertheless often beaten").[88] The two boyars therefore wanted to provide the Prussian duke with enough people, if only there was room. Another example is the information provided by 30 freemen in 1584, who called themselves boyars from *Daugentlaucken* (today Dauglaukis); at that time located directly on the Prussian-Lithuanian border, on the Lithuanian side).[89] They were certainly well aware of the conditions on both sides of the border after the agrarian reforms of 1567 (in Lithuania) under King Sigismund August and 1580 (in Prussia). However, they still wanted to come to the Prussian duke if only he would remit their socage (Germ. *Scharwerk*). It becomes clear from these examples that everywhere in 'royal' Lithuania (i.e. not just Samogitia), the situation was certainly worse than in ducal Prussia.

A very important insight from the Mortensens' manuscript concerns the success of the Lithuanian migration and settlement movements: In their opinion, this was based on the fact that the ducal authorities did not really intervene in the form of state regulations until very late around 1580. It seems to have been the intention of both the Order and later the Duke to allow the new Lithuanian settlers to settle relatively autonomously for many decades since the end of the 15th century. Until the 1540s, absolutely no state regulations for the Lithuanian settlements can be found in the sources, and later only a few. It was not until 1580 that the authorities began to regulate taxes, meadows, livestock, clearing, cultivation, etc., and to enact certain laws for Lithuanian farmers.[90] The Mortensens compared the agrarian reform in the Duchy (in the year 1580) with the first agrarian reform around 1400 in the Order's land (the so-called 'Great Measure' (Germ. *große Maße*))[91] and found that both institutionally and centrally controlled agrarian reforms took place only about 100 years after the start of the respective migration movement (first German, later Lithuanian). They therefore concluded: "Diese lange Vorbereitungszeit war es sicher, die neben der einfühlsamen Durchführung das reibungslose Gelingen der Reformen bewirkte". ("It was certainly this long preparation time, in addition to the sensitive implementation, that ensured the smooth success of the reforms".)[92]

Overall, the Mortensens' observation seems very valuable: The Prussian authorities behaved quite cautiously and loosely towards the migrant groups for many decades, allowing them to quietly cultivate the land and establish themselves before confronting them with regulations. This obviously contributed significantly to the success of the settlement movements.

Finally towards the end of the 16th century, as a result of the massive Lithuanian migration, a Lithuanization of the smaller Prussian and Curonian populations in the north-eastern wilderness districts took place.[93] The Prussian-Curonian population in the Lithuanian districts adapted to the majority in terms of habitus and language.[94] The translation of the Lutheran catechism by Martin Marvidas (Mosvid) into Lithuanian – the first ever printed Lithuanian book – and the translation of the Lutheran Bible into Lithuanian by Johannes Bredtke (provisionally completed in 1590) are good evidence of the increasing importance of the Lithuanian language and culture in north-eastern Prussia.[95]

However, the small economic units, called *Krüge* (inns), in the new settlement areas in the wilderness were predominantly German – this can be consistently proven by the names of the *Krug* owners (e.g. Werner Schwabe, Lorenz Sylvester). In terms of numbers, they can of course be neglected for the expansion of the settlement, as they were often settled on land that had already been cleared and they represented only a small group in general – we can determine an average of 12–15 *Krüge* in the larger districts.[96] However, the importance of the inns for the development of the region for trade and commerce can hardly be overestimated. In addition, the old German centres in the Wilderness (Memel, Tilsit, Ragnit, Insterburg) developed positively as a result of the Lithuanian settlement in the 16th century, so that they were partly elevated to cities (especially Tilsit became a city in 1552 and thus surpassed initially more important Ragnit, which only became a city in 1722).[97] The guild regulations in the 16th century[98] from these towns testify to the predominantly German element in the towns – the newcomers had to be of *deutscher Zunge* ('German tongue'), and also the council had to be German. However, the streetscape of the town of Memel in the 19th century (where there was only one German street name) indicates that earlier there must have been a considerably large Lithuanian or Curonian population. Nevertheless, the general rule (like in the older settlement areas) seems to apply: The elites in the wilderness areas were particularly strongly made up of Germans, even if early modern examples can even be found in which a German name took on Lithuanian suffixes and thus slowly became Lithuanianized.[99]

Finally, there is the question of the economic system and the taxes paid by the Lithuanian peasants. In the old settlement areas the situation was clear: the peasants paid taxes for their land, which was mainly based on arable farming, and the freemen provided military and castle-building services.[100] For both the ruler and the rural population this was largely a productive mutual business. If Lithuanians settled in the old German-Prussian settlement area (as was the case in the early period on the deserted areas), they were included into the given tax system of the respective village.[101]

We have hardly any concrete information from the sources about the Lithuanians' specific levies and services in the Great Wilderness districts in the 15th century.[102] Presumably, the sovereign was initially content for the Lithuanians to gain a foothold and to push ahead with the clearing of the land. In the early days the levies must have mainly consisted of small natural levies (e.g. marten pelts).[103] The Lithuanians are less likely to have been involved in socage (*Scharwerk*, a duty of the Prussian peasants in particular), as there were hardly any sovereign settlements in the wilderness (apart from castles and wilderness houses) where socage could be carried out. Perhaps the Lithuanians were obliged to perform forest and rafting services here and there, as it is known from the 16th century.[104]

It should be noted that the taxes were not paid for the defined plots of land (i.e. according to hides and hooks) but for the wider family units (*Gezinsel/Gesinde* – as explained above). The priority of the Lithuanians was cattle farming (hence the above calculations in *Ochsen* in the Ragnit house book). As they operated in their wider family groups, their numbers probably remained untransparent to the Order and later the Duke's officials, which unfortunately also makes it difficult for us today to compare them with actual figures. For this reason, the later villages in the Lithuanian offices were often not properly recorded administratively. Some of them stretched like a string of pearls along the course of the respective rivers, and in some places they took the form of non-terminating street villages. The village of *Patilsze* (today not existing) in the Ragnit district is a prime example of such a development: The edition of the Turkish tax registers for the districts of Ragnit and Insterburg[105] states that this village had 118 *Brote* ('breads'). However, it was a settlement strip along the river *Tilsze* which later formed an entire *Schulzenamt* (small administrative unit) and was then divided into several villages.

An analysis of the Turkish tax registers of 1539/1540 regarding wider family structures clearly shows that different branches of one extended family lived in one village. The surnames had not yet been fully established, which makes exact assessment difficult. However, if they developed in some villages, it is clear that there were always around two to three peasant families with the same surname, i.e. they must have been related.[106] As the extended family units, from which the levies were initially paid, grew steadily,[107] it could only be in the interests of the Ducal officials to transfer the levies from the bigger *Gesinde* to the smaller *Brote*.[108] The majority of the rural population themselves must also have considered the levies, which were independent of the size of the actually bigger family, i.e. the number of farms and the size of the farms of the individual *Gesinde*, to be antiquated and unjust.[109] But it was only in the second half of the 16th century (with the reform of 1580) that the Duke complied with the requests and complaints and equated a *Brot* with a fixed unit of land of three hides. In the future, taxes were to be paid from these units.[110]

Finally, the *Benders*,[111] who are often mentioned in the Turkish tax registers, played a very significant role in the Lithuanian settlement structures. They were dependent on the main peasant. Research has repeatedly examined the *Bender*-system, and often there are different opinions. Generally spoken, the *Benders* must have been a kind of 'junior partners' to the main peasants, whereby the main host was the first to arrive at a new settlement site and thus provided the *Bender* with assistance in clearing and cultivating his fields to a degree that should not be underestimated. In return, the *Bender* was then called upon to do certain work for the main peasant (harvest help, etc.).[112] In any case, the *Benders* must have been an advantage for the main peasant, as the Ducal administration in the second half of the 16th century demanded fees from the main peasant for a *Bender's* services.[113]

It is not until the 1540s that we have the first source for Lithuanian levies that brings some clarity to the matter of specific levies. A prescription for the *Schulzen* of the main office of Insterburg of 1548 shows that the Lithuanian taxpayers, who lived five miles and more from the house of Insterburg, did not have to perform any socage; in the source they are called *Großzinser*.[114] However, they had to pay three marks *Freigeld*. In addition to this *Freigeld*, they also had to make the following payments to the officials: Three marks of taxes, one mark of *Mardergeld*, two eighths of wood (one hard and one soft sort; in the case of one acre, that is, 8 eighths) to be rafted to Königsberg, half an eighth of wood for the house of Insterburg, a bushel of oats for the guard and (in the event that the Duke should hunt there) a position in front of the garn with a spit. In addition, each taxpayer was to cut, gather and bring in grass one day a year, (if necessary) to do construction work at the fortification, help with rafting the produce of the forest, wood, ashes and the likes according to agreement (thus apparently relatively flexible), also to give honey (the ton for four marks) and two bushels of barley. The *Kleinzinser*, however, who lived within the five-mile radius, had to work on the state property one day a week (*Vorwerk*) but did not have to give any *Freigeld* or honey. They were still expected to carry wood to the house and drive the carts on hunts and journeys. In addition, both tax groups had to pay the *Marziliengeld* ('Martin's money') of half a mark.[115]

It is difficult to make a comparison with the taxes of the other ethnic groups (Prussians and Germans) in terms of the severity of the levies, as although these Lithuanian taxpayers (*Zinser*) paid from their own land, we do not know exactly how large it was. But perhaps their conditions were somewhat better than those of the Prussians.[116] For most Lithuanian settlers and for the majority of the 16th century, however, the taxes were levied on the basis of the *Gezinse* units, as shown above. In the 1539/1540, Turkish tax register we at least find a complete list of the livestock in the Lithuanian offices.[117] The duke's administration set levies for all livestock in the form of *Nachtgeld* – a draught horse or a milking cow, for example, counted as one *Nachtgeld*, while four goats or four pigs also counted as one *Nachtgeld*.[118] There had been attempts by researchers to convert the *Nachtgeld* into measurements of estates (e.g. 10 *Nachtgeld* would correspond to one hide),[119] but there is far too much speculation here.

There were also complaints about the socage (*Scharwerk*) and taxes among the Lithuanian 'new settlers' in the 16th century.[120] When the Lithuanian farmers of the Tilsit district asked in 1572 to be allowed to pay their share of the tax (normally paid in oxen) in the form of money, they were refused with the remark that *S. F. G. können kein geld essen* ("His Ducal Gracious cannot eat money").[121] But the conditions on the other side of the Memel or in 'royal' Lithuania and also in Poland seem to have been much worse at this time, so that the Lithuanians mostly stayed in Prussia (see above).[122] The already mentioned relatively small number of noble peasants compared to the number of sovereign peasants[123] certainly guaranteed the Lithuanians 'fair' treatment by the sovereign because there was almost no pressure of concurrence for the sovereign.

On this last point, one final problem should be addressed which is even of supra-regional significance: the *Gutsherrschaft* (manorial lordship), which has been traditionally associated with the East Elbe regions since the studies of Georg Friedrich Knapp, Werner Wittich and Georg von Below for the early modern period.[124] This has often been the subject of debate

– nowadays people tend to focus more on micro-historical case studies and are wary of making overly general structural statements – but the juxtaposition still plays a major role in modern works.[125] Also the Mortensens dealt with this problem for eastern Prussia, which is associated with an increasing *Gutsherrschaft* from the 16th century onwards.[126] They first found out that the conversion to manorial lordship in the new settlement area of the Lithuanians was considerably less than in the Old-Prussian settlement area. They spotted only one example of a nobleman: Moritz von Perschkau in the Tilsit district in 1540.[127] The low incidence of manorial lordship in the Lithuanian districts was evidently due to the fact that the nobility was much less likely to gain a foothold in these regions (it is assumed to be no more than 8.5% in total).[128] This observation of the minor role of manorial lordship in the 16th century initially only concerned a regional internal distinction (new settlement areas vs. old settlement areas in Ducal Prussia) – on a structural-general level it played no role. However, inspired by their observation, the Mortensens analysed how many servants (i.e. maidservants and farmhands) and gardeners could be identified in eastern Prussia.[129] The number is very small compared to the number of peasants who paid taxes and worked, as Table 6.2 with figures from the Tapiau district shows.

The gardeners, however, who were so immensely important for the maintenance of the estate, were not found to be strongly represented either in the Lithuanian new settlement areas nor in the old settlement areas.[130] In addition, these gardeners not only worked on the noble estates but (as the Turkish tax registers clearly show) also very often assisted ordinary tax paying peasants (e.g. there are 9 peasants and 5 gardeners as assistants in one village).

The Mortensens were thus increasingly convinced that the 'cash rent based rule' (Germ. *Grundrentenherrschaft*) had played still a major role in the 16th century, especially in view of the fact that the socage (*Scharwerk*) is hardly specified in this century – we have more precise information on this only from the 17th century. The Mortensens therefore concluded with the statement: "Der Unterschied zwischen Altdeutschland und dem ostdeutschen Kolonisationsgebiet, der später so ungemein wird und in Gestalt des ostdeutschen Großgrundbesitzes bis heute nachwirkt, hat damals noch gar nicht bestanden, wenn man unser Arbeitsgebiet als repräsentativ betrachtet! Wenn wir nicht wüssten, dass sich aus den sozusagen westdeutsch grundherrlichen Verhältnissen unseres Gebietes später eins der Zentren ostdeutschen Großgrundbesitzes entwickelt, würden wir es aus den damaligen

Table 6.2 Tapiau district in 1539/1540

	Peasants	Gardeners	Inst-people
Sovereign	430	62	8
Nobles	227	15	?

Besitzverhältnissen nicht ahnen können". ("The difference between old German territories and the East German colonization area, which later becomes so immense and continues to have an effect today in the form of the East German manorial regime, did not even exist at that time, if one considers our working area as representative. Had we not known that one of the centers of East German land ownership, our region, would later develop from the West German landlord-like conditions, we would not have been able to guess so from the ownership conditions at the time".)[131]

The Mortensens thus stated that the process of aristocratic *Gutswirtschaft* (manorial regime) took place very late, in a relatively short period between 1630 and 1700.[132] They attributed this to the differing abilities of the peasants and the various phases of desolation in the 16th and 17th centuries. The less productive peasants (usually the former Prussian peasants) were unable to bear the additional burden imposed on them by the sovereign and the noblemen, due to the deserted neighbouring areas. They thus became 'unprofitable', and the respective landlord then slowly incorporated them into his manor, which subsequently grew more and more into the *Gutswirtschaft*. During this period, two-thirds of the originally sovereign-owned Prussian villages fell victim to the manorial process, while most of the *Kulmisch* villages survived.[133] Mortensen's conclusion: The existence of the indigenous villages is therefore the only precondition for the 17th-century process of manorialization (Germ. *Vergüterung*).[134] It may have taken place as early as the 16th century, but the immigration of Lithuanians and Poles, who took over the old places of the Old-Prussian and German peasants, delayed the process by about a century.

This brings us to the end of our considerations with an outlook: Until the beginning of the 17th century, the development of the old Prussian-German settlement area and the new Lithuanian settlement area was quite different: In the east one could see overflowing new settlement and an exponential increase in population, while at the same time in the west (old settlement areas) stagnation and drastic population decline were rampant. From the beginning of the 17th century onwards, this difference becomes much smaller: Both parts were now gripped by the same severe crisis that then afflicts the whole of eastern Prussia. It is only at this time that we can notice a totally new tendency: More and more examples of former Lithuanian or Polish immigrants escaping to Poland and Lithuania or to Ermland/Warmia can be found. The rural population had already been decimated by the many waves of plague in the 17th century. The attempt by the rulers to shift the taxes and burdens onto the remaining population further accelerated depopulation.[135] The Lithuanian peasants were evidently not in a position to take over the deserted farms in the villages and found the attempt by the ruler to assign them a second hide as a burden.[136] The 17th century therefore saw an increase in the number of noblemen among the farmers in the former wilderness areas[137] – a trend that led to the proverbial Prussian *Gutswirtschaft* at the end of the 17th century.

To finally return to Philip von Kreutz and his pejorative statements about the Lithuanians: Lithuanian migration seems to have been a thoroughly peasant phenomenon; we have seen that it was not until the mid-/late 16th century that important institutions such as churches, inns, *Schulzen* offices and finally towns were established. Nevertheless, these peasants were very successful with clearing and settling the land, which, in turn, had far-reaching consequences for eastern Prussia right up to the modern era.

Notes

1 Grzegorz Białunski. 'Stan badań historycznych nad dziejami Prusów po 1945 roku,' *Pruthenia* 1 (2006): 41–78.
2 Older, but still useful: Karl Kasiske, *Die Siedlungstätigkeit des Deutschen Ordens im östlichen Preußen bis zum Jahre 1410*, Einzelschriften der Historischen Kommission für Ost- und Westpreußische Landesforschung 5 (Königsberg: Gräfe & Unzer, 1924). More recently: Heide Wunder, *Siedlungs- und Bevölkerungsgeschichte der Komturei Christburg (13–16. Jahrhundert)*, Marburger Ostforschungen 28 (Wiesbaden: Otto Harrassowitz, 1968); ead., 'Siedlung und Bevölkerung im Ordensstaat, Herzogtum und Königreich Preußen, 13.–18. Jahrhundert,' in *Ostdeutsche Geschichts- und Kulturlandschaften*, vol. 2, *Ost- und Westpreußen*, ed. Hans Rothe (Köln: Böhlau Verlag, 1987), 67–98; briefly but usefully summarizing the state of research at the time: Werner Rutz, 'Phasen staatlicher Raumorganisation im ehemaligen Ostpreussen,' *Nordost-Archiv* 24/102 (1991): 1–25; Grischa Vercamer, *Siedlungs-, Verwaltungs- und Sozialgeschichte der Komturei Königsberg im Deutschordensland Preußen (13.–16. Jahrhundert)*, Einzelschriften der Historischen Kommission für ost- und westpreußische Landesforschung 29 (Marburg/Lahn: N. G. Elwert Verlag, 2010); id., 'Siedlungs-, Verwaltungs- und Sozialgeschichte der Komturei Königsberg im Deutschordensland Preußen (13–16. Jahrhundert). Zusammenfassende Worte über eine landesgeschichtliche Doktorarbeit und ein Plädoyer für mehr gemeinsame Projektarbeit unter Historikern,' *Blätter für deutsche Landesgeschichte* 148 (2012): 313–320. A more recent publication (although the main features date back to 2002): Janusz Małłek, ',Die Wege führen nach Preussen' – Migrationen der deutschen, polnischen (masurischen) und litauischen Bevölkerung in die preussischen Gebiete im 13.–18. Jahrhundert,' in *Studies on the military orders, Prussia, and urban history: essays in honour of Roman Czaja on the occasion of his sixtieth birthday / Beiträge zur Ritterordens-, Preussen- und Städteforschung: Festschrift für Roman Czaja zum 60. Geburtstag*, ed. Jürgen Sarnowsky, Krzysztof Kwiatkowski, Hubert Houben, László Pósán, and Attila Bárány (Debrecen: Printart-Press Kft., 2020), 425–436.
3 Derived from Kulm law, which was fundamental to Prussia, cf. Friedrich Ebel, 'Kulmer Recht – Probleme und Erkenntnisse,' *Beiträge zur Geschichte Westpreußens* 8 (1983): 9–26.
4 Kasiske, *Siedlungstätigkeit*, 56, 59–73.
5 Vercamer, *Siedlungs-, Verwaltungs- und Sozialgeschichte*, 212–216.
6 See also Klaus Militzer, 'Probleme der Migration und Integration sozialer Gruppen im Preußenland,' in *Probleme der Migration und Integration im Preußenland vom Mittelalter bis zum Anfang des 20. Jahrhunderts*, Tagungsberichte der Historischen Kommission für ost- und westpreußische Landesforschung 21, ed. Roman Czaja and Klaus Militzer (Marburg: N. G. Elwert Verlag, 2005), 34.
7 Bernhart Jähnig, 'Der Neustamm der Preußen. Seine Entwicklung von der Teilung Preußens bis zu den Teilungen Polens (1466–1772/93),' in *Zwischen Lübeck und Novgorod. Wirtschaft, Politik und Kultur im Ostseeraum vom frühen Mittelalter*

bis ins 20. Jahrhundert. Norbert Angermann zum 60. Geburtstag, ed. Ortwin Pelc (Lüneburg: Institut Nordostdeutsches Kulturwerk, 1996), 305–328. *Cf.* also Vercamer, *Siedlungs-, Verwaltungs- und Sozialgeschichte*, 281–293 (chap. "Multiethnische Zusammensetzung (im 15. Jahrhundert)"), on the adaptation based on the name material.

8 Wilhelm Guddat, *Die Entstehung und Entwicklung der privaten Grundherrschaften in den Ämtern Brandenburg und Balga (Ostpreußen)*, Wissenschaftliche Beiträge zur Geschichte und Landeskunde Ostmitteleuropas 96 (Marburg/Lahn: J.-G. Herder-Institut, 1975); Thomas Lewerenz, *Die Größenentwicklung der Kleinstädte in Ost- und Westpreußen bis zum Ende des 18. Jahrhunderts*, Wissenschaftliche Beiträge zur Geschichte und Landeskunde Ostmitteleuropas 101 (Marburg/Lahn: J.-G. Herder-Institut, 1976); Roman Czaja, *Miasta Pruskie a zakon krzyżacki. Studia nad stosunkami między miastem a władzą terytorialną w późnym średniowieczu* (Toruń: Wydawnictwo Uniwersytetu Mikołaja Kopernika, 1999).

9 'Verwaltung des Ordenslandes Preußen um 1400' (map), prep. Hans Mortensen, Gertrud Mortensen, and Reinhard Wenskus in *Historisch-geographischer Atlas des Preußenlandes*, issue 1, ed. Hans Mortensen, Gertrud Mortensen, and Reinhard Wenskus (Wiesbaden: Franz Steiner Verlag, 1968).

10 Vercamer, *Siedlungs-, Verwaltungs- und Sozialgeschichte*, 216–221.

11 Darius Baronas and Stephen C. Rowell, *The conversion of Lithuania – from pagan barbarians to late medieval Christians* (Vilnius: Institute of Lithuanian Literature and Folklore, 2015), 261–326. The supplications from the Lithuanian diocese in the 15th century show impressively that many mixed forms were still existing there; *cf.* Monika Saczyńska-Vercamer, *Władza i grzech. Supliki z terenów metropolii gnieźnieńskiej do Penitencjarii Apostolskiej w XV wieku* (Warszawa: Wydawnictwo Instytutu Archeologii i Etnologii PAN, 2021).

12 Premysl Bar, 'The diplomacy of Sigismund of Luxembourg in the dispute between the Teutonic Knights and Poland-Lithuania,' in *Networking in late medieval Central Europe. Friends, families, foes*, ed. Beata Możejko, Anna P. Orłowska, and Leslie Carr-Riegel (London: Routledge, 2023), 77–91.

13 Małłek, 'Die Wege,' 428, 431, summarizes the demographic estimations of German and Polish research of the past decades: Around 1410 in the entire Ordensland Prussia, approx. 270,000 inhabitants (52% Germans, 38% Old-Prussians, 10% Poles). In the mid-17th century, the total population of the Duchy of Prussia (i.e. the successor of the Teutonic Order) was 360,000, with around one-third Poles and a similar number of Lithuanians.

14 Important literature on this subject: Gertrud Mortensen and Uwe Kühl, 'Die Besiedlung der Grossen Wildnis (bis 1618). Erläuterungen zur 8 Lieferung,' in *Historisch-geographischer Atlas des Preussenlandes*, issue 8, ed. Hans Mortensen, Gertrud Mortensen, Reinhard Wenskus, and Helmut Jäger (Wiesbaden: Franz Steiner Verlag, 1982), 1–13; Hans & Gertrud Mortensen, *Die Besiedlung des nordöstlichen Ostpreußens bis zum Beginn des 17. Jahrhunderts*, part II, *Die Wildnis im östlichen Preußen, ihr Zustand um 1400 und ihre frühere Besiedlung*, Deutschland und der Osten. Quellen und Forschung zur Geschichte ihrer Beziehungen 7 (Leipzig: S. Hirzel, 1938), 16–17; Grzegorz Białuński, *Kolonizacja "Wielkiej Puszczy" (do 1568 roku) – starostwa piskie, ełckie, straduńskie, zelkowskie i węgoborskie*, Rozprawy i Materiały Ośrodka Badań Naukowych im. Wojciecha Kętrzyńskiego w Olsztynie 204 (Olsztyn: Ośrodek Badań Naukowych im. Wojciecha Kętrzyńskiego w Olsztynie, 2002); in German translation: id., *Bevölkerung und Siedlung im ordensstaatlichen und herzoglichen Preußen im Gebiet der "Großen Wildnis" bis 1568*, transl. Michael G. Esch, Sonderschriften des Vereins für Familienforschung in Ost- und Westpreussen e.V. 109 (Hamburg: Selbstverlag des Vereins, 2009). Lately: Stefan Striegler,

'Die Große Wildnis im 14. Jahrhundert – Wahrnehmung und Beschreibung eines geografischen Raumes,' in *Viele Welten des Ostseeraumes. Politischer, wirtschaftlicher und kultureller Austausch vom Hochmittelalter bis zum Beginn der Neuzeit*, ed. Paul Srodecki and Ludwig Steindorff (Marburg: Verlag Herder-Institut, 2024), 223–234.

15 Kurt Forstreuter, 'Die Entwicklung der Grenze zwischen Preußen und Litauen seit 1422,' *Altpreußische Forschungen* 18 (1941): 50–70.

16 *Cf.* Dusburg (S/W), 326–327 (book III, cap. 211); 436–437 (book III, cap. 326).

17 Alt-Wartenburg thus offers a rare opportunity for German-Polish urban archaeology to excavate a complete small town; *cf.* Felix Paul Biermann, Christofer Herrmann, and Arkadiusz Koperkiewicz, 'Alt-Wartenburg: Gründung und Untergang einer Lokationsstadt in der ‚Großen Wildnis',' in *Faszination Stadt. Die Urbanisierung Europas im Mittelalter und das Magdeburger Recht*, ed. Gabriele Köster and Cristina Link (Dresden: Sandstein Verlag, 2019), 274–277. The excavation campaigns are still ongoing.

18 *Cf.* Klaus Riel, 'Die Siedlungstätigkeit des deutschen Ordens in Preußen in der Zeit von 1410–1466,' in *Altpreußische Forschungen* 14 (1937): 243–254; confirming this: Grzegorz Białuński, *Przemiany społeczno-ludnościowe południowo-wschodnich obszarów Prus Krzyżackich i Książęcych (do 1568 roku)*, Rozprawy i Materiały Ośrodka Badań Naukowych im. Wojciecha Kętrzyńskiego w Olsztynie 195 (Olsztyn: Ośrodek Badań Naukowych im. Wojciecha Kętrzyńskiego w Olsztynie, 2001), 264–267.

19 Wiesław Długokęcki, 'Die Bildung der Grenze zwischen dem Deutschordensland Preußen und dem Herzogtum Masowien in den Jahren 1343–1422,' in *Grenze und Grenzüberschreitung im Mittelalter. 11. Symposium*, ed. Ulrich Knefelkamp (Berlin: Akademie-Verlag, 2007), 136–151. This border with Lithuania proved to be very stable until 1918, *cf.* Forstreuter, 'Entwicklung der Grenze,' 50–57.

20 *Cf.* Edyta Gawin, 'Miedzy Polską a Zakonem. Polityka Siemowita IV w latach 1386–1426,' *Rocznik Mazowiecki* 14 (2002): 9–25; Wiesław Sieradzan, 'Rozjm mazowiecko-krzyżacki z 1459 roku. Jeszcze o polityce książąt mazowieckich w pierwszych latach wojny trzynastoletniej,' KMW 2/224 (1999): 179–196.

21 *Cf.* Mortensen and Kühl, 'Die Besiedlung der Grossen Wildnis,' 1–13. Obviously based on the earlier works of Mortensen's in the 1920s and 30s.

22 *Cf.* endnote 2, and Grzegorz Białuński, *Siedlungswesen im Bereich der Großen Masurischen Seen vom 14. bis zum 18. Jahrhundert – Ämter Lötzen und Rhein*, transl. Christian Myschor, Sonderschriften des Vereins für Familienforschung in Ost- und Westpreussen e.V. 97 (Hamburg: Selbstverlag des Vereins, 2005).

23 *Cf.* also well summarized: Małek, 'Die Wege,' 430–431.

24 *Cf.* Riel, 'Die Siedlungstätigkeit,' 262.

25 Białuński, *Bevölkerung und Siedlung*, 24–25.

26 GStA PK, XX. HA, OBA, no. 4259.

27 Białuński, *Bevölkerung und Siedlung*, 34–35, 48, and 83 (also for the following figures).

28 Białuński, 48.

29 Białuński, 409–416 (summary of the study).

30 A good first overview: Bernhart Jähnig, 'Litauische Einwanderung nach Preußen im 16. Jahrhundert. Ein Bericht zum ‚dritten Band' von Hans und Gertrud Mortensen,' in *Zur Siedlungs-, Bevölkerungs- und Kirchengeschichte Preußens*, ed. Udo Arnold (Lüneburg: Verl. Nordostdt. Kulturwerk, 1999), 75–94. Here Jähnig also deals with the political contexts in the 1920s to 1940s.

31 Hans & Gertrud Mortensen, *Die Besiedlung*, part I, *Die preußisch-deutsche Siedlung am Westrand der großen Wildnis um 1400.* Deutschland und der Osten. Quellen und Forschung zur Geschichte ihrer Beziehungen 7 (Leipzig: S. Hirzel, 1937); part II (as in endnote 14). *Cf.* also on the situation of the Lithuanian

wilderness offices at the time of the Turkish tax registers 1539/1540: Grischa Vercamer, 'Die Türkensteuerregister von Ragnit, Insterburg, Saalau und Georgenburg (Einführung),' in *Die Türkensteuer im Herzogtum Preußen 1540*, vol. 3, *Ragnit, Insterburg, Saalau, Georgenburg*, Sonderschriften des Vereins für Familienforschung in Ost- und Westpreußen e.V. 88/3, ed. Hans H. Diehlmann (Hamburg: Selbstverlag. des Vereins für Familienforschung in Ost- und Westpreußen, 2008), 7*–31*.

32 The Mortensen estate is to be found at GStA PK, XX. HA, Rep. 300, Nachlass Mortensen (Karton 14, 1–7b) (henceforth: Mortensen, Besiedlung III [Ms.]).

33 The starting point of the dispute was an article by Adalbert Bezzenberger, 'Die litauisch-preussische Grenze,' *Altpreußische Monatsschrift* 19 (1882): 651–655, in which he did not take into account the younger age of these Lithuanian place names.

34 *Cf.* Arthur Hermann, 'Die Besiedlung Preußisch-Litauens im 15.–16. Jahrhundert in der deutschen und litauischen Historiographie. Ein Forschungsbericht,' *Zeitschrift für Ostforschung* 39, no. 2 (1990): 321–341.

35 Martynas Gelžinis, *Musų gimtine Mažoji Lietuva* (Vilnius: Mažosios Lietuvos Fondas: Mokslo ir Enciklopediju Leidykla, 1996), 477–478. On Lithuanian research in general: Hermann, 'Die Besiedlung,' 321–341. For the modern development of 'Prussian Lithuania': Algirdas Matulevičius, 'Deutsch-litauische Beziehung in Preußisch-Litauen,' in *Die Grenze als Ort der Annäherung 750 Jahre deutsch-litauische Beziehungen*, ed. Arthur Hermann (Köln: Mare Balticum, 1992), 25–45. In the 1920s, this debate was indeed a political issue, as attempts were made to fathom the original affiliation of 'Prussian Lithuania' (also called 'Little Lithuania' in Lithuanian works). Today, however, these aspects play a lesser role. All the more surprising is the Lithuanian attitude, which is still based on the erroneous linguistic-historical studies by Adalbert Bezzenberger. For a summary of the research up to 1924, *cf.* Paul Karge, *Litauerfrage in Altpreussen in geschichtlicher Beleuchtung* (Königsberg: Meyer, 1925), 5–35.

36 Gelžinis, *Musų gimtine Mažoji Lietuva*, 477.

37 When editing the manuscript, it became apparent that parts were revised up to three times (there are date notes in the handwritten margins).

38 *Cf.* Kurt Forstreuter, 'Die Entwicklung der Nationalitätenverhältnisse auf der Kurischen Nehrung,' *Altpreußische Forschungen* 8 (1931): 46–63.

39 'Bericht des Philipp von Creutz von 1526,' ed. Theodor Hirsch, in SRP, V: 384. Until 1525 he was *Pfleger* of Insterburg. Philipp von Creutz was then replaced by Johannes Pein in 1526. He had previously, yet very late, paid homage to the new duke (four days he resisted in doing so), *cf.* Grischa Vercamer, 'Ein Hochmeister wird zum Herzog: Reaktionen und Schicksal der letzten Ordensbrüdern in Preußen um das Jahr 1525,' in *Die Ritterorden in Umbruchs- und Krisenzeiten/ The Military Orders in Times of Change and Crisis*, ed. Roman Czaja and Jürgen Sarnowsky, Ordines Militares. Colloquia Torunensia Historica XVI (Toruń: Wydawnictwo Naukowe Uniwersytetu Mikołaja Kopernika w Toruniu, 2011), 213–239.

40 *Cf.* endnote 101. In general on the situation in the Grand Duchy of Lithuania: Werner Conze, *Agrarverfassung und Bevölkerung in Litauen und Weißrußland*, vol. 1, *Die Hufenverfassung im ehemaligen Großfürstentum Litauen*, Deutschland und der Osten 15 (Leipzig: Hirzel 1940); Carsten Goehrke, 'Siedlungsgeschichte des Ostbaltikums,' *Zeitschrift für Ostforschung* 37, no. 4 (1988): 491–492.

41 It turns out that the uninhabited area between Goldap and Marggrabowa, which can be seen on the 1540 map, is the border between the Masurian and Lithuanian settlements. The former border between the two ethnic groups essentially follows

the watershed between the Biebrza–Narew and Pregel (Pregoła) Rivers. Thus Mortensen believed that the Lithuanian settlement in the Angerburg district was only an internal migration from the northern districts, because the Lithuanian settlements there were quite few; *cf.* Mortensen, Besiedlung III [Ms.], chap. 1,88 a.
42 For example, GStA PK, XX. HA, OF 107, fol. 120r (a. 1372): *Sterken dem littowen*.
43 For example, GStA PK, XX. HA, OF 112, fol. 2r (a. 1303): *der czu uns geflogin hat durch beschirmunge cristensgelouben*.
44 Vercamer, *Siedlungs-, Verwaltungs- und Sozialgeschichte*, 286–287.
45 GStA PK, XX. HA, OF 112, fol. 13r (a. 1291), fol. 2r (a. 1303), fol. 2r (a. 1303); GStA PK, XX. HA, OF 91a, fol. 36r, 171r (a. 1305), fol. 38r, 172b (a. 1305).
46 However, these were probably not yet settled at around 1400.
47 Mortensen, Besiedlung III [Ms.], chap. 1, 1.
48 GStA PK, OF 105, fol. 158v–159r (a. 1333).
49 Vercamer, *Siedlungs-, Verwaltungs- und Sozialgeschichte*, 287.
50 LECUB, 1/IX: 620–621 no. 925 (of the year 1443).
51 *Cf.* the compilation in Anton Salys, *Die zemaitische Mundart*, part 1, *Geschichte des zemaitischen Sprachgebiets* (Leipzig: "Spindulio" B-ves Spaustuve, 1930), 132–133.
52 It is significant that in 1426 the captain of Samogitia speaks of only five people who had fled to the Order's land in the previous year (1425), and that six of his people were now living in the Order's land, *cf.* CEVMDL, II: 715 no. 1215 (in the year 1426). As can be seen, these are not large numbers.
53 Mortensen, Besiedlung III [Ms.], chap. 1, 1.
54 GStA PK, XX. HA, Pergamenturkunden, Schiebl. XIV, Nr. 11 (according to the manuscript ca. 1480).
55 ASP, V: 326–327 no. 110. Since after a series of such provisions on freedom of movement, marriage, etc., suddenly comes the text passage: *Item mit den Preussen sal man es halden noch alder gewonheit*, it would appear that the provisions listed before this refer only to new immigrants. It sheds an interesting light on the extent of this new immigration and also confirms the fact that until then (i.e. the 1470s) the old settlement strata included mainly Germans and Prussians.
56 AST, V: 327 no. 110 (in 1478).
57 GStA PK, XX. HA, OBA, no. 17738 (2 November 1492).
58 GStA PK, XX. HA, Ostpr. Fol. 118, fol. 585r (a. 1492).
59 Mortensen, Besiedlung III [Ms.], chap. 1, 7.
60 *Cf. Karte von Ost-Preussen nebst Preussisch Litthauen und West-Preussen nebst dem Netzdistrict*. Aufgenommen unter Leitung des Königlich Preussischen Staatsministers Friedrich Leopold Freiherr von Schroetter 1796 bis 1802, Section 6: Labiau, Königsberg, Wehlau. *Norurhatschen* (today part of Gusev), located directly near *Truszischken* (today not existing), also belongs to *Kalligkehmen* (today Lipovo) in 1554/1556, *cf.* Otto Barkowski, 'Die Besiedlung des Hauptamtes Insterburg unter Herzog Albrecht und Markgraf Georg Friedrich von Ansbach 1525–1603,' *Prussia* 28 (1928): 213. *Pruszischken* originally means 'Pruselkemen' and 'Pruszargkeym', *cf.* Barkowski, 'Die Besiedlung des Hauptamtes Insterburg unter Herzog Albrecht und Markgraf Georg Friedrich von Ansbach 1525–1603,' *Prussia* 30 (1933): 41, so that *Prusella* from *Zamaites* is the namesake of *Pruszischken*.
61 Mortensen, Besiedlung III [Ms.], chap. 1, 7. Unfortunately, the reference source is missing in the manuscript.
62 Mortensen, chap. 1, 7.
63 Mortensen, chap. 1, 8 (Oberratsstube Tilsit (1554)).
64 Mortensen, chap. 1, 8.

65 See also Mortensen and Kühl, 'Die Besiedlung der Grossen Wildnis,' 10. The household visitations of the entire Ordensland 1507/1508 (GStA PK, XX. HA, OF 134, and OF 135) did not include the offices of Memel and Insterburg (for this see GStA PK, XX. HA, OBA, nos. 27658, 27649). For Ragnit, the *Heerschauregister* (muster list) of 1516 is to be used as a substitute. These muster lists from 1519 are only available for Memel and Ragnit. For Tilsit, there is only a brief note that the office contained 321 peasants.
66 Vercamer, 'Die Türkensteuerregister,' 7–31.
67 These and the following figures from Mortensen, Besiedlung III [Ms.], chap. 1, 81.
68 Contrary to this, Małłek, 'Die Wege,' 432, took over from Marian Biskup the false thesis that the settlers moved from the borders along the rivers (i.e. exactly the opposite of Mortensen's research).
69 Mortensen, Besiedlung III [Ms.], chap. 1, 88.
70 Mortensen, chap. 2, 4.
71 Mortensen, chap. 2, 14.
72 *Cf.* Barkowski, 'Die Besiedlung,' *Prussia* 28 (1928): 176, who draws attention to a note from an Insterburg church register from 1544, which begins with the following words: "In 1544 the church [in Insterburg] was the only one in the main office". Gawaiten (today Gavrilovo) was not mentioned in a document as a second church village until 1558. *Cf.* also: 'Der Gang der Kirchengründungen (Pfarrkirchen) in Altpreußen' (map), in *Historisch-geographischer Atlas des Preußenlandes*, issue 3, ed. Hans Mortensen, Gertrud Mortensen, and Reinhard Wenskus (Wiesbaden: Franz Steiner Verlag, 1973). This wave of church foundations in the second half of the 16th century was initiated by Georg von Polentz, who urged Abraham Culvensis, an exiled Lithuanian and doctor of law, to support his people spiritually. Duke Albrecht was also interested in the spiritual welfare of his Lithuanian subjects. On 24 April 1547, he wrote to Georg von Polentz to ask him for an exact list of the Lithuanian inhabitants in the offices of Ragnit, Tilsit and Insterburg, including where exactly churches were located there and how much the pastors had in income, *cf.* Barkowski, 'Die Besiedlung,' *Prussia* 28 (1928): 192–193; and Jochen D. Range, 'Preußisch-Litauen in kulturhistorischer Sicht,' in *Deutsche, Slawen und Balten. Aspekte des Zusammenlebens im Osten des Deutschen Reiches und in Ostmitteleuropa*, ed. Hans Hecker and Silke Spieler (Bonn: Kulturstiftung der deutschen Vertriebenen, 1989), 60–61; Juozas Jurginis, 'Die Beziehungen zwischen dem Großfürstentum Litauen und dem Herzogtum Preußen unter den letzten Jagellonen,' in *Kulturgeschichte Ostpreußens in der Frühen Neuzeit*, ed. Klaus Garber (Tübingen: Niemeyer, 2001), 199–208.
73 In 1539 there were only 6 inns in 145 settlements in Insterburg, *cf.* Horst-Dieter Enzberg, 'Regionalforschung im historischen Längsschnitt am Beispiel der Sied-lungs- und Verwaltungsgeschichte des Hauptamts Insterburg bis zu dessen Neueinteilung 1723,' *Deutsche Studien. Vierteljahreshefte* 131 (1996): 247.
74 It is worth remembering his policy of retablissement. For example, Gumbinnen (today Gusev) (1724), Darkehmen (today Ozjorsk) (1725), Goldap (1570 town), Stallupöhnen (today Nesterov) (1722), Pillkallen (today Dobrovol'sk) (1724), Schirwindt (today Kutuzovo) (1725), Ragnit (1722), *cf.* Fritz Terveen, *Gesamtstaat und Retablissement* (Göttingen: Musterschmidt, 1953), 10–12.
75 Vercamer, *Siedlungs-, Verwaltungs- und Sozialgeschichte*, 232–233. The 13 *Schulzenämter* of *Hauptamt* Insterburg were not yet listed in the *Türkensteuerregister*, but they are already present in the *Amtsrechnung* of 1554, *cf.* Barkowski, 'Die Besiedlung,' *Prussia* 28 (1928): 194
76 *Cf.* 'Als adlig geltenden Familien mit Landbesitz im Herzogtum Preußen 1540' (map), in *Historisch-geographischer Atlas des Preußenlandes*, issue 5, ed. Hans Mortensen, Gertrud Mortensen, and Reinhard Wenskus (Wiesbaden: Franz Steiner Verlag, 1978).

77 Mortensen, Besiedlung III [Ms.], chap. 1, 76.
78 Mortensen, 59–61.
79 GStA PK, XX. HA, OF 124.
80 Hans Mortensen, 'Einwanderung und innerer Ausbau in den Anfängen der Besiedlung des Hauptamtes Ragnit,' in *Acta Prussica. Abhandlungen zur Geschichte Ost- und Westpreussens. Fritz Gause zum 75. Geburtstag*, Beihefte zum Jahrbuch der Albertus-Universität Königsberg/Pr. XXIX (Würzburg: Holzner-Verlag, 1968), 68.
81 *Cf.* Mortensen, 68.
82 Mortensen, Besiedlung III [Ms.], chap. 1, 35, states 10 oxen as the value for 2 large farms in the house book of Ragnit.
83 Antanas Salys, *Die zemaitische Mundart*, 137.
84 Mortensen, Settlement III [Ms.], chap. 1, 89 b.
85 *Cf.* Otto Natau, *Mundart und Siedlung im nordöstlichen Ostpreußen*, Schriften der Albertus-Universität. Geisteswissenschaftl, Reihe 4 (Königsberg/Berlin: Ost-Europa-Verlag, 1937), 105–107. For the year 1580 (the *Ragnitische Vermessung*, *cf.* GStA PK, XX. HA, Ostpr. Fol. 1307, fol. 130r) two Lithuanians are reported, Albertus Hermannus and Hanß Peterwiitz, who accepted 15 *Hufen* (hides) of high and wet forest on the village border in the village of *Aesernicken* (in the *Amt* Georgenburg), later the village was called Jodßen (today not existing) near Willuhnen (today not existing) for 15 years freedom from taxes. Furthermore, it is mentioned, that Albertus could read, write and speak Polish, understood German quite well and had good knowledge of the land in Samogitia and the entire Grand Duchy of Lithuania – so he offered his services. It can be seen from such sources that the Prussian authorities used special trained persons for peasant recruitments in Lithuania and Mazovia.
86 Mortensen, Besiedlung III (Ms.), chap. 1, 81–4.
87 Mortensen, Besiedlung III [Ms.], chap. 1, 85–88.
88 GStA PK, XX. HA, Ostpr. Fol. 1307, fol. 13b; *cf.* also Mortensen, Besiedlung III (Ms.), chap. 1, 85–86.
89 GStA PK, XX. HA, EM 91g, Nr. 1 (Heusarden oder Buden, a. 1584).
90 Mortensen, Besiedlung III [Ms.], chap. 3, 3: Tax system: As a rule, this was based on the previous quality of the land. Lithuanians who had not settled freely in the wilderness but had previously taken over fields from Prussians, paid interest like the Prussians and not according to the Lithuanian system.
91 *Cf.* also Vercamer, *Siedlungs-, Verwaltungs- und Sozialgeschichte*, 185–207. What is interesting about this earlier reform is that around 1400 the Order extended the holdings of the Prussian peasants in the *Komturei* of Königsberg from one hook (11.2 hectares) to 1.5 hooks or one hide (16.8 hectares) and thus – in a positive sense – had a strong regulating effect on the agricultural constitution of the Prussian villages (199). This shows that the smaller Old-Prussian peasants at the end of the 14th century were evidently much more productive than a few generations earlier. The Order could 'trust' them more. This may have been similar with the Lithuanian settlements.
92 Mortensen, Besiedlung III [Ms.], chap. 3, 17.
93 Mortensen, chap. 1, 108.
94 This effect was intensified in favour of the Lithuanians by waves of plague in the 16th century; *cf.* Vercamer, *Siedlungs-, Verwaltungs- und Sozialgeschichte*, 248. The Lithuanians were just as affected by the plague waves as the other ethnic groups but were able to fill the gaps with newcomers.
95 Fritz Gause, 'Johannes Bretke,' in: *Neue Deutsche Biographie*, vol. 2 (Berlin: Duncker & Humblot, 1955), 602. For the general value of 'Prussian-Lithuania's' cultural achievements in modern times *cf.* Range, 'Preußisch-Litauen,' 55–81.

96 Mortensen, Besiedlung III [Ms.], chap. 1, Annex: Krugliste, give a list of the inns founded in the wilderness. In the district of Insterburg: Insterburg (1516), Gaweisten (today Gavrilovo, 1549), *Gaudischkehmen* and *Galugneweis* = Pötschkehmen (today Krasnopol'e, already existing in 1555), Pillupönen (today Nevskoe, 1557, also a second inn there in 1560), Kattenau (today Nezhinskoe, 1562), Kussen (today Vesnovo, 1565), Bratricken (today Malaya Dubrovka, 1565), Tellitzkehmen (today not existing, 1566), Szameithkehmen (today Bolotnikovo, already existing in 1570), Bretschkehmen (today not existing, 1587), Brakupönen (today Kubanovka, before 1587), Schackeln (today Michurinskoe, 1588), Dopönen (today Pokryshkino, proof of ownership 1590) (= 13 inns in total). In the district of Ragnit: Wischwill (today Viešvilė, 1514), 2 inns to Ragnit (1548/1549), to Schirwindt (1548/1549), to Kraupischken (today Ul'janovo, 1551), Lencken (today not existing, 1556), Lasdehnen (today Krasnoznamensk, 1557), Pillkallen (today Dobrovol'sk, 1566), Daynen (today Dainiai, 1572 application for one inn), Kurschen (today Kuršeliai, before 1578 the captain of Ragnit had one inn created there), Kindschen (today not existing, already in existence in 1578), Schwirgallen (today Zavodskoe, already in existence in 1590) (= 12 inns in total). Around 1590 there were a total of 4 inns in Ragnit, 2 inns in Lasdehnen and Schirwindt, one inn in Wisborienen (today not existing), Schwirgallen, Pillkallen, Weszeningken (today Vėžininkai), Daynen, Baiorgallen (= Löbegallen, today Tolstovo), Kl. Warningken (today non existing), Nettschunen (today non existing), Wischwill, Willkischken and Lengken. In the district of Georgenburg 1584 Sesslacken (today Pridorozhnoe). In the district of Labiau: 2 inns at the river Gilge (today Matrosovka) and at the small river Wippe. The Mortensens intended to add the district of Memel (which is proven by a note).
97 Even if Wunder, 'Siedlung,' 90, emphasizes that the Lithuanians made little use of the towns themselves.
98 Mortensen, Settlement III [Ms.], chap. 6, 6.
99 Reinhard Wenskus, 'Namengebung und Namenwechsel im nordöstlichen Ostpreußen in der frühen Neuzeit,' *Altpreußische Geschlechterkunde. Neue Folge* 20 (1990): 34.
100 Vercamer, *Siedlungs-, Verwaltungs- und Sozialgeschichte*, 319, 340–342.
101 *Cf.* Mortensen, Besiedlung III [Ms.], chap. 3, 3.
102 *Cf.* Vercamer, 'Die Türkensteuerregister,' 10–13.
103 *Cf.* Mortensen, Besiedlung III [Ms.], chap. 3, 2–3. This tax was later converted into the *Mardergeld*.
104 *Cf.* Barkowski, 'Die Besiedlung,' *Prussia* 28 (1928): 195.
105 Türkensteuer, 3: 81–83.
106 This analysis was carried out for the Insterburg district in particular. For reasons of space, however, here the analysis results are not presented but only mentioned.
107 *Cf.* Mortensen, Besiedlung III [Ms.], chap. 1, 100. Around 1560 an interest amounted to about 5 loaves.
108 *Cf.* Mortensen, chap. 1, 96.
109 There were numerous complaints and petitions from the population about the injustice of the tax system; see Mortensen, chap. 3, 2–3, where further sources can also be found.
110 Mortensen, chap. 3, 5–6.
111 This term was most probably adopted from Lithuanian, *cf.* Conze, *Agrarverfassung*, 33–34; Mortensen, Besiedlung III [Ms.], chap. 2, 11–12. *Benders* were partners in the settlement project who came from the more distant circle of relatives. They are often attested to in the Turkish tax register. The Lithuanian *Benders* were then obliged to provide certain services to the main landowner (harvest help, etc.). They only appear very occasionally in the older Prussian sources and

only in the second half of the 15th century: for example, in a grandmaster's document from 1467 (GStA PK, XX. HA, OF 94, fol. 287r) for the Prussian Hans Konig, living in Samland, Hans Konigcke, a Prussian living in the Samland, *und haben uns vorczalt wie sie sich zu bender zcu sampne gegeben haben*, or likewise a Grand Master's document of 1465 (OF 94, fol. 337) for the cousins Hans and Michel, living in the Samland, *voreyninget und zcu Bender also vortragen haben*.

112 Mortensen, Besiedlung III [Ms.], chap. 2, 16.
113 Mortensen, chap. 2, 16.
114 In Białuński, *Przemiany*, 195, they are called *Zinser, Littauische Zinser*. He emphasizes that they should not be confused with the later high *Zinsers*. They often farmed on 3–4 hides, with the help of benders or gardeners. Unfortunately, the sources on this group are very scarce.
115 *Cf*. Barkowski, 'Die Besiedlung,' *Prussia* 28 (1928): 195–196 (for all evidence of levies).
116 Thus Białuński, *Przemiany*, 194–196, interprets that the *Zinser* (i.e. Lithuanian peasants) had a slight advantage over the *Zinsbauern* (i.e. Germans and Old-Prussians) but that basically there were hardly any differences. However, he himself hints to the fact that the former (Lithuanians) paid from their entire business, while the latter (*culmische* peasants) paid from each hide. A concise comparison is not possible and remains speculation.
117 *Die Türkensteuer im Herzogtum Preußen 1540*, vol. 2, *Memel – Tilsit*, ed. Hans H. Diehlmann, Sonderschriften des Vereins für Familienforschung in Ost- und Westpreußen e.V. 88/2 (Hamburg: Selbstverlag. des Vereins für Familienforschung in Ost- und Westpreußen, 2006); as well as: Türkensteuer, 3.
118 Vercamer, 'Die Türkensteuerregister,' 12*.
119 Vercamer, 10*, with examples from research.
120 Vercamer, 10*.
121 GStA PK, XX. HA, Ostpr. Fol. 368 II, fol. 41b.
122 *Cf*. Mortensen, Besiedlung III [Ms.], chap. 1, 84–86. For the early phase of Lithuanian settlement in the wilderness he also points to the fact that the Lithuanians not only accepted the cleared areas but even paid for uncleared land.
123 For concrete figures, see also Mortensen, chap. 7b, 115.
124 Georg F. Knapp, *Die Bauern-Befreiung und der Ursprung der Landarbeiter in den älteren Teilen Preußens*, part 1–2 (Leipzig: Duncker & Humblot, 1887); Georg von Below, 'Der Osten und Westen Deutschlands,' in id., *Territorium und Stadt. Aufsätze zur deutschen Verfassungs-, Verwaltungs- und Wirtschaftsgeschichte* (München/Leipzig: Oldenbourg, 1900); Werner Wittich, *Die Grundherrschaft in Nordwestdeutschland* (Leipzig: Duncker & Humblot, 1896).
125 A representative example was the Potsdam Max Planck working team "Ostelbische Gutsherrschaft als sozialhistorisches Phänomen" of the 1990s, *cf*. Carsten P. Rasmussen, 'Ostelbische Gutsherrschaft und nordwestdeutsche Freiheit in einem Land – die Gut des Herzogtums Schleswig 1524–1770,' *Zeitschrift für Agrargeschichte und Agrarsoziologie* 52 (2004): 25.
126 Gustav Aubin, *Zur Geschichte des gutsherrlich-bäuerlichen Verhältnisses in Ostpreussen von der Gründung des Ordensstaates bis zur Steinschen Reform* (Leipzig: Duncker & Humblot, 1910), 64, 67.
127 Mortensen, Besiedlung III [Ms.], chap. 6B, 118; *cf*. Vercamer, *Siedlungs-, Verwaltungs- und Sozialgeschichte*, 240: In the Turkish tax register, Moritz von Perschkau counted 45 gardeners under his command in the Tilsit district, and he also owned 50 peasants in this area – but this finding is unique for the 16th century.
128 Vercamer, *Siedlungs-, Verwaltungs- und Sozialgeschichte*, 239–240. Only about 2% of the villages of the year 1400 had become noble seats in the former territory of Königsberg commandery by 1540, in the sense that a nobleman sat there

and a village no longer existed. However, most early modern noblemen sat in the villages together with the peasants. The number of peasants belonging to the nobility was therefore negligible compared to the number of peasants belonging to the sovereign around 1540.

129 Mortensen, Besiedlung III [Ms.], chap. 6B, 27–33.
130 Supporting: Vercamer, *Siedlungs-, Verwaltungs- und Sozialgeschichte*, 240–241.
131 Mortensen, Besiedlung III [Ms.], chap. 6B, 40. They are particularly opposed to the publication by Friedrich Lütge, *Die mitteldeutsche Grundherrschaft und ihre Auflösung*, Quellen und Forschungen zur Agrargeschichte 4 (Stuttgart: G. Fischer, 1957), 21, like in this quotation (Mortensen, Besiedlung III [Ms.], chap. 6B, 40): "Die Tatsache, dass die west- und süddeutsche Grundherrschaft einen Gutseigenbetrieb, im Sinne Lütges eine Gutswirtschaft, und zwar sogar mit Gutsgesinde statt mit Fronbauern, keineswegs ausschließt, lässt nun auch die früher so klar erscheinende Grenze zwischen Grundherrschaft und Gutsherrschaft undeutlich werden. Die Unterschiede, die Lütge (48 f.) angibt, sind rechtshistorisch sehr wesentlich. Sie erfassen jedoch weder das Erscheinungsbild noch die tatsächliche wirtschaftliche Struktur wirklich voll befriedigend. In der Tat konnte nach Lütge auch außerhalb Ostdeutschlands ‚die Gutswirtschaft, die auf dem herrschaftlichen Eigenland (*terra salica*) der Villikationen getrieben wurde,. .die in unmittelbarerer und enger Beziehung zu diesem Herrensitz stehenden Bauern so intensiv erfassen und ein Herrschaftsgebilde von so ausgeprägter Geschlossenheit darstellen, dass im Hinblick darauf von Gutsherrschaft gesprochen werden kann". ("The fact that the West and South German manorial lordship by no means rules out any estate holding, in Lütge's sense an estate economy, and even with estate servants rather than with front peasants, now also makes the boundary between manorial lordship and estate lordship, which previously seemed so clear, unclear. The differences that Lütge (48 f.) mentions are very important in terms of legal history. However, they do not really capture either the appearance or the actual economic structure in a fully satisfactory way. In fact, according to Lütge, even outside eastern Germany the 'estate economy, which was practised on the manorial land (terra salica) of the villications, […] could encompass the peasants standing in a more direct and close relationship to this manor so intensively and represent a manorial structure of such pronounced unity that one can speak of manorial rule with regard to it". Mortensen, Besiedlung III [Ms.], 26: "According to the previous view, as it is represented for East Prussia, e.g. by Hans Plehn and also by Gustav Aubin in his excellent work on the development of the manorial-peasant relationship in East Prussia (1910, e.g. 64, 67) and most recently by Korth (Diss. 135 note 1), the noblemen in the East have operated a fairly strong manor economy from the colonization period onwards. They relied in part on the labour of peasants from the manor and to a considerable extent on manor employees. Gardeners, servants and free or unfree workers and servants are mentioned as such. What is the situation in our area?"
132 *Cf.* Mortensen, Besiedlung III [Ms.], chap. 7, 52–59. However, the large estates of this period were considerably smaller than the estates in the 19th century. Estates of 10–15 hides make the majority. There was therefore a subsequent expansion of these manors.
133 Mortensen, chap. 7, 52–54, 102–103.
134 Mortensen, chap. 7, 54.
135 Mortensen, chap. 4b, 22–24. Mortensen sees strong processes of assimilation of the Lithuanians with the Germans and Old-Prussians of the old settlement areas in the 17th century, which were expressed less by the language than by the general conditions. In the 17th/18th century, manorial regime spread across the whole of eastern Prussia, including the wilderness areas.

136 Cf. August Skalweit, *Die ostpreussische Domänenverwaltung unter Friedrich Wilhelm I. und das Retablissement Litauens* (Leipzig: Duncker & Humblot, 1906), 223–224.
137 Mortensen, Besiedlung III [Ms.], chap. 7b, 115.

Primary Sources

Berlin. Geheimes Staatsarchiv Preußischer Kulturbesitz, XX. Hauptabteilung, Etats-Ministerium 91g, Nr. 1.
Berlin. Geheimes Staatsarchiv Preußischer Kulturbesitz, XX. Hauptabteilung, Ordensbriefarchiv, nos. 4259, 17738, 27649, 27658.
Berlin. Geheimes Staatsarchiv Preußischer Kulturbesitz, XX. Hauptabteilung, Ordensfolianten 91a, 105, 107, 112, 124, 134, 135, 171, 172b, 185a.
Berlin. Geheimes Staatsarchiv Preußischer Kulturbesitz, XX. Hauptabteilung, Ostpreußische Folianten 118, 368 II, 1307.
Berlin. Geheimes Staatsarchiv Preußischer Kulturbesitz, XX. Hauptabteilung, Pergamenturkunden, Schiebl. XIV, Nr. 11.
Berlin. Geheimes Staatsarchiv Preußischer Kulturbesitz, XX. Hauptabteilung, Rep. 300, Nachlass Mortensen (Karton 14, 1–7b).
Acten der Ständetage Preußens unter der Herrschaft des Deutschen Ordens. Vol. V, 1458–1525, edited by Max Toeppen. Leipzig: Duncker & Humblot, 1886.
'Bericht des Philipp von Creutz von 1526.' Edited by Theodor Hirsch. In SRP, vol. V, edited by Theodor Hirsch, Max Toeppen, and Ernst Strehlke, 362–384. Leipzig: Hirzel, 1874.
Codex epistularis Vitoldi Magni Ducis Lithaniae 1376–1430. Part II. Edited by Antoni Prochaska. Monumenta medii aevi historica res gestas Poloniae illustrantia VI = Wydawnictwa Komisji Historycznej Akademii Umiejętności w Krakowie 23. Cracoviae: Sumptius Academiae Literarum Crac., 1882.
Liv-, est- und kurländisches Urkundenbuch nebst Regesten. Sec. 1, vol. IX, 1436–1443, edited by Hermann Hildebrand. Riga/Moskau: Verlag von J. Deubner, 1899.
Petri de Dusburg Chronica Terre Prussie / Peter von Dusburg, *Chronik des Preußenlandes*, translated and edited by Klaus Scholz and Dieter Wojtecki. Ausgewählte Quellen zur deutschen Geschichte des Mittelalters 25. Darmstadt: Wissenschaftliche Buchgesellschaft, 1984.
Die Türkensteuer im Herzogtum Preußen 1540. Vol. 2, *Memel – Tilsit*. Edited by Hans H. Diehlmann. Sonderschriften des Vereins für Familienforschung in Ost- und Westpreußen e.V. 88/2. Hamburg: Selbstverlag des Vereins für Familienforschung in Ost- und Westpreußen, 2006.
Die Türkensteuer im Herzogtum Preußen 1540. Vol. 3, *Ragnit, Insterburg, Georgenburg, Saalau*, edited by Hans H. Diehlmann. Sonderschriften des Vereins für Familienforschung in Ost- und Westpreußen e.V. 88/3. Hamburg: Selbstverlag des Vereins für Familienforschung in Ost- und Westpreußen, 2008.

Secondary Sources

'Als adlig geltenden Familien mit Landbesitz im Herzogtum Preußen 1540' (map). Prepared by Hans Mortensen, Gertrud Mortensen, Hans Dobbertin, and Heinz Henze. In *Historisch-geographischer Atlas des Preußenlandes*, issue 5, edited by Hans Mortensen, Gertrud Mortensen, Reinhard Wenskus, and Helmut Jäger. Wiesbaden: Franz Steiner Verlag, 1978.
Aubin, Gustav. *Zur Geschichte des gutsherrlich-bäuerlichen Verhältnisses in Ostpreussen von der Gründung des Ordensstaates bis zur Steinschen Reform*. Leipzig: Duncker & Humblot, 1910.

Bar, Premysl. 'The diplomacy of Sigismund of Luxembourg in the dispute between the Teutonic Knights and Poland-Lithuania,' In *Networking in late medieval Central Europe. Friends, families, foes*, edited by Beata Możejko, Anna Paulina Orłowska, and Leslie Carr-Riegel, 77–91. London: Routledge, 2023.

Barkowski, Otto. 'Die Besiedlung des Hauptamtes Insterburg unter Herzog Albrecht und Markgraf Georg Friedrich von Ansbach 1525–1603,' *Prussia* 28 (1928): 159–243; *Prussia* 30 (1933): 3–131.

Baronas, Darius, and Stephen C. Rowell. *The conversion of Lithuania – from pagan barbarians to late medieval Christians*. Vilnius: Institute of Lithuanian Literature and Folklore, 2015.

von Below, Georg. 'Der Osten und Westen Deutschlands,' In id., *Territorium und Stadt. Aufsätze zur deutschen Verfassungs-, Verwaltungs- und Wirtschaftsgeschichte*, 10–23. München/Leipzig: Oldenbourg, 1900.

Bezzenberger, Adalbert. 'Die litauisch-preussische Grenze.' *Altpreußische Monatsschrift* 19 (1882): 651–655.

Białuński, Grzegorz. *Przemiany społeczno-ludnościowe południowo-wschodnich obszarów Prus Krzyżackich i Książęcych (do 1568 roku)*. Rozprawy i Materiały Ośrodka Badań Naukowych im. Wojciecha Kętrzyńskiego w Olsztynie 195. Olsztyn: Ośrodek Badań Naukowych im. Wojciecha Kętrzyńskiego w Olsztynie, 2001.

Białuński, Grzegorz. *Kolonizacja "Wielkiej Puszczy" (do 1568 roku) – starostwa piskie, ełckie, straduńskie, zelkowskie i węgoborskie*. Rozprawy i Materiały Ośrodka Badań Naukowych im. Wojciecha Kętrzyńskiego w Olsztynie 204. Olsztyn: Ośrodek Badań Naukowych im. Wojciecha Kętrzyńskiego w Olsztynie, 2002 (Germ. translation: Bevölkerung und Siedlung im ordensstaatlichen und herzoglichen Preußen im Gebiet der "Großen Wildnis" bis 1568. Hamburg: Selbstverl. des Vereins, 2009).

Białuński Grzegorz. *Siedlungswesen im Bereich der Großen Masurischen Seen vom 14. bis zum 18. Jahrhundert – Ämter Lötzen und Rhein*. Hamburg: Selbstverl. des Vereins für Familienforschung in Ost- und Westpreußen, 2005.

Białuński, Grzegorz. 'Stan badań historycznych nad dziejami Prusów po 1945 roku.' *Pruthenia* 1 (2006): 41–78.

Biermann, Felix P., and Christofer Herrmann, and Arkadiusz Koperkiewicz. 'Alt-Wartenburg: Gründung und Untergang einer Lokationsstadt in der ‚Großen Wildnis',' In *Faszination Stadt. Die Urbanisierung Europas im Mittelalter und das Magdeburger Recht*, edited by Gabriele Köster and Christina Link, 274–277. Dresden: Sandstein Verlag, 2019.

Conze, Werner. *Agrarverfassung und Bevölkerung in Litauen und Weißrußland*. Vol. 1, *Die Hufenverfassung im ehemaligen Großfürstentum Litauen. Deutschland und der Osten 15*. Leipzig: Hirzel 1940.

Czaja, Roman. *Miasta pruskie a zakon krzyżacki. Studia nad stosunkami między miastem a władzą terytorialną w późnym średniowieczu*. Toruń: Wydawnictwo Uniwersytetu Mikołaja Kopernika w Toruniu, 1999.

Długokęcki, Wiesław. 'Die Bildung der Grenze zwischen dem Deutschordensland Preußen und dem Herzogtum Masowien in den Jahren 1343–1422.' In *Grenze und Grenzüberschreitung im Mittelalter. 11. Symposium*, edited by Ulrich Knefelkamp, 136–151. Berlin: Akademie-Verlag, 2007.

Ebel, Friedrich. 'Kulmer Recht – Probleme und Erkenntnisse.' *Beiträge zur Geschichte Westpreußens* 8 (1983): 9–26.

Enzberg, Horst-Dieter. 'Regionalforschung im historischen Längsschnitt am Beispiel der Siedlungs- und Verwaltungsgeschichte des Hauptamts Insterburg bis zu dessen Neueinteilung 1723.' *Deutsche Studien. Vierteljahreshefte* 131 (1996): 234–263.

Forstreuter, Kurt. 'Die Entwicklung der Nationalitätenverhältnisse auf der Kurischen Nehrung.' *Altpreußische Forschungen* 8 (1931): 46–63.

Forstreuter, Kurt. 'Die Entwicklung der Grenze zwischen Preußen und Litauen seit 1422.' *Altpreußische Forschungen* 18 (1941): 50–70.
'Der Gang der Kirchengründungen (Pfarrkirchen) in Altpreußen.' (map) In *Historisch-geographischer Atlas des Preußenlandes*, issue 3, edited by Hans Mortensen, Gertrud Mortensen, and Reinhard Wenskus. Wiesbaden: Franz Steiner Verlag, 1973.
Gawin, Edyta. 'Między Polską a Zakonem. Polityka Siemowita IV w latach 1386–1426.' *Rocznik Mazowiecki* 14 (2002): 9–25.
Gelžinis, Martynas. *Musų gimtine Mažoji Lietuva*. Vilnius: Mažosios Lietuvos Fondas: Mokslo ir Enciklopediju Leidykla, 1996.
Goehrke, Carsten. 'Siedlungsgeschichte des Ostbaltikums.' *Zeitschrift für Ostforschung* 37, no. 4 (1988): 481–554.
Guddat, Wilhelm. *Die Entstehung und Entwicklung der privaten Grundherrschaften in den Ämtern Brandenburg und Balga (Ostpreußen)*. Wissenschaftliche Beiträge zur Geschichte und Landeskunde Ostmitteleuropas 96. Marburg/Lahn: J.-G. Herder-Institut, 1975.
Hermann, Arthur. 'Die Besiedlung Preußisch-Litauens im 15.–16. Jahrhundert in der deutschen und litauischen Historiographie. Ein Forschungsbericht.' *Zeitschschrift für Ostforschung* 39, no. 3 (1990): 321–341.
Jähnig, Bernhart. 'Der Neustamm der Preußen. Seine Entwicklung von der Teilung Preußens bis zu den Teilungen Polens (1466–1772/93).' In *Zwischen Lübeck und Novgorod. Wirtschaft, Politik und Kultur im Ostseeraum vom frühen Mittelalter bis ins 20. Jahrhundert. Norbert Angermann zum 60. Geburtstag*, edited by Ortwin Pelc, 305–328. Lüneburg: Institut Nordostdeutsches Kulturwerk, 1996.
Jähnig, Bernhart. 'Litauische Einwanderung nach Preußen im 16. Jahrhundert. Ein Bericht zum ‚dritten Band' von Hans und Gertrud Mortensen.' In *Zur Siedlungs-, Bevölkerungs- und Kirchengeschichte Preußens*, edited by Udo Arnold, 75–94. Lüneburg: Verl. Nordostdt. Kulturwerk, 1999.
Jurginis, Juozas. 'Die Beziehungen zwischen dem Großfürstentum Litauen und dem Herzogtum Preußen unter den letzten Jagellonen.' In *Kulturgeschichte Ostpreußens in der Frühen Neuzeit*, edited by Klaus Garber, 199–208. Tübingen: Niemeyer, 2001.
Karge, Paul. *Litauerfrage in Altpreussen in geschichtlicher Beleuchtung*. Königsberg: Meyer, 1925.
Kasiske, Karl. *Die Siedlungstätigkeit des Deutschen Ordens im östlichen Preußen bis zum Jahre 1410*. Einzelschriften der Historischen Kommission für ost- und westpreußische Landesforschung 5. Königsberg: Gräfe & Unzer, 1924.
Knapp, Georg F. *Die Bauern-Befreiung und der Ursprung der Landarbeiter in den älteren Teilen Preußen*. Part I–II. Leipzig: Duncker & Humblot, 1887.
Lewerenz, Thomas. *Die Größenentwicklung der Kleinstädte in Ost- und Westpreußen bis zum Ende des 18. Jahrhunderts*. Wissenschaftliche Beiträge zur Geschichte und Landeskunde Ostmitteleuropas 101. Marburg/Lahn: J.-G. Herder-Institut, 1976.
Lütge, Friedrich. *Die mitteldeutsche Grundherrschaft und ihre Auflösung*. Quellen und Forschungen zur Agrargeschichte 4. Stuttgart: G. Fischer, 1957.
Małłek, Janusz. '‚Die Wege führen nach Preussen' – Migrationen der deutschen, polnischen (masurischen) und litauischen Bevölkerung in die preussischen Gebiete im 13.–18. Jahrhundert.' In *Studies on the military orders, Prussia, and urban history: essays in honour of Roman Czaja on the occasion of his sixtieth birthday / Beiträge zur Ritterordens, Preussen- und Städteforschung: Festschrift für Roman Czaja zum 60. Geburtstag*, edited by Jürgen Sarnowsky, Krzysztof Kwiatkowski, Hubert Houben, László Pósán, and Attila Bárány, 425–36. Debrecen: Printart-Press Kft., 2020.
Matulevičius, Algirdas. 'Deutsch-litauische Beziehung in Preußisch-Litauen.' In *Die Grenze als Ort der Annäherung 750 Jahre deutsch-litauische Beziehungen*, edited by Arthur Hermann, 25–45. Köln: Mare Balticum, 1992.

Militzer, Klaus. 'Probleme der Migration und Integration sozialer Gruppen im Preußenland.' In *Probleme der Migration und Integration im Preußenland vom Mittelalter bis zum Anfang des 20. Jahrhunderts*, Tagungsberichte der Historischen Kommission für Ost- und Westpreußische Landesforschung 21, edited by Roman Czaja and Klaus Militzer, 11–38. Marburg: N. G. Elwert Verlag, 2005.

Mortensen, Hans & Gertrud. *Die Besiedlung des nordöstlichen Ostpreußens bis zum Beginn des 17. Jahrhunderts*. Part I, *Die preußisch-deutsche Siedlung am Westrand der großen Wildnis um 1400*. Deutschland und der Osten. Quellen und Forschung zur Geschichte ihrer Beziehungen 7/I. Leipzig: S. Hirzel, 1937. Part II, *Die Wildnis im östlichen Preußen, ihr Zustand um 1400 und ihre frühere Besiedlung*. Deutschland und der Osten. Quellen und Forschung zur Geschichte ihrer Beziehungen 8/II. Leipzig: S. Hirzel 1938.

Mortensen, Hans. 'Einwanderung und innerer Ausbau in den Anfängen der Besiedlung des Hauptamtes Ragnit.' In *Acta Prussica. Abhandlungen zur Geschichte Ost- und Westpreussens. Fritz Gause zum 75. Geburtstag*, 67–77. Beihefte zum Jahrbuch der Albertus-Universität Königsberg/Pr. XXIX. Würzburg: Holzner-Verlag, 1968.

Mortensen, Gertrud, and Uwe Kühl, 'Die Besiedlung der Grossen Wildnis (bis 1618). Erläuterungen zur 8 Lieferung.' In *Historisch-geographischer Atlas des Preussenlandes*, issue 8, edited by Hans Mortensen, Gertrud Mortensen, Reinhard Wenskus, and Helmut Jäger, 1–13. Wiesbaden: Franz Steiner Verlag, 1982.

Natau, Otto. *Mundart und Siedlung im nordöstlichen Ostpreußen*. Schriften der Albertus-Universität. Geisteswissenschaftl, Reihe 4. Königsberg/Berlin: Ost-Europa-Verlag, 1937.

Range, Jochen D. 'Preußisch-Litauen in kulturhistorischer Sicht.' In *Deutsche, Slawen und Balten. Aspekte des Zusammenlebens im Osten des Deutschen Reiches und in Ostmitteleuropa*, edited by Hans Hecker and Silke Spieler, 55–81. Bonn: Kulturstiftung der deutschen Vertriebenen, 1989.

Rasmussen, Carsten P. 'Ostelbische Gutsherrschaft und nordwestdeutsche Freiheit in einem Land – die Güter des Herzogtums Schleswig 1524–1770,' *Zeitschrift für Agrargeschichte und Agrarsoziologie* 52 (2004): 25–40.

Riel, Klaus. 'Die Siedlungstätigkeit des deutschen Ordens in Preußen in der Zeit von 1410–1466.' *Altpreußische Forschungen* 14 (1937): 224–267.

Rutz, Werner. 'Phasen staatlicher Raumorganisation im ehemaligen Ostpreussen,' *Nordost-Archiv* 24/102 (1991): 1–25.

Saczyńska-Vercamer, Monika. *Władza i grzech. Supliki z terenów metropolii gnieźnienskiej do Penitencjarii Apostolskiej w XV wieku*. Warszawa: Wydawnictwo Instytutu Archeologii i Etnologii PAN, 2021.

Salys, Antanas. *Die zemaitische Mundart*. Part 1, *Geschichte des zemaitischen Sprachgebiets*. Leipzig: "Spindulio" B-ves Spaustuve, 1930.

Sieradzan, Wiesław. 'Rozejm mazowiecko-krzyżacki z 1459 roku. Jeszcze o polityce książąt mazowieckich w pierwszych latach wojny trzynastoletniej.' KMW 2/224 (1999): 179–196.

Skalweit, August. *Die ostpreussische Domänenverwaltung unter Friedrich Wilhelm I. und das Retablissement Litauens*. Leipzig: Duncker & Humblot, 1906.

Striegler, Stefan. 'Die Große Wildnis im 14. Jahrhundert – Wahrnehmung und Beschreibung eines geografischen Raumes.' In *Viele Welten des Ostseeraumes. Politischer, wirtschaftlicher und kultureller Austausch vom Hochmittelalter bis zum Beginn der Neuzeit*, edited by Paul Srodecki and Ludwig Steindorff, 223–234. Marburg: Verlag Herder-Institut, 2024.

Vercamer, Grischa. 'Die Türkensteuerregister von Ragnit, Insterburg, Saalau und Georgenburg (Einführung).' In *Die Türkensteuer im Herzogtum Preußen 1540*, vol. 3, *Ragnit, Insterburg, Saalau, Georgenburg*, edited by von Hans Heinz Diehlmann, 7*–31*. Sonderschriften des Vereins für Familienforschung in Ost- und

Westpreußen e.V. 88/3. Hamburg: Selbstverl. des Vereins für Familienforschung in Ost- und Westpreußen, 2008.

Vercamer, Grischa. *Siedlungs-, Verwaltungs- und Sozialgeschichte der Komturei Königsberg im Deutschordensland Preußen (13.–16. Jahrhundert).* Einzelschriften der Historischen Kommission für ost- und westpreußische Landesforschung 29. Marburg/Lahn: N. G. Elwert Verlag, 2010.

Vercamer, Grischa. 'Ein Hochmeister wird zum Herzog: Reaktionen und Schicksal der letzten Ordensbrüdern in Preußen um das Jahr 1525.' In *Die Ritterorden in Umbruchs- und Krisenzeiten/The Military Orders in Times of Change and Crisis*, edited by Roman Czaja and Jürgen Sarnowsky, 213–239. Ordines Militares. Colloquia Torunensia Historica XVI. Toruń: Wydawnictwo Naukowe Uniwersytetu Mikołaja Kopernika w Toruniu, 2011.

Vercamer, Grischa. 'Siedlungs-, Verwaltungs- und Sozialgeschichte der Komturei Königsberg im Deutschordensland Preußen (13–16. Jahrhundert). Zusammenfassende Worte über eine landesgeschichtliche Doktorarbeit und ein Plädoyer für mehr gemeinsame Projektarbeit unter Historikern.' *Blätter für deutsche Landesgeschichte* 148 (2012): 313–320.

'Verwaltung des Ordenslandes Preußen um 1400' (map). Prepared by Hans Mortensen, Gertrud Mortensen, and Reinhard Wenskus. In *Historisch-geographischer Atlas des Preußenlandes*, issue 1, edited by Hans Mortensen, Gertrud Mortensen, and Reinhard Wenskus. Wiesbaden: Franz Steiner Verlag, 1968.

Wenskus, Reinhard. 'Namengebung und Namenwechsel im nordöstlichen Ostpreußen in der frühen Neuzeit.' *Altpreußische Geschlechterkunde. Neue Folge* 20 (1990): 27–142.

Wittich, Werner. *Die Grundherrschaft in Nordwestdeutschland.* Leipzig: Duncker & Humblot, 1896.

Wunder, Heide. *Siedlungs- und Bevölkerungsgeschichte der Komturei Christburg (13–16. Jahrhundert)*, Marburger Ostforschungen 28. Wiesbaden: Otto Harrassowitz, 1968.

Wunder, Heide. 'Siedlung und Bevölkerung im Ordensstaat, Herzogtum und Königreich Preußen, 13.–18. Jahrhundert.' In *Ostdeutsche Geschichts- und Kulturlandschaften*, vol. 2, *Ost- und Westpreußen*, edited by Hans Rothe, 67–98. Köln: Böhlau Verlag, 1987.

7 Polish Nobility in Royal Prussia 1454–1506

Status, Position, and Migrations

Sobiesław Szybkowski

I

The issue of the presence of Polish nobility in Royal Prussia during the first half-century of the area's belonging to the Kingdom of Poland has already been dealt with by a number of Polish researchers[1]. However, a broader discussion of this issue by scholars is lacking. The present chapter will serve to remedy this gap in the research. Before moving on to the main subject, it is necessary to clarify a few points.

The first will be the chronological and territorial scope. The chronological frames of the analysis begin with the year 1454, which saw the incorporation of the entire territory of Prussia into the Kingdom of Poland. It gave way to a war between the Kingdom of Poland and the Teutonic Order, which did not end until 1466 with the Second Peace of Toruń.[2] Incorporating Prussia into Poland on an autonomous basis allowed the possibility for the Polish nobility to migrate to the area. However, it should be emphasized that it was not until 1466 that the boundaries of new Royal Prussia (eventually consisting of the provinces (voivodeships) of Malbork, Pomerania, and Chełmno) were finally formed. These provinces, together with the dominion of the bishops of Warmia (Germ. Ermland), came under the direct authority of King Casimir Jagiellon. The remaining part of the Teutonic Order's dominion in Prussia remained under the rule of the Grand Masters of the Teutonic Order (as so-called 'Order's Prussia', Pol. 'Prusy Zakonne'), who were obliged to swear a personal oath of allegiance to Polish monarchs.[3] The subject of this chapter's research will consist in the presence of the Polish nobility only in Royal Prussia. The year 1506 serves as the terminus ad quem of this study, which constitutes the date of the death of King Alexander Jagiellon and opens the new long era of Sigismund I's reign.

Yet, the term 'Polish nobility' still requires clarification in terms of the issues of interest here. In legal terms, we understand it as all persons enjoying privileges belonging to the noble state, both in the Kingdom of Poland and in its Mazovian fiefdoms (the Duchy of Płock with the Ruthenian Land of Bełz and the Duchy of Czersk-Warsaw). At this point, it is worth noting that already during the Thirteen Years' War and later decades, the dominions of

DOI: 10.4324/9781003502876-7

the Mazovian dukes were gradually incorporated into the direct dominion of the Polish kings.[4]

The period covered in this chapter marked only the beginning of the migration process concerning representatives of the Polish nobility heading for Royal Prussia. A process that had to face (as discussed below) certain limitations. Therefore, in presenting the issue of the influx of this group into the new Kingdom, it was justified to include in our analysis not only those who decided to associate themselves with Prussia permanently, but also those operating there temporarily, though not incidentally. This concerns primarily the Polish nobility, which was active in administrating the Prussian starosties in offices below the starosts. This will avoid including the two other categories of Polish nobles present in Prussia between 1454 and 1506 in the present study. The first one consisted of very numerous mercenaries from Poland and Mazovia, active in the area during the Thirteen Years' War or the later so-called 'War of the Priests' (1478–1479), but not binding themselves permanently to Prussia.[5] The other group comprised participants in the increasingly profitable trade along the Vistula River, which involved visits to Prussia on merchant business.

A few more words must be said about the source base relating to the discussed subject matter. In the case of the migration and activity of the nobility in late medieval and early modern Royal Prussia, there is a lack of nobility courts' books, which for the three above mentioned provinces of Royal Prussia have not survived to the present day at all. This contrasts strongly with the state of preservation of sources of this kind for other lands of the Kingdom of Poland, where numerous records, though not always evenly distributed for all territories, constitute a basic source of information for research concerning the nobles, including their migrations.[6] They are only to a small extent replaced in Prussia by the surviving council and jury books of towns (Puck (Germ. Putzig), Nowe (Germ. Neuenburg), Toruń (Germ. Thorn), Malbork (Germ. Marienburg), Chojnice (Germ. Konitz)), where entries concerning the nobility also occur. Also lost are the late medieval consistory books of the bishoprics of Chełmno/Kulm, Pomesania, and Warmia/Ermland, in which one would also expect to find information concerning potential noble migrants from the Kingdom of Poland and Mazovia. The same is true for the Pomeranian officiate in the bishopric of Włocławek and the Kamień/Cammin officiate in the diocese of Gniezno, whose territories included parts of Royal Prussia.[7] As a result, researchers are forced to draw their knowledge primarily from scattered documents and correspondence[8].

When negotiating the content of the incorporation privilege of 6 March 1454 with King Casimir Jagiellon, the Prussian noble and urban elites tried to look after the interests of the local noblemen and burghers in the best possible way. Although this document included the declaration that Poland's subjection of Prussia merely constituted a restoration of the *status quo*, this connection was in no way intended to jeopardize the rights of the locals, because "all dignities and offices and castles and tenements in Prussia" were to "be entrusted to the local inhabitants (*indigenae*) according to the custom of the other lands of the Kingdom".[9] It was therefore decided that none of the fresh arrivals in Royal Prussia should be granted office in the Prussian land offices hierarchies and should also not take up the office of starost in Prussia. However, the reference to "the custom of other lands of the Kingdom" was only partly true. In practice, after 1454 somewhat different rules were implemented in Royal Prussia compared to the 'old lands' of the Kingdom of Poland. In Polish parts of the Kingdom, in fact, the king could appoint only local inhabitants to land offices,[10] however, this principle did not apply to the starost offices. Indeed, many starosts came from outside the provinces where they held their offices.[11] It should be added that in the 'old lands' of the Kingdom, there were two forms of appointment by the king to the office of starost. The first one involved transferring the office "into faithful hands" (*in fideles manus*), which allowed the monarch to revoke it at any time. The second form pertained to the recording of sums (pledges), whereby the starosts and his heirs held their office until the money was returned by the royal treasury. Both forms were applicable in Royal Prussia. The established rules regarding all Prussian offices (i.e. land offices and starost offices) were therefore beneficial for the locals, who were concerned about political and economic competition from the newcomers. They were indeed intended to hinder the administrative careers of newcomers from Poland and Mazovia. However, they did not deprive the Polish and Mazovian nobleman of the right to reside in Royal Prussia.

In the case of the presence of Polish and Mazovian nobles in the first decades after 1454, another difference arises concerning Prussia and places of their origin. In the Kingdom of Poland and in the Mazovian duchies, regardless of minor territorial differences, the entire nobility was subject to the so-called 'Polish law'. Moreover, when it came to holding hereditary estates (which provided, in practice, strong rights to women to inherit land estates in the absence of male heirs and the right to inherit to relatives in the collateral line) the same was also true.[12] In Royal Prussia, there was a much greater diversity in the legal position of nobility, which lasted for up to twenty years after the incorporation in 1454. The so-called 'knightly law' (possibly of Polish origin), the so-called 'Saxon-Magdeburg simple law' (as a common land law), and the Kulm land law were in operation here, a consequence of the long reign of the Teutonic Order. The first two of these impaired the hereditary rights of women (land estates without male heirs passed to the lord), and all prevented inheritance of estates by relatives in the collateral line.[13] Major changes to the inheritance law were initially not introduced after the incorporation of Prussia in 1454, retaining all types of land law. The matter was finally settled in 1476, when all the nobility of Royal Prussia, by special king's privilege, received the Kulm land law. This legal system was considered the best for nobility in the Teutonic Order's times, especially as the king extended the possibilities of inheritance to collateral relatives.[14] This unified the legal system concerning the Prussian nobility and, in terms of the inheritance rights of women and collateral relatives, made it substantially similar to the inheritance rules known in the land law used in the Polish lands of the Kingdom.

Incorporating Royal Prussia into the Kingdom of Poland in 1454, even if it retained considerable political autonomy, was a necessary condition for the wider migration of representatives of the Polish nobles into the area analysed here. In fact, until 1454, Polish lands and Prussia were separated by a state border. This did not completely prevent permanent migration between the two countries, but it did seriously hinder it. Moreover, much of the first half of the 15th century stood for a period constituting a serious crisis in Poland's relations with the Teutonic Order, which ruled Prussia. This resulted in numerous military conflicts, conducted between 1409–1411, 1414–1422, and 1431–1435.[15] Their streak was only ended by the Peace of Brześć Kujawski in 1435, which ensured almost two decades of peace in Polish-Prussian relations. All this hindered cross-border migrations of Polish nobles to Prussia. Migrations to Prussia therefore occurred only sporadically and from territories directly neighbouring this country.[16]

The premises of the incorporation privilege of 1454 concerning exclusivity of the local inhabitants in nominations for Prussian land offices and Prussian starost offices did not endure. Indeed, the financial and military needs of the Polish Crown quickly resulted in suspending the provisions of the aforementioned privilege concerning the exclusivity of Prussians in manning starosts. A relevant document guaranteeing the Prussian Estates (i.e. Prussian nobles and burghers) that the practice of filling the local starosties also by persons who were not native to Prussia would only last during the ongoing war, was issued by King Casimir Jagiellon as early as 24 June 1454.[17] This made it possible to entrust the Prussian starosts to representatives of the Polish nobility as well as Polish and Bohemian mercenaries. Many of the representatives from these groups obtained bequests from the monarch during the war of 1454–1466, resulting from debts to the royal treasury from loans granted for war purposes or unpaid dues for military service. The lack of funds in the royal treasury led to the fact that the starosts were not paid off and the Prussian starost offices remained in the hands of non-Prussians even after 1466. Moreover, even during the war, King Casimir Jagiellon sought to change the rules resulting from the incorporation privilege. He did this by means of appointments granted also on the basis of a lease "to the faithful hands" (without a bequest concerning the starosts).[18] This trend continued after the war, despite constant protests from the Prussian Estates, suggesting that this was a breach of the principles of the 1454 privilege. This also applied to starosts held by bequest.[19]

It is also worth noting that in the case of the status of Prussian starosts there were significant differences compared to analogous offices in the Polish lands of the Kingdom. In the 'old' territories of the Crown, there were two types of starost offices. The first was the so-called 'judicial starosts' (Pol. *starostowie grodowi*), and the office holders were the real governors of the royal power in the area entrusted to them. This was expressed in, among other things, military power and possessing judicial jurisdiction over the nobility in the special form of a starost court (Pol. *sąd starościński*), namely municipal court (Pol. *sąd grodzki*). The position of the second group, the non-judicial starosts (Pol. *starostowie niegrodowi*) who held no jurisdiction over the nobility, was much weaker. This was because their competences were limited to managing the royal estates in the territory entrusted to them, from which they also derived income.[20]

Meanwhile, in Royal Prussia, military competence and supervision over the noble judiciary belonged to the voivodes. These were land officials appointed after 1454 who could only be appointed from among those native to Prussia. Therefore, the starosts had only the function of managers of royal estates and local Prussian castles with limited order/police functions, and as a result, their position was similar to that of non-judicial starosts in the Polish lands of the Crown.[21] This undoubtedly weakened their political position in Prussia in comparison to the judicial starosts in Poland.

II

The most important starost in Prussia, was the starost of Malbork. Its 'central' character resulted from the fact that Marienburg was, from 1309/1324 until 1457, the main residence of the Grand Masters of the Teutonic Order and its main house. Moreover, it was the best endowed starost in the whole Kingdom as its estate included as many as 76 villages and two towns. The starost of Malbork also resided in the former castle of the Grand Masters of the Teutonic Order. This location was of significant importance to the Prussian Estates, who hoped that the Malbork Castle would become the seat of the Governor of Prussia, who, by virtue of the incorporation privilege, was to function in the new part of the Kingdom of Poland. This office symbolized the autonomy of this new province, alongside a council distinct from the Polish royal council, known as the Prussian council. This was indeed the case following the purchase of the Marienburg castle and town in 1457 by King Casimir Jagiellon from a corporation of unpaid mercenaries in the Teutonic Order's service, whose leader was Oldřich Červenka, originating from Bohemia. He served the Polish king as a starost of Malbork very brief period (1457–1458).[22] However, in 1467 the Polish monarch abolished the governor's office. Attempts to resurrect it on a slightly different basis, namely as a general starost of Prussia or royal governor (Germ. *Anwald*), also failed. However, even the two Prussian governors, Johann/Hans von Baysen (Pol. Jan Bażyński) and his younger brother, Stibor von Baysen (Pol. Ścibor Bażyński), had to share the Malbork residence with the royal starosts managing the estates of the starost and the castle.[23] After Oldřich Červenka's tenure, the office of starost of Malbork was held only by Poles until 1506. These were Ścibor Chełmski z Ponieca (1458–1459),

Prandota Lubieszowski (1459–1460) who was a starost together with Jan Kościelecki (1459–1474), son of the latter, Mikołaj Kościelecki (1475–1478), Piotr Donin z Prawkowic i Ujazdu (1478–1484, Paweł Jasieński (1484–1485), Zbigniew Tęczyński (1485–1496). After Tęczyński left office, from 1496 to 1498, King John Albert did not appoint a new starost of Malbork. Malbork was administered by two governors (vicestarosts) who were, however, also Poles from the Polish lands of the Crown. From 1498 to 1500, the office of starost of Malbork was held by Maciej ze Służewa, and later by Piotr Szafraniec (1501–1504) and Ambroży Pampowski (1504–1510).[24] Of all these officials only Ścibor Chełmski z Ponieca (probably), Jan Kościelecki, and Paweł Jasieński received bequests concerning the starosty of Malbork from King Casimir Jagiellon. The King bequeathed to Jan Kościelecki a very large sum of 80,000 Hungarian florins, inherited by his son Mikołaj.[25] The other starosts of Malbork held office by appointment "into faithful hands", without royal bequests.

Research on the origins and careers of the aforementioned Malbork starosts demonstrates that the majority of them came from the magnate class[26] (the higher rank of Polish nobility).[27] However, only Zbigniew Tęczyński originated from a very prominent magnate family, which had a particularly long duration in a group of this status. However, he received the office at a time when his family was already among the close associates of King Casimir Jagiellon. Jan, his father, was the castellan of Kraków. As such, he could afford to be more politically independent, even remaining the leader of a group in opposition to the king's policy. However, by the 1480s–1490s, this was a thing of the past. Jan and Mikołaj Kościelecki also came from the group of the old magnates with a significant position in Central Poland. However, the representatives of their family were among the particularly close supporters of Casimir Jagiellon. However, it was Piotr Donin z Prawkowic i Ujazdu and Paweł Jasieński who owed their attainment of a magnate position to close cooperation with Casimir Jagiellon. Even though Donin's ancestors belonged to the magnate elite of Kuyavia and Mazovia at the turn of the 14th and 15th centuries, but his family underwent later a temporary decline in political significance. Piotr Donin owed attaining a high position in Casimir Jagiellon's environment to his close cooperation with the monarch as the victorious commander during the Thirteen Years' War and the War of the Priests, as well as his participation in managing the royal estates (he was also a long-time starost of Łęczyca). Paweł Jasieński, who came from the noble local elite of eastern Mazovia, belonged to similar social circles as Donin. He also achieved a high position thanks to his close cooperation with Casimir Jagiellon, as commander during the war 1454–1466 and the military conflicts fought by the Jagiellonians in later years (he was the treasurer of the Kingdom, and starost (not only of Malbork, but also of Bełz and Chełm).

Ambroży Pampowski's career should be considered very similar to the two previous ones, except that the starting point of his career was somewhat weaker compared to that of Donin and Jasieński, as he came from an ordinary noble family from Greater Poland, whose representatives had not previously achieved any significant position even on a local scale.

The career of Piotr Szafraniec z Pieskowej Skały was slightly more complicated. He came from a significant magnate family, which achieved its prominent position during the reign of Władysław II. However, its rapid decline followed his death. It was only Piotr who thanks to his close relations with King John Albert, initiated the return of the Szafraniec family to the ranks of the significant magnate families in the Kingdom of Poland at the end of the 15th century. The position of Ścibor Chełmski z Ponieca (from Greater Poland), was slightly weaker than the aforementioned. As a military commander, royal administrator of Eastern Pomerania, and short-lived starost of Malbork, he failed King Casimir Jagiellon. He was only promoted from the office of chamberlain of Poznań to the office of Poznań land judge.[28] He himself and his descendants, despite their quite considerable wealth, did not even form part of the local magnate elite of Greater Poland.[29] Meanwhile, Prandota Lubieszowski who hailed from Lesser Poland and was the starost of Malbork in the early days of the office, did not belong to the elite circles. As a captain of mercenaries, he possessed significant military experience, which was essential for maintaining the castle during the Thirteen Years' War.[30]

None of the aforementioned starosts acquired hereditary land estates in Prussia. Thus, they did not leverage their position as administrators of the largest and wealthiest Prussian starosty to acquire even the formal right for themselves or their descendants to seek Prussian territorial offices in the future and to become established in the new province of the Kingdom. As holders of land under knightly hereditary law, they would have had the opportunity to be recognized as locals and to attain full rights within the nobility of Royal Prussia. None of them, however, with the exception of the Kościelecki family, established family relations with the local Prussian noble elite which could have led to acquiring hereditary land estates in Royal Prussia. They built their property domain in the 'old' lands of the Kingdom. There, they also acquired further starost offices.

The case was slightly different for the Kościelecki family. The representatives of this family, in addition to starosties in Kuyavia (Bydgoszcz with the holding of Gniewkowo, Nieszawa, and temporarily Inowrocław), acquired starost offices in Royal Prussia (more on this below). Apart from Kościelecki, the Malbork starosts discussed above were only temporary residents of Royal Prussia, whose presence in the area was exclusively linked to managing the most important and richest of the Prussian starosties.

III

In addition to the Malbork starost, representatives of the Polish and Mazovian nobility held other starosties in Royal Prussia. We see a particularly large number of them in the districts located in the southern part of the

Pomeranian voivodeship. Only the Człuchów starosty was administered by newcomers from the Crown. The starosts were, successively, Mikołaj z Łabiszyna (1454–1455), Mikołaj Szarlejski (1455), Włodek z Danaborza (1455–1463), Mikołaj Pieniążek (1481), Mikołaj Kościelecki (1481–1486), Andrzej Górski (1486–1495), and finally, his nephew, Piotr (1496–1508).[31]

The Tuchola starosty was also held exclusively by Poles from 1454: Mikołaj Szarlejski, Jan Kościelecki, and his son Mikołaj.[32] The situation was similar in the case of the Świecie starosty, which, however, after the castle and the town in Świecie were recovered from the hands of the Teutonic Knights in 1461, the king gave to Jan Kościelecki and the town council of Toruń, which lasted until the end of the period of interest.[33]

Jan Kościelecki, and later his son Mikołaj, from 1455 held two small starosties: Jasieniec and Osiek, but in the case of Osiek, the original royal record referred jointly to Jan and Mikołaj Szarlejski (except for the years 1461–1466, when Osiek was occupied by the Teutonic Knights). Mikołaj Kościelecki only temporarily pledged Osiek first to the office of chamberlain of Człuchów, Georg von Dameraw (Pol. Jerzy Dąbrowski) and later to his brother-in-law Otto von Schymelow (nobleman from the Chełmno Land, Pol. Otton Szumiłowski), while Jasieniec to Jerzy Tworkowski, a mercenary from Silesia and his heirs.[34]

The starost of Nowe in 1456 was the aforementioned Prandota Lubieszowski, but the castle was soon conquered by mercenaries in the Teutonic Order's service. After the recovery of Nowe from the hands of the Order (1465), the castle, with the starosty, was given to another captain of the Polish mercenaries: Jan Garbacz Jasieński and his brothers Ninogniew and Mikołaj. This was done on the basis of a royal bequest. The Nowe starosty remained in the hands of the Jasieński family until the end of the period under investigation.[35]

Far fewer starosts originating from the Polish nobility can be recorded in the northern part of Eastern Pomerania. The starost of Gniew from 1464 until his death in 1489 was administered by the captain of the Polish mercenaries, Tomasz (Tomiec) z Młotkowa. He received the office as security for the debts of the royal treasury resulting from dues for military service. After him, the starosty remained in the hands of his widow Agnieszka ze Sławska, whose second husband was a Prussian, Sebastian Legendorf.[36]

The royal creditor was also the captain of mercenaries Piotr Szorc z Obrębu, who as compensation for unpaid wages received the starosty of Kiszewa, held by him until his death in 1503, and inherited by his heirs.[37]

In a similar way, the bequests of the starosty of Kościerzyna transferred to Przecław Słowak z Kłopoczyna, another Polish mercenary captain, in 1471. He was the local starost until his death (he died after 1484). The starosty was later divided, but half of it was in the hands of another Polish mercenary from the years of the Thirteen Years' War, Adam Wilkanowski. His heirs were still administering the starosty in 1502.[38]

The presence of Polish starosts in Starogard was incidental. In 1466, the castle was briefly administered by captain Gotard Bystram z Radlina.

However, in 1467, King Casimir Jagiellon bequeathed the starosty of Starogard to the aforementioned Tomasz Tomiec. Ultimately, however, he never assumed that office. Similarly, in 1505, King Alexander Jagiellon granted permission to Mikołaj Szpot z Krajowa in Lesser Poland to buy the starosty from Gertruda Pilewska. However, this matter was not finalized until 1509.[39]

Within the Chełmno Land, the starosty of Brodnica, directly adjacent to the Dobrzyń Land, was outside the control of the locals throughout the period under study. It was initially administered from 1456–1461 by the voivode of Brześć Kujawski and starost of Dobrzyń, Mikołaj Kościelecki ze Skępego. Kościelecki was assisted in these duties by his son, Wincenty, the chamberlain of Dobrzyń. However, between 1461 and 1462, the town and castle of Brodnica were occupied by Teutonic Order's mercenaries commanded by the captain Bernard von Zinnenberg (who originated from Bohemia). It did not return to king's rule until 1479, after the end of the War of the Priests. It was briefly managed by Wincenty Kościelecki. However, in 1481, on the basis of a royal bequest, Brodnica was granted by Casimir Jagiellon to a burgher from Kraków and captain of the royal mercenaries, Franciszek Gliwicz. It was not until 1485, after his death, that the starosty was bought from Gliwicz's widow by the voivode of Inowrocław, Mikołaj Działyński, a close relative of the Kościelecki family. The Brodnica starosty remained in his hands, and later in those of his heirs, until the early 17th century.[40]

Grudziądz was also mostly under the control of the starosts of Polish origin between 1454 and 1506. Between the years 1455 and 1459, the starosty was held by the pantler of Sandomierz and starost of Lublin Jan (the younger) ze Szczekocin, a native of Lesser Poland, followed by Jan Synowiec z Rzędowic (1459–1463). After his resignation following a royal bequest, Grudziądz starosty was given to Jan Skalski z Valdštejnu, a captain of the Bohemian mercenaries in the king's service (as security for unpaid pay from the time of his military service during the Thirteen Years' War). After his death the office was passed to his heirs. In turn, Wojciech Kiełbasa z Tymieńca, brother of Wincenty, Bishop of Chełmno, a native of Greater Poland, became starost of Grudziądz in 1481. The office was given "to the faithful hands", although he was also a royal mercenary during the 1454–1466 war and afterwards. In 1485, Kiełbasa was replaced by Jałbrzyk Jan Sokołowski, also a native of Greater Poland. He received bequests concerning the starosty, and consequently, after his death, Grudziądz fell into the hands of his brothers. Paweł Sokołowski and his heirs eventually became the starost of Grudziądz, and they administered the starost until 1546.[41] The next office of the starost in the southeastern part of Royal Prussia was held by a newcomer from the Polish lands of the Kingdom, specifically Golub starosty. This office was held briefly from 1472 to 1473 by the castellan of Sandomierz, Jan Hincza z Rogowa.[42]

In 1467, the captain of the king's mercenaries from the years of the Thirteen Years' War, Gotard Bystram z Radlina (in Lesser Poland), became the starost of Rogóźno as a royal pledgee, who soon annexed the castle and town of Łasin to this holding. After Gotard's heirless death, the holdings in question were taken over by his brother, Mikołaj Bystram. It was not until 1500 that the starost passed from the hands of his heirs to the administration of a Prussian, Lukas von Allen (Pol. Łukasz Mełdzyński).[43]

Another captain of the king's mercenaries from the years of the Thirteen Years' War, Adam Wilkanowski, received the starosty of Bratian in 1467 as security for unpaid pay from the time of his military service. However, he did not actually take over the holding until 1469–1470. He managed it until his death, after which his sons and later their heirs took over Bratian. The Wilkanowski family administered the starosty of Bratian until 1521.[44]

In the period under investigation, in the area of the Malbork province attempts by Polish noblemen to acquire only one starosty can be observed: that of Sztum (together with Straszewo). In 1503, permission to buy it out from the heirs of the deceased voivode of Malbork, Nikolaus von Baysen (Pol. Mikołaj Bażyński), was obtained by the aforementioned Mikołaj Szpot z Krajowa. However, the case was not entirely successful, as in 1510 only part of this holding was still in Szpot's hands.[45]

Polish starosts are completely absent from Warmia/Ermland, which was an episcopal dominion. It thus constituted an autonomous administrative unit within Royal Prussia and was administered by the bishops there. Therefore, there were no royal estates and thus no starosts.[46]

The above-discussed Prussian starosts originating from the Crown and Mazovia, and active between 1454 and 1506 can be divided into three groups. The first of these included representatives of the Polish nobility, who were close associates of the Jagiellonian dynasty, actively supporting King Casimir Jagiellon during the Thirteen Years' War (Mikołaj Szarlejski, Włodek z Danaborza, Jan Hincza z Rogowa, Jan ze Szczekocin, and Andrzej and Piotr Górski). A particularly large number of starosts in Royal Prussia came under the administration of the Kościelecki family of Kościelec and Skępe, who belonged to the same group, as well as to their close relatives from the Działyński family. It should be noted that their position in Royal Prussia was based on the use of royal property. There are no traces that they sought to acquire Prussian hereditary estates during the analysed period. Most of them also did not enter familial relations with the Prussian nobility. A different family policy can be observed only in the case of the Kościelecki family of Kościelec and the Działyński family, who married their daughters to Prussian nobles.[47] It must be clearly emphasized that the mentioned magnate families already had a strong property and political position in the Kingdom of Poland, which was also the main arena of their activity. Their striving for and acquisition of royal estates in Prussia was primarily intended to strengthen and consolidate the significance they already possessed.

The second group of starosts in Royal Prussia includes the royal captains of mercenaries who most often obtained Prussian starosties as security for debts owed by the royal treasury because of debts concerning payment of wages for military service during the Thirteen Years' War (Tomasz Tomiec z Młotkowa, Jan Synowiec z Rzędowic, Gotard Bystram z Radlina,

Jan Garbacz Jasieński, Piotr Szorc z Obrębu, Adam Wilkanowski, Przecław Słowak z Kłopoczyna, and their successors). They came from outside the magnate group, with the property position of some of them being extremely poor, as is the case of Tomasz Tomiec z Młotkowa, and Gotard Bystram z Radlina. Their acquisition of sizeable royal estates in Prussia, usually consisting of a castle, a town, and a complex of several or more villages, considerably strengthened their position within the Polish nobility. This resulted in the acquiring of Polish or Mazovian land offices, as most of them retained estates in the Crown or the Mazovian duchies. Their social advancement was also expressed by their entrance into advantageous marriages with women descended from Polish and Mazovian noble families, who were of higher status than them. However, written sources confirm that the main arena of their activity was Royal Prussia and they usually resided in castles which were the centres of the starosties they administered. Two of them, Piotr Szorc and Gotard Bystram, married Prussian noblewomen.[48] As a result of these relationships, they both gained potential rights to the hereditary estates of their wives, which resulted from the binding principles of the Kulm land law, granted to all noblemen of Royal Prussia by Casimir Jagiellon in 1476. In turn, the Jasieński family independently acquired considerable hereditary estates in Eastern Pomerania.[49] The hereditary estate in Chełmno Land (Lniska and half of Sampława) was also acquired by the starost of Bratian, Adam Wilkanowski. After his death, as a result of dividing his estate between his sons, it was inherited by Adam (the younger) Wilkanowski.[50]

A separate group of starosts included Mikołaj Pieniążek z Witowic, Wojciech Kiełbasa z Tymieńca, the Sokołowski family, and Mikołaj Szpot z Krajowa. What they had in common was that they all came from what we would now call middle-class backgrounds. For Pieniążek, relations with Royal Prussia were only occasional. The remaining became associated with Royal Prussia for longer. In the case of Wojciech Kiełbasa and the Sokołowski family, it is characteristic that their families sought social advancement through close cooperation with the Jagiellonian dynasty. For example Wojciech's brother, Wincenty, served as a royal secretary and diplomat for Casimir Jagiellon, and he owed his acquisition of the bishopric of Chełmno and the position of administrator of the Pomesanian diocese to the support of the king. However, Jan Jałbrzyk Sokołowski was a close collaborator of Casimir Jagiellon and his son Władysław (Vladislav), the King of Bohemia.[51] This resulted in Kiełbasa and the Sokołowski family acquiring the Grudziądz starosty. However, there is no source evidence that during the period under investigation, the aforementioned people acquired hereditary estates in Prussia or entered into family relationships with the local nobility. A bequest concerning three Prussian villages was also acquired from King Casimir Jagiellon by Mikołaj Szpot in 1491. However, he married the daughter of the chamberlain of Chełmno, Eberhard von Powersche (Pol. Eberhard Powierski), obtaining rights to her hereditary estate.[52] Only later in his career did he acquire the rights to the starosty of Sztum, by obtaining king's approval for its purchase. However, this was only the beginning of his significant career in Royal Prussia (more on this below).

In addition to the Prussian starosties, which constituted significant complexes of royal estates with castles and a towns, one must also take into account the distribution of smaller complexes of royal estates or even individual villages to newcomers from Poland and Mazovia. There are known examples of this type concerning the villages of Mosiny (Eastern Pomerania) as well as Słończ and Stablewice in the Chełmno Land.[53]

The possession of starosts in Royal Prussia by Poles and Mazovians also enabled them to pledge, with royal consent, royal villages in the estate complexes they managed. This practice was linked to financial needs. Source evidence confirms that the pledging of royal villages was carried out for the benefit of nobles from Poland. The pledging of royal villages concerned both noblemen with no family ties to the starost, as well as that person's relatives and affinities. This resulted, for example, from obligations to repay the dowries of sisters. There are particularly numerous examples of this type in villages belonging to the Tuchola starosty.[54] It seems that royal bequests to individual villages of royal estates and their pledging by starosts should be regarded as another channel that encouraged the permanent or temporary migration of Polish and Mazovian nobility to the area of Royal Prussia. This issue requires further, in-depth research.

IV

The holding of starost offices in Royal Prussia by representatives of the Polish and Mazovian nobility facilitated the migration of additional members of this social group to Royal Prussia This is because Polish and Mazovian starosts could not manage starosties alone. This required taking advantage of officials of the district administration. In accordance with Polish custom, which we also observe in Royal Prussia, the starost individually selected the officials of the board.[55] As a result, in the starosties administered by newcomers from the Crown and the Mazovian duchies, the officials subordinate to them were often their countrymen, not local residents.

The greatest effort was undoubtedly required to manage the largest Prussian and at the same time capital starost of Malbork. Between 1454 and 1506, most of the offices of the starost's administration were developed here. These included the governor of the starost's office – the deputy starost (Germ. *Anwald*), burgraves (Lat. *burgrabii*), treasurer (Lat. *thesaurarius*) of Malbork castle, administrators (Lat. *advocati*) of Wielkie Żuławy and Małe Żuławy (Żuławy Fiszewskie), administrator (Lat. *advocatus*) of Malbork. In addition to the persons performing the duties of these offices, there were also 'people in service' (Lat. *servitores*, Germ. *dienere*, also referred to as the starost's *familia* or his *familiares*) at the disposal of the starost. These people did not have specific functions but were in the service of the starost and carried out his orders.[56]

This group of people was diverse. It included Poles from various districts of the Crown, in addition to people from Mazovia. Some of them came to Prussia as mercenaries during the Thirteen Years' War. Among them were individuals who obtained bequests concerning royal estates in Royal Prussia from starosts who were indebted to them (e.g. Jakub Kostka, ancestor of the Prussian noble line of the Kostka family and his brother Jan Kostka, progenitor of the Mazovian Kostka family) or royal estates directly from Polish kings (e.g. Mikołaj Szczawiński and Krzysztof z Celin i Łodygowa). Some acquired Prussian hereditary estates or through marriage came into possession of their spouses' hereditary estates (e.g. Jakub Kostka and Mikołaj Szczawiński). There were also those who, despite a favourable marriage with a representative of a Prussian elite family, returned to their homeland.[57] It is worth noting here that even the lower offices in the service of the Malbork starosts were considered so prestigious by Polish and Mazovian newcomers that they were also accepted by persons holding simultaneously the starost office in other places of Royal Prussia. The deputy starost in Malbork during the term of office of the starost Zbigniew Tęczyński (and also later, until 1503) was the starost of Kiszewa, Piotr Szorc z Obrębu, and the administrator of Żuławy Wielkie was the starost of Grudziądz, Wojciech Kiełbasa z Tymieńca.[58] The office of Malbork deputy starost in 1496 was held by the starost of Grudziądz, Paweł Sokołowski. The office of Malbork treasurer in the years 1500–1501 and administrator of Malbork in the years 1502–1503 was held by starost of Starogard, Mikołaj Szpot z Krajowa.[59]

It seems that also in the case of other Prussian starosties administered by Poles and Mazovians, it should be expected that their countrymen were present among their administration. The Polish 'people in service' (*familiares*) and officials of the board are mentioned in sources related to the activities of the Polish starosts managing the starosties of Gniew, Tuchola, and Człuchów.[60]

The issue of Polish and Mazovian noblemen serving on the board of Prussian starosts obviously still requires further research. The sources on which it can be based are not satisfactory. However, the presented examples seem to indicate that participation by this group in the starost administration constituted another channel through which temporary or permanent migrations of Poles and Mazovians to the area of Royal Prussia took place. In some of the described cases, it was even an introduction to gaining a prominent position in the modern elite of Royal Prussia in the future.

V

The temporary or more permanent migration of Polish nobility to Royal Prussia was also influenced by the fact that the Polish clergy held bishoprics whose capitals were located on the territory of the former Teutonic Order's dominion, however, such situations were not frequent in the analysed period. Only Wincenty Kiełbasa served as Bishop of Chełmno for an extended period (1457–1479) while also holding the position of administrator of the Pomesanian bishopric from 1466 to 1479, a territory that was under the authority of the Grand Masters of the Teutonic Order.[61] Bishops had courts at their disposal which, at times, could be quite extensive. These courts often included people who shared their same places of origin.[62] There is the source evidence that Wincenty Kiełbasa's courtiers originated from the Crown. It is a list of witnesses to his 1469 document listing his 'courtiers and people in service' (Lat. *curienses et servitores*).[63]

Bishops also had the right to pledge property belonging to their endowment. Therefore, theoretically, as the Bishop of Chełmno, Wincenty Kiełbasa could have mortgaged his episcopal estates to newcomers from Poland. However, at this stage of the research there is no source evidence for this. What is known is that he had demonstrably pledged his estates on the territory of the bishopric of Pomesania to newcomers from the Crown (bequest to Trumiejki Nowe in 1470, in the amount of 200 marks).[64]

Another channel which brought Polish nobility to Royal Prussia can be observed in the disposal of landed estates by Prussian cathedral chapters.[65] The lack of sources prevents this phenomenon from being shown more widely. However, it is known to have occurred at least on one occasion, namely the granting of the village of Słupy in the Kurzętnik estate in 1470.[66] The participation of Polish nobility in the administration of the estates of bishops and cathedral chapters in Royal Prussia may also have played a role in bringing Polish nobility into the region, as in the case of participation in the administration of Prussian starosties. It is known that in the 15th century, the estate of the property of the bishopric of Włocławek in Eastern Pomerania was managed by administrators (*procuratores*) residing in Subkowy near Gdańsk. These were not always representatives of the clergy.[67] Perhaps a similar practice took place during the reign of Wincenty Kiełbasa over the bishopric of Chełmno.

VI

The most glaring problem of the influx of Polish nobility into Royal Prussia consists in identifying noblemen who had no connection with the administration of the Prussian starosties but were linked with this territory only as a result of acquiring landed estates there. The acquisition of land assets in Prussia by newcomers could occur through purchase or exchange, or alternatively through marriage to heiresses of local estates governed by Kulm land law. The primary obstacle consists in the lack of sources documenting the activities of the courts for the noblemen in Royal Prussia. This is only slightly compensated for by the town (jury) books, in which it is possible to find incidental entries concerning the affairs of the nobility.

The analysed materials concerning the Chełmno Land indicate that, indeed, after the end of the war in 1466, noblemen from the neighbouring lands of the Crown began to come into possession of noble estates in the region. These men primarily came from the Dobrzyń Land and Kuyavia, but those living in other Polish and Mazovian lands can also be identified. Polish ownership between 1466 and 1506 can be seen there in the villages: *Jerzmieniec* (near Unisław), Orzechówek, Trzcianka, Trzebcz, Dźwierzno, Święte, Wałdówek, Żygląd, Szewa, Obrąb, Salno, Bursztynów, Klęczkowo, and Zaskocz. The estates located there came into the possession of representatives of the Polish nobility as a result of purchases, marriages with Prussian noblewomen, and under unknown circumstances.[68] However, these estates did not always remain permanently in the hands of the Polish nobility. In fact, it sometimes happened that they were returned to the Prussians due to a sale, or the closest relatives of the wives of Polish noblemen bought their estates.[69]

Far fewer examples of a similar type are also recorded in southern part of Eastern Pomerania (due to the lack of available source material). We have already mentioned the acquisition of estates in the Nowe district by the starosts of Jasieński family (Bąkowo, Płochocin, and Krzewiny). However, it should be added that they bought these estates from, among others, Polish noblemen Włodek (Władysław) Sarnowski (from the Gniezno county) and Szymon Swawola, who came into their possession through marriages with heiresses.[70] Similar activity is to be expected for other territories in Eastern Pomerania; however, this issue requires further research.[71]

The property expansion of the Polish nobility unconnected with the starosty administration in Royal Prussia resulting from acquiring estates through purchases or marriages started from the territories directly bordering the lands of the Polish land of the Crown. In the period analysed here, this phenomenon has not yet occurred in the northern regions of Royal Prussia. This is indicated, for example, by analysing the town (jury) book of Malbork. Polish and Mazovian noblemen non-related to the administration of the Malbork starosty are not recorded at all in this book in the context of acquiring and possessing estates under hereditary law.

To summarize, the process of property expansion of the Polish nobility in Royal Prussia 1454–1506 was only in its early stages. It probably took on intensity in the later period. This is indicated by recent analyses of the origins of landowners in the Chełmno Land in the second half of the 16th century, of whom just over 50% were said to have originated in Poland (although this result seems greatly exaggerated due to the research method used).[72]

VII

The first representatives of the Polish and Mazovian nobility to arrive in Prussia after the incorporation in 1454 were the royal mercenaries, their commanders (captains), and the administrators of the starosties. Most of the mercenaries left the area after the end of the war, although there were again temporary influxes of this category of newcomers due to the conflicts waged with the Bishop of Warmia/Ermland, Nikolaus Tungen, and the Teutonic Order in the 1470s (the 'War of the Priests'). Only a few commanders of the mercenaries permanently allied themselves with Royal Prussia, having received grants of Prussian starosts due to the indebtedness of the royal treasury for their military service during the war of 1454–1466. Similarly, Polish magnates financially supporting the royal treasury during the years of the conflict and afterwards became the owners of Prussian starosties. The unpaid debts of the treasury meant that starosts with bequests became almost hereditary assets of Polish and Mazovian newcomers, as they were inherited by successive generations of their heirs, right into the modern era. They also became the subject of transactions between them resulting from pledges and dowry repayments to women from their families. Polish starosts in the most important Prussian starost of Malbork were also appointed by the king himself, undoubtedly in order to maintain control over the unruly Prussian Estates. This situation continued throughout the period under observation, despite the constant protests of the elites of local origin and their strong pressure on the monarch.

The largest number of Prussian starosts administered by Polish and Mazovian nobles is recorded in the southern part of Eastern Pomerania and in the Chełmno Land. In the northern part of Royal Prussia, the starosts of the Malbork should be highlighted. Poles and Mazovians are also recorded in the northern part of Eastern Pomerania (starost of Gniew, Kiszewa, and Kościerzyna). Some Polish starosts in Royal Prussia also bonded with their new homeland by acquiring hereditary estates and marriages to women descended from Prussian noble families. This resulted in them coming into possession of their spouses' hereditary estates. Poles and Mazovians came into possession of Prussian royal estates of a rank lower than a starosty as a result of royal pledges or pledging by starosts who were indebted to them.

The presence of the starosts of Polish and Mazovian origin in Prussia also resulted in the arrival of their countrymen, who were employed in the administration of the starosties they held. In many cases, this also resulted in newcomers from this category acquiring the right to the Prussian royal estates pledged to them, acquiring the hereditary estates there, and marrying Prussian noblewomen.

The process of acquiring land estates in Royal Prussia through purchases and marriages by Polish and Mazovian nobility not associated with the management of the starosties is less perceptible. This is due to the lack of written sources that could illuminate this problem better. Despite this, it is possible to present quite a few examples of this type in the Chełmno Land directly bordering the Polish land of the Crown, and somewhat fewer in the southern parts of Eastern Pomerania.

As a result of the research conducted in this study, it can cautiously be assumed that in the first fifty years of Royal Prussia's existence, the most significant channel that led to permanent (or longer term) migration of the Polish and Mazovian nobility into this country was the possibility to use the Prussian royal estates. The migration initiated by the incorporation in 1454 appears to be an extended process of a continuous nature, in contrast to a rapid transformation. Polish and Mazovian nobles settled in Royal Prussia and tied themselves more firmly to this territory despite the restrictions imposed on the newcomers by the provisions of the incorporation privilege in terms of holding Prussian Land and starosty offices. They also came across resentment from the local noblemen perceiving them (and rightly so) as economic and political competitors. Despite this, Poles and Mazovians were permanently associated with Royal Prussia, and this phenomenon was one of the elements of the progressive integration of this country with the remaining (Polish) land of the Crown in the following decades.

Notes

1 For example, see Wojciech Kętrzyński, *O narodowości polskiej w Prusach Zachodnich za czasów krzyżackich. Studium historyczno-etnograficzne* (Kraków: Drukarnia Uniwersytetu Jagiellońskiego, 1874), 42–64, 75; id., *O ludności Polskiej w Prusiech niegdyś krzyżackich* (Olsztyn: Ośrodek Badań Naukowych i Towarzystwo Naukowe im. Wojciech Kętrzyński in Olsztyn, 2009, 2nd ed. (1st ed. Lwów: Zakład Narodowy im. Ossolińskich, 1882)); Karol Górski, *Pomorze w wojnie trzynastoletniej* (Oświęcim: Wydawnictwo Napoleon V, 2014, 2nd ed. (1st ed. Poznań: Poznańskie Towarzystwo Przyjaciół Nauk, 1932)), 146–172; id., *Starostowie malborscy w latach 1457–1510. Pierwsze półwiecze polskiego Malborka*, Roczniki Towarzystwa Naukowego w Toruniu 63, no. 1 (Toruń: Towarzystwo Naukowe w Toruniu, 1960); Beata Możejko, 'Gotard z Radlina – działalność w Prusach Królewskich,' in *Społeczeństwo Polski średniowiecznej*, vol. 10, ed. Stefan K. Kuczyński (Warszawa: Wydawnictwo DiG, 2004) 229–253; ead., 'Agnieszka Zarembówna i Sebastian Legendorf a starostwo gniewskie w latach 1489–1504,' *Społeczeństwo Polski średniowiecznej*, vol. 11, ed. Stefan K. Kuczyński (Warszawa: Wydawnictwo DiG, 2011), 225–249; Sobiesław Szybkowski, 'Starostowie z Korony w Prusach Królewskich,' in *Jagiellonowie i ich świat. Centrum a peryferie w systemie władzy Jagiellonów*, eds. Bożena Czwojdrak, Jerzy Sperka, and Piotr Węcowski (Kraków: Towarzystwo Naukowe Societas Vistulana, 2018), 53–100; id., 'Przybysze z Korony i Mazowsza w zarządzie starostwa malborskiego w końcu średniowiecza. Piotr z Rembielina, Mikołaj Szczawiński i Krzysztof z Łodygowa i Celin,' in *Homini, qui in honore fuit. Księga pamiątkowa poświęcona śp. Profesorowi Grzegorzowi Białuńskiemu*, eds. Alina Dobrosielska, Aleksander Pluskowski, and Seweryn Szczepański (Olsztyn: Towarzystwo Naukowe Pruthenia/Uniwersytet Warmińsko-Mazurski w Olsztynie, 2020), 377–390; id., 'Pochodzenie Szczawińskich herbu Dąbrowa z Prus Królewskich,' in *Genealogia, prozopografia i dzieje społeczeństw na historycznych obszarach Pomorza w okresie przedindustrialnym (od średniowiecza po wiek XIX)*, eds. Sławomir Kościelak, Sobiesław Szybkowski, and Tomasz Rembalski (Gdańsk: Wydawnictwo Uniwersytetu Gdańskiego, 2020), 61–76; id., 'Urzędnicy zarządu starostwa malborskiego podczas kadencji starościńskiej Zbigniewa Tęczyńskiego (1485–1496). Studium prozopograficzne,' in *Regnum defendo ense et alis tego stricto – Królestwa bronię dobytym mieczem i osłaniam skrzydłami. Malbork w Prusach Królewskich*, vol. 1, *Prusy Królewskie i Malbork w okresie staropolskim (1454–1772)*, eds. Rafał Panfil and Artur Dobry (Malbork: Muzeum Zamkowe, 2021), 22–37.

2 Marian Biskup, *Zjednoczenie Pomorza Wschodniego z Polską w połowie XV wieku* (Warszawa: Państwowe Wydawnictwo Naukowe, 1959); id., *Trzynastoletnia wojna z zakonem krzyżackim 1454–1466* (Warszawa: Wydawnictwo Obrony Narodowej, 1967); id., 'Rozwój gospodarki czynszowej i utrwalenie ustroju stanowego na Pomorzu Wschodnim pod rządami krzyżackimi (1310–1466),' in *Historia Pomorza*, vol. I, *Do roku 1466*, part II, ed. Gerard Labuda (Poznań: Wydawnictwo Poznańskie, 1969), 727–743; id., *Wojny Polski z zakonem krzyżackim 1308–1521* (Gdańsk: Wydawnictwo Marpress, 1993), 200–259; Marian Biskup, 'Załamanie się państwa krzyżackiego w XV w.,' in Marian Biskup and Gerard Labuda, *Dzieje zakonu krzyżackiego w Prusach. Gospodarka – Społeczeństwo – Państwo – Ideologia* (Gdańsk: Wydawnictwo Morskie, 1988), 404–418; Jacek Wijaczka, 'Prusy Królewskie. Dzieje polityczne do 1660 r.,' in *Prusy Królewskie. Społeczeństwo, kultura, gospodarka 1454–1772*, ed. Edmund Kizik (Gdańsk: Muzeum Narodowe w Gdańsku, 2012), 34–39.

3 Biskup, *Trzynastoletnia wojna*, 703–709; idem, 'Zjednoczenie,' 740–743; id., 'Prusy Królewskie i Krzyżackie (1466–1657),' in *Historia Pomorza*, in *Historia Pomorza*, vol. II, *Do roku 1815*, part I, *1464–66–1648/57*, ed. Gerard Labuda (Poznań: Wydawnictwo Poznańskie, 1976), 42–45; id., *Wojny*, 255–259; Maksymilian Grzegorz, *Analiza dyplomatyczno-sfragistyczna dokumentów traktatu toruńskiego 1466 r.*, Roczniki Towarzystwa Naukowego w Toruniu 75, no. 1 (Toruń: Towarzystwo Naukowe w Toruniu, 1970), 170–215; Biskup, 'Załamanie się państwa,' 415–417; Krzysztof Mikulski, *Urzędnicy Prus Królewskich XV–XVIII wieku. Spisy* (Wrocław: Zakład Narodowy imienia Ossolińskich and Wydawnictwo Polskiej Akademii Nauk, 1990), 6; Edmund Kizik, 'Uwagi wstępne. Prusy Królewskie: środowisko geograficzne, administracja, geografia,' in *Prusy Królewskie*, ed. Kizik, 17, 18; Adam Szweda, 'II pokój toruński,' in *Toruń miastem pokoju. II pokój toruński*, ed. Piotr Oliński and Waldemar Rozynkowski (Toruń: Wydawnictwo Adam Marszałek, 2016), 48–59.

4 Henryk Samsonowicz, 'Dzieje polityczne (połowa XIV – początek XVI w.),' in *Dzieje Mazowsza do 1526 roku*, eds. Aleksander Gieysztor and Henryk Samsonowicz (Warszawa: Wydawnictwo Naukowe PWN, 1994), 226–9; Janusz Grabowski, *Dynastia Piastów mazowieckich* (Kraków: Wydawnictwo Avalon, 2012), 137–141, 174, 175, and 189–191.

5 This issue awaits further research, because it concerns a numerous group of several thousand people, see Górski, *Pomorze*, 139–146; Biskup, *Trzynastoletnia*, 714–719; Marian Biskup, 'Z zagadnień wojskowości polskiej z okresu wojny trzynastoletniej,' in Marian Biskup and Karol Górski, *Kazimierz Jagiellończyk. Zbiór studiów o Polsce drugiej połowy XV wieku* (Warszawa: Państwowe Wydawnictwo Naukowe, 1987), 146–153.

6 Klemens Bruski, *Lokalne elity rycerstwa na Pomorzu Gdańskim w okresie panowania zakonu krzyżackiego. Studium prozopograficzne* (Gdańsk: Wydawnictwo Uniwersytetu Gdańskiego, 2002), 15, 16; Sobiesław Szybkowski, 'Elita rycerska krzyżackich Prus w świetle listy gwarantów pokoju brzeskiego z 1436 r. Próba charakterystyki,' *Studia z Dziejów Średniowiecza* 26 (2023): 238–241.

7 APByd, 1675, 33; APG, 519, nr 41; APG, 508, nr 1329; KŁMN; KŁSMT (1479–1515), I–II; Andrzej Tomczak, *Kancelaria biskupów włocławskich w okresie księgi wpisów (XV–XVIII w.)*, Roczniki Towarzystwa Naukowego w Toruniu 69, no 3 (Toruń, Towarzystwo Naukowe w Toruniu, 1964), 28; Antoni Gąsiorowski and Izabela Skierska, 'Początki oficjalatu kamieńskiego archidiecezji gnieźnieńskiej (wieki XIV–XV),' *Kwartalnik Historyczny* 103, no. 2 (1996): 15, 16. The consistory books of Gdańsk existed from 1468–1500 and still existed at the beginning of the 20th century: *Acta capitulorum nec non iudiciorum ecclesiasticorum*

selecta, vol. 3, part 1, *Acta iudiciorum ecclesiasticorum dioecesum Plocensis, Wladislaviensis et Gneznensis (1422–1533)*, ed. Bolesław Ulanowski (Kraków: Akademia Umiejętności, 1908), vi.

8 Bruski, *Lokalne elity*, 16.
9 *Związek Pruski i poddanie się Prus Polsce*, ed. Karol Górski (Poznań: Instytut Zachodni, 1949), 54–64 (polish translation); *Die Staatsverträge des Deutschen Ordens in Preussen im 15. Jahrhundert*, vol. 2, *1438–1467*, ed. Erich Weise (Marburg: N.G. Elwert Verlag, 1955), 126–133 no. 292; the most recent literature concerning the incorporation privilege is collected by Marcin Grulkowski, 'Recepcja pruskiego przywileju inkorporacyjnego Kazimierza Jagiellończyka w Gdańsku w XV–XVI w.,' *Studia z Dziejów Średniowiecza* 25 (2023): 363–398.
10 Antoni Gąsiorowski, *Urzędnicy zarządu lokalnego w późnośredniowiecznej Wielkopolsce*, Poznańskie Towarzystwo Przyjaciół Nauk, Prace Komisji Historycznej 24, no. 3 (Poznań: Poznańskie Towarzystwo Przyjaciół Nauk, 1970), 97–101; Alicja Szymczakowa, *Urzędnicy łęczyccy i sieradzcy do połowy XV wieku* (Łódź: Wydawnictwo Uniwersytetu Łódzkiego, 1984), 55–56; Sobiesław Szybkowski, *Kujawska szlachta urzędnicza w późnym średniowieczu (1370–1501)* (Gdańsk: Wydawnictwo Uniwersytetu Gdańskiego, 2006), 125–128.
11 Gąsiorowski, *Urzędnicy*, 230, 231; Szybkowski, *Starostowie z Korony*, 55.
12 Juliusz Bardach, *Historia państwa i prawa Polski*, vol. 1 (Warszawa: Państwowe Wydawnictwo Naukowe, 1964), 418–426; Zdzisław Kaczmarczyk and Bogusław Leśnodorski, *Historia państwa i prawa Polski*, vol. 2 (Warszawa, Państwowe Wydawnictwo Naukowe, 1966), 7–24.
13 Bruski, *Lokalne elity*, 19–34; Michał Targowski, *Na prawie polskim i niemieckim. Kształtowanie się ziemskiej własności szlacheckiej na Pomorzu Gdańskim w XIII–XVI wieku* (Warszawa: Wydawnictwo DiG, 2014), 140–164.
14 *Acten der Ständetage Preussens, Königlichen Anteils (Westpreussen)*, vol. I, ed. Franz Thunert (Danzig: A.W. Kafemann, 1896), 413, 414; Kaczmarczyk and Leśnodorski, *Historia państwa i prawa Polski*, 2: 24; Targowski, *Na prawie polskim i niemieckim*, 159, 171, and 172; Beata Możejko, 'An Autonomous Dependency. The Unstable Relationship between Royal Prussia and Polish Crown, 1466–1568,' in *Unions and Divisions. New Forms of Rule in Medieval and Renaissance Europe*, ed. Paul Srodecki, Norbert Kersken, and Rimvydas Petrauskas (London, New York: Routledge, 2023), 174.
15 Biskup, *Wojny Polski*, 38–199; Sławomir Jóźwiak, Krzysztof Kwiatkowski, Adam Szweda and Sobiesław Szybkowski, *Wojna Polski i Litwy z zakonem krzyżackim 1409–1411* (Malbork: Muzeum Zamkowe w Malborku, 2010).
16 Beata Możejko, *Ród Świnków na pograniczu polsko-krzyżackim w średniowieczu* (Gdańsk: Wydawnictwo Uniwersytetu Gdańskiego, 1998), 104–113, 121–127, and 138–212; Szybkowski, *Kujawska szlachta*, 533, 646; id., 'Krzyżacy i ich dobrzyńscy poplecznicy w latach 1405–1413. Z badań nad polsko-pruskimi związkami transgranicznymi na początku XV wieku,' KMW 3/269 (2010): 281–300; id., 'Victims of Political Choice. Noble Refugees from Dobrzyń Land, 1391–1405 and Later,' *East Central Europe* 47 (2020): 89–106.
17 *Acten der Ständetage Preussens unter der Herrschaft des Deutschen Ordens*, vol. IV, ed. Max Toeppen (Leipzig: Verlag von Duncker und Humblot, 1884), 432, 433; Szybkowski, 'Starostowie z Korony,' 54.
18 Beata Możejko, 'Odległe pogranicze. Stanowisko stanów Prus Królewskich, a zwłaszcza Gdańska, wobec problemu zagrożenia tureckiego w latach 1485–1488,' *Średniowiecze Polskie i Powszechne* 3 (2011): 158; Szybkowski, 'Starostowie z Korony,' 54.
19 Możejko, 'Odległe pogranicze,' 154–155, 157, and 158; ead., 'An Autonomous Dependency,' 175; Wijaczka, 'Prusy Królewskie. Dzieje polityczne,' 40; Szybkowski, 'Starostowie z Korony,' 54.

20 Gąsiorowski, *Urzędnicy zarządu lokalnego*, 159, 160; Antoni Gąsiorowski, *Starostowie wielkopolskich miast królewskich w dobie jagiellońskiej* (Warszawa, Poznań: Państwowe Wydawnictwo Naukowe, 1981), 9–14; Michael Ludwig, *Besteuerung und Verpfändung königlicher Städte im spätmittelalterlichen Polen*, Osteuropastudien der Hochschulen des Landes Hessen. Reihe 1, Giessener Abhandlungen zur Agrar- und Wirtschaftsforschung des Europäischen Ostens 126 (Berlin: Duncker und Humblot, 1984); Szybkowski, 'Starostowie z Korony,' 56–58.
21 Szybkowski, 'Starostowie z Korony,' 56–58; Możejko, 'An Autonomous Dependency,' 175.
22 Paweł Czaplewski, *Senatorowie świeccy, podskarbiowie i starostowie Prus Królewskich, 1454–1772*, Roczniki Towarzystwa Naukowego w Toruniu 26–28 (Toruń: Towarzystwo Naukowe, 1921), 127; Górski, *Starostowie malborscy*, 9, 10.
23 Szybkowski, 'Starostowie z Korony,' 59; Możejko, 'An Autonomous Dependency,' 172–174.
24 Czaplewski, *Senatorowie świeccy*, 127–129; Górski, *Starostowie malborscy*, 9–170; Szybkowski, 'Starostowie z Korony,' 59–70; Możejko, 'An Autonomous Dependency,' 175.
25 Górski, *Starostowie malborscy*, 21, 23, 39, 40, and 55; Szybkowski, 'Starostowie z Korony,' 59, 60, 61, and 65.
26 Generally, see Szybkowski, 'Starostowie z Korony,' 59–70, 94, and 95. For Jan and Mikołaj Kościelecki z Kościelca, see Szybkowski, *Kujawska szlachta urzędnicza*, 559, 560, 627, and 628; for Piotr Donin z Prawkowic i Ujazdu, see Szybkowski, 664–666; for Paweł Jasieński, see Górski, *Starostowie malborscy*, 48–55; for Zbigniew Tęczyński, see Janusz Kurtyka, *Tęczyńscy. Studium z dziejów polskiej elity możnowładczej w średniowieczu* (Kraków: Wydawnictwo Secesja, 1997), 563–565; Adam Szweda, 'Tęczyński Zbigniew,' in *Polski słownik biograficzny*, vol. 53 (Warszawa, Kraków: Polska Akademia Nauk/Polska Akademia Umiejętności, 2021), 459–464); for Piotr Szafraniec z Pieskowej Skały, see Jerzy Sperka, *Szafrańcowie herbu Stary Koń. Z dziejów kariery i awansu w późnośredniowiecznej Polsce* (Katowice: Wydawnictwo Uniwersytetu Śląskiego, 2011), 394–407; id., 'Szafraniec Piotr,' in *Polski słownik biograficzny*, vol. 46 (Warszawa, Kraków: Polska Akademia Nauk/Polska Akademia Umiejętności, 2009–2010), 464–468; for Ambroży Pampowski, see Jacek Wiesiołowski, *Ambroży Pampowski – starosta Jagiellonów. Z dziejów awansu społecznego na przełomie średniowiecza i odrodzenia* (Wrocław: Wydawnictwo Polskiej Akademii Nauk, 1976).
27 The holding of high land offices (voivodes and castellans), which conferred the right to participate in the royal council, is regarded as a criterion for belonging to the class of magnates. It is important to exercise caution when equating the terms magnate and political elite.
28 The land judge (*iudex terrestris*) was a very important office within the category of Polish intermediate land offices, which could be held exclusively by the nobles. He received a lifetime appointment from the king and presided over the court for the nobility in the respective region.
29 Karol Piotrowicz, 'Chełmski Ścibor,' in *Polski słownik biograficzny*, vol. 3 (Kraków: Polska Akademia Umiejętności, 1937), 286, 287; Zbyszko Górczak, *Kariery majątkowe rodzin aspirujących do kręgu elity możnowładztwa wielkopolskiego w drugiej połowie XV i początkach XVI w.* (Poznań: Wydawnictwo Naukowe UAM, 2013), 249–283.
30 Adam Boniecki, *Herbarz polski*, vol. 11 (Warszawa: Gebethner i Wolff, 1911), 234, 235; Górski, *Starostowie malborscy*, 10, 21–27.
31 KŁSMT (1479–1515), I: 422–427 nos. 1191–1196; Czaplewski, *Senatorowie świeccy*, 69–73; Szybkowski, 'Starostowie z Korony,' 71, 72.
32 Czaplewski, *Senatorowie świeccy*, 204; Szybkowski, 'Starostowie z Korony,' 73.

33 Czaplewski, *Senatorowie świeccy*, 186–8; Szybkowski, 'Starostowie z Korony,' 73.
34 BCz., TN, t. 24, p. 73–44, 111, and 112; MRPS, IV/2: 30 no. 8841; KŁMN, 323–324 no. 1118; Czaplewski, *Senatorowie świeccy*, 95, 96, 99, 100, and 149–151; Biskup, *Trzynastoletnia*, 738, 739; Szybkowski, 'Starostowie z Korony,' 73–74.
35 Czaplewski, *Senatorowie świeccy*, 142; Szybkowski, 'Starostowie z Korony,' 80, 81.
36 Czaplewski, *Senatorowie świeccy*, 80, 81; Możejko, 'Agnieszka Zarembówna i Sebastian Legendorf,' 225–249; Szybkowski, 'Starostowie z Korony,' 87, 88.
37 Czaplewski, *Senatorowie świeccy*, 102, 103; Szybkowski, 'Starostowie z Korony,' 89, 90.
38 Czaplewski, *Senatorowie świeccy*, 102, 103; Szybkowski, 'Starostowie z Korony,' 88, 89.
39 MRPS, III: 137 no. 2097; IV/1, 37 no. 586; Czaplewski, *Senatorowie świeccy*, 178, 179; Szybkowski, 'Starostowie z Korony,' 87.
40 Czaplewski, *Senatorowie świeccy*, 62–4; Beata Możejko, 'Brodnica, Chełmno i Starogród w czasie wojny popiej (1467–1479),' *Gdańskie Studia z Dziejów Średniowiecza* 7 (2000): 125–144; Szybkowski, 'Starostowie z Korony,' 74–76; idem, *Kościeleccy ze Skępego herbu Ogon i ich protoplaści* (Gdańsk: Wydawnictwo Uniwersytetu Gdańskiego, 2018), 282, 283, 290, and 291.
41 Czaplewski, *Senatorowie świeccy*, 89–91; Szybkowski, 'Starostowie z Korony,' 83–86.
42 Czaplewski, *Senatorowie świeccy*, 85; Szybkowski, 'Starostowie z Korony,' 82.
43 Czaplewski, *Senatorowie świeccy*, 168, 169; Możejko, 'Gotard z Radlina – działalność w Prusach Królewskich,' 229–253; Szybkowski, 'Starostowie z Korony,' 78, 79.
44 Czaplewski, *Senatorowie świeccy*, 59; Szybkowski, 'Starostowie z Korony,' 76, 77.
45 MRPS, III: 3 no. 49, 50 no. 771, 54 no. 860, 59 no. 943, 137 no. 2090; IV/2: 4 no. 8380, 69 no. 9628; Czaplewski, *Senatorowie świeccy*, 184, 193; Szybkowski, 'Starostowie z Korony,' 90.
46 Jerzy Sikorski, *Monarchia polska i Warmia u schyłku XV wieku*, Rozprawy i Materiały Ośrodka Badań Naukowych im. Wojciecha Kętrzyńskiego w Olsztynie 65 (Olsztyn: Wydawnictwo Pojezierze, 1978).
47 Biskup, *Trzynastoletnia*, 171, 270, 412, 458, 521, 540, 548, 552, 571, 591, 592, 615, 632, and 680; Szybkowski, *Kujawska szlachta urzędnicza*, 620, 646, and 647; id., 'Szarlejski Mikołaj,' in *Polski słownik biograficzny*, vol. 47 (Warszawa, Kraków: Polska Akademia Nauk/Polska Akademia Umiejętności, 2010–2011), 99–103; id., 'Starostowie z Korony,' 60, 73, 74, 75, 76, 79–80, and 82; id., *Kościeleccy ze Skępego*, 415, 431, and 436; Renata Trawka, 'Szczekocki Jan,' in *Polski słownik biograficzny*, vol. 47 (Warszawa, Kraków: Polska Akademia Nauk/Polska Akademia Umiejętności, 2010–2011), 238–243; Witold Brzeziński, *Koligacje małżeńskie możnowładztwa wielkopolskiego w drugiej połowie XIV i pierwszej połowie XV wieku* (Wrocław: Wydawnictwo Uniwersytetu Wrocławskiego, 2012), 346, 347.
48 Szybkowski, 'Starostowie z Korony,' 77–79, 81–83, and 87–90; id., 'Tomasz zwany Tomiec z Młotkowa,' in *Polski słownik biograficzny*, vol. 54 (Warszawa, Kraków: Polska Akademia Nauk/Polska Akademia Umiejętności, 2022), 169–172; Tomasz Maćkowski, 'Szorc Piotr,' in *Polski słownik biograficzny*, vol. 48 (Warszawa, Kraków: Polska Akademia Nauk/Polska Akademia Umiejętności, 2012–2013), 560, 561.
49 *Księga ławnicza miasta Nowego nad Wisłą (1416–1527)*, ed. Krzysztof Mikulski and Wiesław Nowosad, FTNT 106 (Toruń: Towarzystwo Naukowe w Toruniu, 2012), 144–150 nos. 626, 627.
50 APG, 508, nr 1329, p. 193; MRPS, III: 1 no. 1; SHGZCh, 113.
51 Szybkowski, 'Starostowie z Korony,' 79, 83, 84–87, and 90–92.
52 Szybkowski, 90–92.

53 AGAD, MK, vol. 12, fol. 217v; MRPS, I: 69 no. 1344, 87 no. 1696; SHGZCh, 118, 121.
54 AGAD, MK, vol. 17, fol. 163v; BCz., TN, t. 21, p. 325, 326; t. 22, p. 153–155, 191–194, 225, 226, and 401–407; t. 23, p. 405–407, 419, and 420; t. 24, p. 309, 310; vol. 27, p. 53, 54, and 63–66; MRPS, II: 77 no. 1222; *Regesta historico-diplomatica Ordinis. S. Mariae Theutonicorum 1198–1525*, pars II, *Regesta Privilegiorum Ordinis S. Mariae Theutonicorum/Regesten der Pergament-Urkunden aus der Zeit des Deutschen Ordens*, eds. Erich Joachim and Walther Hubatsch (Göttingen: Vandenhoeck und Ruprecht, 1948), 387 no. 3494; Paul Panske, 'O Dębnicy, własności Latalskich, gnieździe Żalińskich,' *Zapiski Towarzystwa Naukowego w Toruniu* 1 (1908): 19, 20; Bronisław Nowak, 'Protoplaści Żalińskich z Żalna herbu Poraj. Przyczynek do kwestii osadnictwa na Pomorzu po 1466 roku,' in *Między średniowieczem a nowożytnością. Echa wojny trzynastoletniej na ziemi chojnickiej*, ed. Jacek Knoppek and Bogdan Kuffel (Chojnice: Przedsiębiorstwo Marketingowe "Logo", 2009), 64, 65; id., 'Wielkopolscy spadkobiercy Mościców ze Ściborza,' in *Z dziejów pogranicza kujawsko-wielkopolskiego II*, ed. Dariusz Karczewski (Strzelno: Polskie Towarzystwo Historyczne Oddział w Inowrocławiu, 2009), 68.
55 Gąsiorowski, *Urzędnicy zarządu lokalnego*, 221–223, 270, 271, and 277–279.
56 Szybkowski, 'Urzędnicy zarządu starostwa malborskiego,' 22–37.
57 AGAD, MK, vol. 5, fol. 117v; KŁSMT (1479–1515), II: 579 no. 1701; Górski, *Starostowie malborscy*, 30–32, 57, 88, 89, 95, 98, 93, and 95; Sobiesław Szybkowski, 'Trzy źródła do genealogii i prozopografii Rembielińskich herbu Dołęga,' *Studia z Dziejów Średniowiecza* 16 (2011), 317–332; id., 'Urzędnicy zarządu starostwa malborskiego,' 22–37; id., 'Pochodzenie Szczawińskich 61–76; idem, 'Przybysze z Korony i Mazowsza,' 381–384.
58 Szybkowski, 'Urzędnicy zarządu starostwa malborskiego,' 27–29.
59 Czaplewski, *Senatorowie świeccy*, 128; Górski, '*Starostowie malborscy*,' 122, 123; Witold Szczuczko, 'Szpot (Spot, Spoth, Szpott) Mikołaj z Krajowej,' in *Słownik biograficzny Pomorza Nadwiślańskiego*, vol. 4, ed. Zbigniew Nowak (Gdańsk: Gdańskie Towarzystwo Naukowe/Uniwersytet Gdański, 1997), 319.
60 BCz., TN, t. 21, p. 326; t. 22, p. 401–407; t. 23, p. 405–407, 419, and 420; t. 24, p. 73, 74; KŁSMT (1479–1515), I: 426– 7 nos. 1194, 1196; Górski, *Starostowie malborscy*, 92; Możejko, 'Agnieszka Zarembówna i Sebastian Legendorf,' 238.
61 Błażej Śliwiński, 'Wincenty zwany Kiełbasa,' in *Ludzie Pomorskiego średniowiecza*, eds. Józef Borzyszkowski et al. (Gdańsk: Ossolineum, 1981), 172–174; Teresa Borawska, 'Kiełbasa Wincenty,' in *Słownik biograficzny Pomorza Nadwiślańskiego*, vol. 2, ed. Zbigniew Nowak (Gdańsk: Gdańskie Towarzystwo Naukowe/Uniwersytet Gdański, 1994), 384, 385; Tomasz Pietras, *Oporowscy herbu Sulima. Kariera rodziny możnowładczej w późnośredniowiecznej Polsce* (Łódź: Wydawnictwo Uniwersytetu Łódzkiego, 2013), 165–167.
62 Michał Słomski, *Urzędnicy i personel zamku arcybiskupów gnieźnieńskich w Łowiczu (XIV w. – 1531 r.)* (Warszawa: Instytut Historii PAN, 2017) 6–8; Łukasz Włodarski, *Dwory arcybiskupów gnieźnieńskich do 1493 r. Struktura, urzędy, ludzie* (Toruń: Wydawnictwo Naukowe Uniwersytetu Mikołaja Kopernika, 2023), 55–165.
63 UBBC, II: 539 no. 650.
64 UBBC, II: 545–546 no. 654; UBBP, III: 233–234 no. 169.
65 Stefan Cackowski, 'Wsie szlachty wasalnej w dobrach biskupstwa i kapituły chełmińskiej w XVI/XVII w.,' ZH 57, no. 4 (1982): 153–166.
66 UBBC, II: 545–546 no. 654.
67 Peter Kriedte, *Die Herrschaft der Bischöfe von Włocławek in Pommerellen von den Anfängen bis zum Jahre 1409*, Veröffentlichungen des Max-Planck-Instituts für Geschichte 40 (Göttingen: Vadenhoeck und Ruprecht, 1974), 356–359.

68 KŁSMT (1456–1479), 229–230 no. 862, 231 no. 868, 255, 256 no. 952, 268–269 no. 988, 343–344 no. 1223; KŁSMT (1479–1515), I: 126–128 no. 313, 175 no. 430, 192–193 no. 481, 203, no. 508, 321–322 no. 851; II: 579 no. 1701, 712–713 no. 2132; Kętrzyński, *O narodowości polskiej w Prusach Zachodnich za czasów krzyżackich*, 56, 59, and 60; SHGZCh, 89, 91, 11, 131, 132, 142, and 152; Szybkowski, *Kujawska szlachta urzędnicza*, s. 638, 669.

69 For example, see KŁSMT (1456–1479), 231 no. 868, 255–256 no. 952; KŁSMT (1479–1515), I: 203 no. 508.

70 *Księga ławnicza miasta Nowego nad Wisłą*, 144–150 nos. 626–627, 165 nos. 671–673, 173, 174 no. 700, 188–189 no. 755; Jan Pakulski, *Ród Godziębów w średniowiecznej Polsce. Studium genealogiczne* (Toruń: Wydawnictwo Uniwersytetu Mikołaja Kopernika, 2005), 68.

71 Panske, 'O Dębnicy, własności Latalskich,' 19, 20; Nowak, 'Protoplaści Żalińskich,' 64, 77, and 78; id., 'Wielkopolscy spadkobiercy Mościców,' 68.

72 Bartosz Drzewiecki, *Szlachta województwa chełmińskiego w latach 1545–1772* (Warszawa: Wydawnictwo DiG, 2014), 45–64.

Primary Sources

Bydgoszcz. Archiwum Państwowe w Bydgoszczy, 1675 (Akta miasta Chojnic), nr 33.
Gdańsk. Archiwum Państwowe w Gdańsku, 519 (Akta miasta Pucka), nr 4.
Gdańsk. Archiwum Państwowe w Gdańsku, 508 (Akta miasta Malborka), nr 1329.
Kraków. Biblioteka Czartoryskich w Krakowie, Teki Naruszewicza, t. 21, 22, 23, 24, 27.
Warszawa. Archiwum Główne Akt Dawnych w Warszawie, Metryka Koronna, t. 12, 17.

Acta capitulorum nec non iudiciorum ecclesiasticorum selecta. Vol. 3, pars 1, *Acta iudiciorum ecclesiasticorum dioecesum Plocensis, Wladislaviensis et Gneznensis (1422–1533)*, edited by Bolesław Ulanowski. Kraków: Akademia Umiejętności, 1908.

Acten der Ständetage Preussens, Königlichen Anteils (Westpreussen). Vol. 1, edited by Franz Thunert. Danzig: A.W. Kafemann, 1896.

Acten der Ständetage Preussens unter der Herrschaft des Deutschen Ordens. Vol. 4, edited by Max Toeppen. Leipzig: Verlag von Duncker und Humblot, 1884.

Księga ławnicza miasta Nowego nad Wisłą (1416–1527). Edited by Krzysztof Mikulski and Wiesław Nowosad. FTNT 106. Toruń: Towarzystwo Naukowe w Toruniu, 2012.

Księga ławnicza Starego Miasta Torunia (1456–1479). Edited by Krzysztof Kopiński and Janusz Tandecki. FTNT 99. Toruń: Towarzystwo Naukowe w Toruniu, 2007.

Księga ławnicza Starego Miasta Torunia (1479–1515). Parts I–II. Edited by Krzysztof Kopiński, Krzysztof Mikulski, and Janusz Tandecki. FTNT 113. Toruń: Towarzystwo Naukowe w Toruniu, 2018.

Matricularum Regni Poloniae Summaria, excussis codicibus, qui in Chartophylacio Maximo Varsoviensi asservantur. Edited by Theodorus Wierzbowski. Pars I, *Casimiri regis tempora comlectens (1447–1492)*. Varsoviae: Typis Officinae C. Kowalewski, 1905.

Matricularum Regni Poloniae Summaria, excussis codicibus, qui in Chartophylacio Maximo Varsoviensi asservantur. Edited by Theodorus Wierzbowski. Pars II, *Iohannis Alberti regis tempora complectens (1492–1501)*. Varsoviae: Typis Officinae C. Kowalewski, 1907.

Matricularum Regni Poloniae Summaria, excussis codicibus, qui in Chartophylacio Maximo Varsoviensi asservantur. Edited by Theodorus Wierzbowski. Pars III, *Alexandri regis tempora complectens (1501–1506)*. Varsoviae: Typis Officinae C. Kowalewski, 1908.

Matricularum Regni Poloniae Summaria, excussis codicibus, qui in Chartophylacio Maximo Varsoviensi asservantur. Edited by Theodorus Wierzbowski. Pars IV, *Sigismundi I regis tempora complectens (1507–1548)*, vol. 1, *Acta cancellariorum, 1507–1548.* Varsoviae: Typis Officinae C. Kowalewski, 1910.
Matricularum Regni Poloniae Summaria, excussis codicibus, qui in Chartophylacio Maximo Varsoviensi asservantur. Edited by Theodorus Wierzbowski. Pars IV, *Sigismundi I regis tempora complectens (1507–1548)*, vol. 2, *Acta vicecancellariorum, 1507–1535.* Varsoviae: Typis Officinae C. Kowalewski, 1912. Pars IV, *Sigismundi I regis tempora complectens (1507–1548)*, vol. 2, *Acta vicecancellariorum, 1507–1535.* Varsoviae: Typis Officinae C. Kowalewski, 1912.
Regesta historico-diplomatica Ordinis. S. Mariae Theutonicorum 1198–1525. Pars. II, *Regesta Privilegiorum Ordinis S. Mariae Theutonicorum/Regesten der Pergament-Urkunden aus der Zeit des Deutschen Ordens.* Edited by Erich Joachim and Walther Hubatsch. Göttingen: Vandenhoeck und Ruprecht, 1948.
Die Staatsverträge des Deutschen Ordens in Preussen im 15. Jahrhundert. Vol. 2, *1438–1467*, edited by Erich Weise. Marburg: N.G. Elwert Verlag, 1955.
UBBC = *Urkundenbuch des Bisthums Culm.* Edited by Carl P. Woelky. Vol. II, *Das Bisthum Culm unter Polen 1466–1774.* Neues Preußisches Urkundenbuch. Westpreussischer Theil 2: Urkunden der Bisthümer, Kirchen und Klöster. Danzig: Commisionsverlag von Theodor Bertling, 1885.
UBBP = *Urkundenduch zur Geschiche des vormaligen Bisthums Pomesanien.* Edited by Hermann Cramer. Vol. III. Marienwerder: Im Selbstverlag des Historischen Vereins für den Regierungs-Bezirk, Marienwerder, 1886.
Związek Pruski i poddanie się Prus Polsce. Edited by Karol Górski. Poznań: Instytut Zachodni, 1949.

Secondary Sources

Bardach, Juliusz. *Historia państwa i prawa Polski.* Vol. 1. Warszawa: Państwowe Wydawnictwo Naukowe, 1964.
Biskup, Marian. 'Prusy Królewskie i Krzyżackie (1466–1657).' In *Historia Pomorza.* Vol. II, *Do roku 1815.* Part I, *1464–66–1648/57*, edited by Gerard Labuda, 24–186. Poznań: Wydawnictwo Poznańskie, 1976.
Biskup, Marian. 'Rozwój gospodarki czynszowej i utrwalenie ustroju stanowego na Pomorzu Wschodnim pod rządami krzyżackimi (1310–1466).' In *Historia Pomorza.* Vol. I, *Do roku 1466.* Part I, edited by Gerard Labuda, 581–775. Poznań: Wydawnictwo Poznańskie, 1972.
Biskup, Marian. *Trzynastoletnia wojna z zakonem krzyżackim 1454–1466.* Warszawa: Wydawnictwo Obrony Narodowej, 1967.
Biskup, Marian. *Wojny Polski z zakonem krzyżackim 1308–1521.* Gdańsk: Wydawnictwo Marpress, 1993.
Biskup, Marian. 'Załamanie się państwa krzyżackiego w XV w.' In *Dzieje zakonu krzyżackiego w Prusach. Gospodarka – Społeczeństwo – Państwo – Ideologia*, edited by Marian Biskup and Gerard Labuda, 353–437. Gdańsk: Wydawnictwo Morskie, 1988.
Biskup, Marian. *Zjednoczenie Pomorza Wschodniego z Polską w połowie XV wieku.* Warszawa: Państwowe Wydawnictwo Naukowe, 1959.
Biskup, Marian. 'Z zagadnień wojskowości polskiej z okresu wojny trzynastoletniej.' Edited by Marian Biskup and Karol Górski, *Kazimierz Jagiellończyk. Zbiór studiów o Polsce drugiej połowy XV wieku*, 141–172. Warszawa: Państwowe Wydawnictwo Naukowe, 1987.
Boniecki, Adam. *Herbarz polski.* Vol. 11. Warszawa: Gebethner i Wolff, 1911.
Borawska, Teresa. 'Kiełbasa Wincenty.' In *Słownik biograficzny Pomorza Nadwiślańskiego.* Vol. 2, edited by Zbigniew Nowak, 384–385. Gdańsk: Gdańskie Towarzystwo Naukowe/Uniwersytet Gdański, 1994.

Bruski, Klemens. *Lokalne elity rycerstwa na Pomorzu Gdańskim w okresie panowania zakonu krzyżackiego. Studium prozopograficzne*. Gdańsk: Wydawnictwo Uniwersytetu Gdańskiego, 2002.

Brzeziński, Witold. *Koligacje małżeńskie możnowładztwa wielkopolskiego w drugiej połowie XIV i pierwszej połowie XV wieku*. Wrocław: Wydawnictwo Uniwersytetu Wrocławskiego, 2012.

Cackowski, Stefan. 'Wsie szlachty wasalnej w dobrach biskupstwa i kapituły chełmińskiej w XVI/XVII w.' ZH 57, no. 4 (1982): 153–166.

Czaplewski, Paweł. *Senatorowie świeccy, podskarbiowie i starostowie Prus Królewskich, 1454–1772*. Roczniki Towarzystwa Naukowego w Toruniu 26–28. Toruń: Towarzystwo Naukowe, 1921.

Drzewiecki, Bartosz, *Szlachta województwa chełmińskiego w latach 1545–1772*. Warszawa: Wydawnictwo DiG, 2014.

Gąsiorowski, Antoni. *Starostowie wielkopolskich miast królewskich w dobie jagiellońskiej*. Warszawa, Poznań: Państwowe Wydawnictwo Naukowe, 1981.

Gąsiorowski, Antoni. *Urzędnicy zarządu lokalnego w późnośredniowiecznej Wielkopolsce*. Poznańskie Towarzystwo Przyjaciół Nauk, Prace Komisji Historycznej 24, no. 3. Poznań: Poznańskie Towarzystwo Przyjaciół Nauk, 1970.

Gąsiorowski, Antoni and Izabela Skierska. 'Początki oficjalatu kamieńskiego archidiecezji gnieźnieńskiej (wieki XIV–XV).' *Kwartalnik Historyczny* 103, no. 2 (1996): 3–21.

Górczak, Zbyszko. *Kariery majątkowe rodzin aspirujących do kręgu elity możnowładztwa wielkopolskiego w drugiej połowie XV i początkach XVI w.* Poznań: Wydawnictwo Naukowe UAM, 2013.

Górski, Karol. *Pomorze w wojnie trzynastoletniej*. Oświęcim: Wydawnictwo Napoleon V, 2014. 2nd edition (1st edition: Poznań: Poznańskie Towarzystwo Przyjaciół Nauk, 1932).

Górski, Karol. *Starostowie malborscy w latach 1457–1510. Pierwsze półwiecze polskiego Malborka*. Roczniki Towarzystwa Naukowego w Toruniu 63, no. 1. Toruń: Towarzystwo Naukowe w Toruniu, 1960.

Grabowski, Janusz, *Dynastia Piastów mazowieckich*. Kraków: Wydawnictwo Avalon, 2012.

Grulkowski, Marcin. 'Recepcja pruskiego przywileju inkorporacyjnego Kazimierza Jagiellończyka w Gdańsku w XV–XVI w.' *Studia z Dziejów Średniowiecza* 25 (2023): 363–398.

Grzegorz, Maksymilian *Analiza dyplomatyczno-sfragistyczna dokumentów traktatu toruńskiego 1466 r*. Roczniki Towarzystwa Naukowego w Toruniu 75, no. 1. Toruń: Towarzystwo Naukowe w Toruniu, 1970.

Jóźwiak, Sławomir, Krzysztof Kwiatkowski, Adam Szweda and Sobiesław Szybkowski, *Wojna Polski i Litwy z zakonem krzyżackim 1409–1411*. Malbork: Muzeum Zamkowe w Malborku, 2010.

Kaczmarczyk, Zdzisław and Bogusław Leśnodorski. *Historia państwa i prawa Polski*. Vol. 2. Warszawa, Państwowe Wydawnictwo Naukowe, 1966.

Kętrzyński, Wojciech. *O ludności Polskiej w Prusiech niegdyś krzyżackich*. Olsztyn: Ośrodek Badań Naukowych i Towarzystwo Naukowe im. Wojciech Kętrzyńskiego w Olsztynie, 2009. 2nd edition (1st edition: Lwów: Zakład Narodowy im. Ossolińskich, 1882).

Kętrzyński, Wojciech. *O narodowości polskiej w Prusach Zachodnich za czasów krzyżackich. Studium historyczno-etnograficzne*. Kraków: Drukarnia Uniwersytetu Jagiellońskiego, 1874.

Kizik, Edmund. 'Uwagi wstępne. Prusy Królewskie: środowisko geograficzne, administracja, geografia.' In *Prusy Królewskie. Społeczeństwo, kultura, gospodarka 1454–1772*, edited by Edmund Kizik, 12–32. Gdańsk: Muzeum Narodowe w Gdańsku, 2012.

Kriedte, Peter. *Die Herrschaft der Bischöfe von Włocławek in Pommerellen von den Anfängen bis zum Jahre 1409*. Veröffentlichungen des Max-Planck-Instituts für Geschichte 40. Göttingen: Vadenhoeck und Ruprecht, 1974.
Kurtyka, Janusz. *Tęczyńscy. Studium z dziejów polskiej elity możnowładczej w średniowieczu*. Kraków: Wydawnictwo Secesja, 1997.
Ludwig, Michael. *Besteuerung und Verpfändung königlicher Städte im spätmittelalterlichen Polen*. Osteuropastudien der Hochschulen des Landes Hessen. Reihe 1, Giessener Abhandlungen zur Agrar- und Wirtschaftsforschung des Europäischen Ostens 126. Berlin: Duncker und Humblot, 1984.
Maćkowski, Tomasz. 'Szorc Piotr.' In *Polski słownik biograficzny*. Vol. 48, 560–561. Warszawa, Kraków: Polska Akademia Nauk/Polska Akademia Umiejętności, 2012–2013.
Mikulski, Krzysztof. *Urzędnicy Prus Królewskich XV–XVIII wieku. Spisy*. Wrocław: Zakład Narodowy imienia Ossolińskich and Wydawnictwo Polskiej Akademii Nauk, 1990.
Możejko, Beata. 'Agnieszka Zarembówna i Sebastian Legendorf a starostwo gniewskie w latach 1489–1504.' In *Społeczeństwo Polski średniowiecznej*. Vol. 11, edited by Stefan K. Kuczyński, 225–249. Warszawa: Wydawnictwo DiG, 2011.
Możejko, Beata. 'An Autonomous Dependency. The Unstable Relationship between Royal Prussia and Polish Crown, 1466–1568.' In *Unions and Divisions. New Forms of Rule in Medieval and Renaissance Europe*, edited by Paul Srodecki, Norbert Kersken, and Rimvydas Petrauskas, 172–184. London, New York: Routledge, 2023.
Możejko, Beata. 'Brodnica, Chełmno i Starogród w czasie wojny popiej (1467–1479).' *Gdańskie Studia z Dziejów Średniowiecza* 7 (2000): 125–144.
Możejko, Beata. 'Gotard z Radlina – działalność w Prusach Królewskich.' In *Społeczeństwo Polski średniowiecznej*. Vol. 10, edited by Stefan K. Kuczyński, 229–253. Warszawa: Wydawnictwo DiG, 2004.
Możejko, Beata. 'Odległe pogranicze. Stanowisko stanów Prus Królewskich, a zwłaszcza Gdańska, wobec problemu zagrożenia tureckiego w latach 1485–1488.' *Średniowiecze Polskie i Powszechne* 3 (2011): 151–170.
Możejko, Beata. *Ród Świnków na pograniczu polsko-krzyżackim w średniowieczu*. Gdańsk: Wydawnictwo Uniwersytetu Gdańskiego, 1998.
Nowak, Bronisław. 'Protoplaści Żalińskich z Żalna herbu Poraj. Przyczynek do kwestii osadnictwa na Pomorzu po 1466 roku.' In *Między średniowieczem a nowożytnością. Echa wojny trzynastoletniej na ziemi chojnickiej*, edited by Jacek Knoppek and Bogdan Kuffel, 62–82. Chojnice: Przedsiębiorstwo Marketingowe "Logo", 2009.
Nowak, Bronisław. 'Wielkopolscy spadkobiercy Mościców ze Ściborza.' In *Z dziejów pogranicza kujawsko-wielkopolskiego II*, edited by Dariusz Karczewski, 53–82. Strzelno: Polskie Towarzystwo Historyczne Oddział w Inowrocławiu, 2009.
Pakulski, Jan. *Ród Godziębów w średniowiecznej Polsce. Studium genealogiczne*. Toruń: Wydawnictwo Uniwersytetu Mikołaja Kopernika, 2005.
Panske, Paul. 'O Dębnicy, własności Latalskich, gnieździe Żalińskich.' *Zapiski Towarzystwa Naukowego w Toruniu* 1 (1908): 17–20.
Pietras, Tomasz. *Oporowscy herbu Sulima. Kariera rodziny możnowładczej w późnośredniowiecznej Polsce*. Łódź: Wydawnictwo Uniwersytetu Łódzkiego, 2013.
Piotrowicz, Karol. 'Chełmski Ścibor.' In *Polski słownik biograficzny*. Vol. 3, 286–287. Kraków: Polska Akademia Umiejętności, 1937.
Samsonowicz, Henryk. 'Dzieje polityczne (połowa XIV – początek XVI w.).' In *Dzieje Mazowsza do 1526 roku*, edited by Aleksander Gieysztor and Henryk Samsonowicz, 212–248. Warszawa: Wydawnictwo Naukowe PWN, 1994.
Słownik historyczno-geograficzny ziemi chełmińskiej w średniowieczu. Prepared by Krystyna Porębska and Maksymilian Grzegorz, edited by Marian Biskup. Wrocław, Warszawa, Kraków, Gdańsk: Zakład Narodowy im. Ossolińskich – Wydawnictwo, 1971.

Sikorski, Jerzy. *Monarchia polska i Warmia u schyłku XV wieku*. Rozprawy i Materiały Ośrodka Badań Naukowych im. Wojciecha Kętrzyńskiego w Olsztynie 65. Olsztyn: Wydawnictwo Pojezierze, 1978.

Słomski, Michał. *Urzędnicy i personel zamku arcybiskupów gnieźnieńskich w Łowiczu (XIV w. – 1531 r.)*. Warszawa: Instytut Historii PAN, 2017.

Sperka, Jerzy. 'Szafraniec Piotr.' In *Polski słownik biograficzny*. Vol. 46, 464–468. Warszawa, Kraków: Polska Akademia Nauk/Polska Akademia Umiejętności, 2009–2010.

Sperka, Jerzy. *Szafrańcowie herbu Stary Koń. Z dziejów kariery i awansu w późnośredniowiecznej Polsce*. Katowice: Wydawnictwo Uniwersytetu Śląskiego, 2011.

Szybkowski, Sobiesław. 'Elita rycerska krzyżackich Prus w świetle listy gwarantów pokoju brzeskiego z 1436 r. Próba charakterystyki.' *Studia z Dziejów Średniowiecza* 26 (2023): 233–275.

Szybkowski, Sobiesław. *Kościeleccy ze Skępego herbu Ogon i ich protoplaści*. Gdańsk: Wydawnictwo Uniwersytetu Gdańskiego, 2018.

Szybkowski, Sobiesław. 'Krzyżacy i ich dobrzyńscy poplecznicy w latach 1405–1413. Z badań nad polsko-pruskimi związkami transgranicznymi na początku XV wieku.' KMW 3/269 (2010): 281–300.

Szybkowski, Sobiesław. *Kujawska szlachta urzędnicza w późnym średniowieczu (1370–1501)*. Gdańsk: Wydawnictwo Uniwersytetu Gdańskiego, 2006.

Szybkowski, Sobiesław. 'Pochodzenie Szczawińskich herbu Dąbrowa z Prus Królewskich.' In *Genealogia, prozopografia i dzieje społeczeństw na historycznych obszarach Pomorza w okresie przedindustrialnym (od średniowiecza po wiek XIX)*, edited by Sławomir Kościelak, Sobiesław Szybkowski, and Tomasz Rembalski, 61–76. Gdańsk: Wydawnictwo Uniwersytetu Gdańskiego, 2020.

Szybkowski, Sobiesław. 'Przybysze z Korony i Mazowsza w zarządzie starostwa malborskiego w końcu średniowiecza. Piotr z Rembielina, Mikołaj Szczawiński i Krzysztof z Łodygowa i Celin.' In *Homini, qui in honore fuit. Księga pamiątkowa poświęcona śp. Profesorowi Grzegorzowi Białuńskiemu*, edited by Alina Dobrosielska, Aleksander Pluskowski, and Seweryn Szczepański, 377–390. Olsztyn: Towarzystwo Naukowe Pruthenia/Uniwersytet Warmińsko-Mazurski w Olsztynie, 2020.

Szybkowski, Sobiesław. 'Starostowie z Korony w Prusach Królewskich.' In *Jagiellonowie i ich świat. Centrum a peryferie w systemie władzy Jagiellonów*, edited by Bożena Czwojdrak, Jerzy Sperka, and Piotr Węcowski, 53–100. Kraków: Towarzystwo Naukowe Societas Vistulana, 2018.

Szybkowski, Sobiesław. 'Szarlejski Mikołaj.' In *Polski słownik biograficzny*. Vol. 47, 99–103. Warszawa, Kraków: Polska Akademia Nauk/Polska Akademia Umiejętności, 2010–2011.

Szybkowski, Sobiesław. 'Tomasz zwany Tomiec z Młotkowa.' In *Polski słownik biograficzny*. Vol. 54, 169–172. Warszawa, Kraków: Polska Akademia Nauk/Polska Akademia Umiejętności, 2022.

Szybkowski, Sobiesław. 'Trzy źródła do genealogii i prozopografii Rembielińskich herbu Dołęga.' *Studia z Dziejów Średniowiecza* 16 (2011): 317–332.

Szybkowski, Sobiesław. 'Urzędnicy zarządu starostwa malborskiego podczas kadencji starościńskiej Zbigniewa Tęczyńskiego (1485–1496). Studium prozopograficzne.' In *Regnum defendo ense et alis tego stricto – Królestwa bronię dobytym mieczem i osłaniam skrzydłami. Malbork w Prusach Królewskich. Vol. 1: Prusy Królewskie i Malbork w okresie staropolskim (1454–1772)*, edited by Rafał Panfil and Artur Dobry, 22–37. Malbork: Muzeum Zamkowe w Malborku, 2021.

Szybkowski, Sobiesław. 'Victims of Political Choice. Noble Refugees from Dobrzyń Land, 1391–1405 and Later.' *East Central Europe* 47 (2020): 89–106.

Szymczakowa, Alicja. *Urzędnicy łęczyccy i sieradzcy do połowy XV wieku*. Łódź: Wydawnictwo Uniwersytetu Łódzkiego, 1984.

Szweda, Adam. 'II pokój toruński.' In *Toruń miastem pokoju. II pokój toruński*, edited by Piotr Oliński and Waldemar Rozynkowski, 48–59. Toruń: Wydawnictwo Adam Marszałek, 2016.

Szweda, Adam. 'Tęczyński Zbigniew.' In *Polski słownik biograficzny*. Vol. 53, 459–464. Warszawa, Kraków: Polska Akademia Nauk/Polska Akademia Umiejętności, 2021.

Śliwiński, Błażej. 'Wincenty zwany Kiełbasa.' In *Ludzie Pomorskiego średniowiecza*, edited by Józef Borzyszkowski et al., 172–174. Gdańsk: Ossolineum, 1981.

Targowski, Michał. *Na prawie polskim i niemieckim. Kształtowanie się ziemskiej własności szlacheckiej na Pomorzu Gdańskim w XIII–XVI wieku*. Warszawa: Wydawnictwo DiG, 2014.

Tomczak, Andrzej, *Kancelaria biskupów włocławskich w okresie księgi wpisów (XV–XVIII w.)*. Roczniki Towarzystwa Naukowego w Toruniu 69, no. 3. Toruń: Towarzystwo Naukowe w Toruniu, 1964.

Trawka, Renata. 'Szczekocki Jan.' In *Polski słownik biograficzny*. Vol. 47, 238–243. Warszawa, Kraków: Polska Akademia Nauk/Polska Akademia Umiejętności, 2010–2011.

Wijaczka, Jacek. 'Prusy Królewskie. Dzieje polityczne do 1660 r.' In *Prusy Królewskie. Społeczeństwo, kultura, gospodarka 1454–1772*, edited by Edmund Kizik, 34–70. Gdańsk: Muzeum Narodowe w Gdańsku, 2012.

Włodarski, Łukasz. *Dwory arcybiskupów gnieźnieńskich do 1493 r. Struktura, urzędy, ludzie*. Toruń: Wydawnictwo Naukowe Uniwersytetu Mikołaja Kopernika, 2023.

8 The Functioning of Mendicant Orders in Multi-Ethnic Communities in the Territory of the Teutonic Order in Prussia and in Royal Prussia until the Beginning of the 16th Century[1]

Rafał Kubicki

When considering the issue of the functioning of the mendicant orders in the multi-ethnic communities living in the territory of the state of the Teutonic Order in Prussia, it is necessary at the outset to point out the specific conditions under which they carried out their activities.[2] Firstly, supreme authority in the country was exercised by an ecclesiastical corporation (i.e. the Teutonic Order) which, much like the mendicant communities, was a formal subject of the Holy See. Secondly, at the time of the organisation of the first monastic foundations in Prussia, the process of founding cities was only just under way. Monasteries were therefore established in newly founded centres: Kulm (today Chełmno), Elbing (today Elbląg) and Thorn (today Toruń). Urban parishes were also organised in these centres at the same time.[3] Thirdly, in Western Europe, the Mendicant orders (Dominicans and Franciscans) exercised pastoral care primarily for the new urban dwellers arriving in large numbers in the 13th century.[4] In Prussia, however, in addition to preaching to Christian settlers in the cities, they also carried out missionary action (Christianisation and evangelisation) in the countryside among the local, indigenous Old-Prussian population.[5] Later, there was a gradual formation of alms collection districts (*terminus*), which also included rural areas. This is also where monastic fundraisers regularly reached out to collect alms for the needs of the convent in question.[6] All the circumstances mentioned here required the mendicant orders to adapt to the specific conditions in Prussia. In this connection, an important question concerns the extent of the involvement of Mendicants in rural pastoral care in the area, particularly among the indigenous Old-Prussian population.[7] Importantly, the first missionary activities were undertaken by the Mendicants even before the Teutonic Order appeared here and conquered the Old-Prussian regions. Surviving sources indicate that Dominicans from the convent in Danzig (today Gdańsk), i.e. from the area of Eastern Pomerania (Germ. Pommerellen, Pol. Pomorze Wschodnie) adjacent to Prussia, were already carrying out their activities in Pomesania (Pol. Pomezania) and the land of *Passaluc* in

DOI: 10.4324/9781003502876-8

Pogesania (Pol. Pogezania) (later area around the town Preußisch Holland, today Pasłęk) as early as 1231.[8] The Dominican and Franciscan orders were also involved in the so-called "Prussian mission", i.e. encouraging knights, mainly from the Holy Roman Empire, to participate in the crusades.[9] Let us also add that the problem of the involvement of Mendicants in pastoral work in Prussia can be seen in a wider context, as a process of gradual valorisation of the rural space by removing paganism and religious ignorance and giving it value by joining the Christian world, to *christianitas*.[10] In this connection, the present chapter will discuss the conditions of the mendicant orders in the state of the Teutonic Order in Prussia and Polish Royal Prussia in the late Middle Ages, including the problem of the ethnic origin of the friars in the various convents. Their activities in Prussia's multi-ethnic communities, both in urban and rural areas, will also be presented with selected examples.

Outline of the Foundation of Mendicant Friaries in Prussia

In discussing the conditions under which the mendicant orders in Prussia carried out their activities, let us first recall the chronology of monastery foundations and its relationship to the urbanisation processes of the country. In the first period from the 1230s until the mid-13th century, Dominicans and Franciscans were active here. Both orders managed to run the foundations of their monasteries in the three largest urban centres of Prussia already mentioned: Kulm (Dominicans ca. 1233–1236), Elbing (Dominicans, in 1239) and Thorn (Franciscans 1239). In the second phase of the foundation period, which took place in the late 1250s and early 1260s, further monasteries of both communities were established in Kulm (Franciscans, in 1258) and Thorn (Dominicans, in 1263). At this time in nearby Eastern Pomerania, in addition to the Dominican monastery in Gdańsk established with the support of Świętopełk II Wielki (Svantopolk II the Great), Duke of Eastern Pomerania in 1227, the Franciscans implemented a foundation in Neuenburg (today Nowe) in 1282. The Dominicans likewise founded a monastery in Dirschau (today Tczew) in 1289.[11] By this time, monasteries were steadily appearing in urban centres along the Vistula River, which provided convenient transport over long distances. It was not until 1296, however, that the first monastery of the mendicant order was founded on land belonging to the bishops of Ermland (Pol. Warmia). This was the outpost of the Franciscans in Braunsberg (today Braniewo).[12] We should add that the friars associated with this monastery worked not only in Braunsberg – they were also involved in missionary activities. At the beginning of the 14th century, the friars of Braunsberg were present in the distant land of Semigallia,[13] an area of southern Latvia that bordered on the south with the pagan territories of Samogitia.[14]

With the advances in settlement and urbanisation of Prussia in the 14th century, there were also new monastic foundations in areas in the eastern part of the state of the Teutonic Order.[15] In 1349, another Franciscan monastery was founded. However, it was not located in the well-organised Chełmno Land (Germ. Kulmerland, Pol. ziemia chełmińska), although such plans existed in the early 14th century for the town of Lessen (today Łasin),[16] but in the small town of Wehlau (today Znamiensk) far to the east, close to Königsberg (today Kaliningrad).[17] The Bishops of Ermland/Warmia also decided in 1364 to establish a new monastery of the Friars Minor in Wartenburg (today Barczewo), located at the south-eastern edge of their dominion.[18]

This was not the first monastery of the mendicant order in this part of Ermland/Warmia. Indeed, at this time, representatives of another of the mendicant orders, the Augustinian Eremites,[19] appeared in Prussia. This community as a mendicant order was established by a decision of Pope Alexander IV in 1256, when it was decided to unite several smaller hermit groups, and in 1303 they were formally classified as a mendicant order. The first Augustinian Eremite monastery in Prussia was organised in 1347 on land belonging to the Bishops of Ermland/Warmia, in the small town of Rößel (today Reszel).[20] The friars of this congregation were very active in the area at that time. In 1356, their second monastery was established. However, it was located very far from Rößel, in Konitz (today Chojnice), located at the south-western edge of Prussia.[21] Two more outposts of this congregation were established in the eastern part of Prussia. In 1372, the monastery at Heiligenbeil (today Mamonovo) was founded,[22] while the second was established around 1400 in the knightly estate of Patollen (later the Groß Waldeck estate, today Ossokino).[23] Due to the time of their establishment, all Augustinian Eremite foundations were located in small urban centres, the most significant of which was Konitz. Interestingly, their establishment was not allowed in any of the major cities where Dominicans and/or Franciscans were already present. Let us further emphasise that the friaries in Patollen, Rößel and Heiligenbeil were located in areas with a largely Old-Prussian population. The Patollen convent was not the last planned foundation of the Augustinian Eremites in Prussia. In 1409, Ulrich von Jungingen, the Grand Master of the Teutonic Order, granted the Augustinian Hermits land for the construction of a new monastery in Memel (today Klaipėda).

At the same time, the foundation of the Franciscans in Ragnit (today Neman) was also planned.[24] The two monasteries were intended to be located in towns on the eastern edge of the Order's territories, presumably so that the friars could carry out missionary work from there in the areas of neighbouring Samogitia newly conquered by the Teutonic Order. Moreover, they could also participate in the organisation of Church structures there.[25] Let us add that in 1406 an unknown friar carried out pastoral activities in Samogitia for a year (at that time under the authority of the Teutonic Order), for which he was rewarded by the Grand Master of the Teutonic Order.[26] These plans were thwarted by the outbreak of a new uprising in Samogitia on 30 May 1409 and the subsequent defeat of the Teutonic Order by a combined army of the Kingdom of Poland and the Grand Duchy of Lithuania (15 July 1410).

As a result, the intention to establish a Dominican monastery in Lithuania, which was to involve friars from the Prussian counter-region (*contrata Prussiae*), i.e. a unit within the Polish province of the order, also became obsolete.[27] The Dominicans, however, established a new foundation in Prussia. In 1407, the friars received direct financial support from the coffers of the Grand Master of the Teutonic Order for the organisation of a monastery in Nordenburg (today Krylovo), in what was then the easternmost town of central Prussia.[28] In 1428, however, the convent was relocated to Gerdauen (today Zheleznodorozhny) further to the west, due to the inability of the Mendicant community to sustain itself in such desolate areas.[29]

In addition, the Carmelites began their activities in Prussia around 1380. Their first monastery was established in 1380 near the Young Town Danzig (Germ. Jungstadt Danzig), probably soon after the city was founded. The process of founding the new monastery was crowned by papal confirmation in 1399.[30] In the settlement complex of Danzig in the first half of the 15th century, there was still a Franciscan monastery (1419) located in the suburb of the Main Town Danzig (Germ. Rechtstadt Danzig)[31].

As a result of the Thirteen Years' War (1454–1466) and in accordance with the provisions of the Second Peace of Thorn (1466), the Teutonic Order lost Eastern Pomerania, the Chełmno Land, the area around Elbing and the whole of Ermland/Warmia to Poland. These areas became part of the Kingdom of Poland as its new province, called Royal Prussia. As a result of these changes, only two Augustinian Hermit monasteries and one Dominican monastery remained under the rulership of the Teutonic Order. In addition, there was still the Franciscan monastery in Wehlau, but there were no friars there at the time. However, the Friars Minor made efforts to regain their seat in Wehlau as early as 1467. A new impetus for the development of Mendicant religious structures in the Teutonic Order's jurisdiction was given by the appearance there of Franciscans of the strict rule, called Observants.[32] In 1477, they founded a monastery on the outskirts of the town of Wehlau, and in 1480 another monastery in Saalfeld (today Zalewo).[33] In addition, Observant Franciscans were still present in Eastern Pomerania in Lauenburg (today Lębork),[34] and from 1502 in Löbau (today Lubawa),[35] which was situated outside the territory of the Teutonic Order's dominion, in the territory belonging to the Bishops of Kulm/Chełmno. By contrast, the third Observant Franciscan monastery in Prussia was founded around 1515 at Tilsit (today Soveck), and a fourth in 1517 in Königsberg.[36]

In the second half of the 15th century, the Carmelites, who at that time had only one monastery in Gdańsk, also made efforts to establish new foundations in the area. Even during the Thirteen Years' War, attempts were made to establish the foundation of the Carmelites in Rastenburg (today Kętrzyn) (1457).[37] Their outposts were eventually established in Christburg (today Dzierzgoń) (before 1485) and Riesenburg (today Prabuty) (before 1489), but they operated for a fairly short time.[38]

184 *Societies in Late Medieval Prussia: Ethnicities*

In summary, during the Teutonic Order's rule, including Royal Prussia (which became part of the Kingdom of Poland after 1466), the Franciscans had seven convents, the Dominicans six, the Observant Franciscans five, the Augustinian Hermits four, and the Carmelites one permanent convent along with three others that quickly declined. After 1466, only one Dominican monastery (Gerdauen), two Augustinian hermits (Heiligenbeil and Patollen) and one Franciscan monastery (Wehlau) remained within the state of the Teutonic Order. In the second half of the 15th century, four houses of the Observant Franciscans (Wehlau, Saalfeld, Tilsit, Königsberg) and periodically two of the Carmelites (Rastenburg, Riesenburg) were established there.[39] By the middle of the 15th century, the Teutonic Order had both Mendicant monasteries operating in large towns (Kulm, Thorn, Gdańsk, Elbing, Braunsberg) and small towns, especially those in the eastern part of the state (Wartenburg, Rößel, Gerdauen, Wehlau) within its jurisdiction. Importantly, in the case of the latter, the friars played an important role in pastoral care directed not only to the urban population, but also to the non-German-speaking population living in the surrounding villages (Old-Prussians and perhaps Lithuanians, the latter near the monastery in Tilsit). Perhaps in connection with these tasks, a monastery of Observant Franciscans in Saalfeld was also established in the second half of the 15th century. The town is located on the border between Pomesania and Pogesania, where the countryside was then inhabited in large numbers by the Old-Prussian population.[40] However, the Observant Franciscan monastery in Tilsit was organised in a town adjacent to the areas where the rural settlement of the Lithuanian population developed intensively in the early 16th century.[41]

In attempting to determine more closely the ethnic composition of the population of Prussia in the Middle Ages, we can only refer to rather cursory estimates. Not only did the German-speaking population predominate in the towns, it also made up a large percentage among the rural population of the Chełmno Land and Prussia proper, i.e. excluding Eastern Pomerania and the Chełmno Land (up to 50% of the total population). In contrast, the Slavic-speaking population (Kashubian-Pomeranian and (Old-)Polish) lived mainly in rural areas and accounted for at least two-thirds of the total population of Eastern Pomerania. The Old-Prussian population around 1400 in Prussia proper exceeded 30% of the population,[42] including at least 10% in towns.[43] The indigenous Prussian population lived mainly in rural areas. Mainly in the eastern part of the state, including the southern edge of the jurisdiction of the Bishops of Ermland/Warmia. Very general estimates indicate that in the area of the western Prussian commanderies (Elbing, Christburg), the ratio of Old-Prussian-speaking to German-speaking people was 3:5, in the bishopric of Ermland/Warmia – in the northern part – the Old-Prussians made up 50% of the population, in the southern part up to 75%. Particularly relevant is that it was there (i.e. in the southern part of Ermland/Warmia) that the Franciscan monasteries in Wartenburg and the Augustinian Eremite monasteries in Rößel functioned. The number of Old-Prussians in the

The Functioning of Mendicant Orders in Multi-Ethnic Communities   185

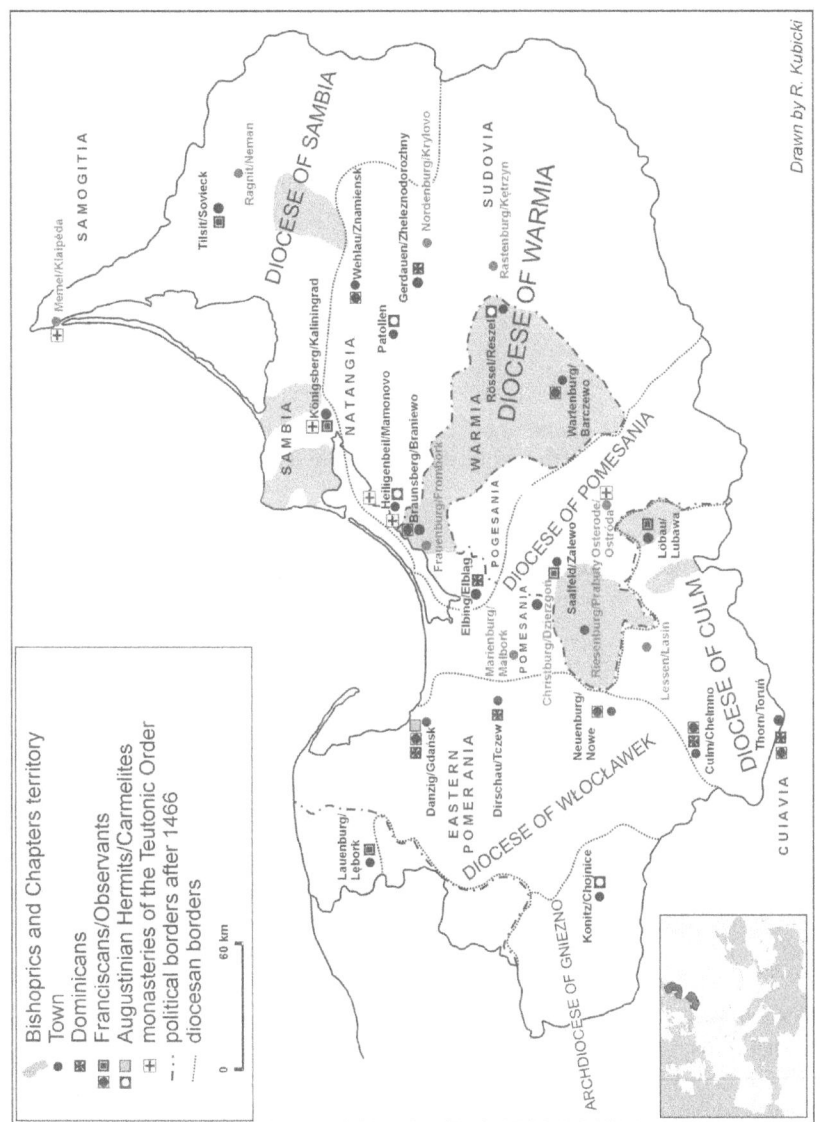

Figure 8.1 Mendicant Friaries in Royal Prussia and in Teutonic Order's Prussia about 1525

commandery to the east was even greater. In the territory of Natangen (Pol. Natangia) (Balga and Brandenburg commanderies), it was up to 90%, and in Samland (Pol. Sambia) (Königsberg commandery) it reached almost 100% in places.[44] In Natangen, the Augustinian Eremites in Heiligenbeil and Patollen were present, while in Samland alms collections were conducted by fundraisers from several mendicant monasteries, including the Dominicans of Elbing.

Thus, the friars did not limit themselves to pastoral work among the German population arriving from the west and the Slavic-speaking (Kashubian-Pomeranian and (Old-)Polish) population living in the western and southern parts of the country (Eastern Pomerania, Chełmno Land). Their activity also extended to the indigenous Prussian population.[45] Unfortunately, we do not know whether the friars in the Prussian monasteries were specifically trained in knowing the Old-Prussian language and conducting pastoral ministry in it.[46] Nor is there any record of them making use of the institution of Old-Prussian interpreters (*tolken*) in this regard, as was customary for diocesan clergy.[47]

The Composition of the Convents – The Ethnicity of the Friars, the Relationship to the District of Activity and the Recruitment of the Convents

The ethnically diverse social background of the monasteries probably also had some influence on the composition of the various Mendicant convents in Prussia. However, in considering this issue, it is also important to bear in mind at the same time a certain cultural and organisational unity in which the Church and the religious orders carried the idea of a universal community of believers, built on the same tradition, with an important unifying factor being the Latin language for the educated religious.

In the case of the Dominicans in the 13th century, friars from Poland played an important role in some convents.[48] In the Dominican monastery of Gdańsk, the prior of the convent was Brother Wojan in 1278. Similarly, the Dominican convent in Elbing at the time recorded the presence of several brothers bearing the Slavic names Primislaus, Pribezlaus and Stenzlaus, who even held the position of prior in 1276. From the few accounts of the convent at Kulm, it is known that Brother V[itus] was the prior there in 1248.[49] In 13th-century sources, a friar bearing the Slavic name Pribezlaus is also recorded in the Thorn monastery.[50] In Dirschau, the prior in 1335 was Wenceslaus. However, at a later stage, probably as early as the first half of the 14th century, German-speaking friars gained a decisive advantage in all Dominican monasteries in Prussia.[51] Despite this, their monasteries operating in Prussia were at all times part of the order's Polish provinces. We should add, however, that in the first half of the 15th century, the Dominicans made an unsuccessful attempt to change provincial affiliation. An important motive for this was a sense of cultural bonding with brothers from other parts of the Order's provinces was based on language, where there were strong German-speaking communities in the towns (Silesia and Western Pomerania).[52]

Despite these changes, (Old-)Polish-speaking friars were also present in Dominican convents in Prussia at a later date. The ethnic composition of the immediate social base of the monasteries, especially in the case of the convents in Danzig, Dirschau (both Eastern Pomerania), Kulm and Thorn (both Chełmno Land), gave rise to the constant need for the presence of friars who knew the (Old-)Polish language and could preach in it to the local Pomeranian community.[53]

The language problem in pastoral work was well known to the religious authorities. In the case of the Dominicans, the provincial chapters always specified that brothers transferred to convents in the province would preach in Polish or German. At the same time, Polish preachers usually came to the Prussian counter usually from the depths of the province, from conventions with a Polish majority.[54] This is confirmed by the practice observed in the 15th century of sending preachers by provincial authorities to individual convents. Among them were not only friars who spoke German, but also Polish preachers who were sent to monasteries in Eastern Pomerania and the Chełmno Land.[55] These brothers came, among others, from the monasteries of Poznań and Lwów (today Lviv), where the Polish element was predominant.

The presence of friars bearing Slavic names and arriving from monasteries in Poland, presumably for the purpose of carrying out pastoral work among the local Poles, was also noted in the various convents (primarily in Eastern Pomerania). In Elbing they were Brother Stanislaus and Paul Glenbicki, and in Thorn a certain Venceslaus. The brothers Crisogonus and Bogislaus were recorded in Dirschau in 1413. In 1505, Mathias Piwko, lector and Polish preacher, was also sent there. The permanent presence in the monasteries of friars who spoke (Old-)Polish was probably also a response to the real needs of their social base, in which the Slavic element (Kashubian-Pomeranian and (Old-)Polish) was not only present, but in the rural environment was sometimes dominant in Eastern Pomerania and in the Chełmno Land, i.e. in the area of activity of the Dominicans of Danzig, Dirschau, Kulm and Thorn, also constituting their potential recruitment base.[56]

Brothers from the local Slavic-speaking population were also present in the Franciscan convents. The custodian of the Prussian custody was Johan Poloni (1431 and 1438), as was the custodian in 1519–1521, Johan Szyłslaw/Żelisławski, who came from the nobility of Kociewie region. Similarly, the guardian at the Franciscans in Braniewo was in 1388 a friar bearing the Polish name 'Ryba' (Eng. fish).[57] Many others may be behind the popular names of the friars Johan, Jacob, whose names are not recorded in extant sources.[58] This seems to have been different in the case of the Carmelite convent in Danzig, where only German-speaking brothers were recorded.[59] Obviously, the nationality relations prevailing in the social background of the Mendicant monasteries and the associated real pastoral needs were reflected in the personal structure of the individual monasteries. This meant that, although there was a preponderance of friars from the German-speaking population in the convents, there also had to be brothers who spoke (Old-)Polish and Old-Prussian.

There are many indications that friars drawn from the indigenous Prussian population were mainly present in the Mendicant monasteries located in the eastern part of Prussia. Despite the prohibitions introduced, the Old-Prussian population migrated to the towns where they assimilated into the suburbs with the dominant German-speaking community. However, they probably did not lose their language too quickly. In the monastery of the Augustinian hermits in Rößel, in 1459, Nikolaus Legyn (from the village of *Legin*, later Legienen) was mentioned, and in 1476, Brother Augustin Tollawke (from the village of *Tollawke*, later Tollack, today Tuławki).[60] The same was true of the Dominican monasteries in Elbing and Gerdauen, which was directly related to their area of operation. In Elbing these were Martin Munter (1458), bearing a patronymic surname derived from the Old-Prussian name Muntir.[61] However, the parents of Jacob Revosze or Rabusa[62] (Rawusen, Raus, Rawos), an Old-Prussian village (in the field of *Raus*), and Bartholomeus Ruscheyszen (from the village of *Ruszaynen*, later *Russchenhain*, Reuschhagen, today Ruszajny)[63] may have come from Old-Prussian settlements. Old-Prussians who were culturally already connected to the German ethnicity may have been Peter Zugelia, possibly from the Sambian village of *Suggelaw* (today not existing), and Johan Bomgart (year 1409) from the village of *Boumgarte* (today not existing).[64] Obviously these friars, thanks to their knowledge of the Old-Prussian language, had a special role to play in the daily pastoral and preaching ministry.[65] Old-Prussian-speaking brothers were also present at the convent in Gerdauen. In 1499, Johan Kenstute, whose surname indicates an Old-Prussian origin, was recorded there. A certain Heinrich Kynstute was recorded around 1440 in the vicinity of Preußisch Holland.[66] Brethren with knowledge of the Old-Prussian language were useful in their contacts with the inhabitants of the fund-raising district where, in addition to the collection of alms, they could also carry out preaching activities there. Most importantly, of course, were the aforementioned Dominicans of Elbing and Gerdauen, the Augustinian hermits of Rößel, Heiligenbeil and Patollen, and the Franciscans of Wartenburg and Wehlau.

As already mentioned, the friars working in the various Mendicant convents in the area were mostly drawn from the German-speaking population that dominated the urban centres of Prussia. They not only preached for the Order, but also prepared texts in German. From the few references available, we know that the Franciscan custodian Claus Cranc translated the prophetic books of the Old Testament into Middle High German at the request of the Grand Marshal of the Teutonic Order Siegfried von Dahenfeld (1346–1360).[67] The Franciscans of the Thorn monastery also kept a yearbook of records.[68] The Franciscans in Gdańsk, however, had a manuscript, written in Middle Low German, of the Saxon Chronicle in their library. The same volume also contains a treatise on mystical theology, *Der Seele Trost*, which was also written in Middle Low German in the 15th century.[69] The works in Middle Low German probably served the brothers who came from North Germany, especially for pastoral work among some of the inhabitants of Danzig and Werder (Pol. Żuławy), who used this language. It was also probably no coincidence that, as a result of requests made to the King of Poland, the Franciscans in Danzig were granted the right to conduct alms collections in 1521 in the Großes Werder (Pol. Żuławy Wielkie) region, which was inhabited by people speaking the Middle Low German language. Perhaps language issues were also behind the decisions regarding the staffing of the new convent of Observant Franciscans that was established in 1517 in Königsberg. In the same year, the Grand Master of the Teutonic Order, Albrecht von Brandenburg-Ansbach, asked Bishop of Pomesanien/Pomezania, Hiob von Dobeneck to write to the friars in the Observant Franciscan convents in Löbau, Saalfeld and Lauenburg. He instructed Hiob to ask them to send two priests each for preaching and confession, for as long as their superiors allowed, and especially from Löbau, a friar from Franconia and Michael Curaw, which may hint to the importance of their knowledge of Middle High German and Middle Low German.[70] However, no texts written in (Old-)Polish or Old-Prussian have been preserved in the monastery libraries.

The Activities of Friars in the Multi-ethnic Communities of Prussia (Towns and Countryside)

When considering the problem of the activities of Mendicants in the ethnically diverse communities of Prussia, we can refer to the relatively few accounts touching directly on the issue of the tasks set by the founder. An interesting clue is provided by the *arenga* of the foundation document of the Dominican monastery in Elbing of 13 January 1239.[71] The Land Master of the Teutonic Order, Herman Balk, in specifying the motive for the decision on the foundation, stated the following: "therefore we declare with the present document that, wishing to protect the souls exposed to many possible dangers, which are mostly born in the newly settled countries, where those fleeing from an honest life and evading exposure are most often hiding, by the complete will of our chapter, to the venerable order, which is called a preacher's order and is recognised as such indeed, to the brothers, namely the prior and the friars [literally: lord and people – R. K.] beloved and effective in works and words in our newly settled town of Elbing, we grant them a place where they can build their monastery".[72] The Dominicans' main task, therefore, was to provide pastoral care for the population of the newly founded town and to assist in caring for the standard of religious life of the numerous settlers arriving in the town. In the charter confirming this foundation of 14 April 1246, Grand Master Heinrich von Hohenlohe additionally mentioned the Dominican activities of the time in Prussia and Livonia (today Latvia and Estonia).[73]

Importantly, according to the contents of the Christburg Treaty of 7 February 1249, concluded between the Old-Prussian tribes and the Teutonic Order through the papal legate Jacobus of Leodium, it was agreed, among other things, that "Prussian boys born of the right bed have full access to the priestly and monastic state (*clerici et religionem*), while neophytes from noble families (*ex nobili prosapia*) may enlist in the armed state and acquire the knight's belt".[74]

Unfortunately, we have no record of whether the Old-Prussians were already joining monasteries of Mendicant orders during this period. However, some testimony has survived regarding the knowledge of the Old-Prussian language among Dominican friars from a later period. A Dominican named Nikolaus, who was a witness in the 1339 Warsaw-Uniejów trial by the Polish side against the Teutonic Order in connection with its occupation of Eastern Pomerania and had previously served as a lector in the Kulm monastery and as prior in Elbing, testified that he was present when the knights of the Teutonic Order destroyed the Dominican monastery in Sieradz. He tried to plead with the commandery of Elbing that the town and the monastery be spared. In response, he heard the Old-Prussian words "ne prest", i.e. "I don't understand", from the commander. Nikolaus therefore knew the meaning of these words in Old-Prussian. He probably formulated his requests in German, but the commander Hermann von Oettingen used the Old-Prussian phrase because he wanted to avoid conversation. This transmission indirectly confirms the knowledge of the Old-Prussian language among at least some of the Dominicans in Elbing.[75]

At the same time, the friars of this monastery were engaged in pastoral activities in the eastern parts of Prussia. Interesting information on the subject is provided by a collection of formulas of the Polish Dominican province, which preserves a specimen of a letter of recommendation from the year around 1338–1344, in which the provincial of the Dominicans presented to the Bishop of Ermland/Warmia, Hermann von Prag (1338–1349), for help in hearing confessions, the friars of the Dominican monastery in Elbing. Although the monastery in question was at the western end of the diocese, its friars must have played an important role in assisting the diocesan clergy with the administration of the sacraments. It is also particularly interesting to note that in the aforementioned letter, the provincial requested that the friars be presented "when convenient" also to the Bishop of Samland/Sambia, Johann von Clare (1320–1344).[76]

Perhaps the Dominicans also reached Samland/Sambia, inhabited by the indigenous Prussians, at this time. The authorities of the Polish Dominican province constantly sought the support of the local bishops for their friars. The tradition of pastoral cooperation is evidenced by a letter written by the Dominican provincial Albert from Siecień on 27 February 1497 to the Bishop of Ermland/Warmia, Lukas Watzenrode, in which he recommended the Dominicans of Elbing to him, pointing to their involvement in pastoral work among the local population.[77] In this way, in agreement with the local bishops, the friars carried out their pastoral activities not only in the cities, but also outside them. It has already been mentioned that, besides hearing confessions, the most important task carried out by the friars was preaching. In areas away from the monastery church, this was obviously of an irregular nature. It seems, however, that it may have taken on greater significance where local vicars did not quite properly carry out this duty themselves.[78]

Local people were also encouraged to establish close ties with the monastery by the indulgences held by the community and the particular church, as well as the relics kept there and the holy images held in special esteem by the faithful.[79] In this context, it is worth mentioning that the Augustinian church in Patollen was an important pilgrimage site because of the icon of the Virgin Mary from the church in Georgenau (today Roschtschino) kept there.[80] In turn, an extremely valuable relic of the Holy Cross was in the possession of the Augustinian Hermits church in Konitz. In 1384 the Archbishop of Gniezno, Bodzanta (Bodzęta), issued a letter of indulgence (establishing a forty-day indulgence) which encouraged pilgrims to visit this church.[81] Important feast celebrations connected with indulgences were also organised at the Franciscan church in Neuenburg. A chronicler's note reports that in 1399, one hundred inhabitants of the surrounding villages of Stangendorf (today Glina) and Nebrow (today Nebrowo) were killed on their way back from the monastery church. They were returning by ferry across the Vistula after visiting the church, associated with the indulgence on the Sunday after the octave of *Corpus Christi* (8 June).[82]

It has already been mentioned that, in addition to the immediate surroundings of the monastery of the city and the suburbs, the mendicants worked in a fund-raising district covering even remote rural areas. This was the case for the Dominicans and Franciscans of Thorn, who had the right to collect alms not only in the state of the Teutonic Order, but also in Kuyavia.[83]

However, monasteries of the Augustinian Hermits had their own rural facilities in the form of estates and villages. Interestingly, the Augustinian Hermits monastery in Rößel, located in a town belonging to the Bishops of Ermland/Warmia, possessed its own estates to the east of the bishop's rule, within the borders of the area under the authority of the Teutonic Order (in the area of the procuratorate in Seehesten (today Szestno)).[84] The estates and villages of the Augustinian Hermits of Patollen and Heiligenbeil, however, were located near their monasteries.[85] The ownership of meadows, estates or even villages meant that the interface with the people of the rural district was not only the collection of alms by itinerant collectors, but also mutual economic interests: agreements on leases and neighbourhood agreements concerning the use of meadows, pastures, streams, etc.

It was not the task of mendicants to take over urban or rural parishes and replace diocesan clergy in their pastoral work.[86] However, there have been some deviations from this general rule. The Dominicans of Thorn had links with the parish of Kaszczorek.[87] Similarly, parish churches were periodically cared for by the Dominicans of Kulm (parish in Althaus (today Starogród

Chełmiński))[88] and by the Augustinian Hermits of Patollen (parish *hinder dem Tyeffe*, so perhaps in Pillau, today Baltiysk).[89] The Augustinian Hermits monastery in Patollen also looked after the nearby parish churches in Almenhausen (today Kaschtanovo) and Abschwangen (today Tischino) in the 15th century, which was reconfirmed by Pope Alexander VI (1492–1503) at the request of the Prior.[90]

In addition to their links with rural parishes, the mendicants also participated in fund-raising organised not only in the immediate vicinity of their monastery. The extent of this phenomenon is indirectly evidenced by the surviving alms collection permits (*Bettelbrief* or *Termineibrief*), mainly in Samland, which were issued to individual monasteries by the Grand Master of the Teutonic Order in the late 15th and early 16th centuries. The alms collection was probably combined with some form of pastoral care to the local population (sermons, confessions). Such activities were carried out both by the Dominicans of Elbing and Gerdauen, the Augustinian Hermits of Rößel, Patollen[91] and Heiligenbeil, the Franciscans of Braunsberg and Wehlau, the Observant Franciscans of Wehlau and Tilsit, and even the hospital congregations: the Antonians of Frauenburg (today Frombork) and the Order of the Holy Ghost of Riesenburg (today Prabuty).[92] This was of particular importance in the case of the territories of the Königsberg commandery and Samland/Sambia, where the parish network was very underdeveloped and did not actually meet the needs of an area inhabited overwhelmingly by an indigenous Prussian population.[93]

Interestingly in 1513, due to the cost of construction and other needs of the convent, the Franciscans of Wehlau asked the Grand Master for the right to have an alms district and conduct alms collections also in the territory of Sudauen (Sudovia, Yotvingia).[94]

These permits not only specified the exact term of their validity (usually one year), but also the area over which the fundraisers could roam. This information is contained in the permission for alms collection that the Dominicans of Gerdauen received on 7 September 1518. They were free to collect donations in Samland/Sambia and in villages along the route to Memel. However, they could not do so along the beach. They were also not allowed to visit certain villages in the north-western part of Samland/Sambia, and these were Thierenberg (today Dunayevka), Germau (today Russkoye), Heiligenkreutz (today Krasnotorovka), Sankt Lorenz (today Sal'skoe) and Pobethen (today Romanovo).[95] The restriction was a ban on the collection and receipt of amber. This was clearly indicated in the analogous permission for the Dominicans in Elbing,[96] with the prohibition covering both the bailiwicks (*Kämmerämter*) belonging to the Teutonic Order (Germau, Sankt Lorenz, Pobethen) and the territory of the bishop of Samland/Sambia (the villages of Heiligenkreutz and Thierenberg).

During these tours led by the fundraisers, interesting events sometimes occurred. A testimony to this was recorded in the chronicle of the Dominican, Simon Grunau. While wandering around the fundraising district, he ended up in a village where he accidentally encountered a large gathering of indigenous Prussians in one of the houses. They had just listened to the teachings preached in Old-Prussian by the old peasant who was their *waidlott*.[97] According to Grunau's account, they initially wanted to kill him, but he pleaded with the *waidlott* to spare his life, addressing him in Old-Prussian, which he confessed to knowing a little (*ich kundt ein wenigk Preusch*).[98] This account obviously describes an extraordinary incident that happened to the chronicler, and he thought it worth noting down. Its authenticity is supported not only by a frank description of the friar's behaviour, which was far from the attitude of a martyr for the faith. As he noted, he took an oath to the pagan god Perkun not to inform the bishop of the incident. It also provides a good characterisation of the progress of Christianisation of the Old-Prussian population, particularly in Samland/Sambia and on the eastern edges of Prussia.[99] Awareness of the actual state of pastoral care for the local population was also one of the motives behind the foundation of the aforementioned Observant Franciscan monastery in Tilsit. In a letter to the house commander of Ragnit and the procurator of Tilsit on 9 August 1515, encouraging them to help complete the monastery as quickly as possible, the surrounding population, whom the friars were to serve, the population was described as: "our poor, ignorant and unbelieving subjects".[100]

Summary

The successful functioning of mendicant orders in the multi-ethnic communities living in Prussia required the need to adapt to local conditions. The friars provided pastoral care in an urban environment in which Polish-speaking people were present alongside the predominantly German-speaking population. This was particularly the case in Eastern Pomerania and in the Chełmno Land, as indicated by the Dominicans' appointment of separate preachers who spoke Polish or German. We should add that among the German-speaking population there were settlers using both Middle Low German (from the northern part of the German lands) and Middle High German (from the southern German lands). Surviving sources indicate that the friars addressed their message to this population in both languages.

Also important is that, from the very beginning, the friars were also involved in missionary activity among the Old-Prussians (Dominicans from Gdańsk). They also participated in this activity in Livonia (Dominicans from an unknown monastery, possibly from Riga, and Franciscans from Braniewo). In the rural areas, especially in the district for collecting alms in the eastern part of the country (Ermland/Warmia, Samland/Sambia), the friars were in constant contact with the indigenous Prussian population and, from the beginning of the 16th century, also with the immigrant Lithuanian population (Observant Franciscans in Tilsit). The various convents thus also had friars from the Old-Prussian population who knew the language well. At the same time, this did not mean that the presence of itinerant collectors, or even the pastoral activity of itinerant preachers, could replace the tasks of village parsons there. Indulgences and feast days organised regularly in the monastery churches, which brought together people coming from the surrounding villages (Augustinian Hermits in Patollen and Konitz), may have played a greater role in this respect. Alongside their work in multi-ethnic urban communities, the friars also reached out to the inhabitants of rural areas, where there was also a strong ethnic diversity of inhabitants. In addition to villages inhabited by German-speaking or Slavic-speaking people (especially in Eastern Pomerania and the Chełmno Land), there were also dense areas settled by Old-Prussians and, from the beginning of the 16th century, Lithuanians.

Notes

1 In the chapter, reference is made to the research results presented in a broader context in the book Rafał Kubicki, *Zakony mendykanckie w Prusach Krzyżackich i Królewskich od XIII do połowy XVI wieku* (Gdańsk: Wydawnictwo Uniwersytetu Gdańskiego, 2018).

2 Regarding the activity of mendicant orders in the Teutonic Order state in Prussia, see Werner Roth, *Die Dominikaner und Franziskaner im Deutsch-Ordenslande Preußen bis zum Jahre 1466* (Königsberg in Pr.: Drewes Buchdruckerei, 1918); Adalbero Kunzelmann, *Geschichte der deutschen Augustiner-Eremiten*, part 3, *Die bayerische Provinz bis zum Ende des Mittelalters* (Würzburg: Augustinus-Verlag, 1972); part 5, *Die sächsisch-thüringische Provinz und die sächsische Reformkongregation bis zum Untergang der Beiden* (Würzburg: Augustinus-Verlag, 1974); Tadeusz Mikołaj Trajdos, *U zarania karmelitów w Polsce* (Warszawa: Instytut Historii PAN, 1993); Jürgen Sarnowsky, 'Die Dominikaner und Franziskaner im Ordensland Preußen,' in *Franciscan Organisation in the Mendicant Context. Formal and informal structures of the friars' lives and ministry in the Middle Ages*, ed. Michael Robson and Jens Röhrkasten, Vita Regularis Ordnungen und Deutungen religiosen Lebens im Mittelalter 44 (Berlin: LIT Verlag, 2010), 43–64; Rafał Kubicki, 'Die Rolle der Bettelorden im Ordensland Preußen,' in *Cura animarum. Seelsorge im Deutschordensland des Mittelalters*, ed. Stefan Samerski (Köln, Weimar, Wien: Böhlau Verlag, 2013), 74–91; Sławomir Zonenberg, *Stosunki krzyżacko-mendykanckie w Prusach do 1466 roku* (Bydgoszcz: Wydawnictwo Uniwersytetu Kazimierza Wielkiego, 2018).

3 Marian Biskup, 'Bemerkung zum Siedlungsproblem und den Pfarrbezirken und Ordenspreußen im 14.–15. Jahrhundert,' in *Die Rollen der Ritterorden in der Christianisierung und Kolonisierung des Ostseegebietes*, ed. Zenon Hubert Nowak, Ordines Militares. Colloquia Torunensia Historica I (Toruń: Wydawnictwo Naukowe UMK, 1983), 45–48; Marian Biskup, 'Parafie w państwie krzyżackim,' in *Państwo zakonu krzyżackiego w Prusach. Podziały administracyjne i kościelne w XIII–XVI wieku*, ed. Zenon Hubert Nowak (Toruń: Wydawnictwo Naukowe UMK, 2000), 81–93.

4 William Aquinas Hinnebusch, *The history of the Dominican Order. Origins and Growth to 1500*, vol. 1 (New York: Alba House, 1966), 119–143; Sławomir Zonenberg, '«Cura animarum» zakonu kaznodziejskiego w średniowieczu na tle rozwoju duszpasterstwa mniszego,' *Lietuvos Istorijos Studijos* 18 (2006): 14–15.

5 Andrzej Radzimiński, *Chrystianizacja i ewangelizacja Prusów. Historia i źródła* (Toruń: Wydawnictwo Adam Marszałek, 2011), 6–10.

6 Jerzy Kłoczowski, 'Klosterkreise in der polnischen Dominikanerprovinz im Mittelalter,' in *Vita Religiosa im Mittelalter. Festschrift für Kaspar Elm zum 70. Geburtstag*, ed. Franz Josef Felten and Nikolas Jaspert, Berliner Historische Studien 31 (Berlin: Duncker & Humblot, 1999), 533–542.
7 Andrzej Radzimiński, 'Udział zakonu krzyżackiego w procesie ewangelizacji Prus. Uwagi na podstawie ustawodawstwa synodalnego,' ZH 70, no. 1 (2005): 7–26.
8 PUB, I/2: 64–65 no. 84. Regarding the activities of Dominicans, see Jan Powierski, 'Dzieje ziemi pasłęckiej do schyłku XIII w.,' in *Pasłęk z dziejów miasta i okolic 1297–1997*, ed. Józef Włodarski (Pasłęk: Urząd Miasta i Gminy, 1997), 162–168 (chapter 18, *Misja dominikańska w ziemi pasłęckiej a rywalizacja Krzyżaków z biskupem Chrystianem*).
9 Compilation of papal bulls concerning calls for crusade preaching addressed to the Franciscan Order, see Hans Niedermeier, 'Die Franziskaner in Preussen, Livland und Litauen im Mittelalter,' *Zeitschrift für Ostforschung* 27, no. 1 (1978): 18. Regarding the activities of the Dominicans, see Berthold Altaner, *Die Dominikanermission des 13. Jahrhunderts* (Halberschwerdt: Franke, 1924). Compilation of papal bulls addressed to the Dominican Order, see Sławomir Zonenberg, 'Stosunki dominikańsko-krzyżackie w Prusach do 1466 roku,' in *Klasztor dominikański w Toruniu w 750. rocznicę fundacji*, ed. Piotr Oliński, Waldemar Rozynkowski, and Juliusz Raczkowski, (Toruń: Wydawnictwo Naukowe UMK, 2013), 49–50 footnote 24.
10 Rafał Simiński, *Od "solitudo" do "terra culta". Przestrzeń jako przedmiot wyobrażeń w Inflantach i Prusach od XIII do początku XV wieku*, Roczniki Towarzystwa Naukowego w Toruniu 92, no. 2 (Toruń: Towarzystwo Naukowe w Toruniu, 2008), 151.
11 Roth, *Die Dominikaner*, 81–82, 136. In 1308–1309, the territories of Eastern Pomerania were conquered by the Teutonic Order. As a result, the mentioned monasteries found themselves in the same state as the convents already existing in Prussia.
12 Roth, *Die Dominikaner*, 61–85, 126–143; Niedermeier, 'Die Franziskaner,' 5–9.
13 He mentioned this in the bull of 19 July 1310, Pope Clement V, *cf.* PUB, II: 8 no. 13; Niedermeier, 'Die Franziskaner,' 8, 14.
14 At that time, the Franciscans had an existing monastery in Riga on this part of the Baltic coast since 1238. Dominicans were also present there earlier, since 1234, *cf.* Rafał Kubicki, 'Mendicant Orders in medieval Prussia and Livonia: Pastoral Activities in Towns,' *Acta Historica Universitatis Klaipedensis* 33 (2016): 130.
15 The comprehensive process of founding villages and towns in these areas was presented by Karl Kasiske, *Die Sieglungstätigkeit des Deutschen Ordens im östlichen Preussen bis zum Jahre 1410* (Königsberg: Kommissionsverlag Gräfe und Unzer, 1934); id., *Das deutsche Siedelwerk des Mittelalters in Pommerellen* (Königsberg: Kommissionsverlag Gräfe und Unzer, 1938).
16 Regarding the unsuccessful foundation in Lessen due to resistance from city authorities, see Roth, *Die Dominikaner*, 116.
17 Roth, *Die Dominikaner*, 144.
18 CDW, II: 382 no. 368.
19 The data regarding the activity of the Augustinian Hermits in Prussia was compiled by Kunzelmann, *Geschichte*, 5: 271–272, 276–282, 288–290, and 300–305.
20 Adolf Poschmann, 'Das Augustinerkloster in Rössel,' *Zeitschrift für die Geschichte und Altertumskunde Ermlands* 24 (1932): 83.
21 Hugo Eysenblätter, 'Die Klöster der Augustiner Eremiten im Nordosten Deutschlands,' *Altpreußische Monatsschrift* 35 (1898): 372–374.
22 Poschmann, *Das Augustinerkloster*, 89.
23 MTB, 83, 97, and 199.

24 *Anno 1409 statim post pasce Ulricus magister cum aliquibus preceptoribus* [...] *dedit locum Augustinensibus in Memela; nobis vero, fratribus minoribus, in Ragnit; sed guerra interveniente nihil pro tunc est factum, cf.* FTAP, 298; Leonhard Lemmens, 'Aus der Geschichte der deutschen Franziskaner im Ordenslande Preußen,' *Mitteilungen des Coppernicus-Vereins für Wissenschaft und Kunst zu Thorn* 20 (1912): 62; Roth, *Die Dominikaner*, 103; Niedermeier, 'Die Franziskaner,' 15.

25 Rafał Kubicki, 'Działalność zakonów mendykanckich na pograniczu krzyżacko-litewskim do początków XVI w.,' in *Litwa i jej sąsiedzi w relacjach wzajemnych (XIII–XVI w.)*, ed. Anna Kołodziejczyk, Rafał Kubicki, and Marek Radoch (Olsztyn, Gdańsk: Wydawnictwo Uniwersytetu Warmińsko-Mazurskiego, 2014), 184–185.

26 On 29 September 1406, expenses from the Grand Master's treasury recorded a payment for a friar who had been in charge throughout the year: *item 2 m. eyme monche gegeben, der zu Samaythen gewest was eyn ganz yar, cf.* MTB, 407.

27 Kubicki, 'Działalność zakonów mendykanckich,' 184, 191–192.

28 MTB, 423.

29 CDW, IV: 267–268 no. 233, 276 no. 242.

30 Trajdos, *U zarania*, 16, 24–25.

31 Rafał Kubicki, *Franciszkanie w Gdańsku w XV–XVI wieku* (Gdańsk: Wydawnictwo Uniwersytetu Gdańskiego, 2022), 25–29.

32 Id., 'Mendicant Friaries in the Dominion of the Teutonic Order in Prussia and in Royal Prussia after 1466 until the Reformation', ZH 81, no. 4 (2016): 84–85.

33 USF, 33 no. 113.

34 Unfortunately, we know nothing about the circumstances of the foundation of the Franciscan Observant monastery in Lauenburg. The first evidence of their presence in this centre is a record of 20 marks for the brothers made in 1492 by the Danzig's alderman and councillor Otto Angermünde, *cf.* Paul Simson, 'Das Testament des Danziger Schöffen und Ratsherrn Otto Angermünde,' *Mitteilungen des Westpreußischen Geschichtsvereins* 14, no. 3 (1915): 45.

35 *Diecezja chełmińska zarys historyczno-statystyczny* (Pelplin: Pielgrzym, 1928), 443.

36 *Spuren franziskanischer Geschichte. Chronologischer Abriß der Geschichte der Sächsischen Franziskanerprovinzen von ihren Anfängen bis zur Gegenwart*, ed. Dieter Berg (Werl: Butzon & Bercker 1999), 251; Kubicki, 'Mendicant Friaries in the Dominion', 86.

37 *Bullarium Poloniae*, vol. 6, ed. Irena Sułkowska-Kuraś and Stanisław Kuraś (Romae, Lublin: Abilgraf – Polski Instytut Kultury Chrześcijańskiej, 1998), 251 no. 1203.

38 Trajdos, *U zarania*, 216; Joachim Smet and Ulrich Dobhan, *Die Karmeliten. Eine Geschichte der Brüder U.L. Frau vom Berg Karmel von den Anfängen (ca. 1200) bis zum Konzil von Trient* (Freiburg, Basel, Wien: Herder Verlag, 1981), 182; Kraków, Archiwum klasztoru oo. karmelitów w Krakowie na Piasku, 92/682 ("Index fundationum monasteriorum provinciae Polonae Carmelitarum Antiquae Regularis Observantiae, Anno 1676"), fol. 41r–43r; Kubicki, 'Mendicant Friaries in the Dominion', 85.

39 The location of mendicant monasteries in Prussia is presented on the map included in this chapter. In total, in the dioceses of Kulm/Chełmno, Pomesanien/Pomezania, Ermland/Warmia, and Samland/Sambia, there were 646 rural parishes in the Middle Ages, and in the entire Prussia, there were 851 rural and 97 urban parishes. See Biskup, 'Parafie,' 91. Interesting observations regarding forms of piety in the rural areas of Prussia and the role of sacred art as a transmitter of religious content were formulated by Monika Jakubek-Raczkowska, *Tu ergo flecte genua tua. Sztuka a praktyka religijna świeckich w diecezjach pruskich państwa zakonu*

krzyżackiego do połowy XV wieku (Pelplin: Wydawnictwo Bernardinum, 2014), 481–571.
40 They discussed the state of Old-Prussian settlement in these areas: Heide Wunder, *Siedlungs- und Bevölkerungsgeschichte der Komturei Christburg (13.–16. Jahrhundert)*, Marburger Ostforschungen 28 (Wiesbaden: Otto Harrassowitz, 1968), 77–143, 165; Peter Germershausen, *Siedlungsentwicklung der preußischen Ämter Holland, Liebstadt und Mohrungen vom 13. bis zum 17. Jahrhundert*, Wissenschaftliche Beiträge zur Geschichte und Landeskunde Ost-Mitteleuropas 87 (Marburg: Johann Gottfried Herder-Institut, 1970), 9–38.
41 Wiesław Długokęcki, 'Odbudowa osadnictwa, kolonizacja i przemiany wsi w państwie krzyżackim (1411–1525),' in *Państwo zakonu krzyżackiego w Prusach. Władza i społeczeństwo*, ed. Marian Biskup and Roman Czaja (Warszawa: Wydawnictwo Naukowe PWN, 2008), 381–383; Leonhard Lemmens, *Die Franziskanerkustodie Livland und Preussen. Beitrag zur Kirchengeschichte der Gebiete des Deutschen Ordens* (Düsseldorf: Kommissionsverlag von L. Schwann, 1912), 24, 35.
42 Marzena Pollakówna, 'Zanik ludności pruskiej,' in *Szkice z dziejów Pomorza. Pomorze wczesnośredniowieczne* (Warszawa: Książka i Wiedza, 1958), 191; Marian Biskup, 'Das Problem der ethnischen Zugehörigkeit im mittelalterlichen Landesausbau in Preussen. Zum Stand der Forschung,' *Jahrbuch für die Geschichte Mittel- und Ostdeutschlands* 40 (1991): 8.
43 Henryk Łowmiański, *Polityka ludnościowa zakonu niemieckiego w Prusach i na Pomorzu* (Gdańsk: Instytut Bałtycki, 1947), 43.
44 Henrich Harmjanz, *Volkskunde und Siedlungsgeschichte Altpreussen* (Berlin: Junker und Dünnhaupt, 1943, 2nd ed.), 32; Biskup, 'Das Problem,' 3–25.
45 Furthermore, it should be added that the Old-Prussian population, upon settling in the towns, rather quickly underwent assimilation under the influence of interactions with the predominantly German settlers there. The issue of assimilation of the Old-Prussian population is addressed by Pollakówna, 'Zanik ludności pruskiej,' 160–207; Grischa Vercamer, 'Der Übergang der prußischen Stammeseliten in die Schicht der ‚Freien' unter der Herrschaft des Deutschen Ordens und der Kulturtransfer von der ‚deutschen' auf die prußische Kultur,' in *Mittelalterliche Eliten und Kulturtransfer östlich der Elbe. Interdisziplinäre Beiträge zu Archäologie und Geschichte im mittelalterlichen Ostmitteleuropa*, ed. Anne Klammt and Sébastien Rossignol (Göttingen: Universitätsverlag, 2009), 169–191.
46 In the case of the diocesan clergy, this issue is discussed by Radzimiński, *Chrystianizacja*, 28–34.
47 Radzimiński, 28.
48 Jerzy Kłoczowski, *Dominikanie polscy na Śląsku w XIII–XIV wieku* (Lublin: TN KUL, 1956), 136.
49 Publishers resolve his name in the document from 1257, *cf.* UBBC, II: 1153 no. 1228.
50 Perhaps identical to Pribezlaus, a friar in Elbing in 1251.
51 Kubicki, *Środowisko*, 137–143.
52 Kubicki, 32–33; Jakub Turek, 'Podział polskiej prowincji dominikanów w czasach prowincjalatu Jana Biskupca w latach 1415–1417,' *Przegląd Historyczny* 106, no. 2 (2015): 287–324. It was different in the case of Franciscan monasteries in Kulm and Thorn, which originally belonged to the Polish province of the order but in the 13th century moved to the Saxon province of the order.
53 The brothers from Thorn conducted alms collections in Kuyavia, in areas inhabited by the Polish population. Also, in the local Franciscan monastery, the presence of Brother Łukasz, a Polish preacher, was noted in 1511. See Marian Biskup, *Historia Torunia*, vol. 2, part 1, *U schyłku średniowiecza i w początkach odrodzenia (1454–1548)* (Toruń: Wydawnictwo TNT, 1992), 205.

54 Kubicki, *Środowisko*, 107–108, 138.
55 Kubicki, 138, 140–141, and 201–202.
56 Kubicki, 136.
57 Regarding the nationality of Prussian Franciscans, with reference to these examples, see Kamil Kantak, *Franciszkanie polscy*, vol. 1, *1237–1517* (Kraków: Prowincja Polska OO. Franciszkanów, 1937), 353–354.
58 Kantak, 353.
59 So accepted by Trajdos, *U zarania*, 198.
60 Poschmann, *Das Augustinerkloster*, 91.
61 Reinhold Trautmann, *Die altpreußischen Personennamen* (Göttingen: Vandenhoeck & Ruprecht, 1974), 63.
62 CDW, I: 221–223 no. 125 (*campus Raus*), 297–298 no. 171 (*campus Rawos*), *cf.* Marzena Pollakówna, *Osadnictwo Warmii w okresie krzyżackim* (Poznań: Instytut Zachodni, 1953), 37, 82, and 133.
63 Pollakówna, *Osadnictwo*, 151.
64 Kubicki, *Środowisko*, 140.
65 Sławomir Zonenberg, *Kronika Szymona Grunaua* (Bydgoszcz: Wydawnictwo Uniwersytetu Kazimierza Wielkiego, 2009), 119 footnote 649; Poschmann, *Das Augustinerkloster*, 93.
66 Trautmann, *Die altpreußischen Personennamen*, 45; Kubicki, *Środowisko*, 143.
67 This information has been preserved thanks to the acrostic placed at the beginning of the book. See Roth, *Die Dominikaner*, 119; Arno Mentzel-Reuters, *Arma spiritualia: Bibliotheken, Bildung und Bücher im Deutschen Orden*, Beiträge zum Buch- und Bibliothekswesen 47 (Wiesbaden: Harrassowitz, 2003), 65, 121, 170, and 263.
68 FTAP, 227; 'Annales Minorum Prussicorum,' ed. Ernst Strehlke, in SRP, V: 647–648.
69 Gdańsk, Polska Akademia Nauk, Biblioteka Gdańska, Ms. 1614; *Katalog der Handschriften der Danziger Stadtbibliothek*, part 2, ed. Otto Günther, Katalog der Danziger Stadtbibliothek 2 (Danzig: Kommissions-Verlag der L. Saunierschen Buch- und Kunsthandlung, 1903), 298–299; Agata Larczyńska, 'Piękno średniowiecznych manuskryptów. Biblioteka gdańskiego klasztoru franciszkanów na nowo odkryta,' *Studia Zamkowe* 4 (2012): 116.
70 Lemmens, *Die Franziskanerkustodie*, 27; USF, I: 54 no. 234.
71 The foundation document of the monastery, dated 13 January 1238, was issued by the Land Master of the Teutonic Order in Prussia, Hermann Balk. Jan Powierski, based on the analysis of Balk's itinerary, concluded that this document is dated according to the Annunciation style, meaning it was actually issued in January 1239. See Powierski, 'Początek walk Krzyżaków o panowanie nad Zalewem Wiślanym i założenie Elbląga,' *Nautologia* 3 (1993): 19–21.
72 [...] *Ea propter presencium testimonio protestamur quod cavere volentes in quantum possumus periculum animarum quod in novellis terrarum plantacionibus fit plerumque ubi latitant a vivendi rectitudine fugitivi noticiam devitantes de capituli nostri plenaria voluntate ordini venerando qui dicitur predicatorum et esse dinoscitur ab effectu, fratrum videlicet domino et hominibus dilectorum potentiumque in opere et sermone in civitate nostra plantacionis novelle Elbinc dicta contulimus aream quondam in qua edificet claustrum suum* [...], *cf.* CDW, I: 1–2 no. 1. The broader context of monastery foundations in the state of the Teutonic Order in Prussia was discussed by Piotr Oliński, 'Motywy fundacji klasztorów przez zakon krzyżacki w Prusach w świetle dokumentów fundacyjnych (ze szczególnym uwzględnieniem dokumentów fundacyjnych żeńskiego klasztoru benedyktyńskiego w Królewcu i klasztoru augustianów-eremitów w Chojnicach),' in *Kancelarie krzyżackie. Stan badań i perspektywy badawcze*, ed. Janusz Trupinda (Malbork: Wydawnictwo Zamkowe, 2002), 191–209.

73 De quorum laboribus et redicacionibus germinare fructus uberes cepit prusia et rigata lyvonia messis habundancia iocundari, cf. CDW, I: 22–23 no. 14. In the case of Livonia, they were probably Dominicans from Riga, where their monastery was established in 1234, cf. Rafał Kubicki, 'Mendicant Orders in medieval Prussia and Livonia,' 130.

74 [...] et ut ipsi et filii eorum legitimi possint esse clerici et religionem intrare; et quod illi ex ipsis neophitis, qui sunt vel erunt ex nobili prosapia procreati, accingi possint cingulo militari, cf. PUB, I/1: 160 no. 218. Regarding the Treaty of Christburg, see Reinhard Wenskus, 'Zur Lokalisierung der Preußenkirchen des Vertrages von Christburg 1249,' in Acht Jahrhunderte Deutscher Orden in Einzeldarstellungen. Festschrift für P. Dr. Marian Tumler O.T. anlässlich seines 80. Geburtstages, ed. Klemens Wieser, Quellen und Studien zur Geschichte des Deutschen Ordens 1 (Bad Godesberg: Verlag Wissenschaftliches Archiv, 1967), 121–136.

75 The entire testimony was quoted and thoroughly discussed by Janusz Bieniak, 'Udział duchowieństwa zakonnego w procesie warszawsko-uniejowskim w 1339 r.,' in Klasztor w kulturze średniowiecznej Polski, ed. Anna Pobóg-Lenartowicz and Marek Derwich (Opole: Wydawnictwo św. Krzyża, 1995), 486–487.

76 Zbiór formuł zakonu dominikańskiego prowincji polskiej z lat 1338–1411, ed. Jacek Woroniecki and Jan Fijałek, Archiwum Komisji Historycznej 12, part 2 (Kraków: Polska Akademia Umiejętności, 1938), 325 no. 164.

77 Kubicki, Środowisko, 48.

78 Examples of admonitions addressed by individual Prussian bishops to diocesan clergy regarding irregularities in their preaching are cited by Radzimiński, 'Udział zakonu,' 17–18.

79 Regarding the documents of indulgences possessed by mendicants in the state of the Teutonic Order in Prussia, see Łukasz Myszka, 'Przywileje odpustowe dla dominikanów toruńskich przyczynek do dziejów życia religijnego średniowiecznego miasta,' Nasza Przeszłość 110 (2008): 329–344; Kubicki, 'Podstawy ekonomiczne,' 210–214.

80 Eysenblätter, 'Die Klöster der Augustiner,' 386; Christofer Herrmann, Mittelalterliche Architektur in Preussenland. Untersuchungen zur Frage der Kunstlandschaft und -geographie, Studien zur internationalen Architektur- und Kulturgeschichte 56 (Petersberg: Michael Imhof, 2007), 432–433. The role of relics and pilgrimage sites in the development of religiousness in the state of the Teutonic Order in Prussia is discussed by Waldemar Rozynkowski, Omnes Sancti et Sanctae Dei. Studium nad kultem świętych w diecezjach pruskich państwa zakonu krzyżackiego (Malbork: Wydawnictwo Zamkowe, 2006), 189–228.

81 Rafał Kubicki, 'Podstawy ekonomiczne funkcjonowania mendykantów w państwie krzyżackim i Prusach Królewskich do połowy XVI w.,' in Inter oeconomiam coelestem et terrenam mendykanci a zagadnienia ekonomiczne, ed. Wiesław Długokęcki a.o. (Kraków: Wydawnictwo Esprit SC, 2011), 214.

82 Roth, Die Dominikaner, 139.

83 Kubicki, 'Działalność dominikanów kontraty pruskiej na pograniczu polsko-krzyżackim – okręg klasztorny konwentu w Toruniu w XV w.,' in Pogranicze polsko-pruskie i krzyżackie II, ed. Kazimierz Grążawski (Włocławek, Brodnica: Oficyna Wydawnicza LEGA, 2007), 373–387.

84 Grzegorz Białuński, 'Dobra za granicą. O pozawarmińskich posiadłościach ziemskich klasztoru w Reszlu w XIV–XVI wieku,' KMW 2/252 (2006): 209–217.

85 Kubicki, 'Podstawy ekonomiczne,' 198–201.

86 Zonenberg, '«Cura animarum»,' 14–15.

87 Waldemar Rozynkowski, 'Księgi metrykalne parafii w Kaszczorku w kontekście ostatnich lat pobytu dominikanów w Toruniu,' in Klasztor dominikański w Toruniu, ed. Oliński, Rozynkowski, and Raczkowski, 149–151.

88 *Formularz z Uppsali. Późnośredniowieczna księga formularzowa biskupstw pruskich*, ed. Radosław Biskup, FTNT 109 (Toruń: Towarzystwo Naukowe w Toruniu, 2016), 131–132 no. 196.

89 [...] *dy pharr hinder dem Tyeffe nach dem sy ein weltlichen prister aws armut nicht vormucht zuhalten gegeben, cf.* GStA PK, XX. HA, OF 127, no. 29; Emil Johannes Guttzeit, 'Das Kloster Patollen (zur heiligen Dreifaltigkeit) innerhalb der Geschichte des Rittergutes Gross Waldeck, Kreis Pr. Eylau,' in *Studien zur Geschichte des Preussenlandes. Festschrift für Erich Keyser zu seinem 70. Geburtstag dargebracht von Freunden und Schülern*, ed. Ernst Bahr (Marburg: Elwert Verlag, 1963), 205.

90 'Sedes archipresbyterales diocesis Warmiensis,' ed. Carl Peter Woelky, in *Scriptores rerum Warmiensium oder Quellenschriften zur Geschichte Ermlands*, vol. I, ed. Carl Peter Woelky and Johann Martin Saage, MHW II (Braunsberg: Verlag von Eduard Peter, 1866), 423–424; Eysenblätter, 'Die Klöster der Augustiner,' 386.

91 Guttzeit, 'Das Kloster Patollen,' 202–203.

92 Grunau, I: 389–390.

93 Regarding the catastrophic state of the parish network in Samland/Sambia, see Biskup, 'Bemerkung zum Siedlungsproblem,' 45–48; Grischa Vercamer, *Siedlungs-, Sozial- und Verwaltungsgeschichte der Komturei Königsberg in Preußen (13.–16. Jahrhundert)*, Einzelschriften der Historischen Kommission für ost- und westpreußische Landesforschung 29 (Marburg: N.G. Elwert Verlag, 2010), 373; id., 'Der Übergang,' 187; Jakubek-Raczkowska, *Tu ergo flecte*, 482. The specific form of rural churches in Sambia, their elongated shape, and distinct spatial separation, symbolically dividing the sphere of the priest from that belonging to the Old-Prussian faithful, were pointed out by Christofer Herrmann, 'Die Architektur der mittelalterlichen Kirchen in den preußischen Bistümern,' in *Cura animarum*, ed. Samerski, 142.

94 *in Sudowe* [...] *zcu terminiren und bethelen vorgunnen, cf.* GStA PK, XX. HA, OBA, no. 19916.

95 Rafał Kubicki, 'Dominikanie w Nordenborku i Gierdawach w XV – początkach XVI w.,' KMW 2/276 (2012): 240.

96 Kubicki, 'Dominikanie w Nordenborku,' 240.

97 The *waidlott* served as a wandering poet, minstrel and storyteller, playing a significant role in the local culture and tradition. *Waidlotts* were especially important in the pre-Christian era when the transmission of oral traditions played a crucial role in the community.

98 *Ich qwam in ein haus eines dorffes und fandt in der stuben viel mennir und frauen, welche in Preuschir sproche predigte ein alter pauer ir waidlott. Sie entpfingen mich ein iglicher mit seinem messer mich zu todten, so gebrach es ag am waidlotten, und er sprach ein wort. Den gobin gottis ich is dancke, und ich kundt ein wenigk Preusch, mit welchin ich bat umb mein leben, ich wolt thun, was sie wolten. Und sie hörten von mir ire sprache, sie wurden irfreuet und schrigen alle sta nossen rickie, nossen rickie* [Der ist unser Herr, unser Herr], *und muste ein eit schweren im namen Perkuno des gottis, und ich is nit wult dem bischoff sogen, der ir herre war, und ich schwur und hilffe mit waidelen, cf.* Grunau, I: 91. For a detailed discussion of this event, see Zonenberg, *Kronika*, 26–27; Julia Możdżeń, 'Synkretyzm religijny Prusów na podstawie kroniki Szymona Grunaua,' *Pruthenia* 6 (2011): 233–234, 236.

99 For information on the progress of the Christianisation of the Old-Prussians up to the Reformation and beyond, see Karol Górski, 'Problemy chrystianizacji w Prusach, Inflantach i na Litwie,' KMW 2/157 (1982): 152–165; Janusz Małłek, 'Ludność staropruska a Reformacja,' *Gdański Rocznik Ewangelicki* 5 (2011): 45–49.

100 *Gothe dem demuthige seiner unbefelkten geberen Marie zu lob und ehr den armen unsern unwissenden und unglaubigen underthannen heyl und seligkeit etc.*, *cf.* GStA PK, XX. HA, OF 127, no. 37; USF, I: 50 no. 212; Lemmens, *Die Franziskanerkustodie*, 24; Erich Joachim, 'Vom Kulturzustande im Ordenslande Preußen am Vorabende der Reformation,' *Altpreußische Forschungen* 1, no. 1 (1924): 16.

Primary Sources

Berlin. Geheimes Staatsarchiv Preußischer Kulturbesitz, XX. Hauptabteilung, Ordensbriefarchiv, no. 19916.

Berlin. Geheimes Staatsarchiv Preußischer Kulturbesitz, XX. Hauptabteilung, Ordensfolianten 29, 37.

Gdańsk. Polska Akademia Nauk, Biblioteka Gdańska, Ms. 1614.

Kraków. Archiwum klasztoru oo. karmelitów na Piasku, 92/682 ("Index fundationum monasteriorum provinciae Polonae Carmelitarum Antiquae Regularis Observantiae, Anno 1676").

'Annales Minorum Prussicorum.' Edited by Ernst Strehlke. In SRP, vol. V, edited by Theodor Hirsch, Max Toeppen, and Ernst Strehlke, 647–648. Leipzig: Verlag von S. Hirzel, 1874.

Bullarium Poloniae. Vol. 6. Edited by Irena Sułkowska-Kuraś and Stanisław Kuraś. Romae–Lublin: Abilgraf – Polski Instytut Kultury Chrześcijańskiej, 1998.

Codex diplomaticus Warmiensis oder Regesten und Urkunden zur Geschichte Ermlands. Vol. I, *Urkunden der Jahre 1231–1340*, edited by Carl Peter Woelky and Johann M. Saage. MHW I/I. Meinz: Franz Kirchheim, 1860.

Codex diplomaticus Warmiensis oder Regesten und Urkunden zur Geschichte Ermlands. Vol. II, *Urkunden der Jahre 1341–1375 nebst Nachträgen von 1240–1340*, edited by Carl Peter Woelky and Johann M. Saage. MHW I/I. Meinz: Franz Kirchheim, 1864.

Codex diplomaticus Warmiensis oder Regesten und Urkunden zur Geschichte Ermlands. Vol. IV, *Urkunden der Jahre 1424–35 und Nachträge*, edited by Victor Röhrich, Franz Lidtke, and Hans Schmauch. MHW I/IX. Braunsberg: Druck der Ermländischen Zeitungs- und Verlagsdruckerei, Selbstverlag des Vereins, 1935.

Formularz z Uppsali. Późnośredniowieczna księga formularzowa biskupstw pruskich. Edited by Radosław Biskup. FTNT 109. Toruń: Towarzystwo Naukowe w Toruniu, 2016.

'Franciscani Thorunensis Annales Prussici (941–1410).' Edited by Ernst Strehlke. In SRP, vol. III, edited by Theodor Hirsch, Max Toeppen, and Ernst Strehlke, 13–388. Leipzig: Verlag von S. Hirzel, 1866.

Katalog der Handschriften der Danziger Stadtbibliothek. Part 2. Edited by Otto Günther. Katalog der Danziger Stadtbibliothek 2. Danzig: Kommissions-Verlag der L. Saunierschen Buch- und Kunsthandlung, 1903.

Das Marienburger Tresslerbuch der Jahre 1399–1409. Edited by Erich Joachim. Königsberg: Verlag von Thomas & Oppermann, 1896.

Preußisches Urkundenbuch. Vol. I, part 1, *1206–1256*, edited by Rudolph Philippi and Carl P. Woelky. Königsberg: Hartungsche Verlagsdruckerei, 1882.

Preußisches Urkundenbuch. Vol. II, *1309–1335*, edited by Max Hein and Erich Maschke. Königsberg: Gräfe and Unzer, 1939.

'Sedes archipresbyterales diocesis Warmiensis.' Edited by Carl Peter Woelky. In *Scriptores rerum Warmiensium oder Quellenschriften zur Geschichte Ermlands*, vol. I, edited by Carl Peter Woelky and Johann Martin Saage, 388–444. MHW II. Braunsberg: Verlag von Eduard Peter, 1866.

Simon Grunau's preussische Chronik. Edited by Max Perlbach. Vol. I. Leipzig: Verlag Duncker & Humblot, 1876.

Urkundenbuch der alten sächsischen Franziskanerprovinzen. Vol. I, *Die Observantenkustodie Livland und Preußen*, edited by Leonhard Lemmens. Düsseldorf: Kommissionsverlag von L. Schwann, 1912.
Urkundenbuch des Bisthums Culm. Edited by Carl P. Woelky. Vol. II, *Das Bisthum Culm unter Polen 1466–1774*. Neues Preußisches Urkundenbuch. Westpreussischer Theil 2: Urkunden der Bisthümer, Kirchen und Klöster. Danzig: Commisionsverlag von Theodor Bertling, 1885.
Zbiór formuł zakonu dominikańskiego prowincji polskiej z lat 1338–1411. Edited by Jacek Woroniecki and Jan Fijałek. Archiwum Komisji Historycznej 12, part 2. Kraków: Polska Akademia Umiejętności, 1938.

Secondary Sources

Altaner, Berthold. *Die Dominikanermission des 13. Jahrhunderts.* Halberschwerdt: Franke, 1924.
Białuński, Grzegorz. 'Dobra za granicą. O pozawarmińskich posiadłościach ziemskich klasztoru w Reszlu w XIV–XVI wieku.' KMW 2/252 (2006): 209–217.
Bieniak, Janusz. 'Udział duchowieństwa zakonnego w procesie warszawsko-uniejowskim w 1339 r.' In *Klasztor w kulturze średniowiecznej Polski*, edited by Anna Pobóg-Lenartowicz and Marek Derwich, 467–490. Opole: Wydawnictwo św. Krzyża, 1995.
Biskup, Marian. 'Bemerkung zum Siedlungsproblem und den Pfarrbezirken und Ordenspreußen im 14.–15. Jahrhundert.' In *Die Rollen der Ritterorden in der Christianisierung und Kolonisierung des Ostseegebietes*, edited by Zenon Hubert Nowak, 35–56. Ordines Militares. Colloquia Torunensia Historica I. Toruń: Wydawnictwo Naukowe UMK, 1983.
Biskup, Marian. 'Das Problem der ethnischen Zugehörigkeit im mittelalterlichen Landesausbau in Preussen. Zum Stand der Forschung.' *Jahrbuch für die Geschichte Mittel- und Ostdeutschlands* 40 (1991): 3–25.
Biskup, Marian. *Historia Torunia.* Vol. 2, part 1, *U schyłku średniowiecza i w początkach odrodzenia (1454–1548)*. Toruń: Wydawnictwo TNT, 1992.
Biskup, Marian. 'Parafie w państwie krzyżackim.' In *Państwo zakonu krzyżackiego w Prusach. Podziały administracyjne i kościelne w XIII–XVI wieku*, edited by Zenon Hubert Nowak and Roman Czaja, 81–93. Toruń: Wydawnictwo Naukowe UMK, 2000.
Diecezja chełmińska zarys historyczno-statystyczny. Pelplin: Pielgrzym, 1928.
Długokęcki, Wiesław. 'Odbudowa osadnictwa, kolonizacja i przemiany wsi w państwie krzyżackim (1411–1525).' In *Państwo zakonu krzyżackiego w Prusach. Władza i społeczeństwo*, edited by Marian Biskup and Roman Czaja, 375–383. Warszawa: Wydawnictwo Naukowe PWN, 2008.
Eysenblätter, Hugo. 'Die Klöster der Augustiner Eremiten im Nordosten Deutschlands.' *Altpreußische Monatschrift* 35 (1898): 357–391.
Germershausen, Peter. *Siedlungsentwicklung der preußischen Ämter Holland, Liebstadt und Mohrungen vom 13. bis zum 17. Jahrhundert.* Wissenschaftliche Beiträge zur Geschichte und Landeskunde Ost-Mitteleuropas 87. Marburg: Johann Gottfried Herder-Institut, 1970.
Górski, Karol. 'Problemy chrystianizacji w Prusach, Inflantach i na Litwie.' KMW 2/157 (1982): 151–168.
Guttzeit, Emil Johannes. 'Das Kloster Patollen (zur heiligen Dreifaltigkeit) innerhalb der Geschichte des Rittergutes Gross Waldeck, Kreis Pr. Eylau.' In *Studien zur Geschichte des Preussenlandes. Festschrift für Erich Keyser zu seinem 70. Geburtstag dargebracht von Freunden und Schülern*, edited by Ernst Bahr, 195–215. Marburg: Elwert Verlag, 1963.
Harmjanz, Heinrich. *Volkskunde und Siedlungsgeschichte Altpreussen.* Berlin: Junker und Dünnhaupt, 1943, 2nd edition.

Herrmann, Christofer. 'Die Architektur der mittelalterlichen Kirchen in den preußischen Bistümern.' In *Cura animarum. Seelsorge im Deutschordensland des Mittelalters*, edited by Stefan Samerski, 132–160. Köln, Weimar, Wien: Böhlau Verlag, 2013.
Herrmann, Christofer. *Mittelalterliche Architektur in Preussenland. Untersuchungen zur Frage der Kunstlandschaft und -geographie*. Studien zur internationalen Architektur- und Kulturgeschichte 56. Petersberg: Michael Imhof, 2007.
Hinnebusch, William Aquinas. *The History of the Dominican Order. Origins and Growth to 1500*. Vol. 1. New York: Alba House, 1966.
Jakubek-Raczkowska, Monika. *Tu ergo flecte genua tua. Sztuka a praktyka religijna świeckich w diecezjach pruskich państwa zakonu krzyżackiego do połowy XV wieku*. Pelplin: Wydawnictwo Bernardinum, 2014.
Joachim, Erich. 'Vom Kulturzustande im Ordenslande Preußen am Vorabende der Reformation.' *Altpreußische Forschungen* 1, no. 1 (1924): 12–17.
Kantak, Kamil. *Franciszkanie polscy*. Vol. 1, *1237–1517*. Kraków: Prowincja Polska OO. Franciszkanów, 1937.
Kasiske, Karl. *Das deutsche Siedelwerk des Mittelalters in Pommerellen*. Königsberg: Kommissionsverlag Gräfe und Unzer, 1938.
Kasiske, Karl. *Die Sieglungstätigkeit des Deutschen Ordens im östlichen Preussen bis zum Jahre 1410*. Königsberg: Kommissionsverlag Gräfe und Unzer, 1934.
Kłoczowski, Jerzy. *Dominikanie polscy na Śląsku w XIII–XIV wieku*. Lublin: TN KUL, 1956.
Kłoczowski, Jerzy. 'Klosterkreise in der polnischen Dominikanerprovinz im Mittelalter.' In *Vita Religiosa im Mittelalter. Festschrift für Kaspar Elm zum 70. Geburtstag*, edited by Franz Josef Felten and Nikolas Jaspert, 533–542. Berliner Historische Studien 31. Berlin: Duncker & Humblot, 1999.
Kubicki, Rafał. *Zakony mendykanckie w Prusach Krzyżackich i Królewskich od XIII do połowy XVI wieku*. Gdańsk: Wydawnictwo Uniwersytetu Gdańskiego, 2018.
Kubicki, Rafał. 'Die Rolle der Bettelorden im Ordensland Preußen.' In *Cura animarum. Seelsorge im Deutschordensland des Mittelalters*, edited by Stefan Samerski, 74–91. Köln, Weimar, Wien: Böhlau Verlag, 2013.
Kubicki, Rafał. 'Dominikanie w Nordenborku i Gierdawach w XV – początkach XVI w.' KMW 2/276 (2012): 227–242.
Kubicki, Rafał. 'Działalność dominikanów kontraty pruskiej na pograniczu polsko-krzyżackim – okręg klasztorny konwentu w Toruniu w XV w.' In *Pogranicze polsko-pruskie i krzyżackie* II, edited by Kazimierz Grążawski, 373–387. Włocławek, Brodnica: Oficyna Wydawnicza LEGA, 2007.
Kubicki, Rafał. 'Działalność zakonów mendykanckich na pograniczu krzyżacko-litewskim do początków XVI w.' In *Litwa i jej sąsiedzi w relacjach wzajemnych (XIII–XVI w.)*, edited by Anna Kołodziejczyk, Rafał Kubicki, and Marek Radoch, 175–192. Olsztyn, Gdańsk: Wydawnictwo Uniwersytetu Warmińsko-Mazurskiego, 2014.
Kubicki, Rafał. 'Mendicant Friaries in the Dominion of the Teutonic Order in Prussia and in Royal Prussia after 1466 until the Reformation.' ZH 81, no. 4 (2016): 83–99.
Kubicki, Rafał. 'Mendicant Orders in Medieval Prussia and Livonia: Pastoral Activities in Towns.' *Acta Historica Universitatis Klaipedensis* 33 (2016): 123–146.
Kubicki, Rafał. 'Podstawy ekonomiczne funkcjonowania mendykantów w państwie krzyżackim i Prusach Królewskich do połowy XVI w.' In *Inter oeconomiam coelestem et terrenam mendykanci a zagadnienia ekonomiczne*, edited by Wiesław Długokęcki a.o., 183–238. Kraków: Wydawnictwo Esprit SC, 2011.
Kubicki, Rafał. *Franciszkanie w Gdańsku w XV–XVI wieku*. Gdańsk: Wydawnictwo Uniwersytetu Gdańskiego, 2022.

Kunzelmann, Adalbero. *Geschichte der deutschen Augustiner-Eremiten.* Part 3, *Die bayerische Provinz bis zum Ende des Mittelalters.* Würzburg: Augustinus-Verlag, 1972.
Kunzelmann, Adalbero. *Geschichte der deutschen Augustiner-Eremiten.* Part 5, *Die sächsisch-thüringische Provinz und die sächsische Reformkongregation bis zum Untergang der Beiden.* Würzburg: Augustinus-Verlag, 1974.
Larczyńska, Agata. 'Piękno średniowiecznych manuskryptów. Biblioteka gdańskiego klasztoru franciszkanów na nowo odkryta.' *Studia Zamkowe* 4 (2012): 111–127.
Lemmens, Leonhard. 'Aus der Geschichte der deutschen Franziskaner im Ordenslande Preußen,' *Mitteilungen des Coppernicus-Vereins für Wissenschaft und Kunst zu Thorn* 20 (1912): 58–64.
Lemmens, Leonhard. *Die Franziskanerkustodie Livland und Preussen. Beitrag zur Kirchengeschichte der Gebiete des Deutschen Ordens.* Düsseldorf: Kommissionsverlag von L. Schwann, 1912.
Łowmiański, Henryk. *Polityka ludnościowa zakonu niemieckiego w Prusach i na Pomorzu.* Gdańsk: Instytut Bałtycki, 1947.
Małłek, Janusz. 'Ludność staropruska a Reformacja.' *Gdański Rocznik Ewangelicki* 5 (2011): 41–56.
Mentzel-Reuters, Arno. *Arma spiritualia: Bibliotheken, Bildung und Bücher im Deutschen Orden.* Beiträge zum Buch- und Bibliothekswesen 47. Wiesbaden: Otto Harrassowitz, 2003.
Możdżeń, Julia. 'Synkretyzm religijny Prusów na podstawie kroniki Szymona Grunaua.' *Pruthenia* 6 (2011): 221–248.
Myszka, Łukasz. 'Przywileje odpustowe dla dominikanów toruńskich przyczynek do dziejów życia religijnego średniowiecznego miasta.' *Nasza Przeszłość* 110 (2008): 329–344.
Niedermeier, Hans. 'Die Franziskaner in Preussen, Livland und Litauen im Mittelalter.' *Zeitschrift für Ostforschung* 27, no. 1 (1978): 1–31.
Oliński, Piotr. 'Motywy fundacji klasztorów przez zakon krzyżacki w Prusach w świetle dokumentów fundacyjnych (ze szczególnym uwzględnieniem dokumentów fundacyjnych żeńskiego klasztoru benedyktyńskiego w Królewcu i klasztoru augustianów-eremitów w Chojnicach).' In *Kancelarie krzyżackie. Stan badań i perspektywy badawcze,* edited by Janusz Trupinda, 191–209. Malbork: Wydawnictwo Zamkowe, 2002.
Pollakówna, Marzena. 'Zanik ludności pruskiej.' In *Szkice z dziejów Pomorza. Pomorze wczesnośredniowieczne,* 160–207. Warszawa: Książka i Wiedza, 1958.
Pollakówna, Marzena. *Osadnictwo Warmii w okresie krzyżackim.* Poznań: Instytut Zachodni, 1953.
Poschmann, Adolf. 'Das Augustinerkloster in Rössel.' *Zeitschrift für die Geschichte und Altertumskunde Ermlands* 24 (1932): 81–189.
Powierski, Jan. 'Dzieje ziemi pasłęckiej do schyłku XIII w.' In *Pasłęk z dziejów miasta i okolic 1297–1997,* edited by Józef Włodarski, 162–168. Pasłęk: Urząd Miasta i Gminy, 1997.
Powierski, Jan. 'Początek walk Krzyżaków o panowanie nad Zalewem Wiślanym i założenie Elbląga.' *Nautologia* 3 (1993): 2–22.
Radzimiński, Andrzej. 'Udział zakonu krzyżackiego w procesie ewangelizacji Prus. Uwagi na podstawie ustawodawstwa synodalnego.' ZH 70, no. 1 (2005): 7–26.
Radzimiński, Andrzej. *Chrystianizacja i ewangelizacja Prusów. Historia i źródła.* Toruń: Wydawnictwo Adam Marszałek, 2011.
Roth, Werner. *Die Dominikaner und Franziskaner im Deutsch-Ordenslande Preußen bis zum Jahre 1466.* Königsberg in Pr.: Drewes Buchdruckerei, 1918.
Rozynkowski, Waldemar. 'Księgi metrykalne parafii w Kaszczorku w kontekście ostatnich lat pobytu dominikanów w Toruniu.' In *Klasztor dominikański w Toruniu w 750. rocznicę fundacji,* edited by Piotr Oliński, Waldemar Rozynkowski, and Juliusz Raczkowski, 145–160. Toruń: Wydawnictwo UMK, 2013.

Rozynkowski, Waldemar. *Omnes Sancti et Sanctae Dei. Studium nad kultem świętych w diecezjach pruskich państwa zakonu krzyżackiego.* Malbork: Wydawnictwo Zamkowe, 2006.
Sarnowsky, Jürgen. 'Die Dominikaner und Franziskaner im Ordensland Preußen.' In *Franciscan Organisation in the Mendicant Context. Formal and informal structures of the friars' lives and ministry in the Middle Ages*, edited by Michael Robson and Jens Röhrkasten, 43–64. Vita Regularis Ordnungen und Deutungen religiosen Lebens im Mittelalter 44. Berlin: LIT Verlag, 2010.
Simiński, Rafał. *Od "solitudo" do "terra culta". Przestrzeń jako przedmiot wyobrażeń w Inflantach i Prusach od XIII do początku XV wieku.* Roczniki Towarzystwa Naukowego w Toruniu 92, no. 2. Toruń: Towarzystwo Naukowe w Toruniu, 2008.
Simson, Paul. 'Das Testament des Danziger Schöffen und Ratsherrn Otto Angermünde.' *Mitteilungen des Westpreußischen Geschichtsvereins* 14, no. 3 (1915): 42–48.
Smet, Joachim, and Dobhan Ulrich. *Die Karmeliten. Eine Geschichte der Brüder U.L. Frau vom Berg Karmel von den Anfängen (ca. 1200) bis zum Konzil von Trient.* Freiburg, Basel, Wien: Herder Verlag, 1981.
Spuren franziskanischer Geschichte. Chronologischer Abriß der Geschichte der Sächsischen Franziskanerprovinzen von ihren Anfängen bis zur Gegenwart. Edited by Dieter Berg. Werl: Butzon & Bercker 1999.
Trajdos, Tadeusz Mikołaj. *U zarania karmelitów w Polsce.* Warszawa: Instytut Historii PAN, 1993.
Trautmann, Reinhold. *Die altpreußischen Personennamen.* Göttingen: Vandenhoeck & Ruprecht, 1974.
Turek, Jakub. 'Podział polskiej prowincji dominikanów w czasach prowincja latu Jana Biskupca w latach 1415–1417.' *Przegląd Historyczny* 106, no. 2 (2015): 287–324.
Vercamer, Grischa. 'Der Übergang der prußischen Stammeseliten in die Schicht der ‚Freien' unter der Herrschaft des Deutschen Ordens und der Kulturtransfer von der ‚deutschen' auf die prußische Kultur.' In *Mittelalterliche Eliten und Kulturtransfer östlich der Elbe. Interdisziplinäre Beiträge zu Archäologie und Geschichte im mittelalterlichen Ostmitteleuropa*, edited by Anne Klammt and Sébastien Rossignol, 169–191. Göttingen: Universitätsverlag, 2009.
Vercamer, Grischa. *Siedlungs-, Sozial- und Verwaltungsgeschichte der Komturei Königsberg in Preußen (13.–16. Jahrhundert).* Einzelschriften der Historischen Kommission für ost- und westpreußische Landesforschung 29. Marburg: N.G. Elwert Verlag, 2010.
Wenskus, Reinhard. 'Zur Lokalisierung der Preußenkirchen des Vertrages von Christburg 1249.' In *Acht Jahrhunderte Deutscher Orden in Einzeldarstellungen. Festschrift für P. Dr. Marian Tumler O.T. anlässlich seines 80. Geburtstages*, edited by Klemens Wieser, 121–136. Quellen und Studien zur Geschichte des Deutschen Ordens 1. Bad Godesberg: Verlag Wissenschaftliches Archiv, 1967.
Wunder, Heide. *Siedlungs- und Bevölkerungsgeschichte der Komturei Christburg (13.–16. Jahrhundert.* Marburger Ostforschungen 28. Wiesbaden: Otto Harrassowitz, 1968.
Zonenberg, Sławomir. '«Cura animarum» zakonu kaznodziejskiego w średniowieczu na tle rozwoju duszpasterstwa mniszego.' *Lietuvos Istorijos Studijos* 18 (2006): 9–38.
Zonenberg, Sławomir. 'Stosunki dominikańsko-krzyżackie w Prusach do 1466 roku.' In *Klasztor dominikański w Toruniu w 750. rocznicę fundacji*, edited by Piotr Oliński, Waldemar Rozynkowski, and Juliusz Raczkowski, 43–77. Toruń: Wydawnictwo Naukowe UMK, 2013.
Zonenberg, Sławomir. *Kronika Szymona Grunaua.* Bydgoszcz: Wydawnictwo Uniwersytetu Kazimierza Wielkiego, 2009.
Zonenberg, Sławomir. *Stosunki krzyżacko-mendykanckie w Prusach do 1466 roku.* Bydgoszcz: Wydawnictwo Uniwersytetu Kazimierza Wielkiego, 2018.

9 Teutonic Order and German Dialects under Special Consideration of the Prussian Branch in the Late Middle Ages

Piotr Gotówko

The Teutonic Order can be described as a multilingual institution in the Late Middle Ages, for its members came from different regions of the Holy Roman Empire (*Reich*) and spoke therefore various German dialects as their mother tongues.[1] The analyses in this chapter are based on the assumption that the Order's brethren used the dialects from their home regions.[2] The aim of this study is to explain these German dialects – which belong either to the Low, to the Middle or to the Upper German group – and to show their distribution among the Prussian brethren during the 13th and the 14th centuries.

Low German Dialects

Low German dialects clearly differed from their Middle and Upper German relatives. This can be traced back to the time between 400 and 800 A.D., as the 'High German consonant shift' ('zweite Lautverschiebung') took place. At its end, the languages spoken in Low Germany did not change much, while in Middle and Upper Germany 'p' mutated to 'pf' or 'f', and 't' to 's' or 'z'.[3] As a result, people in Low Germany still said 'dat', 'wat' or 'Water', further in the south the same words changed to 'was', 'das' and 'Wasser'. Other differences were so common terms as 'ik' and 'maken', pronounced in Middle and Upper German as 'ich' and 'machen'.[4]

In the territories nearest to the North Sea, the people spoke Frisian (*friesisch*), which is the first Western Low German dialect.[5] Only a few miles inland, the very influential Saxon (*sächsisch*) began, today called the Low Saxon (*niedersächsisch*).[6] It also covered the dialectical area of the Ostphalian (*ostfälisch*) dialect, which counts today as an autonomous dialect. Its Western neighbour is the Westphalian (*westfälisch*), which reaches to the Dutch border.[7] In the Southwest, from Xanten to the city of Düsseldorf (Benrath), there is a small territory of the Low Franconian (*niederfränkisch*, also: Low Rheinlandish, *niederrheinisch*).[8] Finally in Schleswig-Holstein, people speak Holsteinian (*holsteinisch*).[9]

A few miles from Lübeck, Eastern Low German begins. In Mecklenburg-Vorpommern settlers from Saxony germanised the Slavic population, which gave rise to a new dialect: Mecklenburgian (*mecklenburgisch*).[10]

DOI: 10.4324/9781003502876-9

In Brandenburgia without its Southeastern part and Berlin, the Brandenburgian (*brandenburgisch*), also called Markian (*märkisch*),[11] originated. On the Eastern shore of the river Oder and further to the east, on the Baltic cost, two different ethnical groups lived: the indigenous Slavs who had spoken (Polish-)Pomeranian and the descendent of German-speaking settlers from Saxony and Low Franconia who had developed as their dialect the Eastern Pomeranian (*ostpommersch*).[12] In Prussia, the Teutonic Order invited its German-speaking countrymen in, who developed on the Northeastern shore of the Vistula and the Baltic Cost the Low Prussian (*niederpreussisch*).[13] The Low German had therefore at least nine distinct dialects in the Middle Ages.

Middle German Dialects

The drift of the German dialects continued during the High Middle Ages. Until approximately 1300 A.D. the Middle German had changed the monopthongs 'i', 'ü' and 'u' to the dipthongs 'ei', 'eu' and 'au'. The sentence *min nü hus* mutated to *mein neues Haus*.[14]

The Western Middle German accounts for six dialects. Around the important cities of Cologne, Aachen and Bonn Ripuarian (*ripuarisch*) starts.[15] Beside of the mutation of 'ik' and 'maken' to 'ich' and 'machen' many other words change, like 'söst' or 'sek' to 'schwäst' and 'sech'.[16] When continuing going up the river Rhine, Koblenz and Trier are the area of the Moselle Franconian (*moselfränkisch*).[17] To the west, in the present-day Duchy of Luxemburg, people speak the Luxembourgian (*luxemburgisch*),[18] which is by many authors considered rather a subdialect of Moselle Franconian than an autonomous dialect. In the present-day Eastern Lothringia in France, Lothringian (also: Lorraine Franconian, *lothringisch*) was at home.[19] When returning to the lands of the Moselle Franconian and going some more up the river Rhine, the dialect changes to Hessian (*hessisch*).[20] Its key territories lie in the East of the Rhine, from Kassel to Frankfurt/Main and Aschaffenburg. Up the river, the Palatine (*pfälzisch*, also: *rheinpfälzisch*), around Kaiserslautern until Speyer is spoken.[21] Palatine, Lothringian and Hessian have so many similarities that are called the Rhinefranconian dialects (*rheinfränkische Mundarten*).[22] The city of Speyer marks the end of the Middle German. This isogloss does not – in contrast to the line of Benrath – stay at the same geographical height and turns after Speyer diagonally to the North to the nowadays Southern Thuringian border.

In present-day Thuringia and the South of Sachsen-Anhalt, one hears Thuringian (*thüringisch*), the first Eastern Middle German dialect.[23] Eastwards, the Slavic tribes had been since the 12th century germanised by the predominantly Middle German-speaking settlers developing in the area of Leipzig und Dresden Meissnian (*meissnisch*; today: *obersächsisch*, also called: *sächsisch*).[24] In the Mountains of Erzgebirge, the Erzgebirgian (*erzgebirgisch*) originated.[25] Between Bautzen and Cottbus one could hear, apart from Sorbian (*sorbisch*), a Western Slavic language, also a German dialect

Lausitanian (*lausitzisch*).²⁶ In the North of the Lausitz with the city of Berlin people spoke Southern Markian (*südmärkisch*).²⁷ In Bohemia, after the mountains, the newcomers from the *Reich* developed a 'tongue' called the Northern Bohemian.²⁸ Also in Silesia the German-speaking settlers formed slowly another dialect, Silesian (*schlesisch*).²⁹ In the lands conquered by the Teutonic Order, especially on the Eastern shore of the Vistula River, between Kulm (today Chełmno) and Marienwerder (today Kwidzyn), the last Middle German dialect, High Prussian (*hochpreussisch*), was in use.³⁰ Therefore, the Middle German had 14 distinct dialects.

Upper German Dialects

The Upper German region was on the one hand not affected by the changes that had happened in the Middle Germany. The sentence *min nü hus* remained there still the same. On the other hand, after the High German consonant shift many words in Upper German mutated. From the Germanic 'appla' became 'Ebfel'.³¹ This isogloss goes through the city of Speyer, marking the end of the Middle German and the beginning of the Upper German.

The Western Upper German starts in the Vogtland, where Vogtlandian (*vogtländisch*), the most Northeastern panhandle of Franconian, is at home.³² Although this area historically and administratively is linked with Thuringia, the dialect spoken there distinguishes itself from the rest of the Thuringian 'tongues', so the contemporaries used to describe it as 'Vogtland' or even as 'Egerlant'.³³ Because the Vogtlanders played an important role in the Teutonic Order, they likely considered themselves as an autonomous group.

On large territories from Würzburg and Nürnberg until near Stuttgart, the people talk Franconian (*fränkisch*, also: Eastern Franconian, *ostfränkisch*).³⁴ In a small area south of Heidelberg to Karlsruhe, one hears Southern Franconian (*südfränkisch*) which is, despite its name, not a Franconian subdialect but rather an autonomous dialect.³⁵ Further to the South, the lands of Swabian (*schwäbisch*) begin.³⁶ In Baden-Württemberg, Alsace, the German-speaking part of Switzerland and in Vorarlberg Alemannic (*alemannisch*) is at home.³⁷

The last subgroup, the Eastern Upper German, starts in the South of Nürnberg until Regensburg with Northern Bavarian (*nordbairisch*),³⁸ then in the large area till Vienna people speak different varieties of Middle Bavarian (*mittelbairisch*, also: Bavarian-Austrian).³⁹ Finally in Tirol, Southern Tirol and Karnten, one hears Southern Bavarian (*südbairisch*).⁴⁰

Contemporary people in the Middle Ages clearly perceived the *Reich* as multilingual. In the early 13th century, a French epic lauded the bravery of 'Alemant et Bavier'.⁴¹ Much finer differentiation was made by the inhabitants of the *Reich* themselves. Hugo von Trimberg (app. 1230–1313) wrote about the many languages of *Swâbe, Franken, Beire, Düringe, Sahsen, Rînliute, Wetereiber,*⁴² *Mîsner, Egerlant, Osterrîch, Stîrlant, Kernde* and *Westfaln.*⁴³ In the Golden Bull of 1356, the Electors of the *Reich* were told to be able of speaking the different tongues (*diversorum ydiomatum et linguarum differenciis instruantur*).[44]

Presence of the Order in the Different German Dialectical Areas

Among how many dialectical areas was the Teutonic Order represented? To answer this question, it is necessary to scrutinise his possessions in the *Reich*, which provided the Order with men and materials for the wars against the 'infidels'.[45] Larger properties were summoned to commanderies governed by the commanders (*Komture*). Commanderies from the same region were summoned to bailiwicks (*Balleien*) administrated by the land commanders (*Balleimeister*). Above them stood the 'German Master' (*Deutschmeister*) which was subordinated to the Grand Master (after 1309/1324 in Prussia) and obligated the gathering of the Great Chapter.[46]

Around 1400, the Order had 16 bailiwicks. Twelve of them were laying in the lands where German-speaking people played an exclusive or predominant role. In the North, the brethren hold the Bailiwick of Saxony (*Ballei Sachsen*) with nine commanderies.[47] Five of them (Bergen, Goslar, Göttingen, Langeln and Lucklum) covered the area of the Saxon and four (Aken, Buro, Dahnsdorf and Dommitzsch) were in the region where nowadays Brandenburgian is spoken. In the Late Middle Ages, the difference might have been fluent.

Going westwards, the possessions of the Order were subordinated to the Bailiwick of Westphalia (*Ballei Westfalen*), whose six commanderies (Brackel, Ootmarsum, Osnabrück, Mühlheim an Möhne, Münster and Welheim) were lying in the Westphalian dialectical zone.[48] Both commanderies (Bremen and Lübeck) in the *Reich* belonging to the Bailiwick of Livonia (*Ballei Livland*) were situated in the Saxon zone.[49]

From all the properties in the Middle Germany, by far the most important was the Bailiwick of Thuringia (*Ballei Thüringen*) with 15 commanderies. Six of them (Halle, Liebstedt, Mühlhausen, Nägelstedt, Weimar and Zwätzen) were situated in the Thuringian zone, another six in the Vogtlandian zone (Adorf, Asch, Plauen, Reichenbach, Saalfeld and Schleiz), two in the Meissnian zone (Altenburg and Wechselburg) and one in the Northern Bavarian zone (Eger).[50]

In the west of Thuringia, the Order had the Bailiwick of Marburg (*Ballei Marburg*) with 10 commandaries. Six of them were Hessian (Felsberg, Fritzlar, Kirchhain, Marburg, Schiffenberg, Wetzlar), two Thuringian (Erfurt, Greifstedt), one Palatine (Ober-Flörsheim) and one on the border between Hessian and Thuringian (Reichenbach) dialect zones.

In the Rhineland was the Bailiwick of Koblenz (*Ballei Koblenz*) with its eight far-flung commanderies. Three of these (Judenrode, Köln and Muffendorf) were in the Ripuarian zone, one (Rheinberg) in the Low Franconian, one (Koblenz) in the Moselle Franconian, one (Ibersheim) in the Palatine and two (Dieren and Mecheln) even in the Dutch zone.[51]

The Bailiwick of Lothringia (*Ballei Lothringen*) possessed eight commanderies. The headquarter was in Trier with Moselle Franconian dialect. In two (Beckingen and Saarbrücken) the local inhabitants spoke Palatine,[52] in one (Luxembourg) Luxembourgian, in two (Metz, Saarburg) Lothringian. One commandery in Thann near the Vosges Mountains was in Alsace, where people spoke an Alemannic dialect. The last commandery (Einsiedel) was situated on the border of Moselle Franconian and Palatine.

The last predominantly Middle German bailiwick was the one under the direct supervision of the 'German Master' with its headquarters in Horneck (*Ballei des Deutschmeisters*).[53] It counted for eight commanderies in the following zones: two in Moselle Franconian (Mainz, Waldbreitenbach), two in Palatine (Speyer, Weissenburg), one in Hessian (Sachsenhausen), one in Southern Franconian (Weinheim), one in Franconian (Horneck), and one on the border between Hessian and Franconian (Prozelten).[54]

The most important unit in the Upper Germany seemed to be the Bailiwick of Franconia (*Ballei Franken*) with its 18 commanderies.[55] In eight of them, the Franconian dialect (Heilbronn, Münnerstadt, Nürnberg, Rothenburg, Schweinfurt, Virnsberg, Winnenden, Würzburg) was spoken, in five the Northern Bavarian (Donauwörth, Ellingen, Karpfenburg, Obermässing, Oettingen), in three Middle Bavarian (Aichach, Gangofen, Regensburg) and in two Swabian (Giengen, Ulm).

To the Southwest was the Bailiwick of Alsace-Burgundy (*Ballei Elsass-Burgund*).[56] In 14 (Andlau, Basel, Bern, Beuggen, Freiburg, Gebweiler, Hitzkirch, Kayserberg, Köniz, Mainau, Mühlhausen, Rufach, Strassburg and Sumiswald) out of its 15 commanderies, different Alemannic dialects were in use and in one (Altshausen) Swabian.[57]

The smallest Bailiwick of Bozen (*Ballei Bozen*), also called Etsch or 'in the Mountains' (*im Gebirge*), had six commandaries in Southern Bavarian (Bozen, Lana, Lengmoos, Schlanders, Sterzing and St. Leonhard) and one (Trient) in Italian zone.[58]

The Bailiwick of Austria (*Ballei Österreich*) counted for seven commandaries.[59] Two of them (Wien and Wiener-Neustadt) spoke the Middle Bavarian (also: Bavarian-Austrian), while in the vicinity of three others (Friesach, Graz and Gross-Sonntag) the local population spoke Southern Bavarian dialect and around of next two (Crnomelij and Lubljana) mostly Slavic (here: Slovenian).

Bailiwicks of the Teutonic Order in Other Linguistical Regions

The Teutonic Order had four more bailiwicks in the lands which were not predominantly German-speaking. In the Northwestern part of the *Reich* was the Bailiwick of Altenbiesen (*Ballei Altenbiesen*) with 13 commanderies. On the territory of six the locals talked Dutch (Altenbiesen, Bekkevoort, Bernissem, Gemert, Gruitrode, Vught). Four could be classified as Low Franconian at least in the further sense (Geleen, Lüttich, Maastricht, Sint Pietersvoeren).

In three people used Ripuarian (Aachen, Ramersdorf, Siersdorf). The other bailiwick in the basically Dutch zone was Utrecht (*Ballei Utrecht*) with another 13 commanderies. All of them were situated in Dutch lands (Bunne, Doesburg, Katwijk, Leiden, Maasland, Middelburg, Nes, Tiel, Rhenen, Schelluinen, Schoonhoven, Schoten and Utrecht).

The Bailiwick of Bohemia-Moravia (*Ballei Böhmen-Mähren*) had its 20 commanderies on the territory of the modern-day Czech Republic.[60] In some regions, there were, of course, German-speaking settlers, but because of their different origins they also talked in different dialects. Nevertheless, three commanderies were lying close to the border, two next to the Erzgebirgian (Bilin, Chomutov), one (Aussig) in the region of Northern Bohemian (German dialect), and at least one could have had the brethren of Silesian tongue. Few possessions in the Northern Burgundy were summoned to two commanderies (Beauvoir, Orbec) under the last Bailiwick of France (*Ballei Frankreich*) with French as the common language.[61]

Brethren from Different Regions of the *Reich* in Prussia until 1309

How did this linguistical variety reflect in the Prussian branch of the Order? According to previous studies of the brethren in Prussia of the 13th century until 1309, the biggest contribution came from the Bailiwick of Thuringia with 40.5%, at the second place ranked the Bailiwick of Saxony with 20%, followed by the Bailiwick of Franconia with 15%, the bailiwicks form Upper Germany with 9%, the Rhineland with 7% and all the other regions, including Slavic territories, with almost 9%.[62]

Nothing is known about conflicts among brethren of different dialects and it is likely that none such existed, because the members of the Teutonic Order lived at that time in Prussia under the constant danger from the Baltic 'pagans'.[63] They were conquered until 1283, but the Order gained a stronger local acceptance around 1300 and established definitively its rule in the region.[64] The Order's brethren probably looked for the most effective people suitable for holding high offices, paying much less attention to linguistic and ethnic differences.

Brethren in Prussia in the First Half of the 14th Century

The time gap of 1310–1351 had been examined by Norbert Delestowicz who allocated 387 brethren to certain regions.[65] On the base of his studies, one can figure out the home dialect of each member. 36.2% (140 brethren) came in that period from the Bailiwick of Thuringia. Most of them (24%, 92 brethren), but by far not all were of Thuringian mother tongue. Some members arrived from Meissen and from Pleissenland (14 and eight brethren). Those two groups with 5.7% (22 brethren) talked Meissnian, today called (Upper) Saxon. A slightly bigger group came with 6.7% (26 brethren) from Vogtland and spoke Vogtlandian, a Franconian subdialect.[66]

The second place was still occupied by the Bailiwick of Saxony with 15% (58 brethren). Delestowicz, however, did not make a finer differentiation. If one bears in mind that this bailiwick reached to the territory of Brandenburgian dialect, it is likely that not all of the brethren spoke Saxon. One can roughly estimate that the Saxons made 12.5–13% (from 15%), the members of Brandenburgian (Markian) dialect less than 2% and those from Mecklenburg-Vorpommern less than 1%.[67]

The third largest group comprised 11.6% (45 brethren) and originated in the Bailiwick of Franconia. Among them, 5.7% (22 brethren) were of Franconian, 2.3% (nine brethren) of Swabian, 1.55% (six brethren) of Hessian, 1.3% (5 brethren) of Northern Bavarian and 0.75% (three brethren) of Southern Franconian mother tongue.[68]

The next group, comprising 10.85% (42 brethren), is called 'from Prussia'.[69] It is particularly difficult to make any predictions about their origins, because either they came from German-speaking families who settled down in Prussia or they were wearing as surnames places in Prussia or they were of Baltic or Slavic origin. 12 brethren appear to have had Old-Prussian roots.[70] In the case of eight brethren, it is not clear whether they were of Old-Prussian or of German ancestry, although the dominant German first names seem to favour the latter possibility.[71] For that reason, it will be assumed that 3.6% (14 brethren) were Old-Prussians. Further six brethren could have been of German or of Polish origin.[72] Two brethren seemed to have been originated from Poland or Pomerania, one brother from a German-speaking family in Silesia and one from Lübeck.[73] In this group of 10 brethren, one can suppose that 1.05% (four brethren) had Polish roots. In such a manner, one can deduce 20 brethren (14 Prussians, four Poles, one Silesian German and one *Lübecker*). The original group of 42 brethren 'from Prussia' therefore decreases to 22 members (5.7%).[74] They were likely of German origins, but it is not possible to determine their mother tongues. Some clues may lie in the general history of the settlement in the country. As mentioned above, in Prussia the German-speaking settlers at the Vistula River talked High Prussian (Middle German dialect) and those on the Baltic coast and around Königsberg Low Prussian (Low German dialect). Because the territories of the Vistula River were colonised first, it is possible that the brethren from High Prussia (*Oberland*) were more numerous than those from Low Prussia (*Niederland*). For that reason, one can estimate the brethren with High Prussian dialect at approximately 2.5–3% and the members of Low Prussian dialect at approximately 2–2.5%. The remaining 0.2–1.2% might have come from various regions of the *Reich* and spoke other dialects.

From the Bailiwick of Koblenz, which corresponded vastly to the 'Rhineland', came 6.2% (24 brethren). This large region accommodated, as shown above, one with Low Franconian one Low German dialect and five Middle German dialects: Ripuarian, Moselle Franconian, Rhinehessian (subdialect of Hessian), Luxembourgian and Palatine. Among the mentioned 24 brethren 3.35% (13 brethren) came from the area of Moselle Franconian,[75] 2.05%

(8 brethren) talked Ripuarian⁷⁶ and 0.8% (3 brethren) another Rhinelander dialect.⁷⁷

The Bailiwick of Marburg, whose possessions were lying in the zone of the Hessian dialect, sent to Prussia in this time 18 brethren. 16 of them (4.15%) spoke in a Hessian dialect and among them at least 2 (0.5%) Rhinehessian, so they also could pass as Rhinelanders.⁷⁸ The remaining 2 (0.5%) were Palatines.⁷⁹

16 brethren (4.15%) came from 'different' places: less than 1% (three brethren) was of Polish ancestry, less than 1% (three brethren), whose parentage was rather German than Slavic, from Lausitz and less than 1% (three brethren) from Silesia.⁸⁰ In the case of the four brethren their origins are not clear, although they might have come from Moravia or Prussia, one was from 'Bohemia or Poland', one (Arnold von Livland) was rather of Westphalian roots and called himself after a conquered region, and one was from Lübeck.⁸¹

Among the smallest groups in the Prussian branch, 3.35% (13 brethren) arrived from Westphalia, and 1.8% (seven brethren) from the Bailiwick of Alsace-Burgundy. Among them 1.3% (five brethren) were of Alemannic and 0.5% (two brethren) of Swabian dialect. For another 1.55% of brethren (six persons), it is possible to indicate origins from the Netherlands, 1.55% (six brethren) from the Bailiwick of Lothringia, five of whom were of Moselle Franconian and one of the Luxembourgian tongue, and another 1.55% (six brethren) from the Bailiwick of Bohemia-Moravia.⁸² In the case of 1.55% (six brethren) from Pomerania, four brethren (1.05%) might have been of German and two were of Slavic heritage.⁸³

Dialectical Representation in the Prussian Branch 1310–1351 in Numbers

The above analysis gives a good impression of the representation of each German dialect in the Prussian branch of the Teutonic Order in the first half of the 14th century. Almost half (48–48.5%) of the Prussian members who are confirmed by historical sources in the years 1310–1351 came from Middle Germany, followed by the Low Germans who made up almost a quarter (22–23.5%) and the Upper Germans (18.5%). It is remarkable that 9% of all the known brethren were in that time of non-Germanic (Baltic or Slavic) ancestry.

From the Low German zone, not a single brother spoke Frisian or Holsteinian. This is not surprising, as those dialects are small and the Order had no commanderies there. Among the Middle German dialects, one finds in Prussia even rare examples such as Lausitanian or Silesian where the Order also did not have any possessions. Only brethren of Lothringian, Southern Markian and Erzgebirgian mother tongues are missing. The biggest surprise arrives from Eastern Upper Germany. Although the Teutonic Order held Bailiwick of Bozen and Bailiwick of Austria, two dialects covering vast geographical areas are missing: the Middle and the Southern Bavarian.

Table 9.1 Representation of different dialects among all the Prussian brethren 1310–1351

Brethren of Low German dialects (including Dutch)	
Saxon (today called Low Saxon)	12.5–13.5%
Low Prussian	2–2.5%
Westphalian[84]	3.6%
Brandenburgian (Markian)	less than 2%
Dutch (Netherlands)	1.55%
Eastern Pomeranian	1.1%
Mecklenburgian	less than 1%
Low Franconian	0.25%
Total	app. 23–24.5%
Brethren of Middle German dialects	
Thuringian	24%
Meissnian (today Saxon)	5.7%
Hessian[85]	5.7%
Moselle Franconian[86]	4.4%
High Prussian	2.5–3%
Ripuarian	2.1%
Lausitanian	1%
Silesian[87]	0.75%
Palatine[88]	0.75%
Luxembourgian	0.75%
(German) Northern Bohemian	0.5%
Total	app. 48.5–49%
Brethren of Upper German dialects	
Vogtlandian	6.7%
Franconian	5.75%
Swabian[89]	2.8%
Alemannic	1.3%
Northern Bavarian	1.3%
Southern Franconian	0.75%
Total	app. 18.5%
Brethren of Slavic and Old-Prussian origins	
Poland/Pomerania/Silesia[90]	2.5%
Bohemia	2.25%
Old-Prussians	4.1%
Total	app. 9%

Different Dialects in the Second Half of the 14th Century

Until today, no prosopographic study of all the Prussian brethren of the Teutonic Order from the second half of the 14th century has been made. Some information can nevertheless be gained by analysing the most important members of the Order – the six high dignitaries and the leaders of at least 21 commanderies.[91] In around 90 cases, their origins are traceable.

The enlistment of those brethren from 1350 to 1400 starts once again with Saxony, from which eight members can be identified.[92] One person might have spoken Mecklenburgian and one to two Dutch.[93] Two brethren came from Westphalia.[94]

The Grand Master Winrich von Kniprode (1352–1382) favoured his countrymen from the Rhineland, so the West Middle German became much better represented among the Order's elite. Twelve of the important brethren were of Ripuarian[95] and another 10 of Moselle Franconian[96] dialect. Three more members came from the Rhineland. In two cases (Johann von Streifen, 1393–1404 and Walrabe von Scharfenberg, 1383–1393) it can be only said that their home region was the Northern Rhineland so it is unclear whether they spoke Low Franconian, Ripuarian, or even another 'tongue' from the borderland, such as Westphalian or Dutch.[97] The small Low Franconian can be rather rejected. Westphalian and Dutch were not spoken in the Rhineland itself, so those two Order's members can be counted among the Ripuarians, increasing that number to 14 brethren. One more (Konrad von Kalemunt, 1368–1381) might have been from the borderland between Ripuarian and Moselle Franconian so he can be counted to the group speaking Moselle Franconian dialect.[98]

One or two brothers were from the area of Luxembourg.[99] One brother likely spoke Palatine.[100] The last group from the Western Middle Germany were Hessians with ten members.[101]

From the Eastern Middle Germany likely five brethren were of Meissnian[102] and five of Thuringian[103] dialect. In one case (Nikolaus von Melin, 1398–1410), it is not sure whether he spoke Thuringian or Vogtlandian.[104] Two brethren (Eckhard Kulling, 1349–1353 and Rüdiger von Ostischau, 1382–1388) were likely from Prussia and according to their first names, they did not originate among the Baltic natives but from the German settlers.[105] It is impossible to say whether they had spoken High or Low Prussian. Because settlers first colonised the lands east of the Vistula, where High Prussian arose, brother Eckhard and brother Rüdiger will be counted to this dialectical group.

The Grand Masters of the late 14th century, Konrad Zöllner, Konrad Wallenrode and Konrad von Jungingen, might have favoured (a.o. through promotion to offices) their countrymen from Upper Germany.[106] From Vogtland, which is administratively part of Thuringia, but dialectically part of Upper Germany, came four persons[107] and ten from Franconia.[108] The Swabian dialect talked three higher brethren.[109] One brother was likely of Northern Bavarian descent.[110] One (Heinrich Harder, 1388–1402) was either of Bavarian-Austrian or of Swabian dialect.[111] Seven to eight members were of different Alemannic mother tongues.[112]

One person (Nicolaus von der Frantz, 1350–1374) was likely of Slavic origin from Pomerania.[113] He might have been the only one commander of non-Germanic roots in Prussia in that period.

Can such a table of the most important members be representative for the entire Order? One only has to look at the numbers of the Ripuarians and Moselle Franconians, who grew from 2.1%, respectively, 4.4% among all the brethren in 1310–1351 to the fabulous 15.6%, respectively, 12.2% among the Teutonic Order's elite in 1350–1400. It is almost impossible that these two fractions increased the same among lower-ranking officials. Therefore, the results for the high dignitaries and the commanders 1350–1400 cannot be valid also for the minor members. The fact that there were

Table 9.2 'Tongues' of the most important members of the Teutonic Order in Prussia 1351–1400

'Tonge' group	'Tonge'	Brethren	Percentage
Low German	Saxon (today Low Saxon)	8	8.9%
	Westphalian	2	2.2%
	Mecklenburgian	1	1.1%
Dutch		1 or 2	1.1% or 2.2%
Middle German	Ripuarian	14	15.6%
	Moselle Franconian	11	12.2%
	Hessian	9	11.1%
	Thuringian	5 or 6	5.6% or 6.7%
	Meissnian	5	5.6%
	Luxemburgian	1 or 2	1.1% or 2.2%
	Palatine	1	1.1%
	High Prussian	2	2.2%
Upper German	Vogtlandian	4 or 5	4.4% or 5.6%
	Franconian	10	11.1%
	Swabian	3 or 4	3.3% or 4.4%
	Northern Bavarian	1	1.1%
	Bavarian-Austrian (Middle Bavarian)	0 or 1	0% or 1.1%
	Alemannic	7 or 8	7.8% or 8.9%
Slavic	Pomeranian	1	1.1%

some struggles for the leadership of the Order in the 14th century makes it inappropriate to simply transfer the data concerning high dignitaries to other brothers who held offices and are recorded in the sources.[114] This issue therefore requires first conducting comprehensive prosopographic research.

Conclusions

In the Middle Ages, German dialects could be divided into at least nine Low German, 14 Middle German and eight Upper German variants. Due to the wide network of commanderies of the Teutonic Order, most of those dialects were also spoken in its Prussian branch. In that region among all the brethren of the 13th and the first half of the 14th centuries, the most common dialects were Thuringian, Low Saxon and Vogtlandian. In the second half of the 14th century, among the Teutonic Order's elite members, brethren, especially from the Rhineland and, to a smaller degree, from Franconia, dominated what is very likely not representative for the minor brethren in Prussia.

Notes

1 Heinrich Löffler, 'Dialekt,' in *Lexikon der Germanistischen Linguistik*, ed. Hans Althaus and Helmut Henne, Herbert Wiegand (Tübingen: Max Niemeyer Verlag, 1980, 2nd ed.), 454.

2 There might have been situation in which fathers sent their sons from their native regions to the relatives in other regions of the *Reich*, where they stayed at least for a dozen of month and learned new dialects.
3 The First Germanic sound shift (also: Grimm's law; erste Lautverschiebung) took place in the first millennium BC, *cf.* Werner Besch and Norbert Wolf, *Geschichte der deutschen Sprache. Längsschnitte – Zeitstufen – Linguistische Studien* (Berlin: Erich Schmidt Verlag, 2009), 47, 191, and 269–272; Guus Kroonen, *Etymological Dictionary of Proto-Germanic* (Leiden, Boston: Brill, 2013), XVI–XXVII; Peter von Polenz and Norbert Wolf, *Geschichte der deutschen Sprache* (Berlin: De Gruyter, 2020, 11th ed.), 44–49; Norbert Wolf, *Geschichte der deutschen Sprache*, vol. I, *Althochdeutsch-Mittelhochdeutsch* (Heidelberg: Quelle & Meyer 1981), 47–51; Gerhard Köbler, *Vom Umfang des Althochdeutschen* in *Verborum Amor*, ed. Harald Burger, Alois Haas, and Peter von Matt (Berlin: de Gruyter, 1992), 130; Jochen Splett, 'Die Wortbildung des Althochdeutschen,' in *Sprachgeschichte. Ein Handbuch zur Geschichte der deutschen Sprache und ihrer Erforschung*, vol. II, ed. Werner Besch, Anne Betten, Oskar Reichmann, and Stefan Sonderegger (Berlin: Walter de Gruyter, 2000, 2nd ed.), 1214–1215.
4 Werner König, *dtv-Atlas zur deutschen Sprache. Tafeln und Texte. Mit Mundart-Karten* (München: Deutscher Taschenbuch Verlag, 1994, 10th ed.), 64; Wolf, *Geschichte*, I: 41–42.
5 König, *dtv-Atlas*, 56; Oebele Vries, 'Geschichte der Friesen im Mittelalter: West- und Ostfriesland,' in *Handbuch des Friesischen – Handbook of Frisian Studies*, ed. Horst Munske, in collaboration with Nils Århammar, Volkert Faltings, Jarich Hoekstra, Oebele Vries, Alastair Walker, and Ommo Wilts (Tübingen: Max Niemeyer Verlag, 2001), 538–542; Thomas Johnston, 'The Old Frisian Law Manuscripts and Law Texts,' in Vries, 573; Theodor Siebs, *Helgoland und seine Sprache* (Wiesbaden: Dr. Martin Sändig, 1968), 29–34.
6 König, *dtv-Atlas*, 56; Wolf, *Geschichte*, I: 41; Hermann Niebaum, *Westniederdeutsch*, in *Lexikon*, ed. Althaus, Henne, and Wiegand, 463; Andreas Bieberstedt, Jürgen Ruge, and Ingrid Schröder, 'Kontaktinduzierte sprachliche Variation in der Hamburger Peripherie. Ein Modell zur Messung sprachlicher Konvergenz,' in *Hamburgisch. Struktur, Gebrauch, Wahrnehmung der Regionalsprache im urbanen Raum*, ed. Andreas Bieberstedt, Jürgen Ruge, and Ingrid Schröder (Frankfurt/Main, Internationaler Verlag der Wissenschaften, 2016), 21–32; Jürgen Ruge, 'Dialekttiefe durch lexikalische Analyse messbar machen,' in *Hamburgisch*, ed. Bieberstedt, Ruge, Schröder, 77; Richard Brill, 'Aus der Geschichte der niederdeutschen Sprache,' in *Niederdeutsch. Ein Handbuch zur Pflege der Heimatkunde*, ed. Richard Mehlem and Wilhelm Seedorf (Hannover: Hermann Schroedel Verlag, 1957), 66; Walter Niekerken, 'Von den Lauten der niederdeutschen Sprache,' in *Niederdeutsch*, ed. Mehlem and Seedorf, 75–79;
7 The subgroups are: Eastern, Southern Westphalian, Munsterlandian and Western Munsterlandian, *cf.* Niebaum, *Westniederdeutsch*, 459–462; Jakob Heinzerling and Hermann Reuter, *Siegerländer Wörterbuch* (Siegen: Verlag Vorländer, 1968, 2nd ed.), 579; Ferdinand Holthausen, 'Das Alter der südwestfälischen Diphthone,' *Zeitschrift für Mundartforschung* 18, no. 1/4 (1942): 106–107.
8 It has three subdialects: Northern, Southern Low Franconian and Eastern Bergish, *cf.* Hans-Dietrich Hammel, *Bedeutung, Wortschatz und Weltbild der niederfränkischen Mundart von Mülheim an der Ruhr*, Freiburg/Breisgau: Selbstverlag, 1967, 37–45; König, *dtv-Atlas*, 230.
9 Peter Jørgensen, *Zum Schleswiger Niederdeutsch. Kritik und Forschung* (København: Ejnar Munksgaard, 1954), 54–60; Klaus Kamp and Wolfgang Lindow, *Das Plattdeutsche in Schleswig-Holstein. Eine Erhebung des Statistischen Landesamtes Schleswig-Holstein* (Neumünster: Karl Wachtholz Verlag, 1967), 9–15.

10 This area was in the Late Middle Ages vastly germanised, cf. Erhard Riemann, 'Niederdeutsche Sprachlandschaften,' in *Niederdeutsch. Ein Handbuch zur Pflege der Heimatkunde*, ed. Richard Mehlem and Wilhelm Seedorf (Hannover: Hermann Schroedel Verlag, 1957), 24–25; Karl Nerger, *Grammatik des meklenburgischen Dialekts älterer und neuerer Zeit. Laut- und Fexionslehre* (Wiesbaden: Dr. Martin Sändig, 1966), 1–10; Hans Gernentz, *Niederdeutsch – gestern und heute. Beiträge zur Sprachsituation in den Nordbezirken der Deutschen Demokratischen Republik in Geschichte und Gegenwart* (Rostock: Hinstorff, 1980), 28–34.

11 König, *dtv-Atlas*, 74; Gernentz, *Niederdeutsch*, 31–34; Riemann, *Niederdeutsche*, 26–7; Gerard Labuda, *Pierwsze wieki monarchii piastowskiej* (Poznań: Nauka i Innowacje, 2012), 21–30; Günther Bellmann, 'Slawische Sprachen und deutsche Gesamtsprache,' in *Lexikon*, ed. Althaus, Henne, and Wiegand, 680–681; Dieter Stellmacher, *Ostniederdeutsch*, in *Lexikon*, ed. Althaus, Henne, and Wiegand, 465.

12 Robert Holsten, 'Der Kampf der niedersächsichen und niederfränkischen Mundart um Pommern,' *Zeitschrift für Mundartforschung* 18, no. 1/4 (1942): 123–128; id., *Sprachgrenzen im pommerschen Plattdeutsch* (Pyritz: Druck der Backeschen Buchdruckerei, 1913), 5–10; Alexander Hilferding, 'Die Ueberreste der Slaven auf der Südküste des baltischen Meeres,' *Zeitschrift für slavische Literatur, Kunst und Wissenschaft* 1, no. 1 (1862), 82–86.

13 G. Th. Hoffheinz, 'Ueber den ostpreuß. hochdeutschen Dialect. Vortrag, gehalten in der Königl. Deutschen Gesellschaft zu Königsberg,' *Altpreußische Monatsschrift* 9 (1872), 450, 457–458; König, *dtv-Atlas*, 74, 230–231.

14 Besch and Wolf, *Geschichte*, 292–6; von Polenz and Wolf, *Geschichte*, 63, 84; König, *dtv-Atlas*, 62, 72; Thorsten Roelcke, *Typologische Variation im Deutschen. Grundlagen – Modelle – Tendenzen* (Berlin: Erich Schmidt Verlag, 2011), 19, 22; Alois Walde, *Die germanischen Auslautgesetze. Eine sprachwissenschaftliche Untersuchung mit vornehmlicher Berücksichtigung der Zeitfolge der Auslautsveränderungen* (Halle/Salle: Max Niemeyer, 1900), 54–60; Carl Martens and Peter Martens, *Phonetik der deutschen Sprache. Praktische Aussprachlehre* (München: Max Heuber Verlag, 1961), 17–21, 108–111; Siegfried Grosse, 'Morphologie des Mittelhochdeutschen,' in *Sprachgeschichte*, ed. Besch, Betten, Reichmann und Sonderegger, 1333–1334.

15 Hartmut Beckers, 'Westmitteldeutsch,' in *Lexikon*, ed. Althaus, Henne, and Wiegand, 469; Theodor Frings, *Sprache und Geschichte*, vol. I (Haale: Max Niemeyer Verlag, 1956), 14–18, 108; Adolf Steins, *Grammatik des Aachener Dialekts*, ed. Klaus-Peter Lange (Köln: Böhlau Verlag, 1998), 31–35; Ferdinand Münch, *Grammatik der ripuarisch-fränkischen Mundart* (Bonn: Verlag von Friedrich Cohen, 1904), 6–12.

16 Another good exemple is 'dorp' changing around Bonn to 'dorf', cf. König, *dtv-Atlas*, 150, 155; Rolf Bergmann, *Mittelfränkische Glossen. Studien zu ihrer Ermittlung und sprachgeographischen Einordnung* (Bonn: Ludwig Röhrscheid Verlag, 1966), 93.

17 Peter Gilles, Phonologie der n-Tilgung im Moselfränkischen (Eifer Regel). Ein Beitrag zur dialektologischen Prosodieforschung,' in *Perspektiven einer linguistischen Luxemburgistik. Studien zu Synchronie und Diachronie*, ed. Claudine Moulin and Damaris Nübling (Heidelberg: Winter, 2006), 30–40; König, *dtv-Atlas*, 64; Britta Weimann, *Moselfränkisch. Der Konsonantismus anhand der frühesten Urkunden* (Köln: Böhlau Verlag, 2012), 93–100; Matthias Katerbow, *Spracherwerb und Sprachvariation. Eine phonetisch-phonologische Analyse zum regionalen Erstspracherwerb im Moselfränkischen* (Berlin: de Gruyter, 2013), 7–20; Walter Henzen, *Schriftsprache und Mundarten. Ein Überblick über ihr Verhältnis und ihre Zwischenstufen im Deutschen* (Zürich: Max Niehans Verlag, 1938), 42.

18 Luxembourgian will be nevertheless seen as autonomous. It has four different regional apparitions: *Elz-, Mosel-, Sauer-* and *Öslingermundart, cf.* Nico Weber, 'Sprachen und ihre Funktionen in Luxemburg,' *Zeitschrift für Dialektologie und Linguistik* 61, no. 2 (1994): 130, 149–151; J. P. Bourg, 'Die Luxemburger Mundart,' *Ons Hémecht* 1, no. 7 (1895): 206; 2, no. 12 (1896): 41 (online: http://engelmann.uni.lu/lux-PDFs/Bourg%20j.P.%20-%20Die%20Luxemburger%20Mundart%20-Ons%20H%C3%A9mecht%20-%201895-96.pdf, accessed 23 January 2023).

19 Albert Hudlett, *Morphologie verbale dans les parlers du Pays de Bitche (Moselle germanophone). Essai de représentation graphique automatique de la dynamique des variations géolinguistiques* (Bern: Peter Lang, 1989), 21–30; Hélène Nicklaus, *Le Platt. Le francique rhénan du Pays de Sarreguemines jusqu'à l'Alsace. Dictionnaire dialectical Platt – Allemand – Français* (Sarreguemines: Editions Pierron, 2001), 5–30; Hans Witte, *Das deutsche Sprachgebiet Lothringens und seine Wandelungen von der Feststellung der Sprachgrenze bis zum Ausgang des 16 Jahrhunderts* (Stuttgart: Verlag von J. Engelhorn, 1894), 9–17.

20 It has four subdialects: Northern, Middle, Eastern and Southern Hessian, *cf.* Bernd Strauch, *Dialekt in Mittelhessen. Oberhessisches Taschenwörterbuch* (Giessen: Offset Köhler, 2005), 9, 44–45; Hans Friebertshäuser, *Kleines hessisches Wörterbuch* (München: C. H. Beck, 1990), 13: Karte 1.

21 Palatine consists of two subgroups: Vorder- and Western Palatine, *cf.* Rudolf Post, 'Die Mundarten in Rheinhessen. Erforschung – Grenzen – Besonderheiten,' *Alzeyer Geschichtsblätter* 38 (2010): 53–59; König, *dtv-Atlas*, 230; Rahel Beyer, *Der pfälzische Sprachinseldialekt am Niederrhein. Eine generationsbedingte Variablenanalyse* (Mannheim: Institut für Deutsche Sprache, 2017), 13–21, 48–54; Kurt Bräutigam, *Die Mannheimer Mundart* (Walldorf: Fr. Lamade, 1934), 27, 39–42.

22 Jochen Müller, *Der mittelschwäbische Dialekt am Beispiel der Urbacher Mundart* (Stuttgart: ibidem-Verlag, 2003), 29; Bräutigam, *Mundart*, 27; Ernst Christmann, *Der Lautbestand des Rheinfränkischen und sein Wandel in der Mundart von Kaulbach (Pfalz)* (Speyer/Rhein: Pfälzische Gesellschaft zur Förderung der Wissenschaften, 1927), 1–11.

23 It has nine subdialects: Northern, Northeastern, Central, Western, Eastern, Southeastern and Ilm Thuringian, Hennebergian and Itzgrundian, *cf.* Karl Spangenberg, *Die Umgangssprache im Freistaat Thüringen und im Südwesten des Landes Sachsen-Anhalt* (Rudolfstadt, Jena: Hain Verlag, 1998), 16–17; Karl Spangenberg, *Laut- und Formeninventar thüringischer Dialekte. Beiband zum Thüringischen Wörterbuch* (Berlin: Akademie-Verlag, 1993), 6–10.

24 Theodor Frings, *Sprache und Siedlung im mitteldeutschen Osten* (Leipzig: Verlag von S. Hirzel, 1932), 24; Horst Becker and Gunter Bergmann, *Sächsische Mundartenkunde. Entstehung, Geschichte und Lautstand der Mundarten des obersächsischen Gebietes* (Halle: Max Niemeyer Verlag, 1969), 30–39; Wolf, *Geschichte*, I: 41; Theodor Frings, *Die Grundlagen des Meißnischen Deutsch. Ein Beitrag zur Entstehungsgeschichte der deutschen Hochsprache* (Halle/Saale: Max Niemeyer Verlag, 1936), 7–11; Karl Albrecht, *Die Leipziger Mundart. Grammatik und Wörterbuch der Leipziger Volkssprache* (Leipzig: Arnoldische Buchhandlung, 1881), 3–12; Ernst Schwarz, 'Probleme der Stammeskunde im deutsch-slawischen Berührungsgebiet,' *Zeitschrift für Ostforschung* 11, no. 1 (1962): 115; Labuda, *Pierwsze*, 21: Map 1, 30: Map 5.

25 It divides itself in the Northern, Western and Eastern Erzgebirgian, *cf.* Waltraud Krannich, *Wörterbuch der erzgebirgischen Mundart* (Zwickau: Chemnitzer Verlag, 2018), 14–16; Gunter Bergmann, *Das Vorerzgebirgische. Mundart und Umgangssprache im Industriegebiet um Karl-Marx-Stadt–Zwickau* (Haale: Max Niemeyer Verlag, 1965), 35–40; Oswin Böttger, *Der Satzbau der erzgebirgischen*

Mundart (Leipzig: Buchdruckerei von Heinrich John, 1904), 15–19. It will be seen as part of Upper Saxon by: Wolfgang Putschke, 'Ostmitteldeutsch,' in *Lexikon*, ed. Althaus, Henne and Wiegand, 477: Abb. 2.

26 Hans Klecker, *Oberlausitzer Wörterbuch* (Spitzkunnersdorf: Oberlausitzer Verlag, 2003), 5–10.

27 Norbert Dittmar, Peter Schlobinski, and Inge Wachs, *Berlinisch. Studien zum Lexikon, zur Spracheinstellung und zum Stilrepertoire* (Berlin: Verlag Arno Spitz, 1986), 9–20; Jan Eik, *Der Berliner Jargon*, with a foreword of Jutta Voigt (Berlin: Jaron Verlag, 2018, 3rd ed.), 12–13.

28 Putschke, *Ostmitteldeutsch*, 477; Bernd Kesselgruber, 'Die deutschen Mundarten Böhmens, Mährens und Schlesiens in der Bearbeitung des Sudetendeutschen Wörterbuches,' in *Deutsche und tschechische Dialekte im Kontakt*, ed. Albrecht Greule and Marek Nekula (Regensburg: Verlag für Literatur- und Sprachwissenschaft, 2003), 89–94.

29 Barbara Suchner, *Schlesisches Wörterbuch* (Husum: Husum Druck- und Verlagsgesellschaft, 1996), 7–15, 231; Putschke, *Ostmitteldeutsch*, 478: Karte 5; Frings, *Sprache und Siedlung*, 30; Reinhold Olesch, 'Zur schlesischen Sprachlandschaft. Ihr alter slawischer Anteil,' *Zeitschrift für Ostforschung* 27, no. 2 (1978): 33–40; Walter Mitzka, 'Altschlesische Vokabulare,' in *Volk – Sprache – Dichtung. Festgabe für Kurt Wagner* (Gießen: [s.n.], 1960), 131–134; Walter Mitzka, 'Niederdeutsch-schlesische Siedel und Sprachgemeinschaft,' in *Jahrbuch des Vereins für niederdeutsche Sprachforschung* 83 (1960): 33–37; Kesselgruber, *Mundarten*, 92.

30 König, *dtv-Atlas*, 231; Putschke, *Ostmitteldeutsch*, 477–478.

31 Harald Noth, *Alemannisches Dialektbuch vom Kaiserstuhl und seiner Umgebung* (Freiburg/Breisgau: Schillinger Verlag, 1993), 24; König, *dtv-Atlas*, 230–231.

32 Gunter Bergmann and Volkmar Hellfritzsch, *Kleines vogtländisches Wörterbuch* (Leipzig: Bibliographisches Institut Leipzig, 1990), 9; Erich Straßner, 'Nordoberdeutsch,' in *Lexikon*, ed. Althaus, Henne and Wiegand, 480: Karte.

33 Egerland has another dialect, similar to the Vogtlandian, *cf.* Josef Schiepek, 'Der Satzbau der Egerländer Mundart, erster Theil,' in *Beiträge zur Kenntnis deutschböhmischer Mundarten*, ed. Hans Lambel (Prag: Verlag des Vereins für Geschichte der Deutschen in Böhmen, 1899), 3–9; Michael Kollmer, *Wesenszüge des Bairischen, nachgewiesen an der Mundart Niederbayerns und der südlichen Oberpfalz, insbesondere des Bayrischen Waldes*, (Prackenbach: [s.n.], 1985), 8–14.

34 Oskar Brenner, *Mundarten und Schriftsprache in Bayern* (Bamberg: Buchnersche Verlagsbuchhandlung, 1890), 13; Sabine Krämer, *Die Steigerwaldschranke. Zum Aufbau einer ostfränkischen Dialektgrenze* (Würzburg: Königshausen & Neumann, 1995), 16–21; Klaus Trukenbrod, *Dialektgeographie des Obermainraumes und der nördlichen Fränkischen Schweiz* (Kulmbach: Freude der Plassenburg, 1973), 11–16; Müller, *Dialekt*, 29; Eberhard Wagner, 'Sprachproben aus Mittel-, Ober und Unterfranken,' in *Bayerns Mundarten. Dialektproben mit Kommentaren und einer Einführung in die Verbreitung und Verwendung des Dialekts in Bayern*, ed. Wolfgang Küpper, with a foreword of Hans Zehetmair (München: TR-Verlagsunion, 1991), 160–167; Ludwig Zehetner, *Sprachproben aus Ostbayern. Niederbayern, Oberpfalz und angrenzende Gebiete*, in *Bayerns Mundarten*, ed. Küpper, 97–101; Theodor Diegritz, *Lautgeographie des westlichen Mittelfrankens* (Neustadt/Aisch: Degener & Co., 1971), 33–41.

35 Müller, *Dialekt*, 30; König, *dtv-Atlas*, 230–231; Peter Ernst, *Deutsche Sprachgeschichte: Eine Einführung in die diachrone Sprachwissenschaft des Deutschen* (Wien: Facultas, 2021), 76.

36 It has five subdialects: Western, Middle and Eastern Swabian, Southern Eastswabian and Southern Middleswabian, *cf.* Müller, *Dialekt*, 32–65; Karl Bohnenberger, *Zur Geschichte der schwäbischen Mundart im XV. Jahrhundert* (Tübingen, J. C.

B. Mohr, 1892), 2–12; Fritz Rahn, *Der schwäbische Mensch und seine Mundart. Beiträge zum schwäbischen Problem* (Stuttgart: Hans-Günther-Verlag, 1962), 4–10.

37 Konrad Kunze, 'Alemannisch – was ist das? Grenzen, Geschichte, Merkmale eines Dialekts,' in *Kleiner Dialektatlas. Alemannisch und Schwäbisch in Baden-Württemberg*, ed. Hubert Klausmann, Konrad Kunze, and Renate Schrambke (Bühl (Baden): Konkordia, 1993), 30–35; Hubert Klausmann, *Alemannisch in einzelnen Regionen Baden-Württembergs*, in *Kleiner Dialektatlas*, ed. Klausmann, Kunze, and Schrambke, 76–86; Christian Bader, *Lexique des Parlers Sundgauviens* (Mulhouse: éditions du Rhin, 1997), 5–15; Michael Frank, 'Das Elsässerditsch – Merkmal einer eigenständigen Kultur,' in *Burgund Elsass*, ed. Thorsten Droste, Michael Frank, Haug von Kuenheim, and Heinz-Gert Woschek (München, Luzern: Verlag C. J. Bucher, 1984), 157; Werner Hodler, *Berndeutsche Syntax* (Bern: Francke, 1969), 5–20; Leo Jutz, *Die Mundart von Südvorarlberg und Liechtenstein* (Heidelberg: Carl Winter's Universitätsbuchhandlung, 1925), 45–49.

38 Rudolf Freudenberg, 'Ostoberdeutsch,' in *Lexikon*, ed. Althaus, Henne and Wiegand, 487–488; Michael Kollmer, *Wesenszüge des Bairischen, nachgewiesen an der Mundart Niederbayerns und der südlichen Oberpfalz, insbesondere des Bayrischen Waldes* (Prackenbach: [s.n.], 1985), 8–11; Roland Wolff, *Wie sagt man in Bayern. Eine Wortgeographie für Ansässige, Zugereiste und Touristen* (München: C. H. Beck, 1980), 56–59; Manfred Renn, *Die Mundart im Raum Augsburg. Untersuchungen zum Dialekt und zum Dialektwandel im Spannungsfeld großstädtisch-ländlicher und alemannisch-bairischer Gegensätze* (Heidelberg: Universitätsverlag C. Winter, 1994), 14–19.

39 Kurt Rein, 'Bayerns Mundarten. Eine Einführung in Verbreitung und Verwendung,' in: *Bayerns Mundarten*, ed. Küpper, 16; König, *dtv-Atlas*, 230–231; Ludwig Zehetner, *Das bairische Dialektbuch* (in cooperation with Ludwig Eichinger, Reinhard Rascher, Anthony Rowley, and Christopher Wickham) (München: C. H. Beck, 1985), 41–44; Freudenberg, *Ostoberdeutsch*, 487; Wolff, *Wie sagt*, 27–31; Johann Schmeller, *Die Mundarten Bayerns grammatisch dargestellt* (München: Karl Thienemann, 1821), 7–15; Stefan Dollinger, *Österreichisches Deutsch oder Deutsch in Österreich? Identitäten im 21. Jahrhundert* (Wien, Hamburg: new academic press, 2021), 178.

40 Freudenberg, *Ostoberdeutsch*, 487; Rein, *Bayerns Mundarten*, 24; Josef Schatz, *Die tirolische Mundart* (Innsbruck: Wagner'sche Univ.-Buchdruckerei, 1903), 18–38; Franz Lanthaler, *Zur Morphologie der Verben in der Mundart des Passeiertales (Südtirol)* (Innsbruck: [s.n.], 1971), 65–69, 113–119; Bernhard Wurzer, *Die deutschen Sprachinseln in Oberitalien* (Bozen: Athesia, 1983), 12–15.

41 Werner Maleczek, 'Das Reich im 14. Jahrhundert – Blicke von außen,' in *Die Goldene Bulle. Politik – Wahrnehmung – Rezeption*, vol. I, ed. Ulrike Hohensee, Mathias Lawo, Michael Lindner, Michael Menzer, and Olaf Rader (Berlin: Akademie Verlag, 2009), 584.

42 Wetterau lies between Taunus, Lahn and Main and was sometimes perceived as a separate region, *cf.* Gerhard Köbler, *Historisches Lexikon der deutschen Länder. Die deutschen Territorien und reichsunmittelbaren Geschlechter vom Mittelalter bis zur Gegenwart* (München: C. H. Beck'sche Verlagsbuchhandlung, 1999, 6th ed.), 716; Hans Limburg, *Die Hochmeister des Deutschen Ordens und die Ballei Koblenz*, Quellen und Studien zur Geschichte des Deutschen Ordens 8 (Bad Godesberg: Verlag Wissenschaftliches Archiv, 1969), 192.

43 *Der Renner von Hugo von Trimberg*, vol. III, ed. Gustav Ehrismann (Tübingen: Druck H. Laupp Jr., 1909), 220–221 lines 22256–22297; Adolf Socin, *Schriftsprache und Dialekte im Deutschen nach Beugnissen alter und neuer Zeit* (Heilbronn: Verlag von Gebr. Henninger, 1888), 117.

44 *Quellen zur Verfassungsgeschichte des Römisch-Deutschen Reiches im Spätmittelalter (1250–1500)*, ed. Lorenz Weinrich (Darmstadt: Wissenschaftliche Buchgesellschaft 1983), chap. XXXI.
45 *Die Statuten des Deutschen Ordens nach den ältesten Handschriften*, ed. Max Perlbach (Halle/Salle: Max Niemeyer, 1890), 30: Rule 2; Nicholas Morton, *The Teutonic Knights in the Holy Land 1190–1291* (Woodbridge: Boydell Press, 2009), 144–147.
46 Klaus Militzer, *Die Entstehung der Deutschordensballeien im Deutschen Reich*, Quellen und Studien zur Geschichte des Deutschen Ordens 16 (Bonn, Bad Godesberg: Wissenschaftliches Archiv, 1970), 34–39.
47 Till 1287 this bailiwick went together with Thuringia, *cf.* Janusz Tandecki, 'Organizacja wewnętrzna zakonu krzyżackiego i jego członkowie,' in *Państwo zakonu krzyżackiego w Prusach. Władza i społeczeństwo*, ed. Marian Biskup and Roman Czaja (Warszawa: Wydawnictwo Naukowe PWN, 2009), 409; Klaus Militzer, *Historia zakonu krzyżackiego* (Kraków: Wydawnictwo WAM, 2007), 72; Jürgen Sarnowsky, *Der Deutsche Orden* (München: C. H. Beck, 2007), 27; Udo Arnold, 'Agrarwirtschaft im Deutschen Orden. Besitzverwaltung und Bewirtschaftungsformen des landwirtschaftlichen Besitzes im Deutschen Reich bis zum Reformzeitalter,' in *Beiträge zur Geschichte des Deutschen Ordens*, vol. 1, ed. id., Quellen und Studien zur Geschichte des Deutschen Ordens 36 = Veröffentlichungen der Internationalen Historischen Kommission zur Erforschung des Deutschen Ordens 1 (Marburg: N. G. Elwert Verlag, 1986), 53: Karte.
48 The commandery of Ootmarsum was rather in the Dutch zone but the linguistical differences were effusive, so it will be counted as a Westphalian, *cf.* Hans Dorn, *Die Deutschordensballei Westfalen von der Reformation bis zu ihrer Auflösung im Jahre 1809*, Quellen und Studien zur Geschichte des Deutschen Ordens 26 (Marburg: N. G. Elwert Verlag, 1978), 6–11; Militzer, *Historia*, 322; Militzer, *Entstehung*, 107–112; Arnold considers the commandery of Bremen to be part of the Bailiwick of Westphalia, *cf.* Arnold, *Agrarwirtschaft*, 53: Karte.
49 Bernhart Jähnig, *Verfassung und Verwaltung des Deutschen Ordens und seiner Herrschaft in Livland* (Berlin: W. Hopf, 2011), 182–183; Militzer, *Historia*, 322.
50 Dieter Wojtecki, *Studien zur Personalgeschichte des Deutschen Ordens im 13. Jahrhundert*, Quellen und Studien zur Geschichte des östlichen Europa 3 (Wiesbaden: Franz Steiner Verlag, 1971), 74–75; Militzer, *Historia*, 322; König, *dtv-Atlas*, 231.
51 Limburg, *Die Hochmeister*, 16–22; Militzer, *Entstehung*, 91–92; Sarnowsky, *Orden*, 58; Johannes Voigt, *Geschichte des Deutschen Ritter-Ordens in seinen zwölf Balleien in Deutschland*, vol. I (Berlin: Druck und Verlag von Georg Reimer, 1857), 75–76. The Rhineland was even in its most important parts politacally split, *cf.* Peter Moraw, 'Über Rahmenbedingungen und Wandlungen auswärtiger Politik vorwiegend im deutschen Spätmittelalter,' in *Auswärtige Politik und internationale Beziehungen im Mittelalter (13. bis 16. Jahrhundert)*, ed. Dieter Berg, Martin Kintzinger, and Pierre Monnet (Bochum: Verlag Dr. Dieter Winkler, 2002), 42.
52 Wilhelm Will, *Saarländische Sprachgeschichte*, with a foreword of Adolf Bach (Saarbrücken: Saarbrücker Druckerei und Verlag, 1932), 21–37. According to Arnold there was no commandery in Saarbrücken, *cf.* Arnold, *Agrarwirtschaft*, 53: Karte.
53 Klaus Militzer, Heinz Henze, and Stefan Mielke, 'Die Balleien des Deutschen Ordens in ‚Deutschen und Welschen Landen'um 1400 I,' in *Historisch-geographischer Atlas des Preussenlandes*, issue 11, ed. Hans Mortensen, Gertrud Mortensen, Reinhard Wenskus, and Helmut Jäger (Stuttgart: Franz Steiner Verlag, 1986), Karte 1; Klaus Militzer, 'Erläuterungen zu den Karten: Die Balleien des Deutschen Ordens in ‚Deutschen und Welschen Landen'um 1400 I,' in

Historisch-geographischer Atlas, ed. Mortensen, Mortensen, Wenskus, and Jäger, 5; Sarnowsky, *Orden*, 27.
54 Militzer, *Historia*, 322.
55 Dieter Weiß, *Die Geschichte der Deutschordens-Ballei Franken im Mittelalter* (Neustadt/Aisch: Degener, 1991), 1–10; Josef Hopfenzitz, *Kommende Oettingen Deutschen Ordens (1242–1805). Recht und Wirtschaft im terrtorialen Spannungsfeld*, Quellen und Studien zur Geschichte des Deutschen Ordens 33 (Bonn, Bad Godesberg: Verlag Wissenschaftliches Archiv, 1975), 7–15; Militzer, Henze, and Mielke, 'Die Balleien,' Karte 4; Militzer, 'Erläuterungen,' 5; Sarnowsky, *Orden*, 58.
56 The opinion that Alsace-Burgundy was the second most important bailiwick in the Reich after Franconia: Hopfenzitz, *Kommende Oettingen*, 82.
57 Militzer, Henze, and Mielke, 'Die Balleien,' Karte 3; Arnold, *Agrarwirtschaft*, 53; Voigt, *Geschichte*, 77–82.
58 Militzer, Henze, and Mielke, 'Die Balleien,' Karte 5; Militzer, 'Erläuterungen,' 5; Militzer, *Historia*, 322; Voigt, *Geschichte*, 84–88.
59 Militzer, Henze, and Mielke, 'Die Balleien,' Karte 6; Militzer, *Historia*, 322.
60 Militzer, Henze, and Mielke, 'Die Balleien,' Karte 7; Josef Hemmerle, *Die Deutschordens-Ballei Böhmen in ihren Rechnungen 1382–1411*, Quellen und Studien zur Geschichte des Deutschen Ordens 22 (Bonn, Bad Godesberg: Verlag Wissenschaftliches Archiv, 1967), 11–17.
61 These were commanderies in Beauvoir and Orbec, *cf.* Karol Polejowski, 'Kryzys krzyżackiej komendy Beauvoir we Francji pod koniec XIV w.,' *Studia z Dziejów Średniowiecza* 15 (2009), 133–136; Militzer, *Historia*, 322.
62 Klaus Militzer, *Von Akkon zur Marienburg. Verfassung, Verwaltung und Sozialstruktur des Deutschen Ordens 1190–1309*, Quellen und Studien zur Geschichte des Deutschen Ordens 56 = Veröffentlichungen der Internationalen Historischen Kommission zur Erforschung des Deutschen Ordens 9 (Marburg: N. G. Elwert Verlag, 1999), 427; Maciej Dorna, *Bracia Zakonu krzyżackiego w Prusach w latach 1228–1309* (Poznań: Wydawnictwo Poznańskie, 2004), 55–60; Tandecki, 'Organizacja,' 409; Wojtecki, *Studien*, 123–128; Klaus Scholz, *Beiträge zur Personengeschichte des Deutschen Ordens in der ersten Hälfte des 14. Jahrhunderts* (Münster: Westfälischen Wilhelms-Universität, 1971), 10–18.
63 Wenta supposes nevertheless that such a phenomenon existed already in the 13th century, *cf.* Jarosław Wenta, 'Studium, Arbeit, Intrige – die Karriere im Deutschen Orden in Preußen,' in *La vie quotidienne des moines et chaniones réguliers au Moyen Âge et Temps modernes. Actes du Premier Colloque International du L.A.R.H.C.O.R., Wrocław–Książ, 30. novembre – 4. decembre 1994*, ed. Marek Derwich (Wrocław: Publications de l'Institut d'Histoire de l'Université de Wrocław, 1995), 194.
64 Dusburg (S), book III, cap. 221; Militzer, *Historia*, 96–104; Karol Górski, *Państwo krzyżackie w Prusach* (Gdańsk, Bydgoszcz: Instytut Bałtycki, 1946), 48.
65 In the table the author talks about 382 brethren and he specifies at the last place 17 brethren of unclear origin, *cf.* Delestowicz, *Bracia*, 39. A check in the later schedules (pages: 65–67) reveals that there were 22 (instead of 17) such brethren (six from Pomerenia, thee from Poland, one from Livonia, 12 of undefined provenance) what makes all together 387 (instead of 382) brethren.
66 Delestowicz, *Bracia*, 36, 45–52; Bergmann and Hellfritzsch, *Kleines vogtländisches Wörterbuch*, 9.
67 Among those 58 brethren from the Bailiwick of Saxony Hermann von Oppen and Otto von Oppen came surely from Brandenburgia and must have spoken Markian. Nicolaus von Gutow came from Rostock so he talked Mecklenburgian. Konrad Kesselhut had also family name from Northeastern Germany and according

to Weichbrodt was from Mecklenburg-Vorpommern. Delestowicz counts him to the Thuringians and Militzer lets the question open, cf. Ernst Weichbrodt, 'Erläuterungen zur Karte: Gebietiger des Deutschen Ordens in Preußen nach ihrer Herkunft,' in *Historisch-geographischer Atlas des Preußenlandes*, issue 1, ed. Hans Mortensen, Gertrud Mortensen, and Reinhard Wenskus (Wiesbaden: Franz Steiner Verlag, 1968), 3; Delestowicz, *Bracia*, 47, 220, 254, 281, and 288; Klaus Militzer, 'Kesselhut, Konrad, Ritterbruder des Deutschen Ordens, Großkomtur,' in APB, vol. V, ed. Klaus Bürger and Bernhart Jähnig (Marburg/Lahn: N. G. Elwert Verlag, 2015), 2119. The estimation of 1% matches with the 13th century when 1.16% of the high dignitaries came from Mecklenburgia, cf. Militzer, *Von Akkon*, 443.

68 Delestowicz defines 25 brethren from Franconia, two from Bavaria, one from 'Upper Pfalz' which belongs to Bavaria, and two from 'Bavaria-Franconia'. One of them will be given to the fraction of Franconians and one to that of Bavarians. Johann Nothaft counted by Delestowicz to the Franconians was rahter a Bavarian. This makes 25 Franconians and five Bavarians. Among those 25 Franconians three came from the region of Southern Franconian. Nine brethren are defined as Swabians, four are from 'Taunus' and two from 'Rhineland' in the further sense. Those six brethren might have spoken Hessian dialect, cf. Delestowicz, *Bracia*, 55–57, 179, 296, and 316. Discutable is Heinrich Dusemer, counted by the majority opinion and herein as Franconian, by the minority (Paweł Pizuński) as Swabian and by the older opinion (Johannes Voigt) as Pomeranian, cf. Klaus Conrad, 'Heinrich Dusemer (13. oder 18. XII. 1345 – Ende 1351),' in *Die Hochmeister des Deutschen Ordens 1190–1994*, ed. Udo Arnold, Quellen und Studien zur Geschichte des Deutschen Ordens 40 = Veröffentlichungen der Internationalen Historischen Kommission zur Erforschung des Deutschen Ordens 6 (Marburg: N. G. Elwert Verlag, 1998), 81; Delestowicz, *Bracia*, 101; Paweł Pizuński, *Poczet wielkich mistrzów krzyżackich* (Skarszewy: Arenga, 2017, 4th ed.), 97; Johannes Voigt, *Geschichte Preussens von den ältesten Zeiten bis zum Untergange der Herrschaft des Deutschen Ordens*, vol. V (Königsberg: Bei den Gebrüdern Bornträger, 1832), 38.

69 Delestowicz, *Bracia*, 57–60.

70 Old-Prussians were surely because of their names: Albert Prusse, Glabune, Gobelo, Johann Prusse, Johann Wernkonis, Leykot, Zancirmo. It is also likely in the cases of: Albert von Schaaken, Heinrich Cleycz, Heinrich von Thymau, Nicolaus Pechwinkel and Peter von Thymau, cf. Delestowicz, *Bracia*, 117, 123, 170–171, 183, 230–232, 266, 280, 292, 314–315, and 333; Rozalia Przybytek, *Ortsnamen baltischer Herkunft im südlichen Teil Ostpreussens*, Hydronomia Europaea, Sonderband (Stuttgart: Franz Steiner Verlag, 1993), 10–4.

71 They are Bartolomeus von Radam, Eberhard von Schalmey, Eckhard Kulling, Friedrich von Lanzin, Jakob von Radam, Johann von Geidau, Johann von Lessen and Reinhard von Leitisch, cf. Delestowicz, *Bracia*, 147, 149, 236, 293, 322, 327, 345, and 373. Because four first names are clerly German, it will be supposed that these members were German-speaking brethren. Four remaining first names are Biblical, so two of them will be counted to the Prussians (who grow from 12 to 14) and two to the German-speaking people.

72 These are: Friedrich von Senskau, Heinrich von Orlow, Heinrich von Senskau, Johann von Neuteich, Kunemund von Malken, Nicolaus von Senskau, cf. Delestowicz, *Bracia*, 161, 207, 212, 264, 345, and 352.

73 From Poland: Jan Swiercin; from Pomerania: Nicolaus von der Frantz. In his case it is unclear if he was from a Polish or German-speaking family; from Silesia: Friedrich von Goldberg who might have been a German-speaking man; from Lübeck: Tilo Lubecke. He likely spoke Saxon. As this city lies close to Mecklenburgian

dialect it is also possible that he came from this region and only called himself after the famous town, *cf.* Delestowicz, *Bracia*, 281, 300, 327, and 342.
74 This group of 22 brethren will increase to 26, because under the brethren from 'different places', there are four unclear persons who might have come either from Moravia or from Prussia.
75 Moselle Franconian talked: Eberhard von Virneburg, Friedrich von Boppard, Friedrich von Veldenz, Friedrich von Wildenberg, Gerhard Nayl, Gottfried von Sayn, Johann von Lahnstein, Ludwig von Isenburg, Reimbold von Isenburg, Richwin Specht von Bubenheim, Salentin von Isenburg, Wilhelm Lander von Sponheim, Wilhelm von Helfenstein, *cf.* Delestowicz, *Bracia*, 148, 155, 162–166, 172, 237, 272, 293, 310, and 382–385.
76 Ripuarian talked Christian von Binsfeld, Heinrich von Rondorf, Johann Overstolz von der Bach, Kirsilie von Kindswulie, Ludwig von Wolkenburg, Schweder von Pellant, Werner von Rondorf, Winrich von Kniprode. Their number might have been slightly bigger as Johann von Köln whose name shows on Colonia was counted as indiffiniable, *cf.* Delestowicz, *Bracia*, 132, 210, 229, 236, 251, 273–274, 297, and 309–311.
77 Andreas Hecht came fron the area of Geldern, near Cleve in Low Franconia, Marquart von Lindelbrunn from the area of Vorweidenthal so he spoke Palatine and Dietrich von Pirmont from the mountains of Eifel probably Luxemburgian, *cf.* Delestowicz, *Bracia*, 142, 277, and 362.
78 They were Kuno von Hattstein and possibly Gerhard von Runkel, *cf.* Klaus Militzer, 'Rheinländer im mittelalterlichen Livland,' in id., *Zentrale und Region. Gesammelte Beiträge zur Geschichte des Deutschen Ordens in Preussen, Livland und im Deutschen Reich aus den Jahren 1968 bis 2008*, Quellen und Studien zur Geschichte des Deutschen Ordens 75 = Veröffentlichungen der Internationalen Historischen Kommission zur Erforschung des Deutschen Ordens 13 (Weimar: Verlag und Datenbank für Geisteswissenschaften, 2015), 266; Militzer, *Historia*, 147; Delestowicz, *Bracia*, 168, 266; Tomasz Kruszewski, 'Przedstawiciele rodu von Hattstein jako urzędnicy zakonu krzyżackiego w Prusach. Studium historycznoprawne i genealogiczne,' KMW 1/287 (2015): 19, 29.
79 Two brethren of Palatine mothertongue were Johann and Werner von Bolanden. Delestowicz lists under the Pfalz two more brethren, Dietrich and Heinrich von Blumenstein. They came from the area of Zierenburg, near Kassel in the Northern Hessia and spoke rather Hessian, *cf.* Delestowicz, *Bracia*, 61, 138, 192, 233, and 305.
80 It is possible that very few brethren from the group of 92 Thuringians came from Lausitz. That would make grow this region from three brethren to four–five brethren which gives more than 1%. In case of Silesians 1 brother (Jan von Brieg) was rather of Polish origin, one (Heinrich von Schlewitz) of German origin and one (Hugo von Wratislawia) of unclear origin, *cf.* Delestowicz, *Bracia*, 67, 223, 342, and 371; Tomasz Jurek, *Obce rycerstwo na Śląsku do połowy XIV wieku* (Poznań: Poznańskie Towarzystwo Przyjaciół Nauk, 1996), 327; Marek Cetwiński, *Rycerstwo śląskie do końca XIII w. Biogramy i rodowody* (Wrocław: Zakład Narodowy im. Ossolińskich, 1982), nos. 10, 70, 574, 787, and 832.
81 From those four brethren two will be counted in the following to the Prussians so that their number grows from 14 to 16 (4.1%) and the other two to the Bailiwick of Bohemia-Moravia. Arnold von Livland will be considered as a Westphalian because this team dominated in the Livonian branch of the Order, and the brother from Lübeck as Saxon, *cf.* Delestowicz, *Bracia*, 66–67.
82 According to Jähnig among the six brethren from Bailiwick of Lothringia two (Johann von Falkenstein, Dietrich von Brandenburg) came from Luxembourg. Delestowicz accepts also the disputable brother von Falkenstein. This version will

be taken in the following, *cf.* Bernhart Jähnig, 'Zur Herkunft von Dietrich von Brandenburg, Komtur von Thorn,' in id., *Zum Innenleben des Deutschen Ordens in Preußen* (Münster: Nicolaus-Copernicus-Verlag, 2021), 195; Delestowicz, *Bracia*, 139, 235; Among six brethren from the Bailiwick of Bohemia-Moravia four (Jesko von Böhmen, Jesko von Schönburg, Johann von Troppau and Scislaus) were of Czech origin and in two cases (Siegfried von Wobitz and Friedrich von Tuchelsdorf) the ethnical ancestry remains unclear. Because of their names they may be counted to (German) Northern Bohemian, *cf.* Delestowicz, *Bracia*, 162, 246–247, 315, 347, and 360.

83 Eberhard von Borne and Wilhelm von Borne came from the Neumark. Their first names reveals clearly German ancestery, which in this region spoke Eastern Pomeranian (*ostpommersch*). Nicolaus Holste was from (German-speaking) Pomeranians. The family of Albert von Massou immigrated to Pomerania from Saxony so he also might have spoken Pomeranian, *cf.* Delestowicz, *Bracia*, 146, 362, and 380; Christian Gahlbeck, 'Zur Herkunft und Zusammensetzung des neumärkischen Adels bis zur Mitte des 14. Jahrhunderts,' in *Landesherr, Adel und Städte in der mittelalterlichen und frühneuzeitlichen Neumark*, ed. Klaus Neitmann (Berlin: Berliner Wissenschafts-Verlag, 2015), 122–125; Roman Czaja, 'Die Städte und der Deutsche Orden in der Neumark und in Preußen,' in *Landesherr*, ed. Neitmann, 239; Georg von Mülverstedt, 'Die Beamten und Konventsmitglieder in den Verwaltungsbezirken des Deutschen Ordens innerhalb des Oberländischen Kreises,' *Oberländische Geschichtsblätter* 2 (1900): 19; Dieter Heckmann, *Amtsträger des Deutschen Ordens in Preußen und in den Kammerballeien des Reiches (oberste Gebietiger, Komture, Hauskomture, Kumpane, Vögte, Pfleger, Großschäffer)* (online: accessed 4 March 2024), 98.

84 From the Bailiwick of Westphalia came 13 brethren. To this group was added Arnold von Livland from unclear brethren as in the Livonian branch Westphalians had the most powerful position. Fourteen brethren make 3.6%.

85 Sixteen brethren came from the Bailiwick of Marburg and six brethren from the Bailiwick of Franconia, what gives 22 brethren and 5.7%.

86 Five brethren came from Lothringia and 12 brethren from the Bailiwick of Koblenz which makes 17 brethren and 4.4%.

87 Together three brethren: In best case two brethren from Silesia and one (Friedrich von Golberg) from German-speaking family who settled down in Prussia from Silesia.

88 Two brethren came from the Bailiwick of Marburg and one from the Bailiwick of Koblenz.

89 9 Swabian brethren came from the Bailiwick of Franconia and two from the Bailiwick of Alsace-Burgundy, giving 11 brethren and 2.8%.

90 From Poland, Pomerania and (Polish speaking) Silesia came nine or ten (2.35% or 2.58%) brethren and from Bohemia eight or nine (2 or 2.3%) brethren.

91 In Prussia, the Order in the years 1350–1400 held 21 commanderies consistently: in Althaus, Balga, Birgelau, Brandenburg, Danzig, Engelsburg, Gollub, Graudenz, Memel, Mewe, Nessau, Osterode, Papau, Ragnit, Rehden, Schlochau, Schönsee, Schwetz, Strasburg, Thorn and Tuchel, *cf.* Helmut Hartmann, 'Hochmeister, Deutschmeister, Landkomtur, Komtur, Hauskomtur, Ritter, Priester – Ämter und Lebensweise der Deutschordensangehörigen (bis etwa 1809),' in *Der Deutsche Orden und die Ballei Elsaß-Burgund*, ed. Hermann Brommer (Bühl (Baden): Konkordia Verlag, 1996), 79; Piotr Gotówko, 'Rotacje osobowe w Zakonie Krzyżackim w Prusach między przeniesieniem siedziby Wielkiego Mistrza do Malborka a bitwą pod Grunwaldem (1310–1409),' KMW 3/322 (2023): 488–490.

92 Burkhart von Asseburg (years as a commander or as high dignitary: 1358–1376), Burkhart von Wobeke (1393–1411), Heinrich von Bovenden (1338–1359), Heinrich von Schöningen (1362–1364), Gebhard von Ampleben (1360–1379), Gottfried von der Kuhle (1398–1409), Johann von Barkenfelde (1336–1350). The eight member from Saxony was the commander of Papau in the year 1382, who was mentioned without name by the annals of Thorn as *commendator in Papow Saxo*. In Papau there is a gap 1349–1386, so the brother from Saxony remains unknown by his name, *cf.* FTAP, 121; Weichbrodt, 'Erläuterungen',1–5; Heckmann, *Amtsträger*, 31, 39, 44, 52–54, 65–67, and 70–73; Delestowicz, *Bracia*, 194, 233.
93 From Mecklenburgia arrived Friedrich von Wenden (1381–1407), from Holland Johann Langerak (1346–1356) and possibly Heinrich von Rechter (1348–1351), who according to Delestowicz remains undefinable, *cf.* Weichbrodt, 'Erläuterungen', 3–4; Delestowicz, *Bracia*, 209, 238, 281; Heckmann, *Amtsträger*, 39, 45–49, 76, and 160.
94 Rabe von Pappenheim (1363–1364) and Kirstan von Bernsfelde (1363), *cf.* Weichbrodt, 'Erläuterungen', 1, 3; Heckmann, *Amtsträger*, 41, 60.
95 Ripuarian dialect spoke: Baldwin von Frankenhofen (1375–1393), Daniel von Menden (1362–1374), Dietrich von Elner (1374–1382), Gottfried von Troisdorf (1391–1398), Kirsilie von Kindswulie (1352–1355), Ludwig von Wolkenburg (1347–1363), Reinhard von Elner (1374–1387), Rüdiger von Elner (1383–1396), Schweder von Pellant (1351–1375), Thomas von Merheim (1378–1392), Werner von Rondorf (1354–1372) and Winrich von Kniprode (1338–1382), *cf.* Weichbrodt, 'Erläuterungen', 2–5; Heckmann, *Amtsträger*, 3, 31-3, 38–42, 49, 52–54, 65–67, and 72–27.
96 Moselle Franconian brethren were: Erwin von Kruftele (1393–1398), Johann Rübsamen (1370–1377), Johann von Sayn (1398–1410), Konrad von Eltz (1386–1402), Kuno von Liebenstein (1380–1387), Ortluf von Trier (1346–1371), Siegfried Walpot von Bassenheim (1370–1396), Wilhelm von Helfenstein (1387–1410). Two came from the area where Moselle Franconian borders on Luxembourgian: Johann von Beffart (1382–1399) and Winrich von Ryndorf (1384–1387), *cf.* Weichbrodt, 'Erläuterungen', 1–4; Heckmann, *Amtsträger*, 31, 35, 38, 41–42, 49, 52–54, 60, 63, 65–67, 73, and 76–77; Delestowicz, *Bracia*, 282, 311; Christian Krollmann, 'von Helfenstein, Wilhelm,' in APB, vol. I, ed. Christian Krollmann (Marburg/Lahn: N. G. Elwert Verlag, 1974), 263; Georg von Mülverstedt, 'Die Beamten und Conventsmitglieder in den Verwaltungs-Districten des Deutschen Ordens innerhalb des Regierungsbezirks Danzig,' *Zeitschrift des Westpreußischen Geschichtsvereins* 24 (1888): 8 with footnote 10.
97 Weichbrodt, 'Erläuterungen', 4; Heckmann, *Amtsträger*, 38, 41, 44–55, 49, 54, and 77.
98 Weichbrodt, 'Erläuterungen', 3; Heckmann, *Amtsträger*, 73, 76; Militzer, *Historia*, 147.
99 It was surely Dietrich von Brandenburg (1352–1374) and maybe Johann von Falkenstein (1347–1359), although brother Johann might have come also from the area of the Bailiwick of Alsace-Burgundy, *cf.* Weichbrodt, 'Erläuterungen', 1–2; Jähnig, 'Zur Herkunft,' 195; Delestowicz, *Bracia*, 139, 235; Heckmann, *Amtsträger*, 60, 76.
100 Johann von Bolanden (1373–1376), not identical with Johann von Bolanden (Low Compagnon of Grand Master 1348–1352), *cf.* Delestowicz, *Bracia*, 233; Weichbrodt, 'Erläuterungen', 1; Heckmann, *Amtsträger*, 4, 53.
101 Arnold von Bürgeln (1387–1402), Giselbrecht von Dudelsheim (1357–1363), Hartmann von Königstein (1381–1392), Johann von Rumpenheim (1384–1404), Konrad von Bruningisheim (1335–1355), Kuno (der Jüngere) von Hattstein

(1374–1382), Kuno (der Mittlere) von Hattstein (1356–1370), Marquart von Sulzbach (1396–1410), Wigand von Beldersheim (1380–1384) and Wolfram von Beldersheim (1357–1374). At least one person, Johann von Rumpenheim, came from a Rheinhessian family, cf. Weichbrodt, 'Erläuterungen', 1–4; Heckmann, *Amtsträger*, 31–33, 38, 42–49, 53, 60, 65–66, and 71–72; Delestowicz, *Bracia*, 258, 266, and 313; Karl Lampe, 'von Rumpenheim, Johann,' in APB, vol. II, ed. Christian Krollmann (Marburg/Lahn: N. G. Elwert Verlag, 1969), 576. Although the family of Beldersheim is considered to be Rhinelandian and Hessian, they were basically from Hessia, cf. *Die Urkunden des Deutschordens-Zentralarchivs in Wien. Regesten II*, ed. Udo Arnold, vol. II, *März 1313 – November 1418*, Quellen und Studien zur Geschichte des Deutschen Ordens 60 = Veröffentlichungen der Internationalen Historischen Kommission zur Erforschung des Deutschen Ordens 11 (Marburg: N. G. Elwert Verlag, 2007), 692 no. 2237; Klaus Militzer, 'Bellersheim, Wolfram von,' in APB, V: 2005.

102 Meissnian dialect spoke likely Albrecht von Sachsen (1380–1383), Gotebold von Korwitz (1376–1383), Johann von Reddern (1391), Petzolt von Korwitz (1363–1370) and likely Johann von Schönfeld, cf. Weichbrodt, 'Erläuterungen', 3–4; Georg von Mülverstedt, 'Die Beamten und Konventsmitglieder in den Verwaltungsbezirken des Deutschen Ordens innerhalb Masurens,' *Mitteilungen der Litterarischen Gesellschaft Masovia* 6 (1900): 53.

103 Thuringians were Alexander von Körner (1338–1354), Burkhart von Mansfeld (1365–1379), Günther von Hohenstein (1338–1380), Heinrich Gans von Weberstedt (1377–1387) and Henning Schindekop (1350–1370), cf. Weichbrodt, 'Erläuterungen', 2–4; Heckmann, *Amtsträger*, 35–38, 45, 52, 63, 66–67, 72, and 76; Delestowicz, *Bracia*, 124, 127–128, 165, and 181.

104 According to von Mülverstedt he was rather Vogtlandian, cf. Weichbrodt, 'Erläuterungen', 3; Heckmann, *Amtsträger*, 41, 67; von Mülverstedt, 'Die Beamten und Konventsmitglieder in den Verwaltungsbezirken des Deutschen Ordens innerhalb des Oberländischen Kreises,' 18.

105 Delestowicz, *Bracia*, 149; Weichbrodt, 'Erläuterungen', 3–5; Heckmann, *Amtsträger*, 96.

106 Udo Arnold, 'Gründung, Wirksamkeit und Bedeutung des Deutschen Ordens bis 1525,' in *Der Deutsche Orden*, ed. Brommer, 26.

107 Engelhard Rabe von Wildstein (1383–1397), Heidenreich Rabe (1352), Marquart von Raschau (1380 – ca. 1392) and Nikolaus von Viltz (1399–1410), cf. Weichbrodt, 'Erläuterungen', 3–5; Heckmann, *Amtsträger*, 44, 59, 67, 71, and 76; Delestowicz, *Bracia*, 188; von Mülverstedt, 'Die Beamten und Konventsmitglieder in den Verwaltungsbezirken des Deutschen Ordens innerhalb des Oberländischen Kreises,' 24.

108 Friedrich von Egloffstein (1383–1387), Friedrich von Wallenrode (1394–1410), Hermann von Kudorf (1338–1353), Johann von Egloffstein (1398–1402), Johann von Lengenfeld (1357), Johann von Lichtenstein (1391–1398), Karl von Lichtenstein (1387–1396), Konrad von Wallenrode (1377–1393), Konrad/Kuno von Lichtenstein (1392–1410) and Siegfried von Dahenfeld (1342–1360), cf. Weichbrodt, 'Erläuterungen', 2–4; Heckmann, *Amtsträger*, 3, 31–35, 41–42, 45, 59–62, 65–68, 70, and 73; Hans Koeppen, 'Wallenrodt, Konrad von,' in APB, II: 772; Delestowicz, *Bracia*, 185, 218, and 316.

109 Konrad von Jungingen (1391–1407), Ulrich von Jungingen (1396–1410) and Wolf von Zolnhart (1383–1392), cf. Weichbrodt, 'Erläuterungen', 3–5; Heckmann, *Amtsträger*, 3, 33–42, 49, 52, and 76.

110 It was Ulrich von Hachenberg (1360–1398), described as *Ulricu*[s] *de Achenberg*, *thesaurariu*[s] *Bavariu*[s]. It is likely that he came from the Northern Bavaria as this region lay the closest to the commandaries in the Bailiwick of Franconia, cf. FTAP, 120.

111 According to Schön he came from Württemberg, according to Weichbrodt from the area of Linz in Austria, *cf.* Theodor Schön, 'Beziehungen Württembergs zum Deutschen Orden in Preußen,' *Diözesan-Archiv von Schwaben: Organ für Geschichte, Altertumskunde, Kunst und Kultur der Diözese Rottenburg und der angrenzenden Gebiete* 21 (1903): 47; Weichbrodt, 'Erläuterungen', 2; Heckmann, *Amtsträger*, 59, 62.

112 Johann Marschalk von Frohburg (1387–1390), Johann von Pfirt (1396–1407), Konrad von Königsegg (Kunseckeln) (1374–1376), Konrad von Kyburg (1388–1402), Ludwig von Benfeld (1383–1386), Rudolf von Kyburg (1391–1402), Werner von Tettingen (1387–1412) and possibly Johann von Falkenstein (1347–1359), *cf.* Weichbrodt, 'Erläuterungen', 1–4; Heckmann, *Amtsträger*, 33–38, 42, 59–67, and 72; Piotr Gotówko, 'Der Aufstieg der Landsmannschaft aus Elsass-Burgund im preußischen Zweig des Deutschen Ordens im späten 14. Jahrhundert,' in *Ordines Militares Colloquia Torunensia Historica. Yearbook for the Study of the Military Orders* 28 (2023): 202.

113 Delestowicz, *Bracia*, 281; Weichbrodt, 'Erläuterungen', 2; Heckmann, *Amtsträger*, 42.

114 Arnold, 'Gründung,' 26; Militzer, *Historia*, 147. This situation continued during the 15th century. In the years 1436–1437 the Order was shaken by the conflict between the 'German Master' and the Grand Master and in spring 1440 by the tensions with the local Prussian Estates, *cf.* Jürgen Sarnowsky, 'Sancta obedientia. Die Rolle des Gehorsams in den geistlichen Ritterorden des ausgehenden Mittelalters', *Ordines Militares Colloquia Torunensia Historica. Yearbook for the Study of the Military Orders* 27 (2022): 288; Carl Lückerath, 'Paul von Rusdorf (10. III. 1422 – 2. I. 1441)', in *Die Hochmeister*, ed. Arnold, 126; id., 'Saunsheim, Eberhard von', in *Neue Deutsche Biographie*, vol. 22 (Berlin: Duncker & Humblot, 2005), 465 (online: https://www.deutsche-biographie.de/pnd139579206.html#ndbcontent, accessed 23 January 2023); Klaus Neitmann, 'Die "Hauptstädte" des Ordenslandes Preussen und ihre Versammlungstage. Zur politischen Organisation und Repräsentation der preußischen Städte unter der Landesherrschaft des Deutschen Ordens', *Zeitschrift für Historische Forschung* 19, no. 2 (1992): 137, 141; Sven Ekdahl, 'Einstellung der Bevölkerung Preussens zur Herrschaft der Ordensritter,' *Miscellanea Historico-Archivistica* 23 (2016): 111; ASP, IV: 21–33, no. 17. In the same year (1440), among the Prussian brethren a riot in the convents of Königsberg, Brandenburg and Balga broke out, *cf.* Sophie Meyer, 'Paul von Russdorf und die Konvente von Königsberg, Balga und Brandenburg,' *Altpreußische Monatsschrift* 46 (1909): 383–390; Sławomir Jóźwiak, 'Kryzys władzy terytorialnej,' in *Państwo zakonu krzyżackiego*, ed. Biskup and Czaja, 334; Simon Helms, 'Der Aufstand der Deutschordenskonvente Königsberg, Balga und Brandenburg (1440) – ein landsmannschaftlich motivierter Konflikt?,' *Mrągowskie Studia Humanistyczne* 4–5 (2002–2003), 17–22.

Primary Sources

Acten der Ständetage Preussens unter der Herrschaft des Deutschen Ordens. Edited by Max Toeppen, Bd. IV, *August 1453 bis September 1457*. Leipzig: Duncker & Humblot, 1884.

'Franciscani Thorunensis Annales Prussici (941–1410).' Edited by Ernst Strehlke. In SRP, vol. III, edited by Theodor Hirsch, Max Toeppen, and Ernst Strehlke, 13–388. Leipzig: Verlag von S. Hirzel, 1866.

Peter von Dusburg. Chronik des Preussenlandes. Edited and translated by Klaus Scholz and Dieter Wojtecki. Darmstadt: Wissenschaftliche Buchgesellschaft, 1984.

Quellen zur Verfassungsgeschichte des Römisch-Deutschen Reiches im Spätmittelalter (1250–1500). Edited and translated by Lorenz Weinrich. Darmstadt: Wissenschaftliche Buchgesellschaft, 1983.
Der Renner von Hugo von Trimberg. Vol. III, edited by Gustav Ehrismann. Tübingen: Druck von H. Laupp Jr., 1909.
Die Statuten des Deutschen Ordens nach den ältesten Handschriften. Edited by Max Perlbach, Halle/Salle: Max Niemeyer, 1890.
Die Urkunden des Deutschordens-Zentralarchivs in Wien. Regesten II. Edited by Udo Arnold. Vol. II, *März 1313 – November 1418*. Quellen und Studien zur Geschichte des Deutschen Ordens 60 = Veröffentlichungen der Internationalen Historischen Kommission zur Erforschung des Deutschen Ordens 11. Marburg: N. G. Elwert Verlag, 2007.

Secondary Sources

Albrecht, Karl. *Die Leipziger Mundart. Grammatik und Wörterbuch der Leipziger Volkssprache*. Leipzig: Arnoldische Buchhandlung, 1881.
Arnold, Udo. 'Agrarwirtschaft im Deutschen Orden. Besitzverwaltung und Bewirtschaftungsformen des landwirtschaftlichen Besitzes im Deutschen Reich bis zum Reformzeitalter.' In *Beiträge zur Geschichte des Deutschen Ordens*, Vol. I, edited by Udo Arnold, 47–70. Quellen und Studien zur Geschichte des Deutschen Ordens 36 = Veröffentlichungen der Internationalen Historischen Kommission zur Erforschung des Deutschen Ordens 1. Marburg: N. G. Elwert Verlag, 1986.
Arnold, Udo. 'Gründung, Wirksamkeit und Bedeutung des Deutschen Ordens bis 1525.' In *Der Deutsche Orden und die Ballei Elsaß-Burgund*, edited by Hermann Brommer, 17–32. Bühl (Baden): Konkordia Verlag, 1996.
Bader, Christian. *Lexique des Parlers Sundgauviens*. Mulhouse: éditions du Rhin, 1997.
Becker, Horst, and Gunter Bergmann. *Sächsische Mundartenkunde. Entstehung, Geschichte und Lautstand der Mundarten des obersächsischen Gebietes*. Halle/Saale: Max Niemeyer Verlag, 1969.
Beckers, Hartmut. 'Westmitteldeutsch.' In *Lexikon der Germanistischen Linguistik*, edited by Hans Althaus, Helmut Henne, and Herbert Wiegand, 468–473. Tübingen: Max Niemeyer Verlag, 1980, 2nd edition.
Bellmann, Günther. 'Slawische Sprachen und deutsche Gesamtsprache.' In *Lexikon der Germanistischen Linguistik*, edited by Hans Althaus, Helmut Henne, and Herbert Wiegand, 680–685. Tübingen: Max Niemeyer Verlag, 1980, 2nd edition.
Bergmann, Gunter. *Das Vorerzgebirigische. Mundart und Umgangssprache im Industriegebiet um Karl-Marx-Stadt–Zwickau*, Haale/Saale: Max Niemeyer Verlag, 1965.
Bergmann, Gunther, and Volkmar Hellfritzsch. *Kleines vogtländisches Wörterbuch*. Leipzig: Bibliographisches Institut Leipzig, 1990.
Bergmann, Rolf. *Mittelfränkische Glossen. Studien zu ihrer Ermittlung und sprachgeographischen Einordnung*. Bonn: Ludwig Röhrscheid Verlag, 1966.
Besch, Werner, and Norbert Wolf. *Geschichte der deutschen Sprache. Längsschnitte – Zeitstufen – Linguistische Studien*. Berlin: Erich Schmidt Verlag, 2009.
Beyer, Rahel. *Der pfälzische Sprachinseldialekt am Niederrhein. Eine generationsbedingte Variablenanalyse*. Mannheim: Institut für Deutsche Sprache, 2017.
Bieberstedt, Andreas, Jürgen Ruge, and Ingrid Schröder. 'Kontaktinduzierte sprachliche Variation in der Hamburger Peripherie. Ein Modell zur Messung sprachlicher Konvergenz.' In *Hamburgisch. Struktur, Gebrauch, Wahrnehmung der Regionalsprache im urbanen Raum*, edited by Andreas Bieberstedt, Jürgen Ruge, and Ingrid Schröder, 21–66. Frankfurt/Main: Internationaler Verlag der Wissenschaften, 2016.

Bohnenberger, Karl. *Zur Geschichte der schwäbischen Mundart im XV. Jahrhundert.* Tübingen: J. C. B. Mohr, 1892.
Bourg, J. P. 'Die Luxemburger Mundart.' *Ons Hémecht* 1, no. 7 (1895): 205–207, 229–231, 258–262, 287–290, 315–319, 351–355; 2, no. 12 (1896): 40–42, 68–72, 127–129, 172–175, 210–213, 228–231, 300–303, 332–335, 361–365, 403–407, 423–425 (online: http://engelmann.uni.lu/lux-PDFs/Bourg%20j.P.%20-%20Die%20 Luxemburger%20Mundart%20-Ons%20H%C3%A9mecht%20-%201895-96. pdf, accessed 23 January 2023).
Böttger, Oswin. *Der Satzbau der erzgebirgischen Mundart.* Leipzig: Buchdruckerei von Heinrich John, 1904.
Bräutigam, Kurt. *Die Mannheimer Mundart.* Walldorf: Druck von Fr. Lamade, 1934.
Brenner, Oskar. *Mundarten und Schriftsprache in Bayern.* Bamberg: Buchnersche Verlagsbuchhandlung, 1890.
Brill, Richard. 'Aus der Geschichte der niederdeutschen Sprache.' In *Niederdeutsch. Ein Handbuch zur Pflege der Heimatkunde*, edited by Richard Mehlem and Wilhelm Seedorf, 66–74. Hannover: Hermann Schroedel Verlag, 1957.
Cetwiński, Marek. *Rycerstwo śląskie do końca XIII w. Biogramy i rodowody.* Wrocław: Zakład Narodowy im. Ossolińskich, 1982.
Christmann, Ernst. *Der Lautbestand des Rheinfränkischen und sein Wandel in der Mundart von Kaulbach (Pfalz)*, Speyer/Rhein: Pfälzische Gesellschaft zur Förderung der Wissenschaften, 1927.
Conrad, Klaus. 'Heinrich Dusemer (13. oder 18. XII. 1345 – Ende 1351).' In *Die Hochmeister des Deutschen Ordens 1190–1994*, edited by Udo Arnold, 81–84. Quellen und Studien zur Geschichte des Deutschen Ordens 40 = Veröffentlichungen der Internationalen Historischen Kommission zur Erforschung des Deutschen Ordens 6. Marburg: N. G. Elwert Verlag, 1998.
Czaja, Roman. 'Die Städte und der Deutsche Orden in der Neumark und in Preußen.' In *Landesherr, Adel und Städte in der mittelalterlichen und frühneuzeitlichen Neumark*, edited by Klaus Neitmann, 235–243. Berlin: Berliner Wissenschafts-Verlag, 2015.
Diegritz, Theodor. *Lautgeographie des westlichen Mittelfrankens.* Neustadt/Aisch: Degener & Co., 1971.
Dittmar, Norbert, Peter Schlobinski, and Inge Wachs. *Berlinisch. Studien zum Lexikon, zur Spracheinstellung und zum Stilrepertoire.* Berlin: Verlag Arno Spitz, 1986.
Dollinger, Stefan. *Österreichisches Deutsch oder Deutsch in Österreich? Identitäten im 21. Jahrhundert.* Wien, Hamburg: New Academic Press, 2021.
Dorn, Hans. *Die Deutschordensballei Westfalen von der Reformation bis zu ihrer Auflösung im Jahre 1809.* Quellen und Studien zur Geschichte des Deutschen Ordens 26. Marburg: N. G. Elwert Verlag, 1978.
Dorna, Maciej. *Bracia Zakonu krzyżackiego w Prusach w latach 1228–1309.* Poznań: Wydawnictwo Poznańskie, 2004.
Eik, Jan. *Der Berliner Jargon*, with a foreword of Jutta Voigt. Berlin: Jaron Verlag, 2018, 3rd edition.
Ekdahl, Sven. 'Einstellung der Bevölkerung Preussens zur Herrschaft der Ordensritter.' *Miscellanea Historico-Archivistica* 23 (2016): 109–114.
Ernst, Peter. *Deutsche Sprachgeschichte: Eine Einführung in die diachrone Sprachwissenschaft des Deutschen.* Wien: Facultas, 2021.
Frank, Michael. 'Das Elsässerditsch – Merkmal einer eigenständigen Kultur.' In *Burgund Elsass*, edited by Thorsten Droste, Michael Frank, Haug von Kuenheim, and Heinz-Gert Woschek, 157–159. München, Luzern: Verlag C. J. Bucher, 1984.
Freudenberg, Rudolf. 'Ostoberdeutsch.' In *Lexikon der Germanistischen Linguistik*, edited by Hans Althaus, Helmut Henne, and Herbert Wiegand, 486–491. Tübingen: Max Niemeyer Verlag, 1980, 2nd edition.

Friebertshäuser, Hans. *Kleines hessisches Wörterbuch*. München: C. H. Beck, 1990.
Frings, Theodor. *Die Grundlagen des Meißnischen Deutsch. Ein Beitrag zur Entstehungsgeschichte der deutschen Hochsprache*. Halle/Saale: Max Niemeyer Verlag, 1936.
Frings, Theodor. *Sprache und Geschichte*. Vol. I. Haale/Saale: Max Niemeyer Verlag, 1956.
Frings, Theodor. *Sprache und Siedlung im mitteldeutschen Osten*. Leipzig: Verlag von S. Hirzel, 1932.
Gahlbeck, Christian. 'Zur Herkunft und Zusammensetzung des neumärkischen Adels bis zur Mitte des 14. Jahrhunderts.' In *Landesherr, Adel und Städte in der mittelalterlichen und frühneuzeitlichen Neumark*, edited by Klaus Neitmann, 115–181. Berlin: Berliner Wissenschafts-Verlag, 2015.
Gernentz, Hans. *Niederdeutsch – gestern und heute. Beiträge zur Sprachsituation in den Nordbezirken der Deutschen Demokratischen Republik in Geschichte und Gegenwart*. Rostock: Hinstorff, 1980.
Gilles, Peter. 'Phonologie der n-Tilgung im Moselfränkischen (Eifer Regel). Ein Beitrag zur dialektologischen Prosodieforschung.' In *Perspektiven einer linguistischen Luxemburgistik. Studien zu Synchronie und Diachronie*, edited by Claudine Moulin and Damaris Nübling, 28–68. Heidelberg: Winter, 2006.
Gotówko, Piotr. 'Der Aufstieg der Landsmannschaft aus Elsass-Burgund im preußischen Zweig des Deutschen Ordens im späten 14. Jahrhundert.' *Ordines Militares Colloquia Torunensia Historica. Yearbook for the Study of the Military Orders* 28 (2023): 197–265.
Gotówko, Piotr. 'Rotacje osobowe w Zakonie Krzyżackim w Prusach między przeniesieniem siedziby Wielkiego Mistrza do Malborka a bitwą pod Grunwaldem (1310–1409).' KMW 3/322 (2023): 463–502.
Górski, Karol. *Państwo krzyżackie w Prusach*. Gdańsk, Bydgoszcz: Instytut Bałtycki, 1946.
Grosse, Siegfried. 'Morphologie des Mittelhochdeutschen.' In *Sprachgeschichte. Ein Handbuch zur Geschichte der deutschen Sprache und ihrer Erforschung*, vol. II, edited by Werner Besch, Anne Betten, Oskar Reichmann, and Stefan Sonderegger, 1332–1339. Berlin: Walter de Gruyter, 2000, 2nd edition.
Hammel, Hans-Dietrich. *Bedeutung, Wortschatz und Weltbild der niederfränkischen Mundart von Mülheim an der Ruhr*. Freiburg/Breisgau: Selbstverlag, 1967.
Hartmann, Helmut. 'Hochmeister, Deutschmeister, Landkomtur, Komtur, Hauskomtur, Ritter, Priester – Ämter und Lebensweise der Deutschordensangehörigen (bis etwa 1809).' In *Der Deutsche Orden und die Ballei Elsaß-Burgund*, edited by Hermann Brommer, 73–96. Bühl (Baden): Konkordia Verlag, 1996.
Heckmann, Dieter. *Amtsträger des Deutschen Ordens in Preußen und in den Kammerballeien des Reiches (oberste Gebietiger, Komture, Hauskomture, Kumpane, Vögte, Pfleger, Großschäffer)* (online: https://hiko-owp.eu/wp-content/uploads/2024/12/Amtstraeger-DO-Preussen.pdf, accessed 4 March 2024).
Heinzerling, Jakob, and Hermann Reuter. *Siegerländer Wörterbuch*. Siegen: Verlag Vorländer, 1968, 2nd edition.
Helms, Simon. 'Der Aufstand der Deutschordenskonvente Königsberg, Balga und Brandenburg (1440) – ein landsmannschaftlich motivierter Konflikt?.' *Mrągowskie Studia Humanistyczne* 4–5 (2002–2003): 14–28.
Hemmerle, Josef. *Die Deutschordens-Ballei Böhmen in ihren Rechnungen 1382–1411*. Quellen und Studien zur Geschichte des Deutschen Ordens 22. Bonn, Bad Godesberg: Verlag Wissenschaftliches Archiv, 1967.
Henzen, Walter. *Schriftsprache und Mundarten. Ein Überblick über ihr Verhältnis und ihre Zwischenstufen im Deutschen*. Zürich: Max Niehans Verlag, 1938.
Hilferding, Alexander. 'Die Ueberreste der Slaven auf der Südküste des baltischen Meeres.' *Zeitschrift für slavische Literatur, Kunst und Wissenschaft* 1, no. 1 (1862): 81–97.

Hodler, Werner. *Berndeutsche Syntax*. Bern: Francke, 1969.
Hoffheinz, G. Th. 'Ueber den ostpreuß. hochdeutschen Dialect. Vortrag, gehalten in der Königl. Deutschen Gesellschaft zu Königsberg.' *Altpreußische Monatsschrift* 9 (1872): 447–461.
Holsten, Robert. 'Der Kampf der niedersächsichen und niederfränkischen Mundart um Pommern.' *Zeitschrift für Mundartforschung* 18 no. 1/4 (1942): 122–134.
Holsten, Robert. *Sprachgrenzen im pommerschen Plattdeutsch*. Pyritz: Druck der Backeschen Buchdruckerei, 1913.
Holthausen, Ferdinand. 'Das Alter der südwestfälischen Diphthone.' *Zeitschrift für Mundartforschung* 18, no. 1/4 (1942): 105–107.
Hopfenzitz, Josef. *Kommende Oettingen Deutschen Ordens (1242–1805). Recht und Wirtschaft im terrtorialen Spannungsfeld*. Quellen und Studien zur Geschichte des Deutschen Ordens 33. Bonn, Bad Godesberg: Verlag Wissenschaftliches Archiv, 1975.
Hudlett, Albert. *Morphologie verbale dans les parlers du Pays de Bitche (Moselle germanophone). Essai de représentation graphique automatique de la dynamique des variations géolinguistiques*. Bern: Peter Lang, 1989.
Jähnig, Bernhart. *Verfassung und Verwaltung des Deutschen Ordens und seiner Herrschaft in Livland*. Berlin: W. Hopf, 2011.
Jähnig, Bernhart. 'Zur Herkunft von Dietrich von Brandenburg, Komtur von Thorn.' In idem, *Zum Innenleben des Deutschen Ordens in Preußen*, 171–200. Münster: Nicolaus-Copernicus-Verlag, 2021.
Johnston, Thomas. 'The Old Frisian Law Manuscripts and Law Texts.' In *Handbuch des Friesisischen – Handbook of Frisian Studies*, edited by Horst Munske, in collaboration with Nils Århammar, Volkert Faltings, Jarich Hoekstra, Oebele Vries, Alastair Walker, and Ommo Wilts, 571–587. Tübingen: Max Niemeyer Verlag, 2001.
Jørgensen, Peter. *Zum Schleswiger Niederdeutsch. Kritik und Forschung*. København: Ejnar Munksgaard, 1954.
Jóźwiak, Sławomir. 'Kryzys władzy terytorialnej.' In *Państwo zakonu krzyżackiego w Prusach. Władza i społeczeństwo*, edited by Marian Biskup and Roman Czaja, 332–356. Warszawa: Wydawnictwo Naukowe PWN, 2009.
Jurek, Tomasz. *Obce rycerstwo na Śląsku do połowy XIV wieku*. Poznań: Poznańskie Towarzystwo Przyjaciół Nauk, 1996.
Jutz, Leo. *Die Mundart von Südvorarlberg und Liechtenstein*. Heidelberg: Carl Winter's Universitätsbuchhandlung, 1925.
Kamp, Klaus, and Wolfgang Lindow. *Das Plattdeutsche in Schleswig-Holstein. Eine Erhebung des Statistischen Landesamtes Schleswig-Holstein*. Neumünster: Karl Wachtholz Verlag, 1967.
Katerbow, Matthias. *Spracherwerb und Sprachvariation. Eine phonetisch-phonologische Analyse zum regionalen Erstspracherwerb im Moselfränkischen*. Berlin: de Gruyter, 2013.
Kesselgruber, Bernd. 'Die deutschen Mundarten Böhmens, Mährens und Schlesiens in der Bearbeitung des Sudetendeutschen Wörterbuches.' In *Deutsche und tschechische Dialekte im Kontakt*, edited by Albrecht Greule and Marek Nekula, 89–94. Regensburg: Verlag für Literatur- und Sprachwissenschaft, 2003.
Klausmann, Hubert. 'Alemannisch in einzelnen Regionen Baden-Württembergs.' In *Kleiner Dialektatlas. Alemannisch und Schwäbisch in Baden-Württemberg*, edited by Hubert Klausmann, Konrad Kunze, and Renate Schrambke, 59–117. Bühl (Baden): Konkordia Verlag, 1993.
Klecker, Hans. *Oberlausitzer Wörterbuch*. Spitzkunnersdorf: Oberlausitzer Verlag, 2003.
Kollmer, Michael. *Wesenszüge des Bairischen, nachgewiesen an der Mundart Niederbayerns und der südlichen Oberpfalz, insbesondere des Bayrischen Waldes*. Prackenbach: s.n., 1985.

Koeppen, Hans. 'Wallenrodt, Konrad von.' In APB, vol. II, edited by Christian Krollmann, 772–773. Marburg/Lahn: N. G. Elwert Verlag, 1969.
Köbler, Gerhard. *Historisches Lexikon der deutschen Länder. Die deutschen Territorien und reichsunmittelbaren Geschlechter vom Mittelalter bis zur Gegenwart.* München: C. H. Beck'sche Verlagsbuchhandlung, 1999, 6th edition.
Köbler, Gerhard. 'Vom Umfang des Althochdeutschen.' In *Verborum Amor. Studien zur Geschichte und Kunst der deutschen Sprache*, edited by Harald Burger, Alois Haas, and Peter von Matt, 129–155. Berlin: de Gruyter, 1992.
König, Werner. *dtv-Atlas zur deutschen Sprache. Tafeln und Texte. Mit Mundart-Karten.* München: Deutscher Taschenbuch Verlag, 1994, 10th edition.
Krannich, Waltraud. *Wörterbuch der erzgebirgischen Mundart.* Zwickau: Chemnitzer Verlag, 2018.
Krämer, Sabine. *Die Steigerwaldschranke. Zum Aufbau einer ostfränkischen Dialektgrenze.* Würzburg: Königshausen & Neumann, 1995.
Krollmann, Christian. 'von Helfenstein, Wilhelm.' In APB, vol. I, edited by Christian Krollmann, 263. Marburg/Lahn: N. G. Elwert Verlag, 1974.
Kroonen, Guus. *Etymological Dictionary of Proto-Germanic.* Leiden, Boston: Brill, 2013.
Kruszewski, Tomasz. 'Przedstawiciele rodu von Hattstein jako urzędnicy zakonu krzyżackiego w Prusach. Studium historycznoprawne i genealogiczne.' KMW 1/287 (2015): 3–33.
Kunze, Konrad. 'Alemannisch – was ist das? Grenzen, Geschichte, Merkmale eines Dialekts.' In *Kleiner Dialektatlas. Alemannisch und Schwäbisch in Baden-Württemberg*, edited by Hubert Klausmann, Konrad Kunze, and Renate Schrambke, 15–57. Bühl (Baden): Konkordia Verlag, 1993.
Labuda, Gerard. *Pierwsze wieki monarchii piastowskiej.* Poznań: Nauka i Innowacje, 2012.
Lampe, Karl. 'von Rumpenheim, Johann.' In APB, vol. II, edited by Christian Krollmann, 576. Marburg/Lahn: N. G. Elwert Verlag, 1969.
Lanthaler, Franz. *Zur Morphologie der Verben in der Mundart des Passeiertales (Südtirol).* Innsbruck: s.n., 1971.
Limburg, Hans. *Die Hochmeister des Deutschen Ordens und die Ballei Koblenz.* Quellen und Studien zur Geschichte des Deutschen Ordens 8. Bad Godesberg: Verlag Wissenschaftliches Archiv, 1969.
Löffler, Heinrich. 'Dialekt,' In *Lexikon der Germanistischen Linguistik*, edited by Hans Althaus, Helmut Henne, and Herbert Wiegand, 453–458. Tübingen: Max Niemeyer Verlag, 1980, 2nd edition.
Lückerath, Carl. 'Paul von Rusdorf (10. III. 1422 – 2. I. 1441).' In *Die Hochmeister des Deutschen Ordens 1190–1994*, edited by Udo Arnold, 122–128. Quellen und Studien zur Geschichte des Deutschen Ordens 40 = Veröffentlichungen der Internationalen Historischen Kommission zur Erforschung des Deutschen Ordens 6. Marburg: N. G. Elwert Verlag, 1998.
Lückerath, Carl. 'Saunsheim, Eberhard von.' In *Neue Deutsche Biographie*, vol. 22, 464–465. Berlin: Duncker & Humblot, 2005 (online: https://www.deutsche-biographie.de/pnd139579206.html#ndbcontent, accessed 23 January 2023).
Maleczek, Werner. 'Das Reich im 14. Jahrhundert – Blicke von außen.' In *Die Goldene Bulle. Politik – Wahrnehmung – Rezeption*, vol. I, edited by Ulrike Hohensee, Mathias Lawo, Michael Lindner, Michael Menzer, and Olaf Rader, 563–598. Berlin: Akademie Verlag, 2009.
Martens, Carl, and Peter Martens. *Phonetik der deutschen Sprache. Praktische Aussprachlehre.* München: Max Heuber Verlag, 1961.
Meyer, Sophie. 'Paul von Russdorf und die Konvente von Königsberg, Balga und Brandenburg.' *Altpreußische Monatsschrift* 46 (1909): 363–417, 543–591.
Militzer, Klaus. 'Bellersheim, Wolfram von.' In APB, vol. V, edited by Klaus Bürger and Bernhart Jähnig, 2005–2006. Marburg/Lahn: N. G. Elwert Verlag, 2015.

Militzer, Klaus. *Die Entstehung der Deutschordensballeien im Deutschen Reich.* Quellen und Studien zur Geschichte des Deutschen Ordens 16. Bonn, Bad Godesberg: Wissenschaftliches Archiv, 1970.
Militzer, Klaus. 'Erläuterungen zu den Karten: Die Balleien des Deutschen Ordens in ‚Deutschen und Welschen Landen' um 1400 I.' In *Historisch-geographischer Atlas des Preussenlandes,* issue 11, edited by Hans Mortensen, Gertrud Mortensen, Reinhard Wenskus, and Helmut Jäger, 1–8. Stuttgart: Franz Steiner Verlag, 1986.
Militzer, Klaus. *Historia zakonu Krzyżackiego.* Translated by Ewa Marszał and Jerzy Zakrzewski. Kraków: Wydawnictwo WAM, 2007.
Militzer, Klaus. 'Kesselhut, Konrad, Ritterbruder des Deutschen Ordens, Großkomtur.' In APB, vol. V, edited by Klaus Bürger and Bernhart Jähnig, 2119. Marburg/Lahn: N. G. Elwert Verlag, 2015.
Militzer, Klaus. 'Rheinländer im mittelalterlichen Livland.' In id., *Zentrale und Region. Gesammelte Beiträge zur Geschichte des Deutschen Ordens in Preussen, Livland und im Deutschen Reich aus den Jahren 1968 bis 2008,* 262–278. Quellen und Studien zur Geschichte des Deutschen Ordens 75 = Veröffentlichungen der Internationalen Historischen Kommission zur Erforschung des Deutschen Ordens 13. Weimar: Verlag und Datenbank für Geisteswissenschaften, 2015.
Militzer, Klaus. *Von Akkon zur Marienburg. Verfassung, Verwaltung und Sozialstruktur des Deutschen Ordens 1190–1309.* Quellen und Studien zur Geschichte des Deutschen Ordens 56 = Veröffentlichungen der Internationalen Historischen Kommission zur Erforschung des Deutschen Ordens 9. Marburg: N. G. Elwert Verlag, 1999.
Militzer, Klaus, Heinz Henze, and Stefan Mielke. 'Die Balleien des Deutschen Ordens in ‚Deutschen und Welschen Landen' um 1400 I.' In *Historisch-geographischer Atlas des Preussenlandes,* issue 11, edited by Hans Mortensen, Gertrud Mortensen, Reinhard Wenskus, and Helmut Jäger, Stuttgart: Franz Steiner Verlag, 1986.
Mitzka, Walter. 'Altschlesische Vokabulare.' In *Volk – Sprache – Dichtung. Festgabe für Kurt Wagner,* 131–142. Gießen: s.n., 1960.
Mitzka, Walter. 'Niederdeutsch-schlesische Siedel und Sprachgemeinschaft.' *Jahrbuch des Vereins für niederdeutsche Sprachforschung* 83 (1960): 33–40.
Moraw, Peter. 'Über Rahmenbedingungen und Wandlungen auswärtiger Politik vorwiegend im deutschen Spätmittelalter.' In *Auswärtige Politik und internationale Beziehungen im Mittelalter (13. bis 16. Jahrhundert),* edited by Dieter Berg, Martin Kintzinger, and Pierre Monnet, 31–45. Bochum: Verlag Dr. Dieter Winkler 2002.
Morton, Nicholas. *The Teutonic Knights in the Holy Land 1190–1291.* Woodbrigde: Boydell Press, 2009.
Müller, Jochen. *Der mittelschwäbische Dialekt am Beispiel der Urbacher Mundart.* Stuttgart: ibidem-Verlag, 2003.
von Mülverstedt, Georg. 'Die Beamten und Conventsmitglieder in den Verwaltungs-Districten des Deutschen Ordens innerhalb des Regierungsbezirks Danzig.' *Zeitschrift des Westpreußischen Geschichtsvereins* 24 (1888): 1–73.
von Mülverstedt, Georg. 'Die Beamten und Konventsmitglieder in den Verwaltungsbezirken des Deutschen Ordens innerhalb des Oberländischen Kreises,' *Oberländische Geschichtsblätter* 2 (1900): 1–59.
von Mülverstedt, Georg. 'Die Beamten und Konventsmitglieder in den Verwaltungsbezirken des Deutschen Ordens innerhalb Masurens,' *Mitteilungen der Litterarischen Gesellschaft Masovia* 6 (1900): 48–67.
Münch, Ferdinand. *Grammatik der ripuarisch-fränkischen Mundart.* Bonn: Verlag von Friedrich Cohen, 1904.
Neitmann, Klaus. 'Die "Hauptstädte" des Ordenslandes Preussen und ihre Versammlungstage. Zur politischen Organisation und Repräsentation der preußischen Städte unter der Landesherrschaft des Deutschen Ordens.' *Zeitschrift für Historische Forschung* 19, no. 2 (1992): 125–158.

Nerger, Karl. *Grammatik des meklenburgischen Dialekts älterer und neuerer Zeit. Laut- und Fexionslehre.* Wiesbaden: F. A. Brockhaus 1869.
Nicklaus, Hélène. *Le Platt. Le francique rhénan du Pays de Sarreguemines jusqu`à l`Alsace. Dictionnaire dialectical Platt – Allemand – Français.* Sarreguemines: Editions Pierron, 2001.
Niebaum, Hermann. 'Westniederdeutsch,' In *Lexikon der Germanistischen Linguistik*, edited by Hans Althaus, Helmut Henne, and Herbert Wiegand, 458–464. Tübingen: Max Niemeyer Verlag, 1980, 2nd edition.
Niekerken, Walter. 'Von den Lauten der niederdeutschen Sprache.' In *Niederdeutsch. Ein Handbuch zur Pflege der Heimatkunde*, edited by Richard Mehlem and Wilhelm Seedorf, 75–84. Hannover: Hermann Schroedel Verlag, 1957.
Noth, Harald. *Alemannisches Dialektbuch vom Kaiserstuhl und seiner Umgebung.* Freiburg/Breisgau: Schillinger Verlag, 1993.
Olesch, Reinhold. 'Zur schlesischen Sprachlandschaft. Ihr alter slawischer Anteil.' *Zeitschrift für Ostforschung* 27, no. 2 (1978): 32–45.
Pizuński, Paweł. *Poczet wielkich mistrzów krzyżackich.* Skarszewy: Arenga, 2017, 4th edition.
Polejowski, Karol. 'Kryzys krzyżackiej komendy Beauvoir we Francji pod koniec XIV w.' *Studia z Dziejów Średniowiecza* 15 (2009): 131–147.
von Polenz, Peter, and Norbert Wolf. *Geschichte der deutschen Sprache.* Berlin: De Gruyer, 2020, 11th edition.
Post, Rudolf. 'Die Mundarten in Rheinhessen. Erforschung – Grenzen – Besonderheiten.' *Alzeyer Geschichtsblätter* 38 (2010): 51–74.
Przybytek, Rozalia. *Ortsnamen baltischer Herkunft im südlichen Teil Ostpreussens.* Hydronomia Europaea, Sonderband. Stuttgart: Franz Steiner Verlag, 1993.
Putschke, Wolfgang. 'Ostmitteldeutsch,' In *Lexikon der Germanistischen Linguistik*, edited by Hans Althaus, Helmut Henne, and Herbert Wiegand, 474–479. Tübingen: Max Niemeyer Verlag 1980, 2nd edition.
Rahn, Fritz. *Der schwäbische Mensch und seine Mundart. Beiträge zum schwäbischen Problem.* Stuttgart: Hans E. Günther Verlag, 1962.
Rein, Kurt. 'Bayerns Mundarten. Eine Einführung in Verbreitung und Verwendung.' In *Bayerns Mundarten. Dialektproben mit Kommentaren und einer Einführung in die Verbreitung und Verwendung des Dialekts in Bayern*, edited by Wolfgang Küpper, with a foreword of Hans Zehetmair, 8–35. München: TR-Verlagsunion, 1991.
Renn, Manfred. *Die Mundart im Raum Augsburg. Untersuchungen zum Dialekt und zum Dialektwandel im Spannungsfeld großstädtisch-ländlicher und alemannisch-bairischer Gegensätze.* Heidelberg: Universitätsverlag C. Winter, 1994.
Riemann, Erhard. 'Niederdeutsche Sprachlandschaften.' In *Niederdeutsch. Ein Handbuch zur Pflege der Heimatkunde*, edited by Richard Mehlem and Wilhelm Seedorf, 20–28. Hannover: Hermann Schroedel Verlag, 1957.
Roelcke, Thorsten. *Typologische Variation im Deutschen. Grundlagen – Modelle – Tendenzen.* Berlin: Erich Schmidt Verlag, 2011.
Ruge, Jürgen. 'Dialekttiefe durch lexikalische Analyse messbar machen.' In *Hamburgisch. Struktur, Gebrauch, Wahrnehmung der Regionalsprache im urbanen Raum*, edited by Andreas Bieberstedt, Jürgen Ruge, and Ingrid Schröder, 67–90. Frankfurt/Main: Internationaler Verlag der Wissenschaften, 2016.
Sarnowsky, Jürgen. *Der Deutsche Orden.* München: C. H. Beck, 2007.
Sarnowsky, Jürgen. 'Sancta obedientia. Die Rolle des Gehorsams in den geistlichen Ritterorden des ausgehenden Mittelalters.' *Ordines Militares Colloquia Torunensia Historica. Yearbook for the Study of the Military Orders* 27 (2022): 275–294.
Schatz, Josef. *Die tirolische Mundart.* Innsbruck: Wagner'sche Univ.-Buchdruckerei, 1903.
Schiepek, Josef. 'Der Satzbau der Egerländer Mundart, erster Theil.' In *Beiträge zur Kenntnis deutsch-böhmischer Mundarten*, edited by Hans Lambel, Prag: Verlag des Vereins für Geschichte der Deutschen in Böhmen, 1899.

Schmeller, Johann. *Die Mundarten Bayerns grammatisch dargestellt*. München: Karl Thienemann, 1821.
Scholz, Klaus. *Beiträge zur Personengeschichte des Deutschen Ordens in der ersten Hälfte des 14. Jahrhunderts. Untersuchungen zur Herkunft livländischer und preußischer Deutschordensbrüder*. Münster: Westfälischen Wilhelms-Universität, 1971.
Schön, Theodor. 'Beziehungen Württembergs zum Deutschen Orden in Preußen.' *Diözesan-Archiv von Schwaben: Organ für Geschichte, Altertumskunde, Kunst und Kultur der Diözese Rottenburg und der angrenzenden Gebiete* 21 (1903): 45–48.
Schwarz, Ernst. 'Probleme der Stammeskunde im deutsch-slawischen Berührungsgebiet.' *Zeitschrift für Ostforschung* 11, no. 1 (1962): 90–123.
Siebs, Theodor. *Helgoland und seine Sprache*. Wiesbaden: Dr. Martin Sändig, 1968.
Socin, Adolf. *Schriftsprache und Dialekte im Deutschen nach Beugnissen alter und neuer Zeit*. Heilbronn: Verlag von Gebr. Henninger, 1888.
Spangenberg, Karl. *Die Umgangssprache im Freistaat Thüringen und im Südwesten des Landes Sachsen-Anhalt*. Rudolfstadt, Jena: Hain Verlag, 1998.
Spangenberg, Karl. *Laut- und Formeninventar thüringischer Dialekte. Beiband zum Thüringischen Wörterbuch*. Berlin: Akademie Verlag, 1993.
Splett, Jochen. 'Die Wortbildung des Althochdeutschen.' In *Sprachgeschichte. Ein Handbuch zur Geschichte der deutschen Sprache und ihrer Erforschung*, vol. II, edited by Werner Besch, Anne Betten, Oskar Reichmann, and Stefan Sonderegger, 1213–1221. Berlin: Walter de Gruyter, 2000, 2nd edition.
Steins, Adolf. *Grammatik des Aachener Dialekts*. Edited with an afterword by Klaus-Peter Lange. Köln: Böhlau Verlag 1998.
Stellmacher, Dieter. 'Ostniederdeutsch.' In *Lexikon der Germanistischen Linguistik*, edited by Hans Althaus, Helmut Henne, and Herbert Wiegand, 464–468. Tübingen: Max Niemeyer Verlag, 1980, 2nd edition.
Straßner, Erich. 'Nordoberdeutsch.' In *Lexikon der Germanistischen Linguistik*, edited by Hans Althaus, Helmut Henne, and Herbert Wiegand, 479–482. Tübingen: Max Niemeyer Verlag, 1980, 2nd edition.
Strauch, Bernd. *Dialekt in Mittelhessen. Oberhessisches Taschenwörterbuch*. Giessen: Offset Köhler, 2005.
Suchner, Barbara. *Schlesisches Wörterbuch*. Husum: Husum Druck- und Verlagsgesellschaft, 1996.
Tandecki, Janusz. 'Organizacja wewnętrzna zakonu krzyżackiego i jego członkowie.' In *Państwo zakonu krzyżackiego w Prusach. Władza i społeczeństwo*, edited by Marian Biskup and Roman Czaja, 405–411. Warszawa: Wydawnictwo Naukowe PWN, 2009.
Trukenbrod, Klaus. *Dialektgeographie des Obermainraumes und der nördlichen Fränkischen Schweiz*. Kulmbach: Freude der Plassenburg, 1973.
Voigt, Johannes. *Geschichte des Deutschen Ritter-Ordens in seinen zwölf Balleien in Deutschland*. Vol. I. Berlin: Druck und Verlag von Georg Reimer, 1857.
Voigt, Johannes. *Geschichte Preussens von den ältesten Zeiten bis zum Untergange der Herrschaft des Deutschen Ordens*. Vol. V. Königsberg: Bei den Gebrüdern Bornträger, 1832.
Vries, Oebele. 'Geschichte der Friesen im Mittelalter: West- und Ostfriesland.' In *Handbuch des Friesischen – Handbook of Frisian Studies*, edited by Horst Munske, in collaboration with Nils Århammar, Volkert Faltings, Jarich Hoekstra, Oebele Vries, Alastair Walker, and Ommo Wilts, 538–549. Tübingen: Max Niemeyer Verlag, 2001.
Wagner, Eberhard. 'Sprachproben aus Mittel-, Ober und Unterfranken.' In *Bayerns Mundarten. Dialektproben mit Kommentaren und einer Einführung in die Verbreitung und Verwendung des Dialekts in Bayern*, edited by Wolfgang Küpper, with a foreword of Hans Zehetmair, 158–242. München: TR-Verlagsunion, 1991.

Walde, Alois. *Die germanischen Auslautgesetze. Eine sprachwissenschaftliche Untersuchung mit vornehmlicher Berücksichtigung der Zeitfolge der Auslautsveränderungen.* Halle/Salle: Max Niemeyer, 1900.
Weber, Nico. 'Sprachen und ihre Funktionen in Luxemburg.' *Zeitschrift für Dialektologie und Linguistik* 61, no. 2 (1994): 129–169.
Weichbrodt, Ernst. 'Erläuterungen zur Karte: Gebietiger des Deutschen Ordens in Preußen nach ihrer Herkunft.' In *Historisch-geographischer Atlas des Preussenlandes*, issue 1, edited by Hans Mortensen, Gertrud Mortensen, and Reinhard Wenskus, 1–6. Wiesbaden: Franz Steiner Verlag, 1968.
Weimann, Britta. *Moselfränkisch. Der Konsonantismus anhand der frühesten Urkunden.* Köln: Böhlau Verlag, 2012.
Weiß, Dieter. *Die Geschichte der Deutschordens-Ballei Franken im Mittelalter.* Neustadt/Aisch: Degener, 1991.
Wenta, Jarosław. 'Studium, Arbeit, Intrige – die Karriere im Deutschen Orden in Preußen.' In *La vie quotidienne des moines et chaniones réguliers au Moyen Âge et Temps modernes. Actes du Premier Colloque International du L.A.R.H.C.O.R., Wrocław–Książ, 30. novembre – 4. decembre 1994*, edited by Marek Derwich, 193–202, Wrocław: Publications de l'Institut d'Histoire de l'Université de Wrocław, 1995.
Will, Wilhelm. *Saarländische Sprachgeschichte*, with a foreword of Adolf Bach. Saarbrücken: Saarbrücker Druckerei und Verlag, 1932.
Witte, Hans. *Das deutsche Sprachgebiet Lothringens und seine Wandelungen von der Feststellung der Sprachgrenze bis zum Ausgang des 16. Jahrhunderts.* Stuttgart: Verlag von J. Engelhorn, 1894.
Wojtecki, Dieter. *Studien zur Personalgeschichte des Deutschen Ordens im 13. Jahrhundert.* Quellen und Studien zur Geschichte des östlichen Europa 3. Wiesbaden: Franz Steiner Verlag, 1971.
Wolf, Norbert. *Geschichte der deutschen Sprache.* Vol. I, *Althochdeutsch-Mittelhochdeutsch.* Heidelberg: Quelle & Meyer, 1981.
Wolff, Roland. *Wie sagt man in Bayern. Eine Wortgeographie für Ansässige, Zugereiste und Touristen.* München: C. H. Beck, 1980.
Wurzer, Bernhard. *Die deutschen Sprachinseln in Oberitalien.* Bozen: Verlagsanstalt Athesia, 1983, 5th edition.
Zehetner, Ludwig. 'Sprachproben aus Ostbayern. Niederbayern, Oberpfalz und angrenzende Gebiete.' In *Bayerns Mundarten. Dialektproben mit Kommentaren und einer Einführung in die Verbreitung und Verwendung des Dialekts in Bayern*, edited by Wolfgang Küpper, with a foreword of Hans Zehetmair, 96–156. München: TR-Verlagsunion, 1991.
Zehetner, Ludwig. *Das bairische Dialektbuch* (in cooperation with Ludwig Eichinger, Reinhard Rascher, Anthony Rowley, and Christopher Wickham). München: Verlag C. H. Beck, 1985.

Index

Aachen 207, 211
Åbo 61
Abraham Culvensis 142
Abschwangen (Rus. Tischino) 192
Acketel/Akutte 87, 89, 102; see also Eketė
Adam Wilkanowski 159, 161, 162
Adam (the younger) Wilkanowski 162
Adorf 209
Aesernicken 143
Agnieszka ze Sławska 159
Aichach 210
Aken 209
Albert, Bishop of Pomesania 48
Albert (Wajsyl?) 50
Albert from Siecień 190
Albert Prusse 224
Albert von Massou 226
Albert von Schaaken 224
Albertus 51
Albertus Hermannus 143
Albertus Pruthenus 50
Albrecht von Brandenburg-Ansbach, Grand Master of the Teutonic Order, Duke of Prussia 142, 189
Albrecht von Sachsen 228
Alexander IV, Pope 182
Alexander VI, Pope 192
Alexander Jagiellon (Aleksander Jagiellończyk), King of Poland 152, 160
Alexander Vytautas, Grand Duke of Lithuania 125
Alexander von Körner 228
Allenburg (Rus. Druzhba) 114
Allenstein (Pol. Olsztyn) 50, 67, 117
Almenhausen (Rus. Kaschtanovo) 192
Alsace 208, 210; Bailiwick of Alsace-Burgundy 210, 213, 223, 226, 227

Altdeutschland see Germany
Altenbiesen 210; Bailiwick of 210
Altenburg 209
Althaus (Pol. Starogród Chełmiński) 191, 226
Althausen 210
Alt-Wartenburg (Pol. Barczewko) 65, 70, 117, 139
Alt Wehlau (Rus. Znamensk) 65, 68, 69, 71
Ambroży Pampowski 157, 171
America 34, 38
Americans see Native Americans
Ampilten (Germ. Impelt, Lit. Ipiltis) 101
Andlau 210
Andreas Hecht 225,
Andrzej Górski 159,
Angerapp river 127
Angerburg (Pol. Węgorzewo) 117, 118, 120, 122, 141
Antonians 192
Ankrehnen (Rus. Perovo) 125
Arnold von Bürgeln 227
Arnold von Livland 213, 225, 226
Asch 209
Aschaffenburg 207
Aubin, Gustav 146
Augustin Tollawke 188
Augustinian Eremites 182–184, 186, 188, 191, 192, 194–196
Aukštaitija 130
Aussig 211
Austria 45, 229; Bailiwick of 210, 213

Baden-Württemberg 208; see also Württemberg
Baiorgallen (Löbegallen, Rus. Tolstovo) 144
Bąkowo 166

Balduin of Alna 101
Baldwin von Frankenhofen 227
Balga (Rus. Bal'ga) 46, 49, 51, 114, 115, 186, 226, 229
Balkans 60
Baltic 31, 32, 60, 116
Baltic Sea 8, 44, 60, 85, 100, 114, 195, 207, 212
Baltiysk *see* Pillau
Balts/Baltic people 1, 2, 4–6, 66, 81, 85, 92, 93, 102, 212, 213, 215; West Balts 61
Bando 50
Barczewko *see* Alt-Wartenburg
Barczewo *see* Wartenburg
Barten (Pol. Barciany) 117
Bartenstein (Pol. Bartoszyce) 48–51
Barthia 27, 46
Bartholomeus Ruscheyszen 188
Barthus Nyvirgalt 50
Bartolomeus von Radam 224
Bartoszyce *see* Bartenstein
Basel 210
Bäslack (Pol. Bezławki) 65, 66, 68, 70
Bautzen 207
Bavaria 224; *see also* Northern Bavaria
Beauvoir 211, 223
Beckingen 210
Beisleiden (Pol. Bezledy) 48
Bekkevoort 210
von Beldersheim family 228
von Below, Georg 134
Bełz 157; Land of 152
Benrath 206, 207
Bergen 209
Berlin 118, 121, 207
Bern 210
Bernard von Zinnenberg 160
Bernhard von Balzhofen 62
Berthold von Brühaven 45
Bernissem 210
Beuggen 210
Bezławki *see* Bäslack
Bezledy *see* Beisleiden
Bezzenberger, Adalbert 121, 140
Biała Piska 118
Białuński, Grzegorz 117, 118, 120
Biebrza river 44, 141
Bilin 211
Birgelau (Pol. Bierzgłowo) 226
Biskup, Marian 142
Blomkvist, Nils 61
Bodzanta (Bodzęta), Archbishop of Gniezno 191

Bogislaus 187
Bohemia 45, 156, 160, 208, 213, 226; Bailiwick of Bohemia-Moravia 211, 213, 225, 226
Bohemians 155, 160, 226
Bolotnikovo *see* Szameithkehmen
Bonn 207
Boockmann, Hartmut 21, 22
Boumgarte 188
Bozen 210; Bailiwick of 210, 213
Brackel 209
Brakupönen (Rus. Kubanovka) 144
Brandenburg 45
Brandenburg (Rus. Ushakovo) 31, 63, 114, 115, 186, 226, 229
Brandenburgia 207, 223
Bratian 161, 162
Bratricken (Rus. Malaya Dubrovka) 144
Braunsberg (Pol. Braniewo) 50, 51, 114, 181, 184, 187, 192, 193
Brecon 30
Bremen 209, 222
Bretschkehmen 144
Brodnica *see* Strasburg
Brulando 50
Brześć Kujawski 160; Peace of 155
Bunne 211
Burgundy *see* Northern Burgundy
Burkhart von Asseburg 227
Burkhart von Mansfeld 228
Burkhart von Wobeke 227
Buro 209
Bursztynów 166
Buschinger, Danielle 37
Bydgoszcz 158

Cammin/Kamień, officiate of 153
Candeyn family 45
Carmelites 183, 184, 187
Casimir Jagiellon (Kazimierz Jagiellończyk), King of Poland 152, 153, 155–158, 160–162
Ceclis (*Cecklis*) 83, 100
Central Poland 157
Chełm 157
Chełmno/Kulm, bishopric of 153, 162, 165, 196; voivodship 152
Chełmno Land *see* Culmer Land
Chełmża *see* Kulmsee
Chernyakhovsk *see* Insterburg
Chester 26
Chojnice *see* Konitz
Chomutov 211

Christburg (Pol. Dzierzgoń) 20, 21, 28–31, 35, 46, 49–51, 183, 184; Treaty of 32, 190, 199
Christian, Bishop of Prussia 25, 27
Christian von Binsfeld 225
Christiansen, Eric 24
Claus Cranc 188
Claus Witing 50
Clement V, Pope 195
Cleve 225
Cologne (Köln) 48, 207, 209
Constance 116
Cottbus 207
Creten 87, 102; *see also* Ėgliškiai-Anduliai
Crisogonus 187
Crnomelij 210
Culmer Land (Pol. ziemia chełmińska) 1, 2, 25, 26, 159, 160, 162, 163, 166, 167, 182–184, 186, 187, 193, 194
Curonia/Courland 82, 83, 85, 87–90, 93, 95, 100, 101, 103, 104; bishop of 82, 87, 89, 100; diocese of 83; *Vogt* of 86, 102
Curonian Lagoon 82
Curonians 3, 6, 7, 48, 81–83, 85–95, 100–104, 122, 127, 131, 132
Curonian Spit 3, 93
Czaja, Roman 20, 22, 23, 28, 38
Czarnowo 36
Czech Republic 211
Czersk-Warsaw, Duchy of 152
Człuchów *see* Schlochau
Czyprki 64

Dahnsdorf 209
Dainiai *see* Daynen
Dange (Lit. Dangė) river 82, 87
Daniel von Menden 227
Danzig (Pol. Gdańsk) 3, 50, 114, 165, 169, 180, 181, 183, 184, 186–189, 193, 196, 226; Main Town Danzig 183; Young Town Danzig 183
Darkehmen (Rus. Ozjorsk) 142
Daugava river 82
Daugentlaucken (Lit. Dauglaukis) 130
Daynen (Lit. Dainiai) 144
Delestowicz, Norbert 211, 212, 224, 225, 227
Denbigh 26
Detmar von Lübeck 88
von Diebes family 49
Dieren 209
Dietrich Skomand *see* Skomand

Dietrich von Altenburg, Grand Master of the Teutonic Order 48, 118
Dietrich von Blumenstein 225
Dietrich von Brandenburg 225, 227
Dietrich von Elner 227
Dietrich von Pirmont 225
Dirschau (Pol. Tczew) 181, 186, 187
Dobre Miasto *see* Guttstadt
Dobrosielska, Alicja 6, 22, 27, 34
Dobrovol'sk *see* Pilkallen
Dobrzyń 160
Dobrzyń Land 7, 160, 166
Doesburg 211
Dominicans 180–184, 186–193, 195, 199
Dommitzsch 209
Donauwörth 210
Dopkiewitsch, Helene 89, 102
Dopönen (Rus. Pokryshkino) 144
Dresden 207
Druzhba *see* Allenburg
Drwęca river 44
Dubissa river 130
Dulsyenkysys (Germ. Dulsen/Dulzen, Pol. Dulsin) 48
Dunayevka *see* Thierenberg
Durbe, battle of 47, 48
Düsseldorf 206
Dutch settlers 3
Duvzare 83
Duwirstene/*Dwiristis* 87, 102; *see also* Groß Wirsteniken; Virkštininkai
Dygo, Marian 25
Działyński family 161
Dzierzgoń *see* Christburg; Stary Dzierzgoń
Dźwierzno 166

East 5
Eastern Lothringia 207
Eastern Pomerania (Germ. Pommerellen, Pol. Pomorze Wschodnie) 3, 33, 158, 159, 162, 163, 165–167, 180, 181, 183, 184, 186, 187, 190, 193, 194, 195
East Prussia 122, 146
Eberhard von Borne 226
Eberhard von Powersche (Eberhard Powierski) 162
Eberhard von Schalmey 224
Eberhard von Virneburg 225
Eckhard Kulling 215, 224
Eger 209
Egerland 220

Ėgliškiai-Anduliai (Germ. Krottingen) 102; *see also* Creten
Eifel mountains 225
Einsiedel 210
Eisermühl *see* Staświny
Ekete (Germ. Ekitten) 89, 102; *see also* Acketel*Akutte*
Elbe river 134
Elbing (Pol. Elbląg) 22, 28, 29, 36, 49, 50, 65, 114, 180, 181, 183, 184, 186–190, 192, 197, 198; Elbląg group 61; Old Town Elbing 51, 62; New Town Elbing 28, 50, 51; *see also* Lastadie
Ełk *see* Lyck
Ellingen 210
Engelbert I von der Mark 47
Engelhard Rabe von Wildstein 228
Engelsburg (Pol. Pokrzywno) 226
English people 3, 22
Erfurt 209
Ermland/Warmia 46, 114, 117, 136, 152, 161, 181, 183, 184, 193; bishop/bishopric of 20, 51, 153, 167, 182, 184, 190, 191, 196; *Vogt* of 60
Erwin von Kruftele 227
Erzgebirge, mountains 207
Estonia 60, 69, 189
Eszeruppen 130
Etsch *see* Bozen, Bailiwick of
Europe 33, 60, 68; Western Europe 31, 66, 180; *see also* 'West'
Eywon Spandenne/Spandeme 104

Felsberg 209
Finland 60
Finno-Ugric people 66
Flint 29
France, Bailiwick of 211
Franciscans 180–184, 187–189, 191–193, 195–198
Franciszek Gliwicz 160
Franconia 189, 215, 216, 224; Bailiwick of 210–212, 223, 226, 228; *see also* Low Franconia
Frankfurt/Main 207
Frankish people 32
Frauenburg (Pol. Frombork) 114, 192
Freiburg 210
Friedland (Rus. Pravdinsk) 50
Friedrich Wilhelm I, King in Prussia 129
Friedrich von Boppard 225
Friedrich von Egloffstein 228
Friedrich von Goldberg 224, 226

Friedrich von Lanzin 224
Friedrich von Senskau 224
Friedrich von Tuchelsdorf 226
Friedrich von Veldenz 225
Friedrich von Wallenrode 228
Friedrich von Wenden 227
Friedrich von Wildenberg 225
Friesach 210
Fritzlar 209
Frombork *see* Frauenburg

Galindia 61
Galms 47
Galugneweis see Pötschkehmen
Gangofen 210
Gawaiten/Gaweisten (Rus. Gavrilovo) 142, 144
Gaudischkehmen see Pötschkehmen
Gayline 104
Gdańsk *see* Danzig
Gebhard von Ampleben 227
Gebweiler 210
Gedete 47
Gedethe 48, 53
Gedune 45
Geisseln 49
Gelayne (Germ. Gallehnen, Pol. Gałajny) 48
Geldern 225
Geleen 210
Gelžinis, Martynas 121
Gemert 210
Georg von Dameraw (Jerzy Dąbrowski) 159
Georg von Polentz 142
Georgenau (Rus. Roschtschino) 191
Georgenburg (Rus. Mayovka) 117, 127, 143, 144
Gerald of Wales 26
Gerdauen (Rus. Zheleznodorozhny) 37, 49, 66, 114, 116, 117, 124, 183, 184, 188, 192
Gerhard Nayl 225
Gerhard von Runkel 225
German people 2, 4, 5, 8, 19–23, 25–27, 29, 31–35, 58, 60–62, 95, 113, 114, 116, 117, 120, 122, 125, 128, 131, 132, 134, 136, 138, 145, 146, 184, 186–188, 193, 194, 197, 207, 209–213, 215, 224–226
Germany 60, 122, 135, 136, 146, 189, 193, 223; *see also* Low Germany; Middle Germany; *Reich*; Upper Germany

Germau (Rus. Russkoye) 192
Gertruda Pilewska 160
Giengen 210
Gilge river (Rus. Matrosovka) 144
Gintil 104
Girdaw 27, 28, 37, 49
Girdowia 27
Giruliai (Germ. Plantage) 102; see also Poys
Giselbrecht von Dudelsheim 227
Giżycko *see* Lötzen
Glabune 49, 50, 224
Glappo 49
Glausote 49
Glina *see* Stangendorf
Glinde Pruthenus 50
Gniew *see* Mewe
Gniewkowo 158
Gniezno 25, 166; archbishops of/ bishopric of 153, 191
Gobelo 224
Goldap (Pol. Gołdap) 122, 128, 140, 142
Goldingen (Lat. Kuldīga) 83, 101, 102
Gollub (Pol. Golub) 160, 226
Goslar 209
Gotard Bystram z Radlina 159–162
Gotebold von Korwitz 228
Gotówko, Piotr 8
Gottfried 87
Gottfried von der Kuhle 227
Gottfried von Sayn 225
Gottfried von Troisdorf 227
Göttingen 209
Górowo Iławeckie *see* Landsberg
Górski, Karol 2
Grande 47
Gratz 210
Graudenz (Pol. Grudziądz)160, 162, 164, 226
Great Wilderness (Germ. *Große Wildnis*) 58, 64, 83, 91–93, 114, 116, 117, 119, 121–129, 132, 140
Greater Poland 3, 7, 25, 158, 160
Greifstedt 209
Gresen 101
Greyne 104
Groß Wirsteniken 102
Große Wildnis see Great Wilderness
Großes Werder (Pol. Żuławy Wielkie) 3, 163, 164, 189
Gross-Sonntag 210
Grudziądz *see* Graudenz
Gruitrode 210

Gruta 36
Guillbert de Lannoy 88, 102
Gumbinnen (Ros. Gusev) 142
Günther von Hohenstein 228
Gusev 141
Guttstadt (Pol. Dobre Miasto) 69
Gvardeysk *see* Tapiau

Halle 32, 33, 209
Hannus Merun 50
Hannus Schayboth 49
Hans Konig 145
Hans Konigcke 145
Hansa 60
Hanß Peterwiitz 143
Harlech 29
Hartmann von Königstein 227
Heidelberg 208
Heidenreich Rabe 228
Heilbronn 210
Heilige Aa river 83, 89, 90
Heiligenbeil (Rus. Mamonovo) 182, 184, 186, 188, 191, 192
Heiligenkreutz (Rus. Krasnotorovka) 192
Heilsberg (Pol. Lidzbark Warmiński) 50
Heinrich Botel 47
Heinrich Cleycz 224
Heinrich Crattegalbe 50
Heinrich Dusemer, Grand Master of the Teutonic Order 224
Heinrich Gans von Weberstedt 228
Heinrich Harder 215
Heinrich Kynstute 188
Heinrich Monte 27
Heinrich von Blumenstein 225
Heinrich von Bovenden 227
Heinrich von Hohenlohe, Grand Master of the Teutonic Order 189
Heinrich von Orlow 224
Heinrich von Rechter 227
Heinrich von Rondorf 225
Heinrich von Schlewitz 225
Heinrich von Schöningen 227
Heinrich von Senskau 224
Heinrich von Thymau 224
Heinrich Zuckschwert 46
Henniko Pruthenus 50
Henning Schindekop 228
Henry de Lacy, Earl of Lincoln 26
Henry the Bearded (Henryk Brodaty), Duke of Krakow and of Wrocław 25
Henry the Pious (Henryk Pobożny), Prince of Silesia 25

Hermann Balk, Land Master of the
    Teutonic Order in Prussia 189, 198
Hermann von Kudorf 228
Hermann von Oettingen 190
Hermann von Oppen 223
Hermann von Prag, Bishop of Ermland/
    Warmia 190
Hessia *see* Northern Hessia
Hiob von Dobeneck, Bishop of
    Pomesania 189
Hitzkirch 210
Hojko of Konojady 50
Holland 227
Holy Roman Empire (*Reich*) 1, 8, 64, 114,
    116, 181, 206, 208–212, 217, 223
Holy See 180
Horneck 210
Hrodna 47
Hugo von Trimberg 208
Hugo von Wlatislawia 225

Iberia 60
Ibersheim 209
Inowrocław 158, 160
Inster river 127
Insterburg (Rus. Chernyakhovsk) 114,
    116, 117, 122, 124, 127–129,
    132–134, 140, 142, 144
Ireland 23, 26, 28, 29, 32
Irish people 32

Jacob 51
Jacob Revosze/Rabusa 188
Jacob Zamehl 50
Jacobus of Leodium 190
Jäger, Eckhard 117
Jähnig Bernhart 139, 225
Jakob von Radam 224
Jakub Kostka 164
Jałbrzyk Jan Sokołowski 160, 162
Jan Garbacz Jasieński 159, 162
Jan Hincza z Rogowa 160, 161
Jan Kościelecki 157, 159, 171
Jan Skalski z Valdštejnu 160
Jan Swiercin 224
Jan Synowiec z Rzędowic 160, 161
Jan (the younger) ze Szczekocin 160, 161
Jan von Brieg 225
Jasieniec 159
Jasieński family 159, 162, 166
Jerzmieniec 166
Jerzy Tworkowski 159
Jesko von Böhmen 226
Jesko von Schönburg 226

Jewish people 3, 60
Jodßen 143
Jodute 48, 49
Jogaila *see* Władysław II
Johan Bomgart 188
Johan Kenstute 188
Johan Poloni 187
Johan Szyłsław (Żelisławski) 187
Johann Langerak 227
Johann Marschalk von Frohburg 229
Johann Nothaft 224
Johann Overstolz von der Bach 225
Johann Prusse 224
Johann Rübsamen 227
Johann Wernkonis 224
Johann von Barkenfelde 227
Johann/Hans von Baysen (Jan Bażyński)
    156
Johann von Beffart 227
Johann von Bolanden 225, 227
Johann von Bolanden 227
Johann von Clare, Bishop of Sambia/
    Samland 190
Johann von Egloffstein 228
Johann von Falkenstein 225, 227, 229
Johann von Geidau 224
Johann von Köln 225
Johann von Lahnstein 225
Johann von Lengenfeld 228
Johann von Lessen 224
Johann von Lichtenstein 228
Johann von Neuteich 224
Johann von Ochtenhausen 101
Johann von Pfirt 229
Johann von Reddern 228
Johann von Rumpenheim 227, 228
Johann von Sayn 227
Johann von Schönfeld 228
Johann von Streifen 215
Johann von Troppau 226
Johannes Bredtke 131
Johannes Pein 140
Johannes Peytune 51
Johannes von Waplitz 50
Johannisburg (Pol. Pisz) 117, 118, 120
John Albert (Jan Olbracht), King of
    Poland 157, 158
John (*Johann Prutenus*) 50
John Zamehl 50
Jończyk, Ludwika 75
Józef Naronowicz-Naroński 63
Judenrode 209
Juncter 50
Jurbarkas 130

Kaiserslautern 207
Kalaten (Germ. Kollaten, Lit. Kalotė) 87
Kaliningrad *see* Königsberg
Kaliningrad Oblast 121
Kalkstein familiy 50
Kalligkehmen see Kulligkehmen
Kamenskoe *see* Saalau
Kamień *see* Cammin
Karczewska, Małgorzata 6
Karczewski, Maciej 6
Karl von Lichtenstein 228
Karlsruhe 208
Karnten 208
Karpfenburg 210
Kaschtanovo *see* Almenhausen
Kashubians/Pomeranians 5, 59, 184, 186, 187, 226
Kassel 207, 225
Kaszczorek 191
Kattenau (Rus. Nezhinskoe) 144
Katwijk 211
Kayserberg 210
Kazimierz, Duke of Kuyavia 25
Kerse 49
Kertene 48
Kętrzyn 117; Kętrzyn County 67
Kiełbasa family 162
Kildare 26
Kindschen 144
Kirchhain 209
Kirsilie von Kindswulie 225, 227
Kirstan von Bernsfelde 227
Kisch, Guido 20, 22, 30
Kiszewa 159, 164, 167
Klaipėda *see* Memel
Klęczkowo 166
Klein Warningken 144
Knapp, Georg Friedrich 134
Koblenz 207, 209; Bailiwick of 209, 212, 226
Kociewie 187
Köln *see* Cologne
Königsberg (Rus. Kaliningrad) 20, 23, 27, 28, 30, 35, 45–47, 50, 53, 68, 114, 115, 121, 124, 125, 127, 134, 143, 145, 182–184, 186, 189, 192, 229
Könitz 210
Konitz (Pol. Chojnice) 153, 182, 191, 194
Konopki 64
Konrad, Duke of Masovia 25, 26
Konrad Kessellnut 223
Konrad von Bruningisheim 227
Konrad von Eltz 227

Konrad von Jungingen, Grand Master of the Teutonic Order 215, 228
Konrad von Kalemunt 215
Konrad von Königsegg (Kunseckeln) 229
Konrad von Kyburg 229
Konrad/Kuno von Lichtenstein 228
Konrad von Thierberg, Land Master of the Teutonic Order in Prussia 47
Konrad von Wallenrode, Grand Master of the Teutonic Order 228
Konrad Zöllner, Grand Master of the Teutonic Order 215
Korth, Leonard 146
Kostka family 164
Kościelec 161
Kościelecki family 158, 160, 161
Kościerzyna 159, 167
Kowalewo Pomorskie *see* Schönsee
Krakow (Kraków) 25, 157, 160
Krasnoe *see* Schöntritten
Krasnopol'e *see* Pötschkehmen
Krasnotorovka *see* Heiligenkreutz
Krasnoznamensk *see* Lasdehnen
Kraupischken (Rus. Ul'janovo) 126, 144
Krewo (Lit. Krėva) 116
Krollmann, Christian 2
Krupin 50
Krylovo *see* Nordenburg
Krzewiny 166
Krzysztof z Celin z Łodygowa 164
Kubanovka *see* Brakupönen
Kubicki, Rafał 7, 8
Kuldīga *see* Goldingen
Kulligkehmen/Kalligkehmen (Prussischken, Rus. Lipovo) 126
Kulm (Pol. Chełmno) 19, 21, 23, 25, 26, 32, 33, 71, 180, 181, 184, 186, 187, 190, 191, 197, 208; Kulm land law 154, 162, 165; Kulm law 26, 27, 30, 154; *see also* Chełmno/Kulm, bishopric of
Kulmerland *see* Culmer Land
Kulmsee (Pol. Chełmża) 26
Kunemund von Malken 224
Kuno (der Jüngere) von Hattstein 225, 227
Kuno (der Mittlere) von Hattstein 228
Kuno von Liebestein 227
Kurortnoye *see* Wohnsdorf
Kurschen (Lit. Kuršeliai) 144
Kurzętnik 165
Kussen (Rus. Vesnovo) 144
Kutuzovo *see* Schirwindt
Kuyavia 3, 7, 25–27, 157, 158, 166, 191, 197

246 Index

Kwiatkowski, Krzysztof 6
Kwidzyn *see* Marienwerder

Labalaucs 47
Labiau (Rus. Polessk) 116, 117, 124, 144
Labuda, Gerard 2
Lahn river 221
Laistai 89, 90
Lake Mełno 83; Treaty of 83, 116, 117
Lake Rensen 32; battle of 32
Lake Spirding 118
Lake *Stasswin* 63
Lake *Swinteseyte* 63
Lake Święcajty 63
Łąki Staświńskie *see* Lake *Stasswin*
Lamotina 83
Lana 210
Landsberg (Pol. Górowo Iławeckie) 47
Langeln 209
Laptau (Rus. Muromskoye) 47
Lasdehnen (Rus. Krasnoznamensk) 144
Łasin *see* Lessen
Lassiten see Laistai
Lastadie (part of Elbing) 36
Latvia 60, 69, 181, 189
Lauenburg (Pol. Lębork) 183, 189, 196
Lausitz 208, 213, 225
Łęczyca 157
Legin (Legienen) 188
von Lehndorf family 49
Leiden 211
Leighton, Gregory 18
Leipzig 207
Lencken (Lengken) 144
Lengmos 210
Leonard von Sparw(e) 51
Lesgewang family 50
Lessen (Pol. Łasin) 182, 195
Lesser Poland 160
Letzen see Lötzen
Levant 32, 38
Leykot 50, 224
Lębork *see* Lauenburg
Lidzbark Warmiński *see* Heilsberg
Liebstedt 209
Lilley, Keith 19
Linkuhnen (Rus. Rschewskoje) 126
Linz 229
Lipińskie 64
Lipovo *see Kulligkehmen/Kalligkehmen*
Litauen *see* Lithuania
Litauischdorf (Rus. Zorino) 125
Lithuania 48, 58, 64, 69, 84, 94, 116, 117, 121, 122, 125, 130, 131, 134, 136, 143; Grand Duchy of 59, 83–85, 116, 117, 124, 128, 140, 143, 182; Lithuania Minor (Prussian Lithuania, 'Little Lithuania') 121, 128, 140, 143
Lithuanians/Lithuanian people 4, 7, 30, 31, 65, 84, 86, 89, 90, 92, 93, 113, 116, 117, 120–122, 124–138, 140–146, 184, 193, 194
Livonia 23, 24, 31, 60, 65, 69, 75, 82–84, 88, 99–101, 130, 189, 193, 199, 223; Bailiwick of 209
Livonian Order 83, 101
Lniska 162
Löbau (Pol. Lubawa) 183, 189
Löbegallen *see* Baiorgallen
Logvino *see* Medenau
Łomża 64
Lorenz Allmann 120
Lorenz Sylvester 131
Lothringia 226; Bailiwick of 210, 213, 225; *see also* Eastern Lothringia
Lötzen (Pol. Giżycko) 63, 117
Low Franconia 225
Low Germany 206
Łowmiański, Henryk 2, 27
Lubawa *see* Löbau
Lübeck 206, 209, 212, 213, 224, 225
Lublin 116, 160
Lubljana 210
Lucas von Allen (Łukasz Mełdzyński) 161
Lucklum 209
Ludwig von Benfeld 229
Ludwig von Isenburg 225
Ludwig von Wolkenburg 225, 227
Lukas Watzenrode, Bishop of Ermland/Warmia 190
Łukasz 197
Lütge, Friedrich 146
Luther von Braunschweig, Grand Master of the Teutonic Order 24, 118
Lüttich 210
Luxemburg (Luxembourg) 210, 215, 225; Duchy of 207
Lwów (Ukr. Lviv) 187
Lyck (Pol. Ełk) 117, 118

Maasland 211
Maastricht 210
Maciej ze Służewa 157
Madog Crach 29
Magdeburg 25; Magdeburg law 48; *see also* Saxon-Magdeburg simple law
Main river 221

Mainau 210
Mainz 210
Malaya Dubrovka *see* Bratricken
Malbork *see* Marienburg
Malbork voivodship 152
Maldenne/Moltenne Eywan 104
Malinovka *see* Wargenau
Małe Żuławy (Żuławy Fiszewskie) 163
Mamonovo *see* Heiligenbeil
Manchester 18
Marburg 209; Bailiwick of 209, 213, 226
Marggrabowa (later Treuburg, Pol. Olecko) 122, 140
Marienburg (Pol. Malbork) 18, 20, 24, 50, 51, 153, 156–158, 161, 163, 164, 167
Marienwerder (Pol. Kwidzyn) 25, 208
Marquart von Lindelbrunn 225
Marquart von Raschau 228
Marquart von Sulzbach 228
Martin Mařvidas (Mosvid) 131
Martin Munter 188
Martin Truchsess von Wetzhausen, Grand Master of the Teutonic Order 125
Masuria 59, 68, 120
Mathias Piwko 187
Matrosovka *see* Gilge river
Matthäus Prätorius 59
Matto Hermann 47, 48, 49, 53
Mayovka *see* Georgenburg
Mažeika Rasa 24, 36
Mazovia 25, 64, 71, 117, 143, 153, 154, 157, 161–164; Duchy of 116–118, 122, 152, 162, 166
Mazovians/Mazovian people 3, 5, 7, 25, 59, 116–118, 120, 122, 128, 140, 142, 144, 154, 158, 163, 164, 166–168
Mecheln 209
Mecklenburgia 224, 227
Mecklenburg-Vorpommern 206, 212, 224
Medenau (Rus. Logvino) 45
Mediterranean 39
Megowe (Lit. Mėguva) 83, 87
Mehlauken (Rus. Zales'e) 126
Meissen 45, 211
Mełno *see* Lake Mełno
Memel 3, 6, 62, 81–94, 97–101, 104, 116, 127, 132, 134, 182, 192, 196, 226
Memel river *see* Nemunas river
Mendicants/Mendicant orders 180, 181, 183–190
Merun/Marune Nakie 50

Metz 210
Mewe (Pol. Gniew) 159, 167, 226
Michael Curaw 189
Michel 145
Michurinskoe *see* Schackeln
Middelburg 211
Middle Germany 206, 208, 209, 213, 215
Mikołaj Bystram 161
Mikołaj Działyński 160
Mikołaj Jasieński 159
Mikołaj Kościelecki 157, 159, 160, 171
Mikołaj Pieniążek z Witowic 159, 162
Mikołaj Szarlejski 159, 161
Mikołaj Szczawiński 164
Mikołaj Szpot z Krajowa 160–162, 164
Mikołaj z Łabiszyna 159
Miligedo 48, 49
Militzer, Klaus 22, 29, 32, 34, 224
Milken (Pol. Miłki) 64
Milutin 50
Minge river 83
Möhne 20
Montemin family 48
Moravia 213, 225
Moritz von Perschkau 135, 145
Mortensen, Gertrud 7, 117, 120–122, 125, 127–131, 135, 136, 140–142, 144
Mortensen, Hans 7, 117, 120–122, 125, 127–131, 135, 136, 140–142, 144, 146
Mosiny 163
Muffendorf 209
Mühlhausen 209, 210
Mühlheim 209
Münnerstadt 210
Münster 209
Muromskoye *see* Laptau
Mutina/Mutine/Mutene/Mutone 87, 102; *see also* Purmaliai

Nadrauen/Nadrovia 124
Nadrovians 48
Nadruve 49
Nägelstedt 209
Nalub 48, 53
Nameda 48
Namile *see* Samile
Narcko/Narckaw 126
Narew river 44, 141
Narva 31
Natangia/Natangen 46, 186
Natangians 27, 44
Native Americans 34, 38

Naudiota 48
Nebrow (Pol. Nebrowo) 191
Neidenburg (Pol. Nidzica) 116
Nekarkis 49
Neman *see* Ragnit
Nemunas river 1, 44, 81, 82, 130
Nes 211
Nessau (Pol. Nieszawa) 158, 226
Nesterov *see* Stallupöhnen
Netherlands 213
Nettschunen 144
Neuenburg (Pol. Nowe) 153, 159, 166, 181, 191
Neuhoff (Pol. Zelki) 118
Neumark 226
Nevėžis river 130
Nevskoe *see* Pillupönen
Nezhinskoe *see* Kattenau
Nicolasu von der Frantz 215, 224
Nicolaus Holste 226
Nicolaus Pechwinkel 224
Nicolaus von Jeroschin 18, 23, 24, 28, 30, 32–34, 38, 44, 47, 89, 90
Nicolaus von Senskau 224
Nidzica *see* Neidenburg
Niederland 31, 212
Nieszawa *see* Nessau
Nikolaus 190
Nikolaus Kunras *de Kyrpeyn* 50
Nikolaus Legyn 188
Nikolaus Tungen, Bishop of Ermland/Warmia 167
Nikolaus von Baysen (Mikołaj Bażyński) 161
Nikolaus von Melin 215
Nikolaus von Viltz 228
Ninerik 26
Ninogniew Jasieński 159
Noer 49
Nordenburg (Rus. Krylovo) 114, 117, 183
North 5
North Sea 206
Northern Bavaria 228
Northern Burgundy 211
Northern Hessia 225
Norurhatschen 141
Nowe *see* Neuenburg
Nürnberg 208, 210
Nycolaus *dictus Pyrgune* 50

Ober-Flörsheim 209
Oberland 212
Obermässing 210

Obrąb 166
Oder river 207
Oettingen 210
Old-Prussians 1–2, 4, 6, 8, 18–25, 27–35, 37, 38, 44–52, 58–66, 68–71, 95, 113, 114, 117, 122, 124, 125, 127, 130–132, 134–136, 138, 143, 145, 146, 180, 182, 184, 186, 188, 190, 193, 194, 197, 200, 212, 224; Second ("Great") Prussian Uprising 21, 25–30, 48, 49, 53; *see also* Prussian law
Oldřich Červenka 156
Olecko *see* Marggrabowa
Olivier, Mathieu 37
Olsztyn group 61
Olsztyn *see* Allenstein
Ootmarsum 209, 222
Orbec 211, 223
Order of the Holy Ghost 192
Orneta *see* Wormditt
Ortelsburg (Pol. Szczytno) 116, 117
Ortulf von Trier 227
Orzechówek 166
Osiek 159
Osnabrück 209
Ossokino *see* Patollen
Osterode (Pol. Ostróda) 226
Otto, Bishop of Courland 100
Otto Angermünde 196
Otto von Oppen 223
Otto von Russen 50
Otto von Schymelow (Otto Szumiłowski) 159
Ottokar II, King of Bohemia 45
Owain Glyndŵr 30
Ozjorsk *see* Darkehmen

von Packmohr family 50
Palangen (Germ. Palangen, Lit. Palanga) 87, 89, 90, 102; Birutė Hill in (Lit. Birutės kalnas) 90
Palatine 207, 209, 210, 215, 225
Papau (Pol. Papowo) 36, 226, 227
Pasłęk *see* Preußisch Holland
Passaluc 180
Patilsze 133
Patollen (Groß Waldeck, Rus. Ossokino) 182, 184, 186, 188, 191, 192, 194
Paul Glenbicki 187
Paweł Jasieński 157, 171
Paweł Sokołowski 160, 164
Penkoweo 47

Perbandt family 50
Perdor 48, 53
Perkun 193, 200
Perkunas 68
Perovo *see* Ankrehnen
Peter Zugelia 188
Peter von Dusburg 6, 18, 23–34, 36–38, 44–49, 58, 71, 89, 90, 117
Peter von Thymau 224
Petzold von Korwitz 228
Pfalz 225; *see also* Upper Pfalz
von Pfeilsdorf family 49
Philipp von Creutz 122, 137, 140
Pillau (Rus. Baltiysk) 192
Pillkallen (Rus. Dobrovol'sk) 142, 144
Pillupönen (Rus. Nevskoe) 144
Pilsaten (Lit. Pilsotas) 83, 87
Piotr Donin z Prawkowic i Ujazdu 157, 171
Piotr Górski 159, 161
Piotr Szafraniec z Pieskowej Skały 157, 158, 171
Piotr Szorc z Obrębu 159, 162, 164
Pipin 49
Pisz *see* Johannisburg
Pizuński, Paweł 224
Plauen 209
Plehn, Hans 146
Pleissenland 211
Płochocin 166
Płock 36; bishop of 36; Duchy of 152
Pluskowski, Alekander 6
Pobethen (Rus. Romanovo) 192
Pogesania 46, 181, 184; *Vogt* of 50
Pogesanians 28, 49
Pokryshkino *see* Dopönen
Poland 59, 62, 116, 130, 134, 136, 153–156, 162, 163, 165, 186, 212, 213, 223, 224, 226; king of 7; Kingdom of 83, 116, 117, 152–158, 160, 166, 182–184, 187; Poland-Lithuania 64; Polish Crown 155–157, 159, 161–168; *see also* Central Poland; Greater Poland; Lesser Poland
Poles/Polish people 3, 5, 7, 8, 19, 20, 22, 24–29, 32–34, 58, 59, 113, 120, 122, 136, 138, 152–159, 161–168, 184, 186, 187, 193, 197, 212, 213, 224–226; Polish law 154
Polessk *see* Labiau
Pomanda 46, 49

Pomerania 1, 59, 212, 213, 215, 223, 224, 226; *see also* Eastern Pomerania; Western Pomerania
Pomerania voivodship 152, 159
Pomeranian people *see* Kashubians/Pomeranians
Pomerelia *see* Eastern Pomerania
Pomesania 48, 49, 58, 165, 180, 184; bishop/bishopric of 58, 153, 162, 165, 189, 196
Pomesanians 28, 29, 30, 44
Pommern *see* Pomerania
Pomorze *see* Eastern Pomerania; Pomerania
Posdraupot 48
Pötschkehmen (Rus. Krasnopol'e) 144
Potsdam 145
Powierski, Jan 198
Poys 87, 102
Poznań 158, 187
Prabuty *see* Riesenburg
Prandota Lubieszowski 157–159
Pravdinsk *see* Friedland
Pregel (Pol. Pregoła) river 141
Preußisch Holland (Pol. Pasłęk) 3, 50, 181, 188
Pribezlaus (in Elbing) 186, 197
Pribezlaus (in Thorn) 186
Pridorozhnoe *see* Saszlaucken
Primislaus 186
Prozelten 210
Prusella from *Colicklaucken* 126
Prusella from *Zamaites* 141
Prussia 1–9, 18, 19, 21–25, 31, 33, 34, 51, 58–62, 64–66, 68–71, 81, 83, 84, 88, 94, 99, 103, 113, 115, 116, 121, 122, 124–127, 129–131, 134–138, 141, 146, 152–156, 158, 161, 162, 164–168, 180–184, 186–190, 193–196, 199, 207, 209, 211–213, 215, 216, 225, 226; Ducal Prussia 122, 135; Duchy of 116, 127–131, 138; Order's Prussia (Prusy Zakonne) 152, 185; Royal Prussia 4, 7, 152–156, 158, 160–168, 180, 181, 183–185; *see also* East Prussia; *Niederland*; *Oberland*; Prussian-Samogitian-Lithuanian Transition Zone
Prussian Estates 155, 156, 167, 229
Prussian Land *see* Prussia
Prussian law 50, 59, 124
Prussian Lithuania *see* Lithuania, Lithuania Minor

250 *Index*

Prussian starosties 7, 153, 155, 158, 161, 163–165, 167
Prussians 113, 114, 116, 136, 143, 145, 154, 158, 159, 161, 162, 164, 166, 167; *see also* Old-Prussians
Prussian-Samogitian-Lithuanian transition zone (frontier) 83–85, 88
Pruszischken 141; *see also* Kulligkehmen/Kalligkehmen
Przecław Słowak z Kłopoczyna 159, 162
Purmaliai 89, 102
Putzig (Pol. Puck) 153

Quednau (Rus. Severnaya Gora) 48, 53

Rabe von Pappenheim 227
Ragnit (Rus. Neman) 3, 7, 83–86, 90, 91, 114, 116, 117, 125, 127–129, 132, 133, 142–144, 182, 193, 196, 226
Ramersdorf 211
Rapoto 50
Rastenburg (Pol. Kętrzyn) 117, 183, 184
Raus 188, 198
Rawos 188, 198
Regensburg 208, 210
Reginald de Grey 26
Rehden (Pol. Radzyń Chełmiński) 226
Reich see Holy Roman Empire
Reichenbach 209
Reimbold von Isenburg 225
Reinhard von Elner 227
Reinhard von Leitsch 224
Rendalia family 27, 37
Rensen *see* Lake Rensen
Reszel *see* Rößel
Reval (Est. Tallinn) 31
Rhein (Pol. Ryn) 116–118
Rheinberg 209
Rhenen 211
Rhine river 207
Rhineland 209, 211, 212, 215, 216, 222, 224
Richwin Specht von Bubenheim 225
Riesenburg (Pol. Prabuty) 48, 183, 184, 192
Riga (Lat. Rīga) 29, 31, 61, 101, 193, 195, 199; Riga law 32
Rigby, Stephen 18
Robert FitzStephen 26
Rogóźno 160
Romanovo *see* Pobethen

Roschtschino *see* Georgenau
Rößel (Pol. Reszel) 182, 184, 188, 191, 192
Rossitten (Rus. Rybachi) 93, 116
Rostock 223
Rothenburg 210
Równina Dolna (Germ. Unterplehn) 65–68, 71
Rschewskoje *see* Linkuhnen
Rüdiger von Elner 227
Rudolf von Kyburg 229
Rufach 210
Rukals 47
Rus' 117
Russkoye *see* Germau
Ruszaynen (Reuschhagen, Pol. Ruszajny) 188
Ruthenians 3, 31
Ruthin 26
Ryba 187
Rybachi *see* Rossitten
Ryn *see* Rhein

Saalau (Rus. Kamenskoe) 117
Saalfeld 209
Saalfeld (Pol. Zalewo) 183, 184, 189
Saarbrücken 210, 222
Saarburg 210
Sachsen-Anhalt 207
Sachsenhausen 210
Sacred Hill *see* Święta Góra
Salentin von Isenburg 225
Salno 166
Sal'skoe *see* Sankt Lorenz
Salys, Anton 129, 130
Sambia/Samland 45, 49, 58, 59, 68, 69, 124, 125, 145, 186, 188, 190, 192, 193, 200; bishops/bishopric of 190, 192, 196; Sambian Peninsula 71; Sambian-Natangian group 61
Sambians 30, 35, 44, 45, 47, 48, 53, 61, 66
Samile (Namile) 46, 47, 49, 50
Samogitia (Žemaitija) 59, 83, 88, 89, 126, 130, 131, 141, 143, 181, 182, 196
Samogitians 31, 84, 89, 90, 98, 100, 104, 125
Sampława 162
Sandomierz 160
Sankt Lorenz (Rus. Sal'skoe) 192
Santung 48, 53
Sarden 87, 89, 102; *see also* Žardė

Saszlaucken (Sesslacken, Rus. Pridorozhnoe) 126, 144
Saul 50
Saxo 227
Saxon-Magdeburg simple law 154
Saxony 45, 206, 214, 226, 227; Bailiwick of 209, 211, 212, 223; *see also* Sachsen-Anhalt; Upper Saxony
Scalovia 85, 94
Scalovians/Schalvians 1, 6, 48, 61, 81–86, 89, 90–95, 100, 117
Scandinavians 49, 85
Schackeln (Rus. Michurinskoe) 144
Schalauer see Scalovians/Schalvians
Schelluinen 211
Schiffenberg 209
Schirwindt (Rus. Kutuzovo) 142, 144
Schlanders 210
Schlauerburg 85
Schleitz 209
Schleswig-Holstein 206
Schlochau (Pol. Człuchów) 50, 159, 226
Schlubutt family 50
Schön, Theodor 229
Schönsee (Pol. Kowalewo Pomorskie) 50, 226
Schöntritten (Rus. Krasnoe) 125
Schoomhoven 211
Schoten 211
Schumacher, Bruno 2
Schweder von Pellant 225, 227
Schweinfurt 210
Schwetz (Pol. Świecie) 159, 226
Schwirgallen (Rus. Zavodskoe) 144
Ścibor Chełmski z Ponieca 156–158
Scislaus 226
Sebastian Legendorf 159
Seehesten (Pol. Szestno) 117, 191
Selart, Anti 31
Semigallia 101, 104, 181
Sesslacken *see Saszlaucken*
Severnaya Gora *see* Quednau
Siegfried Walpot von Bassenheim 227
Siegfried von Dahenfeld 188, 228
Siegfried von Wobitz 226
Sieradz 190
Siersdorf 211
Sigismund I, King of Poland 152
Sigismund II August, King of Poland 131
Silesia 25, 62, 159, 187, 208, 212, 213, 224, 226
Silesians 3
Simon Grunau 59, 192, 193

Sint Pietersvoeren 210
Sirenes 29, 30
Skępe 161
Sklodo 48, 53
Skomand 26, 47, 49, 52
Slavs/Slavic people 3–6, 21, 25, 29, 36, 49, 59, 64, 184, 186, 187, 194, 206, 207, 212, 213, 215
Słończ 163
Słupy 165
Sobieraj, Jarosław 67
Sobis 48
Sokołowski family 162
Sorge river 28
South 5
Southern Tirol 208
Sovetsk *see* Tilsit
Speyer 207, 208, 210
Spirding (Pol. Jezioro Śniardwy) *see* Lake Spirding
St. Leonhard 210
Stabławki (Germ. Stablack) 69
Stablewice 163
Stallupöhnen (Rus. Nesterov) 142
Stangendorf (Pol. Glina) 191
Stanislaus 187
Stanteko 47
Starogard 159, 164
Starogród Chełmiński *see* Althaus
Stary Dzierzgoń 62
Stasswienen See *see* Lake *Stasswin*
Stasswin (Pol. Staświnka) river 63
Stasswin see Lake *Stasswin*
Stasswinnen see Eisermühl
Staświnka *see Stasswin* river
Staświny (Germ. Eisermühl) 62–64, 70
Stenion 50
Stenzlaus 186
Sterzing 210
Stevens, Matthew Frank 6, 22, 23
Steynio 47
Stibor von Baysen (Ścibor Bażyński) 156
Stradaunen (Pol. Straduny) 117, 118, 120, 122
Strasburg (Pol. Brodnica) 160, 226
Strassburg 210
Straszewo 161
Stuttgart 208
Subkowy 165
Sudovia (Sudauen) *see* Yotvingia
Sudovians *see* Yotvingians/Sudovians
Suggelaw 188
Sumiswald 210

Święcajty *see* Lake Święcajty
Świecie *see* Schwetz
Święta Góra (Germ. *Heiliger Berg/Pruzzenhöhe*) 63, 64, 70
Święte 166
Świętopełk II Wielki, Duke of Eastern Pomerania/Pomerelia 33, 181
Swinteseyte see Lake *Swinteseyte*
Switzerland 208
Szameithkehmen (Rus. Bolotnikovo) 144
Szczytno *see* Ortelsburg
Szestno *see* Seehesten
Szewa 166
Sztum 161, 163
Szybkowski, Sobiesław 7
Szymon Swawola 166

Tallinn *see* Reval
Talpaki *see* Taplacken
Tandecki, Janusz 22
Tannenberg/Grunwald/Žalgiris, battle of 113, 116
Tapiau (Rus. Gvardeysk) 114, 124, 135
Taplacken (Rus. Talpaki) 117
Tatars 3
Taunus mountains/region 221, 224
Tczew *see* Dirschau
Tellitzkehmen 144
Tessim 49
Tessymid family 50
Teutonic Order 1–4, 6, 7, 9, 18–21, 23–31, 35, 37, 44–53, 58, 59, 62–64, 66, 68, 70, 71, 81–95, 97–101, 103, 104, 113, 114, 116–118, 120, 121, 124–132, 138, 141, 143, 152, 154–156, 159, 160, 164, 165, 167, 180–184, 188–192, 194, 195, 198, 199, 206–211, 213–216, 225, 226, 229; Teutonic Knights 24, 26, 45–47, 49, 159
Thann 210
Thierenberg (Rus. Dunayevka) 192
Thitmar 87
Thomas ap David 30
Thomas von Merheim 227
Thomas Westval Polonus 22
Thorn (Pol. Toruń) 19, 21–23, 25, 36, 153, 159, 180, 181, 184, 186–188, 191, 197, 226, 227; New Town Thorn 28; Old Town Thorn 22; Second Peace of 21, 114, 152, 183

Thuringia 45, 62, 207–209, 215; Bailiwick of 209, 211, 222
Tiel 211
Tilo Lubecke 224
Tilsit (Rus. Sovetsk) 116, 126–128, 132, 134, 135, 141, 142, 145, 183, 184, 192, 193
Tilsze river 133
Tirol 208; *see also* Southern Tirol
Tischino *see* Abschwangen
Tollawke (Tollack, Pol. Tuławki) 188
Tolstovo *see* Baiorgallen
Tomasz Tomiec z Młotkowa 159–162
Torpine (Germ. Topprienen, Pol. Toprzyny) 48
Toruń *see* Thorn
Trampe 48
Trient 210
Trier 207, 210
Trisko 47, 49
Trist 48
Tropo 48, 49
Trumiejki Nowe 165
Truszischken 141
Trzcianka 166
Trzebcz 166
Tuchel (Pol. Tuchola) 159, 163, 226
Tuławki *see Tollack*
Turku *see* Åbo
Tyrune 49

Ul'janovo *see* Kraupischken
Ulm 210
Ulrich von Hachenberg 228
Ulrich von Jungingen, Grand Master of the Teutonic Order 182, 228
Ulricus 196
Unisław 166
Unterplehn *see* Równina Dolna
Upper Germany 206, 210, 211, 213, 215
Upper Pfalz 224
Upper Saxony 62
Urban, William 26
Ushakovo *see* Brandenburg
Utrecht 211; Bailiwick of 211

Venceslaus 187
Venta river *see* Windau
Vercamer, Grischa 7
Vesnovo *see* Kussen
Vesselnoe *see* Balga

Index   253

Vėžininkai *see* Weszeningken
Vienna (Wien) 208, 210
Viešvilė *see* Wischwill
Virkštininkai 102
Virnsberg 210
Vistula river 1, 44, 153, 181, 191, 207, 208, 212, 215
V[itus] 186
Vogtland 208, 215
Voigt, Johannes 224
Vorarltberg 208
Vorweidenthal 225
Vosges mountains 210
Vught 210

Waldbreitenbach 210
Wałdówek 166
Wales 22–24, 26, 28, 29, 32
Wallachia 126
Walrabe von Scharfenberg 215
Waplitz (Pol. Waplewo) 50
Wargenau (Rus. Malinkovka) 125
Wargule 49
Warmia *see* Ermland
Warsaw (Warszawa) 50; Warsaw Trial 50, 190
Wartenburg (Pol. Barczewo) 182, 184, 188
Wechselburg 209
Węgorzewo *see* Angerburg
Wehlau (Rus. Znamensk) 47, 49, 124, 182–184, 188, 192
Weichbrodt, Ernst 224, 229
Weimar 209
Weinheim 210
Weissenburg 210
Welheim 209
Welsh people 26, 30, 32
Wenceslaus 186
Wendish lands 60
Wenskus, Reinhard 6, 20, 117
Wenta, Jarosław 223
Werner Schwabe 131
Werner von Bolanden 225
Werner von Orseln, Grand Master of the Teutonic Order 82
Werner von Rondorf 225, 227
Werner von Tettingen 229
'West' 4, 5; 'Western' countries 83
Western Pomerania 187
Westphalia 213, 214; Bailiwick of 209, 222, 226
Westphalians 3

Weszeningken (Lit. Vėžininkai) 144
Wetterau 221
Wetzlar 209
Wexford 26
Wien *see* Vienna
Wiener-Neustadt 210
Wigand von Beldersheim 228
Wildnis *see* Great Wilderness
Wilhelm IV von Jülich 47
Wilhelm Lander von Sponheim 225
Wilhelm von Borne 226
Wilhelm von Helfenstein 225, 227
Wilkanowski family 161, 162
William of Modena 82
Willkischken 144
Willuhnen 130, 143
Wincenty Kiełbasa, Bishop of Kulm/ Chełmno 160, 162, 165
Wincenty Kościelecki 160
Windau (Lit. Venta) river 101
Windenburg 93
Winnenden 210
Winrich von Kniprode, Grand Master of the Teutonic Orders 215, 225, 227
Winrich von Ryndorf 227
Wippe river 144
Wisborienen 144
Wischwill (Lit. Viešvilė) 144
Wisna Land 64
Wissegaud 45
Wittich, Werner 134
Władysław (Vladislav), King of Bohemia 162
Władysław II (Jogaila), King of Poland 116, 158
Władysław Odonic, Prince of Great Poland 25
Włocławek, bishopric of 153, 165
Włodek (Władysław) Sarnowski 166
Włodek z Danaborza 159, 161
Wohnsdorf (Rus. Kurortnoye) 47, 49
Wojan 186
Wojciech Kiełbasa z Tymieńca 160, 162, 164
Wolf von Zolnhart 228
Wolfram von Beldersheim 227
Wolkeniten 125
Wormditt (Pol. Orneta) 50
Wrocław 25
Württemberg 229
Würzburg 208, 210
Wyszowate 64